Mauritius, Réunion & the Seychelles

Seychelles
p275

Madagascar

Mauritius
p50

Rodrigues
p150

Réunion
p174

Matt Phillips, Jean-Bernard Carillet, Anthony Ham

Contents

LA DIGUE, SEYCHELLES
P307

MARKET, MAHÉBOURG,
MAURITIUS P104

Contents

SPECIAL FEATURES

Welcome to Mauritius, Réunion & Seychelles

Blessed with superlative landscapes and idyllic beaches, rich in activities and culinary experiences, Mauritius, Réunion and the Seychelles offer the best cure for the blues.

From Beach to Adventure

Believe it or not, a day will come during your stay when you decide you've had enough with the beach lounging. Mauritius, Rodrigues, Réunion and the Seychelles aren't just about pampering and relaxation; when it comes to recharging adrenaline levels, they have big surprises up their sleeves. Hike the footpaths that criss-cross the islands, ranging from meandering trails to trudges up mountains; scuba dive in enticing warm waters, marvelling at more than 300 species of fish (and the odd shipwreck or two); catch the wind and waves on a kiteboard; take a boat tour; explore magnetic canyons; or discover the countryside on horseback.

Life's a Beach

The Seychelles (and, to a lesser extent, Mauritius) is home to perhaps the sexiest beaches in the world. From intimate, hard-to-reach coves to mile-long crescents of white sand, the choice is endless. They're so consistently perfect that it's hard not to become blasé about them. That's why people come here to spend days on the beach under the bright tropical sun, swinging in hammocks, splashing in the sea and sipping a cocktail. Even Réunion, which doesn't fit the cliché of a sun-soaked paradise, has a few good stretches of sand.

To Luxe or Not to Luxe

It's hardly surprising that the Seychelles and Mauritius are choice destinations for honeymooners: here the world's most exclusive hotels compete with each other to attain ever-greater heights of luxury, from personal butlers and private lap pools to in-room massages and pillow menus – not to mention sensuous spas. But if this is not in your budget, don't let that dissuade you from buying a ticket to these destinations. Small, family-run hotels, bed and breakfasts and self-catering establishments offer a closer-to-the-culture experience at prices that won't require you to remortgage the house.

Cultural Gems

Don't for a second assume that these islands are for beach holidays, nature and adrenaline only – there's so much more to each destination that any trip will be an unforgettable and exciting experience. Across the region, you can explore a fascinating colonial past in myriad mansions and museums, attend a music festival or a fire-walking ceremony, visit an old sugar factory or a restored Creole villa, or simply soak up the atmosphere of a picturesque village. One thing's for sure, culture buffs won't be disappointed.

Why I Love Mauritius, Réunion & Seychelles

By Anthony Ham, Writer

I'm with Mark Twain: Mauritius may have been the model for heaven. The first time I laid eyes on the place, I fell in love with the beaches, but I also love the melting-pot cultural mix, beautiful forests and wildlife, and the opportunities for hiking the mountainous interior, all on one small island. Rodrigues, with its refreshingly retro lack of development, is another favourite – a real Mauritius-as-it-once-was experience. And the Seychelles, even down to its name, carries echoes of luxury and superb natural beauty, its islands dropped like pearls into a remote, tropical corner of the Indian Ocean.

For more about our writers, see p352

Above: Le Morne Peninsula (p102), Mauritius

Mauritius, Réunion & Seychelles

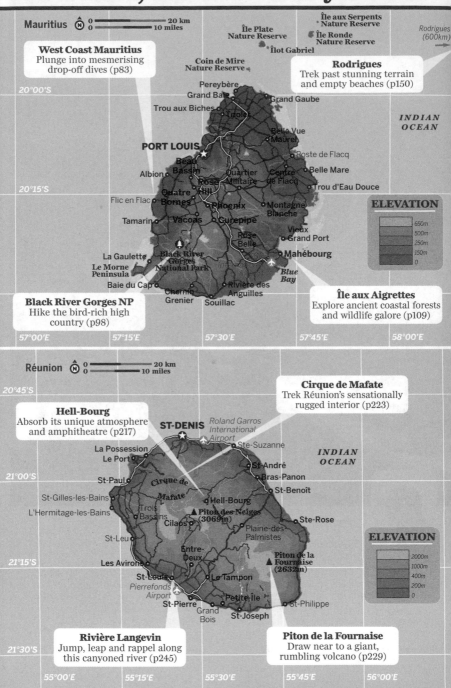

Mauritius 〔N〕 0 —— 20 km / 0 —— 10 miles

Île aux Serpents Nature Reserve

Île Plate Nature Reserve

Île Ronde Nature Reserve

Îlot Gabriel

Rodrigues (600km)

West Coast Mauritius
Plunge into mesmerising drop-off dives (p83)

Coin de Mire Nature Reserve

Pereybère

Grand Baie

Grand Gaube

Trou aux Biches

Triolet

Rodrigues
Trek past stunning terrain and empty beaches (p150)

INDIAN OCEAN

20°00'S

Belle Vue Maurel

PORT LOUIS

Beau Bassin

Albion

Rose Hill

Quartier Militaire

Centre de Flacq

Poste de Flacq

Belle Mare

Quatre Bornes

Flic en Flac

Phoenix

Trou d'Eau Douce

20°15'S

Tamarin

Vacoas

Curepipe

Montagne Blanche

Vieux Grand Port

Rose Belle

ELEVATION
650m
500m
250m
150m
0

La Gaulette

Le Morne Peninsula

Black River Gorges National Park

Mahébourg

Baie du Cap

Chemin Grenier

Rivière des Anguilles

Blue Bay

Île aux Aigrettes
Explore ancient coastal forests and wildlife galore (p109)

Black River Gorges NP
Hike the bird-rich high country (p98)

Souillac

57°00'E   57°15'E   57°30'E   57°45'E   58°00'E

Réunion 〔N〕 0 —— 20 km / 0 —— 10 miles

20°45'S

Cirque de Mafate
Trek Réunion's sensationally rugged interior (p223)

Hell-Bourg
Absorb its unique atmosphere and amphitheatre (p217)

ST-DENIS

Roland Garros International Airport

La Possession

Le Port

Ste-Suzanne

INDIAN OCEAN

21°00'S

St-Paul

St-André

Bras-Panon

Cirque de Mafate

St-Benoît

St-Gilles-les-Bains

Trois Bassins

Hell-Bourg

▲ Piton des Neiges (3069m)

L'Hermitage-les-Bains

Cilaos

Ste-Rose

St-Leu

Plaine-des-Palmistes

ELEVATION
2000m
1000m
400m
200m
0

Entre-Deux

21°15'S

Les Avirons

Piton de la Fournaise (2632m)

St-Louis

Le Tampon

Pierrefonds Airport

Petite-Île

St-Philippe

St-Pierre

Grand Bois

St-Joseph

21°30'S

Rivière Langevin
Jump, leap and rappel along this canyoned river (p245)

Piton de la Fournaise
Draw near to a giant, rumbling volcano (p229)

55°00'E   55°15'E   55°30'E   55°45'E   56°00'E

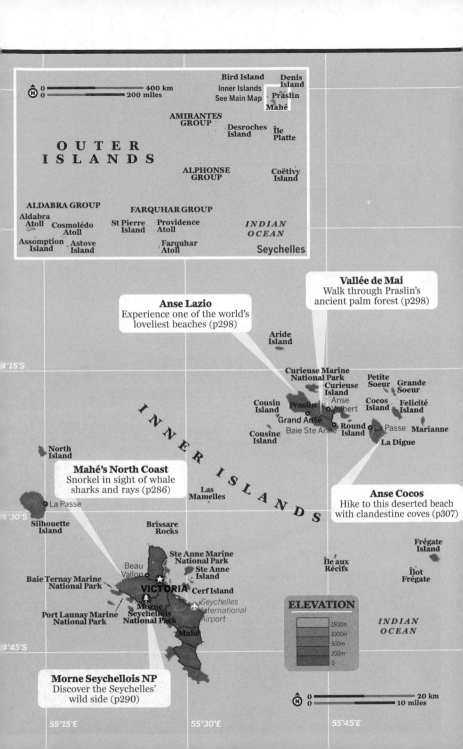

Vallée de Mai
Walk through Praslin's ancient palm forest (p298)

Anse Lazio
Experience one of the world's loveliest beaches (p298)

Mahé's North Coast
Snorkel in sight of whale sharks and rays (p286)

Anse Cocos
Hike to this deserted beach with clandestine coves (p307)

Morne Seychellois NP
Discover the Seychelles' wild side (p290)

ELEVATION

1500m
1000m
500m
200m
0

0 ——— 400 km
0 ——— 200 miles

Bird Island
Denis Island
Inner Islands
See Main Map
Praslin
Mahé

AMIRANTES GROUP
Desroches Island
Île Platte

OUTER ISLANDS

ALPHONSE GROUP
Coëtivy Island

ALDABRA GROUP
Aldabra Atoll
Cosmolédo Atoll
Assomption Island
Astove Island

FARQUHAR GROUP
St Pierre Island
Providence Atoll
Farquhar Atoll

INDIAN OCEAN

Seychelles

Aride Island

Curieuse Marine National Park
Curieuse Island
Petite Soeur
Grande Soeur

Cousin Island
Praslin
Anse Volbert
Cocos Island
Felicité Island

Grand Anse
Baie Ste Anne
Round Island
La Passe
Marianne

Cousine Island
La Digue

North Island

Las Mamelles

INNER ISLANDS

La Passe
Silhouette Island

Brissare Rocks

Frégate Island

Île aux Récifs

Îlot Frégate

Ste Anne Marine National Park
Ste Anne Island

Beau Vallon

VICTORIA

Cerf Island

Baie Ternay Marine National Park

Port Launay Marine National Park

Morne Seychellois National Park

Seychelles International Airport

Mahé

INDIAN OCEAN

0 ——— 20 km
0 ——— 10 miles

4°15'S

4°30'S

4°45'S

55°15'E

55°30'E

55°45'E

Mauritius, Réunion & Seychelles'
Top 17

Reaching the Summit of Piton de la Fournaise (Réunion)

1 Piton de la Fournaise (p229) is Réunion's crowning glory. Seen from the viewpoint at Pas de Bellecombe, *le volcan* (as it's known to locals) broods black and beautiful, its shapely form towering over the island. Even though this is an active volcano, it's still possible to climb up to the crater rim and stare down into the abyss – a seriously memorable sight. Hiking and horse trails lead to the summit, while a scenic helicopter flight offers the ultimate bird's-eye view down into the caldera.

Anse Lazio (Seychelles)

2 On the northwest tip of Praslin, Anse Lazio (p298) is a reminder of just why the Seychelles has become one of the most alluring destinations in the Indian Ocean. The beach here is near perfect, a stereotype come to life, with golden sands, granite boulders at either end, palm trees and unbearably beautiful waters somewhere between turquoise and lapis lazuli. Ideal for hours spent lying on the beach, snorkelling or eating in the beachfront restaurant, Anse Lazio is the sort of place you'll never want to leave.

ERIC VALENNE GEOSTORY/SHUTTERSTOCK ©

HAVESEEN/SHUTTERSTOCK ©

RICARDO STEPHAN/SHUTTERSTOCK ©

The Northeastern Coastal Walk (Rodrigues)

3 There are few finer trails in the Indian Ocean than the coastal path (p157) on east-coast Rodrigues between Graviers and St François. There are no roads in this corner of the island, and you'll want to linger at Trou d'Argent, one of the prettiest beaches anywhere in Mauritius. At the end of the trail (or the beginning, depending on where you start), St François has some fine informal restaurants, such as the fabulously fishy and breezy Chez Robert et Solange for lunch, and the tranquil St François beach.

Diving for Wildlife Treasures (Mauritius)

4 Some of the Indian Ocean's best dives are found off the west coast of Mauritius (p83). The architecture of the underwater rock formations and the substantial schools of fish make the waters off Flic en Flac in particular a world-class dive destination and there are numerous dive schools on hand to take you out, regardless of your level of experience. The best sites are the walls and drop-offs on the edge of the turquoise lagoon, and La Cathédrale, near Flic en Flac, is simply marvellous.

Trekking the Cirque de Mafate (Réunion)

5 Perhaps the finest set of multiday hikes anywhere in the Indian Ocean, the Cirque de Mafate (p222) feels like you're traversing the end of the earth. Wild and remote, watched over by fortress-like ridges and riven with deep valleys, this is an extraordinary experience. A four-day hike through the Haut Mafate can be combined with the four-day, even-more-secluded Bas Mafate. Best of all, these hikes take you through quiet mountain hamlets where you'll find lodges where the welcome is warm and genuine.

Île aux Aigrettes (Mauritius)

6 Lying offshore from the dramatically beautiful southeastern coast, Île aux Aigrettes (p109) is one place where time has moved in reverse. With an ancient ebony forest and extensive programs to restore to the island wildlife species that were, in the not-too-distant past, in danger of extinction on the mainland, the nature reserve can feel like a return to the pre-contact time before Dutch sailors arrived in 1598. Highlights include the rather lovely pink pigeon, the vivid Mauritian fody and free-ranging wild tortoises

Chambres & Tables d'Hôtes (Mauritius)

7 Whether on Mauritius' west coast or in the quiet highlands of Rodrigues, staying in a *chambre d'hôte* (p143) is a wonderful way to learn about local life. Rooms in these family-run guesthouses are often simple, but the warmth and personal nature of the welcome you'll receive and the nightly table d'hôte, where the guests and hosts gather together for a traditional meal, make for the kind of experience you'll remember long after the luxury resorts have faded in your memory.

YGGDRASILL/SHUTTERSTOCK ©

Canyoning in Rivière Langevin (Réunion)

8 One of the top spots for canyoning in the region is the Rivière Langevin (p246) valley that slithers into the mountains. What to expect? Jumps, leaps in natural pools and scrambling over rocks. And rappelling. Serious rappelling: the Cascade de la Grande Ravine (also known as Cascade de Grand Galet; pictured) is a striking waterfall that tumbles down a vertical basaltic cliff. Fear not, your guides will give you a thorough safety briefing and provide high-quality, easy-to-use climbing gear, making the thrill safe and immensely fun.

Morne Seychellois National Park (Seychelles)

9 In their quest for the perfect beach, many travellers are oblivious to the fact that there are fantastic experiences to be had in this lush and splendid national park (p290) that rises in a series of peaks to crown the island of Mahé. Take a guided hike through dense forest, coastal mangroves and rugged mountains and you'll soon believe that the world and its clamour belong to another planet. While exploring, you'll come across rare species of birds, reptiles and plants, not to mention some breathtaking views.

Snorkelling & Diving (Seychelles)

10 Anyone who loves the water will adore the Seychelles. Whatever your abilities, you'll experience sensory overload while diving off Mahé, Praslin and La Digue, as well as off the other inner islands. Mahé's north coast (p286) offers the greatest variety, with a good balance of healthy reefs, fascinating shipwrecks and dense marine life and the unmistakable cachet of swimming in sight of whale sharks and massive rays. Each island also caters to avid snorkellers, with gin-clear waters and a smattering of healthy coral gardens around.

Dining & Drinking in Chamarel (Mauritius)

11 High in the hills that rise dramatically from the west coast, the village of Chamarel (p94) is quietly gathering a reputation as one of Mauritius' best places to eat. Lining the road through town, and along the steep climb towards Black River Gorges National Park, are all manner of restaurants, from informal family-run places to fine-dining establishments. Other attractions include a fascinating rum distillery (pictured), the famous Terres de 7 Couleurs (coloured earths), and a quirky museum.

Anse Cocos (Seychelles)

12 If you're suffering from visions of tropical paradise, here is your medicine. On the east coast of La Digue, Anse Cocos (p307) is the sort of place you'll never want to leave. The beach here is near perfect, a stereotype come to life with blindingly white sand, casuarina trees and palms arching gracefully to shade beachgoers, shapely boulders forming clandestine coves at either end and startlingly blue waters. Ideal for hours spent lazing on the beach, far from the crowds.

Black River Gorges National Park (Mauritius)

13 One of Mauritius' most underrated attractions, Black River Gorges National Park (p98) has the island's most beautiful scenery. Well-maintained and clearly signposted hiking trails weave among forested hills, vertiginous waterfalls and deep gorges where you might see some of the island's signature bird species, including the distinctive white-tailed tropicbird and endangered Mauritian kestrel. Even if you don't hike, a good road leads through the park to some of its prettier viewpoints.

Hell-Bourg (Réunion)

14 Deep in the heart of the Cirque de Salazie, Hell-Bourg (p217) takes its curious name from the former governor Amiral de Hell; the town itself is anything but! It's a supremely picturesque place blessed with a wealth of appealing Creole houses and a splendid setting in the centre of a natural amphitheatre. For those who've got itchy feet, a number of hiking trails await. Even if you're not a walker, it's worth lingering in Hell-Bourg a couple of days to make the most of the laid-back atmosphere. Below: Colonial architecture in Hell-Bourg

Hindu & Creole Festivals

15 Hindu festivals are a wonderful way to liven up your visit to Mauritius and catch a glimpse of the island's fascinating cultural mosaic. The biggest festival of all, in February or March, is the 500,000-strong Hindu pilgrimage to the sacred lake of Grand Bassin (p228). March is also the month of colourful Holi festivities, October means Divali, and Teemeedee in December or January is all about firewalking wherever Hindus are found. For celebrations of Creole culture, December is particularly exuberant in Rodrigues.

Above: Hindu temple statue at Grand Bassin

Forêt de Bébour-Bélouve (Réunion)

16 If you want to decompress in forested mountains, head to Forêt de Bébour-Bélouve (p233), which lies right in the centre of the island. This vast primary forest is a magical spot for naturalists. Reached after a 20km-long secondary road, it is an exceptional ecosystem, with a mix of giant ferns, silvery tamarind trees and Japanese cryptomeria. Unsurprisingly, Forêt de Bébour-Bélouve is a walker's paradise, with a mesh of interpretative trails of varying levels of difficulty. It is also a great spot to see birdlife.

Vallée de Mai (Seychelles)

17 If you can tear yourself away from the beach, Vallée de Mai (p298) is a paradise of a different kind. Inscribed by Unesco, and home to the rare and beautiful coco de mer palms and a host of other endemic plants, the park is all about being immersed in lush tropical forest, serenaded by birdsong, and losing yourself along quiet hiking trails that meander agreeably through a verdant miniwilderness. Keep your eyes peeled for the endemic Seychelles bulbul, the lovely blue pigeon, the Seychelles warbler and the endangered black parrot.

Accommodation

Find more accommodation reviews throughout the On the Road chapters (from p50)

Accommodation Types

B&Bs These small, family-run houses provide good value. More luxurious versions are like boutique hotels.

Gîtes Limited to Réunion, these range from basic mountain lodges to more comfortable options. Great for budget travellers and those trekking the cirques.

Guesthouses The most personal option, these places are often family-run, offering simple rooms, but a warm welcome. In Mauritius, Rodrigues and Réunion many are called *chambres d'hôtes* (French equivalent of B&Bs).

Hotels & resorts The choice here is seemingly endless. Many resorts offer all-inclusive packages and a range of activities, spas and restaurants. Top-end resorts can be exclusive and spectacularly luxurious.

Meublés de Tourisme & Locations Saisonnières Rental houses in Réunion. A great choice for self-caterers.

Private island resorts These ultra-exclusive options fulfil desert-island fantasies, and the pampering on offer is legendary. All have an eco bent.

Self-catering accommodation or vacation rentals Self-catering villas or apartments can be excellent alternatives to hotels. Many are by the sea and range from basic to luxurious.

PRICE RANGES

The following price ranges refer to a double room with bathroom, but without breakfast.

€ less than €75

€€ €75–€150

€€€ more than €150

Best Places to Stay

Best on a Budget

Mauritius is perhaps the best destination for those seeking the tropics on a budget, with a choice of inexpensive guesthouses and self-catering apartments. For the mountains, Réunion has a great selection of B&Bs and walkers' lodges *(gîtes)*. For the Seychelles, your best bet is the island of La Digue.

➡ Sous Le Badamier (p71), Grand Baie

➡ Maison Papaye (p101), La Gaulette

➡ Matilona (p259), Ste-Rose

➡ Dan'n Tan Lontan (p249), St-Philippe

➡ La Cour Mont Vert (p241), St-Pierre

➡ Pension Michel (p311), La Digue

Best for Families

There are plenty of resorts in Mauritius that cater for families, with kids clubs and heaps of activities on the menu, while in Réunion families can take advantage of the *meublés de tourisme* and *saisonnières* (private houses/lodges and apartments) to rent for self-catering holidays. With the lack of cars, profusion of bicycles, child-friendly beaches and some self-catering options, La Digue is a great option in the Seychelles.

➡ Outrigger Mauritius Beach Resort (p116), Bel Ombre

➡ Le Saint Géran (p124), Belle Mare

➡ Senteur Vanille (p191), St-Gilles-les-Bains

➡ Les Lataniers (p203), Les Hauts de St-Leu

➡ La Maison de Rosalie (p260), Ste-Rose

➡ Anse Sévère Beach Villas (p314), La Digue

Best for Solo Travellers

Whether looking for somewhere social, quiet or away from honeymooners, there are plenty of options. Réunion's *gîtes* provide the sole dorm rooms, while some of the hotels and resorts in Mauritius and the Seychelles provide the ability both to hunker down in private or to join fellow guests in welcoming communal areas. On-site dining and activities are also widespread.

➡ Émeraude Beach Attitude (p125), Belle Mare

➡ La Belle Rodriguaise (p159), Rodrigues

➡ Esprit Libre (p72), Grande Baie

➡ Gîte de la Chapelle (p211), Cilaos

➡ La Villa de la Plage (p198), La Saline-les-Bains

➡ Le Nautique (p314), La Digue

Best for Private Island Escapes

With more than 150 islands making up the Seychelles, it's unsurprising that it's home to some of the world's best private island escapes. The most basic may lack TV, aircon, phones and a pool, but even these come with astoundingly beautiful beaches, a plethora of water-based activities and endless azure sea. The other end of the scale is barefoot luxury beyond measure.

➡ North Island (p318), North Island

➡ Fregate Island Private (p320), Frégate

➡ Six Senses Zil Pasyon (p320), Félicité

➡ Denis Private Island (p319), Denis

➡ Bird Island Lodge (p319), Bird Island

➡ Desroches Island Resort (p322), Desroches

Booking

It's wise to book well in advance, particularly for stays in July and August and from mid-December to mid-January. For the island of La Digue in the Seychelles, early reservations are crucial any time of the year. And if hiking in Réunion between September and November, it's imperative to book *gîtes* as early as possible.

Six Senses Zil Pasyon (p320), Félicité, Seychelles

Lonely Planet (lonelyplanet.com/hotels) Find independent reviews, as well as recommendations on the best places to stay – and then book them online.

Centrale d'Information et de Réservation Régionale – Île de la Réunion Tourisme (www.explorelareunion.com) Wide range of options from the official website in Réunion, and good for booking *gîtes de montagne*.

CG Villas (www.villas-maurice.com) Booking for villas and apartments in Mauritius.

Seychelles Bons Plans (www.seychellesbonsplans.com) A selection of well-run and well-priced establishments in the Seychelles.

Seychelles Travel (www.seychelles.travel) Has a list of accommodation options.

Seyvillas (www.seyvillas.com) Hotels and self-catering villas in the Seychelles, placing the accent on originality and authentic hospitality.

If You Like...

Beaches

Anse Marron, Seychelles A La Digue stunner backed by granite boulders and palm trees. (p307)

Anse Source d'Argent, Seychelles Another La Digue slice of paradise with perfect sand, stone and water. (p307)

Anse Lazio, Seychelles On Praslin and simply as gorgeous as you'll find in the Indian Ocean. (p298)

Anse Cocos, Seychelles Secluded and blissfully beautiful on La Digue. (p307)

Anse Soleil, Seychelles On the west coast of Mahé and somewhere close to heaven. (p294)

Le Morne & Tamarin, Mauritius Pretty beaches with dramatic mountainous backdrops in western Mauritius. (p83)

Trou d'Argent, Rodrigues Pick any beach on this island's east coast, but this cliff-surrounded cove is our favourite. (p155)

Plage de Grande Anse, Réunion Cliffs and white sand in the wild south of the island. (p239)

Plage de L'Hermitage, Réunion The longest and most appealing white-sand beach in Réunion. (p195)

Hiking

Piton de la Fournaise, Réunion Climb to the rim of an active volcano – a classic hike. (p229)

Haut Mafate, Réunion A four-day hike that takes you through some of the island's wildest cirques. (p224)

Bas Mafate, Réunion Four-day trek across the roof of Réunion. (p223)

Piton des Neiges, Réunion Ascend the island's highest summit and enjoy sensational views. (p211)

The Northeastern Coastal Walk, Rodrigues Lovely coastal walk from Graviers to St François past Rodrigues' best beaches. (p157)

Black River Gorges National Park, Mauritius Hiking trails through bird-rich wilderness and the island's last great forest. (p98)

Le Morne Peninsula, Mauritius A steep climb up Le Morne Brabant with extraordinary views and a soulful backstory. (p102)

Tea Factory to Morne Blanc, Seychelles Climb to the Seychelles' summit for superlative views. (p291)

Morne Seychellois National Park, Seychelles The Seychelles' best hiking. (p291)

Wildlife

Île aux Aigrettes, Mauritius An island Noah's ark where tortoises and pink pigeons live free. (p109)

Vallée de Ferney, Mauritius Go looking for the Mauritius kestrel, once the world's most endangered bird. (p105)

Grande Montagne Nature Reserve, Rodrigues A chance to pick up some of birding's biggest Indian Ocean prizes. (p155)

Curieuse Island, Seychelles A veritable Galápagos of giant Aldabra tortoises. (p305)

Vallée de Mai, Seychelles Birdlife, rich and endangered, in a forest filled with endemic trees. (p298)

Spectacular Landscapes

Piton de la Fournaise, Réunion The single most dramatic landform in the Indian Ocean, bar none. (p229)

Cirque de Cilaos, Réunion Perfect hiking country amid a landscape that reaches magnificently for the sky. (p207)

Cirque de Salazie, Réunion Another beguiling mountain kingdom. (p217)

Le Morne Peninsula, Mauritius
World Heritage Site with stunning beauty and a tragic story to match. (p102)

Black River Gorges National Park, Mauritius Waterfalls off the high plateau, dense forest and a deep river canyon. (p98)

Cap Malheureux, Mauritius The main island's northernmost tip has dramatic views out to the islands. (p80)

Silhouette, Seychelles The most dramatic island in the Seychelles archipelago. (p317)

Morne Seychellois National Park, Seychelles Stunning mountainous, forested crown on Mahé. (p290)

Romantic Getaways

North Island, Seychelles A mix of heavenly paradise, royal glamour and the last word in luxury. (p318)

Alphonse Island Resort, Seychelles Low-key resort on a remote island, with phenomenal fishing and diving. (p321)

Diana Dea Lodge & Spa, Réunion Get away from it all at this gem of a hotel hidden in the hills on the east coast. (p258)

Grand Bassin, Réunion As remote as it gets, a great place to decompress. (p228)

Le Saint Géran, Mauritius The ultimate in luxury with beach butlers, indulgent beauty treatments and glorious accommodation. (p124)

Le Prince Maurice, Mauritius There's something in the air at Belle Mare and this sublime complex is heavenly. (p124)

Lux Le Morne, Mauritius Luxury at every turn in the shadow of Mauritius' most beautiful mountain. (p103)

Top: Cap Malheureux (p80), Mauritius

Bottom: Aldabra giant tortoise, Curieuse Island (p305), Seychelles

Month by Month

January

Warm temperatures are guaranteed, but rain and even cyclones (in Mauritius and Réunion) are possibilities. Hotel prices soar over Christmas and New Year, but taper off after mid-January.

✨ Chinese New Year

Chinese New Year falls in late January or early February. On New Year's Eve homes are spring cleaned and decked in red, the colour of happiness. Firecrackers are *very* big here and Port Louis in particular crackles with noise and energy. Resorts often have themed dinners.

February

February weather is much like January. With the New Year peak past and the rest of the world no longer on holidays, crowds are rare.

✨ Maha Shivaratri

This massive February or March pilgrimage sees up to 500,000 Hindus make their way by all means possible to the holy lake of Grand Bassin, close to Black River Gorges National Park. The lake's waters are said to come from the sacred Ganges River. (p96)

March

March continues the trend of warm temperatures with possible rain. Chances of cyclones in Mauritius and Réunion is diminished. Festivals across the islands add plenty of local colour.

✗ Fish Festival

Rodrigues lives and breathes fish, and the Fête du Poisson, held in the first week of March, marks the opening of the fishing season. It is celebrated with all sorts of festivities, including fishing expeditions... and lots of eating. (p158)

✨ Holi Hindu

Holi, the festival of colours in Mauritius, is known for the exuberant throwing of coloured powder and water. The festival symbolises the victory of divine power over demonic strength. The night before Holi, bonfires are built to symbolise the destruction of the evil demon Holika.

April

If Easter falls in April, expect prices to peak and accommodation to fill. Otherwise, enjoy calm seas, great diving and low-season prices. April is typically the last month when cyclones affect weather patterns across Mauritius and Réunion.

✨ Tamil New Year

Wherever there are large Indian communities (Mauritius and Réunion), the Tamil New Year is marked with great gusto, with dance displays often forming the centrepiece of the celebrations. The New Year can ensure that things grind to a halt for a few days in predominantly Tamil areas.

May

Although this can change depending on the timing of French school holidays, May is generally a great time to visit – fewer tourists, moderate prices, milder temperatures and rain and wind are rarely a problem.

⭐ FetAfrik

The Seychelles is possibly the most African of the Indian Ocean islands, and it celebrates its African origins with FetAfrik, a weekend of music and dance in late May. It's one of the more exuberant festivals in the region.

June

June is generally low season and some hotels drop their prices. Winter has arrived, but not so you'd notice if you've arrived from Europe.

July

A fairly quiet month with relatively mild temperatures, little rain to speak of and lower hotel prices (unless French school holidays fall in July).

🏃 Rodrigues Kitesurfing

Some of the world's best kitesurfers descend on Rodrigues in late June or early July for the Rodrigues International Kitesurfing Festival, which has been running since 2013. (p157)

Top: Festival Kréol (p24)

Bottom: Maha Shivaratri

August

August is one of the driest months, and neither temperatures nor humidity reach the heights of later in the year. In Réunion it may even be cold in the Cirques and around the volcano. European school holidays often push prices upwards.

September

An extension of the Indian Ocean winter, September remains cooler and generally dry, although in the Seychelles temperatures are getting warmer and more humid, with rain being a possibility.

✹ Père Laval Feast Day

The most important date for many Mauritian Christians is 9 September, Père Laval Feast Day, which marks the anniversary of the priest's death. Pilgrims from around the world come to his shrine at Ste-Croix, on the outskirts of Port Louis, to pray for miracle cures. (p53)

October

Generally dry and calm, this is a great month to visit, particularly for hiking in Réunion. It's a month when visitor numbers and prices start to creep up everywhere.

✹ Divali

Both Mauritius and Réunion mark the Tamil festival of light Divali (Dipavali) in late October or early November. It celebrates the victory of Rama over the evil deity Ravana, and to mark this joyous event countless candles and lamps are lit to show Rama the way home from his period of exile.

✹ Festival Kréol

Creole culture comes to the fore in late October in the Seychelles, with the Festival Kréol's explosion of local cuisine, theatre, art, music, street processions and dance. The Festival Kréol in Rodrigues, however, takes place over three days in December and entails particularly vibrant traditional Creole ceremonies.

November

November is an especially good time to visit the islands, especially Mauritius and Réunion. The weather's warming up, the rains usually don't begin until later in the year and the crowds of December have yet to arrive.

December

The first half of December is much like November, although the rains can make an appearance to dampen things a little. As Christmas approaches, prices soar.

✹ Teemeedee

Teemeedee is a Hindu and Tamil fire-walking ceremony to honour various gods. Held throughout the year, most celebrations are in December and January when participants walk over red-hot embers scattered along the ground. Asking your hotel's staff can help you access this predominantly local affair.

✹ Christmas

Around one-quarter of Mauritius' population (and almost everyone in Rodrigues) is Christian (the Franco-Mauritians and predominantly Roman Catholic Creole population), and Christmas is an important celebration, both at a family level and publicly. Most resorts will put on some form of Christmas celebration (usually through food).

Itineraries

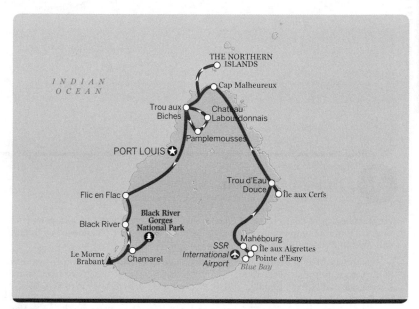

2 WEEKS Essential Mauritius

From the stunning coast of Mauritius' southeast to the dramatic mountain landscapes of the interior and southwest, you'll visit some of the country's prettiest islands, see stunning botanical gardens and explore Black River Gorges.

Start on the sands of **Pointe d'Esny**, snorkel the sparkling azure lagoon at **Blue Bay**, eco-explore **Île aux Aigrettes**, then slip up to sleepy **Mahébourg** for the Monday market. Drive north along the coast to embrace the fisherfolk lifestyle in **Trou d'Eau Douce**, then glide through the crystal lagoon to **Île aux Cerfs**. Pass through the sugar cane before emerging at gorgeous **Cap Malheureux**. In Grand Baie hop on a catamaran for the scenic **northern islands**, then treat yourself to a meal in **Trou aux Biches**. A day-trip loop then takes in the botanical gardens at **Pamplemousses** and lovely **Chateau Labourdonnais**.

Next is a spot of diving in **Flic en Flac**, then base yourself around **Black River** for hiking and canyoning in **Black River Gorges National Park**, mountain biking in **Chamarel** or climbing **Le Morne Brabant**.

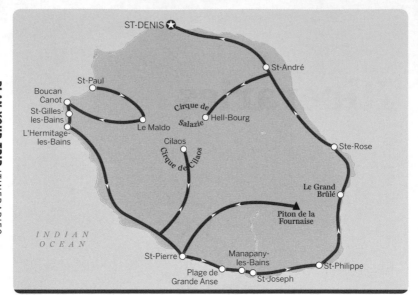

Tour of Réunion

From sophisticated beach resorts to mountain villages, art galleries to volcanoes, two weeks is a minimum to sample the variety Réunion has to offer. Get hooked on hiking and you could easily fill a month.

Kick things off in **St-Paul**, before heading inland to **Le Maïdo** for a bird's-eye view of the Cirque de Mafate. Then drive down to the coast for some beach action in **Boucan Canot**, one of Réunion's trendiest towns. A five-minute drive takes you to **St-Gilles-les-Bains**, a classic Indian Ocean resort with fine beaches and rowdy nightlife. The best beach to recover from it all is **L'Hermitage-les-Bains**. Allow three days to make the most of the area's botanical gardens, museums and water sports.

Next detour to **Cilaos** for at least two days to soak up the rugged mountain scenery and the laid-back atmosphere. Hiking and canyoning opportunities will immerse you in some unparalleled views, while there are also thermal springs, wine to taste and ecotourism possibilities. The bright lights of **St-Pierre** follow – if possible, get here for the huge Saturday market. From St-Pierre, it's a long but scenic drive up to Bourg-Murat, which is the launch pad for the **Piton de la Fournaise**, one of earth's most accessible volcanoes.

Return to St-Pierre and follow the RN2 that hugs along the scenic south coast. You may want to enjoy a picnic lunch at **Plage de Grande Anse** or unwind in **Manapany-les-Bains** before spending the night near **St-Joseph**. Proceeding east, you'll pass charmingly rural **St-Philippe** and the lunar landscapes of **Le Grand Brûlé** before reaching **Ste-Rose**, where hot lava once lapped at the door, narrowly missing the Virgin Mary.

As you head to the island's north, go inland and stay at least two nights in **Hell-Bourg**, exploring the Cirque de Salazie. Take in the Indian-influenced **St-André** before ending your trip sampling cafe culture and Creole architecture in the capital, **St-Denis**, which can also serve as a return to civilisation (without the clamour of a big city) if you've been climbing volcanoes and hiking the Cirques.

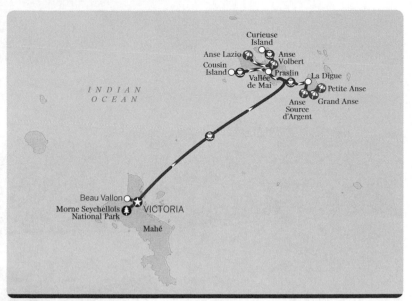

 Essential Seychelles

Two weeks is fine for a taster of the Seychelles' islands – allowing plenty of time for enjoying the very best of the country's superb beaches.

On the first day, tune into island life in the capital, **Victoria**, checking out the market and strolling among the palm trees in the botanical gardens. Move on to **Beau Vallon**, where three days can easily be spent messing around in and on the water. Devote the next two days to the beaches and byways of Mahé and to visiting the **Morne Seychellois National Park**, which has a little bit of everything: a colonial-era ruin, a tea factory and some fabulous hiking.

Next, cruise over to Praslin, which closely resembles paradise. Ogle curvaceous coco de mer nuts in the Unesco World Heritage–listed **Vallée de Mai**, hike amid massive palm fronds and then flake out on the perfect, sugar-white sands at **Anse Lazio**, one of the prettiest beaches we know. Fill the next four days with snorkelling, diving and swimming off **Anse Volbert**, getting up close and personal with giant tortoises on **Curieuse Island** – home to a large breeding farm of giant Aldabra tortoises – and walking among cacophonous clouds of seabirds on **Cousin Island**. With more than 300,000 birds and numerous endemic species – even amateur bird-watchers will want to spend more time here than most tours allow.

From Praslin, make sail for La Digue; if you thought Praslin was paradise, just wait until you lose yourself on La Digue. Three days is the perfect amount of time to lapse into the island's slow vibe. Visit **Anse Source d'Argent** – the archetypal idyllic beach, although it's by no means the only one on the island. Get there late afternoon for the best atmosphere and try to avoid high tide, when the beach all but disappears. Take a snorkelling trip around nearby islands, then find solitude on the beaches of **Grand Anse** and **Petite Anse**. Grand Anse is incredibly scenic and has a great restaurant, Loutier Coco, where you can enjoy a superb lunch buffet. Petite Anse, which is accessible on foot only, feels wilder and more secluded. All too soon, it will be time to tear yourself away for the trip back to Victoria.

Top: Curieuse Island
(p305), Seychelles

Bottom: Market in
Mahébourg (p104),
Mauritius

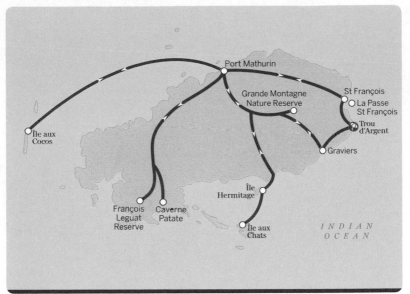

Rodrigues – The Other Mauritius

A week is ample time to discover the delights of this small, mountainous island. You can pass the days walking, diving and taking boat trips to nearby islands, as well as kicking back on the beach and indulging in seafood feasts at Rodrigues' great family-run restaurants.

First, spend half a day strolling the streets of **Port Mathurin** – make sure you come on a Saturday, when the island's endearingly sleepy 'capital' springs into life and it seems the entire population descends on the weekly market. Devote another day to two of the island's not-to-be-missed sights: the giant tortoises at **François Leguat Reserve** and the caves at **Caverne Patate**. Another day could be taken up by the classic coastal hike from **Graviers to St François**, passing en route a gem of a beach at **Trou d'Argent** – this is perhaps our favourite coastal walk anywhere in Mauritius. Linger over lunch at one of St François' excellent restaurants, then walk back the way you came or take a bus to Port Mathurin. Another day should be dedicated to the boat excursion to **Île aux Cocos**, with its quiet beaches and lively seabird colonies. Set aside a couple of hours on the same day for a hike in search of endangered species in the **Grande Montagne Nature Reserve**.

You're spoilt for choice when it comes to diving. Start your Rodrigues diving experience by exploring the channel off St François, **La Passe St François**, on the edge of the lagoon, with more options beyond the reefs. Follow up the diving with the good snorkelling around the little-visited **Île aux Chats and Île Hermitage** off the south coast – it's a bit less exciting than the dive, but a marvellous day trip nonetheless.

And of course, along the way you'll want to dedicate as much time as you can to simply kicking back on the beach for hours at a stretch and indulging in seafood feasts at the island's family-run restaurants scattered around the island. Perhaps reserve your spot at Graviers' La Belle Rodriguaise for lunch on your final day – it's an excellent choice to round off your week on Rodrigues.

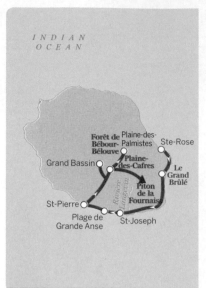

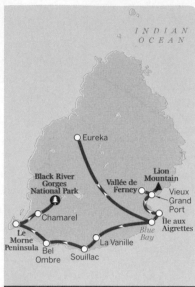

1 WEEK Réunion's Sud Sauvage & Hautes Plaines

Réunion's 'Wild South' and central plains offer volcanic landscapes, massive ravines, wave-lashed cliffs and sensational hiking trails. You can discover the best of the region in a reasonably leisurely week.

Start at **Ste-Rose** and head south to find the first tongues of lava tumbling down to the sea. Cross the threatening lava fields of **Le Grand Brûlé** to spend a night or two near **St-Joseph**; stay in the hills for a real taste of rural life. From here you can explore the picturesque **Rivière Langevin** valley – bring a picnic.

Continuing west, take a dip in **Plage de Grande Anse** before spending the night in **St-Pierre** and partying up at its buzzing nightlife. The next morning, head to the high plateau of **Plaine-des-Cafres** to visit the Cité du Volcan. Take the magnificent forest road up to **Piton de la Fournaise**, Réunion's restless volcano. Now drop back down to Plaine-des-Cafres, where you could spend a couple of days hiking to **Grand Bassin**, a village at the end of the world. Finally, head for **Plaine-des-Palmistes**, where the hikes through the **Forêt de Bébour-Bélouve** provide unforgettable experiences.

1 WEEK Southern Mauritius

The south of Mauritius offers the perfect combination of outstanding beaches and glorious natural scenery.

Blue Bay is everything its name suggests, and its proximity to a host of postcard-pretty landscapes makes it the perfect base for the island's southeast. Don't miss the excursion to **Île aux Aigrettes**, where you can spy pink pigeons and giant tortoises. Just north, **Vieux Grand Port** is where Mauritius' human story began centuries ago. The challenging but rewarding hike up **Lion Mountain** provides sweeping views of the bay. There's an untouched feel to the nearby forests of **Vallée de Ferney**, home to the iconic Mauritius kestrel, which you can see being fed most mornings. From your Blue Bay base, consider a day trip inland to **Eureka** in Moka.

Now head west, pausing at **La Vanille** in Rivière des Anguilles, then in **Souillac** and **Bel Ombre** to enjoy the pretty coast. Continue on to **Le Morne**, where dramatic hiking trails await. Climb into the hills to **Chamarel**, with its terrific eating scene and rum distillery – it's the perfect base for scenic drives and hikes through **Black River Gorges National Park**.

Plan Your Trip
Diving

Though largely overshadowed by the iconic Maldives, scuba diving in Mauritius, Réunion and the Seychelles is increasingly popular. Beneath the clear turquoise waters is a trove of unbelievable riches: rainbow-coloured fish and large pelagic species (yes, sharks are part of the package), a dramatic seascape and a host of drop-offs and reefs. It's not the cheapest place on earth to dive (Thailand or the Red Sea it ain't), but it's a great place to learn, and in turn love, scuba diving. Good news: bar a few areas, the dive sites are never crowded.

Mauritius

So you want variety? Abundant marine life, dramatic seascapes, atmospheric wrecks – Mauritius has it all, not to mention well-established, high-quality dive operators. Mauritius is almost entirely surrounded by a barrier reef, creating turquoise lagoons that provide great possibilities for snorkellers, swimmers and novice divers. And then there's the pièce de résistance: Rodrigues, which has virgin sites and outstanding fish life.

Where to Dive
North

The north coast is a magnet for divers of all levels, and it's no wonder: there's a good combination of thrilling dives, wrecks, drop-offs and easy dives.

The islands off the coast (Île Plate, Coin de Mire) are the main highlights, with splendid sites and diverse marine life – not to mention a sense of wilderness. To the northwest, Trou aux Biches is the main jumping-off point for a variety of superb dives.

La Fosse aux Requins (Map p66) Iconic site famous for its congregations of blacktip reef sharks.

The Wall (Map p66) Dramatic underwater cliff.

Best Dives for...

Wrecks
Stella Maru (Mauritius)

Kei Sei 113 (Mauritius)

Antonio Lorenzo (Réunion)

Aldebaran (Seychelles)

Beginners
Tug II (Mauritius)

Le Jardin des Kiosques (Réunion)

Anse Sévère (Seychelles)

Experienced Divers
Manioc (Mauritius)

Shark Bank (Seychelles)

Haï Siang (Réunion)

Tombant de la Pointe aux Canonniers (Mauritius)

THE FIRST TIME

You've always fancied venturing underwater on scuba? Now's your chance. Mauritius, Réunion and the Seychelles are perfect starting points for new divers, as the warm waters and shallow reefs are a forgiving training environment. Most dive centres offer courses for beginners and employ experienced instructors.

Just about anyone in reasonably good health can sign up for an introductory dive, including children aged eight and over. It typically takes place in shallow (3m to 5m) water and lasts about 30 minutes, escorted by a divemaster.

If you choose to enrol in an Open Water course, count on it taking about four days, including a few classroom lectures and Open Water training. Once you're certified, your C-card is valid permanently and recognised all over the world.

Djabeda (Map p66) Atmospheric wreck dive.

Holt's Rock (Map p72) Domes and boulders in 25m of water.

Tombant de la Pointe aux Canonniers (Map p72) Has an exhilarating drop-off to about 60m.

Kingfish (Map p72) Drift diving down to 28m.

Waterlily & Emily (Map p68) Good wreck diving for beginners.

Stella Maru (Map p68) A not-to-be-missed wreck in 25m of water.

West

The Flic en Flac area ranks among the best in Mauritius for diving. Conditions are optimal year-round – it's protected from the prevailing winds – and visibility is usually excellent.

Along the southwest coast, the area between Le Morne Peninsula and Black River (Rivière Noire) has a few diving hotspots, but they lack the wow factor, with average visibility and fairly dull topography.

Rempart Serpent (Snake Rampart; Map p88000) Sinuous rock in 25m, attracting a huge number of fish.

La Cathédrale (p85) A scenic, memorable seascape.

Couline Bambou (Map p88) Less crowded than La Cathédrale; a kaleidoscope of changing scenery.

Manioc (Map p88) A deep, atmospheric dive beloved by seasoned divers.

Kei Sei 113 (Map p88) Good wreck diving for experienced divers.

Tug II (Map p84) Good wreck diving with brilliant fish life.

Passe St Jacques (Map p84) One of Mauritius' best drift-dive sites, with depths of 3m to 30m.

Southeast

Off the southeast coast it's the dramatic underwater terrain that impresses more than anything, making for unique profiles. You'll be rewarded with a profusion of caves, tunnels and giant arches – it's very scenic – as well as large numbers of pelagics thrown in for good measure. The hitch? From June to August most sites are exposed to the prevailing winds – expect choppy seas in rough weather.

Colorado (Map p116) A 400m-long canyon pocked with chasms and crevices.

Roches Zozo (Map p116) Like Colorado, which it's close to, this is another must-dive site.

Grotte Langouste (Map p116) A cave brimming with lobsters.

Sirius (Map p116) Great for wreck buffs.

Blue Bay (p110) A safe, lovely spot to learn to dive, with a parade of reef fish to be observed.

East

The east is not known for its diving, but there are two standout sites if you don't fancy a trip elsewhere on the island.

Belmar Pass (Map p122) Stunning seascapes and a good chance to see grey reef or bull sharks because of the strong currents.

Passe de Trou d'Eau Douce (Map p122) Worth visiting, though less spectacular than Belmar.

Rodrigues

This is the Indian Ocean at its best. A true gem, Rodrigues boasts numerous untouched sites for those willing to experience something different. There's a profusion of coral that you won't see anywhere else in Mauritius, and the density of fish life is astounding. The underwater scenery is another pull, with a smorgasbord of canyons, arches and caves.

La Passe St François (Map p152) A 1km-long channel down to 30m, offering the full gamut of reef species.

Le Canyon (Map p152) A truly atmospheric site: a canyon that runs under the reef.

La Basilique (The Basilica; Map p152) Tunnels, caves and some fabulous underwater topography.

Karlanne (Map p152) Dense marine life and healthy coral formations.

La Grande Passe (Map p152) Considered by many dive instructors to be among the best medium-depth reefs in the area.

Practicalities

Diving Conditions

Although Mauritius is diveable year-round, the most favourable periods are October to December, March and April (January and February are peak months for cyclone activity). During July and August, when the southeastern trade winds are at their strongest, the seas are too rough and murky for diving all along the south and east coasts and around Rodrigues. Visibility is heavily dependent on weather and thus varies a lot – from a low of 10m at certain sites at certain periods to 40m at others.

Current conditions vary greatly, from imperceptible to powerful. Water temperatures range from a low of 22°C in August to a high of 28°C between December and February.

Dive Operators

There are at least 40 professional dive centres in Mauritius. Most belong to the **Mauritius Scuba Diving Association** (MSDA; ☑454 0011; www.msda.mu), which is affiliated with the Confédération Mondiale des Activités Subaquatiques (CMAS) and makes regular and rigorous checks. Most dive centres are also affiliated with one or more of the internationally recognised certifying agencies, usually the Professional Association of Diving Instructors (PADI) or CMAS.

Many dive centres in Mauritius are hotel-based, but all welcome walk-in clients. In general you can expect well-maintained equipment, good facilities and professional staff, but standards may vary from one centre to another, so it pays to shop around.

PLAN YOUR TRIP DIVING

SNORKELLING

If the idea of total immersion doesn't appeal to you, snorkelling is also possible in Mauritius, Réunion and the Seychelles. It's a great way to explore the underwater world with minimal equipment and without the costs associated with diving. Even the shallowest reefs are home to many colourful critters. In all three destinations, rental gear is widely available from dive centres.

Mauritius

Top snorkelling spots include the marine park at Blue Bay and along the west coast off Flic en Flac and Trou aux Biches, not forgetting the lagoon around Rodrigues.

Réunion

The lagoon along the west coast between St-Gilles-les-Bains and La Saline-les-Bains offers great snorkelling, with particularly good marine life off L'Hermitage-les-Bains. Take advice before leaping in as the currents can be dangerous and stick to supervised areas.

Seychelles

The sheltered lagoons provide safe havens for swimming and snorkelling. The Ste-Anne and Port Launay Marine National Parks are firm favourites in the waters around Mahé. In September and October you have a chance to snorkel respectfully alongside whale sharks. Around Praslin, try just off Anse Lazio and Anse Volbert beaches, or take a boat trip from Anse Volbert to Curieuse Island or St Pierre Islet. Close to La Digue, the submerged granite boulders around Cocos, Grande Soeur and Marianne islands teem with fish life.

Réunion

Who said that diving in Réunion wasn't interesting? OK, the island is mostly famous for its trekking, but its dive sites are nothing to sneeze at. You'll be positively surprised: there's a wide choice of shallow dives inside the lagoon for novices and deeper dives (mostly 25m to 40m) just outside for more experienced divers, as well as a few purpose-sunk wrecks thrown in for good measure.

Where to Dive

Most dive sites are located off the west coast between Boucan Canot and St-Pierre.

St-Gilles-les-Bains

If you want relaxed diving, St-Gilles will appeal to you. Diving here is focused on the reefs, which slope gently away in a series of valleys to a sandy bottom in about 25m – very reassuring. Pelagics are rare, but small reef species are prolific.

Tour de Boucan (Map p186) A fantastic site suitable for all levels. Super underwater terrain, with a massive boulder that provides shelter to numerous species.

Le Pain de Sucre (Map p186) The setting is the strong point, with a contoured terrain and lots of small critters in the recesses (damselfish, parrotfish, triggerfish, lobsters), as well as a few seafans. Great for beginners.

Petites Gorgones (Map p186) Also known as Saliba, this is an easy site suitable for all levels. Keep an eye out for leaf scorpion fish and turtles.

La Passe de L'Hermitage (Map p195) An exciting dive. The terrain is nicely sculpted, with little canyons and large boulders that act as magnets for a wealth of species. Sadly, visibility is often reduced.

Haï Siang (Map p186) With a maximum depth of 55m, this atmospheric wreck is accessible to very experienced divers only. Fish life is scarce.

Navarra (Map p186) This wreck is not in good shape but it acts as a magnet for lots of reef species. The catch? It lies in 55m of water and is accessible to experienced divers only.

La Barge (Map p186) Off St-Paul, a relaxing wreck dive in less than 22m. The wreck is not in good shape but it's home to plenty of small fish. Beginners will love it!

St-Leu

St-Leu features splendid wall diving and good coral fields, but fish life is said to be less abundant than off St-Gilles-les-Bains. Here walls tumble steeply to several dozen metres.

Tombant de la Pointe au Sel (Map p186) South of St-Leu, this is widely regarded as Réunion's best all-round dive site. In addition to great scenery, this stunning drop-off offers a fabulous array of fish life and seldom fails to produce good sightings of pelagics, especially tuna, barracudas and jacks. Suitable for experienced divers.

Le Jardin des Kiosques (Map p200) With a depth ranging from 3m to 18m, it's very secure yet atmospheric for beginners. It's all about little canyons and grooves.

La Maison Verte (Map p200) A relaxing site, blessed with good coral formations in less than 6m.

Antonio Lorenzo (Map p186) Wreck enthusiasts will make a beeline for this well-preserved vessel that rests in about 38m on a sandy bottom off Pointe des Chateaux. Fish life is dynamic, and penetration in the hull is possible.

St-Pierre

Savvy divers, this area is for you. This area is unhyped and that's why we enjoy it so much. There are a host of untouched sites between St-Pierre and Grand Bois. The main drawcard is the topography, with numerous ridges, canyons and drop-offs.

Les Ancres & Le Tombant aux Ancres (Map p240) A sloping reef festooned by healthy coral formations. You'll also see some old anchors dotted around the reef.

Demhotel (Map p240) A lovely dive off Grand Bois along a contoured plateau with plenty of protruding basaltic formations and arches. Fish life is usually dense.

Practicalities
Diving Conditions

While it is possible to dive all year, the best time is October to April, when the water is at its warmest (about 28°C). However, you might want to avoid February and March, which is cyclone season. Water temperatures can drop to about 21°C in August.

WHAT YOU'LL SEE

Let's be honest: the western Indian Ocean is not the richest marine realm in the world – some parts of the Caribbean, the South Pacific and the Red Sea boast more prolific fish life. But it's far from being poor – in fact, it has everything from tiny nudibranchs (sea slugs) to huge whale sharks.

Reef Fishes

Like technicolour critters? You'll encounter a dizzying array of species darting around the reef, including clownfish, parrotfish, angelfish, emperor fish, butterflyfish and various types of grouper. Moray eels are also frequently encountered.

Pelagics

Pelagic fish – larger beasts that live in the open sea, such as tuna and barracuda – sometimes cruise quite close to the reef in search of prey. Of the shark species inhabiting these waters, the most common are the whitetip reef shark, the hammerhead shark and the reasonably docile nurse shark. Whale sharks are also regularly encountered.

Rays

The most common species of ray found around the Seychelles and Mauritius is the manta ray. One of the larger stingray species, often encountered at Shark Bank off Mahé, is the round ribbontail ray. It can grow up to 2m across. The blue-spotted stingray is quite common in the sandy areas between the granite boulders of the Seychelles.

Turtles

The best place to see turtles in the wild is the Seychelles, which has a number of important breeding grounds for hawksbill and green turtles.

Coral

Coral is not the strongest point here. The Indian Ocean's shallow-water reefs were badly hit by coral bleaching in 1997 and '98. In parts of the Seychelles, up to 90% of hard corals (the reef-building corals) were wiped out. They're still struggling, but there are encouraging signs of new growth.

Dive Operators

The dive centres are concentrated around St-Gilles-les-Bains, St-Leu, Étang-Salé-les-Bains and St-Pierre. The standard of diving facilities is high. You'll find professional dive centres staffed with qualified instructors catering to divers of all levels. Staff members usually speak English. Most dive centres are affiliated with PADI, Scuba Schools International (SSI) or CMAS – all internationally recognised dive organisations.

Take note that a simple medical certificate stating you are fit enough to dive is compulsory for diving in France. You can get one from your doctor in your home country or have it faxed or emailed to the dive centre. Otherwise, you can get one from any doctor in Réunion.

Seychelles

Billed as one of the Indian Ocean's great diving destinations, the Seychelles almost rivals the Maldives, though it's much less hyped – all the better for you. You don't need to be a strong diver – there are sites for all levels and plenty of places to learn.

There's excellent diving off Mahé, Praslin and La Digue, the three main islands, as well as off the other inner and outer islands. The strong point is the underwater scenery, complete with big granite boulders and seamounts – it's as atmospheric as on land.

Top: Brissare Rocks, Mahé, Seychelles

Bottom: Hawksbill turtle, Seychelles

Where to Dive

Mahé

Shark Bank (Map p278) Mahé's signature dive, for experienced divers only. The name is misleading, because there are very few sharks around this 30m-tall granite plateau 9km off Beau Vallon. Instead, you'll encounter round ribbontail rays the size of a small car, eagle rays, barracuda, batfish, and abundant yellow snappers and bigeyes. This site nearly always has a strong current.

Îlot (Map p278) This granite outcrop, just off north Mahé, consists of several large boulders topped by a tuft of palm trees. The current in the channel can be quite strong, but the cluster of boulders yields one of the highest densities of fish life in the Seychelles. Golden-cup coral festoons the canyons and gullies, and gorgonians and other soft corals abound. Îlot is about a 15-minute boat ride from Beau Vallon.

Brissare Rocks (Map p276) About 5km north of Mahé, this granite pinnacle is accessed from Beau Vallon. The site features abundant fire coral and great concentrations of yellow snappers, wrasses, parrotfish and fusiliers, as well as groupers and eagle rays. It's covered with bright-orange sponges and white gorgonians.

Twin Barges (Map p287) If you need a break from offshore dives, these two adjoining shipwrecks will keep you happy. They sit upright on the seabed in about 20m in Beau Vallon bay.

Aldebaran (Map p278) This boat was scuttled in 2010 off Anse Major; the maximum depth is 40m. It shelters moray eels, groupers and rays.

Alice in Wonderland (Map p280) Famous for its healthy coral formations. Off Anse à la Mouche.

Jailhouse Rock (Map p280) A high-voltage drift dive for experienced divers, with prolific fish life. Off Pointe Lazare.

Shark Point (Map p280) Whitetip reef sharks, nurse sharks and grey reef sharks are commonly sighted here. Off Pointe Lazare.

Praslin & La Digue

Aride Bank Off Aride Island, this pristine site can be accessed from Praslin if you don't mind the 30-minute boat trip to get to the site. A hot fave among local divemasters, it features rays, snappers, nurse sharks, jacks, barracudas and Napoleon wrasses as well as magnificent seafans.

Booby Islet (Map p300) Approximately halfway between Aride Island and Praslin, this exposed seamount consistently sizzles with fish action.

In less than 20m of water, you'll come across parrotfish, Napoleon wrasses, moray eels, turtles, eagle rays and nurse sharks.

Anse Sévère (Map p309) An easy site, close to the shore of La Digue with potential sightings including parrotfish, eagle rays and turtles. Good for drift dives.

Cousin (Map p300) An easy site in the waters off Cousin Island.

Marianne Island An islet east of La Digue famous for its dense fish life (including grey sharks, stingrays, barracudas, eagle rays, nurse sharks and moray eels) and contoured seascape.

White Bank Stunning seascape (tunnels, arches) and prolific fish life, including shoals of jacks and the occasional whitetip shark.

Ave Maria Rocks A seamount northwest of La Digue. Noted for its shark sightings and Napoleon wrasses.

Other Inner Islands & Outer Islands

The private islands of Frégate, North, Silhouette and Denis offer fantastic, but expensive, diving options, with absolutely pristine sites and only one dive boat: yours. One step beyond, you'll find Aldabra, Cosmoledo and Astove, the stuff of legend. They feature the best sites in the eastern Indian Ocean, with electric fish action in a totally virgin territory and high-voltage drift dives. The catch? They are not accessible because of piracy in the area.

Napoleon (Alphonse Group) One of Alphonse's iconic dives, Napoleon is always full of action. You're sure to see Napoleon wrasses, giant sweetlips, snappers, skipjack tuna, huge turtles, bluefin trevallies, barracudas and triggerfish in less than 20m. The seascape is incredibly scenic, with a clutch of massive coral pinnacles dotted on a vast plateau.

The Abyss (Alphonse Group) This scenic stretch of reef is peppered with ledges and overhangs that are coated with photogenic coral formations and seafans. You'll come across oriental sweetlips, spotted eagle rays, turtles, giant groupers and dogtooth tuna.

The Arcade (Alphonse Group) One of Alphonse's most magical dives, the Arcade is known for its sheer abundance of underwater life and healthy coral gardens. Divers are bedazzled by the incredible variety of fish, including shoals of giant sweetlips and fusiliers, bigeye and bluefin trevallies, batfish, snappers, triggerfish and pufferfish. Huge sea turtles are also frequently seen in the area.

MARINE CONSERVATION

The main pressures on the marine environment are pollution, over-exploitation and inappropriate activities such as the use of drag anchors and explosives for fishing. In recent years Mauritius, Réunion and the Seychelles have introduced laws banning destructive practices, such as shell and coral collection, shark finning and spearfishing. Each has also established marine reserves to protect at least some of their coral reefs. If you're interested in helping, there are good volunteering opportunities, especially in Mauritius (p146) and the Seychelles (p331).

The Pinnacles (Alphonse Group) This site consistently sizzles with fish action. Here the reef plunges into an incredible abyss along a steep slope decorated with large seafans, but you don't need to go deep: frequently observed in less than 25m are anthias, blue-striped and two-spotted snappers, honeycombed moray eels, groupers, bluefin trevallies and even silvertip sharks.

Morane A 50-minute boat ride from Silhouette, Morane features an array of boulders dotted around a sandy floor in about 20m. It's an oasis of life, with huge stingrays, eagle rays, manta rays, scorpionfish, trevallies and lionfish, among others. Because of strong currents, this site is suitable for experienced divers only. Well worth the lengthy boat ride.

Sprat City This atmospheric dive site centres on a large reef north of Silhouette. It acts as a magnet for all sorts of fish life, including barracudas, wahoos, fusiliers and batfish, and is overgrown with various species of coral. During the southeast monsoon, it's famous for its incredible concentration of sprats.

Turtle Rock (Map p317) Just off the northeastern tip of Silhouette, Turtle Rock features a series of atmospheric coral formations at around 10m. Keep your eyes peeled for eagle rays, barracudas, trevallies, fusiliers and green turtles.

Barracuda Rock The underwater scenery is the main draw here, with a profusion of small caves, arches and fissures. They shelter hosts of small, colourful fish that provide photographers with great opportunities in clear water. Eagle rays, tuna, giant trevallies, nurse sharks and stingrays can also be spotted.

Lion Rock Frégate's signature dive, Lion Rock is a tiny islet visible from the main island. The varied underwater terrain acts as a magnet for a host of species, including nurse sharks, eagle rays, lionfish and lobsters. Bull sharks and tiger sharks also regularly patrol the area.

Îlot Frégate Famous for its astoundingly dense fish life and its varied underwater terrain (at 5m to 15m).

Practicalities

Diving Conditions

Diving in the Seychelles heavily hinges on the weather conditions, currents and direction of the wind. However, diving can be sampled during all seasons as there are always sheltered conditions. The seas are calmest from April to May and October to November. Due to currents and wind, visibility is temperamental and can drop to 5m. But in normal conditions you can expect 25m visibility.

Dive Operators

The Seychelles' 15-odd dive centres have first-rate personnel and facilities. You'll find dive centres in Mahé, Praslin, La Digue, Ste-Anne, Silhouette, Frégate, Denis, North and Alphonse. Most centres are affiliated with PADI.

Piton de la Fournaise (p229), Réunion

Plan Your Trip

Hiking in Réunion

Hiking is the very best of what Réunion has to offer. Formed from one mighty dead volcano (Piton des Neiges) and one active volcano (Piton de la Fournaise), the island is a paradise for hikers, adventure-sports enthusiasts or indeed anyone who is receptive to the untamed beauty of a wilderness environment.

Hiking Tips

Safety is basically a matter of common sense and being prepared.

Before You Leave

➡ Get a detailed and up-to-date map (or GPS).

➡ Double-check the state of the paths before setting out.

➡ Check the weather report.

➡ Tell someone where you're going.

➡ Leave early enough to reach your destination before dark.

Take Along

➡ Comfortable hiking boots.

➡ Wet-weather gear.

➡ Plenty of water and energy-rich snacks.

➡ A basic medical kit.

When to Hike

The best time to hike is during the dry season, from around late April to the end of October. May and June, as well as September and October, are probably the best months of all. July and August are a bit chilly, and during the rainy months (December to March) a number of paths are not accessible. The weather is extremely changeable from one part of this small island to the other.

The weather in Réunion has a tendency to become worse as the day goes on. As the hours pass, the island's uplands seem to delight in 'trapping' any cloud that happens to come their way. An early start is therefore one of the best defences against the vagaries of the elements.

The next day's weather forecast is shown on the two main TV channels after the evening news. You can also get the forecast by telephoning the Météo France voice service on ☎0892 68 02 00 (per minute €0.35). Cyclone bulletins are available on ☎0897 65 01 01 (€0.60 per call). Both these services are in French. Also check out the website www.meteofrance.re.

What to Bring

Good shoes are essential for hiking the trails of Réunion, which are made of gravel and stone and are often very steep, muddy or slippery.

Be sure to carry water (at least 2L for a day's hiking), wet-weather gear, a warm top, a hat, sunscreen, sunglasses, insect repellent, a whistle, a torch and a basic medical kit including plasters, elastic bandages and muscle balm for blisters and minor muscle injuries. The *gîtes* (lodges) provide sheets and blankets (but no towels), but if you intend on sleeping out at altitude, you'll need a decent sleeping bag, as temperatures in the Cirques can fall rapidly at night.

In most places to stay and places to eat, payment will be expected in cash, so bring a stash of euros with you. The only places to get euros in the Cirques are the ATMs at the post offices in Salazie, Hell-Bourg and Cilaos, and these can't be depended on.

You will be able to buy most last-minute supplies at a sporting-goods store or one of the big supermarkets in Cilaos or elsewhere in Réunion.

Hiking Trails

There are countless trails in Réunion, with two major 'official' hiking trails, known as Grande Randonnée® Route 1 (GR® R1) and Grande Randonnée® Route 2 (GR® R2), with numerous offshoots. The GR® R1 does a tour of Piton des Neiges, passing through Cilaos, the Forêt de Bébour-Bélouve, Hell-Bourg and the Cirque de Mafate. The GR® R2 makes an epic traverse of the island all the way from St-Denis to St-Philippe via the three Cirques, the Plaine-des-Cafres and Piton de la Fournaise. A third trail, the Grande Randonnée® Route 3 (GR® R3), does a tour of Cirque de Mafate and overlaps with some sections of the GR® R1 and GR® R2.

You don't need to follow these trails entirely – your best bet is to tweak your own itinerary, combining various trails and variants according to your time constraints, level of fitness and own interests. Three great sample hiking itineraries include the Haut Mafate (p43), the Bas Mafate (p45) and the Tour des Cirques (p46).

The trails are well maintained, but the tropical rainfall can eat through footpaths and wash away steps and handrails. Even experienced hikers should be prepared for tortuous ascents, slippery mud chutes and narrow paths beside sheer precipices. The routes are well signposted on the whole, but it's essential to carry a good map or GPS and you should check locally on the current situation; trails are occasionally closed for maintenance, especially following severe storms.

Information

Hiking information is provided by the Plateforme de Réservation – Île de la Réunion (p224) and by associated tourist offices, including those in Cilaos, Salazie, Hell-Bourg, Ste-Suzanne, St-Gilles-les-Bains, St-Pierre, St-Leu, Plaine-des-Palmistes, Ste-Anne, St-Joseph and Bourg-Murat. All these offices organise bookings for *gîtes d'étape et de randonnée* (walkers' lodges) and can give advice on which paths are currently closed.

The official tourism website (www.reunion.fr) is by far the most useful website for hikers. It allows you to book your accommodation online. The websites www.randopitons.re and http://randotectec.reunion-parcnational.fr are also helpful.

For information on *état des sentiers* (closed trails) check the website www.onf.fr/la-reunion/sommaire/loisirs_en_foret/randonner/organiser.

The **Fédération Française de la Randonnée Pédestre** (FFRandonnée; www.ffrandonnee.fr) is responsible for the development and upkeep of the GR® walking tracks.

The definitive guide to the GR® R1, GR® R2 and GR® R3 is the TopoGuides GR® Grande Randonnée *L'Île de la Réunion* (2018), published by the FFRandonnée. It uses 1:25,000 scale IGN maps and details the itineraries. The GR® R1 is described in six *étapes* (stages), the GR® R2 in 12 stages and the GR® R3 in five stages.

The FFRandonnée also publishes the TopoGuide PR® *Sentiers forestiers de L'Île de la Réunion* (2011), which covers 25 walks varying from one-hour jaunts to six-hour hikes.

Published locally by Orphie, *52 Balades et Randonnées Faciles* is designed with

Cirque de Mafate (p223), Réunion

children in mind and describes outings that can be covered in less than four hours. A broader range of walks is covered by *62 Randonnées Réunionnaises* (also by Orphie).

Maps

Réunion is covered by the six 1:25,000 scale maps published by the Institut Géographique National (www.ign.fr). These maps are reasonably up to date and show trails and *gîtes*. Map number 4402 RT is one of the most useful for hikers, since it covers Cirque de Mafate and Cirque de Salazie as well as the northern part of the Cirque de Cilaos.

Tours & Guides

Réunion's hiking trails are well established and reasonably well signposted, but you may get more information about the environment you are walking through if you go with a local guide.

Fully qualified mountain guides can be contacted through the local tourist offices.

Cirque de Cilaos (p207), Réunion

Rates are negotiable and vary according to the length and degree of difficulty of the hike; an undemanding one-day tour should start at around €50 per person (minimum four people).

Aparksa Montagne (p210)

Kokapat Rando (☑0262 33 30 14, 0692 69 94 14; www.kokapatrando-reunion.com; tours from €50)

Réunion Mer et Montagne (☑0692 83 38 68; www.reunionmeretmontagne.com)

Run Evasion (p211)

Sleeping & Eating

Most of the accommodation for hikers consists of *gîtes de montagne* (mostly found in isolated locations on the trails themselves) or privately run *gîtes d'étape* along the walking trails. Both offer dorm beds of varying levels of comfort and, increasingly, doubles (sometimes with private facilities). They also provide meals. Almost all *gîtes* provide hot showers (they're solar heated). A third option consists of small, family-run *chambres d'hôtes* (mostly found in the vil-

lages at the ends of the hiking trails). Your choice of where to stay will most likely be based on where you can find a room. There are also a few hotels in Hell-Bourg and Cilaos for that last night of luxury (and central heating) before you set out on your hike.

One night's accommodation without food costs between €16 and €18. For half board, budget around €45 per person.

You can also camp for free in some areas in the Cirques, but only for one night at a time. Setting up camp on Piton de la Fournaise (the volcano) is forbidden for obvious reasons.

Most *gîtes* offer Creole meals, which are normally hearty, though a little rustic for some palates. The standard fare is *carri poulet* (chicken curry), *boucané* (smoked pork) or *rougail saucisses* (sausage with spices and rice), often with local wine or *rhum arrangé* (rum punch) thrown in. Breakfast usually consists of just a cup of coffee with *biscottes* (rusks) – or, if you're lucky, bread – and jam.

If you plan to self-cater, you will need to bring plenty of carbohydrate-rich food. Note that only a few *gîtes* are equipped with cooking facilities; better to bring a camping stove. Bear in mind that you are not allowed to light fires anywhere in the forest areas. Some villages in the Cirques have shops where you can purchase a very limited variety of food.

Bookings

Book your accommodation before arriving in Réunion, especially during the busiest months (July, August, October, November and around Christmas). At other times it's best to book at least a couple of months in advance, particularly for popular places such as the *gîtes* at Caverne Dufour (for Piton des Neiges) and Piton de la Fournaise.

Some *gîtes de montagne* are managed by the Plateforme de Réservation – Île de la Réunion (p224) and must be booked and paid for in advance. This can be done through the website or at tourist offices. When you pay, you will receive a voucher to be given to the manager of the *gîte* where you will be staying. You must call the *gîte* to book your meals at least one day in advance; this can be done at the same time as the original booking if you'd rather, but meals still have to be paid for on the spot.

For the privately owned *gîtes*, things are less restrictive in terms of logistics; you can book directly through the *gîte*.

Best Multiday Hikes
The Haut Mafate

Hiking in the Haut Mafate is truly stupendous, with a vast network of well-maintained trails, which allows you to build your own itinerary. The most popular route consists of completing a four-day loop that takes in the hamlets of La Nouvelle, Roche-Plate and Marla, but, if your time is limited, you can simply spend a day in the Haut Mafate, in La Nouvelle (and Marla). From the Haut Mafate it's also easy to rejoin the hamlets of the Bas Mafate.

IGN's 1:25,000 topographic map 4402 RT covers the area.

Itinerary

Day one (two hours, 100m ascent, 520m descent) is a breeze. The trail to La Nouvelle starts at the car park below Col des

---

> ### EMERGENCIES
> In a real emergency out on the trail, lifting both arms to form a 'V' is a signal to helicopter pilots who fly over the island that you need help. If you have a mobile phone, call the emergency services on ☎112.

Bœufs, from where you'll get your first glimpse of the Cirque de Mafate. Ahead, the trail plunges steeply to the forested Plaine des Tamarins. Follow the path signposted to La Nouvelle (the other branch heads south to Marla), which meanders through the forest in a fairly leisurely fashion before dropping rapidly to the village of La Nouvelle.

Day two (about three hours, 450m ascent, 795m descent) is a bit more energetic. The trail to Grand Place, Cayenne and Roche-Plate via Le Bronchard turns downhill just after the La Nouvelle chapel and heads into the maize fields before plummeting into the valley of the Rivière des Galets. This steep and often treacherous descent is not for the faint-hearted, though reassuring handrails are provided for some of the steeper sections. An exhilarating two hours or so will get you to Fond de Mafate (the bottom of the Cirque), where you can take a well-deserved splash in the river. Then starts the arduous ascent up the far side of the valley. When you reach the white metal cross at Le Bronchard after roughly one hour from the floor of the valley, the worst is over. The final stretch descends slowly down to the village of Roche-Plate (count on about 15 minutes). The village of Roche-Plate sits at the foot of the majestic Le Maïdo (2205m).

Day three (five hours, 900m ascent, 370m descent), which will get you to Marla via Trois Roches, is the most demanding.

> ### THE HAUT MAFATE HIKE AT A GLANCE
> **Duration** Four days
>
> **Distance** 20.4km
>
> **Difficulty** Moderate
>
> **Start/finish** Col des Bœufs car park
>
> **Nearest town** Grand Îlet

Top: Piton des Neiges (p211), Réunion

Bottom: Hiker on Réunion

ECOWALKING

To help preserve the ecology and beauty of Réunion, consider these tips when hiking.

Rubbish

➡ Carry out all your rubbish. Don't overlook easily forgotten items, such as silver paper, orange peel, cigarette butts and plastic wrappers. Empty packaging should be stored in a dedicated rubbish bag.

➡ Never bury your rubbish: digging disturbs soil and ground cover and encourages erosion. Buried rubbish will likely be dug up by animals, who may be injured or poisoned by it.

➡ Minimise waste by taking minimal packaging and no more food than you will need. Take reusable containers or stuff sacks.

➡ Sanitary products, condoms and toilet paper should be carried out despite the inconvenience. They burn and decompose poorly.

Human Waste Disposal

➡ Contamination of water sources by human faeces can lead to the transmission of all sorts of nasties. Where there is a toilet, use it. Where there is none, bury your waste.

Erosion

➡ Hillsides and mountain slopes, especially at high altitudes, are prone to erosion. Stick to existing tracks and avoid shortcuts.

➡ If a well-used track passes through a mud patch, walk through the mud so as not to increase the size of the patch.

➡ Avoid removing any plant life – it keeps the topsoil in place.

The first section rises steadily through a dry landscape with *choka* (an agave species). Towering overhead are the peaks of Le Grand Bénare and Le Gros Morne. Apart from one significant drop, the path stays fairly level before descending to the waterfall at Trois Roches (about 2¾ hours from Roche-Plate). This curious waterfall drops through a narrow crack in a bed of grey granite that has been perfectly polished into ripple patterns by aeons of erosion. Marla is about 2¼ hours beyond the falls. The trail crosses the river and then follows the left bank, passing through a rather arid landscape of eroded volcanic cinders from Piton des Neiges. At an altitude of 1640m, Marla is the highest village in Cirque de Mafate.

The last day (three hours, 540m ascent, 280m descent) is a fairly easy one. Take the trail signposted to La Nouvelle, Col de Fourche and Col des Bœufs. After about 30 minutes, follow the GR R3 signposted to Col des Bœufs, which cuts straight back up (northward) to the Plaine des Tamarins. Before reaching the relatively flat Plaine des Tamarins, you'll have to tackle a very

steep and tedious ascent from Rivière des Galets. Past the Plaine des Tamarins, you'll rejoin the main trail that climbs up to Col des Bœufs.

The Bas Mafate

Hiking is exceptional in the Bas Mafate, with a superb network of well-defined trails that connect the various *îlets* (hamlets). One of the most popular options is to walk around the Bas Mafate Route in four days.

If time allows, you can rejoin the *îlets* in the Haut Mafate. A path connects Îlet des Orangers and Roche-Plate. From Les Lataniers, you can also get to Roche-Plate via the Sentier Dacerle.

IGN's 1:25,000 topographic map 4402 RT covers the area.

Itinerary

This popular circuit starts from the Rivière des Galets valley and takes in all the *îlets* (hamlets) of Bas Mafate, including Aurère, Îlet à Malheur, La Plaque, Îlet à Bourse, Grand Place Les Hauts, Grand

---

THE BAS MAFATE HIKE AT A GLANCE

....

Duration Four days

Distance 30km

Difficulty Moderate

Start Deux Bras

Finish Sans Souci

Nearest towns Rivière des Galets and Sans Souci

Place, Cayenne, Les Lataniers and Îlet des Orangers. It's a four-day hike, but you can design a longer or shorter itinerary depending on how much time you have and how energetic you are. Expect plenty of spectacular landscapes consisting of precipitous mountain slopes and steep-sided valleys.

On day one (three hours, ascent 705m), starting from Deux Bras, you'll follow the riverbed for about 30 minutes before tackling the arduous ascent to Bord Bazar and Aurère.

Day two (four hours, ascent 470m, descent 560m) starts with a short but steep 20-minute descent to the Ravine du Bras Bémale, then a hike up to Îlet à Malheur and La Plaque. You'll cross Grande Ravine before arriving in the hamlet of Îlet à Bourse. After another sharp descent to Bras d'Oussy and steep ascent to a forested ridge, Grand Place Les Hauts comes into view.

Day three (3½ hours, ascent 645m, descent 500m) is particularly challenging, with one major descent to the floor of the Rivière des Galets via Grand Place and Cayenne, followed by one long, difficult ascent to Les Lataniers and Îlet des Orangers.

On day four (four hours, ascent 50m, descent 600m), you'll walk along the Canalisation des Orangers – along the flank of the mountain on a narrow ledge above the Rivière des Galets. After the Canalisation des Orangers, a dirt track leads downhill to Sans Souci, where you can take the bus down to the coast.

Tour des Cirques

The Tour des Cirques (Round the Cirques) is a classic Réunion hike that is sure to leave you with indelible memories. Combining the best of the three Cirques, it offers three distinct atmospheres and varied landscapes. As a bonus, you'll cross a few towns that are well equipped with cosy accommodation facilities.

The walk is best started in Cilaos, which has excellent facilities for walkers and the added advantage of a health spa where you can unwind after your hike. The walk covers 51.5km and is usually completed in five days, taking in the Piton des Neiges, Hell-Bourg, Grand Îlet, La Nouvelle (via Col des Bœufs) and Col du Taïbit.

Day Hikes

If you don't have time for a multiday trek, there are also plenty of great day hikes that will give you a taste of life in rural Réunion. A not-to-be-missed day hike is the climb up the Piton de la Fournaise (p229) (the volcano) from Pas de Bellecombe. Réunion's highest point, Piton des Neiges, can also be done in a day if you're super fit, but most people choose to stay overnight at Gîte de la Caverne Dufour (p211).

Another popular hiking activity is exploring the lava tubes on the southeast coast. You'll walk (make it scramble) over slippery wet rocks through tunnels and caves that were formed by the volcanic eruptions.

Tourist offices have plenty of recommendations for short, easy walks.

TOUR DES CIRQUES HIKE AT A GLANCE

....

Duration Five days

Distance 51.5km

Difficulty Demanding

Start/finish Cilaos

Islands at a Glance

Four unique island destinations cast adrift in the warm azure waters of the Indian Ocean; Mauritius, Rodrigues, Réunion and the Seychelles can all stake a convincing claim to being a piece of paradise. Mauritius achieves perfect balance with its blend of culture and coast, offering terrific activities, landscapes and wildlife, while Réunion, with its surreal mountainous terrain, is heaven on earth for hiking and adrenaline enthusiasts. Beach bums will be better off in the Seychelles, which is blessed with some of the most alluring beaches in the world. Rodrigues is a gem that time forgot, a languid Indian Ocean outpost fast developing impeccable credentials as an ecotourism destination. Visit one and you'll never want to leave. Visit all four and you'll be among the luckiest people on the planet.

Mauritius

Culture
Beaches
Activities

Past & Present

Visitors are often overwhelmed by the sense of devotion that emanates from the incredibly colourful festivals – whether Hindu, Christian, Chinese or Muslim – held throughout the island. Architecture buffs should make a point of visiting the country's historic buildings, especially the colonial plantation houses.

Mind-Blowing Beaches

When it comes to beaches, you'll be spoilt for choice. Most resorts and guesthouses have access to perfect white sand and amazing sapphire water. Good news: despite the crowds, it's easy to find your own slice of paradise.

Watersports & Hiking

Mauritius is the place to be if you want to get your feet (and the rest of you) wet. Pretty much everything's on offer here, from kitesurfing and kayaking to windsurfing and excellent snorkelling and diving. Oh, and beachcombing counts, too. Fabulous hiking also.

p50

Rodrigues

Diving
Village Life
Walking

Pristine Underwater World

The lack of resorts and a remarkably well-preserved marine environment make Rodrigues one of the best places to dive in the Indian Ocean. Sharks, giant trevallies and barracudas galore!

Lost in Time

Slip into island time in Port Mathurin, Rodrigues' somniferous capital, and savour the unhurried pace of life. Accessible homestays, small markets, stuck-in-time villages and welcoming smiles – you'll be hard pressed to find a mellower destination to maroon yourself for a languid holiday.

Coast Walks

The coastline between Graviers and St François in the island's east is extremely alluring: a string of hard-to-reach inlets and coves lapped by azure water, with the mandatory idyllic beach fringing the shore, and vast expanses of rocks. Who knows, you may find a pirate's hidden booty!

p150

Réunion

Outdoors
Scenery
Food

Adrenaline Fix

With its extraordinarily varied terrain, Réunion is an incredible stage for the action seeker in search of anything from canyoning and paragliding to whitewater rafting and whale watching. And when it comes to hiking, Réunion is in a league of its own.

Scenic Mountains

Soaring peaks, lush valleys, majestic summits, sensational lookouts, waterfalls taller than skyscrapers, stunning forests and one of the world's most active volcanoes: Réunion's rugged topography will take your breath away.

Bon Appétit

Foodies of the world, rejoice. In Réunion, even the simplest meal has a flavour you're unlikely to forget. Imagine French gastronomy, prepared with the freshest ingredients, add a dash of Creole, a smidgen of Indian, and *voilà*!

p174

Seychelles

Beaches
Wildlife
Resorts

Perfect White Sand

Many think the eye-catching brochure images of turquoise seas and shimmering white sands are digitally enhanced but, once here, they realise the pictures barely do them justice. The Seychelles is the tropical paradise you've always dreamed about.

Wildlife Riches

The country is a nature-lover's dream. A variety of charismatic species can easily be approached and photographed. Scratch the neck of a giant tortoise, swim respectfully alongside a massive whale shark, observe thousands of nesting sooty terns or look for the smallest frog on earth. Don't forget your camera!

Lap of Luxury

Few islands have the concentration of world-class resorts that can be found in the Seychelles. Whether it's small and romantic, superglamorous or back-to-nature luxury, you'll find the right resort here.

p275

On the Road

Mauritius

📞 230 / POP 1.36 MILLION

Best Places to Eat

➡ La Clef des Champs (p63)

➡ Le Café des Arts (p123)

➡ L'Alchimiste (p97)

➡ Le Château Bel Ombre (p117)

➡ Restaurant Le Barbizon (p97)

Best Places to Stay

➡ Le Saint Géran (p124)

➡ Le Prince Maurice (p124)

➡ Lux Le Morne (p103)

➡ Le Paradise Cove (p80)

➡ La Maison d'Été (p126)

Why Go?

Mark Twain once wrote that 'Mauritius was made first and then heaven, heaven being copied after Mauritius'. For the most part, it's true: Mauritius is rightly famed for its sapphire waters, powder-white beaches and luxury resorts. But there's so much more attraction to Mauritius than the beach, and it's the kind of place that rewards even the smallest attempts at exploration. There's hiking in the forested and mountainous interior and world-class diving and snorkelling offshore. There are boat trips to near-perfect islets and excursions to botanical gardens and colonial plantation houses. Mauritius is a fabulous culinary destination with great wildlife watching thrown in. And the real Mauritius away from the beach resorts – a hot curry of different cultures and quiet fishing villages – is never far away.

When to Go

➡ Mauritius enjoys a typically tropical climate with year-round heat. The summer months are December to April, when it can be extremely humid, and the cooler winter, such as it is, runs from May to November. Coastal temperatures range between 25°C and 33°C in summer and between 18°C and 24°C in winter. On the plateau it will be some 5°C cooler.

➡ Peak cyclone months are January and February, with cyclones possible until April.

➡ High season roughly runs from November to April, with a Christmas–New Year peak, although other factors (French school holidays; for example) can also cause spikes in prices and visitor numbers.

Mauritius Highlights

1 Black River Gorges National Park (p98) Hiking through forested gorges and past waterfalls.

2 Chamarel (p94) Pausing for lunch and rum in this foodie mountain village.

3 Île aux Aigrettes (p109) Discovering how Mauritius once looked.

4 Flic en Flac (p83) Diving and snorkelling epic underwater sites.

5 Pamplemousses (p81) Exploring a botanical garden, a sugar museum and a fine colonial relic.

6 Tamarin & Black River (p89) Searching for whales and dolphins.

7 Eureka (p60) Enjoying colonial plantation architecture.

8 Blue Bay (p109) Snorkelling off fantastic beaches.

9 East Coast Beaches (p120) Finding your perfect patch of sand.

without being really interesting – the calamari vindaloo caught our eye, but the grilled fish is also appealing. People often stay around for a drink or two afterwards.

Brasserie Chic
BRASSERIE €€

(Map p54; ☑ 202 4017; www.labourdonnais.com; mains from Rs 450; ⏰ 6.30am-10.30pm) The Labourdonnais Waterfront Hotel (p56) boasts this cool and classy brasserie serving up salads, bagels, pasta, casseroles and prime cuts of steak. There's even a curry bar with six curries to choose from. It's just as popular as a classy place for a coffee or business meeting as it is for its food.

Namaste
INDIAN €€

(Map p54; ☑ 211 6710; mains Rs 350-500, set menu Rs 850-1800; ⏰ 11.30am-3pm & 6.30-10.30pm) Atmospheric Namaste serves up excellent North Indian specialities such as tandooris, tikkas and butter chicken – the set menus are outstanding and worth getting your head around before ordering. Try for a balcony table. The place gets lively on Saturday evening, when meals are followed by Bollywood tunes.

★ Yuzu
ASIAN €€€

(Map p54; ☑ 202 4000; www.labourdonnais.com; 4-/5-/6-course tasting menu Rs 1700/ 2100/3700, mains Rs 670-1900; ⏰ 11am-11pm Mon-Fri, to 3.40pm Sat) Thai, Vietnamese, Chinese and Japanese fusion cooking fuse seamlessly at this swish and sophisticated restaurant at Labourdonnais Waterfront Hotel. The set menus are a wonderful culinary journey, but everything on the menu is fresh and innovative.

☆ Entertainment

Caudan Arts Centre
ARTS CENTRE

(Map p54; ☑ 211 9430; www.caudanartscentre. com/shows; Le Caudan Waterfront; ⏰ vary) Port Louis' newly minted arts centre, which opened at the end of 2018, is a terrific concert and multi-use venue where you can catch the country's best live performances, from theatre to music concerts and more. Check the website for the full program.

🔒 Shopping

Most of the main streets have clusters of merchants selling similar items. Bourbon St has swarms of flower sellers, Coderie St (aka Corderie St) has silk and fabric vendors, and La Chaussée St is where locals go to buy electronics.

Le Caudan Waterfront offers trendy knick-knacks, designer boutiques, books, handicrafts and souvenirs. For an earthier experience, there's the Central Market (p52).

★ MAST
ARTS & CRAFTS

(Map p54; ☑ 5423 8959, 211 7170; Le Caudan Waterfront; ⏰ 9.30am-5.30pm Mon-Sat) The model-ship manufacturer Voiliers de l'Océan (p62) has an outlet just outside the Craft Market with dozens of model ships, large and small, on display and for sale.

Craft Market
MARKET

(Map p54; ☑ 210 0139; Le Caudan Waterfront; ⏰ 9.30am-5pm Mon-Sat) The Craft Market is less fun but also less hassle than the Central Market (p52). You'll find better-quality souvenirs, such as Mauritius glass, artworks and essential oils from the stalls arrayed over two floors inside the shopping mall.

ℹ️ Information

DANGERS & ANNOYANCES

Port Louis is generally not safe at night just about anywhere south of the motorway; most of the streets empty as the workday ends. After dark all travellers should stick to well-lit main streets and avoid the Jardins de la Compagnie (p54), a favoured hang-out for all manner of unsavoury types (but fine during the day). If you don't know your exact route, take a taxi. Le Caudan is fine as long as there are lots of people around.

By day, Port Louis is a very safe city, but beware of pickpockets anywhere, particularly in the central market (p52) and around the bus stations.

EMERGENCY & IMPORTANT NUMBERS

Ambulance	☑ 114
Police	☑ 999

MEDICAL SERVICES

Dr Jeetoo Hospital (☑ 203 1001; Volcy Pougnet St) Provides 24-hour medical and dental treatment and has a 24-hour pharmacy. Staff speak English and French.

Medical Training Pharmacy (☑ 210 4146; La Chaussée St; ⏰ 9am-4.30pm Mon-Fri, to noon Sat) One of the best pharmacies in the city. Close to Jardins de la Compagnie.

TOURIST INFORMATION

Mauritius Tourism Promotion Authority (MTPA; Map p54; ☑ 210 1545; www.tourismmauritius.mu; 4th & 5th fl, Victoria House, St Louis St; ⏰ 9am-4pm Mon-Fri, to noon Sat) Only moderately useful. Distributes maps of Port Louis and Mauritius.

SHOPPING IN MAURITIUS

Mauritius is increasingly promoting itself as a shopping destination. While clothing is a mainstay of any shopping experience here, other possibilities include the island's signature model ships, glasswork, artwork and basketware. Port Louis generally has the widest range of souvenirs and handicrafts, and there's a daily market in Port Louis and weekly markets in Mahébourg and Port Mathurin (Rodrigues).

Handicrafts & Souvenirs

Locally produced basketry, essential oils, sugar, spices, rums, teas and T-shirts all make very portable souvenirs. The Craft Market in Port Louis' Caudan Waterfront complex offers perhaps the widest choice. Most of the crafts and souvenirs sold at Port Louis' Central Market (p52) and the Grand Baie Bazaar (p76), such as leather belts and bags, masks, embroidery and semiprecious-stone solitaire sets, are from Madagascar.

Model Ships

It's difficult not to be impressed by the skill that goes into producing Mauritius' famous model ships. Small-scale shipbuilding has become a huge business and you'll see intricate replicas of famous vessels, such as the *Bounty, Victory, Endeavour, Golden Hind* and even *Titanic,* for sale all over the island. Model shipbuilding dates back to only 1968, when an unknown Mauritian carved a model ship for fun and launched a whole new industry.

The models are made out of teak or mahogany (cheaper camphor wood is liable to crack), and larger ships take up to 400 hours to complete. Men usually work on the structure and women do the rigging and sails, which are dipped in tea to give them a weathered look.

One of the best model-ship builders is Voiliers de l'Océan (p62), in Curepipe. The company also has an outlet, MAST, in Port Louis' Caudan Waterfront complex.

To get your goods home safely, shops will pack the models for carry-on luggage or in sturdy boxes to go in the hold, and deliver them to your hotel or the airport, often at no extra charge.

Central Post Office (Map p54; ☑ 208 2851; Sir William Newton St; ⊗ 8.15am-4pm Mon-Fri, to 11.45am Sat) The last 45 minutes before closing are for stamp sales only.

ⓘ Getting There & Away

BUS

Port Louis' two bus stations are both located in the city centre. Buses for northern and eastern destinations, such as Trou aux Biches, Grand Baie (Rs42, one hour) and Pamplemousses (Rs36, 1.5hr), leave from **Immigration Square bus station** (Map p54), northeast of the Central Market. Buses for southern and western destinations, such as Mahébourg (Rs42, 1.25 hr), Curepipe (Rs42, one hour) and Flic en Flac, use the **Victoria Square bus station** (Map p54) just southwest of the city centre.

The first departure on most routes is at about 6am; the last leaves at around 6pm.

FERRY

Ferries to Rodrigues and Réunion dock beside the passenger terminal on Quai D of Port Louis harbour, 1km northwest of town.
Mauritius Shipping Corporation (Map p60; ☑ 217 2285; www.mauritiusshipping.net; Nova

Bldg, 1 Military Rd, Port Louis) runs services to Rodrigues.

TAXI

Taxis from Port Louis to Grand Baie cost Rs 1200. To Flic en Flac it's Rs 1200, to Mahébourg it's Rs 1800 and to Belle Mare it's Rs 2000. If you'd prefer a private vehicle, contact any of the island's rental agencies – they'll deliver a car to your hotel. After dark, expect to pay Rs 100 to Rs 200 for a short taxi ride across town. Always agree on a price beforehand.

CENTRAL PLATEAU

Home to a large majority of Mauritians, the cool and rainy centre of the island feels, for the most part, like a continuation of the urban chaos in Port Louis. There's very little to see in the corridor of towns that runs almost unbroken from the capital to Curepipe; in fact, it's pretty much the opposite of that postcard your friends sent you from their trip here last year.

Even so, for tourists interested in learning about life on the island beyond the sand and

Central Plateau

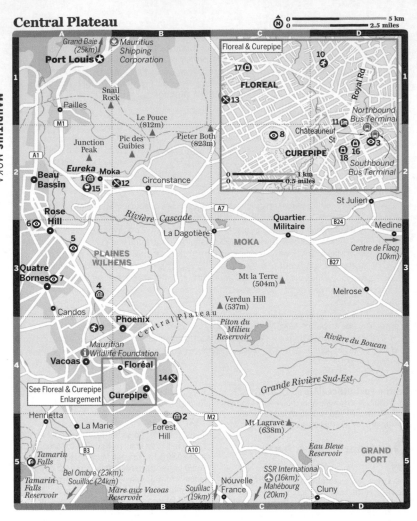

sun, there are a few worthwhile attractions, among them the dormant volcano Trou aux Cerfs (p62); Eureka, a charming plantation home and museum in Moka; and the shopping possibilities in Curepipe, Floréal and elsewhere.

Moka

POP 8570

The most interesting of the Central Plateau towns, the country's academic centre and the official home of the president of Mauritius, Moka is a great place to visit for a taste of national history. The scenery is dramatic here, too, with waterfalls, valleys and the towering Le Pouce in the background. Moka's main attraction, though, is the captivating colonial mansion of Eureka. Almost perfectly preserved from the mid-19th century, it provides a window onto the island's plantation past.

⊙ Sights

★Eureka   HISTORIC BUILDING
(Map p60; ☏ 433 8477; Moka; Rs 300; ⊙ 9am-5pm Mon-Sat, to 3pm Sun) If you're only going to visit one attraction related to Mauritius' rich colonial history, choose Eureka. This perfectly

Central Plateau

MAURITIUS CUREPIPE

preserved Creole mansion was built in the 1830s and today it's a museum and veritable time machine providing incredible insight into the island's vibrant plantation past. The main manor house is a masterpiece of tropical construction, which apparently kept the interior deliciously cool during the unbearably hot summers, and boasts 109 doors and more rooms than a Cluedo board.

Rooms are adorned with an impeccably preserved collection of period furniture imported by the French East India Company – take special note of the antique maps, a strange shower contraption that was quite the luxury some 150 years ago and the mildewed piano with keys like rotting teeth.

The courtyard behind the main mansion contains beautifully manicured grounds surrounded by a set of stone cottages – the former servants' quarters and kitchen. Follow the trail out the back for 15 minutes and you'll reach the lovely **Ravin waterfall**.

The estate's unusual name is believed to have been the reaction of Eugène Le Clézio when he successfully bid to purchase the house at auction in 1856.

✗ Eating

★ **Escale Créole**   MAURITIAN €€
(Map p60; ✆ 5422 2332; www.escalecreole.net; off Bois Cheri Rd; mains Rs 250-600, set menu Rs 750-950; ☺ noon-2.45pm Mon-Fri) Around 1km from Eureka, and well signposted along the main road through Moka, this charming garden *table d'hôte* (privately hosted meal) serves up Mauritian specialities such as homemade Creole sausages and octopus bouillon with coconut chutney. Your hosts are the charming mother-daughter team of Majo and

Marie-Christine. Book at least a day in advance. Warmly recommended.

Eureka Table d'Hôte   MAURITIAN €€
(Map p60; ✆ 433 8477; meals Rs 805; ☺ noon-3pm) To deepen your Eureka experience we recommend planning your visit around noon to enjoy a relaxing repast at the in-house *table d'hôte*. Sample an assortment of Mauritian classics like marlin *fumée* (smoked fish), lentils and curried fish while enjoying the delightful historical atmosphere. Call ahead, as sometimes the restaurant is closed for tour groups.

❶ Getting There & Away

To get to Eureka, take a bus from Curepipe, or Victoria Sq in Port Louis, and get off at Moka. Eureka is signposted about 1km north of the bus stop. Otherwise, many hotels and most tour operators can organise half-day excursions here from anywhere on the island, and all taxi drivers know it.

Curepipe
POP 84,200

Effectively Mauritius' second city, Curepipe (pronounced *kew-re-peep*) has only limited appeal to visitors. It's a bustling highland commercial centre famous for its rainy weather, milder temperatures, volcanic crater (p62) and shopping. Its strange name reputedly stems from the malaria epidemic of 1867, when people fleeing lowland Port Louis would 'cure' their pipes of malarial bacteria by smoking them here (although it's more likely that the area was named after a fondly remembered town in France).

Curepipe is the highest of the plateau towns. At 550m above sea level, it has refreshingly cool summer temperatures, but according to lowlanders, Curepipe has two seasons: the little season of big rains and the big season of little rains. The damp climate gives the buildings an ageing, mildewed quality. Bring an umbrella.

◉ Sights & Activities

Trou aux Cerfs   VOLCANO
(Map p60) About 1km west of central Curepipe, the Trou aux Cerfs is a dormant volcanic crater some 100m deep and 1km in circumference. The bowl is heavily wooded and from the road around the rim – a favourite spot for joggers and walkers – you get lovely views of the plateau. There are benches where you can rest and reflect, and a radar station that keeps an electronic eye on cyclone activity.

Domaine des Aubineaux   HISTORIC BUILDING
(Map p60; ☑ 676 3089; www.saintaubinloisirs.com; Royal Rd; adult/child Rs 300/150, incl lunch Rs 1000/500; ⊙ 9am-5pm) The manor house of the Domaine des Aubineaux was built in 1872 in a classic colonial style; in 1889 it was the first residence on the island to be outfitted with electricity. The plantation was transformed into a museum in 2000, and today it marks the first stop on the historic Route du Thé (p114). Exotic plants fill the garden under the shade of camphor trees, and you can sip savoury teas in the converted billiard parlour.

Hôtel de Ville   ARCHITECTURE
(Town Hall; Map p60; Châteauneuf St) Overlooking a small park in the centre of Curepipe, the Hôtel de Ville is one of Mauritius' best surviving structures from its colonial era. Notice the gable windows, veranda and decorative wooden friezes known as *dentelles* – all are signature traits of the island's early plantation architecture. The building was moved here from Moka in 1903.

Otélair   ADVENTURE SPORTS
(Map p60; ☑ 5251 6680, 696 6750; www.otelair.com; 83 Charles Regnaud St) Otélair organises hiking, climbing, abseiling and canyoning trips, many of which take place inside Black River Gorges National Park.

🛏 Sleeping

Auberge de la Madelon   GUESTHOUSE €
(Map p60; ☑ 670 1885; www.auberge-madelon.com; 10 Sir John Pope Hennessy St; s/d/tw from Rs 1250/1500/1600; ❄@🛜) Excellent value and centrally located, this well-run place is simple, small and surprisingly stylish, boasting comfy en suite rooms and a very helpful management.

🍴 Eating

La Potinière   MAURITIAN €€
(Map p60; ☑ 670 2648; www.facebook.com/la potiniererestaurant; Charles Lees St; mains Rs 330-725; ⊙ 11.30am-3pm Mon, 11.30am-3pm & 7-9.30pm Tue-Sat) Curepipe's most obviously upmarket restaurant is all starched linen and gleaming tableware. The menu features a selection of quintessential Mauritian eats: hearts of palm, wild boar and seafood – the palm heart and prawn soufflé is superb.

🛍 Shopping

Beauté de Chine   ANTIQUES
(Map p60; ☑ 676 3270; Arcade Currimjee, Châteauneuf St; ⊙ 10am-5.30pm Mon-Fri, to 1pm Sat) Beauté de Chine, one of the longest-running stores on the island, sells an assortment of old-world relics including copper, jade, silk and antique porcelain.

Voiliers de l'Océan   ARTS & CRAFTS
(Map p60; ☑ 676 6986, 674 6764; Winston Churchill St; ⊙ 9am-6pm Mon-Sat) Travellers looking for model-ship showrooms and workshops

HIKING THE CENTRAL PLATEAU

The mountain ranges fringing the Central Plateau offer some memorable rambles and hikes. Two of the best introductions to hiking in Mauritius are **Le Pouce** (812m), a thumb-shaped peak on the plateau's northern edge, and **Corps de Garde** (719m), a wedge-like ridge to the southwest that makes for a slightly more challenging endeavour.

Both hikes offer resplendent views down to the coastal plains but are best appreciated when tackled with a local guide, who can annotate the hike with detailed information about the flora and history. If you decide to go it alone, check out Fitsy (www.fitsy.com), a brilliant website that has mapped out the walks with extensive GPS and satellite detail. For planning purposes, allow about two hours for each hike if you're starting at the trailhead.

A TOUR OF THE CENTRAL PLATEAU

The area southeast of and inland from Port Louis can seem like one great conurbation, and in a sense it is. While most travellers pass right on by en route from coast to coast, there are enough sights to warrant a half-day excursion by taxi – we suggest you don't drive yourself or you'll waste valuable time trying to find each place.

The Central Plateau's main attractions are Eureka (p60), the two culinary options (p61) in Moka, and the Trou aux Cerfs volcano in Curepipe. They're probably the only attractions worth visiting in their own right.

Elsewhere, attractions relate mostly to architecture or shopping. **Rose Hill** (pronounced *row-zeel* by locals), wedged between Beau Bassin and Quatre Bornes in the heart of the Central Plateau's urban sprawl, is virtually a suburb of Port Louis. Here, architecture buffs will appreciate the unusual Creole structure housing the **Municipality of Beau Bassin-Rose Hill** (Map p60; Royal Rd, Beau Bassin-Rose Hill). The building was constructed in 1933 as a municipal theatre. The attractive Creole manse next door – **Maison Le Carne** (Map p60; Royal Rd, Beau Bassin-Rose Hill) – houses the Mauritius Research Council.

Another satellite of Port Louis, **Quatre Bornes** has little to detain you, other than on Thursday and Sunday, when scores of locals flock to the city to rummage through stall upon stall at the bustling produce and textile **market** (Map p60; St Jean Rd, Quatre Bornes; ☉8am-4pm Tue-Sun); there's also a popular veggie market on Saturday. It's also the home of the **MCB Building** (Map p60; M1), which is perhaps Mauritius' most striking modern architectural creation – you'll see the eye-like structure by the M1 motorway as you approach Port Louis from the south.

In **Phoenix**, the **Mauritius Glass Gallery** (Map p60; ☎696 3360; www.facebook.com/pg/MauritiusGlassGallery; Pont Fer, Phoenix; adult/child Rs 80/40; ☉8am-5pm Mon-Fri, to noon Sat) produces unusual souvenirs made from recycled glass. You can see pieces being made using traditional methods in the workshop, which doubles as a small museum.

The neighbouring town of **Vacoas** is home to the oldest golf course in the Indian Ocean, **Mauritius Gymkhana Club** (Map p60; ☎696 1404; www.mgc.mu; Suffolk Close, Vacoas; 9-/18-hole green fees per person Rs 1350/1850, equipment hire Rs 1000). It's the fourth-oldest fairway in the world (the three older courses are in Britain and India).

Another possibility is **Floréal**, the 'Beverly Hills' of Mauritius and a rather posh suburb northwest of Curepipe. Fill your suitcase with clothes at **Floréal Square** (Map p60; Swami Sivananda Ave, Floréal; ☉9.30am-5.30pm Mon-Fri, to 4pm Sat), on the main road from Curepipe.

If you're in the neighbourhood, we highly recommend seeking out **La Clef des Champs** (Map p60; ☎686 3458; www.laclefdeschamps.mu; Queen Mary Ave, Floréal; set menu per person from Rs 1250; ☉11am-3pm & 6-10pm Mon-Fri, 6-10pm Sat), the *table d'hôte* – and pet project – of Jacqueline Dalais, chef to the stars. Known for her impressive library of self-created recipes, Jacqueline has earned quite the reputation on the island for her unparalleled cuisine: she is regularly called upon to cater for government functions, especially when foreign dignitaries are in town. Dishes served in her quaint dining room lean towards Provençal flavours; the presentation is exquisite.

should stop by Voiliers de l'Océan. Roughly 200 models are produced per month.

Galerie des Îles   MALL
(Map p60; ☎670 7516; 1st fl, Arcade Currimjee, Châteauneuf St; ☉9.30am-5.30pm Mon-Sat) Galerie des Îles has a generous selection of local designs and artisans across more than a dozen shops.

❶ Getting There & Away

Curepipe is an important transport hub, with frequent bus services to Port Louis (Victoria Sq), Mahébourg, Centre de Flacq, Moka and just about anywhere else on the island. There are two terminals: the **northbound** (Map p60) and the **southbound** (Map p60). Most services go from the northbound (Port Louis, Rose Hill, Quatre Bornes); Mahébourg is served from the southbound. The terminals lie on either side of Châsteauneuf St, at the junction with Jerningham St.

From Curepipe, expect to pay Rs 1100 for a taxi ride to the airport, Rs 1850 to Grand Baie, Rs 1750 to Belle Mare, Rs 1100 to Port Louis, Rs 1100 to Flic en Flac and Rs 700 to Black River (Rivière Noire).

The North

INDIAN
OCEAN

7

8 Coin de Mire
(Nature Reserve)

Cap
Malheureux

Bain Baeuf
Beach

Cap 5
Malheureux
15 18 9

Bassin
Paquet

14 10

See Pereybère
Map (p78)

Pointe aux
Canonniers

Pointe Église

Pereybère

See Pointe aux
Canonniers Map
(p72)

Pointe aux
Canonniers

Grand
Baie

See Grand Baie
Map (p74)

Petit
Raffray

See Trou aux
Biches & Mont
Choisy Map
(p68)

Mont
Choisy

A4

A5

Trou aux Biches

Goodlands

17

Triolet

M2

A5

Fond
du Sac

Plaine des
Papayes

RIVIÈRE DU
REMPART

Pointe aux
Piments

A4

PAMPLEMOUSSES

1 Château
Labourdonnais

12 Balaclava

Solitude

Baie de
l'Arsenal

11

Piton

B41

Arsenal

4

M2

Baie du
Tombeau

3 Sir Seewoosagur Ramgoolam
Pamplemousses Botanical Gardens

A6

Baie du
Tombeau

A4

16

A6

Mt Piton
(267m)

Rivière Citrons

A2

A2

D'Epinay

Terre Rouge

Rivière du Tombeau

M2

6

2 Père Laval's
Shrine

PORT
LOUIS

La
Nicolière

A2

Quatre Bornes (18km);
Curepipe (26km);

Valton

decked out in a Moorish style that's matched by inventive apartment layouts. It's also pleasantly small and feels very relaxed. You have to cross the road to get to the beach and the cheaper rooms are a little over-priced, but otherwise this place is great.

★ Le Sakoa
HOTEL €€€

(Map p68; ☎ 265 5244; www.lesakoa.com; Royal Rd, Trou aux Biches; d incl breakfast/half board from €180/233; ✳@🛜🌊) Easily the most stylish option in Trou aux Biches, Le Sakoa is instantly recognisable by its high-pitched roofs that match the neighbouring palms

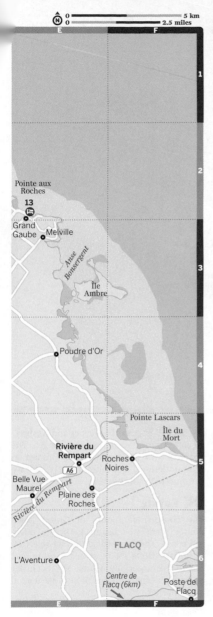

★ Trou aux Biches Resort & Spa
HOTEL €€€

(Map p68; ☎204 6565; www.beachcomber-hotels.com/hotel/trou-aux-biches-resort-spa; Royal Rd, Trou aux Biches; r incl half board from €350; ❄@🛜≋) Uber-luxury is the name of the game at five-star Trou aux Biches Resort & Spa, with its clutch of traditionally inspired beachside suites and villas. The design scheme incorporates such rustic elements as thatch, wicker and hand-cut boulders into the unquestionably modern surrounds. Spas, pools and 2km of sand make this the most desirable address in Trou aux Biches.

Veranda Pointe aux Biches Hotel
HOTEL, RESORT €€€

(Map p68; ☎266 9736; www.veranda-resorts.com; Royal Rd, Trou aux Biches; r from €232; P❄🛜≋) Extremely good value, this outpost of the Veranda chain mixes simplicity in the rooms (think pine bunk beds in the family rooms) with the reassuringly tropical surrounds of an upmarket resort: infinity pool, spa centre, water sports, kids club, more palm trees than we cared to count and hanging wicker

in both height and grandeur. Spacious accommodation is in wonderful two-storey thatched blocks radiating out from the fantastic beach. A charming dark-marble infinity pool anchors the hotel's centre, providing a luxurious setting for couples and families.

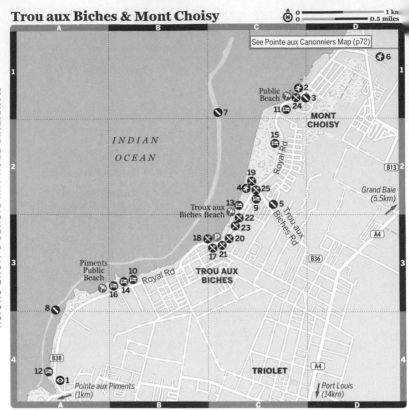

See Pointe aux Canonniers Map (p72)

INDIAN OCEAN

Public Beach

MONT CHOISY

Grand Baie (5.5km)

Troux aux Biches Beach

Trou aux Biches Rd

Piments Public Beach

Royal Rd

TROU AUX BICHES

TRIOLET

Pointe aux Piments (1km)

Port Louis (14km)

---

swing-chairs. Beware of add-ons like paying for the activities.

Bon Azur APARTMENT €€€
(Map p68; ☑204 6565; www.innlov.com/bon-azur-beachfront-suites---penthouses.html; Royal Rd, Trou aux Biches; apt from €232; P✳🛜☒) These stylish, modern apartments, each with an expansive balcony overlooking the pool and small beach, are a fine choice. The beach isn't really for swimming, but the whole set-up is excellent: numbers are kept to a minimum, families are welcome and it's a short drive (or a longish walk) to the town's restaurants; you'll need a car for the supermarket.

Plage Bleue APARTMENT €€€
(Map p68; ☑265 6507; www.plage-bleue-appar tements.com; Royal Rd, Trou aux Biches; 3-bedroom apt from €325; P✳🛜☒) Large and luxurious serviced apartments on a quiet stretch of beach are what Plage Bleue is all about.

Each has Weber gas barbecues and Nespresso coffee machines, and all face the sea. The beach is not really for swimming (it's lagoon mud underfoot), but that's the only fault we can find with this place.

🍴 Eating

The competitive nature of Grand Baie's dining scene has begun to trickle down the coast. The increasingly broad selection of outlets caters for most tastes, with Trou aux Biches especially notable for its cluster of fine midrange options. It also has a good supermarket.

Chez Popo SUPERMARKET
(Map p68; ☑265 5463; Royal Rd, Trou aux Biches; ⊙7.30am-7.30pm Mon-Sat, to 12.30pm Sun) In an area where self-catering apartments rule, a supermarket really matters. Chez Popo has improved dramatically, getting a makeover, expanding in size and there's even off-street parking.

Trou aux Biches & Mont Choisy

★ **Chez Meung**   CHINESE €
(Map p68; Royal Rd, Trou aux Biches; mains from Rs 100; ⊙9.30am-4pm) Join the queue and watch a master reap the whirlwind. Every lunchtime, Meung cooks and serves up some of the simplest and best Chinese food on the island. You put your own meal together by pointing to the pots you wish to try – boiled or fried noodles, beef, *boulettes* (small steamed dumplings in a variety of flavours) or soup.

Costs rarely jump above Rs 100 for a filling meal and the small shopfront is just across the road from the beach, ideal for takeaway.

Kafé La Zétée   CAFE €
(Map p68; ☑5767 4300; off Royal Rd, Trou aux Biches; mains Rs 230-450; ⊙9am-4pm Mon-Sat) A fresh and breezy alternative to its sister restaurant, Le Pescatore (p70), next door, Kafé La Zétée does breakfast, paninis, sandwiches, smoked-marlin salads and daily specials that might include ceviche (raw fish marinated in lemon and garlic) or grilled fish. Great coffee too.

**Cabanne
des Fruits de Mer**   MAURITIAN €
(Map p68; Trou aux Biches; mains Rs 275-550; ⊙11am-9pm) With a better-than-average range of meals – from sandwiches, salads and fried noodles to grilled fish and seafood – this is the pick of the beachfront shacks along this stretch of coast. It's in the car park at the southern end of Trou aux Biches public beach.

La Vogla Matta   ITALIAN €
(Map p68; ☑265 7091; Royal Rd, Trou aux Biches; mains/pizzas from Rs 350/290; ⊙6.30am-9.30pm Tue-Sun, plus noon-2.30pm Fri-Sun) With so many good places to choose from, it takes a lot to catch our attention in Trou aux Biches when it comes to food. La Vogla Matta, next to Chez Popo supermarket, does some of the best pizzas on Mauritius' west coast. The word is out – it's already popular.

★ **Café International -
The Flame Grill**   INTERNATIONAL €€
(Map p68; ☑5765 8735; Royal Rd, Trou aux Biches; mains Rs 250-900; ⊙5-10pm Tue-Fri, noon-10pm Sat & Sun; ⊕) This popular South African–run spot serves up an excellent assortment of dishes from around the world. Burgers here come in many forms with the quality of the meat paramount, but the highlights are the ribs and South African steaks that are so good we would (and, on at least one occasion, did) cross the island just to have them.

It's all watched over by friendly Deon, a former bodyguard for Nelson Mandela. There's a secondhand bookshop as well.

★ **1974**   ITALIAN, SEAFOOD €€
(Map p68; ☑265 7400; Royal Rd, Trou aux Biches; mains Rs 350-600; ⊙6.30-11pm Tue-Sat, plus noon-2.30pm Fri & Sat, noon-5pm Sun) This fabulous place in warm terracotta hues is the work of Italians Antonio and Giulia. The food includes pasta and seafood with an emphasis on fresh local produce – try the cannelloni with crab and fish, or the mixed seafood spaghetti. We're yet to hear a bad word about this place.

OFF THE BEATEN TRACK

BOAT TRIPS TO THE NORTHERN ISLANDS

Coin de Mire, Île Plate & Îlot Gabriel

The distinctive Coin de Mire (Gunner's Quoin), 4km off the coast, was so named because it resembles the *quoin* (wedge) used to steady the aim of a cannon. The island is now a nature reserve and home to a number of rare species, such as the red-tailed tropicbird and Bojer's skink. None of the major catamarans stop here, as landing is often difficult. Despite the island's striking shape, there's not much to see here anyway – it's the kind of place that looks much better from far away.

Most operators take you to the lagoon between Île Plate and Îlot Gabriel, 7km further north, which offers good snorkelling. Barbecue lunches are served on a sandy patch of Îlot Gabriel.

Boats to the islands depart from Grand Baie. You can book online at www.catamaran-cruisesmauritius.com, through any local tour agent or directly with the cruise companies. Prices are Rs 1200 to Rs 1700 per person, including lunch. If you travel by speedboat, the price increases to around Rs 2300.

Île Ronde & Île aux Serpents

Île Ronde (Round Island) and Île aux Serpents (Snake Island) are two significant nature reserves about 20km and 24km, respectively, from Mauritius. It is not possible to land on them. Ironically, Île Ronde is not round and has snakes, while Île aux Serpents is round and has no snakes; the theory is that an early cartographer simply got them confused.

Île Ronde covers roughly 170 hectares and scientists believe it has more endangered species per square kilometre than anywhere else in the world. Many of the plants, such as the hurricane palm (of which one lonely tree remains) and the bottle palm, are unique to the island. The endemic fauna includes the keel-scaled boa and the burrowing boa (possibly extinct), three types of skink and three types of gecko. Among the seabirds that breed on the island are the wedge-tailed shearwater, the red-tailed tropicbird and the gadfly (or Round Island) petrel. Naturalist Gerald Durrell gives a very graphic description of the island in his book *Golden Bats and Pink Pigeons*.

The smaller Île aux Serpents (42 hectares) is a renowned bird sanctuary. The birds residing on the island include the sooty tern, the lesser noddy, the common noddy and the masked (blue-footed) booby. Nactus geckos and Bojer's skinks are also found here.

Cabanne de la Prise du Pêcheur　　　MAURITIAN €€

(Map p68; ☑ 5711 2729; Royal Rd, Trou aux Biches; mains from Rs 450; ☺ noon-10pm) You just don't get experiences like this if you never leave your resort. Run by Nathalie and her all-female crew, this seaside kiosk serves fabulous local specialities, among them prawns or fish in red Creole sauce and fish curry with eggplant. Servings are large and the ramshackle tables by the water could be our favourites along this stretch of coast.

Restaurant Souvenir　　　MAURITIAN, INTERNATIONAL €€

(Map p68; ☑ 5291 1440; cnr Royal Rd & Trou aux Biches Rd, Trou aux Biches; mains Rs 250-550; ☺ 9am-11pm) A wildly popular addition to the Trou aux Biches eating scene, Souvenir does everything from bog-standard Mauritian fried noodles to steaks. The food is generally excellent, although service does go missing when things are busy (which is often). Reservations are recommended at peak lunch and dinner times. There's a well-stocked bar.

Le Pescatore　　　SEAFOOD €€€

(Map p68; ☑ 265 6337; off Royal Rd, Trou aux Biches; set menus Rs 2600-4200, mains Rs 900-1325; ☺ noon-2pm & 7-9pm Mon-Sat) Wonderfully light decor and a great terrace overlooking the fishing boats set the scene for a truly superior eating experience. Dishes such as grilled lobster in ginger and sake sauce should give you an idea of what to expect, but the fine set menus are all worth considering.

ⓘ Information

Shibani Foreign Exchange (☑ 265 5306; www.shibanifinance.com; Royal Rd, Mont Choisy; ☺ 8am-5.30pm Mon-Sat, 8-11.30am Sun) Small forex bureau handily located along the main road.

ℹ️ Getting There & Away

Trou aux Biches and Mont Choisy are served by nonexpress bus services running between Port Louis' Immigration Square bus station and Cap Malheureux via Grand Baie. There are bus stops about every 500m along the coastal highway.

A taxi to Grand Baie starts at around Rs 600, but fares depend on where your journey begins. It's Rs 750 to Pereybère.

ℹ️ Getting Around

Count on Rs 250 for a taxi ride in the Trou aux Biches/Mont Choisy area.

Grand Baie

POP 9560

At once Mauritian town and leading tourist resort set on a gorgeous stretch of coast, Grand Baie is classic Mauritian tourism, for good and for ill. In the 17th century, the Dutch used to call Grand Baie 'De Bogt Zonder Eynt', which means 'The Bend Without End'. Today it appears as though it's the development – not the bay – that's without end. Grand Baie has all the vices and virtues of beach resorts the world over. The virtues include good accommodation, bars and restaurants, while the vices can be found in water frontages consumed by concrete and touts, although the latter, in true Mauritian style, nudge rather than push. To escape the downtown scene, head for charming and quiet Pointe aux Canonniers.

🏃 Activities

Croisières Australes BOATING
(Map p74; ☑202 6660; www.croisieres-australes.mu; per person per day from Rs 2000) Arguably the most professional outfit in town, with a range of full- and half-day catamaran cruises.

Solar Sea Walk ADVENTURE SPORTS
(Map p74; ☑5253 4411, 263 7819; www.solarseawalk.com; Royal Rd; per person Rs 2000; ⊙9am-4.30pm) For nondivers, Solar Sea Walk provides the unique experience of walking underwater while wearing a diver's helmet and weight belt. Solar-powered pumps on the boat above feed oxygen to you during the 25-minute 'walk on the wet side'. Walks are available to everyone aged over seven. In peak season it's advisable to book a day ahead. Last walk at 3pm.

Grand Bay Travel & Tours BOATING
(Map p74; ☑5757 8754, 263 8771; www.gbtt.com; Royal Rd; per person from Rs 1600) One of the

more reliable operators in Grand Baie, this place offers full-day catamaran cruises to the northern islands, plus a range of other excursions. Contact them in advance by phone or online.

Sportfisher FISHING
(Map p74; ☑263 8358; . Royal Rd; half/full day per boat from US$488/569; ⊙7am-6pm) Based beside the Sunset Blvd jetty, Sportfisher has four boats, each taking up to six people (three anglers and three companions). Remember its policy: 'All fish belong to the boat. However, should you wish to sample your fish we will gladly oblige'.

Grand Baie Gym & Hydro Spa GYM, SPA
(Map p72; ☑263 9290; www.grandbaiegymandspa.com; X Club Rd; day membership Rs 700; ⊙6am-9pm Mon-Fri, 7am-7.30pm Sat, 9am-1pm Sun) The Grand Baie Gym & Hydro Spa has a fabulous pool and gym, and you can indulge in a huge range of spa treatments, steam yourself in the hammam (Turkish bath) or enjoy low-fat dishes at the cafe across the street.

Yacht Charters BOATING
(Map p72; ☑263 8395) Magnificent sailing ship the *Isla Mauritia* was built in 1852 and is claimed to be the world's oldest active schooner. Rates vary depending on season, itinerary and number of people.

🛏️ Sleeping

Grand Baie has two distinct classes of hotels: the grandiose resorts and the budget studios and apartments set back from the main drag. There are fewer luxury resorts in the area than one might think, although a clutch of smart hotels occupies the east side of the bay. Those for whom Grand Baie is just a little too busy might want to consider Pereybère nearby.

★ Sous Le Badamier GUESTHOUSE €
(Map p72; ☑263 4391; www.souslebadamier.com; X Club Rd, Pointe aux Canonniers; incl breakfast s €55-70, d €60-85; ❄@🛜) Once known as Chez Vaco for the artist's enchanting paintings adorning almost every wall, this wonderful guesthouse now takes its name from the *badamier* trees that shade the charming entrance cloister. The delightful rooms are sponge painted in soothing tones and furnishings are accented with rattan – there's a warm minimalism here that feels stylish yet homely. This place is a real find.

Pointe aux Canonniers

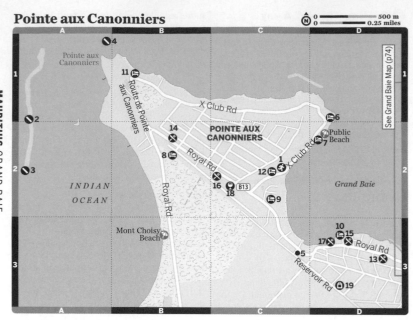

Pointe aux Canonniers

Résidence Peramal APARTMENT €
(Map p72; ☏ 263 8109; www.residence-peramal.
com; Royal Rd; studio with fan Rs 1500-1800, with
air-con Rs 1800-2100, apt Rs 2500-3100; ❄) Excellent-value self-catering accommodation
on a little promontory at the western entrance to Grand Baie. Prices rise depending
on the view. You're close to Grand Baie but
back from the main road.

★**Esprit Libre** GUESTHOUSE €€
(Map p72; ☏ 269 1159; www.espritlibremaurice.
com; Rue Bourdet, Pointe aux Canonniers; r/ste

from €82/150; ❄ 🛜 ⛱) Easily among the
best-value options on the island, this charming and warmly inviting guesthouse has one
mantra in mind: customer service. Rooms
are simple and tastefully decorated and the
restaurant offers up an inventive menu that
has lured in a faithful crowd of locals. It's
well signposted off Royal Rd.

**Azure Beach
Boutique Hotel** BOUTIQUE HOTEL €€
(Map p74; ☏ 263 5900; Royal Rd; s/d incl breakfast
€79/90, with sea view from €92/105; ❄ @ 🛜)

Right in the heart of town, this place is an excellent choice, especially if you get a sea-facing room on the upper floors. S ervice is warm and the decor tries to be contemporary and mostly succeeds, with strategic photos and nice bathrooms. Breakfasts are terrific, but the absence of a pool will matter for some.

Ocean Villas
HOTEL €€

(Map p72; ☑263 6788; www.ocean-villas.com; Royal Rd, Pointe aux Canonniers; r incl breakfast €80-220; ✸@🛜🌊) Ocean Villas is recommended for its broad range of accommodation, from straightforward hotel rooms to self-catering units for up to eight people, sleek honeymoon suites with sunken baths, and the love nest – a private house on the beach. Facilities include an excellent pool plus a small strip of beach (with limited watersports on offer), plus a restaurant.

★Seapoint Boutique Hotel
HOTEL €€€

(Map p72; ☑209 1055; www.seapointboutique hotel.com; Route de Pointe aux Canonniers; s/d incl breakfast €264/352; ✸🛜🌊) Right out near the tip of Pointe aux Canonniers, this lovely place has stunningly turned out rooms, suites and villas, with subtle aquamarine colours and a tasteful use of driftwood furnishings in some rooms. You couldn't be closer to the beach.

★20° Sud
HOTEL €€€

(Map p72; ☑263 5000; www.20degressud.com; X Club Rd, Pointe aux Canonniers; d from €386; ✸@🛜🌊) Perhaps the boutiquiest resort on the island, 20° Sud has a cache of chic, plantation-inspired rooms. Walls are lavished with prim white paint, accented by draped linen and elegant dark-wood mouldings. Palatial oak doors initiate guests into the vine-draped public area, a lush palm grove with an inviting swimming pool and a cosy lodge-style library. Children under 12 not allowed.

Baystone Hotel & Spa
BOUTIQUE HOTEL €€€

(Map p72; ☑209 1900; www.baystone.mu; X Club Rd, Pointe aux Canonniers; r from €689; 🅿✸@🛜🌊) On a lovely quiet stretch of beach that looks across the bay, this classy boutique hotel is one of our favourite upmarket places in Grand Baie. Intimate where so many high-end hotels sprawl impersonally, this is luxury with a personal, discreet touch. The rooms are flooded with natural light and are supremely comfortable.

Royal Palm
HOTEL €€€

(Map p74; ☑209 8300; www.beachcomber-hotels.com/hotel/royal-palm; off Royal Rd; r per person incl breakfast from €776; ✸@🛜🌊) The flagship of the Beachcomber group, the Royal Palm is the pinnacle of luxury and a veritable playground for the rich and famous. Staff don safari-butler uniforms (stylish pith helmets!), and meticulously arranged bouquets are the centrepiece of every room.

✕ Eating

While the centre of town is packed with eateries, some of the better places are slightly outside the heart of Grand Baie, particularly towards Pointe aux Canonniers and Pereybère. Street vendors and vegetable stands can be found all along Royal Rd. They tend to be concentrated near the public beaches.

★Domaine
MAURITIAN €

(Map p66; ☑263 5286; Narainen St, Upper Vale, The Vale; mains Rs 75-200; ⏱4-11pm Mon, 11am-11pm Tue-Sun) 'Domaine' is the answer every local offers when travellers ask where to go to savour some Mauritian home cookin'. The best dishes are those starred on the menu as local specialities – offerings such as *our-ite safrané* (octopus cooked in ginger, garlic and turmeric) and chilli lamb. It can be hard to find and you'll need a private vehicle or taxi.

Take the M2 towards Port Louis, then turn left off the motorway at the first

---

GRAND BAIE VILLAS FOR RENT

As in most resort areas of Mauritius, Grand Baie has its share of agents offering seaside villas and apartments for rent. There are some excellent apartment deals around, especially if you arrive with friends at a quiet time of year.

Grand Bay Travel & Tours (Map p74; ☑263 8771; www.gbtt.com; Royal Rd) Several multi-apartment properties in the Grand Baie area, from basic digs to luxury sleeps. Contact them online before visiting, or they're unlikely to have much.

CG Villas (☑262 5777; www.villas-maurice.com) This accommodation booking service offers villas and apartments directly on the bay.

Grand Baie

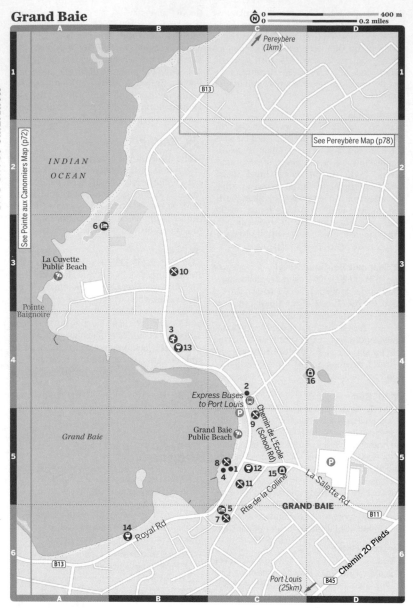

See Pointe aux Canonniers Map (p72)

See Pereybère Map (p78)

Pereybère
(1km)

B13

INDIAN
OCEAN

6

La Cuvette
Public Beach

Pointe
Baignoire

10

3

13

16

2

Express Buses
to Port Louis

Chemin de L'Ecole
(School Rd)

9

Grand Baie
Public Beach

Grand Baie

8 1 12
4 11 15

5
7

14

Royal Rd

Rte de la Colline

GRAND BAIE

La Salette Rd

B11

B13

Chemin 20 Pieds

Port Louis
(25km)

B45

roundabout and follow the signs to The Vale. Once in the village, look for the 'Snack Mustapha' sign where the main road dog-legs left – turn hard right and then take the second paved road on the left, around 250m down the hill.

★ **Boulette Ti Kouloir**   MAURITIAN **€**
(Map p74; School Rd; boulettes Rs 9, noodles Rs 85-95; ⊗ 11.30am-4pm & 6-9.30pm Mon-Sat) Off Royal Rd, this is one of Grand Baie's best places for street food. As the name suggests, this microscopic place really is just a *ti couloir* (li'l hallway), where Yvonne and friends cook

Grand Baie

up *boulettes* (small steamed dumplings) and piled-high bowls of fried noodles to lines of locals. For the *boulettes*, choose among chicken, pork, fish, calamari and lamb.

To get here from the coast road, follow the low-slung billboard for La Rougaille Créole, pass the car park for the Sunset Boulevard shopping centre, then turn right – it's around 50m further along on the right, next to La Rougaille Créole.

La Fournil   PASTRIES, CAFE €
(Map p72; 📱 263 3030; Royal Rd, Pointe aux Cannoniers; mains from Rs 80; ⊙ 6.30am-7pm Mon-Sat, to 1pm Sun) People come from all over the north for the pastries on offer here at this charming little patisserie-cafe. It does some bagels and sandwiches, as well as breakfasts, with the enticing sweet stuff calling out to you from behind the glass. Tables can be tough to snaffle on weekends.

Luigi's   ITALIAN €
(Map p74; 📱 269 1125; Royal Rd; pizza Rs 200-380, mains Rs 350-600; ⊙ 6-10.30pm Tue-Thu, 6-11pm Fri, noon-2.30pm & 6-11pm Sat, 6-10pm Sun; 🛜) There are no frilly adornments at this place, just good wood-fired pizzas, excellent pasta dishes and a breezy dining area. No wonder it's full most of the time.

★ Cafe Roots   CAFE €€
(Map p72; 📱 269 1544; Royal Rd, Pointe aux Cannoniers; light meals from Rs 180, mains Rs 380-480; ⊙ 8.30am-4.30pm Mon-Sat) This fabulous little courtyard cafe with white-wood furnishings does gorgeous salads and antipasto, paninis and sandwiches, a few pasta dishes and a full board of daily specials. Terrific coffee too.

★ Sauterelle   MAURITIAN, FRENCH €€
(Map p74; 📱 263 8836; www.sauterelle.restaurant.mu; Royal Rd; mains Rs 290-510; ⊙ noon-2.30pm & 7-10pm Tue-Sat) Rising above the Sunset

Boulevard shopping precinct, this oasis of sophistication is a fine choice. Dishes range far and wide, and might include roasted red snapper fillet with grapefruit-and-rosemary sauce and prawn curry with green tea–infused noodles, although the menu changes regularly. Service is attentive and the food rarely misses a beat. Check their weekly set menu – excellent value.

Café Müller   CAFE €€
(Map p72; 📱 263 5230; www.facebook.com/kaffeehausmauritius/; Royal Rd; Sat brunch buffet Rs 500, Fri buffet & grill adult/child Rs 450/225, light meals from Rs 150; ⊙ 8am-5pm Tue-Sat) This charming German-run option is a great place for cakes, crêpes, coffee and juices; from mid-September to mid-June, it also offers an excellent Saturday brunch in its lovely grassy garden and a daily breakfast buffet. On Friday it does a buffet and grill from noon to 2pm.

Garden by Happy Rajah   INDIAN €€
(Map p78; 📱 263 8817; www.facebook.com/TheGardenByHappyRajah/; Royal Rd; mains Rs 320-890; ⊙ 11.30am-2.30pm & 6-10pm Mon-Sat; 🍴) Making the most of its busy roadside setting, this fine Indian restaurant does the simple things well – excellent rogan josh, curries, butter chicken and biryani, served up with a smile. We'll be back.

Café de Grand Baie Plage   INTERNATIONAL €€
(Map p74; 📱 263 7041; Royal Rd; breakfast from Rs 250, mains Rs 450-1100; ⊙ 7am-10pm) The food here's a good, if unexceptional, selection of grilled meats, seafood dishes and other local and international staples, and their octopus curry isn't bad, but you come for the uninterrupted views of the bay from a perch right above the water. Reservations are essential for lunch and dinner, especially if you'd like a front-row seat.

Cocoloko INTERNATIONAL €€
(Map p74; ☑ 263 1241; Royal Rd; breakfast from Rs 260, pizza from Rs 265, mains Rs 310-795; ☺ 9am-11pm; ☎) Arranged around an inviting pebble-strewn courtyard across the street from the beach, Cocoloko brings a slice of cool and wannabe sophistication to downtown Grand Baie. Familiar international fare won't inspire devotion, but the atmosphere is very conducive to coffee, cocktails and outdoor dining. There are salads, steaks, burgers, a few other mains and pizza (or 'pizzaloko', as it's known).

Throw in free wi-fi, live music most nights and a happy hour that generously runs from 4pm to 8pm, and there's a lot to be said for letting a long, lazy afternoon here segue effortlessly into the evening.

Coolen – Chez Ram MAURITIAN, SEAFOOD €€
(Map p72; ☑ 263 8569; Royal Rd; mains Rs 150-690; ☺ 11.30am-2pm & 6.30-10pm Thu-Tue) The clear favourite among Royal Rd's parade of restaurants, Coolen is often filled with locals. Customers are welcomed with a splash of rum while they thumb through the menu of Creole, North Indian and seafood staples. The octopus curry is terrific, and save room for the banana flambé.

Le Capitaine SEAFOOD €€€
(Map p72; ☑ 263 6867; www.lecapitaine.mu; Royal Rd; mains Rs 650-1800; ☺ noon-3pm & 6-10.30pm) This popular place serves good, standard seafood dishes in a convivial space that combines style with informality and partial bay views. Fresh lobster is the pick of a menu that ranges across island specialities, while other delicious mains include whole crab cooked with braised palm heart, and lobster ravioli with mushroom and bok choy. Reservations are essential in the evening.

🍸 Drinking & Nightlife

If you're looking for a party in Mauritius, you'll find it in Grand Baie. Many of the area's restaurants – including Cocoloko – have buzzing nightlife as well. Out near Luigi's (p75) just north of the town centre, nightclubs wax and wane with the seasons, but it's always worth checking what's happening.

★ Les Enfants Terribles CLUB
(Ferrari Club; Map p72; ☑ 263 8117; Royal Rd, Pointe aux Canonniers; ☺ 7pm-3am Fri & Sat) The top pick for a night out on the town, the 'little terrors' has a roaring dance floor, a chilled-out lounge and a special VIP section that overflows with champagne. Walls bedecked with hundreds of crinkled photos of partiers confirm the sociable local vibe.

Beach House BAR
(Map p74; ☑ 263 2599; www.thebeachhouse.mu; Royal Rd; ☺ 11.30am-late) Owned until recently by Kabous van der Westhuisen, a South African former rugby player, this lively joint bustles with about as much energy as a sports match in overtime. The unbeatable location is a major draw: the bar is smack-dab along the lapping waves of Grand Baie's emerald lagoon.

B52 COCKTAIL BAR
(Map p74; ☑ 263 0214; cnr La Salette & Royal Rds; ☺ 10am-midnight Mon-Sat) This large, popular spot serves up great cocktails all day long in its open-air setting in the heart of town.

Banana Bar BAR
(Map p74; ☑ 263 0326; www.bananabeachclub.com; Royal Rd; admission Rs 150; ☺ 10am-late Mon-Sat) In a petrol-station car park, this is one of the best spots for a drink and a chat. There's live music most nights and a generous 4pm to 7pm happy hour to kick things off.

🛍 Shopping

Coton des Îles CLOTHING
(Map p74; ☑ 263 2444; www.facebook.com/CotonDeslles/; La Salette Rd; ☺ 10am-5pm) All-natural, 100% cotton, 100% made in Mauritius – what's not to like about this fine shop a block back from the water. It's an all-white look – perfect for summer.

Françoise Vrot ART
(Map p72; ☑ 5754 7976, 263 5118; Reservoir Rd; ☺ 10am-1pm & 3-6.30pm) To purchase some original art, visit the studio of Françoise Vrot to see her expressive portraits of women fieldworkers. Opening hours vary, so you may need to call to get someone to come and open up if ringing the bell doesn't work.

Grand Baie Bazaar ARTS & CRAFTS
(Map p74; off Royal Rd; ☺ 9.30am-4.30pm Mon-Sat, to noon Sun) Hidden down an inland street away from Royal Rd, this market has a broad range of touristy Mauritian and Malagasy crafts. Prices aren't fixed, but wares aren't expensive and there's minimal hassling from vendors.

ⓘ Getting There & Away

There are no direct buses to Grand Baie from the airport, so it's necessary to change in Port Louis and transfer between two bus stations to do so. Almost all people will have a transfer provided by their hotel; for everyone else, we definitely suggest taking a taxi – or, better still, order one in advance via your hotel if your hotel is not one of the big players.

Express buses (Map p74; Royal Rd) run directly between Immigration Square bus station (p59) in Port Louis and Grand Baie every half-hour. The terminus for express buses to/from Port Louis (Rs 42) is on Royal Rd about 100m north of the intersection of Royal and La Salette Rds. Nonexpress buses en route to Cap Malheureux will also drop you in Grand Baie. Buses between Pamplemousses and Grand Baie leave roughly every hour. Nonexpress services via Trou aux Biches stop every few hundred metres along the coast road.

Expect to pay Rs 2200 to Rs 2300 for a taxi to/from the airport. A return trip to Pamplemousses, including waiting time, should set you back Rs 650 or so.

ⓘ Getting Around

BICYCLE

Many hotels and guesthouses can arrange bicycle hire, and some even do so for free. Otherwise, rates vary, but expect to pay between Rs 150 and Rs 250 per day, less if you hire for several days. Most of the local tour operators have bikes for rent; just walk down Royal Rd and see what's on offer.

CAR & MOTORCYCLE

There are numerous car-hire companies in Grand Baie, and there's ABC (p79) in nearby Pereybère, so you should be able to bargain, especially if you're renting for several days. Prices generally start at around Rs 1000 per day for a small hatchback. Find out if your hotel or guesthouse has a special discount agreement with a local company. Motorbikes of 50cc and 100cc are widely available in Grand Baie; rental charges begin at around Rs 500 per day, less if you rent for several days.

Pereybère
POP 8615

As development continues to boom along the north coast, it's becoming rather difficult to tell where Grand Baie ends and Pereybère (peu-ray-bear) begins. This area is very much the second development on the north coast after Grand Baie and has found the sweet spot between being a bustling tourist hub and a quiet holiday hideaway, although it leans more towards the former with each passing year. Its appeal is built around a good public beach.

◉ Sights & Activities

Galerie du Moulin Cassé GALLERY
(Map p78; ☑ 263 0672; www.facebook.com/GalerieDuMoulinCasse/; Old Mill Rd (Chemin de Vieux Moulin Cassé); ⊙ hours vary) FREE Housed in a charmingly restored sugar mill, the Galerie du Moulin Cassé features the vibrant floral scenes of painter Malcolm de Chazal (1902–82) and a collection of photographs by Diane Henry. The most impressive display, however, is the collection of over 20,000 terracotta pots lining the vaulted arcs of the ceiling. Ring ahead to check when they're open.

Ocean Spirit Diving DIVING
(Map p78; ☑ 263 4428; www.osdiving.com; Royal Rd; 1/3 dives Rs 1200/3400; ⊙ 8am-4.30pm) French-run and with an office on the main road through town, this recommended outfit is the pick of the dive centres in Pereybère itself.

Orca Dive Club DIVING
(Map p78; ☑ 5716 3167; www.facebook.com/Orca DiveClubMauritius/; Royal Rd) This professional, German-run dive centre is based at the Merville Hotel, between Pereybère and Grand Baie.

🛏 Sleeping

While there are a few larger hotels on the beach side of the main road, most accommodation here consists of guesthouses and little hotels in the backstreets, all a short walk from the town centre and public beach.

Casa Florida Hotel & Spa HOTEL €
(Map p78; ☑ 263 0080; http://web.casaflorida.net; Mt Oreb Lane; s/d incl breakfast Rs 1925/2350; ✴ ຈ ☎) Friendly staff and attractive rooms swathed in earth tones make this place a well-priced Pereybère option. It's a five-minute walk to the beach.

★ Bleu de Toi GUESTHOUSE €€
(Map p78; ☑ 269 1761; www.bleudetoi.mu; Coastal Rd; r from €75; ✴ @ ຈ ☎) Owned by friendly Belgians, this lovely B&B is the area's only worthy contender in the guesthouse category. Rooms feature simple yet tasteful furnishings, and adorable arched doorways abound. Don't miss the charming *table*

Pereybère

Pereybère

◉ Sights
1 Galerie du Moulin Cassé.................... C4

◆ Activities, Courses & Tours
2 Ocean Spirit Diving..............................C2
3 Orca Dive Club......................................A4
4 Reef Conservation D1

◎ Sleeping
5 Bleu de Toi...B3
6 Casa Florida Hotel & Spa....................C2

7 Flowers of Paradise Hotel.....................C3
8 Hibiscus Hotel B3
9 Le Beach Club..C2
10 Ocean Beauty C2

⊗ Eating
11 Caféteria Pereybère C2
12 Garden by Happy Rajah.........................A4
13 Le Poivrier...A4
14 Wang Thai C2

d'hôte (€12 to €18) in the evenings. Things also get cheaper the longer you stay. No children are allowed.

Flowers of Paradise Hotel HOTEL €€
(Map p78; ☑5934 5320; www.hotel-paradise-mauritius.mu; Beach Lane; s incl breakfast €90-110, d incl breakfast €100-140; ❋ 🛜 ☒) Set back from the main road, but a short walk from the beach, this gorgeous hotel has a vaguely bou-

tique feel, with beautifully appointed rooms and good service. Highly recommended.

Ocean Beauty HOTEL €€
(Map p78; ☑263 6039; www.ocean-beauty.com; Pointe d'Azur; r incl breakfast €70-250; ❋ @ 🛜 ☒) Aimed squarely at honeymooners, this hotel is boutique in the sense of having an intimate feel, but it's also basic: the rooms are stylish and atmospheric, but there's very lit-

tle else to the hotel. Despite this, it's a great spot for romance – breakfast is served on your balcony and there's direct access to the lovely town beach.

Le Beach Club
HOTEL €€

(Map p78; ☑ 263 5104; www.le-beach-club.com; Royal Rd; r from €98; ✳ ☎) This complex of studios and two-bedroom apartments is one of the few places on the seafront and has a great little beach perfect for swimming. Rooms have festive tropical colours and the location's brilliant. Complaints? We're nitpicking, but the common areas are so tiny they feel like storage spaces for stacked furniture.

Hibiscus Hotel
HOTEL €€

(Map p78; ☑ 263 8554; www.hibiscushotel.com; Royal Rd; s incl half board €90-140, d incl half board €130-195; ✳ ☎ ⊠) Hibiscus boasts a stone path that wends past thick jungle-like gardens, a super pool and a private beach of sorts (although there's quite a bit of rock to negotiate). Accommodation is in clean, comfortable rooms in three-storey blocks.

Oasis Villas
VILLAS €€€

(☑ 5791 6225; www.oasisvillasmauritius.com; villas from €205; ✳ ☎ ⊠) They take the use of the word 'oasis' seriously here. Trendy Asian-inspired decor enhances the lavish open-air floor plans at these villas with private pools spread around Pereybère in the blocks back from the beach.

✕ Eating

Pereybère has a handful of good places to eat, although the choice is much larger in Grand Baie.

Caféteria Pereybère
CAFE €

(Map p78; ☑ 263 8700; Royal Rd; mains Rs 160-650; ⊙ 11am-10pm) This friendly all-day, no-frills cafe-restaurant behind the public beach offers uninspired grilled fish, curries, and steak and chips from an extensive menu. Portions are on the small side and it's cash only. Come for the proximity to the beach and the low prices, rather than the quality of the cooking.

★ Le Poivrier
INTERNATIONAL €€

(Map p78; ☑ 263 3251, 5702 5956; www.lepoivrier.mu; Royal Rd; mains Rs 310-630; ⊙ 11.30am-2.30pm Tue-Sat, plus 7-10pm Thu-Sat) This charming, French-run place does a thoughtfully prepared European menu with fresh salads backed up with bruschettas, risottos, pastas and steak tartare. It all takes place in a lovely garden setting with a well-stocked wine shop on the premises. Bookings are recommended for dinner.

★ Wang Thai
THAI €€

(Map p78; ☑ 263 4050; www.thai.mu; Royal Rd; mains Rs 220-900, set menus Rs 450-550; ⊙ 6-10pm daily, plus noon-2.30pm Sat & Sun) Long the best restaurant in town and a pioneer of authentic Thai food in Mauritius, Wang Thai is a sophisticated, airy place with Buddha statues and raw silks setting the scene for surprisingly affordable cuisine. Treat your taste buds to such classics as *tom yum thalay* (lemongrass-laced seafood soup), green curry, fish in tamarind sauce or pad thai.

ⓘ Getting There & Away

Buses between Port Louis and Cap Malheureux stop in Pereybère as well as Grand Baie. Services run roughly every 30 minutes.

ⓘ Getting Around

You can rent cars, motorbikes and bicycles through local tour agencies. Cars start at Rs 1000 per day and motorbikes at Rs 500 for a 50cc or 100cc bike. Bicycles cost upwards of Rs 150 per day. Most of Grand Baie's car-hire companies will also drop off and pick up cars in Pereybère.

ABC Car Rental (☑ 263 1888; www.abc-carrental.com; off Royal Rd) Northern outpost of this reliable chain.

Ara Tour (☑ 262 7158; www.aratoursmauritius.com; off Royal Rd) Local car-rental agency.

PEREYBÈRE'S SAND SCULPTOR

There are many reasons to visit Pereybère's main beach, but one of the more unusual is to witness the extraordinarily skilful sand sculptures of local resident Sanjay Jhowry. Twice a week for the past 12 years, the friendly Sanjay has sculpted sand to the finest of forms, from above-average sand castles to 6m-high masterpieces that take two days to complete. On one day when we visited he had produced a wonderful rendition of the Eiffel Tower. On most days, the tide washes away his handiwork, but ask to see his photo album, which contains the hundreds of sculptures he has created over the years. You can also see some of his work online: www.artonsand.com.

Cap Malheureux

POP 5150

The northern edge of Mauritius has stunning views out to the islands off the coast, most obviously the dramatic headland of Coin de Mire. Although it feels like rather a backwater today, Cap Malheureux (Cape Misfortune; named for the number of ships that foundered on its rocks) is a place of great historical importance for Mauritius: it was here that the British invasion force finally defeated the French in 1810 and took over the island. A little past the cape lies the minuscule, picturesque fishing village also known as Cap Malheureux.

◉ Sights

Notre Dame Auxiliatrice   CHURCH
(Map p66; Royal Rd) Cap Malheureux's much-photographed church, the red-roofed Notre Dame Auxiliatrice, is worth a quick peek inside for its intricate woodwork and a holy-water basin fashioned out of a giant clamshell. A sign strictly prohibits newlyweds 'faking' a church wedding for the photographers here, but newlyweds – genuine or otherwise, photographers in tow – are a common sight in the church grounds. You can attend Mass here at 6pm on Saturday and 9am on Sunday.

🛏 Sleeping & Eating

★Le Paradise Cove   RESORT €€€
(Map p66; ☑204 3820; www.paradisecovehotel.com; Anse la Raie; d/ste with half board from €345/458; ❋@🛜🛉) A five-star, adults-only boutique resort aimed at honeymooners, understated Paradise Cove is as luxurious as its name suggests – it won first prize for the Indian Ocean's Leading Boutique Hotel at the 2016 World Travel Awards and inhabits an attractive small cove. The beach is at the end of an inlet, which gives it remarkable privacy.

Other great touches include a golf course, tennis courts, free watersports, a dive centre and 'love nests' on the promontory overlooking the northern islands. With four restaurants, a Cinq Mondes spa and award-winning gardens, this stylish place is a great destination for couples.

Helena's Cafe   CAFE €
(Map p66; ☑5978 1909; Royal Rd; mains Rs 250-560; ⊙9am-4pm Sun-Fri) Across the road from the church car park near the island's northernmost tip, this appealing little cafe is all decked out in marine blue and white, and serves up sandwiches, paninis and a few mains such as grilled chicken or fish, noodles or rice. Strangely, they're closed on Saturday.

★Amigo   SEAFOOD €€
(Map p66; ☑262 6248; www.facebook.com/restaurantamigoseafood; Le Pavillon, Royal Rd; mains Rs 250-950; ⊙noon-3pm & 6-10pm Mon-Sat) Everyone adores this friendly joint tucked behind Cape Malheureux township near the sugar cane farms. The writing's on the wall (literally): contented customers have left myriad messages of love and affection on every flat surface in the restaurant. The tables, however, are graffiti-free – they're reserved for the excellent seafood specialities.

❶ Getting There & Away

Buses run roughly every half-hour between Port Louis' Immigration Square bus station (p59) and Cap Malheureux (Rs 42), via Grand Baie. A taxi to Port Louis will cost Rs 1200, to Grand Baie Rs 500 to Rs 600, and to the airport Rs 2200.

Grand Gaube

POP 7700

Grand Gaube, about 6km east of Cap Malheureux, is where the development of northern Mauritius currently ends and the big blue takes over. The town remains a tiny fishing village with a good beach. Beyond the small rocky bays of Grande Gaube there are almost no beaches until a long way down the east coast, making any trip beyond here an illuminating glimpse into traditional Mauritian life without the tourists. In 1744 the *St Géran* foundered off Grand Gaube in a storm, inspiring the famous love story *Paul et Virginie* by Bernardin de St-Pierre.

🏃 Activities

Yemaya Adventures   KAYAKING
(www.yemayaadventures.com; half-/full-day from Rs 1600/2200) It's possible to explore Île Ambre offshore on a sea-kayaking trip with Yemaya. It also arranges rental, does longer expeditions and can organise mountain biking.

🛏 Sleeping

★Veranda Paul & Virginie   HOTEL €€€
(Map p66; ☑266 9736; www.veranda-resorts.com; off Royal Rd; r from €238; ❋@🛜🛉) The longest-established hotel in Grande Gaube is a

pleasant surprise. It's small enough not to be overwhelming, yet offers all the amenities required for luxury: two pools, a couple of restaurants, a Seven Colours spa, plenty of activities and a kids club. The spacious four-star rooms, all with sea views, are stylishly fitted out and there's a small but attractive beach.

Zilwa Attitude RESORT €€€
(Map p66; ☑ 204 9800; https://hotels-attitude.com/en/zilwa-attitude/; Royal Rd, Calodyne; r incl half-board from €336) Zilwa Attitude is a lovely four-star place with all the features you'd expect from this excellent chain. These include an infinity pool with fabulous views, good restaurants, rooms with rustic wooden furnishings, and plenty of water sports – from kitesurfing and stand-up paddling to boat excursions to the offshore islands.

Lux* Grand Gaube HOTEL €€€
(Map p66; ☑ 698 9800; www.luxresorts.com; off Royal Rd; r from €273; ✴@🛜🐾) This very large, stylish establishment enjoys an idyllic location miles from the mass tourism found further down the coast. Guests have the run of the pretty bay and the hotel's well-appointed surroundings. The hotel is feng shui themed, and romance is key. Standard rooms are attractive, but the designer private villas with a plunge pool are gorgeous.

❶ Getting There & Away

Buses run roughly every 15 minutes between Port Louis' Immigration Square bus station and Grand Gaube (Rs 48). A taxi to Port Louis will cost Rs 1250, to Grand Baie Rs 700 and to the airport Rs 2300.

Pamplemousses

POP 9570

Just off the motorway between Port Louis and Grand Baie, Pamplemousses (named for the grapefruit-like citrus trees that the Dutch introduced to Mauritius from Java) has a rich concentration of attractions – worth a day of your holiday in Mauritius.

One of the island's main attractions, the botanical gardens are soothing, tranquil and brimful of endemic and foreign plant species. Also of interest is the decommissioned Beau Plan sugar factory nearby, which has been converted into a fascinating museum. Not far away is one of the island's most beautiful colonial-era mansions, Château Labourdonnais. Throw in a couple of excel-

---

WORTH A TRIP

CHÂTEAU LABOURDONNAIS

One of the loveliest examples of colonial architecture on the island, restored **Château Labourdonnais** (Map p66; ☑ 266 9533; www.chateaulabourdonnais.com; adult/child Rs 400/250; ☺9am-5pm, last entry 4.15pm) was completed in 1859. Built in teak and sporting an Italian neoclassical style, the perfectly proportioned chateau is filled with sober Victorian furnishings interspersed with some exceptionally lovely design flourishes. Compulsory guided tours last 45 minutes. The Labourdonnais Express (adult Rs 250, child Rs 175) is a train that does a 45-minute tour of the gardens and orchards at 10.30am and 2pm.

To get here, follow the signs off the M2 motorway, around 3km north of Pamplemousses.

---

lent culinary options and you can realistically make a day of it.

Otherwise, the town is typically Mauritian in a quiet, untouristy and slightly decaying kind of way, and feels a million miles from Grand Baie or nearby Trou aux Biches.

◎ Sights

★ Sir Seewoosagur Ramgoolam Botanical Gardens GARDENS
(Jardins de Pamplemousses, Royal Botanical Gardens; Map p66; ☑ 243 9401; http://ssrbg.govmu.org; admission Rs 200, guide per person Rs 50; ☺8.30am-5.30pm) After London's Kew Gardens, the SSR Gardens is one of the world's best botanical gardens. It's among the most popular tourist attractions in Mauritius and easily reached from almost anywhere on the island. Labelling of the plants is a work in progress, and you can hire one of the knowledgeable guides who wait just inside or use the maps for a self-guided tour. Golf-buggy tours (adult Rs 250, child Rs 100) are available on request for those with limited mobility.

The centrepiece of the gardens is a pond filled with giant *Victoria amazonica* water lilies, native to South America. Young leaves emerge as wrinkled balls and unfold into the classic tea-tray shape up to 2m across in a matter of hours. The flowers in the centre of the huge leaves open white one day and close red the next. The lilies are at their biggest and best in the warm summer months, notably January.

Palms constitute the most important part of the horticultural display, and they come in an astonishing variety of shapes and forms. Some of the more prominent are the stubby bottle palms, the tall royal palms and the talipot palms, which flower once after about 40 years and then die. Other varieties include the raffia, sugar, toddy, fever, fan and even sealing-wax palms. There are many other curious tree species on display, including the marmalade box tree, the fish poison tree and the sausage tree.

Another highlight is the abundant birdlife – watch for the crimson hues of the Madagascar fody – while there are populations of deer and around a dozen giant Aldabra tortoises near the park's northern exit.

The gardens were named after Sir Seewoosagur Ramgoolam, the first prime minister of independent Mauritius, and were started by Mahé de Labourdonnais in 1735 as a vegetable plot for his Mon Plaisir Château (which now contains a small exhibition of photographs). Close to the chateau is the funerary platform where Sir Seewoosagur Ramgoolam was cremated (his ashes were scattered on the Ganges in India). Various international dignitaries have planted trees in the surrounding gardens, including Nelson Mandela, Indira Gandhi and a host of British royals.

The landscape came into its own in 1768 under the auspices of French horticulturalist Pierre Poivre. Like Kew Gardens, the gardens played a significant role in the horticultural espionage of the day. Poivre imported seeds from around the world in a bid to end France's dependence on Asian spices. The gardens were neglected between 1810 and 1849 until British horticulturalist James Duncan transformed them into an arboretum for palms and other tropical trees.

L'Aventure du Sucre   MUSEUM
(Map p66; ✆243 7900; www.aventuredusucre. com; Pamplemousses; adult/child Rs 400/200; ⊙9am-5pm) The former Beau Plan sugar factory houses one of the best museums in Mauritius. It not only tells the story of sugar in great detail but also covers the history of Mauritius, slavery, the rum trade and much, much more. Allow a couple of hours to do it justice.

The original factory was founded in 1797 and only ceased working in 1999. Most of the machinery is still in place, and former workers are on hand to answer questions about the factory and the complicated process of turning sugar cane into crystals. There are also videos and interactive displays as well as quizzes for children. At the end of the visit you can taste some of the 15 varieties of unrefined sugar, two of which were invented in Mauritius. If you're interested in their cane-cutting tour (Rs 460 per person) you'll need to reserve in advance.

✖ Eating

There are a couple of excellent lunch options in Pamplemousses, while the cheaper restaurants that lie scattered along the western perimeter of the gardens are your best (perhaps only) bet if you're here for dinner. Otherwise, head to Grand Baie or Trou aux Biches.

★Chez Tante Athalie   MAURITIAN €€
(Map p66; ✆243 9266; Centre de Flacq Rd, Mont Gout; menu Rs 530; ⊙noon-2.30pm Mon-Sat) The best-known *table d'hôte* in the area, open-sided Chez Tante Athalie offers fresh, simple, wonderful Creole tastes overlooking a garden filled with vintage cars. There's an oasis-like feel to the place. From the entrance to the botanical gardens, follow the signs around 500m to the T-junction, turn left and then watch for a signposted driveway 2km further on your left.

Le Fangourin   MAURITIAN €€
(Map p66; ✆243 7900; www.aventuredusucre. com; L'Aventure du Sucre; mains Rs 380-860; ⊙11.30am-5pm; ✐) If all the sugar in L'Aventure du Sucre museum has set your taste buds working, you could sup a glass of sugar-cane juice at Le Fangourin, a stylish cafe-restaurant in the museum grounds. It specialises in sophisticated Creole cuisine (from seafood to steaks and a fine shellfish risotto) and all sorts of sugary delights. It also does a fine vegetarian platter.

❶ Getting There & Away

Pamplemousses can be reached by bus from Grand Baie, Trou aux Biches, Grand Gaube and Port Louis. Services from Grand Baie and Trou aux Biches run approximately every hour and stop near the sugar museum on the way to the botanical gardens.

Buses from Port Louis' Immigration Square bus station and Grand Gaube operate every 10 to 15 minutes. These buses only stop at the botanical gardens, from where it takes about 15 minutes to walk to the museum.

THE WEST

Mauritius' western coast and hinterland is the nation's most diverse region. Underwater diving treasures lie just off the bustling tourist hub of Flic en Flac, and further south are the sandy bays and mountainous backdrops of Black River (Rivière Noire) and Tamarin. Capping the coastline's southern tip is the dramatic beauty of Le Morne Brabant, an awesomely photogenic (and hikeable) crag. Nor far inland, Mauritius rises steeply; this part of the island encompasses fauna-filled Black River Gorges National Park and beguiling Chamarel, one of the loveliest towns anywhere on the island.

ⓘ Getting There & Away

The main bus routes in western Mauritius are those from Port Louis down to the southern end of Black River (Rivière Noire). There is also a regular service between Quatre Bornes, on the Central Plateau, and Chamarel.

Your hotel or guesthouse should be able to arrange bike and car hire.

Note that there are only two petrol stations in the west: one at **Flic en Flac** (Royal Rd; ⊘ 6am-9pm) and one in **Rivière Noire** (⊘ 24 hr).

Flic en Flac

POP 2620

As wonderful and whimsical as the name sounds, Flic en Flac isn't quite the picture of paradise you saw on your travel agent's website. The area's moniker is thought to be a corruption of the old Dutch name Fried Landt Flaak (Free and Flat Land); the endless acreage of shoreline was undoubtedly striking when explorers arrived in the 18th century. Today the area is exploding with apartment complexes, souvenir shops, moneychangers and pinchpenny holiday rentals. Although development in Flic en Flac has gone the way of Grand Baie, the town's still a dozen clubs and restaurants short of attracting a party crowd.

All is not lost, however. The beach is still one of the best in Mauritius, and if you stay at any of the high-end resorts in the Wolmar area outside the town, you'll uncover some stellar stretches of sand, glorious diving and a small handful of palate-pleasing restaurants.

◉ Sights

Casela World of Adventures ZOO
(Map p84; ☑ 5727 6076, 401 6500; www.caselapark.me; adult/child Rs 770/520; ⊘9am-5pm)

When you arrive at this 14-hectare nature park, you're greeted with a bewildering range of options – in addition to being a zoo (with big cats, rhinos, giraffes and other African mammals), the beautifully landscaped reserve offers a giant slide, animal interactions, and a variety of heart-pumping activities like ziplining, canyoning and quad-bike 'safaris' around a neighbouring home to zebras, impalas, waterbucks, rhinos and monkeys. Casela is on the main road, 1km south of the turn-off to Flic en Flac.

Children are well catered for with a petting zoo, a playground, giant tortoises, fishing and minigolf. Check out the website for a full list of prices or spend some time at the information desk before the main entrance to get a handle on how to spend your day.

If you simply pay the admission fee, you'll be free to wander the grounds, where you'll see tortoises, a huge range of exotic birds and a few primate species in cages. And make sure you pass by the Mirador restaurant, which has fabulous sweeping views of the coastal plain. Also included in the price is a trip in a safari vehicle, during which you get out and look at lions, cheetahs and hyenas from viewpoints overlooking large, grassy enclosures, and another driving through a much larger area roamed by zebras, ostriches etc.

The park is famous for offering 'interactions' with the big cats – which means you're actually in the enclosure with them, accompanied by a guide armed with nothing more than a large stick – and the hour-long 'walking with lions' experience. We don't recommend either of these two options. These are wild animals, despite having been bred in captivity. Incidents in which visitors have been mauled by big cats in similar places in Africa aren't common, but they do occur; participants here are asked to sign an indemnity form before they draw near to the animals. Questions have also been raised by animal rights groups about the quality of life for big cats in such establishments, as well as about the animals' future when they are too old to take part in activities. Any claims that these captive cats contribute in some way to conservation are incorrect.

Bolom Ng Metal Art Gallery GALLERY
(Map p88; ☑ 453 5277; Royal Rd; adult/child Rs 100/50; ⊘10am-4pm Tue-Sun) Once a hotel, now an eclectic gallery of sculptures shaped in wrought iron and tile mosaics, this place is a fun place to pass half an hour.

The West

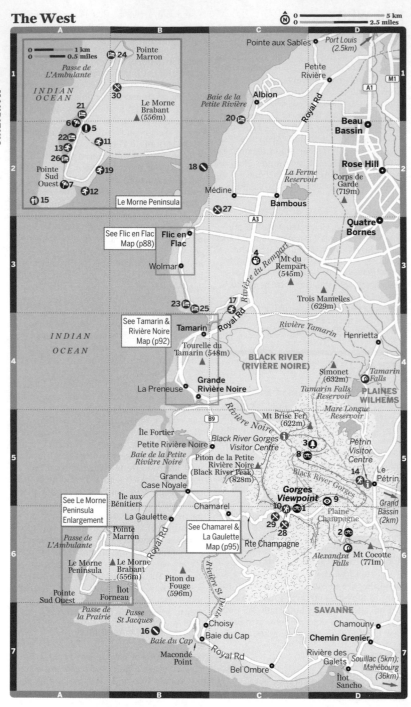

The West

MAURITIUS FLIC EN FLAC

🏃 Activities

Some of Mauritius' best dive sites (p32) can be found just beyond the emerald lagoon near Flic en Flac, where the shallow waters suddenly give way to the deep. The most popular site in the area is **La Cathédrale** (The Cathedral; Map p88), with its signature stone arches and tucked-away cavern.

In addition to the dive shops, most of the upmarket hotels in Wolmar have their own diving operators, all of which are open to nonguests. Check out www.msda.mu for a list of licensed and insured dive operators.

Sun Divers   DIVING
(Map p88; 📞5972 1504; www.sundivers mauritius.com; La Pirogue, Wolmar; 1/3 dives Rs 1800/4700; ⊙8am-5pm Mon-Sat, dives 9am, noon & 2.30pm daily) Based at La Pirogue hotel (p86), Sun Divers is one of the better dive operators in the area and among the oldest outfits on the island. It also runs PADI courses and sessions on underwater photography. Dives have a minimum of three participants. There are discounts for those who have their own equipment. Ring ahead if you're not staying at the hotel.

Sea Urchin Diving Centre   DIVING
(Map p88; 📞453 8825; www.sea-urchin-diving. com; Royal Rd; dive for beginners/experienced divers Rs 2000/1200; ⊙office 8am-4pm Mon-Sat, dives 9am, 11.30am & 1.30pm) This German-run

centre is professionally run and, conveniently, you'll find it along the main road.

La Pirogue Big Game Fishing   FISHING
(Map p88; 📞483 8054; www.lapiroguebiggame. com) Fishing outings and other boat excursions can be arranged with La Pirogue Big Game Fishing, based at La Pirogue hotel.

🧭 Tours

⭐**Taxi à Maurice**   TOURS
(Turquoise Voyages; Map p88; 📞5759 8806; www. taxiamaurice.com; Ave des Flamingos) Primarily a reliable place to arrange taxis around the island, this excellent place also runs tours by boat and by road around Mauritius. It consistently gets glowing reports from travellers.

🛏 Sleeping

Central Flic en Flac is decidedly *not* upmarket, with condos and apartment complexes lining every street. South of Flic en Flac, in the Wolmar area, you'll find several charming luxury options directly on the sand.

As always, if you're considering one of the pricier choices, it is best to book through a travel agent, which should get you significant discounts.

Villas Caroline   HOTEL €€
(Map p88; 📞453 8411; www.facebook.com/Villas-CarolineBeachHotel/; Royal Rd; s/d from €125/140; ❄🛜🏊) Less pretentious than other

DOLPHIN-WATCHING

Swimming with dolphins is one of the most popular activities anywhere along the west coast of Mauritius, with bottlenose and spinner dolphins frolicking in the sea off Flic en Flac and Tamarin. They can be found in the bay most mornings – most boat operators head out by 8am to spend an hour or two dolphin-watching and sending their paying guests into the water with snorkels when the creatures draw alongside.

Watching the dolphins is one thing, but we have travelled on these boats and observed them in action and we have serious concerns about the impact of these excursions.

The boats – sometimes more than 20, all with outboard motors – mount a lookout and then race in the direction of a pod whenever one is sighted. The aim is clearly to get in as near as possible and then offload their clients into the water so that they can get as close as possible to the dolphins. But in our experience, the practice of most operators amounts to nothing less than harassment and carries the possibility of causing significant stress to these gentle creatures. We wonder how long it is before the dolphins leave and don't come back.

Guidelines from scientists for interacting with wild dolphins suggest that it is very difficult to ensure that it is not an intrusive or stressful experience for the animals. When done badly, such interactions can disrupt dolphins' feeding, resting, nursing and other behaviours. Pursuing dolphins in this way may also have long-term impacts on the health and well-being of individual dolphins and whole populations. There are also the risks of injury to dolphins by boat propellers and of dolphins becoming dependent on humans for food – some operators try to lure the animals towards their boat by throwing scraps into the water.

If you do decide to swim with dolphins, please keep your distance from them, do not touch them if they come near, and encourage your operator to keep an appropriate distance from the pods. One local operator we recommend for its sustainable approach is Dolswim (p90).

---

places around here and popular with families, Villas Caroline has attractive rooms, many of which front right onto the beach. It also has a dive centre and a more-than-adequate portfolio of swimming pools.

Aanari
HOTEL €€

(Map p88; ☑ 453 9000; www.aanari.com; Royal Rd; r from €145; ❄ @ ⎋ ⎘) Perched atop Pasadena Village, Aanari attempts boutique sophistication with a clutch of oriental statues and it does a pretty good job of removing itself from the tacky downtown milieu. Rooms feel distinctly Asian, with lacquered furnishings, errant flower petals and silk bed-runners. The hotel's biggest drawcard is the window-filled spa and fitness centre on the roof.

★ Maradiva
HOTEL €€€

(Map p84; ☑ 403 1500; www.maradiva.com; off Royal Rd, Wolmar; villas from €580; ❄ @ ⎋ ⎘) Perfectly manicured grounds sprinkled with luxurious villas lie at Maradiva. The place oozes charm, serenity and impeccable service, from the entry gate to the sleek seaside resto-lounge. Rooms are large and

beautifully presented and come with private plunge pools.

La Pirogue
HOTEL €€€

(Map p88; ☑ 403 3900; www.lapirogue.com; r incl half board from €275; ❄ @ ⎋ ⎘) Mauritius' oldest resort shares the same management as Sugar Beach next door, but there's a completely different feel here. Rather than a colonial-manse theme, La Pirogue opts for a charming fishing-village vibe, with semi-circular clusters of hut-villas arranged along the 500m of spectacular sandy beach.

Sands Suites Resort & Spa
RESORT €€€

(Map p84; ☑ 403 1200; www.sands.mu; Royal Rd, Wolmar; d incl half board from €315; ❄ @ ⎋ ⎘) With gorgeous views from the beachside pool onto Tamarin Bay and towards Le Morne, this sophisticated yet unpretentious option has an airy, tropical elegance that permeates the open, timber-framed lobby. The rooms sport subtle tones, generous bathrooms and sea-view balconies. There are two restaurants, a spa and plenty of activities, including a dive centre.

✖ Eating

Wealthier vacationers tend to take advantage of their upmarket hotels' half board holiday packages, while budgetarians usually self-cater or go for cheap street fare. Thus there's a noticeable lack of out-of-this-world establishments in central Flic en Flac. That said, there are some fabulous budget restaurants serving authentic local cooking if you know where to look.

Spar Supermarket   SUPERMARKET
(Map p88; Royal Rd, Pasadena Village; ⊙8am-8pm Mon-Sat, to 7pm Sun) Well-stocked supermarket for self-caterers.

★Creole Shack   CREOLE €
(Map p88; ✐5736 1523; Ave Radar; mains Rs 400; ⊙noon-9pm) Set just back from the beach so that passers-by don't even know it's there, this wood-lined place does authentic Creole cooking like coconut prawns, traditional Mauritian curries and *rougáilles* (tomato-based ratatouille), tuna steaks and a well-priced seafood platter. Friendly service, reasonable prices, authentic cooking – what more could you want?

★Roti Aka Vinoda   INDIAN €
(Map p88; Royal Rd; mains Rs 12-40; ⊙11am-6pm) It's all very simple here - rotis or farata (Indian flatbreads) filled with whatever you like – fish, beef, chicken etc. The quality puts many Indian restaurants to shame and, not surprisingly, queues form early on weekends.

Jeanno Burger   BURGERS €
(Map p88; ✐5202 4500; Royal Rd; mains Rs 75-240; ⊙11am-9pm Tue-Sun) The pick of the food vans just back from the beach (the places selling fresh pineapple give it a run for its money), Jeanno's serves up good burgers, paninis, hot dogs and sandwiches to a long line of devotees. It's a one-man show, so things can take a while, but no one minds. There are worse places to wait.

★Canne à Sucre   MAURITIAN €€
(Chez May; Map p88; ✐453 9448; Royal Rd; meals Rs 800; ⊙by appointment) Now here's something special: an authentic slice of Mauritian life in the midst of touristy Flic en Flac. May has converted her roadside bar-restaurant into a cosy space that captures the essence of coastal Mauritius. She offers multicourse Creole dinner feasts – rice, chicken, octopus, Creole sausages and 'some vegetables you've never heard of' – with dessert and rum thrown in.

You'll need to order the day before you plan to visit, but *don't* let that put you off and *don't* miss it.

★Domaine Anna   CHINESE, SEAFOOD €€
(Map p84; ✐453 9650; http://domaineanna.mu/; Médine; mains Rs 350-975; ⊙11.30am-2.30pm & 6.30-10.30pm Tue-Sun) You'll need a taxi or rental car to get here, but you'll be glad you made the trip: this is Flic en Flac's most refined dining experience, set in colonial-style pavilions. The predominantly Chinese menu is the brainchild of chef Hang Leung Pah Hang, and the food is excellent – locals come from all over for their fix of crab, calamari and lobster.

Paul & Virginie   MAURITIAN €€
(Map p88; ✐403 3900; www.lapirogue.com; La Pirogue; mains from Rs 590; ⊙12.30-2.30pm & 7.30-10pm Mon-Sat, 12.30-2.30pm Sun) With lovely thatched platforms extending over swimming pools and towards the ocean, Paul & Virginie makes for a romantic meal. The food – grilled fish, palm-heart salads, curries and seafood in many guises – matches the setting and the service rarely misses a beat. You don't need to be staying at La Pirogue to eat here, but you will need to reserve.

Zub Express   INDIAN, CHINESE €€
(Map p88; ✐453 8868, 5757 9355; www.zub-express.com; 286 Coastal Rd; mains Rs 125-950; ⊙10.30am-9.30pm Fri-Wed) Indian-Chinese fusion cooking sounds rather fancy, but the reality is far simpler, featuring dishes like

---

CLUB MED OR CLUB MING DYNASTY?

Forget what you know about the Club Med chain: **Club Med La Plantation d'Albion** (Map p84; ✐206 0700; www.clubmed.com; Avenue Du Club Med, Albion; r incl half-board €580; ❂@🛜🏊) is one of the finest resorts on the island, with acres of groomed gardens and savvy design that fuses African and Zen motifs. The beach isn't tops, but the luxurious swimming pools more than make up for that.

Quirky side note: during particularly tumultuous rainstorms guests often find fragments of Ming dynasty china from a merchant vessel that ran aground in the reef many moons ago.

Flic en Flac

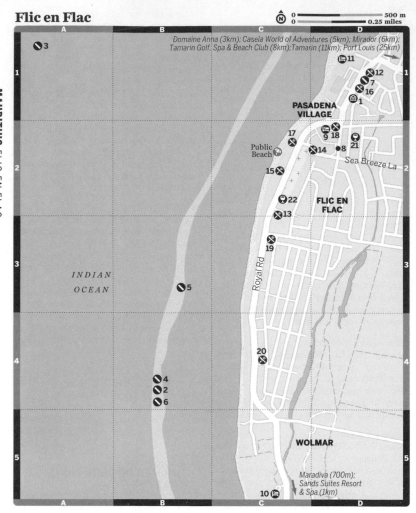

Flic en Flac

N 0 ___ 500 m
0 ___ 0.25 miles

Domaine Anna (3km); Casela World of Adventures (5km); Mirador (6km);
Tamarin Golf, Spa & Beach Club (8km);Tamarin (11km); Port Louis (25km)

PASADENA
VILLAGE

Public
Beach

Sea Breeze La

FLIC EN
FLAC

INDIAN
OCEAN

Royal Rd

WOLMAR

Maradiva (700m);
Sands Suites Resort
& Spa (1km)

---

excellent biryanis and noodle dishes alongside more creative dishes such as lobster butter masala. Throw in friendly service and it's no wonder this place gets rave reviews from travellers and locals alike. They also do a limited number of dishes for take-away.

The Beach Shack   INTERNATIONAL, SEAFOOD €€
(Map p88; ☑ 453 9080; www.facebook.com/The. Beach.Shack.Mauritius/; Royal Rd; mains Rs 310-800; ☉ noon-10pm) We thought this place wouldn't last, with its faddish designer seating and lounge-bar atmosphere. The reason it has is that it's classier than other places

along the coastal strip, and the menu has some fab choices, from fish and chips to burgers (wagyu burgers from Kyoto, for example), prime cuts of steak cooked to your liking and fresh seafood.

Restaurant Carrí Massalé   MAURITIAN €€
(Map p88; ☑ 5777 3545; www.restaurantcarrimassale.com; Royal Rd; mains Rs 195-695; ☉ 10am-3pm & 6-10pm Thu-Tue, 10am-3pm Wed) The roadside setting isn't Flic en Flac's finest, but this place does good local specialties which are much needed in this catch-all town. Curries, *rougaílles* (a tomato-based dish not

Flic en Flac

unlike ratatouille) and dishes with Creole inflections. The emphasis on local ingredients is another highlight.

Chez Pepe ITALIAN €€
(Map p88; ☑ 453 9383; Royal Rd; mains Rs 350-600; ⊙11.30am-late) Chez Pepe is a lively spot serving up Italian favourites like pizza, seafood spaghetti and rustic Tuscan meats, as well as local specialities like smoked-marlin salad. It won't be a particularly memorable meal, but it's still one of the best places for a bite along Flic en Flac's beachside road.

 Drinking & Nightlife

KenziBar BAR
(Map p88; ☑ 453 5259; Ave des Nenuphars; ⊙6pm-midnight Mon-Sat) KenziBar, a block or two back from the waterfront, is your best bet for nightlife in Flic en Flac, and one of few places where it's about more than just noise. There's tongue-tingling *rhum arrangés* (rum punch), fire-spurting torches, live music (Friday from 9pm and Sunday from 7pm) and a mangy, pat-hungry dog that calls the bar home – welcome to Mauritius!

Shotz BAR, CLUB
(Map p88; ☑ 453 5626; http://shotz.mu; Royal Rd; ⊙9pm-2am Mon-Thu, 10pm-5am Fri & Sat) Both lounge bar and nightclub, Shotz is about as glamorous as things get beyond the high walls of the upmarket resorts. Drink early with happy hour before midnight on weekends, then dance til nearly dawn. Not every night works, but when it does you'll find yourself waving your arms in the air like you just don't care.

❶ Getting There & Away

There is a bus from Port Louis to Flic en Flac and Wolmar every 15 minutes or so. Public buses constantly ply the coastal route in Flic en Flac and many tourists use them as a cheap and quick hop-on, hop-off service. A taxi from Port Louis to Flic en Flac will cost Rs 1200. Count on Rs 2000 for a taxi to the airport, Rs 1500 to Le Morne and Rs 1800 to Belle Mare. A ride to Black River costs Rs 650.

❶ Getting Around

All accommodation and travel agencies in the area can help arrange bicycle and car hire. Count on Rs 250 for a bike. Cars start at Rs 900 for a manual and Rs 1200 for an automatic. Agencies line the main road through town and most offer the exact same products and swipe identical commission.

Tamarin & Black River

POP 12,200

The beach-fringed land between Flic en Flac and Le Morne is known to most Mauritians as Black River (Rivière Noire). One of the island's last coastal areas to witness development, this constellation of townships has grown in leaps and bounds over the last few years. Despite the sudden appearance of modern structures, Black River offers a more active yet quieter experience – resorts are few and far between and you have a choice of sea and mountains when it comes to getting out and exploring. Sensational hiking, scenic shorelines, top-notch fishing and interesting historical relics are all within arm's reach.

MAURITIUS TAMARIN & BLACK RIVER

◎ Sights

★ Tamarin Beach
BEACH

(Map p92) Locals like to wax nostalgic about Tamarin Beach and its surfing heyday, and in many ways this sandy cove still feels like a throwback to earlier times, although things are changing. Tamarin remains a popular place and its beach has one of the most spectacular backdrops (looking north) in the country.

Les Salines de Yémen
HISTORIC SITE

(Map p92; ☑484 0430; salinesdeyemen@gmail. com; Royal Rd; tour per person Rs 200; ◎8.30am–4pm Mon–Fri, to 11.30am Sat) On the site of the old salt flats of Black River, this place runs 15-minute tours that take in old and new salt production techniques and this striking-looking site. There's a small gift shop.

Martello Tower
MUSEUM, FORT

(Map p92; ☑471 0178; Allee des Pêcheurs; adult/child Rs 80/40; ◎9.30am-5pm Tue-Sat, to 1pm Sun) In the 1830s the British built five 'Martello' towers – copies of the tower at Mortella Point in Corsica (vowel order was apparently not a priority for the British) – to protect their young colony from predators (namely the French, who were suspected of supporting a slave rebellion). The one at La Preneuse is now a small museum where captions explain the tower's ingenious design – 3m-thick walls are crowned by a copper cannon that could apparently destroy a target 2km away.

✦ Activities

Deep-sea fishing is the main activity here. Although hiking in Black River (Rivière Noire) itself is is next to impossible, it serves as an ideal base for the ample hiking opportunities at Black River Gorges National Park further inland and Le Morne Peninsula to the south.

Tamarina Golf Club
GOLF

(Map p84; ☑401 3006; http://tamarina.mu/golf/en/; Tamarin Bay; ◎9-/18-hole green fees Rs 3200/5500) The magnificent Tamarina Golf Club has a par-72, 18-hole course designed by Rodney Wright. It sprawls across 206 hectares along an old hunting estate situated between the coastal townships and the looming spine of the inland hills – fabulous views.

Dolswim
WILDLIFE WATCHING

(Map p92; ☑5422 9281; www.dolswim.com; La Jetée Rd, Black River; whale-watching adult/ child Rs 2200/1375, dolphin-watching from Rs 1900/1175) ✐ Dolswim bucks the trend of dolphin-watching operators along the west coast by taking a more sustainable approach to excursions – its staff have been trained by local marine and conservation authorities. Unusually, it also runs whale-watching excursions from July to October or November, when humpback whales migrate north along the west coast.

⌷ Sleeping

Noticeably devoid of monstrous upmarket resorts, Black River (Rivière Noire) prefers old-school inns, quiet villas, low-slung apartment complexes and welcoming *chambres d'hôtes* tucked down narrow lanes.

The residential vibe in Black River means that there's a wide selection of private apartments and villas for rent.

Chez Jacques
HOTEL €

(Map p92; ☑5715 5108; www.guesthousechezjacques.com; Tamarin Beach Ave; s/d with fan Rs 1300/1800, with air-con Rs 1500/2200; ❋@☞) Squeeze down a side road on the way to Tamarin Beach and you'll uncover the famous Chez Jacques. Forty years ago Jacques' parents opened their home to visiting surfers and, although the number of wave hunters has dwindled, there's still a laid-back vibe here – this is as close as you'll get on the island to a backpacker's hostel.

Jacques can help water sports enthusiasts get kitted up; he also hosts regular guitar jam sessions.

Tamarin Hotel
HOTEL €€

(Map p92; ☑483 3100; www.veranda-resorts.com/en/mauritius-hotel-tamarin; Tamarin Beach; r from €110; ❋@☞☲) Recently reopened after a major and much-needed overhaul, this is now a modern resort hotel on a prime patch of beachfront real estate. The rooms are smart and contemporary (some with wall murals) and attempts have been made to incorporate some of the original features with exposed beams and white-wood furnishings. If they keep these prices, it's a steal.

La Mariposa
APARTMENT €€

(Map p92; ☑483 5048, 5728 0506; www.lamariposa.mu; Allée des Pêcheurs, La Preneuse; r/apt incl breakfast €110/180; ❋☞☲) Set directly along the sea and surrounded by a wild tropical garden, this quiet option features an L-shaped row of double-decker apartments. Rooms are breezy and simple, with cream-coloured walls, scarlet drapes and rounded balconies promising memorable sunset views. This is one of few hotels in Mauritius that openly advertises its gay-friendly credentials.

Marlin Creek Residence GUESTHOUSE €€
(Map p92; ☑5491 9727; 10 Colonel Dean Ave; d/bungalows incl breakfast €95/170; ⚙🞯🛜⛱) This worthy member of Black River's sleeping scene sits along the cerulean bay just a stone's throw from the jetty. The buzzing fisherfolk next door give the property a wonderfully local feel. Rooms are attractive, if a little wood-heavy, and it has an unusually long and narrow pool. Travellers give consistently glowing reviews.

★ Bay Hotel BOUTIQUE HOTEL €€€
(Map p92; ☑483 7042; www.thebay.mu; Ave des Cocotiers, La Preneuse; r €130-250; ⚙@🛜⛱) What a find! The Bay comes pretty darn close to boutique chic while still keeping prices relatively low. The thoughtfully decorated rooms (bright pillows, fresh tropical flowers, pristine white linen and arty wall hangings) are arranged on two floors around a white-walled courtyard. Don't miss the seaside restaurant and pool out the back.

**Latitude Seafront
Apartments** APARTMENT €€€
(Map p92; ☑403 5308; www.horizon.mu/accommodation/latitude/; Royal Rd; 2-bedroom apt €175-200, 3-bedroom apt €180-380; 🅿⚙🛜⛱) Opened in late 2015, this fine South African–run complex has stunning, spacious, contemporary apartments, many with their own splash pool, and a real sense of minimalist style. There's a lovely infinity pool, barbecues and coffee machines in each apartment, and a boat jetty, but no beach. Avoid the row of apartments at the back that overlook the car park.

Belle Crique APARTMENT €€€
(Map p92; ☑403 5304; www.belle-crique-mauritius.com; Coastal Rd; apt from €265; 🅿⚙🛜⛱) Beautiful modern apartments with understated flair make this place one of the best complexes along this stretch of road. Contemporary art, designer furnishings, Nespresso coffee machines and Weber barbecues all make this feel like home. There's usually a three-night minimum stay.

Les Lataniers Bleus GUESTHOUSE €€€
(Map p92; ☑483 6541; www.leslataniersbleus.com; ⚙@🛜⛱) If you're hoping to partake in the

DEEP-SEA FISHING
•••••••••••••••••••••••••••••••
The estuary at Black River suddenly plunges 700m down to the ocean floor, making it one of the island's deep-sea-fishing hubs. Peak season is between November and March, when you can catch blue marlin. Black marlin and barracuda can be caught throughout the year, the yellowfin season is from March to May and the wahoo season is around September to December.

The better operators include:

Le Morne Anglers' Club (Map p92; ☑483 5801; www.morneanglers.com; Colonel Dean Ave; ⊙6.30am-8.30pm)

Zazou Fishing (Map p92; ☑5729 9222, 5788 3804; www.zazoufishing.com; Ave des Rougets, Tamarin)

JP Henry Charters Ltd (Map p92; ☑5729 0901; www.blackriver-mauritius.com; Royal Rd)

Mauritian *chambre d'hôte* experience, look no further – Les Lataniers Bleus offers local hospitality at its finest. Josette Marchal-Vexlard is the head of the household, and she dotes on her guests with effortless charm and an infectious smile. Major renovations were undertaken in 2018.

Every comfort has been considered – there's even a power point hidden in a tree trunk so that you can update your blog while sitting in the sand. The evening *table d'hôte* on the veranda is a great way to meet other guests and learn about life on the island from the affable hostess.

**Tamarina Golf &
Spa Boutique Hotel** RESORT €€€
(Map p92; ☑404 0150; www.tamarina.mu; Tamarin; villas €250-750; 🅿⚙🛜⛱) Golf enthusiasts should consider leasing a luxurious villa here – rental packages include golfing privileges on its golf cours. As the four-star resort is protected from the main road by tall trees and has no passing traffic, you might just feel as if you've found your Mauritian idyll. The rooms have wicker-and-wood furnishings and either beach or garden views.

West Island Resort RESORT €€€
(Map p92; ☑403 5308; www.horizon.mu/accommodation/west-coast-marina; apt €200-715, villa €430-1050; 🅿⚙🛜⛱) Is this a vision of the future? The luxury apartments at La Balise

Tamarin & Black River

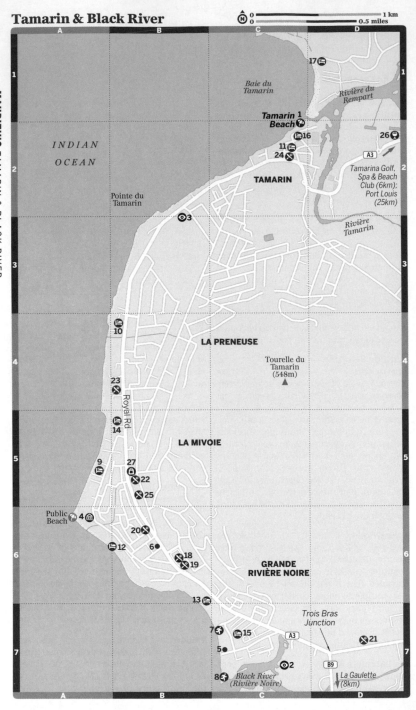

0 1 km
0 0.5 miles

Baie du Tamarin

INDIAN OCEAN

Rivière du Rempart

17

Tamarin Beach 1

16

26
A3

11
24

Tamarina Golf, Spa & Beach Club (6km); Port Louis (25km)

TAMARIN

Pointe du Tamarin

3

Rivière Tamarin

LA PRENEUSE

10

Tourelle du Tamarin (548m)

23

Royal Rd

14

LA MIVOIE

9

27

22

25

Public Beach 4

20

12 6

18
19

GRANDE RIVIÈRE NOIRE

13

Trois Bras Junction

7

15
A3

21

5

2
B9

La Gaulette (8km)

8 Black River (Rivière Noire)

Tamarin & Black River

Marina may be the first signs of an upmarket-tourism surge in the area. You've all the facilities of a resort, plus there's the chance to rub shoulders with the country's great and good. Rooms are luxurious and it can feel more residential than resort.

✕ Eating

The townships have a terrific selection of dining choices strung out along the main road. In general, prices are high relative to the rest of the island – as the target customers are expat South Africans and wealthy Franco-Mauritians – but so is quality.

Those in search of street eats will usually find vendors of *boulette* (small steamed dumplings) at Tamarin Beach on weekends between noon and 7.30pm. Locals say that these are among the best *boulettes* on the island.

London Way   SUPERMARKET
(Map p92; ☑ 483 8888; Royal Rd, La Mivoie; ⊙ 8.30am-7pm Mon-Thu, to 7.45pm Fri & Sat, 8.30am-12.30pm Sun) London Way looks a bit worn out, but it has the widest selection of items in Black River – ideal if you're in a self-catering apartment.

Crêperie Bretonne   CRÊPES €
(Mam Gouz; Map p92; ☑ 5732 8440; Coastal Rd; crêpes Rs 80-280; ⊙ 6.30-9.30pm Tue, noon-2.30pm & 6.30-9.30pm Mon & Wed-Sat) The sweet and savoury crêpes, served in a prim, white-wood dining area, are a welcome (and

rather tasty) alternative to curries and seafood platters.

La Cosa Nostra   ITALIAN €
(Map p92; ☑ 483 6169; cnr Anthurium Lane & Royal Rd, Tamarin; pizzas Rs 285-515, mains Rs 295-460; ⊙ 10am-3pm & 6-10pm Tue-Sun) Two things make this popular pizza joint famous: the whisper-thin crust (you'll swear that you're just eating toppings) and the turtle-speed service (you'll think the servers went back to Italy to fetch your slice). The wine list includes bottles from Italy, France and South Africa. Parking can be difficult; head down to the beach car park and walk back.

Al Dente   ITALIAN €
(Map p92; ☑ 483 7919; Royal Rd, Ruisseau Créole Shopping Complex, Grande Rivière Noire; pizza Rs 180-460, mains Rs 260-470; ⊙ 10.30am-2.30pm & 5.30-11pm) Well-prepared Italian dishes like homemade pasta and osso bucco are a virtual trip to the mother country. There are a few nods to local ingredients, such as the smoked marlin carpaccio with palm-heart salad. The restaurant's down some steps at the back of the hip Ruisseau Créole shopping complex (www.ruisseaucreole.com).

★ Frenchie Café   CAFE €€
(Map p92; ☑ 483 6125; www.frenchiecafe.mu; breakfast from Rs 170, tapas from Rs 150, mains Rs 400-880, brunch Rs 650; ⊙ 8am-midnight Mon-Fri, from 9am Sat) One of the coolest places on the island, French-run Frenchie does quick

bites and more substantial (but reasonably priced) mains, as well as breakfasts and an outstanding Sunday brunch (11am to 4pm). It's also a stylish cocktail bar with Saturday-night DJs. On the road to the Black River Gorges Visitor Centre (p100); the turn-off is almost opposite La Balise Marina.

★ **La Bonne Chute**   MAURITIAN, SEAFOOD €€
(Map p92; 5257 7981, 483 6552; Royal Rd, La Preneuse; mains Rs 450-795; 11am-3pm & 6.30-10.30pm Mon-Sat, bar until midnight) Don't be dissuaded by its location adjacent to a petrol station; La Bonne Chute has been around since 1969 (!) and has built its reputation on expertly prepared dishes served in an attractive garden setting. From duck confit to prawn cassoulette to the best palm-heart salads we tasted, the kitchen always seems to get it right.

Chez Philippe   DELI €€
(Map p92; 483 7920, 5250 8528; chez.phil ippe@intnet.mu; Royal Rd, Ruisseau Créole Shopping Complex, Grande Rivière Noire; mains from Rs 380, light meals from Rs 140; 9.30am-6.30pm Tue-Sat, 9am-noon Sun) Take-away-only Chez Philippe is a fabulous little deli serving up pre-prepared takeaway meals, such as salads, lasagne and creative interpretations of local dishes. There's also foie gras, cheeses and exceptional desserts – the tiramisu is a local institution. A recent move to the Ruisseau Créole shopping complex is a marked improvement on its former roadside location.

Hidden Garden   TAPAS, INTERNATIONAL €€
(Map p92; www.facebook.com/HiddenGarden.res taurant/; Coastal Rd; mains Rs 350-600, tapas from Rs 150; 9.30am-midnight Mon-Sat) This very cool designer spot with a funky cocktail bar and poolside seating is one of the trendier eating experiences in the west. The tapas bar is open all day, but the restaurant mains are only available at lunch and dinner; try the assortment of tapas (Rs 500). And bring your swimmers.

🍷 Drinking & Nightlife

Noticeably quieter than the scene in Grand Baie or Flic en Flac, the communities of Black River (Rivière Noire) prefer house parties to loud club nights. Still, there are a couple of places to go in the evening, and many of the area's restaurants, such as Hidden Garden or La Bonne Chute, have a great after-hours vibe. Do keep in mind, though, that Flic en Flac is only a 15- to 25-minute taxi ride up the coast.

Le Dix-Neuf   BAR
(Map p92; 483 0300; Tamarina Golf & Spa Boutique Hotel, Tamarin Bay; noon-8pm) Hidden behind the walls of Tamarina's exclusive golfing grounds, this classy lodge-like venue, situated at the clubhouse, is a great place for a sundown snifter. Notice how the pentagonal window behind the dark-wood bar perfectly frames the sharp, roof-like ridges of the nearby hills.

Big Willy's   BAR, CLUB
(Map p92; 483 7400; www.bigwillys.mu; Royal Rd, Tamarin; 10pm-2am Wed, to 5am Fri & Sat) Owned by a South African and perennially popular with the expat crowd, Big Willy's is *the* it spot for DJ-ed dance beats and rugby on TV. It's all good, clean fun.

🛍 Shopping

Tutti Frutti   HOMEWARES
(Map p92; 483 6467; www.tuttifrutti.mu; Royal Rd; 9.30am-6pm Mon-Sat) Designer homewares and furnishings that capture the refinement of island chic and Mauritian coastal living are arrayed around a number of showrooms next to the lovely Hidden Garden tapas bar.

ℹ Getting There & Away

Buses headed for Tamarin leave Port Louis roughly every hour and Quatre Bornes every 20 minutes. These buses also stop in La Preneuse. A taxi from Port Louis costs Rs 1100. Expect to pay Rs 1800 for the airport, Rs 650 for Flic en Flac, Rs 750 for Le Morne and Rs 1800 to reach Belle Mare.

Chamarel
POP 820

Known throughout the island for its hushed, bucolic vibe, cool breezes and world-class rum, Chamarel is a wonderful mountain hamlet and an alternative to coastal Mauritius and all those beaches. The town has an excellent culinary scene that's worth crossing the island for, it's home to the famous Terres de 7 Couleurs and Rhumerie de Chamarel, and it's the western gateway to Black River Gorges National Park and the precipitous Chamarel Waterfall.

◉ Sights

★ **Ebony Forest of Chamarel**   FOREST
(Map p95; 460 3030; http://ebonyforest.com/; Seven-Coloured Earth Rd; adult/child Rs 450/270;

Chamarel & La Gaulette

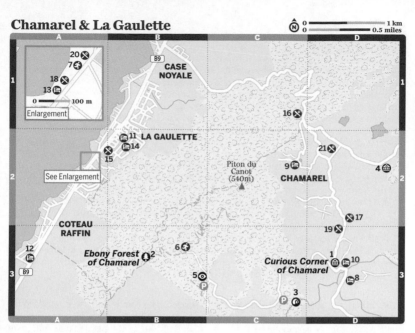

Chamarel & La Gaulette

⊙ 9am-5.30pm Nov-Mar, to 5pm Apr-Oct) One of the most exciting conservation initiatives in Mauritius in the last few years, the Ebony Forest seeks to recreate a small pocket of indigenous native forest, the likes of which covered the entire island just 250 years ago. When finished the forest will cover 45 hectares; around a third has been completed. There are 7km of hiking routes, two raised walkways that climb into the mid-canopy,

safari jeeps, and an interpretation centre with a small shop.

Mauritius Wildlife Foundation has begun introducing two of Mauritius' most endangered signature species: the pink pigeon and echo parakeet. Other bird species to watch out for along the Ebony Forest's trails are the Mauritius paradise flycatcher, grey white-eye, Mauritius black bulbul, white-tailed tropicbird, Mascarene swiftlet and Mascarene swallow.

GRAND BASSIN

According to legend, Shiva and his wife Parvati were circling the earth on a contraption made from flowers when they were dazzled by an island set in an emerald sea. Shiva, who was carrying the Ganges River on his head to protect the world from floods, decided to land. As he did so a few drops of water dripped from his head and landed in a crater to form a lake. The Ganges expressed unhappiness about its water being left on an uninhabited island, but Shiva replied that dwellers from the banks of the Ganges would one day settle there and perform an annual pilgrimage, during which water from the lake would be presented as an offering.

The dazzling island is, of course, Mauritius; the legendary crater lake is known as Grand Bassin (Ganga Talao). It is a renowned **pilgrimage site**, to which up to 500,000 of the island's Hindu community come each year to pay homage to Shiva during the Maha Shivaratri celebrations. This vast festival takes place over three days in February or March (depending on the lunar cycle) and is the largest Hindu celebration outside India.

The most devoted pilgrims walk from their village to the sacred lake carrying a *kanvar* (a light wooden frame or arch decorated with paper flowers). This is no easy feat – February is Mauritius' hottest month and it almost always rains during the festivities. Once the pilgrims arrive, they perform a *puja* (act of reverence), burning incense and camphor at the lakeshore and offering food and flowers.

Ask about the special packages, which include birdwatching, guided hikes, and even a package for honeymooners called the 'Love Tree'.

To get here, you need to enter through the gate for Terres de 7 Couleurs.

★ **Curious Corner of Chamarel** MUSEUM
(Map p95; ☑ 483 4200; www.curiouscornerofchamarel.com; Baie du Cap Rd; adult/child Rs 375/225; ☺9.30am-5pm, last entry 4.15pm) This eclectic place is utterly unlike anywhere else on the island. Essentially an interactive gallery of illusions and art, it has an upside-down room, a laser room and plenty of other attractions that play on your curiosity (and wreak havoc with your sense of perspective). There's a pizza cafe, the Puzzles & Things Shop and an overarching sense of playful originality. It's opposite the turn-off to Terres de 7 Couleurs.

Rhumerie de Chamarel MUSEUM
(Map p95; ☑483 4980; www.rhumeriedechamarel.com; Royal Rd; adult incl tasting Rs 400, child Rs 175; ☺9.30am-4.30pm Mon-Sat) Set among the vast hillside plantations of Chamarel, the *rhumerie* is a working distillery that doubles as a museum showcasing the rum-making process. The project of the Beachcomber hotel tycoon, the factory opened in 2008 and uses a special ecofriendly production method ensuring that all materials are recycled. The rum is quite well regarded by experts, and makes for a pleasant coda to a guided tour of the plant. Time your visit to enjoy lunch at the museum's restaurant, L'Alchimiste.

Chamarel Waterfall WATERFALL
(Map p95) About halfway (1.5km) between the entrance gate to Terres de 7 Couleurs and the colourful sands is a scenic viewpoint over the waterfall, which plunges more than 95m in a single drop. With a reservation, you can abseil with Vertical World (p98) from the top of Chamarel Waterfall all the way into the pool at its base. Note that you can only get to the waterfall by paying the entrance fee to Terres de 7 Couleurs.

Terres de 7 Couleurs LANDMARK
(Chamarel Coloured Earths; Map p95; ☑483 8298; adult/child Rs 450/270; ☺9am-5pm Jun-Sep, to 5.30pm Oct-May) Chamarel Coloured Earths have become one of the sights on the island's usual tourist circuit. Some travellers (and we're among them) find them quite underwhelming but the queues to enter continue. If you temper your expectations, there's a greater chance of enjoying the variations of colourful sand – a result of the uneven cooling of molten rock. The site is 2km southwest of Chamarel. On your way through the reserve, stop at Chamarel Waterfall.

✦ Activities

La Vieille Cheminée
HORSE RIDING
(Map p95; ✒ 483 4249; www.lavieillecheminee.
com/horse-riding; Main Rd; 1hr trail ride per person Rs 2000; ☺ Mon-Sat) La Vieille Cheminée offers beautiful guided horseback rides through the hilly countryside and along shady ravines. It also offers beginner rides for 20 minutes (Rs 650) in which the horses are led by their handlers, which is only available to their lodge guests. Otherwise, advance bookings essential.

Lavilléon Natural Forest
ADVENTURE SPORTS
(Map p95; ✒ 5983 5491; www.facebook.com/laville-onnaturalforest/; entry adult/child Rs 150/100, archery Rs 300, zipline Rs 600; ☺ 9am-5pm) Inside the Terres de 7 Couleurs reserve, this adventure forest has a Nepalese rope bridge, a thrilling zipline, an archery range and hiking trails. Advance bookings essential.

Yemaya Adventures
MOUNTAIN BIKING
(✒ 283 8187, 5752 0046; www.yemayaadventures.
com) Full- and half-day mountain-biking adventures can be arranged with professional 'cycle-path' Patrick Haberland at his outfit, Yemaya. It also arranges hikes through Black River Gorges National Park, and sea kayaking.

🛏 Sleeping

Chamarel's sleeping options are far outweighed by restaurants, which may be why many visitors come here on day trips. There are, however, a couple of excellent choices.

Chalets en Champagne
CABIN €
(Map p84; ✒ 5988 7418; www.leschaletsenchampagne.mu; 110 Plaine Champagne Rd, Chamarel; d/q Rs 4000/8000; ❀) These beautiful log cabins sleep between four and eight people and are tucked into the mountainside amid gnarled tropical trees. The decor stays true to the wooded theme (think thatch roofs and stone-lined bath-tubs) while gently incorporating modern touches (air-con, DVD players etc). Hikers will appreciate the surrounding network of marked trails that weaves across the tree-lined terrain.

Le Coteau Fleurie
GUESTHOUSE €€
(Map p95; ✒ 5733 3963; www.coteaufleurie.com; Royal Rd, Chamarel; r per person incl breakfast €50; ◉) Plucked from the sky-scraping ridges of Réunion, this lovely *chambre d'hôte* feels miles away from anything else in Mauritius. A quaint Creole-style option, it embraces its traditional roots, and owners Geneviève and Gérard offer travellers a welcome retreat among fruit and coffee trees and thick jungle trunks.

La Vieille Cheminée
B&B €€
(Map p95; ✒ 483 4249; www.lavieillecheminee.
com; r €93-225; 🏠) A farm and rustic lodge, La Vieille Cheminée has six pretty Creole-style, self-catering rooms on a lovely sloping property. It offers a range of activities including horse riding, farm visits, nature walks and bike rides.

★ Lakaz Chamarel
LODGE €€€
(Map p95; ✒ 483 5240; www.lakazchamarel.com; Piton du Canot; incl half board s €150-355, d €210-535; P ❀ 🏊 📶) This 'exclusive lodge' in the countryside around Chamarel is a wonderfully conceived collection of rustic (yet oh-so-elegant) cabins offering a blissful getaway amid gorgeous forests, gardens and streams. Rooms are tastefully decorated, with chic safari-style trimmings. Not to be missed are the serene spa and the charming swimming pool adorned with stone goddess statues.

🍴 Eating

Chamarel has gained an island-wide reputation for the charming *tables d'hôtes* sprinkled around its hilltops. Unscrupulous taxi drivers have been known to capitalise on the area's newfound popularity with foodies by overcharging tourists and demanding hefty commissions from local restaurants. We recommend navigating the area with a private vehicle and choosing a dining option at your leisure. Note that most places open only for lunch.

★ Restaurant Le Barbizon
MAURITIAN €€
(Map p95; ✒ 483 4178; lebarbizon@yahoo.fr; Ste-Anne Rd; meals Rs 450, with wild boar Rs 650; ☺ noon-4pm) Barbizon may not look like much, but it's a fabulous place. Marie-Ange helms the kitchen, whipping up traditional Mauritian flavours from her family's cookbook, while Rico L'Intelligent (what a name!) entertains at the tables. He doesn't give you a menu. Instead, he offers a feast of rum punch, rice, five vegetables, and fish or chicken.

★ L'Alchimiste
MAURITIAN €€
(Map p95; ✒ 483 7980; www.rhumeriedecham arel.com; Royal Rd, Rhumerie de Chamarel; mains Rs 550-1200, set menus Rs 1325-1800; ☺ 11.30am-3.30pm Mon-Sat) The Rhumerie de Chamarel's restaurant boasts an impressive menu that promises to satisfy, with

seafood and palm heart from the surrounding hills the highlights. The chef's philosophy is definitely gourmet: Mauritian favourites are whipped into eye-pleasing concoctions such as braised palm heart with king prawn, with a hollandaise sauce and a leek emulsion.

Varangue sur Morne MAURITIAN €€
(Map p84; ☑483 6610, 5421 2510; Plaine Champagne Rd; mains Rs 400-1050; ☺noon-4pm) This former hunting lodge is an institution, and it's not hard to see why. Its stunning location offers great views over the forested hillsides towards the ocean, and the superb menu is pricey but excellent: braised wild boar, prawns flambéed in Île de France rum, palm-heart salad with smoked marlin and a laundry list of clever cocktails.

Le Domaine de Saint-Denis MAURITIAN €€
(Map p84; ☑5728 5562; www.domainedesaintdenis.com; Chamarel; mains from Rs 750, set menu from Rs 1500; ☺by reservation only) Le Domaine features recipes from the kitchen of Jacqueline Dalais, the unofficial First Lady of Mauritian cuisine, who oversees this gem of a restaurant. Order the scallop carpaccio with olive oil and lime if it's on the menu. The restaurant is signposted off the road from Chamarel to Black River Gorges National Park.

Les Palmiers INDIAN, MAURITIAN €€
(Map p95; ☑483 8364; Main Rd; mains from Rs 500; ☺noon-4pm) This popular place does a roaring trade with curries and *faratas* (panfried flat breads) served in a pleasant dining area.

★ Mich Resto MAURITIAN, INTERNATIONAL €€€
(Map p95; ☑438 4158; www.michresto.mu; Main Rd; mains Rs 750-1850; ☺11am-4pm) Consistently glowing reviews from travellers, a classier setting than most in the area, friendly waiters, one of the best palm-heart salads we've tasted, excellent seafood... Mich Resto is a fine place for lunch. Try the crab with Creole sauce, lobster curry or grilled fish in lemon sauce.

Le Chamarel Panoramic Restaurant MAURITIAN, INTERNATIONAL €€€
(Map p95; ☑483 4421; www.lechamarelrestaurant.com; Main Rd, La Crête; set menu per person Rs 995; ☺11.30am-3pm) Perched atop the escarment 1km northwest of Chamarel just before the road plunges down to Black River, this pleasing place has breathtaking views all the way to the coast – get there early or book ahead for the tables with a front-row

vantage point. Dishes vary with the seasons, but could include clear fish soup scented with Moringa leaves or profiteroles with pineapple jam.

ⓘ Getting There & Away

Although there's a bus service from Quatre Bornes to Chamarel, we highly recommend using private transport. Do not visit Chamarel by taxi – drivers are given exorbitant commissions for bringing tourists to the various attractions and *tables d'hôtes*.

Black River Gorges National Park

Mauritius' biggest and best **national park** (Map p84; ☑507 0128; guides per day from Rs 1250) FREE is a wild expanse of rolling hills and thick forest covering roughly 2% of the island's surface. It's difficult to overstate the importance of this park – it's the last stand for Mauritian forests and many native species. It's also the most spectacular corner of the island, so if you make only one day trip from the coast, make it here, perhaps combining it with Chamarel.

Once prime hunting grounds, the area became a protected reserve in 1994 after scientists identified over 300 species of flowering plant, nine endemic species of bird and a 4000-strong population of giant fruit bats. It remains an important habitat for three of the island's most endangered bird species: the Mauritius kestrel, the echo parakeet and the pink pigeon. Introduced wild boar, macaque monkeys and deer also wander through the vast swathes of old-growth ebony, and sightings are not uncommon.

⚹ Activities

Hiking is the main drawcard here, but it's also possible to mountain-bike down some trails. Contact Yemaya Adventures (p97) for the latter.

Vertical World ADVENTURE SPORTS
(☑697 5430; www.verticalworldltd.com) For a truly unique and unforgettable experience, adventurers can abseil from chute to chute on a half- or full-day canyoning excursion with Vertical World.

ⓘ Information

Staff at both visitor centres might be able to offer advice on the trails and hand out (fairly sketchy) maps.

HIKING THE BLACK RIVER GORGES

Numerous trails crisscross Black River Gorges National Park (p98) like unravelling shoe-strings. While all of the trailheads are clearly marked along one of the two roads running through the park, many of the paths can quickly get obscured in the brush, leaving hikers confused. It's worth stopping at one of the visitor centres to grab a crude map and check in about the current state of the trails. We recommend hiring a guide if you're serious about exploring the park and uncovering the better viewpoints. You can also contact the visitor centres ahead of time to enquire about hiring a ranger.

If you choose one of the one-way trails that ends at the Black River Gorges Visitor Centre, you may need to pre-arrange a time with a taxi to pick you up, as it's a long, one-to two-hour walk to the coast road where buses pass by.

The best time to visit the park is during the flowering season between September and January. Look for the rare *tambalacoque* (dodo tree), the black ebony trees and the wild guavas. Bird-watchers should keep an eye out for Mauritius kestrels (best seen from September to February), pink pigeons, echo parakeets and Mauritius cuckoo-shrikes.

Trails

The main trails are as follows. If you only have time to make one trek, choose between the Macchabée Trail, the Macchabée Loop and the Parakeet Trail.

Macchabée Trail (Map p84) (10km one way, strenuous, four hours) Begin at the Pétrin Visitor Centre (p100), hiking along the plateau to the stunning **Macchabée Viewpoint** (Map p84), then down to the Black River Gorges Visitor Centre (p100). Keep an eye out for the Mauritius kestrel, echo parakeet and soaring tropic birds.

Macchabée Forest Trail (Map p84) (8km return, moderate, three hours) Begin at the Pétrin Visitor Centre, but remain on the plateau with a loop through some lovely tropical forest. Watch for black-trunked ebony trees.

Macchabée Loop (Map p84) (8km return, moderate, three hours) Hike along the plateau to the Macchabée Viewpoint, then return along the same path to the Pétrin Visitor Centre.

Parakeet Trail (Map p84) (8km one way, strenuous, three hours) Begin at the **Plaine Champagne Police Post** (Map p84), which is halfway between the Gorges Viewpoint and Alexandra Falls along the tarred road from Chamarel, following a ridge down into the gorge and then along the river to the Black River Gorges Visitor Centre. Echo parakeets are the real prize.

Mare Longue Reservoir (Map p84) (12km return, moderate, four hours) Begin and end at the Pétrin Visitor Centre, taking in a dwarf native forest and a large reservoir at the little-visited northern tip of the park. Sightings of the pink pigeon and echo parakeet are possible.

Black River Peak (Map p84) (6km return, moderate, three hours) Hike to the island's highest point (Piton de la Petite Rivière Noire or Black River Peak; 828m) for extraordinary views. The trail begins along the Chamarel road, 300m west of the car park for Gorges Viewpoint.

Pre-hike Preparations

If you decide to attempt a trip under your own steam, you'll need a private vehicle, as getting to the trailheads can be near impossible with public transport. The best option is to get a taxi to drop you off at a trailhead and then pick you up at the lower end of the park.

We suggest checking Fitsy (https://fitsy.com) before you head out into the wild. This handy website features detailed trail information using GPS and satellite coordinates.

Note that there is nowhere to buy food or drinks in the park. Make sure you bring plenty of water and energy-boosting snacks. You'll also need insect repellent, wet-weather gear and shoes with good grip – no matter how hot and sunny the coast may be, it is usually wet and humid within the park. Consider binoculars for wild-life-watching.

WORTH A TRIP

BLACK RIVER GORGES SCENIC DRIVE

Although we strongly recommend that you explore the Black River Gorges National Park on foot, if that's not possible you can still get a taste for this beautiful region by car. Before we get started, a word of advice: avoid making this trip on weekends if you can, as the otherwise quiet roads are flooded with locals driving slowly and stopping by the roadside while they hunt for wild berries.

Begin along the coast road on Mauritius' western coast at Grand Case Noyale (around 1.5km north of La Gaulette and around 7km south of Black River), where a signpost points inland towards Chamarel. If you're looking for a landmark, there's a cream church set back from the corner. After crossing the coastal plain, the road begins to climb steeply through increasingly dense forest. Around 4km after leaving the coast road, close to the top of the first ridge line, a lookout on your right offers fine, sweeping views of the coastal plain and out to sea.

Passing through Chamarel, ignore for now the signs to Terres de 7 Couleurs (p96) and bear left through Chamarel. After passing Rhumerie de Chamarel (p96), continue climbing through the forest for around 6km to the **Gorges Viewpoint** (Map p84). On a clear day the views from here across the gorge rank among the best on the island. Look for the **Piton de la Petite Rivière Noire** (Black River Mountain peak; 828m) on your left, and keep an eye out for the Mauritius kestrel, tropic birds and fruit bats.

A further 2km along the paved road, you pass the Plaine Champagne Police Post (p99) trailhead for the Parakeet Trail, with the turn-off for **Alexandra Falls** a further 2km on. Turn right off the main road, passing beneath a pretty honour guard of trees, then follow the short path out to the falls' **viewpoint** (Map p84). While there, you can admire the cloud forest of Mt Cocotte (771m) and the view down to the south coast.

Back on the main road, turn right towards Chamouny at the roundabout 2.5km beyond the Alexandra Falls turn-off and follow the road down the hill through the thinning forest. After around 3km, pull into the unpaved parking area on the right (west) side of the road – from the low ridge of dirt and rock there are good views down into the crater lake called **Bassin Blanc**.

Return up the hill and continue straight ahead at the roundabout. After just over 2km, turn right and follow the signs to **Grand Bassin**, an important pilgrimage site for the island's Hindus 2.5km from the turn-off. Long before you arrive, you'll see the massive and curiously hypnotic Shiva, one of two statues that watch over this sacred spot.

Return the 2.5km to the main road and at the T-Junction you'll see the Pétrin Visitor Centre. Even if you're not planning to hike, park your car and wander around the back to an enclosure where pink pigeons are being prepared for release into the wild.

Black River Gorges Visitor Centre (Map p84; ☑ 258 0057; ☺ 7am-5pm Mon-Fri, 9am-5pm Sat & Sun) At the park's western entrance, about 7.5km southeast of Black River's Trois Bras Junction.

Pétrin Visitor Centre (Map p84; ☑ 5507 0128, 471 1128; ☺ 8am-3.15pm Mon-Fri) At the eastern entrance to the park.

ⓘ Getting There & Away

There is little public transport through the park. Semi-regular buses pass the Pétrin Visitor Centre en route between Souillac and Vacoas or Curepipe, with similarly infrequent services from Curepipe or Quatre Bornes to Chamarel. You're much better visiting with your own wheels or hiring a taxi to get you to the trailheads. Buses run along the coastal road, a one- to two-hour walk from the Black River Gorges Visitors Centre.

La Gaulette

POP 2500

South of Black River, the mountains draw ever closer to the coast. You'll find pinewoods and mangroves mingling with the lapping waves but little in the way of habitation besides the ramshackle settlements along the road. Then, a small township emerges under the shade of the nearby hills – it's a quiet, transitory sort of place where the laid-back fisherfolk lifestyle coexists with the carefree surfer vibe. Welcome to La Gaulette.

🏄 Activities

Son of Kite KITESURFING
(Map p95; ☑ 451 6155, 5972 9019; www.sono fkite.com; Royal Rd; 2-hour group class per person

€90, rental per 1/2/7 hours €30/60/90) Kiteboarders of every ilk (from newbies to pros) can sign up for a class with the recommended professionals at Son of Kite. Although you're free to explore the lagoon if renting, they keep a close eye on you to make sure you're OK.

Ropsen TOURS
(Map p95; ☑451 5763, 5902 8000; www.ropsen. net; Royal Rd) La Gaulette's top tour operator, Ropsen organises catamaran excursions, dolphin-watching tours and island tours, as well as accommodation. Ropsen also has a good portfolio of rental cars of all sizes; prices start at Rs 1200 per day.

🛏 Sleeping

Gaining popularity among the kitesurfing crowd, La Gaulette represents excellent value for money. There is currently a handful of decent accommodation options in the village.

★ Rusty Pelican GUESTHOUSE €
(Map p95; ☑5978 9140; www.rusty-pelican.com; apt from €61; ❄@🛜🛏) This fabulous place at the northern end of town is one of La Gaulette's best sleeping options. The rooms are flooded with natural light and have excellent bathrooms. The owners give you a mobile to use for the duration of your visit (you just pay for calls) and they love helping you plan your stay.

★ Maison Papaye GUESTHOUSE €
(Map p95; ☑451 5976, 5752 0918; www.maison papaye.com; 21 Morcellement La Flèche; r incl breakfast €55-98; ❄@🛜🛏) Set among imposing homes on a residential street away from the sea, this stately *chambre d'hôte* is a real find. Although the whitewashed facade, gabled roof and periwinkle shutters may hint at a colonial past, the building is only a few years old – the owners designed their retirement getaway to invoke the island's plantation past.

The owners keep tradition alive every evening with their Creole-inspired *table d'hôte* dinners (€15), served on the shaded veranda. There's a four-night minimum stay.

Pingo Studios APARTMENT €
(Map p95; ☑5755 9773; Royal Rd; r from €45; P❄🛜) Around halfway between La Gaulette and Le Morne, these self-catering apartments get the thumbs up from travellers – budget prices within sight of Le Morne are, after all, difficult to come by. Rooms are large and unpretentious but extremely comfortable.

Ropsen ACCOMMODATION SERVICES €
(Map p95; ☑451 5763, 5255 5546; www.ropsen. net; Royal Rd; studio & apt €30-60, 4-bed villa €100-125; ❄@🛜) From modern studios to large multibedroom apartments, friendly Ropsen proffers such a vast array of high-quality options that you'll start to think every building in La Gaulette is a rentable villa under his name! Almost all of Ropsen's properties have wi-fi. Insist on a sea view.

🍴 Eating & Drinking

The small *superettes* (small self-service grocery stores) that line the main street through town serve the legions of self-caterers. There are only a few restaurants in the area. For more options, drive up to Chamarel or Black River.

Both Enso and Ocean Vagabond offer a little night-time fun, which is more than most other towns can muster in this corner of the country.

La Gaulette Supermarket SUPERMARKET
(Map p95; ☑451 5218; www.facebook.com/LaGau letteSupermarket/; Royal Rd, Village Walk Supermarket Centre; ◉8am-7pm Mon-Sat, to noon Sun) The best supermarket you'll find anywhere in La Gaulette or Le Morne, with a good general selection of food and alcohol.

TAMARIN FALLS

Positioned on the outskirts of the Black River Gorges, roughly 8km southwest of Curepipe in central Mauritius, this set of seven scenic cascades (some say 11) is a wonderful reward for those willing to take on a challenging hike.

Attempts to access the falls should not be made without a guide. Local guides (charging Rs 500 to 1000) usually wait around the bus station at Henrietta, a township near Curepipe, although we prefer linking up with **Yanature** (Trekking Île Maurice; ☑5251 4050, 5785 6177; www.trekkingmauritius. com; 3-4hr hike per person Rs 1500; ◉7am Mon-Sat Apr-Oct, 6am Mon-Sat Nov-Mar).

For a truly unique and unforgettable experience, adventurers can abseil from chute to chute on a half- or full-day canyoning excursion with Vertical World (p98) or Otélair (p62). Both operators start their trips from Henrietta.

WORTH A TRIP

ÎLE AUX BÉNITIERS

The area's most notable attraction is the lovely Île aux Bénitiers, which floats just above sea level in the reef offshore. The islet is considerably larger than many of the other outcrops in the lagoon (keep an eye out for the interesting rocky projection that looks like the top half of an hourglass) and sports a beautiful picnic-worthy beach, a small coconut farm and a colony of migratory birds.

The island's keeper is quite the local character – he travels around with an ever-growing pack of chipper dogs. Note that while the beach is publicly accessible, the island's interior is largely off-limits.

Most of the fishers docked at La Gaulette offer small excursions to the island. The number of boat operators that visit the island continues to grow each year and most of the products are identical: crowded catamarans and a picnic lunch on the sand. Check out www.catamarancruisesmauritius.com and expect to pay €60 per person for a full day's outing. Note that many cruise operators combine a trip to Île aux Bénitiers with dolphin-watching (p86).

Liverpool Snack
INTERNATIONAL €

(Map p95; ☑ 5777 3047; Royal Rd; mains Rs 80-200; ⊙ 11am-10pm) Simple meals, friendly service and an occasional sea breeze – the recipe here is time-honoured with no frills and no complaints from us. Expect rice and noodle dishes as well as fish and a few other staples.

Enso
MEDITERRANEAN €€

(Map p95; ☑ 451 5907; 1st fl, Village Walk Supermarket Centre; mains Rs 390-1500; ⊙ 8.30am-late Tue-Sat; ☎) Styling itself as a lounge bar and restaurant, this place does cool very well, with its laid-back pool table and Saturday-night DJs. The food itself is generally good without being spectacular – think pizzas, pasta and seafood – but it's better when they keep it simple, as with the mixed grill or seafood platter. The home-made bread's a highlight.

Ocean Vagabond
PIZZA €€

(Map p95; ☑ 451 5910; www.facebook.com/ocean vagabondmauritius/; Royal Rd; mains & pizza Rs 350-850; ⊙ 5-10pm Wed-Mon) Ocean Vagabond has good pizzas and something of a surfer's vibe, with DVDs and a Saturday-evening happy hour. It all falls a bit flat when things are quiet, but that changes when a crowd's in. Good orders include the seafood salad and the chicken curry, and the pizzas aren't bad.

❶ Information

MCB ATM (⊙ 24hr) This ATM from Mauritius Commercial Bank handles international cards and can even handle some foreign exchange transactions.

❶ Getting There & Away

Buses (every 20 minutes) between Quatre Bornes and Baie du Cap stop in La Gaulette. There are no direct buses from Port Louis; instead, you have to go via Quatre Bornes or take the bus from Port Louis to Black River and change.

A taxi between Port Louis and La Gaulette will cost around Rs 1200; it's Rs 1800 to the airport. Do not take a taxi to Chamarel as many drivers work on commission with restaurants there – rent a vehicle (p101) instead.

Le Morne Peninsula

Visible from much of southwestern Mauritius, the iconic Le Morne Brabant (556m) is a stunning rocky crag from which this beautiful peninsula takes its name. Shaped like a hammerhead shark, the peninsula itself has some of the island's best beaches, now home to a number of upmarket hotels.

The coastline from the peninsula along to Baie du Cap is some of the most beautiful in the country, and it's blissfully free of development.

◉ Sights

Although the area's upmarket hotels have gobbled up most of the peninsula's beachfront property, the beaches themselves are still open to the public, and there are two public beaches, one at the tip of the peninsula, and the other between the Lux Le Morne and Dinarobin hotels.

International Slavery
Route Monument   MONUMENT

(Map p84; Royal Rd) This modest roadside monument of stone sculptures recognises Le Morne's connection to the story of slavery.

🏃 Activities

Hiking

Added to the Unesco World Heritage list in 2008, Le Morne Brabant is the star of many postcards, as it slopes through the sky and then plunges back into the blue. Few tourists, however, realise that the view from the top is even more spectacular. As you ascend the crag you'll pass through an indigenous forest that's the only place on the island where you'll find Mauritius' national flower, the *boucle d'oreille* ('earring'). When you reach 500m, you'll be treated to unobstructed vistas of the colourful reefs to the west and south. The trail increases in difficulty the higher up you go – those with limited mobility can still take in the views from a midway point (around 260m).

Although you can climb without a guide, the going is difficult in places and we strongly recommend the experienced guides at Ya-nature (p101).

Windsurfing & Kitesurfing

The combination of Indian Ocean winds (the claim is 300 days of ideal winds a year, a claim we were, sadly, unable to verify), sheltered western waters and a fine backdrop make Le Morne ideal for windsurfing and kitesurfing. For the latter, beginners should start at **Kite Lagoon** (Map p84) off the west coast; the southern winds are much more severe and unpredictable. Expect to pay around €90 for a two-hour group lesson, and roughly €30 per hour or €90 per day for equipment rental

ION Club   KITESURFING, WINDSURFING
(Map p84; ☑450 4112; www.ionclubmauritius. com/en) The worldwide surfing organisation ION Club operates intensive kitesurfing and windsurfing courses from its school at Le Morne; equipment rental is also possible for those who know what they're doing. Figure on around €75 for a one-hour private course.

Yoaneye Kite Centre   KITESURFING
(Map p84; ☑5737 8296; www.yoaneye.com; 114 Villa Mona, Le Petit Morne; 2hr group/private class per person from €90/210, 2hr rental €50) Yoaneye Kite Centre, an IKO-affiliated centre, offers

kitesurfing classes for beginners and more experienced kitesurfers, as well as stand-up paddle boarding.

Surfing

The area is home to the ultimate surfing spot in all of Mauritius: **One Eye** (Map p84).

Horse Riding
Haras du Morne   HORSE RIDING

(Map p84; ☑450 4142; www.harasdumorne. com; off Royal Rd; 60/90/120-min ride Rs 3000/3500/4500) Expensive horse rides are on offer at this upmarket equestrian centre, but the landscape through which they go (the forest and beaches around Le Morne) is among the prettiest on the island. The centre is off Royal Rd.

🛏 Sleeping

⭐**Lux Le Morne**   RESORT €€€
(Map p84; ☑401 4000; www.luxresorts.com; Coastal Rd; r from €400; ⓟ❊@☂☀) When you dream of a Mauritian idyll, this might be the place you're thinking of. This resort does everything and does it well: uber-luxurious rooms, top-notch restaurants, dreamy swimming pools, a high-class spa, water sports... Those who've stayed here rave about the experience.

LE MOURNE:
THE MOURNFUL ONE

Although almost totally uninhabited by locals, Le Morne has deep resonance in Mauritian culture. According to legend, a group of escaped slaves fled to the peninsula in the early 19th century, hiding out on top of the mountain to remain free. The story goes that the slaves, ignorant of the fact that slavery had been abolished just before their escape, panicked when they saw a troop of soldiers making their way up the cliffs. Believing they were to be recaptured, the slaves flung themselves from the clifftops to their deaths in huge numbers. And thus the crag earned its name – Le Morne means Mournful One. Although there are no historical records to substantiate the story, it's an important tale for Mauritians and was critical in Le Morne being granted Unesco World Heritage status in 2008.

The St Regis
Mauritius Resort LUXURY HOTEL €€€
(Map p84; ☑ 403 9000; Royal Rd; r incl half board from €780) It's difficult to find fault with this uber-luxurious place, where the rooms have lovely hardwood floors and ceilings, a marvellous sense of light and space, and memorably personalised service. It has all the usual add-ons for Le Morne – terrific restaurants, numerous activities and a blissful beach.

Dinarobin
HOTEL €€€
(Map p84; ☑ 401 4900; www.beachcomber-hotels.com/en/hotel/dinarobin-golf-resort-spa; Coastal Rd; d incl half board from €375; ✳ @ 🗢 ☲) A ravishing Beachcomber beauty, with a sprawling campus of 172 suites, this property is named after the first moniker given to the island by Arab merchants in the 10th century. Rated 'five star plus', it lives up to expectations, with five swimming pools, four restaurants, a golf course and a pampering spa.

Paradis
HOTEL €€€
(Map p84; ☑ 401 5050; www.beachcomber-hotels.com/en/hotel/paradis-golf-resort-spa; d incl half board from €275; ✳ @ 🗢 ☲) Stunning sea views, luxurious accommodation, a golf course and endless activities. What more could you ask for? Not to be missed is the fresh seafood at Blue Marlin, one of the in-house restaurants.

Eating

★ Wapalapam
Island Eatery CAFE €€
(Map p84; ☑ 450 5641; Royal Rd, Centre Commercial De L'Harmonie; breakfast mains Rs 100-250, lunch & dinner mains Rs 350-890; ☺ 8am-10pm) The sort of chilled place you'd expect to find in a downtempo Mauritius beach town, Wapalapam Island Eatery is actually quite the rarity in this part of the country. It's a fabulous mix of breakfast, dishes from wok and grill, curries, cocktails and even a kids menu.

❶ Getting There & Away
Buses en route between Quatre Bornes and Baie du Cap stop on the main road by the junction for Le Morne, but it's a long walk from there. These buses run roughly every hour. A taxi from Port Louis to the hotels in Le Morne costs Rs 1800; figure on Rs 2000 to the airport, Rs 1500 to Flic en Flac and Rs 2500 to Belle Mare.

THE SOUTHEAST
With many charms, the sultry southeast of Mauritius is a seductress. This dramatic stretch of coast, watched over by landforms like Lion Mountain (p113), has lovely turquoise bays (such as Blue Bay), long stretches of sand (Pointe d'Esny) and some of Mauritius' best wildlife-watching at Île aux Aigrettes (p109) and Vallée de Ferney. The main settlement, Mahébourg, combines grit with a somnambulent seaside appeal and a fabulous Monday market, while Vieux Grand Port is where Mauritius' human story began some 400 years ago.

Mahébourg
POP 17,740
There is something relentlessly charming (if a little ramshackle) about bite-size Mahébourg (my-boor), where it's all about simple pleasures: an excellent museum, a buzzing market, spicy street food, good budget lodgings, a pretty backdrop and beautiful beaches to the north and south. We still hear talk of ambitious plans to transform Mahébourg's waterfront into a mammoth complex like Le Caudan in Port Louis, but it will be years before this takes shape. In the meantime, they've repaved the waterfront promenade and added historical plaques, which has improved the experience and is much more in line with Mahébourg's gentler atmosphere.

Founded in 1805, the town was named after French governor Mahé de Labourdonnais. Once a busy port, these days it's something of a backwater, with a small fleet of fishers and a grid of dilapidated buildings.

◉ Sights
You can cover Mahébourg's smattering of sights in a couple of hours, leaving plenty of time to wander the backstreets and stroll along the seafront. Everything can be tackled on foot, though you might want to hire a bike or taxi to get out to the biscuit factory.

★ Monday Market
MARKET
(Map p106; ☺ 7am-5.30pm Mon-Sat, to noon Sun) Don't miss the central *foire de Mahébourg*, near the waterfront. The initial focus was silks and other textiles, but these days you'll find a busy produce section, tacky bric-a-brac and steaming food stalls. It's the perfect place to try some local snacks – *gâteaux piments* (chilli cakes), *dhal puri*

VALLÉE DE FERNEY

Protecting a 400-year-old forest, the **Vallée de Ferney** (Ferney Valley; Map p116; 634 0440, 5729 1080; www.facebook.com/valleedeferney; tours per adult/child Rs 800/450, kestrel feeding (free if part of tour) Rs 500/300, 4WD guided tour Rs 1250/1000; 10am-3pm) reserve is an important habitat for the Mauritius kestrel, one of the world's most endangered raptors, and a visit here is far and away your best chance of seeing one. Guides take you along a 3km trail, pointing out fascinating flora and fauna. At noon (arrive no later than 11.30am, or 10am if you're also doing the hike), staff feed otherwise wild kestrels at the trailhead. Bookings for the tour are essential.

As an important habitat for endemic species, Vallée de Ferney is a hugely important conservation and ecotourism area. The Mauritian Wildlife Foundation (p138), which helps to train the reserve's guides and provides important input into its policies, has reintroduced a number of other endangered species, including the pink pigeon and echo parakeet, here. Keep an eye out for them if on a hike. There are currently 14 to 15 pairs of Mauritian kestrels in the reserve.

The Vallée de Ferney is also well known as the site of a conservation demonstration that ignited when a Chinese paving company sought to construct a highway directly through the protected hinterland. Attempts at development were unsuccessful, but scars remain: trees daubed with red paint alongside the walking trail were to be chopped down to make way for the road.

The turn-off to the 200-hectare reserve is clearly marked along the coastal road, around 2km south of Vieux Grand Port.

(lentil pancakes) and *samousas* (samosas) – usually dispensed from boxes on the backs of motorcycles. The market is open every day but doubles in size on Monday.

★ National History Museum   MUSEUM
(Map p116; 631 9329; Royal Rd; 9am-4pm Mon, Tue & Thu-Sat, from 11am Wed, 9am-noon Sun) This terrific museum is one of Mauritius' best. It contains fascinating early maps of the island and Indian Ocean region, paintings from colonial times, model ships from important episodes in Mauritian history, archive photographs, and a rare, intact skeleton of the dodo and another disappeared species, the Rodrigues solitaire. One real curio is an engraving of Dutch gentlemen riding in pairs on the back of a giant tortoise, a species that also went the way of the dodo.

The colonial mansion housing this museum used to belong to the Robillard family and played an important part in the island's history. It was here in 1810 that the injured commanders of the French and English fleets were taken for treatment after the Battle of Vieux Grand Port (the only naval battle in which the French got the upper hand over their British foes). The story of the victory is retold in the museum, along with salvaged items – cannons, grapeshot and the all-important wine bottles – from the British frigate *Magicienne,* which sank in the battle.

The bell and a cache of Spanish coins from the wreck of the *St Géran* are also on display. The ship's demise in 1744, off the northeast coast of Mauritius, inspired the famous love story *Paul et Virginie* by Bernardin de St-Pierre.

Recent additions to the museum include a retrofitted train carriage out the back and a replica of Napoleon's boat used in the infamous battle that defeated the English.

Rault Biscuit Factory   MUSEUM
(Map p116; 631 9559; www.biscuitmanioc.com; Fabian Rd; adult/child Rs 160/120, incl tasting Rs 200/140, tasting only Rs 110/80; 9am-3pm Mon-Fri) In 1870 the Rault family started producing manioc biscuits at its little biscuit factory on the northern outskirts of Mahébourg, and the factory has changed hardly a jot since. The crispy square cookies are made almost entirely by hand using a secret recipe passed down from generation to generation and baked on hotplates over stoves fuelled with dried sugar-cane leaves. The 20-minute tour ends with a chance to sample the finished product – with a nice cup of tea, of course.

The factory is on the far side of the Cavendish Bridge; when you cross the bridge, turn left at the brown-and-white factory sign and then follow the further signs. Packets of the biscuits in seven flavours (we recommend

Mahébourg

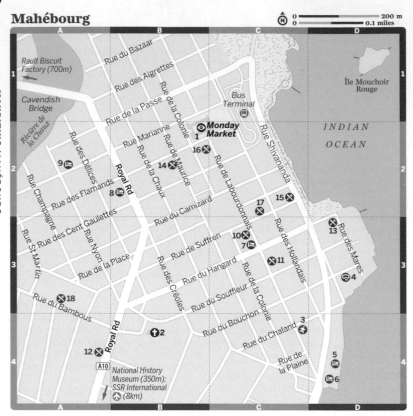

Mahébourg

the butter flavour; reaching this decision involved pleasurable research...) are on sale for Rs 79 (wafers cost Rs 75).

Notre Dame des Anges   CHURCH
(Map p106; Rue du Souffleur) The butter-coloured tower of Notre Dame des Anges dominates the Mahébourg skyline. The original church was built in 1849, but it has been restored several times over the years. Take a quick peek inside at the baronial roof timbers. Local people visit throughout the day to make offerings to beloved missionary Père Laval

(p53), whose statue stands to your right immediately inside the door.

🏃 Activities

The most popular activity is a boat excursion to the offshore islands (Île aux Aigrettes, Île de la Passe, Île aux Vacoas and Île au Phare) or the über-popular Île aux Cerfs (p121) further north. Most trips involve snorkelling and include lunch. Scores of boatswains park along the shores of Mahébourg and Blue Bay awaiting customers; they all offer similar experiences.

Jean-Claude Farla BOATING
(☑ 423 1322, 631 7090) Our operator of choice is local legend Jean-Claude Farla, a six-time national swimming champion who competed in the Indian Ocean games. He is the only person to offer outings on a traditional 22ft pirogue (others have souped-up boats with motors). Figure on €20 for a half-day trip, gliding through the blue and stopping periodically to snorkel and free dive.

It's €50 for a full-day excursion to Île aux Cerfs, with a stop at Île de Flamant and a BBQ lunch on Île aux Mangénie. It's best to call at least two days ahead to ensure that he's available (there's a six-person minimum).

Croisières Turquoise SNORKELLING
(Map p106; ☑ 631 1640; www.croisieres-turquoise. com; Rue du Bouchon; per person Rs 2000) This outfit runs day-long boat trips to Île aux Cerfs, departing from the Pointe Jerome embarkation point close to Le Preskîl hotel (Map p116) at 9.30am and returning at 4.30pm. The price includes snorkelling and a barbecue lunch. Advance bookings are essential.

Case Nautique OUTDOORS
(Map p106; ☑ 631 5613, 5251 8271; www.facebook.com/CaseNautiqueMahebourg; cnr Rue du Chaland & Rue de Labourdonnais; kayak hire per day Rs 500, snorkelling per 2hr Rs 750) Good for equipment hire if your hotel can't help, as well as snorkelling excursions to Île aux Cerfs and other islands, and kayaking expeditions.

🛏 Sleeping

You won't come across any grand hotels in quaint Mahébourg, but you will find a proliferation of good, simple guesthouses, making the town an ideal base for budget travellers.

LOCAL TOURS TO TRY

My Moris (☑ 5775 5516, 5723 1755; https://mymoris.mu) These fabulous tours put local experiences front and centre, with everything from a behind-the-scenes look at a sugar plantation or a visit to a Hindu temple to foodie or music-focused experiences. The emphasis is on exploring on foot or by bicycle and getting a taste of a Mauritius that very few visitors see.

Taste Buddies (☑ 266 7496; www. tastebuddies.mu) To really get under the skin of Mauritius's street-food scene, consider taking a three- to four-hour culinary tour of Mahébourg or Port Louis; in the latter there's also the chance of a Chinatown food tour.

Staying in Pointe d'Esny (p110) further down the coast is a quieter alternative.

Nice Place Guesthouse GUESTHOUSE €
(Map p106; ☑ 631 9419; Rue de Labourdonnais; s/d from Rs 650/750, with shared bathroom Rs 400/500; ❄🛜) As the name suggests, this unfussy guesthouse has nice rooms – if simple and a bit faded – tended by a lovely Indian couple. For this price, it's the best in town.

Chill Pill B&B €
(Map p106; ☑ 5787 4000; www.chillpillmauritius. com; Rue Shivananda 6; d incl breakfast from €60; ❄🛜🏊) Simple but bright rooms with tiled floors and sea views make this a good choice. The location, where Mahébourg begins to peter out and the wide horizons of the ocean take hold, is ideal for those who like the best of both worlds.

ONS Motel GUESTHOUSE €
(Map p106; ☑ 5918 0811; www.onsmotel.com; Royal Rd; s/d/f €30/34/65; ❄🛜) If you had a Mauritian grandmother, this might be the sort of guesthouse she'd run, with its slightly flowery decor and homey sense of welcome. The rooms are simple but a good size, and the hotel gets consistently positive reviews from travellers.

Tyvabro GUESTHOUSE €
(Map p106; ☑ 631 9674; www.tyvabro.com; Rue Marianne; d incl breakfast €27; ❄🛜) This family-run operation earns high marks for friendly and eager service. Little perks like in-room DVD players and a welcoming roof deck with

LA FALAISE ROUGE

Reached through an attractive honour guard of palm trees between Mahébourg and View Grand Port, **La Falaise Rouge** (Map p116; ☑5729 1080, 634 0440; B28; mains Rs 395-650; ☺noon-3pm) combines good food with stunning views – a surprisingly rare combination in Mauritius outside the resorts. Their speciality is venison, but they also do Creole pork sausages, seafood, salads and soups. The views from the clifftop are exceptional.

a hammock more than make up for the past-their-prime furnishings in the rooms.

Coco Villa
GUESTHOUSE €
(Map p106; ☑631 2346; www.mahecocovilla.net; Rue Shivananda; s/d incl breakfast Rs 1000/1500; ❄️ 🛜 ❄️) Simple, light-filled spaces right by the water are what this place is all about. Most of the rooms have unobstructed sea views, and the location on Mahébourg's southern outskirts combines proximity to the town and all it offers with a quiet coastal atmosphere.

✖ Eating

Mahébourg has dozens of back alleys riddled with hidden eateries known only to locals. If you're planning to swing by for a visit, make sure you come on Monday, when the local market (p104) is in full force – you'll be treated to the colourful clanging of street stalls as vendors hawk savoury snacks to shoppers.

London Way
SUPERMARKET
(Map p116; ☑696 0088; Pointe d'Esny Rd; ☺8.30am-7pm Mon-Thu, to 7.30pm Fri & Sat, to 12.30pm Sun) The modern London Way supermarket is on the main road heading towards Pointe d'Esny.

★ Chez François
MAURITIAN €
(Map p106; Rue de Labourdonnais; mains Rs 70-400; ☺8.30am-6pm) For a bowl of noodles served fresh off the boat, this simple family-run place is wildly popular with locals. The *mine bouille* (boiled noodles) with mangoak (a mussel-type seafood that's rarely seen on menus) is a highlight, but every dish follows the same formula – fresh ingredients, local crowd-pleasers and low prices. Well on the way to becoming a Mahébourg classic.

★ Le Bazilic
INTERNATIONAL €
(Map p106; ☑5254 8191; www.facebook.com/LeBazilic; Rue de Maurice; mains Rs 75-300; ☺10am-8pm; ✖) What a fabulous place this is, with sandwiches both simple and gourmet, rice and noodle dishes such as pad thai, pasta, and a range of vegetarian options. There's nothing remarkable here – just good old-fashioned cooking, and warm, friendly service. It's a winning combination.

★ La Vielle Rouge
SEAFOOD €
(Map p106; ☑631 3980; cnr Rue du Hangard & Rue des Mares; mains Rs 285-650; ☺10am-11pm) Fish and seafood cooked fresh or with a few Asian inflections make Le Vielle Rouge one of the standout options in town. Service is friendly and signature dishes include the calamari with ginger sauce or fresh lobster with garlic sauce.

Pyramid Snack
MAURITIAN €
(Map p106; ☑631 9731; Rue de Labourdonnais; kebabs Rs 60-70, small/large biryani Rs 90/120; ☺9.30am-4pm Mon-Sat) This hero of the street-food scene is beside the petrol station just across from the market. Delicious *biryani* (rice cooked in a steel pot with various eastern spices and meat or fish) and 'kebabs' (salad, meat and sauce in a baguette) seem to emerge from the kitchen in factory proportions as fishers and hawkers queue for a midday meal.

Shyam
MAURITIAN €
(☑5764 2960; rotis & dhal puris Rs 14; ☺11am-4pm) For the best *dhal puri* in town, look no further than Shyam (you can call him 'Sam'). He scoots around scooping out flavourful snacks from an empty aquarium tank on the back of his motorbike. On Monday he's at the market (p104), but if you're desperate for *dhal puri* at other times, give him a ring and he'll come find you.

Café de Labourdonnais
CAFE €
(Map p106; ☑5886 8840; www.facebook.com/cafedelabourdonnais; Rue de Labourdonnais; mains from Rs 80; ☺8.30am-7pm Mon-Sat, to 3pm Sun; 🛜) We're starting to see these cool little cafes popping up in smaller Mauritian towns, and it's a most welcome development. With free wi-fi and a full board of hot and cold drinks, you could just come here for some down time, but they also do appealing light meals including wraps, paninis, felafel and burgers; the grilled lamb burger is ace.

Tabagi Bambous MAURITIAN €
(Map p106; ☑ 5796 0070; Rue du Bambous; rotis Rs 12; ⊘ 7.30am-9.30pm) Dark and dimly lit, *tabagis* (convenience stores) line the streets of every town in Mauritius. If you've yet to visit one, the unusually popular Bambous is the perfect place to lose your *tabagi* virginity. Proprietor Amrita dishes out her signature *rotis* while Bollywood heroines clink their bejewelled costumes on the TV screen.

Saveurs de Shin ASIAN €
(Map p106; ☑ 5751 5932, 631 3668; Rue de Suffren; mains Rs 200-450; ⊘ 11am-2pm & 6.30-10pm Wed-Mon) This place a block back from the water may not look like much, but the quality is high, the prices are low and the servings are large – a winning combination in anyone's language. The half/full Peking duck is outrageously good value at Rs 650/1200, but you could choose anything from this extensive menu and not be disappointed.

Chez Patrick MAURITIAN €
(Map p106; ☑ 631 9298; Royal Rd; mains Rs 95-550, set menus Rs 575-900; ⊘ 11.30am-3pm & 6-10pm) Patrick's is popular with locals and tourists for its unpretentious atmosphere and authentic Creole cooking. There's everything from octopus curry to Creole clams, and the set menu feasts are terrific value.

Les Copains d'Abord MAURITIAN €€
(Map p106; ☑ 631 9728; www.facebook.com/lescopainsdabordMaurice; Rue Shivananda; mains Rs 395-995, snacks Rs 90-225; ⊘ 10am-3pm & 6-9pm) Occupying an enviable position along the seafront promenade on the south side of town, Les Copains d'Abord serves tasty Mauritian dishes of fresh seafood curry, prawn croquettes, palm-heart salad, flavourful *rougaille saucisses* (spicy sausages) and wildboar ribs in Rodrigues honey. Smart decor and occasional fits of live music will quickly help you forget that the menu is at times overpriced.

ⓘ Information

HSBC (☑ 631 5224; Royal Rd; ⊘ 9am-3.30pm Mon-Thu, to 4pm Fri)
Mauritius Commercial Bank (MCB; ☑ 631 2879; Rue des Délices; ⊘ 9am-3.15pm Mon-Thu, to 5pm Fri)

ⓘ Getting There & Away

Mahébourg's **bus station** (Map p106) is an important transport hub. There are express buses every half-hour to/from Port Louis (Rs 42, two hours), from where there are connections to Grand Baie and other destinations. Most but not all of these buses stop at the airport en route; check before boarding. A shuttle from Mahébourg to Blue Bay runs roughly every 30 minutes.

Buses running north from Mahébourg go to Centre de Flacq via Vieux Grand Port every 20 minutes or so. Heading south, there are less frequent services to Souillac via Rivière des Anguilles.

A taxi for the 15-minute hop from SSR International Airport (p146) to Mahébourg costs Rs 500. From Mahébourg, you'll pay Rs 1800 to reach Port Louis, Rs 1800 to reach Flic en Flac and Rs 1400 to reach Belle Mare.

ⓘ Getting Around

You'll find a variety of local car hire agencies who also offer rides to the airport. Your accommodation can hook you up with a vehicle.

Pointe d'Esny & Blue Bay

Pointe d'Esny and Blue Bay have some of the most beautiful stretches of beach on the entire island and they're many travellers' favourite corners of the country. Pointe d'Esny is also the jumping-off point for those interested in visiting the nature reserve on Île aux Aigrettes.

⊙ Sights

★**Île aux Aigrettes** ISLAND
(Map p116; www.mauritian-wildlife.org/Ileauxaigrettes) ✦ This popular ecotourism destination is a 26-hectare nature reserve on an island roughly 800m off the coast. It preserves very rare remnants of the coastal forests of Mauritius and provides a sanctuary for a range of endemic and endangered wildlife species (p111). Visits are only possible as part of a guided tour, and these leave from Pointe Jérome (p113), close to Le Preskîl (p107). Highlights include Aldabra giant tortoises, ebony trees, wild orchids, and the endangered pink pigeon and other rare bird species.

As the guides to Île aux Aigrettes rightly point out, this is the last place in Mauritius where you can see it as the first explorers did almost five centuries ago – everywhere else, the land has been tamed. The Mauritian Wildlife Foundation (p110) manages the reserve and conducts tours.

VISITING ÎLE AUX AIGRETTES

The **Mauritian Wildlife Foundation Booking Office** (MWF; Map p116; 631 2396, 5258 8139; www.mauritian-wildlife.org; Coastal Rd, Pointe Jérome; short tour incl boat transfer adult/child Rs 800/400; ☉ office 9am-4pm Mon-Sat, to noon Sun, tours 9.30am, 10am, 10.30am, 1.30pm, 2pm & 2.30pm Mon-Sat, 9.30am, 10am & 10.30am Sun) manages and conducts tours of Île aux Aigrettes (p109); tour revenues go towards its conservation efforts). The usual tours take between 1½ and two hours and start from Pointe Jérome, around 250m southeast of Le Preskîl hotel (Map p116). Bookings can be made by phone or email, or in person at the office opposite the embarkation point.

Longer 'eco tours' of two to 2½ hours are also available. These allow you more time on the island and let you meet some members of the scientific teams working there. Tours involve a good deal of walking; wear comfortable shoes and bring a hat, sunscreen and water. At the end of the tour you can visit a small museum and shop.

★ **Blue Bay Marine Park**   WILDLIFE RESERVE
(Map p116) In an effort to protect the area's rich underwater forest of rare corals from encroaching development, the government has given Blue Bay 'marine park' status. Besides a mandate barring high-speed watercraft, though, it seems that conservation plans are a bit laissez-faire. Local environmentalists fear that irreversible coral bleaching is inevitable, which is a shame as this is the best snorkelling spot on the island.

There are no 'official' tours of the marine park like those on Île aux Aigrettes (p109), but the protected patches of coral can be easily explored on a snorkelling outing or during an excursion aboard a glass-bottomed boat (figure on around Rs 250 per person for one hour).

Île des Deux Cocos   ISLAND
(Map p116; www.iledesdeuxcocos.com) Île des Deux Cocos sits at the edge of the azure lagoon and was once used by flamboyant British governor Sir Hesketh Bell to entertain guests. Today the Lux hotel group has maintained this hospitable tradition by offering tourists a relaxing day of swimming, beach lazing and snorkelling. Welcome drinks, an immense buffet lunch and rum tasting are also included. Transport to the island can be arranged by any of the Lux hotels or via the website.

🏃 Activities

Boat Trips

Like Mahébourg to the north, Blue Bay is home to numerous operators offering journeys on glass-bottomed boats and excursions to the nearby islands. Travellers should be careful, however, when choosing a boatswain here – the area has seen an in-creased number of drug dealers and addicts in recent years and a handful of them have been drawn to tourism. Always seek a recommendation from a local or your hotel before handing over any money. Also, the tides vary greatly in this part of the island; only a knowledgeable tour leader will know the optimal times for going to sea. Recommended operators include Jean-Claude Farla (p107), Case Nautique (p107) and Croisières Turquoise (p107).

Diving
Coral Diving   DIVING
(Map p116; 604 1084; www.coraldiving.com; Astroea Beach Hotel, Coastal Rd; lagoon/sea dive Rs 1800/2000; ☉8.30am-4.30pm) Friendly Tony, one of the most knowledgeable divers in Mauritius, runs Coral Diving, the southeast's main scuba operator. It is primarily located on the sandy grounds of Astroea Beach but is open to those not staying at the hotel. The sea dive includes pool training for beginners.

🛏 Sleeping

Pointe d'Esny and Blue Bay are among the epicentres of tourism in the south and there's a lot to be said for staying here. Close to the airport and to the charms of Mahébourg, the area also has a good mix of upmarket resorts, private villas, apartment complexes and charming *chambres d'hôtes*.

Le Jardin de Beau Vallon   HISTORIC HOTEL €
(Map p116; 631 2850; Rue de Beau Vallon; s/d from €49/61; ❋ 🛜) Beau Vallon is primarily known for its charming restaurant (p112), set on the ground floor of an 18th-century colonial manor house. There are, however, several suites and bungalows on the property that make for a memorable vacation

experience, as long as you don't mind being a 10-minute drive to the beach.

Perched above the restaurant, the two welcoming suites draw their decorative inspiration from Madagascar and East Asia – vibrant tapestries tumble down the walls and four-poster beds are ensconced in a tornado of silky streamers. Several newer bungalows are arranged in a row just beyond the main building and are adorned with plantation-style incarnations of wood and wicker.

Chez Henri GUESTHOUSE €
(Map p116; ☑631 9806; www.henri-vacances.com; Coastal Rd; r incl breakfast Rs 1800; ❋@) Staying at Henri and Majo's welcoming *chambre d'hôte* feels like a trip to the countryside to visit your long-lost uncle and aunt. Rooms are lovingly filled with loads of wood and wicker, and each one sports a useful kitchenette. Don't miss the excellent three-course dinners (Rs 500 to Rs 600), served on the patio.

Blue Beryl GUESTHOUSE €€
(Map p116; ☑631 9862; www.blueberyl.com; Coastal Rd; s incl breakfast €27-102, d incl breakfast €32-120) Despite what you might expect, many – perhaps even most – of the lodgings in Pointe d'Esny and Blue Bay are divided from the beach by a road. Blue Beryl bucks that trend with simply furnished studios, some in aquamarine blue, and most of which face right onto the beach. You can upgrade to half board for an additional €13 per person.

Noix de Coco GUESTHOUSE €€
(Map p116; ☑5772 9303; www.noixdecocoguesthouse.com; Coastal Rd; r incl breakfast €67-95; ❋) Dorette has opened her charming home to travellers. Several rooms have sea views, though you'll spend most of your time lounging on the sand-swept terrace.

Astroea Beach BOUTIQUE HOTEL €€€
(Map p116; ☑631 4282; www.southerncrosshotels.mu; Coastal Rd; s/d with half board from €155/225; P❋@ ﹫) Fronting onto the beach in Pointe d'Esny, this fine spot styles itself as a luxury boutique hotel without the prohibitive price tag. Rooms, all decked in white and aquamarine blue, are large and lovely, and many have ocean views. There's the Ylang Spa, an excellent restaurant with sea views and a full suite of water sports activities and excursions.

THE WILDLIFE OF ÎLE AUX AIGRETTES

In 1985, the Mauritian Wildlife Foundation took out a lease on Île aux Aigrettes and began the difficult task of ridding it of introduced plants and animals, including rats and feral cats. It also began a massive planting program, removing introduced species and reintroducing native plants. Until the foundation began its work, the island was a popular place for day trips and most native plant species had been cut down for firewood. One exception was a small but significant stand of ebony forest. The forest survives, including some trees that may be 400 years old, and most guided tours pass through it.

The foundation was able to bring some of the most endangered species in Mauritius to the island in the hope that they would find refuge and breed in a suitable natural habitat free from predators. Along with other sites, such as Round Island (off the north coast) and Black River Gorges National Park (in the southwest), the island has become a bulwark against extinction, not to mention a stunning conservation success story. Île aux Aigrettes is now home to around 30 pink pigeons (out of just 470 left in the wild today), 55 olive white-eye pairs (out of 100 to 150 pairs) and 450 Mauritian fodies (out of 800). On most guided visits there's a good chance of seeing the pink pigeon, but you'll need luck to see the other species.

Interestingly, not all endangered species made it here – the Mauritian kestrel was introduced but didn't find the habitat to be suitable (the canopy was too low and there was not enough prey), and so the birds crossed the water and found more suitable habitats on the main island, including Black River Gorges National Park (p98) and nearby Vallée de Ferney (p105).

Other stars of the show include around 20 adult Aldabra or Seychelles tortoises (as well as a number of young), the last of the giant Indian Ocean tortoise species. This is the only place in Mauritius to see these soulful creatures in the wild. Note also the five or so caged (and endangered) Mauritian fruit bats and around 450 Telfair's skinks (important competitors for the introduced – and undesirable – Indian shrews, the only remaining mammal species on Île aux Aigrettes).

DON'T MISS

DOMAINE DE L'ÉTOILE

Teetering between the east and south-east realms of the island, the popular forest reserve **Domaine de l'Étoile** (TerrOcean; Map p116; ☑ 729 1050, 448 4444; www.terrocean.mu; off B27) is set on more than 2000 hectares of un-spoilt hinterland – the perfect terrain to explore by horse, on foot or by quad bike. Mountain biking, guided hikes and archery are also on offer. Enjoy a bite at the restaurant while you're here.

If you're lucky, you'll spot Javanese stags hiding in the forest – there are over 1000 living in the reserve.

Shandrani
RESORT €€€

(Map p116; ☑ 601 9000; www.beachcomber-hotels.com; r from €148; ✸@🛜🏊) On the southern side of Blue Bay, this relaxed, fam-ily-friendly resort rambles across a private peninsula with luscious jungle foliage. It has three beaches and boasts all the facilities you'd expect from a heavy hitter in the top-end category, but with a far more reasonable price tag than you might think.

Le Peninsula Bay Hotel
HOTEL €€€

(Map p116; ☑ 631 9046; www.lepeninsulabay.com; Coastal Rd; s/d with half board from €133/166; 🅿✸🛜🏊) The only hotel to sit right on Blue Bay itself, Le Peninsula underwent renova-tions in 2015, and it shows, particularly in the rather lovely bathrooms. Rooms are still comfortable rather than luxurious but the location is excellent, there's an on-site spa and guests have plenty of waterborne activi-ties to choose from.

Eolia Beachfront Villas
VILLA €€€

(Map p116; ☑ 263 3069; Coastal Rd; villa from €240; 🅿✸🛜🏊) The name says it all here – the stylish, contemporary villas all sit right upon the beach in a quiet corner or Blue Bay. If you went sleepwalking, you'd end up in the lagoon – you're that close.

Paradise Beach
APARTMENT €€€

(Map p116; ☑ 403 5308; www.paradisebeach.mu; Coastal Rd; apt from €255; 🅿✸🛜🏊) Right on the beach yet closed off from the rest of the world. Beautiful modern apartments with kitchens. What's not to like at this well-run place?

✗ Eating

Despite the palpable residential vibe, Pointe d'Esny and Blue Bay have a few noteworthy options spread along the coastal road – Blue Bay in particular has some fine choices. And if you're here for a while and in need of a little variety, Mahébourg is rarely more than a 10-minute drive away.

Chez Maryse
MAURITIAN €

(Map p116; ☑ 978 8211; Coastal Rd; mains from Rs 250; ⊙ 11.30am-3pm & 6-9pm) After winning a 'women's empowerment' grant from the Mauritian government many years back, friendly Maryse and her family opened a small restaurant in her backyard. Savoury Creole eats are stewed under the yellow tin roof and served to contented customers gathered around the haphazard collection of tables.

★ Le Jardin de Beau Vallon
MAURITIAN €€

(Map p116; ☑ 631 2850; Rue de Beau Vallon; mains Rs 200-650; ⊙ noon-3pm & 6.30-10pm) Emerg-ing from an inland thicket of trees and sky-scraping cane leaves, Beau Vallon is an enchanting colonial estate that has been lov-ingly refurbished over the last few decades. Romantic dark-wood panelling, flavourful island spices and the lazy spin of frond-shaped ceiling fans make for an atmospheric setting. Unfortunately, when we visited the staff weren't as charming as the surrounds...

La Belle Créole
MAURITIAN €€

(Assiette du Pêcheur; Map p116; ☑ 631 1069; Royal Rd; mains Rs 400-950) Excellent Creole cook-ing – such as venison or wild boar curry or seafood vindaloo – combined with an attrac-tive lagoon-side, open-air setting (bring the mosquito repellent) make this one of our fa-vourite choices in the area. It's around half-way between Mahébourg and Pointe d'Esny.

Blue Bamboo
ITALIAN, MAURITIAN €€

(Map p116; ☑ 631 5801; Coastal Rd; pizza Rs 270-440, mains Rs 380-650; ⊙ 10am-3pm & 6-11pm Tue-Sun) Blue Bamboo has many charms: a cosy plant-filled cloister, delicious pan piz-za, friendly owners and an inviting lounge on the 2nd floor. The upstairs bar is open 6pm to midnight every day except Monday. It's usually best to call ahead if you'd like a table in the bamboo-lined courtyard. Dishes include some intriguing options, including vanilla chicken.

Le Bougainville
MAURITIAN €€

(Map p116; ☑ 631 8299; Coastal Rd; mains Rs 250-450, pizza from Rs 325; ⊙10am-10pm) Worth a mention for its breezy terrace, friendly atmosphere and convenient location across from **Blue Bay Beach**, Le Bougainville is a popular hang-out for locals and tourists alike. The menu is vast, with salads, pizza, fish, curries etc.

❶ Getting There & Away

Buses to and from Mahébourg run every 30 minutes. A taxi there will cost Rs 350, and it's Rs 500 to Rs 600 to the airport.

❶ Getting Around

All of the area's guesthouses can arrange car hire. Try Henri at **JH Arnulphy** (Chez Henri; ☑ 631 9806; www.henri-vacances.com; Coastal Rd), who offers cars from Rs 1450 per day. Arnulphy can also help with bicycle rental; rates start at Rs 150 per day.

Pointe Jérome Embarkation Point (Île aux Aigrettes Departure Point, Pointe Jérome; Map p116) Ferries leave from here to go to Île aux Aigrettes.

Vieux Grand Port
POP 3270

'Old Grand Port', north of Mahébourg, is the cradle of Mauritian history: the place where the first human inhabitants of the island landed on 9 September 1598 under the command of Wybrandt Van Warwyck. The Dutch later built a fort 3km further north in what is now the town of Vieux Grand Port. It was the local headquarters of the Dutch East India Company until 1710, when the Dutch abandoned the island. The site was then taken over by the French.

Most travellers stop here as they travel along the east coast. You won't need more than an hour or two to take in all the sights.

◉ Sights

Frederik Hendrik Museum & Vieux Grand Port Historic Site
MUSEUM

(Map p116; ☑ 634 4319; Royal Rd; ⊙9am-4pm Mon, Tue & Thu-Sat, from 11am Wed, 9am-noon Sun) **FREE** The battered ruins of Fort Frederik Hendrik stand in a park near the church at the northern end of Vieux Grand Port and include the remains of an old Dutch church, a bakery, a prison, a forge, a powder magazine and a dispensary. A few clay pipes, wine bottles and other items left behind by Dutch and French occupants are now on display in the Frederik Hendrik Museum. The museum also outlines the history of the Dutch in Mauritius.

Monument to Dutch Landing
MONUMENT

(Map p116; Royal Rd) A monument marks the site where the Dutch (and indeed the first people ever) first landed on the island on 20 September 1598. It's a fairly low-key site for what is claimed to be the cradle for Mauritian civilisation, but interesting nonetheless.

🏃 Activities

★ Lion Mountain
HIKING

(Map p116) Recognisable by its sphinx-like profile, Lion Mountain offers a challenging, rewarding half-day hike with stunning coastal views. The walk climbs the lion's 'back' to finish on the 'head'. We recommend hiring a local guide or joining an organised hike with Otélair (p62) or Vallée de Ferney (p105). The trailhead is beside the police station at the north of Vieux Grand Port.

Check out www.fitsy.com for detailed GPS information about the hike, though the main trail is fairly obvious and runs straight along the ridge and up over a rocky area to the peak. There are a few hairy scrambles over the rocks before you reach the flat area on the lion's head. From here you can see right across the interior of the island. Return the same way you came up. Allow three to four hours for the return trip.

🛌 Sleeping

★ La Hacienda
VILLA €€

(Map p116; ☑ 263 0914; www.lahaciendamauritius. com; Mosque Rd, Vieux Grand Port; 1-/2-bedroom villa €81/122; ⏻ ❄ @ 🛜 ≋) On the slopes of Lion Mountain, La Hacienda has four stunning villas with some of the best views on this side of the island. The self-contained villas have kitchens, decks with fine views and plenty of space, not to mention a real sense of blissful isolation from all the clamour.

❶ Getting There & Away

The best way to explore around Vieux Grand Port is by private vehicle; most tour operators can hook you up with a half- or full-day visit to any part of the southeast region. Public transport is also available, though it's significantly less convenient. Buses between Mahébourg and Centre de Flacq ply the coast road, passing through Vieux Grand Port, Anse Jonchée and Bambous Virieux. There are departures every 20 minutes or so.

SOUTH COAST

Mauritius' southern coast, known as Savanne, features some of the country's wildest and most attractive scenery. Here you'll find basalt cliffs, sheltered sandy coves, hidden falls and traditional fishing villages. Beyond the shoreline lie endless sugar-cane fields and forests that clothe the hillsides in a patchwork of vibrant greens. Long considered too harsh to develop due to its rugged topography, the region staved off developers until quite recently.

The region is devoid of any prominent towns save Rivière des Anguilles and Souillac. Both can be used as bases from which to explore the nearby parks and preserves, while Bel Ombre, a small village, is best known for its string of upmarket coastal resorts.

❶ Getting There & Away

Most people hire a car to explore the south coast or charter a taxi for the day. It can be slow going if you're driving down here – consisting of back roads with the usual Mauritius traffic that slows to a crawl as it passes through the many little towns – but the rewards are worth it.

Regular buses connect Souillac with Mahébourg, Port Louis and Curepipe; most go via Rivière des Anguilles. From Souillac, buses travel along the coast almost hourly.

WORTH A TRIP

LA ROUTE DU THÉ

La Route du Thé (www.saintaubinloisirs. com) offers tourists a window onto the island's plantation past by linking three of the island's remaining colonial estates. The first stop is the Creole manse turned museum at the Domaine des Aubineaux (p62) near Curepipe. Then the route veers south to the vast Bois Chéri Tea Plantation (p119). The final stop is the stately St Aubin (p118), with its lush gardens and rum distillery. Despite the itinerary's name, the focus of the trip extends far beyond tea – each stop has a charming *table d'hôte* and a museum, and the St Aubin even offers period-style accommodation.

True architecture buffs and historians should consider doing the route backwards and tacking on the resplendent Eureka (p60) estate at the end of the journey.

Souillac

POP 4450

The largest settlement along the south coast is Souillac, 7km from Rivière des Anguilles. Most travellers come here on a day trip along the south coast or as an add-on to a visit to La Vanille zoo (p118). The town itself has little to offer, but the clutch of (somewhat) interesting sights close by and some decent restaurants just about make it worth the detour.

◎ Sights

Gris Gris Beach   BEACH

(Map p116) Around 2.5km southeast of central Souillac, a grassy clifftop affords fine views of the black-rock coastline. A path leads down to the wild Gris Gris beach; a sign warns of the dangers of swimming. The term *gris gris* traditionally refers to 'black magic' and, looking at the tortuous coastline, you can see how the area got its name. Then again, another story suggests that the beach was named after the puppy (!) of a French cartographer who visited in 1753.

Rochester Falls   WATERFALL

(Map p116) Rochester Falls are by no means the country's most spectacular falls, but they're worth a detour if you're in the area. Follow the makeshift signs from the main road through Souillac – the route is rather circuitous but it's reliable nonetheless, although it's a rough ride along the stone-strewn track. Prepare yourself for hawkers who'll want a tip for telling you where to park. The gushing cascade emerges from the cane fields after a five-minute walk from your car.

La Roche Qui Pleure   LANDMARK

(The Crying Rock; Map p116) Right at the end of the headland beyond Gris Gris beach, 600m further on and well signposted, La Roche Qui Pleure resembles a crying man – you'll have to stand there puzzling it out for quite some time, and the waves really have to crash for the 'tears' to come out, but it's oddly satisfying when you finally get it.

✖ Eating

Eating choices are best east and west of the town centre, with especially good options out in the Gris Gris district. If you're eating by the sea, opt for something with seafood – it was probably caught within sight of your table.

LE SOUFFLEUR

A hidden attraction known only to locals, **Le Souffleur** (Map p116) requires a bit of gumption (and a 4WD) to tackle. But if you ask anyone in the know, they'll say that it's well worth the adventure.

Situated on the coast about halfway between Souillac and Blue Bay, this geological anomaly is a half-formed grotto on the side of a cliff that spouts a geyser-like fountain of water (up to 20m high!) when the seas are rough. As the waves crash against the cliff the seawater pushes through a crack in the bluffs like a blowhole on a whale. If the seas aren't particularly rough during your visit, there's a natural land bridge nearby that's worth a camera click or two. It was formed when the roof collapsed on another naturally formed grotto.

To reach the super-secret *souffleur* (grotto), head for the Savannah sugar estate near the village of L'Escalier, cross the estate, then follow the snaking track once you reach the sea. Even if you don't seek permission to cross the sugar estate, which you probably should, we highly recommend bringing a local with you – otherwise you may never find the place.

★ **Le Gris Gris** MAURITIAN €
(Chez Rosy; Map p116; ☑ 625 4179; Gris Gris Beach; mains Rs 275-380; ☻11.30am-4pm) Rosy's place is a simple affair with a motley assortment of wicker and plastic furniture. The food, however, never misses the mark – locals and tourists rave about the home-cooked Mauritian and Chinese dishes. We thoroughly enjoyed the octopus stew.

Zoza PASTRIES €
(Map p116; ☑5253 7774; www.facebook.com/zo zapatisserie125; Off B9; snacks Rs 17-30; ☻6am-7pm) This lovely little spot serves real coffee, tasty sweet pastries, and a handful of savoury pastries (such as pies) and simple sandwiches. There are a few stools inside and a couple of tables outside. We've heard it described by one local as the best pastry shop in Mauritius' south. We wouldn't disagree.

Le Rochester Restaurant MAURITIAN €
(Map p116; ☑ 625 4180; mains Rs 325-650; ☻noon-3pm & 6-9pm Wed-Mon, noon-3pm Tue) The charming Madame Appadu runs her restaurant in an old colonial building by the bridge to Surinam. A delightful mix of Creole, Indian and Chinese staples is served on a shady terrace situated atop a gushing ravine. We enjoyed the grilled calamari with garlic butter sauce. Upstairs you'll find three small guest rooms, but they're nothing to write home about.

Le Batelage MAURITIAN €€
(Map p116; ☑ 625 6083; Village des Touristes, Royal Rd, Port Souillac; mains Rs 600-950; ☻noon-3pm & 6-9pm) Drop down off the main road at the western end of Souillac for a lovely waterside eating experience. The food (the usual mix of Mauritian staples and seafood) is a touch overpriced, but it's still worth it for the setting, which is the best in the area. Service can be hit or miss, especially when there are big groups in.

❶ Getting There & Away

There are buses roughly every half-hour from Mahébourg to Souillac via the airport and Rivière des Anguilles. From Port Louis, buses run hourly, calling at Rivière des Anguilles en route. There are also frequent services to/from Curepipe, with three buses a day taking the coast road via Pointe aux Roches. Buses heading along the coast to Baie du Cap (from where you can pick up onward transport to the west coast) depart hourly.

Bel Ombre

POP 2440

Despite being miles away from the bucket-and-spade atmosphere of Flic en Flac or Grand Baie, Bel Ombre has quickly developed into a cosy tourist bubble along the wild southern shores. It's very much an upmarket crowd, but the public beaches still get popular with locals.

🏃 Activities

In addition to what's on offer at the individual resorts, there's golf, quad-biking, hiking and 4WD safaris on land. Out on the lagoon, you can go windsurfing, diving or snorkelling, or simply float around in a glass-bottomed boat.

Heritage Nature Reserve OUTDOORS
(Map p116; ☑ 623 5615; www.heritagebelombre. com; Bel Ombre; ☻8.30am-4.30pm) The main attraction in Bel Ombre is this open nature reserve set on a sugar plantation developed

The South & Southeast

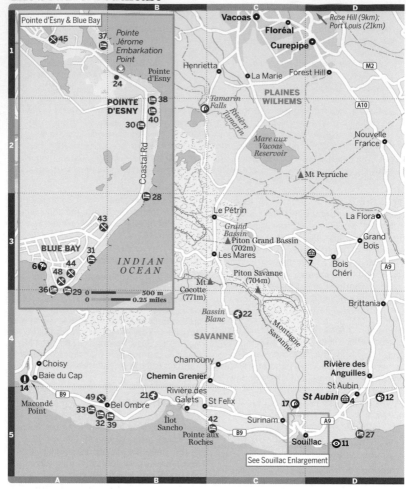

by Charles Telfair between 1816 and 1833. Today it's a multifaceted venture with quad biking, hiking and touring on 4WDs.

🛏 Sleeping & Eating

⭐ Outrigger Mauritius Beach Resort
LUXURY HOTEL €€€

(Map p116; ☎ 623 5000; www.outrigger.com; Allee des Cocotiers; r from €300; 🅿✳@🛜🏊) A high-class resort with a range of restaurants, a poolside bar perfectly sited to frame the sunset, a spa complex and large and lovely rooms – Outrigger is an excellent choice and rates can be surprisingly reasonable. Families are made to feel welcome here.

⭐ Heritage Awali
LUXURY HOTEL €€€

(Map p116; ☎ 601 1500; www.heritageresorts.mu; Domaine de Bel Ombre; r from €275; 🅿✳@🛜🏊) The Awali celebrates an African heritage, with abounding masks, drums and tribal art. There's also a golf course and a spa complex for the ultimate indulgence, as well as the usual prime beachfront location.

Heritage Le Telfair
HERITAGE HOTEL €€€

(Map p116; ☎ 601 5500; www.heritageresorts.mu; Domaine de Bel Ombre; r from €415; 🅿✳@🛜🏊)

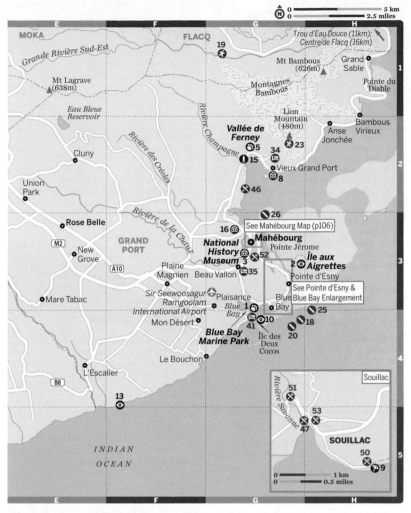

The Heritage Le Telfair has perfectly captured the luxury and grandeur of the island's colonial yesteryear, with stately rooms, expansive grounds, exceptional service and unrelenting attention to detail. Natural fibres, soothing earth tones and a classic style of wood and whitewash make this a sophisticated choice.

★ **Le Château Bel Ombre** MAURITIAN €€€
(Map p116; ☑ 623 5522; www.heritageresorts.mu/le-chateau-de-bel-ombre; mains from Rs 1200; ⊙ noon-3pm Mon-Thu, noon-3pm & 6.30-9pm Fri & Sat) Le Château, set in a stunning conversion of the old Bel Ombre plantation house,

is the place for an exceptional, atmospheric meal of traditional Franco-Mauritian cuisine with contemporary flourishes. Try the squid in its own ink with lemongrass and jackfruit or the lobster cappuccino with salted butter and Rodrigues honey. The menu is overseen by French celebrity chef, David Toutain.

ⓘ Getting There & Away

To range beyond Bel Ombre, most travellers hire a car or taxi from their hotel. A regular bus service runs from Curepipe to Bel Ombre via Nouvelle France and Chemin Grenier.

The South & Southeast

Around the South Coast

The hinterland has enough fascinating attractions to fill at least a day, with a wildlife park, some fine examples of colonial architecture and a take on the coloured-earth phenomenon, not to mention some fine hotels.

◎ Sights & Activities

★St Aubin   HISTORIC BUILDING
(Map p116; ☑ 676 3089; www.saintaubinloisirs.com; off A9, Rivière des Anguilles; adult/child Rs 525/250, incl lunch Rs 1350/700; ⊙ 9am-5pm) St Aubin is an elegant plantation house that dates back to 1819; it originally sat alongside the factory but was moved in the 1970s so that its owner could get a quieter night's sleep. The estate no longer produces sugar, but in the gardens of the house there is a traditional rum distillery and a nursery growing anthurium flowers and vanilla – you'll learn all about the fascinating history of vanilla production on the tour.

The height of the St Aubin experience is a meal at the wonderfully charming **table d'hôte** (Map p116; ☑ 626 1513; Off A9, Rivière des Anguilles; mains Rs 300-900; ⊙ noon-3pm) in the main manor house. The dining room is one of the best throwbacks to colonial times: dainty chandeliers cast ambient light over the white tablecloths and antique wooden furniture. The set menu showcases the fruits of the plantation: hearts of palm, pineapple, mango and chilli, to name a few. Reservations are recommended.

La Vanille   ZOO
(Réserve des Mascareignes; Map p116; ☑ 626 2503; www.lavanille-naturepark.com; Rivière des Anguilles; adult/child Rs 500/270; ⊙ 8.30am-5pm May-Oct, to 5.30pm Nov-Apr) This busy zoo and reserve makes for a fantastic field trip with kids. The park has the greatest number of giant tortoises in captivity in the world (over 1000). It's worth coming to La Vanille

just to check out the immense collection of mounted insects (over 23,000 species!). There's also a farm of Nile crocodiles (population 2000), which can grow up to 7m, and a dodo museum.

The tortoises are the undoubted highlight, the result of a wildly successful breeding program for the Aldabra and *radiata* species. Chances are that you'll see the former breeding in front of your eyes.

The on-site **Hungry Crocodile Restaurant** (La Crocodile Affamé; Map p116; La Vanille, Rivière des Anguilles; mains Rs 280-550; ⊘11am-5pm) specialises in all things crocodilian – croc curry, croc burger, croc fried rice, croc cooked in a vanilla sauce... (It also does more conventional dishes such as spaghetti bolognese and beef burgers.) Don't forget your mozzie repellent – you won't be the only one feasting at the lunch table.

La Vanille is a few kilometres northwest of Souillac or 2km south of Rivière des Anguilles.

Bois Chéri Tea Plantation　　　MUSEUM
(Map p116; ☑676 3089, restaurant 471 1216; www.saintaubinloisirs.com; Grand Bassin; adult/child Rs 525/250, incl lunch Rs 1350/700; ⊘9am-5pm, restaurant 10.30am-3.30pm) This 250-hectare tea factory and museum is located about 12km north of Rivière des Anguilles amid a vast expanse of cane. Hour-long tours of the tea-processing facility end with a stop at a small exhibition space detailing the island's tea history by means of machines and photos. The best part of the visit is undoubtedly the sampling session at the end. It's advisable to visit in the morning, as most of the action takes place before noon.

La Vallée des Couleurs　　ADVENTURE SPORTS
(Map p116; ☑5869 7777; www.lvdc.mu; Chamouny; adult/child Rs 350/200; ⊘10am-5pm) Despite

having 23 colours, as opposed to seven at Chamarel (p96), La Vallée des Couleurs is the less impressive of the island's two 'coloured earths'. The reserve does, however, have a scenic nature trail that passes trickling waterfalls, memorable vistas, crawling tortoises and blossoming tropical flowers. It takes about an hour to complete the reserve's circuit. Other highlights include a 350m Nepalese suspension bridge and the world's third-longest zipline (1.5km).

🛏 Sleeping

★**Auberge de St Aubin**　　HISTORIC HOTEL €€
(Map p116; ☑626 1513; www.saintaubin.mu/fr/auberge_st_aubin.aspx; off A9, Rivière des Anguilles; s/d/f Rs 3300/4400/6500; ❄) The Auberge de St Aubin has three rooms in the plantation manse across from the main building of the estate. The bedroom at the front perfectly captures the charming colonial ambience, with creaky wooden floors and cotton gauze over the four-poster bed. The two rooms out the back are more modern, with a little less character.

Andréa Lodges　　COTTAGE €€
(Map p116; ☑1111 1111; www.andrea-lodge.com; Union Ducray; s/d with half board €78/119; ❄≋) Andréa's 10 lovely cottages, along the sea, have gabled roofs and glass-panelled walls facing the rugged Ireland-esque coast. There's also a swimming pool and a reputable restaurant. Rates include a guided hike through the forest beyond the sugar cane. Guests can arrange 4WD excursions and quad biking; tours of the neighbouring sugar estate are possible between December and June.

★**Shanti Maurice**　　HOTEL €€€
(Map p116; ☑603 7200; www.shantimaurice.com; St Felix; r incl breakfast from €450; ℗❄@⩥≋)

BAIE DU CAP

Baie du Cap marks the eastern end of one of the island's most stunning coastlines (running west to Le Morne Peninsula). It's more a place to admire as you drive along the coast than somewhere to visit as a destination in its own right, but there is a low-key sight here – the **Matthew Flinders Monument** (Map p116).

The monument stands on the shore 500m west of Baie du Cap and was erected in 2003 to honour the 200th anniversary of the arrival of English navigator and cartographer Matthew Flinders. He was less warmly received at the time; the poor bloke didn't know that England and France were at war and he was swiftly imprisoned for six years. For an interesting read on the subject, take a look at Huguette Ly-Tio-Fane Pineo's book *In the Grips of the Eagle: Matthew Flinders at the Île de France, 1803–1810*.

Bus services along here are limited. Baie du Cap is the terminus for buses from Souillac and Quatre Bornes (via Tamarin). Buses run approximately every 20 minutes.

One of the loveliest places to stay along the south coast, and among the island's signature resorts, the Shanti Maurice oozes luxury. All of the expansive rooms face the sea, the beach is superb, and the tropical, 14-hectare grounds are gorgeous. There's also yoga, a kids' club, water sports, gym, spa, and attentive staff to make possible your every whim.

THE EAST

Known by the rather romantic sobriquet La Côte Sauvage (The Wild Coast), the island's east coast is a world away from the touts, nightclubs and souvenir shacks of Flic en Flac in the west and Grand Baie in the north. It does have its resorts, but the eastern face of Mauritius feels blissfully untouched by mass tourism. Best of all, some of the island's very best beaches line this quiet coast. Not surprisingly, this most exclusive side of the island attracts the kind of visitor likely to take a helicopter transfer from the airport when they arrive.

The closest the east comes to a resort town is Trou d'Eau Douce, which has retained the feel of a sleepy fishing village despite rubbing shoulders with the grand hotels next door. It's the jumping-off point for the wildly popular Île aux Cerfs.

❶ Getting There & Away

The main public transport hub for eastern Mauritius is the inland town of Centre de Flacq. You'll have to change here if you're arriving by bus from Port Louis, the Central Plateau towns or Mahébourg in the south.

There are onward connections from Centre de Flacq to villages along the east coast, although some services are pretty infrequent. You can bank on bus transport from Centre de Flacq to

FALLING FOR MAURITIUS?

'Wanna get high?' asks **Skydive Mauritius** (Map p122; ☑ 5499 5551; www. skydivemauritius.com; Belle Vue Maurel; sky dives Rs 14,000) with a wink. This outfit offers travellers a whole other way to check out the island – from 3000m in the air as you zoom towards the earth after jumping from a plane. It's based in a clearing towards Roches Noires in the east, but touts and transfers make Grand Baie a good departure point.

Palmar and Poste Lafayette (with continuing service to Rivière du Rempart), but there are no buses to Belle Mare. Figure on at least Rs 600 to Rs 700 for a taxi between the coastal towns and Centre de Flacq.

❶ Getting Around

Most hotels and guesthouses have bikes for hire. Otherwise, you can hire them from any of the travel agencies in Trou d'Eau Douce. Car hire can easily be arranged through your accommodation.

Trou d'Eau Douce

POP 5800

'Sweet waterhole' sits at a set of major crossroads, making it the tourism hub on this side of the island. From some perspectives, it's a lovely little place, if a bit melancholy, where fishers unravel their nets after a morning at sea and women walk around with baskets of veggies balanced on their heads.

But the place is a draw for other reasons: the sea is a stunning shade of blue here and Trou d'Eau Douce boasts easy access to the massively popular Île aux Cerfs, a favoured destination for day-tripping tourists.

As a result, this seaside township can attract a few touts, but they don't persist for long and it makes a great base for exploring the east coast – especially for those on a tighter budget.

◉ Sights & Activities

★ **Victoria 1840**   GALLERY
(Map p122; ☑ 480 0220; www.maniglier.com; Victoria Rd; ☉ 7.30pm-1am) Worth a look, Victoria 1840 is an old sugar mill that has been lovingly refurbished to house some of the works of Yvette Maniglier, a bewitching French painter who spent a year under the wing of Henri Matisse. The juxtaposition of industrial brick and splashy modern art works surprisingly well. The gallery can only be visited while dining at the in-house restaurant, Le Café des Arts (p123).

Johaness Entertainment   BOATING
(Map p122; ☑ 5825 6903, 5705 4944; www.joha ness.com; Royal Rd; excursions to Île aux Cerfs per person Rs 1500) One of the more professional operators, Johaness runs speedboat or catamaran trips to Île aux Cerfs that leave Trou d'Eau Douce at 9.30am and return around 3pm, including a barbecue lunch, a visit to a waterfall, and time for snorkelling and exploring the island. If things are quiet,

EXCURSIONS TO ÎLE AUX CERFS

Île aux Cerfs, encircled by gin-clear waters, is many people's idea of a postcard-perfect tropical island. It's overrun by tourists and touts during peak season, when it becomes a victim of its own popularity, yet it remains one of the most picturesque island excursions for visitors to Mauritius. There's a world-class golf course, 4km of sandy bliss and a real sense of paradise beneath the palm trees.

Guests of Le Touessrok, including those who have reserved a round of golf, get whisked over to the island for free on the hotel launch. For everyone else, every boat owner in Trou d'Eau Douce seems ready to take you out to the island at a moment's notice. Ask at your accommodation to be set up with a reliable option, or try **Bateaux Vicky** (Map p122; ☏ 5808 7736; info@bateau-vicky.mu; Royal Rd; Île aux Cerfs return per person Rs 450), a ferry or water-taxi service that runs from Trou d'Eau Douce to Île aux Cerfs every half-hour, with the first boat at 9am and the last returning at 4.30pm.

The other way to reach the island is on a popular catamaran or speedboat day trip, which usually includes snorkelling, sunbathing and an expansive barbecue lunch (Rs 1200 to Rs 1800 per person depending on your choice of food). The day trip usually begins around 9.30am and runs until 3pm (if you're leaving from Trou d'Eau Douce).

Most coastal hotels across the island also offer day trips to Île aux Cerfs, or check out www.catamarancruisesmauritius.com for a list of possibilities. In Trou d'Eau Douce, try Johaness Entertainment.

they're quick to offer a discounted rate, but don't count on it.

🛌 Sleeping

Le Dodo APARTMENT €
(Map p122; ☏ 480 0034; christa0307@hotmail.com; Royal Rd; apt €25-40; ❄ 🔊) Le Dodo is an excellent choice in the heart of town, especially if you get a room on an upper floor – although there's no elevator, the views over the cluttered village and azure sea are memorable. The decor has some quirky moments, but somehow it all seems to work. The owner is kind and apartments come outfitted with retro fixtures.

★Four Seasons Resort at Anahita RESORT €€€
(Map p122; ☏ 402 3131, 402 3100; www.fourseasons.com/mauritius; Beau Champ; villas incl breakfast €650-5000; Ⓟ❄@🔊🏊) Located in Beau Champ, slightly south of Trou d'Eau Douce, the Four Seasons Resort is part of a vast luxury complex known as Anahita and features a beautiful assortment of holiday villas. The design scheme plays with local materials including tropical timber and volcanic rock while seamlessly integrating every modern convenience.

Four stone-cut pools, a spa and the stunning Ernie Els–designed golf course are also big draws, while most rooms have private plunge pools.

★Le Touessrok RESORT €€€
(Map p122; ☏ 402 7400; www.shangri-la.com/mauritius/shangrila; r from €350; Ⓟ❄@🔊🏊) Le Touessrok has one of the best reputations on the island, and the accolades are well deserved. Rambling across a sandy peninsula, it blends Moorish architecture and thick patches of jungle. The resort distinguishes itself from the rest of the five-stars with its two offshore islands: the famous Île aux Cerfs and the exclusive Robinson Crusoe–style hideaway Îlot Mangénie.

Tropical Hotel Attitude HOTEL €€€
(Map p122; ☏ 480 1300; https://hotels-attitude.com/en/tropical-attitude/; Royal Rd; s/d with half board from €178/210; ❄@🔊🏊) Part of the smart but reasonably priced Attitude chain, this place on Trou d'Eau Douce's northern outskirts is a refreshingly accessible slice of semi-luxury right on the waterfront. The rooms have a white-linen look and most face the sea.

🍴 Eating

Gilda's Restaurant INTERNATIONAL €
(Map p122; ☏ 428 0498; Royal Rd; mains Rs 150-650; ◷ 8am-10pm Wed-Mon) Pasta, South Indian curries and *ceviche* (raw fish marinated in lemon and garlic) all appear on this varied menu, which can be enjoyed with fine views on the elevated terrace out the back.

The East

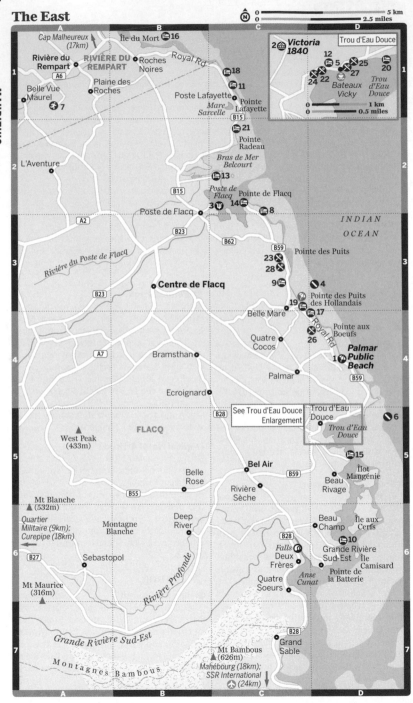

The East

MAURITIUS BELLE MARE & PALMAR

Snack Pelouse   SEAFOOD €
(Map p122; ☎5702 8604; Royal Rd; mains Rs 200-400; ⊗9am-9pm Tue-Sun) You could easily walk past this small eatery, a few steps down off the main road, but it's an appealing choice for its informal surrounds and some of the freshest fish in town, plus Indian thalis, octopus salad and bowls of noodles.

★**Chez Tino**   MAURITIAN €€
(Map p122; ☎480 2769; Royal Rd; mains Rs 250-900; ⊗10am-10pm Mon-Sat, to 4pm Sun) Head for the wonderful terrace on the 1st floor for great views and good food. Chez Tino keeps it simple, dishing up Mauritian cooking with an emphasis on seafood, as well as pizza and pasta. Standout dishes include traditional octopus curry with green pawpaw and grilled fish with lemon. There's live local music at 8.30pm on Saturdays.

Green Island Beach Restaurant   INTERNATIONAL €€
(Map p122; ☎251 7152; Royal Rd; mains Rs 250-550; ⊗noon-10pm Tue-Sun) The friendly staff here serve a delicious assortment of international and local favourites, often in surprising juxtaposition. Have fish curry with eggplant or prawns with Thai curry paste. There's also Aussie beef on what could be the town's most varied menu.

★**Le Café des Arts**   MAURITIAN €€€
(Map p122; ☎480 0220; www.maniglier.com; Victoria Rd; set menu Rs 2900-3600; ⊗7.30pm-1am) This intriguing dining option is located within an old mill that has been transformed into Victoria 1840 (p120), an oddly charming gallery space, with canvases of wicked brushstrokes adorning the cracked brick walls. The food, an exquisite, modern nod to traditional island flavours, mirrors the old-meets-new surrounds. Lunch can be reserved for groups with 24 hours' notice.

ⓘ Getting There & Away

There are no direct buses between Port Louis and Trou d'Eau Douce – you'll need to change at Centre de Flacq, from where onward services to Trou d'Eau Douce run roughly every half-hour. Taxis cost Rs 600 to Rs 700 from Centre de Flacq, Rs 2000 to the airport and Rs 2200 to Port Louis.

Belle Mare & Palmar

North of Trou d'Eau Douce as far as Pointe de Flacq, a 10km-long beach includes some of the best white sand and azure ocean in Mauritius. The towns of Belle Mare and Palmar may pass in the blink of an eye, but the area is also home to an impregnable string of luxury resorts. There are stretches of public beach, including around 4km and 8km north of Trou d'Eau Douce.

⊙ Sights & Activities

★**Palmar Public Beach**   BEACH
(Map p122; Royal Rd) Small, perfectly formed and lapped by waters a near-perfect shade of turquoise on a sunny day, this is the pick of the public beaches on Mauritius' east coast.

WORTH A TRIP

SCENIC DRIVE: THE HEART OF THE ISLAND
....

The divide between coastal Mauritius and the island's interior can be stark, but the small scale of everything here means that it's easy enough to experience both on a rather short drive.

Begin anywhere in the east and make your way to the regional centre of **Rivière du Rempart**. From there, head southwest, passing through small towns (some barely discernible) such as **Belle Vue Maurel** and **Barlow**; the signage can be a little confusing, but until you pass Barlow, follow the signs to Port Louis along the B21. After Barlow, the vistas open up, with some decent views of the inland mountains where you're headed. At the crossroads around 11km after leaving Rivière du Rempart, turn left towards 'La Nicolière'. A lovely honour guard of trees arcs over you for around 2km, whereupon you make a right turn, again following the signs for **La Nicolière**.

The traffic thins as you pass through more sugar-cane fields (no Ashok Hino buses at last!), before crossing the dam wall. After the wall, the road climbs, alternating between lovely thick forest and some fine views out over the coastal plains to the east. After around 4.5km of climbing, the road crosses a plateau haired with agriculture. At the T-junction around 2km further on (look for the 'Selazi Forest Service' sign), turn left, following signs for St Pierre. You're largely back in civilisation with all the attendant construction, sugar cane and traffic, but it's worth it for the views away to the west from **Ripailles** and its approach – **Calebasses** (632m), **Pieter Both** (823m), **Grand Peak** (326m) and **Le Pouce** (812m) are all stunning.

From Ripailles it's downhill all the way – literally. In St Pierre, you could turn left (east) and return to the east of the island via Quartier Militaire. An alternative is to pause in Moka to visit the tranquil tropical mansion of Eureka (p60).

Sagar Shiv Mandir   HINDU SITE
(Map p122; ☉ dawn-dusk) This white Hindu temple sits on a teeny islet tenuously tethered to the mainland by a thin land bridge. The views of the dazzling bastion are best appreciated from Indian Pavilion, the restaurant at Le Saint Géran.

Pedi:Mani:Cure Studio   SPA
(Map p122; ☎ 401 1688; www.oneandonlyresorts. com/one-and-only-le-saint-geran-mauritius/ spa-and-fitness; Le Saint Géran, Pointe de Flacq; ☉ 10am-7pm) This spa at Le Saint Géran was developed by renowned French podiatrist Bastien Gonzalez. The not-to-be-missed signature treatment (Rs 5500) invigorates and revives tired hands and feet, giving them a radiant glow.

🛏 Sleeping

★ **Le Prince Maurice**   LUXURY HOTEL €€€
(Map p122; ☎ 413 9130; www.constancehotels.com; Pointe de Flacq; s/d with half board from €480/625; P ❄ @ 🛜 ≋) The sense of perfect tranquillity is immediately striking as you pass through the entryway – this is a world unto itself that knows no limit to luxury. The lobby's marble architecture and flowing infinity pools can only be described as sublime, and the opulent suites, hidden just beyond, continue the timeless elegance. One of the most beautiful hotels in Mauritius.

The abundance of open-air pavilions and trim thatch is meant to evoke the ancient days of the spice trade – modern amenities are cleverly hidden and butlers are dressed in muted tones as they move across the grounds catering to every whim. Swimming pools, spas, access to Belle Mare Plage's golf courses and a floating restaurant (you'll see) round out the amenities list.

★ **Le Saint Géran**   LUXURY HOTEL €€€
(Map p122; ☎ 401 1688; www.oneandonlyresorts. com; Pointe de Flacq; ste with half board from €425; ❄ @ 🛜 ≋) Le Saint Géran is classic Mauritian luxury at its finest. And the clientele seems to agree. The resort sees more repeat customers than most top-end hotels on the island, the guest list a veritable who's who of movie stars and celebrities. Spacious rooms, under the signature bright-blue roofs, are arranged along the seemingly endless oceanfront – everyone has a to-die-for view.

Water sports are plenty, there's a charming kids' club, and the top-notch butler service caters to every request. Le Saint Géran has set the bar unmatchably high in the dining category as well. Of its numerous restaurants, world-class Indian Pavilion is the pick.

The golf course here, too, is world-class; it was designed by Gary Player.

★ Émeraude Beach Attitude
RESORT €€€

(Map p122; ✏ 415 1107; https://hotels-attitude.com/en/emeraude-beach-attitude/; Belle Mare; s/d with half board from €177/198; ❄ @ 🖥 🌊) Set in a breezy garden across the road from the public beach in Belle Mare, Émeraude is a breath of fresh air compared to the sky-high walls of the neighbouring five-star compounds. Some 20 semi-detached and extremely comfortable cottage units with gabled roofs frame a sociable pool area, an open-air restaurant and a bar.

Lux Belle Mare
LUXURY HOTEL €€€

(Map p122; ✏ 402 2000; www.luxresorts.com/en/hotel-mauritius/luxbellemare; Royal Rd; r with half board from r from €425; P ❄ @ 🖥 🌊) Elegance and luxury as we've come to expect from the Lux team, with the full range of superb rooms, fine dining, cocktails with a view and plenty of activities, from golf to horse-riding. There are many reasons to stay to here, and we can't think of a single reason why you wouldn't want to.

Belle Mare Plage
LUXURY HOTEL €€€

(Map p122; ✏ 402 2600; www.constancehotels.com; Pointe de Flacq; r with half board from €440; ❄ @ 🖥 🌊) One of Mauritius' most delightful hotels, the Belle Mare Plage ticks most boxes. Pass through the inviting lobby – scented with vanilla and ylang-ylang, no less – before uncovering an enviable beach and a cache of top-notch amenities. Golfers relish the two championship-level courses and well-respected academy, while you can also enjoy expert massage therapy and then dine at the superb restaurants.

Residence
LUXURY HOTEL €€€

(Map p122; ✏ 401 8888; www.cenizaro.com/theresidence/mauritius; Belle Mare; s/d incl breakfast from €325/500; ❄ @ 🖥 🌊) Evoking the forgotten grandeur of colonial India, the Residence's vast complex of hotel rooms occupies an enviable stretch of sand. Rooms are simply decorated – with white drapery everywhere and framed Darwin-esque animal sketches on the walls – and perfectly capture the idea of this being a home away from home rather than a hotel.

✖ Eating

Emperor Restaurant
CHINESE €

(Map p122; ✏ 415 1254; Royal Rd, Belle Mare; mains Rs 250-450; ⊙ 11am-10pm) This roadside Chinese restaurant never seems to be full but gets consistently good reviews for authentic Chinese cooking.

Seasons Restaurant & Bar
SEAFOOD €€

(Map p122; ✏ 5729 9967, 415 1350; www.orchidvillas.mu/en/seasons; Royal Rd, Belle Mare; mains Rs 200-625; ⊙ 11am-3pm & 6-9.30pm Tue-Sat, 11am-3pm Sun) Part of the Orchid Villas complex, this roadside restaurant doesn't have sea views, but the food and service are both surprisingly good and the menu is varied. Try the grilled calamari in garlic butter sauce.

Symon's Restaurant
INTERNATIONAL €€

(Map p122; ✏ 415 1135; Royal Rd, Belle Mare; mains Rs 250-850; ⊙ 9.30am-10pm) One of the better options in Belle Mare beyond the all-star line-up of hotel restaurants, Symon's serves up a variety of Indian and Mauritian and Chinese dishes. The views are ho-hum, but some dishes – such as octopus curry with coconut milk, and the grilled catch of the day – stand out.

ⓘ Getting There & Away

Buses connect Palmar with Centre de Flacq and Poste Lafayette, but there are no buses to Belle Mare. Count on Rs 600 for a taxi to the bus station in Centre de Flacq, or Rs 2000 for a taxi all the way to Port Louis.

Poste de Flacq & Roches Noires

POP 8650

Even quieter and more rugged than the sandy shores of Belle Mare, this calm area bordering the island's north still has a distinctive Creole vibe and is generally untouched by upmarket developers. Holidaymakers seeking tranquillity should look no further than the lovely selection of private villas dotting the stone-strewn coast.

🛏 Sleeping

With a noticeable lack of resorts, Poste de Flacq is a haven for upscale villa rentals that work out to be a much better deal than many of the luxury-hotel packages (especially if you're travelling with friends and/or family). Contact CG Villas (✏ 5728 8812; www.villas-maurice.com) to organise your stay – they manage a sizeable collection of beach houses in the area.

★ **La Maison d'Été** BOUTIQUE HOTEL €€€
(Map p122; ☑ 410 5039; www.lamaisondete.com; Poste Lafayette; r incl breakfast €195-290; ❄ @ 🛜 🌊) We're yet to hear a bad word about La Maison d'Été, one of Mauritius' top B&Bs, and we can understand why. The Franco-Mauritian owners have hit the nail on the head: an effortless charm pervades the poolside rooms, each decorated with tasteful tributes to island life. The property also has an inviting restaurant, two pools and a private beach.

★ **L'Ilot** VILLA €€€
(Map p122; www.lilot.biz; Royal Rd, Roches Noires; villa €300-1600; ❄ 🛜) Go one better than staying at a five-star resort and rent your own private island! This four-bedroom masterpiece sits on its own islet attached to the mainland by a concreted bridge made from boulders. The villa is faultlessly decorated and you'll never have to fight for a sun lounge.

Radisson Blu
Poste Lafayette LUXURY HOTEL €€€
(Map p122; ☑ 402 6200; www.radissonblu.com/en/hotel-mauritius-postelafayette; Royal Rd; r from €215; 🅿 ❄ @ 🛜 🌊) With everything you'd expect from this reliably luxurious chain, the Radisson combines large-hotel facilities with a sense of quiet intimacy. The pretty white rooms look onto the garden or the beach, and there are enough bars and restaurants here that you'll never have to leave, if that's the kind of holiday you're after.

Villa La Mauricienne VILLA €€€
(Map p122; ☑ 5728 8812; www.villas-maurice.com; Royal Rd, Poste Lafayette; villa from €655; ❄ 🛜 🌊) Sheltered by a massive roof of thatch and bamboo, this opulent retreat feels decidedly Asian in theme with abounding bursts of fuchsia and orange. The master suite is lofted above the open-air terrace, which looks out over the enormous swimming pool and giant strip of private sand.

🍽 Eating

★ **La Maison d'Été** MAURITIAN €€
(Map p122; ☑ 410 5039; Poste Lafayette; set menus & buffets per person €23-62, pizza Rs 300-550, mains Rs 300-950; ⊙ noon-3pm & 7-9.30pm) The restaurant at La Maison d'Été (p126) is run like a stand-alone establishment, serving an enticing assortment of Mauritian and fusion food of the highest quality. The inn's owner often moonlights as the chef and takes special care when preparing locally sourced

dishes matched with international wines. There's also a Mauritian Sunday lunch buffet that's a local institution.

ℹ Getting There & Away

Most bus services along the east coast pass through Roches Noires.

UNDERSTAND MAURITIUS

Mauritius Today

Mauritius remains an Indian Ocean success story, quietly going about its business far from international headlines and emerging relatively unscathed from uncertain economic times. Mauritius' politics remain robust and, where scandals occur, the country emerges with credit for its handling of things, though there is creeping concern about growing political dynasties and a need for new talent. The impact of tourism on island life and fears about climate change and weather extremes remains at the forefront of public debate.

Economic Progress

Mauritius' economic success wasn't inevitable. Diversification has been key – away from sugar cane, then away from textile manufacturing in the face of competition from China, and so on. Tourism remains a major money earner, and the country's stability and distance from world trouble spots has insulated it from the ups and downs of recent years. As a result the economy continues to tick along nicely, with growth rates of around 4% for most of the past decade, and unemployment stable at a respectable 7.1%. A 2017 jump in inflation from 1% to 3.7% raised eyebrows, but it's still a figure many countries would love to see. The focus now is on banking, with the government announcing in 2018 that it hoped to double the size of the country's financial sector by 2030. The challenge in doing so in the aftermath of international scandals such as the Panama Papers, is how to offer conditions that are attractive to international investors while ensuring transparency and that big global companies meet their tax obligations back home.

Political Dynasties

Mauritius has a proud democratic record, with changes in government arising from the ballot box, never the barrel of a gun. But some things stay very much the same, most notably the family names of those who rule. Take current prime minister, Javind Jugnauth. He became prime minister in 2017 when his father Sir Anerood Jugnauth (who served six terms as prime minister and nine years as president) resigned. It was a seamless transition, and one that Mauritians will, in turn, get to vote upon, but it's not quite the generational change that many Mauritians had in mind.

One of the leading opposition figures, Paul Bérenger, is another of the old guard who has been in and out of power for decades, though the surprise 2014 defeat of Navin Ramgoolam, a former prime minister and son of founding prime minister Sir Seewoosagur Ramgoolam, was taken as a sign of important change – he went from being prime minister from 2004 to 2015, to losing his seat entirely. Even so, talk to many Mauritians and you may sense a growing cynicism about the country's political class.

Political Scandals

If the constant recycling of the same old faces in the country's top political jobs is a sign of political stagnation, recent political scandals suggest that the system may not be theirs to own. The most dramatic case relates to long-serving prime minister, Navin Ramgoolam, who was arrested in Port Louis in 2015, a year after losing power. A police raid on his home uncovered Rs 220 million as well as prohibited drugs such as Viagra. He has since been charged with money laundering. He denies the charges and has promised to fight them, while his supporters claim the charges are politically motivated.

Then in 2018 the country's president, Ameenah Gurib-Fakim (at the time Africa's only female head of state), resigned after accusations that she spent thousands of dollars for her own personal use on a credit card given to her by a charity. She, too, denied all allegations. Both cases remain before the courts, but the episodes have caused much anger in Mauritius, even as analysts suggest that bringing such high-profile defendants to court shows the system is working well.

Small Voices

Sometimes it's not easy being small, and Mauritius has found this to its chagrin in recent years. The most obvious case is that of the Chagos Archipelago. Long a part of Mauritius, but appropriated by the UK just prior to independence then leased to the US for its top-secret Diego Garcia military base, the fate of the Chagos is something of a cause célèbre in Mauritius – many Chagos Islanders live in poor conditions in Mauritius, and the government has been the major and persistent voice of protest in international courts and forums. Even when the International Court of Justice ruled in favour of Mauritius and the Chagos Islanders in 2019, the general consensus remained that little was likely to change.

So, too, for climate change. In 2017 then finance minister (now prime minister) Pravind Jugnauth warned that Mauritius was one of the countries 'most exposed to the adverse effects of climate change'. Like most island nations Mauritius is vulnerable to rising sea levels, extreme weather systems (such as more intense cyclones) and increasing droughts (especially on Rodrigues). The country has made small steps towards moving away from fossil fuels, but far more difficult is the task of making its voice heard in international debates about the planet's future.

History

Mauritius had no indigenous population predating the European colonisers, and so – unlike many other small islands, for which colonisation resulted in the savage destruction of the original population a short time later – its history is pleasantly free of episodes of brutality, at least until the advent of slavery. This historical point is key to understanding the country's culture of tolerance and easy acceptance of all people – there's nobody in the ethnic melting pot able to claim precedence over others.

The First Colonisers

Although Arab traders knew of Mauritius – which they rather unfairly called Dina Arobi (Isle of Desolation) – as early as the 10th century, the first Europeans to discover these uninhabited islands were the Portuguese, around 1507. They, too, were more interested in trade and never attempted to settle.

In 1598 a group of Dutch sailors landed on the southeast coast, at what is now called Vieux Grand Port (p113), and claimed the island for the Netherlands. For the next 40 years the Dutch used Mauritius as a supply base for Batavia (Java), before deciding to settle near their original landing spot. Settlement ruins and a museum (p113) can still be seen at Vieux Grand Port, near Mahébourg, as can a monument (p113) to the first landing.

The colony never really flourished, however, and the Dutch abandoned it in 1710. Nevertheless they left their mark: in the short time they were here, the Dutch were responsible for the extinction of the dodo and for introducing slaves from Africa, deer from Java, wild boar, tobacco and, above all, sugar cane.

Île de France

Five years after the Dutch abandoned Mauritius, it was the turn of the French, when in 1715 Captain Guillaume Dufresne d'Arsel sailed across from what is now Réunion and claimed Mauritius for France. The island was rechristened Île de France, but nothing much happened until the arrival in 1735 of dynamic governor Bertrand François Mahé de Labourdonnais, Mauritius' first colonial hero. He not only transformed Port Louis into a thriving seaport, but also built the first sugar mill and established a road network.

It was around this time that Mauritius' best-known historic event occurred: the *St Géran* went down during a storm off the northeast coast in 1744. The shipwreck inspired Bernardin de St-Pierre's romantic novel *Paul et Virginie,* an early bestseller.

As the English gained the upper hand in the Indian Ocean in the late 18th century, Port Louis became a haven for pirates and corsairs – mercenary marines paid by a country to prey on enemy ships. The most famous Franco-Mauritian corsair was Robert Surcouf, who wrought havoc on British shipping.

In 1789 French settlers in Mauritius recognised the revolution in France and got rid of their governor. But some policies were a bridge too far: they refused to free their slaves when the abolition of slavery was decreed in Paris in 1794.

British Rule

In 1810, during the Napoleonic Wars, the British moved in on Mauritius as part of their grand plan to control the Indian Ocean. Things started badly when they were defeated at the Battle of Vieux Grand Port. Just a few months later, however, British forces landed at Cap Malheureux on the north coast and took over the island.

The new British rulers renamed the island Mauritius but allowed the Franco-Mauritians to retain their language, religion, legal system and the all-important sugar-cane plantations on which the economy depended. Slaves were finally freed in 1835, by which time there were more than 70,000 on the island. They were replaced or supplemented by labour imported from India and China. As many as 500,000 Indians took up the promise of a better life in Mauritius, often to find themselves living and working in appalling conditions on minimum pay.

By sheer weight of numbers, the Indian workforce gradually achieved a greater say in the running of the country. Their struggle was given extra impetus when Indian political and spiritual leader Mahatma Gandhi visited Mauritius in 1901 to push for civil rights. The key event, however, was the introduction of universal suffrage in 1958, and the key personality was Dr (later Sir) Seewoosagur Ramgoolam. Founder of the Labour Party in 1936, Seewoosagur Ramgoolam led the fight for independence, which was finally granted in 1968.

Independence

The first prime minister of newly independent Mauritius was, not surprisingly, Sir Seewoosagur Ramgoolam. He remained in office for 13 years and continued to command great reverence until his death in 1985. A host of public buildings have been named in his honour.

The political landscape since Sir Seewoosagur's death has largely been dominated by the trio of Anerood Jugnauth, the Indian leader of the Mouvement Socialiste Militant (MSM); the Franco-Mauritian Paul Bérenger, with his leftist Mouvement Militant Mauricien (MMM); and Navin Ramgoolam, son of Sir Seewoosagur and leader of the Mauritian Labour Party. The former two parties formed their first coalition government in 1982, with Jugnauth as prime minister and Bérenger as finance minister. In the years that followed, the two men were in and out of government, sometimes power sharing, at other times in opposition to each other, according to the complex and shifting

DIEGO GARCIA & THE CHAGOSSIAN BETRAYAL

One of the most prolonged betrayals in British colonial history is that surrounding the secret exile of the Chagos Islanders from their homeland in the 1960s and 1970s, in order to lease the main island, Diego Garcia, to the USA for use as a military base.

The Chagos Islands were excised from Mauritian territory by the British prior to independence in 1965, and Mauritius and the UK continue to dispute the sovereignty of the islands. The islanders were 'resettled' in Mauritius and the Seychelles between 1965 and 1973. Some 5000 now live in abject poverty in the slums of Port Louis, where they continue to fight for their right to return home. The islanders won derisory compensation of £4 million from the British in 1982, which was paid out to the poverty-stricken islanders in return for them signing away their rights – many did not realise what the legal documents they were signing meant.

In 2000 the UK High Court ruled that the Chagossians had been evicted illegally and upheld their right to be repatriated. Nothing happened, so the Chagossians went back to court. In October 2003 the judge rejected their claim for further compensation, though he acknowledged that the British government had treated the islanders 'shamefully' and that the compensation had been inadequate. In May 2007 the Chagossians won a further case at the Court of Appeal in London, in which the government's behaviour was condemned as unlawful and an abuse of power. The judges in the case also refused to place a stay on the ruling, meaning the Chagossians were free to return to all islands (with the exception of Diego Garcia itself) with immediate effect. In 2008 the case was overturned.

The court cases rolled on. In 2015 the international Permanent Court of Arbitration in The Hague unanimously held that the UK's proclamation of a Marine Protected Area (MPA) around the Chagos Archipelago in 2010 was in violation of international law. In 2016 the British Government confirmed that it would not allow the Chagossians to return to their islands. In 2017 the UN General Assembly voted 94 to 15 to refer the case to the International Court of Justice (ICJ) in order to clarify the islands' legal status.

The resulting ICJ judgment in favour of Mauritius and the Chagos Islanders in 2019 was scathing in its criticism of the UK. One judge described the situation as 'an unlawful act of continuing character' and concluded that the UK was 'under an obligation to bring an end to its administration of the Chagos Archipelago as rapidly as possible'.

Despite the ruling, the ICJ's decisions are not legally binding and the British government has given every indication that it will resist any calls for it to hand back the islands.

Author and documentary film-maker John Pilger gave his angle on the story in his documentary *Stealing a Nation* (2004). You can watch it online. Further information and ways to help the Chagossians can be found at www.chagossupport.org.uk. For additional information on the Chagos Islanders, check out David Vine's book *Island of Shame* (2009).

web of allegiances that enlivens Mauritian politics. In 1995 and again in 2005, Navin Ramgoolam beat the MSM-MMM coalition with his Alliance Sociale coalition.

On the economic front, Mauritius was undergoing a minor miracle. Up until the 1970s the Mauritian economy could be summed up in one word: sugar. It represented more than 90% of the country's exports, covered most of its fertile land and was its largest employer by far. Every so often a cyclone would devastate the cane crop, or a world drop in sugar prices would have bitter consequences.

From the 1970s the government went all out to promote textiles, tourism and financial services, much of it based on foreign investment. Soon Mauritius was one of the world's largest exporters of textiles, with clothes by Ralph Lauren, Pierre Cardin, Lacoste and other famous brands all manufactured on the island. Income from tourism also grew in leaps and bounds as the government targeted the luxury end of the market.

The strategy paid off. The 1980s and 1990s saw the Mauritian economy grow by an extremely healthy 5% a year. Unemployment fell from a whopping 42% in 1980 to less than 6% by 2000 and overall standards of living improved. Even so, rates of unemployment and poverty remained high among the Creole population (people of mixed Afro-European origin), many of whom also felt frustrated at their lack of political power in the face of the Indian majority. These tensions spilled onto the streets of Port Louis in 1999, triggered by the death in police custody of the singer Kaya, an ardent campaigner for the rights of the disadvantaged Creole population. The riots brought the country to a standstill for four days and forced the government to make political concessions.

The post-independence back and forth between the Labour Party and the MSM has continued in recent times. In elections to the national assembly in 2010, an alliance between the two won nearly 50% of the vote, and carried 45 of the 69 seats. Navin Ramgoolam, who had been prime minister since 2005, continued in the post after the elections until he was deposed in 2014. He was succeeded by Aneerood Jugnauth, who was in turn succeeded by his son three years later.

Culture

Mauritius is often cited as an example of racial and religious harmony, and compared with most countries it is, as on the surface there are few signs of conflict. However, racial divisions are still apparent between the Hindu majority and the Muslim and Creole minorities, and these tensions constitute one of the few potential political flashpoints. Such issues usually only surface during elections, when parties aren't averse to playing the race card.

Living Standards

As a result of the ongoing economic boom and political stability, overall living standards have improved in recent years and the majority of houses now have mains water and electricity. The gap between rich and poor, however, is widening. It's estimated that the top 20% of the population earns 45% of the total income and that around 10% of people live below the poverty line. A labourer's wage is just Rs 6000 per month, while a teacher might earn Rs 12,000. You'll see a few people begging around the markets and mosques, but the visible presence of poverty on the streets is relatively discreet.

Mauritians place great importance on education – not just to get a better job but as a goal in its own right. Lawyers, doctors and teachers are regarded with tremendous respect. The pinnacle of success for many is to work in the civil service, though this is beginning to change as salaries rise among business people.

A National Identity?

Despite being a relatively young country with a diverse population, and although ethnicity is often a primary touchstone of identity for many Mauritians, a strong sense of national identity continues to transcend racial and cultural ties.

Of the various forces binding Mauritians together, the most important is language – not the official language of English, but Creole, which is the first language of an estimated 86% of the population and understood by virtually all Mauritians. Another common bond is that everyone is an immigrant or descended from immigrants – there were no First People in Mauritius. Food and music are other unifiers, as is the importance placed on family life.

Mauritius is also a small, tight-knit community. Living in such close proximity

---

ⓘ ETIQUETTE IN MAURITIUS

The people of Mauritius have a well-deserved reputation for tolerance. That said, there are a few 'rules' of behaviour that you should abide by.

Clothing Although beachwear is fine for the beaches, you will cause offence and may invite pestering if you dress skimpily elsewhere. Nude bathing is forbidden.

Greetings Mauritians generally greet each other by shaking hands, or with a kiss on both cheeks for close friends and relatives. In most circumstances for visitors, a simple 'bonjour', 'hello' or 'namaste' will suffice.

Temples and mosques Miniskirts and singlet tops are no-nos, and it is normal to remove your shoes. Many temples and mosques also ask you not to take photos. Some Hindu temples request that you remove all leather items, such as belts. At mosques you may be required to cover your head, so remember to take along a scarf. Never touch a carving or statue of a deity.

breaks down barriers and increases understanding between different groups. Respect for others and tolerance are deeply ingrained in all sectors of society, despite the occasional flare-up of racial tension.

Family & the Role of Women

In general, each ethnic group maintains a way of life similar to that found in their countries of origin, even if they are second- or third-generation Mauritian.

Often several generations live together under one roof and the main social unit is the extended family – as evidenced by the size of family parties at a Sunday picnic. There is minimal social-security provision in Mauritius; people rely on their family in times of need. Mauritians are usually married by the age of 25 and the majority of wives stay home to raise the family, while husbands earn the daily bread. Arranged marriages are still the norm among many Indian families, while the Hindu caste system has also been replicated to some degree. Among all groups, religion and religious institutions continue to play a central role in community life.

As with elsewhere this very traditional pattern is starting to break down as the younger generation grows more individualistic and more Westernised. Young people are far more likely to socialise with people from other communities, and intermarriage is on the rise. The fertility rate of 1.74 children per woman is one of the lowest outside of Western countries, suggesting that young Mauritians are taking longer to marry and are having fewer children once they do.

Other forces for change are the growth of consumerism and the emergence of a largely Indian and Chinese middle class. Middle-class couples are more likely to set up their own home and have fewer children, while the wife may go out to work. Statistics also show a slight decline in the number of marriages, while the divorce rate has doubled over the last 25 years.

Women's equality still has a long way to go in Mauritius. Many women have to accept low-paid, unskilled jobs, typically in a textile factory or as cleaners. Even highly qualified women can find it hard to get promotions in the private sector, though they do better in the public service. In 2003 the government passed a Sex Discrimination Act and set up an independent unit to investigate sex-discrimination cases, including

WOMEN IN MAURITIUS

➡ Maternal mortality rate per 100,000 live births: 53

➡ Life expectancy for men/women: 72.6/79.7 years

➡ Adult literacy for men/women: 94.9/90.7%

➡ Fertility rate: 1.74 children per woman

sexual harassment at work. The unit is also charged with raising awareness levels and educating employers about equal opportunity. Results have, so far, been mixed.

Adult literacy rates are similar for men (94.9%) and women (90.7%), while female students tend to remain longer at school than boys. The unemployment rate for women under 25 years of age (31.2% in 2016) was considerably higher than for men of the same age (18.3%).

People of Mauritius

Figures on ethnicity are difficult to come by – Mauritius has deliberately not included such questions on its census since 1972. The country is made up of five ethnic groups: Indo-Mauritian (roughly 68%), Creole (27%), Sino-Mauritian (3%), Franco-Mauritian (1%) and the new kids on the block – South African expats (1%). Another small group you might come across are the Chagos Islanders.

Indo-Mauritians

The Indian population (the majority of which is Hindu) is descended from the labourers who came to the island to work the cane fields. Nowadays Indians form the backbone of the labouring and agricultural community and own many of the island's small- and medium-sized businesses, typically in manufacturing and the retail trade. Central Plateau towns such as Rose Hill have a definite Indian character.

Indians also tend to be prominent in civic life. Local elections are often racially aligned, and since Indo-Mauritians are in the majority, they tend to win at the polls. The prime minister between 2003 and 2005, Franco-Mauritian Paul Bérenger, was the first (and still only) non-Indian at the helm in the country's history.

Creoles

After the Indo-Mauritians, the next largest group is the Creoles, descendants of African slaves, with varying amounts of European ancestry. Creoles as a whole form the most disadvantaged sector of society. Despite the fact that all forms of discrimination are illegal under the Mauritian constitution, it is widely recognised that the Creole minority has been socially, economically and politically marginalised.

The majority work in low-paid jobs or eke out a living from fishing or subsistence farming, and it's a vicious circle. Creoles find it harder to get work, partly because of low levels of literacy, but few Creole children complete secondary school because they're needed to help support the family. Expectations are also lower – and so it goes on.

Rodrigues, where Creoles make up 98% of the population, is the epicentre of Mauritian Creole culture.

Sino-Mauritians

Mauritius' 30,000 Sino-Mauritians are involved mostly in commerce. Despite their small numbers the Chinese community plays a disproportionate role in the country's economy, though they tend to avoid politics. Most came to the country as self-employed entrepreneurs and settled in the towns (particularly Port Louis), though many villages have at least one Chinese-run store.

Franco-Mauritians & South Africans

Franco-Mauritians are the descendants of the *grands blancs* (rich whites), who were the first European settlers in Mauritius and who quickly parcelled the best arable land out among themselves in the 18th century. Franco-Mauritians own most of the sugar mills, banks and other big businesses, and tend to live in palatial private residences in the hills around Curepipe. They also own almost all the luxurious holiday houses along the coast. Many have decamped completely to live in South Africa, Australia and France. In fact there are now more South African expats living on the island (congregated on the west coast) than there are Franco-Mauritians.

Religion

There is a close link between religion and race in Mauritius and a remarkable degree of religious tolerance. Mosques, churches and Hindu temples can be found within a stone's throw of each other in many parts of the country and we know of one case in Floréal where they are separated only by a shared wall.

Official figures put the number of Hindus at 48.5% of the population, and all are Indian in origin or ethnicity. Festivals play a central role in the Hindu faith and the calendar is packed with colourful celebrations.

There's a certain amount of resentment towards Hindus in Mauritius, not for religious reasons but because the Hindu majority dominates the country's political life and its administration. Up until now, with the economy in full swing, this has merely resulted in grumbling about discrimination and 'jobs for the boys', but there's a fear this might change if the economy really begins to falter.

Around one-quarter of the population is Roman Catholic. Catholicism is practised by most Creoles, and it has picked up a few voodoo overtones over the years. Most Franco-Mauritians are also Catholic and a few Chinese and Indians have converted, largely through marriage.

Muslims make up roughly one-fifth of the population. Like the Hindus, Mauritian Muslims originally came from India. In Mauritius, where Islam exists in close proximity to other religions, it tends to be fairly liberal. Attendance at mosque is high and many Muslim women wear the hijab.

Sino-Mauritians are the least conspicuous in their worship. The one big exception is Chinese New Year, which is celebrated in Port Louis with great gusto. There are also a few Chinese temples scattered around the capital.

POPULATION STATS

➡ Population: 1.36 million

➡ Growth rate: 0.57%

➡ Proportion under 15 years old: 19.9%

➡ Average age: 35.7

➡ Proportion living in urban areas: 40.8%

THE LEGACY OF KAYA

It was a black day for Mauritius, and a blacker one still for the Creole community. On 21 February 1999, singer Joseph Topize (aka Kaya) was found dead in his police cell, seemingly a victim of police brutality, after being arrested for smoking cannabis after a pro-legalisation rally.

As the pioneer of *seggae*, a unique combination of reggae and traditional *séga* beats, Kaya provided a voice for disadvantaged Creoles across the country. His death in the custody of Indian police split Mauritian society along racial lines, triggering four days of violent riots that left several people dead and brought the country to a standstill.

An autopsy cleared the police of wrongdoing, but the events forced the Indian-dominated government to acknowledge *le malaise Créole* – Creoles' anger at their impoverished status in a country that has been dominated by Indians since independence. It's an anger that still simmers two decades after the singer's death.

In contrast to these violent scenes, Kaya's music is full of positive energy. The classic album *Seggae Experience* is a tribute to the singer's unique vision.

Arts

Mauritian literature and fine arts are firmly based in the French tradition. The country's music, however, is African in origin and is very much alive and kicking.

Literature

Mauritius has provided the backdrop for a number of historical novels, but it's the growing profile of local writers that makes Mauritians most proud.

BOOKS BY MAURITIAN WRITERS

Those who want to read a 20th-century Mauritian novel should try something by Malcolm de Chazal, whose most famous works are *Sens-Plastique* (1945), available in translation, and *Petrusmok* (1951), which is available only in French. Chazal was an eccentric recluse, but he inspired a whole generation of local writers. His works are a highly original blend of poetry and philosophy, and are peppered with pithy statements, such as 'Avoid clean people who have a dirty stare'.

Of living writers perhaps the best known internationally is Carl de Souza, though most of his works have not been translated into English. In his novel *Le Sang de l'Anglais* (1993) he looks at the often ambivalent relationship between Mauritians and their countries of origin, while *La Maison qui Marchait Vers le Large* (1996), set in Port Louis, takes inter-community conflict as its theme. *Les Jours Kaya* (2000) is a coming-of-age book set against the violence following Kaya's death.

Other contemporary novelists to look out for include Ananda Devi, Shenaz Patel and Nathacha Appanah-Mouriquand. Unfortunately their works as yet are only available in French, which is regarded as the language of culture.

BOOKS SET IN MAURITIUS

Mauritius' most famous contribution to world literature – one that has become entangled in the island's history – is the romantic novel *Paul et Virginie* by Bernardin de St-Pierre, which was first published in 1788. An English translation of the novel is widely available in Mauritius. The author captures the landscapes beautifully, though his ultra-moralistic tear-jerker is less likely to appeal to modern tastes.

Joseph Conrad's oblique love story *A Smile of Fortune,* collected in '*Twixt Land and Sea* (1912), is set in Mauritius, though it's hardly very flattering about the place. Set in the late 19th century, it does, however, give a taste of the mercantile activity of the time and the curious mix of 'negroes', Creoles, 'coolies' and marooned Frenchmen who populated the island. Visitors to the island will certainly identify with Conrad's

JMG LE CLÉZIO

Mauritius can lay claim (sort of) to a winner of the Nobel Prize for Literature. French author JMG Le Clézio, the 2008 Nobel laureate, has a Mauritian father and set a number of his novels in Mauritius, of which *Le Chercheur d'Or* (The Prospector; 1985) has been translated into English.

SÉGA!

Séga is the powerful combination of music and dance originally conceived by African slaves as a diversion from the injustice of their daily existence. At the end of a hard day in the cane fields, couples danced the *séga* around campfires on the beach to the accompaniment of drums.

Because of the sand (some say because of the shackles), there could be no fancy footwork. So today, when dancing the *séga*, the feet never leave the ground. The rest of the body makes up for it and the result, when the fire is hot, can be extremely erotic. In the rhythm and beat of *séga*, you can see or hear connections with Latin American salsa, Caribbean calypso and the music of Africa. It's a personal, visceral dance where people let the music take over and abandon themselves to the beat.

The dance is traditionally accompanied by the beat of the *ravanne*, a goatskin drum. The beat starts slowly and builds into a pulsating rhythm, which normally carries away performers and onlookers alike. You may be lucky enough to see the dance being performed spontaneously at beach parties or family barbecues. Otherwise you'll have to make do with the less authentic *séga* soirées offered by some bars and restaurants and most of the big hotels, often in combination with a Mauritian buffet.

description of Mauritius as the 'Pearl of the Ocean...a pearl distilling much sweetness on the world', but will undoubtedly find the current inhabitants far more pleasant to deal with than the characters described in the story.

Music & Dance

You'll hear *séga,* the music of Creole culture, everywhere nowadays, but in the early 20th century it fell seriously out of fashion. Its revival in the early 1950s is credited to the Creole singer Ti Frère, whose song 'Anita' has become a classic. Though he died in 1992, Ti Frère is still the country's most popular *séga* star. More recent Creole groups and singers with a wide following include Cassiya, Fanfan and the prolific Jean-Claude Gaspard.

Séga evolved slightly differently in Rodrigues. Here the drum plays a more prominent role in what's known as *séga tambour.* The island's accordion bands are also famous for their surprising repertoire, which includes waltzes, polkas, quadrilles and Scottish reels. Over the years these were

MALCOLM DE CHAZAL

Few figures loom as large over the arts in 20th-century Mauritius as Malcolm de Chazal. Aside from being the father of modern Mauritian literature, the surrealist de Chazal produced paintings full of light and energy – the most famous is *Blue Dodo*. Pereybère's Galerie du Moulin Cassé features his work.

learned from passing European sailors and gradually absorbed into the local folk music. They're now an essential part of any Rodriguan knees-up.

A newer Mauritian musical form – *seggae,* which blends elements of *séga* and reggae – was invented by Creole musician Kaya. With his band Racine Tatane, Kaya gave a voice to dissatisfied Creoles around the island. Tragically the singer died in police custody in February 1999. Following in Kaya's footsteps, Ras Natty Baby and his Natty Rebels are one of the most popular *seggae* groups; sales gained an extra boost when Ras Natty Baby was imprisoned for heroin trafficking in 2003.

Recently *ragga,* a blend of house music, traditional Indian music and reggae, has been gaining a following. Mauritian *ragga* groups include Black Ayou and the Authentic Steel Brothers.

Visual Arts

Historically Mauritian artists took their lead from what was happening in Europe, particularly France. Bizarrely some of the 18th- and 19th-century engravings and oils of Mauritian landscapes you see could almost be mistaken for European scenes. The classical statue of Paul and Virginie in Port Louis' Blue Penny Museum and the one of King Edward VII at the city's Champ de Mars Racecourse were both created by Mauritius' best-known sculptor, Prosper d'Épinay.

Contemporary Mauritian art tends to be driven by the tourist market. One artist you'll find reproduced everywhere is Vaco

Baissac, whose work is instantly recognisable by the blocks of colour outlined in black, like a stained-glass window.

Other commercially successful artists include Danielle Hitié, who produces minutely detailed renderings of markets as well as rural scenes, and Françoise Vrot, known for her very expressive portraits of women fieldworkers. Both artists are exhibited in galleries in Grand Baie, where Vrot also has her studio (p76).

Keep an eye out for exhibitions by more innovative contemporary artists, such as Hervé Masson, Serge Constantin, Henry Koombes and Khalid Nazroo. All have had some success on the international scene, though they're less visible locally.

Architecture

Much of Mauritius' architectural heritage has become buried under a sea of concrete, but thankfully a handful of colonial-era mansions survive, and it's these that provide the architectural highlights for visitors to the country.

Colonial Architecture

In 2003 the government set up a National Heritage Fund charged with preserving the country's historic buildings. The plantation houses from the 18th and 19th centuries have fared best, and you'll still see them standing in glorious isolation amid the cane fields. Many are privately owned and closed to the public. One such is Le Réduit, near Moka, which is now the president's official residence. Others have been converted into museums and restaurants.

The first French settlers naturally brought with them building styles from home. Over the years the architecture evolved until it became supremely well suited to the hot, humid tropics. It's for this reason that so many of the grand plantation houses have survived the ravages of time.

In many of these buildings, flourishes that appear to be ornamental – vaulted roofs and decorative pierced screens, for example – all serve to keep the occupants cool and dry. The most distinctive feature is the shingled roof with ornamental turrets and rows of attic windows. These wedding-cake touches conceal a vaulted roof, which allows the air to circulate. Another characteristic element is the wide, airy *varangue* (veranda), where raffia blinds, fans and pot plants create a cooling humidity.

The roofs, windows and overhangs are usually lined with delicate, lace-like *lambrequins* (decorative wooden borders), which are purely ornamental. They vary from simple, repetitive floral patterns to elaborate pierced friezes; in all cases a botanical theme predominates.

Lambrequins, shingled roofs and verandas or wrought-iron balconies are also found in colonial-era town houses. The more prestigious buildings were constructed in brick, or even stone, and so are better able to withstand cyclones and termites. In Port Louis, Government House and other buildings lining Place d'Armes are all fine examples.

BEST COLONIAL ARCHITECTURE

The following colonial-era mansions are all open to the public (with the exception of Government House) and well worth visiting. The buildings have innate historical and aesthetic values, but visiting them also makes a statement that these are places of beauty *and* value, which may just lead to more of them being preserved.

➡ Eureka (p60), Moka

➡ Government House **(Map p54; Place d'Armes)**, Port Louis

➡ Château Labourdonnais (p81), Mapou

➡ National History Museum (p105), Mahébourg

➡ Hôtel de Ville (p62), Curepipe

➡ Le Jardin de Beau Vallon (p110), near Mahébourg

➡ Domaine des Aubineaux (p62), Curepipe

➡ St Aubin (p118), Rivière des Anguilles

➡ Le Château Bel Ombre (p117), Bel Ombre

Contemporary Architecture

A few attempts at daring contemporary structures have been made, but the most prestigious in recent times has been Port Louis' Le Caudan Waterfront development, which remains a work in progress. Given its location at the very heart of the capital, the architects decided to incorporate elements of the traditional architecture found around the city's Place d'Armes. Further inspiration came from the nearby stone-and-steel dockyard buildings.

Perhaps Mauritius' most striking modern architectural creation is the MCB Building (p63) in Quartre Bornes, an eye-like structure by the M1 motorway as you approach Port Louis from the south. Completed in 2010, it's a model of sustainability with abundant solar panels and clever use of natural air flows.

Food & Drink

Mauritian cuisine is very similar across the island – a rich and delicious mix of Indian spices and fresh local ingredients prepared with strong influences from Chinese, French and African cuisine. The food of Rodrigues is quite different – less spicy but with more fresh fruit and beans as ingredients.

Staples & Specialities

Rice and noodles are two staples of everyday life, though to a great extent what people eat

DHAL PURI
....

Mauritius has many candidates for the title of the country's national dish, but few have the mass appeal of dhal puri (also spelled dholl puri). Inspired by the Indian bread known as paratha, its divergence from the mother country came about because not all of the ingredients were available here. The Mauritian version, using a thin flat bread known as farata, can be rolled around whatever you like, but the staple version is filled with ground yellow split peas and prepared with curries, rougaille (tomato-based stew or hotpot) and pickles or chutney. The best ones are crowned with chillies. You'll find them everywhere along the streets wherever Mauritians live and work, though less so in tourist areas.

depends on their ethnic background. A Sino-Mauritian may well start the day with tea and noodles, a Franco-Mauritian with a café au lait and croissant, and an Indo-Mauritian with a chapatti. Come lunchtime, however, nearly everyone enjoys a hot meal, whether it be a spicy seafood carri (curry) or mines (noodles), and a cooling beer. Dinner is the main meal of the day and is usually eaten en famille (with family).

While meat is widely eaten, especially in Chinese and French cuisine (venison and wild boar are mainstays around Mahébourg, and the distinctive Creole sausages are ever-popular), the mainstays of Mauritian cuisine (regardless of culture) are fish and seafood. Marlin, often smoked, is a big favourite, as are mussels, prawns, lobster and calamari. Octopus (ourite) is a special highlight and appears in all manner of guises – salads, cooked in saffron, or in a curry (sometimes with green papaya). The fish of the day is nearly always a good order.

When it comes to street food, boulettes (tiny steamed Chinese dumplings) are fantastic, and there's always dhal puri.

Drinks

Mauritians love their cocktail hour, and so you'll nearly always have access to an apéro (aperitif) or a ti punch (small punch) – usually a rum-based fruit cocktail.

Unsurprisingly the national drink is rum. Although most experts agree that Mauritian rum isn't up to the standard of the Caribbean equivalent, there are still some excellent brands, particularly Green Island, the dark variety of which is superb. An excellent way to gain an insight into local rums is the Rhumerie de Chamarel (p96), where you can see how it's made, have a wonderful meal and try the product. Despite Mauritius' long history of rum production, the socially preferred spirit tends to be whisky – a hangover from the 150-year British rule.

The national beer is Phoenix (https://phoenixbev.mu), an excellent Pilsner produced since the 1960s and a regular prize-winner at festivals around the world. The brewery's other premium brand, Blue Marlin, is also very good.

Mauritians are also great tea drinkers – you shouldn't miss trying the range of Bois Chéri teas on sale throughout the country. The vanilla tea is the most famous and is quite delicious and refreshing even in the heat of the day. You'll have a chance to see it being made and can taste it at the Bois Chéri tea plantation (p119) in southern Mauritius.

During Hindu and Muslim festivals, deliciously flavoured drinks such as lassi (Indian yogurt drink) and almond milk (almond- and cardamom-flavoured milk) are prepared.

Where to Eat & Drink

There tends to be quite a bit of segregation between 'tourist' restaurants and 'local' ones, particularly around bigger resort areas. In places such as Port Louis and the Central Highlands this is a lot less pronounced, and most places have a mixed clientele.

Nearly all restaurants have menus in English, or at least staff who speak English, so communication difficulties are rare.

Most restaurants have several cuisines served up cheek by jowl, though they're nearly always separated from each other on the menu. While in better restaurants this will mean each cuisine is prepared by a different expert chef, on the whole most chefs are decent at cooking one cuisine but prepare the remaining dishes with something approaching indifference. The rule is a fairly obvious one – don't go to a Chinese restaurant for a good curry.

The best places to eat throughout the country tend to be *tables d'hôtes* (privately hosted meals); these are often given by people who run guesthouses as well, but they're just as often offered alone. Offering a unique insight into local life, you'll usually dine with the host couple and often their children, plus any other travellers who've arranged to come by (or people staying in the guesthouse), and you'll enjoy traditional dishes spread over a number of courses. It's nearly always necessary to book a *table d'hôte,* preferably a day in advance, though it's always worth asking – bigger operations will sometimes be able to accommodate last-minute additions, but smaller places may not even open without a reservation.

It's the Creole element that shines through most strongly at the *tables d'hôtes.* If you don't eat at a *table d'hôte* at least once in Mauritius, you've missed an essential part of its gastronomic culture.

QUICK EATS

Places to enjoy eats on the run are in plentiful supply in Mauritius. Street vendors are at every bus station and town square, and takeaway shops can be found in numerous shopping centres and markets; both offer inexpensive local treats, including Indian, French and Chinese delicacies. Almost all restaurants, except the most upmarket, will do takeaway.

In Mauritius roadside stalls serving dinner dishes such as biryani, Indian rotis and *faratas* (unleavened flaky flour pancakes) are popular. Street eats cost around Rs 5 to Rs 10 for snacks such as rotis, *dhal puris* (lentil pancakes) and *boulettes* (tiny steamed Chinese dumplings) served at markets, along public beaches and in the capital.

The atmospheric markets are worth visiting for the popular *gâteaux piments* (chilli cakes), which are cooked on the spot. You should also try the delicious *dhal puris,* rotis, samosas and *bhajas* (fried balls of besan dough with herbs or onion).

Indian and Chinese restaurants offer quick and inexpensive meals and snacks. Remember to buy some Indian savouries such as *caca pigeon* (an Indian nibble) or the famous Chinese char siu (barbecued pork).

Vegetarians & Vegans

Vegetarians will fare well in Mauritius, though they may be disappointed by the lack of variety. Indian restaurants tend to offer the best choice, but often this is limited to a variation on the theme of *carri de légumes* (vegetable curry). Chinese restaurants are also good for vegetarians, while Creole and French places are much more limiting. That said, almost everywhere has a vegetable curry on the menu. Pescatarians will be spoilt for choice, as almost every eatery in the country offers fresh seafood and freshly caught fish cooked to perfection.

Vegans will find things harder, but not unassailably so – most resorts will be able to offer vegan options with notice, and Indian restaurants will again offer the most choice.

Habits & Customs

Eating habits vary across ethnic groups. Some groups eat with their fingers, others don't eat meat on Fridays and some abstain from eating pork – it's hard to generalise across the community.

Other than in hotels and *chambres d'hôtes,* where buffets are the norm, breakfasts are normally very quick and informal. Lunch is also a fairly casual affair, though at the weekend it tends to be more formal, with family and friends gathering to share

MAURITIUS FOOD & DRINK

the pleasures of the table. In restaurants special menus are offered for weekend lunches. Before dinner, which is a very formal occasion, *gajacks* (predinner snacks) and an *apéro* (aperitif) or a *ti punch* (small punch) is commonly served; during the meal, wine or beer is usually available.

As eating and drinking are important social activities, behaviour at the table should be respectful. Locals can be strict about table manners, and it's considered rude to pick at your food or mix it together. You are also expected to be reasonably well dressed. Unless you are in a beach environment, wearing beachwear or other skimpy clothing won't be well received – casual but neat clothing is the norm. Some upmarket hotels require neat dress for guests – for men that usually includes trousers or long pants, and perhaps even a collared shirt. When invited to dine with locals, bring a small gift (maybe some flowers or a bottle of wine).

If you're attending a traditional Indian or Chinese meal, or a dinner associated with a religious celebration, follow what the locals do. Generally your hosts will make you feel comfortable, but if you are unsure, ask about the serving customs and the order of dishes. Definitely attend an Indian or a Chinese wedding if you get the opportunity – these celebrations are true culinary feasts.

Environment

Mauritius packs a lot into quite a small space, and the beauty of its landforms – the coral reefs, the dramatic rocky outcrops – plays a key role in so many of the country's attractions, either as a stirring backdrop or as destinations worth exploring. But wildlife is where Mauritius' environmental story gets really interesting, from giant tortoises to critically endangered bird species making a comeback.

The Land

Mauritius is the peak of an enormous volcanic chain that also includes Réunion, though it is much older and therefore less rugged than its neighbour.

The island's highest mountains are found in the southwest, from where the land drops slightly to a central plateau before climbing again to the chain of oddly shaped mountains behind Port Louis and the Montagne Bambous to the east. Beyond these mountains a plain slopes gently down to the north coast.

Unlike Réunion, Mauritius has no active volcanoes, though remnants of volcanic activity abound. Extinct craters and volcanic lakes, such as the Trou aux Cerfs crater (p62) in Curepipe and the Grand Bassin holy lake (p96), are good examples. Over the aeons the volcanoes generated millions of lava boulders, much to the chagrin of indentured farm labourers who had to clear the land for sugar cane. Nonetheless, heaps of boulders still dot the landscape and some that have been piled into tidy pyramids are listed monuments!

Mauritius also includes a number of widely scattered inhabited islands, of which the most important is Rodrigues, 600km to the northeast. Rodrigues is another ancient volcanic peak and is surrounded by a lagoon twice the size of the island itself.

Mauritius stakes territorial claim to the Chagos Archipelago (p129), unilaterally declared the British Indian Ocean Territory by the UK and controversially ceded to the US military, despite international courts ruling in favour of Mauritius and the islands' former inhabitants.

Wildlife

The story of Mauritian wildlife certainly didn't end with the dodo. In fact the island's reputation for extinction has been transformed in recent years by its dramatic success in saving endangered species.

The best source of information is the **Mauritian Wildlife Foundation** (MWF; Map p60; ☑ 697 6117; www.mauritian-wildlife.org; Ratharethnum Mudaliar Ave, Vacoas; ☺ 9am-5pm Mon-Fri), which was founded in 1984 to protect and manage the country's many rare species. The MWF vigorously supports the creation of national parks and reserves. It has had significant success in restoring the populations of several endangered bird species and in conserving endemic vegetation. While you're welcome to visit its office to get information, it can be difficult to find. In any event its website is a useful resource and contacting it by email with specific questions usually elicits a response. A visit to MWF-run Île aux Aigrettes (p109) is a highlight of any visit to the island, while Grande Montagne Nature Reserve (p155) on Rodrigues is a growing ecotourism destination.

Birds

The dodo may be Mauritius' most famous former inhabitant (other bird species that were driven to extinction during the early colonial period include the red rail in Mauritius and the solitaire on Rodrigues), but Mauritius should be just as famous for the birds it has saved. In fact an academic review in 2007 found that Mauritius had pulled more bird species (five) back from the brink of extinction than any other country on earth. You can see these birds on Ile aux Aigrettes (p109), Black River Gorges National Park (p98), Vallée de Ferney (p105) and Ebony Forest of Chamarel (p94).

The birds you're most likely to see, however, are the introduced songbirds, such as the little red Madagascar fody, the Indian mynah and the red-whiskered bulbul. Between October and May the Rivulet Terre Rouge Bird Sanctuary (p64), north of Port Louis, provides an important wintering ground for migratory waterbirds such as the whimbrel, the grey plover and the common and curlew sandpipers.

MAURITIUS KESTREL

In 1974 the rather lovely Mauritius kestrel (which once inhabited all corners of the island) was officially the most endangered bird species on the planet, with just four known to survive in the wild, including, crucially, one breeding female. There were a further two of the raptors in captivity. The reasons for its dire situation were all too familiar: pesticide poisoning, habitat destruction and hunting. A captive-breeding program and an intensive project building predator-proof nesting boxes in the wild has led to an amazing recovery, with numbers now around 350, split between a population in the southeast (250) and one in the west and southwest (100).

Your best chance to see them is during their breeding season (August to February in the southeast; September to February in the southwest). The likeliest spots are Vallée de Ferney (p105), where there is kestrel feeding daily at noon, and Lion Mountain (p113). Black River Gorges National Park (p98) is also a possibility, though a more remote one.

PINK PIGEON

Like a number of other Mauritian bird species, the pretty pink pigeon has also been pulled back from the brink. In 1986 this once-widespread bird was down to just 12 individuals in the wild, living close to Bassin Blanc in the southern reaches of Black River Gorges National Park. In that year all five nesting attempts were unsuccessful due to predators such as rats. The species appeared doomed. An intensive program of captive breeding and reintroduction into the wild has seen numbers soar, with around 470 thought to be present throughout Black River Gorges National Park and on Île aux Aigrettes (where there were around 30 at last count). The Mauritian Wildlife Foundation is seeking to ensure that captive pink pigeons in European zoos will form part of

DEAD AS A DODO

Illustrations from the logbooks of the first ships to reach Mauritius show hundreds of plump flightless birds running down to the beach to investigate the newcomers. Lacking natural predators, these giant relatives of the pigeon were easy prey for hungry sailors, who named the birds *dodo*, which, in one interpretation at least, means 'stupid'. It took just 30 years for passing sailors and their pets and pests (dogs, monkeys, pigs and rats) to drive the dodo to extinction; the last confirmed sighting was in the 1660s.

Just as surprising as the speed of the dodo's demise is how little evidence remains that the bird ever existed. A few relics made it back to Europe during the 18th century – a dried beak ended up at the University of Copenhagen in Denmark, while the University of Oxford in England managed to get hold of a whole head and a foot – but until recently our knowledge of the dodo was mainly based on sketches by 17th-century seamen.

In 1865, however, local schoolteacher George Clark discovered dodo bones in a marshy area called Mare aux Songes, close to what is now the international airport. The skeleton was reassembled by scientists in Edinburgh, and has formed the basis of most subsequent dodo reconstructions, one of which is on display in Mahébourg's National History Museum (p105). The only other dodo skeleton is a nearly complete one in the Natural History Museum in Durban, South Africa. All other dodo displays are replicas. There is also an accurate reconstruction of a dodo in bronze in the ebony forest on Île aux Aigrettes.

the program as a means of enhancing the species' genetic diversity.

ECHO PARAKEET

The vivid colours of the echo parakeet were almost lost to Mauritius. In 1986 only about 20 survived. To make matters worse it was the last of six endemic parrot species that once inhabited the Mascarene Islands. Captive breeding, reintroduction and intensive conservation management have seen the species recover to around 800; the echo parakeet project has been one of the world's most successful parakeet conservation projects. The echo parakeet is restricted almost entirely to the Black River Gorges National Park (p98). Recent attempts to establish new sub-populations have been initiated in private reserves, one in Ebony Forest of Chamarel (p94) in the southwest and the other in the southeast in the Vallée de Ferney (p105). Note that the echo parakeet closely resembles the introduced ring-necked parakeet, which is far more common and widespread throughout the island.

Your best chance to see echo parakeets is along Parakeet Trail (p99) and Macchabée Trail (p99), and around Mare Longue Reservoir (p99).

OTHER SPECIES

The olive white eye, a small Mauritian songbird, now numbers no more than 150 pairs in the wild, with 60 to 70 birds on Île aux Aigrettes (p109). The Mauritian fody has also found a refuge on Île aux Aigrettes, which will serve as a base for future reintroduction programs.

Over on Rodrigues the recovery of the Rodrigues warbler (from 30 birds in the 1970s to more than 4000 today) and the Rodrigues fody (six pairs in 1968; more than 8000 individuals today) is almost unparalleled in the annals of wildlife conservation.

Offshore islands such as Île Plate and Îlot Gabriel, and the waters off Coin de Mire, Île Ronde and Île aux Serpents, are good places to see seabirds. Note that boats cannot land at the latter three islands.

Mammals

The only mammals native to Mauritius are the Mauritian cave bat and the wonderful fruit bat. The latter are a common sight at twilight as they come to life and begin their night's foraging.

All other mammals on the island were introduced by colonists, with varying degrees of success. Mongooses are typical of the slapdash ecological management of the past – they were introduced from India in the early 20th century to control plague-carrying rats. The intention was to import only males, but some females slipped through and they bred like, well, mongooses. Soon they were everywhere. They remain fairly common, as are the bands of macaque monkeys that hang out around Grand Bassin and the Black River Gorges. Java deer, imported by the Dutch for fresh meat, and wild pigs, also introduced, roam the more remote forests.

There is one further bat species – the grimly named Mauritius tomb bat.

Marine Creatures

Marine mammals are most commonly seen along the west coast of Mauritius. Spinner dolphins are the most common species in the bay off Tamarin, while bottlenose dolphins are also present. Dolphin-watching boat excursions set out from many places along the west coast, but we have serious concerns (p86) about their impact on the local populations, especially trips that encourage swimming with dolphins.

Numerous shark species inhabit Mauritian waters, though you're only likely to encounter them if you're diving on the outer reaches of the reef; few stray into the shallow waters of the lagoon. Common species include grey reef and bull sharks (east coast), blacktip and leopard sharks (north), and whitetip reef sharks (west).

From July or August through to October or November, humpback whales migrate along the west coast of Mauritius en route between the Antarctic and the warmer waters near the equator where they reproduce and calve. Sperm whales are believed to be resident off Mauritius' west coast and hence are present year-round, though they're generally considered more elusive than humpbacks.

Whale watching is surprisingly low-key in Mauritius when compared to neighbouring Madagascar. This is for two main reasons: first, the main (but by no means the only) season is considered low season, with far fewer visitors in the country; second, unlike dolphin watching, whale viewing takes place out in the open ocean, beyond the lagoon, and therefore requires full-day excursions.

Tortoises & Reptiles

Mauritius, along with Réunion and Seychelles, once had the largest number of giant tortoises on the planet. It was a veritable Galapagos of distinct species, of which Mauritius and Rodrigues had two each – Rodrigues once had the highest density of tortoises on earth. Such abundance didn't last long, however, and all tortoise species on Mauritius and Rodrigues were driven to extinction during the colonial period, when sailors and settlers favoured them as an easy-to-catch and long-lasting source of meat – tortoises could be kept alive on very little food, which was ideal for long-distance ocean journeys.

The only surviving species in the region, the Aldabra giant tortoise from the Seychelles, was introduced onto Île aux Aigrettes in 2000 and elsewhere in the years that followed. The number of wild tortoises has since grown dramatically. The best places to see them are Île aux Aigrettes (p109); La Vanille (p118), near Souillac; and Rodrigues' François Leguat Reserve (p155) and Grande Montagne Nature Reserve (p155).

Native reptiles include the beautiful turquoise-and-red ornate day gecko and Telfair's skink (a clawed lizard), both of which can be seen on Île aux Aigrettes. You can rest easy if you see a slithering critter – there are no dangerous reptiles in Mauritius.

National Parks

Since 1988 several international organisations have been working with the government to set up conservation areas in Mauritius. About 3.5% of the land area is now protected either as national parks, managed mainly for ecosystem preservation and recreation, or as nature reserves.

The largest park is Black River Gorges National Park (p98), established in 1994 in the island's southwest. It covers 68 sq km and preserves a wide variety of environments, from pine forest to tropical scrub, and includes the country's largest area of native forest.

Two of the most important nature reserves are Île aux Aigrettes (p109) and **Île Ronde** (the latter is closed to the public), both of which are being restored to their natural state by replacing introduced plants and animals with native species.

In 1997 marine parks were proclaimed at Blue Bay (p110), near Mahébourg on the southeast coast, and Balaclava (on the west coast), but the number of visitors to the areas makes it difficult to establish rigorous controls and there is a need to encourage local fishers to use less destructive techniques.

There is also the tiny national park of **Bras d'Eau**, close to Poste Lafayette on Mauritius' east coast.

Environmental Issues

The natural environment of Mauritius has paid a heavy price for the country's rapid development, and the government seems keener than ever to encourage more tourists to plug the gap left by declining sugar and textile industries. The expansion of tourist facilities, however, is straining the island's infrastructure and causing environmental degradation and excessive demand on services such as electricity, water and transport.

One area of particular concern is construction along the coast – almost every beach has been developed, and most of the development is tourist related. Many Mauritians, however, are very keen to put environmental concerns first – a proposal for a hotel

IMPORTANT NATIONAL PARKS & RESERVES

PARK	FEATURES	ACTIVITIES	BEST TIME TO VISIT
Balaclava Marine Park	lagoon, coral reef, turtle breeding grounds	snorkelling, diving, glass-bottomed boat tours	all year
Black River Gorges National Park (p98)	forested mountains, Mauritian kestrels, echo parakeets, pink pigeons, black ebony trees	hiking, birdwatching	Sep–Jan for flowers
Blue Bay Marine Park (p110)	lagoon, corals, fish life	snorkelling, diving, glass-bottomed boat tours	all year
Île aux Aigrettes Nature Reserve (p109)	coral island, ebony forests, pink pigeons, olive white eyes, Aldabra giant tortoises, Telfairs skinks	ecotours, birdwatching	all year

on Île des Deux Cocos in Blue Bay, for example, met with such fierce resistance that it was abandoned. Conservationists also fervently (and successfully) combated plans to construct a highway through the old forests in the southeast at Vallée de Ferney (p105), which has now been turned into a conservation hub. Many grassroots organisations and NGOs are fighting against pillaging of the island's natural resources for construction and hotel development, with the Mauritian Wildlife Foundation (p138) at the forefront of campaigns.

The government now requires an environmental-impact assessment for all new building projects, including coastal hotels, marinas and golf courses, and even for activities such as undersea walks. Planning regulations for hotel developments on both Mauritius and Rodrigues require that any developments are 81m from the high-tide mark at spring tide and 30m from wetlands on the main island. Since water shortages are a problem on Rodrigues, new hotels must also recycle their water.

To combat littering and other forms of environmental degradation, the government has established a special environmental police force charged with enforcing legislation and educating the local population. To report wrongdoers there is even a hotline (☑ 210 5151), though enforcement of environmental regulations remains a concern.

If anything the marine environment is suffering even more from over-exploitation than the land. The coast off Grand Baie is particularly affected by the number of divers and boats concentrated in a few specific locations. In addition silting and chemical pollution are resulting in extensive coral damage and falling fish populations. Unregulated dolphin watching (p86) off the west coast is also causing concern for its impact upon dolphin populations.

SLEEPING PRICE RANGES

The following price ranges refer to a double room with bathroom. Unless otherwise stated, breakfast is not included in the price.

€ less than €75 (around Rs 3000)

€€ €75–150 (Rs 3000–6000)

€€€ more than €150 (Rs 6000)

SURVIVAL GUIDE

ⓘ Directory A-Z

ACCESSIBLE TRAVEL

Mauritius makes relatively decent provision for those with mobility problems. Modern buildings conform to international standards for disabled access, though public toilets, footpaths and lifts tend not to be as good. Most top-end hotels have wheelchair access, lifts and a handful of rooms with specially equipped bathrooms. In big hotels there are always plenty of staff around to help and it's often possible to hire an assistant if you want to go on an excursion or a boat trip. With a bit of extra notice some riding stables, dive centres and other sports operators can cater for people with disabilities.

None of the public-transport systems offer wheelchair access. Anyone using a wheelchair will be reliant on private vehicles.

Download Lonely Planet's free Accessible Travel guides from https://shop.lonelyplanet.com/categories/accessible-travel.

ACCOMMODATION

Accommodation should always be booked in advance, particularly during the November-to-April high season.

Vacation rentals Self-catering villas or apartments can be excellent alternatives to the hotel experience. Many are right by the sea and can be quite luxurious.

Guesthouses The most personal option, these places are often family-run, offering simple rooms but a warm welcome. Many are called *chambres d'hôtes*.

Hotels & resorts The choice here is seemingly endless. Many resorts offer all-inclusive packages and a range of activities, spas and restaurants. Top-end resorts can be exclusive and spectacularly luxurious.

Seasons

In general, high season runs from around October to March, with a focus on the European winter months. Prices soar at the end of December and the beginning of January. Travellers can expect prices to dip during the low season (May to September), often called 'green season'.

Apartments & Villas

Renting a holiday apartment or villa is by far the most economical option in Mauritius, especially if there are several people in your travelling party. There are hundreds of rental options, ranging from small studios in factory-sized complexes to lavish seaside mansions fit for a movie star. If you're travelling with family or friends, a large high-end property can cost as little as €25 per person, which more than rivals the island's hostel-esque relics from an earlier era of travel.

But remember, even though rentals represent a better price-to-value ratio on the whole, you always get what you pay for and meals are never included.

Most of the accommodation in this category is privately owned and managed by an umbrella agency that markets a large pool of crash pads. While choices can vary greatly, you should expect (in all but the cheapest places) that your home away from home comes with daily maid service, a fully equipped kitchen, air-con and concierge service provided by the property manager (make sure to double-check).

A few of the larger agencies:
➡ CG Villas (p73)
➡ Ropsen (p101)
➡ Grand Bay Travel & Tours (p73)

Guesthouses & Chambres d'Hôtes

If you're looking for an island experience that doesn't involve the term 'all-inclusive', Mauritius' guesthouses and *chambres d'hôtes* (B&Bs) are well worth considering. This category of accommodation is managed by locals – often families – who as a rule dote on their guests with genuine hospitality. It's a fantastic way to learn about the *real* Mauritius. You'll sometimes even have the chance to dine with your accommodation's proprietors at their *tables d'hôtes,* which can be equally rewarding experiences.

Over the last few years the government has been increasing regulations for all tourism-related properties. Panic buttons and 24-hour security have, for example, become a compulsory expense for owners, forcing guesthouses to jack up their prices beyond the budget range to pay the bills. As a result the island's *chambres d'hôtes* are starting to be under threat, especially since all-inclusive resorts have been known to offer bargain-basement prices to stay competitive during economic downturns. Nonetheless there's still a scattering of charming spots sprinkled around the island that are, now more than ever, promoting a 'local experience'. You'll find a cluster in Pointe d'Esny, and *chambres d'hôtes* are particularly popular in Rodrigues.

Hotels & Resorts

Mauritius' best-known brand of accommodation is the sort of dreamy resorts found on the pages of magazines and in TV commercials for credit cards. Mauritius has hundreds of these opulent properties.

There are, however, two distinct categories of hotel in Mauritius: the luxury resorts that stretch along the coast, and the old-school midrangers that need some serious TLC. It's best to avoid the latter, as many of the top-end properties offer vacation incentives that rival the has-beens, and guesthouses (which are often cheaper) are generally in better shape.

BOOK YOUR STAY ONLINE

For more accommodation reviews by Lonely Planet authors, check out hotels. lonelyplanet.com. You'll find independent reviews, as well as recommendations on the best places to stay. Best of all, you can book online.

Upscale properties come in various tiers of luxury – there are three-, four- and five-star resorts. You'll do perfectly well with a three-star charmer, and while the five-star price tags may be high, it's well worth checking with travel agents about hotel-and-flight packages. In fact no upmarket sleeps should be booked with the public rates – agency rates are always cheaper. If you have your sights set on a luxury holiday, expect to pay €120 per person per night (including half board) at the very minimum. Prices can quickly climb all the way up to €1000 per person per night and beyond.

CHILDREN

Travelling with children in Mauritius presents no particular problems. To put their holiday in context, there's a wonderful series of English-language cartoon books by Henry Koombes (published locally by Editions Vizavi Ltd), including *In Dodoland, SOS Shark* and *Meli-Melo in the Molasses.*

For more information, see Lonely Planet's *Travel with Children.*

Practicalities

Most high-end hotels have dedicated facilities (like 'kids clubs') for children, and those that don't sometimes have a small playground. Most top-end hotels also include babysitting services. The proliferation of villa leases has made it easy to bring the entire family on holiday, while many hotels and even some *chambres d'hôtes* offer family rooms. Most hotels have cots, though usually only a limited number, so always request one when making your reservation and send a reminder some weeks in advance of your arrival.

Remember that some top-end resorts market themselves as 'adults only'. This is less an indication of risqué behaviour than an attempt by hotels and resorts to appeal to the honeymoon or romantic-getaway market. In other words, kids are not welcome. If you're making a reservation online and there's no option of adding kids to your booking, chances are that's the reason.

Disposable nappies are widely available in supermarkets, and most car-hire companies have a limited number and range of child safety seats available (the smaller the company, the fewer options you'll have). Baby-changing facilities in

> **TOP ATTRACTIONS FOR CHILDREN**
> ➡ La Vanille (p118), Rivière des Anguilles
> ➡ Île aux Aigrettes (p109), Pointe d'Esny
> ➡ Casela World of Adventures (p83), Flic en Flac
> ➡ Mauritius Aquarium (p64), Pointe aux Piments
> ➡ Snorkelling, anywhere...

restaurants and other public areas are almost nonexistent. Breastfeeding in public is not really the done thing (though it's usually fine within hotel or resort grounds), but you're unlikely to feel uncomfortable as long as you're discreet.

ELECTRICITY

The supply is 220V, 50Hz; both British-style three-pin sockets (type G) and the Continental two-pin variety (type C) are commonly used, sometimes in the same room – bring both.

EMBASSIES & CONSULATES

Many countries do not have representatives in Mauritius and usually refer their citizens to embassies in Pretoria (South Africa).

Australian High Commission (📋 202 0160; www.mauritius.embassy.gov.au; 2nd fl, Rogers House, 5 President John Kennedy St, Port Louis; ☺ 8.30am-3.30pm Mon-Fri)

Canadian Consulate (📋 212 5500; pretoria-im-enquiry@international.gc.ca; 18 Jules Koenig St, Port Louis; ☺ 9am-noon Mon-Fri)

French Embassy (📋 202 0100; https://mu.ambafrance.org; 14 St Georges St, Port Louis; ☺ 8am-noon Mon-Fri)

Italian Honorary Consulate (📋 686 4233; consolatoitalia2@myt.mu; Nicholson Rd, Vacoas; ☺ 8.30am-noon Tue & Thu, 8-9am Fri)

Seychelles Honorary Consulate (📋 211 1688; gfok@intnet.mu; 616 St James Ct, St Denis St, Port Louis)

UK High Commission (📋 202 9400; www.gov.uk/world/organisations/british-high-commission-port-louis; 7th fl, Les Cascades Bldg, Edith Cavell St, Port Louis; ☺ 7.45am-3.45pm Mon-Thu, to 1.45pm Fri)

US Embassy (📋 202 4400; https://mu.usembassy.gov; 4th fl, Rogers House, President John Kennedy St, Port Louis; ☺ 7.30am-4.45pm Mon-Thu, to 12.30pm Fri)

INTERNET ACCESS

Most towns have at least one internet cafe. Wi-fi connections are almost universal in hotels, resorts and guesthouses, though wi-fi signals sometimes don't extend beyond public areas.

LEGAL MATTERS

Foreigners are subject to the laws of the country in which they are travelling and will receive no special consideration because they are tourists. If you find yourself in a sticky legal predicament, contact your embassy. Drug offences are taken extremely seriously here.

In general travellers have nothing to fear from the police, who rarely harass foreigners and are very polite if you do need to stop them. Talking on your mobile phone while driving will definitely get you pulled over, but if you're in any sort of minor trouble you'll most likely be let off the hook if it's obvious that you're a tourist (speaking in English helps even more).

LGBT+ TRAVELLERS

Mauritius has a paradoxical relationship to homosexuality. On one hand much of the population is young and progressive, gays and lesbians are legally protected from discrimination and individuals have a constitutionally guaranteed right to privacy, and Mauritius has signed the UN Declaration on Sexual Orientation and Gender Identity. At the same time 'sodomy' is illegal and there remains a rigidly conservative streak to Mauritian public debate.

As a result of the latter, gay life remains fairly secretive, mainly existing on the internet, in private and at the occasional party. While there were no gay or lesbian bars or clubs on the island at the time of writing, there were monthly underground club nights organised by text message. La Mariposa (p90), close to Tamarin, is the only place we found that openly advertises itself as gay friendly.

For gay and lesbian travellers there's little to worry about. We've never heard of any problems arising from same-sex couples sharing rooms during their holidays. You're still best to avoid public displays of affection outside your hotel and generally to be aware that what might be entirely standard at home may not be viewed in the same light here.

MONEY

ATMs Widespread on the main island, less common on Rodrigues.

Cash While the Mauritian rupee is the island's currency, almost all villas, guesthouses and hotels (and several high-end restaurants usually affiliated with hotels) tether their prices to the euro to counterbalance the rupee's unstable fluctuations, and it is possible (and sometimes required) to pay in euros at such places.

Credit cards Major credit cards widely accepted by hotels, restaurants, shops and tour companies.

Local currency The Mauritian unit of currency is the rupee (Rs), which is divided into 100 cents (¢). There are coins of 5¢, 20¢, 50¢, Rs 1, Rs 5 and Rs 10. The banknote denominations are Rs 25, Rs 50, Rs 100, Rs 200, Rs 500, Rs 1000 and Rs 2000

Tipping Not generally practised in Mauritius and is never an obligation.

Exchange Rates

For current exchange rates, see www.xe.com.

Australia	A$1	Rs 24.8
Canada	C$1	Rs26.11
Europe	€1	Rs 27.17
Japan	¥100	Rs 33.74
NZ	NZ$1	Rs 23.2
UK	UK£1	Rs 43.34
USA	US$1	Rs 35.96

OPENING HOURS

Hours below are the general rule. Shops in larger seaside resort towns are usually open longer, while on Rodrigues shops and offices generally close earlier than stated below.

Banks 9am–3.15pm Monday to Friday (extended hours in tourist hubs such as Grand Baie and Flic en Flac)

Government offices 9am–4pm Monday to Friday, 9am–noon Saturday (closed during religious and public holidays)

Post offices 8.15am–4pm Monday to Friday, 8.15am–11.45am Saturday (the last 45 minutes are for stamp sales only, and many offices close for lunch from 11.15am to noon on weekdays)

Restaurants noon–3pm and 7pm–10pm; many restaurants close on Sunday

Shops 9am–5pm Monday to Friday, 8am–noon Saturday; many close around 1pm Thursday

PUBLIC HOLIDAYS

New Year 1 and 2 January

Thaipoosam Cavadee January/February

Chinese Spring Festival January/February

Abolition of Slavery 1 February

Maha Shivaratri February/March

Ougadi March/April

National Day 12 March

Labour Day 1 May

Eid al-Fitr May/June

Assumption of the Blessed Virgin Mary 15 August

Ganesh Chaturthi August/September

Divali (Dipavali) October/November

Arrival of Indentured Labourers (Indian Arrival Day) 2 November

Christmas Day 25 December

SAFE TRAVEL

Your biggest annoyances here are likely to be mosquitoes, sunburn and the occasional upset stomach.

➡ There are several aquatic nasties, though few travellers encounter anything more serious than the odd coral cut.

➡ Lying under a coconut palm may seem like a tropical idyll, but there have been some tragic accidents. Take care when walking under coconut trees and don't lie (or park your car) beneath them.

➡ Cyclones can occur between December (or more commonly, January) and March, though they are not unheard of as late as April.

➡ The risk of theft in Mauritius is small, but nonetheless it's worth being cautious.

TELEPHONE

The island's telephone services are reliable and mobile coverage is generally excellent.

If you have a GSM phone and it has been unlocked, you can keep costs down by buying a local SIM card from either Mauritius Telecom (www.mauritiustelecom.com) or Emtel (www.emtel.com).

When phoning Mauritius from abroad, you'll need to dial the international code for Mauritius (🖉 230), followed by the seven-digit local number (unless it's a mobile phone, which has eight digits and begins with '5').

TIME

Mauritius is on GMT plus four hours, both on the mainland and on Rodrigues. When it's noon in Port Louis, it's 8am in London, 9am in Paris, 3am in New York and 6pm in Sydney, though this can vary when other countries change their clocks for daylight savings. Mauritius does not operate a system of daylight saving; being equatorial its sunset and sunrise times vary only slightly throughout the year.

TOURIST INFORMATION

Although independent travellers are definitely in the minority, two corporate entities are dedicated to those who don't fall into the package-getaway category. Both have desks in the airport arrivals hall, and they can assist with hotel bookings (though this is increasingly rare as few travellers arrive in the country without a booking), basic tourist maps and quite general island information.

EATING PRICE RANGES

The following price ranges refer to a standard main course. Unless otherwise stated, service charges and taxes are included in the price.

€ less than Rs 400

€€ Rs 400–800

€€€ more than Rs 800

PRACTICALITIES

Newspapers French-language *L'Express* (www.lexpress.mu) and *Le Mauricien* (www.lemauricien.com); English-language weeklies *News on Sunday* and the *Mauritius Times* (www.mauritiustimes.com).

Radio There's a huge number of local commercial stations broadcasting in Creole and Hindi, and the BBC World Service and Voice of America are readily available. The most popular stations include Kool FM 89.3 Mhz and Taal FM 94.0 Mhz.

Smoking Prohibited in indoor public places and on public transport; allowed in outdoor restaurants, on beaches, in some hotel rooms and at some workplaces.

TV Three free TV channels – MBC1, MBC2 and MBC3 – are run by the state Mauritius Broadcasting Corporation (MBC), and there are numerous pay channels. Programming is mainly in Creole, but there are foreign imports in French, English and Indian languages.

Weights & Measures Mauritius uses the metric system.

Also useful is Mauritius Telecom's 24-hour phone service, **Tourist Info** (☑152). At any time of day or night you can speak to someone (in English) who will at least try to answer your questions.

Mauritius Tourism Promotion Authority (MTPA; www.tourism-mauritius.mu) The Mauritius Tourism Promotion Authority is a government-run body essentially responsible for promoting the island and its virtues to foreign markets. MTPA has a constellation of kiosks across the island, though, to be perfectly frank, many were empty during prime business hours when we visited, and when we did find someone staffing a booth they tossed us an outdated island map and offered very limited information. You're better off asking tour operators, hotel staff or anyone else accustomed to dealing with travellers' queries.

Association des Hôteliers et Restaurateurs de l'Île Maurice (AHRIM; www.mauritius-tourism.org) The recommended AHRIM is an association of high-quality hotels, guesthouses and restaurants. It's starting to offer guesthouse-plus-airfare packages – an attempt to empower tourists to have a local experience while also benefiting from discounted airfares. Check out its website for details.

VISAS

Not required for most nationalities for stays of up to three months.

VOLUNTEERING

There aren't that many volunteering opportunities in Mauritius, but there are some possibilities in the area of wildlife or marine conservation.

DEPARTURE TAX

Departure tax is included in the price of a ticket.

Six-month placements on Île aux Aigrettes are possible through the Mauritian Wildlife Foundation (p138) – there's a volunteering page on its website where you can register. Volunteering at coral reef conservation projects for one week to six months can be arranged through Working Abroad (www.workingabroad.com), **Reef Conservation** (Map p78; ☑262 6775; www.reefconservation.mu; off Les Flamants Rd, Pereybére) and others.

ⓘ Getting There & Away

ENTERING THE COUNTRY/REGION

Entering Mauritius is usually hassle free, with no visas required for many nationalities. Customs searches are generally quick and easy, if they occur at all, but rules are necessarily strict on importing food, especially fruit.

AIR

Direct flights connect Mauritius with Australia, Asia, the Middle East, Africa and Europe. From further afield you may need to take a connecting flight from South Africa, the Middle East or Europe.

Airports & Airlines

Mainland Mauritius' only airport is **Sir Seewoosagur Ramgoolam International Airport** (SSR; Map p116; ☑603 6000; http://aml.mru.aero; Royal Rd, Plaine Magnien).

Air Mauritius (☑207 7212; www.airmauritius.com; Air Mauritius Centre, President John Kennedy St) is the national carrier. It has a good safety record and a decent international network.

SEA

The **Mauritius Shipping Corporation** (☑217 2284, 831 0640; www.mauritiusshipping.net; Rue François Leguat; ⊙8.15am-3pm Mon-Fri, to 11am Sat) operates long-haul ferry services between Réunion and Mauritius at least once a week. The journey takes about 11 hours. We're yet to meet a traveller who arrived in or left Mauritius in this way, but the option does exist. There are no scheduled shipping services to Mauritius from other countries.

ⓘ Getting Around

AIR

The only regular domestic air connections are those between Sir Seewoosagur Ramgoolam International Airport on mainland Mauritius and Sir Gaetan Duval Airport (p163) on Rodrigues. There are at least two daily flights on this route, operated by Air Mauritius, and flying time is around 1½ hours. This is an extremely popular route, so always book ahead as early as you can.

Air Mauritius offers helicopter tours and charters from SSR International Airport to a number of major hotels. A hotel transfer anywhere on the island costs Rs 25,000, while a full one-hour island tour costs Rs 43,000 for up to two passengers; a quick 15-minute jaunt will set you back Rs 17,000. For information and reservations contact **Air Mauritius Helicopter Services** (☑ 603 3754; www.airmauritius.com/helicopter.htm; Sir Seewoosagur Ramgoolam International Airport) or ask your hotel to organise a transfer or trip.

BICYCLE

Cycling isn't really a practical means of long-distance transport in Mauritius – there is simply too much traffic, roads are narrow and drivers rarely take cyclists into consideration – but bikes are fine for short hops along the coast. Given that the coast is pleasantly flat, it's amazing how much ground you can cover in a day. The coast roads are also generally (though not always) quieter than those in the interior.

In general the roads are well maintained, but look out for potholes along country lanes, especially in the western part of the island. Avoid cycling anywhere at night, as most roads are poorly lit.

Most hotels and guesthouses can help you arrange bike rentals (usually mountain bikes). Although many offer this as a complimentary service for guests, expect to pay around Rs 250 per day for a quality bike at those places that don't. You'll usually be asked for a deposit of Rs 5000, either in cash or by taking an imprint of your credit card. Most bikes are in reasonable condition, but be sure to check the brakes, gears and saddle (some are mighty uncomfortable) before riding off into the blue beyond. The bike should have a lock; use it, especially if you leave your bike at the beach or outside shops.

BOAT

Various private operators offer cruises to offshore islands, or snorkelling and fishing excursions. Most commonly this is aboard a catamaran, but speedboat excursions are also possible. For the former check out www.catamarancruisesmauritius.com.

Otherwise two boats, the M/V *Anna* and the M/S *Mauritius Trochetia*, have two to four monthly passenger services in both directions between Port Louis (Maurltlus) and Port Mathurin (Rodrigues). The journey takes close to 36 hours. On board you'll find four classes ranging from 2nd class up to deluxe cabins. Services are operated by the Mauritius Shipping Corporation.

BUS

Bus travel is cheap and fun – you'll usually find yourself chatting to gregarious locals – and though some drivers go a little fast, it's generally a fairly easy and reliable way to get around. There is no countrywide bus service. Instead there are several large regional bus companies and scores of individual operators.

The buses are almost always packed, especially on the main routes, but turnover is quick at all the stops. If you start the trip standing, you're likely to end up sitting.

Be warned that you could have problems taking large bags or backpacks on a bus. If it takes up a seat, you will probably have to pay for that extra seat. A few travellers have even been refused entry to a full bus if they have a large bag, though this is rare.

It's best to stick to express buses whenever possible, as standard buses seem to stop every few metres and can take up to twice as long to reach the same destination. It takes approximately an hour by standard services from Mahébourg to Curepipe, an hour from Curepipe to Port Louis, and an hour from Port Louis to Grand Baie.

The buses are single-deck vehicles bearing dynamic names such as 'Road Warrior', 'Bad Boys' and 'The Street Ruler'. Thus encouraged,

---

ARRIVING IN MAURITIUS

Semi-regular buses between Port Louis or Curepipe and Mahébourg go via the Sir Seewoosagur Ramgoolam International Airport and pick up passengers from outside the arrivals hall; if nothing turns up, you may need to head upstairs to departures. For all other destinations you'll need to change in one of these three cities. Most travellers get where they're going by hiring a taxi – there's a taxi desk with set prices in the arrivals hall. Sample fares are Rs 1600 to Port Louis, Rs 500 to Mahébourg and Rs 2000 to Grand Baie.

it's perhaps not surprising that some drivers harbour Formula 1 racing fantasies; fortunately the frequent stops slow things down a touch. Though the buses are in varying states of disrepair, the fleet is gradually being upgraded.

CAR & MOTORCYCLE

By far the easiest and quickest way to get around Mauritius and Rodrigues is to hire a car. Prices aren't as low as they could be, considering the numbers of visitors who rent vehicles, but you should be able to negotiate a discount if you're renting for a week or more.

Road Conditions & Hazards

Most roads are in reasonable condition, though be wary of potholes and poorly signed speed humps on minor or residential roads. The main concern for first-time drivers is that, apart from the motorway that links the airport with Grand Baie (albeit with roundabouts), many roads can be quite narrow – fine under normal conditions, but slightly trickier when buses, trucks and meandering cyclists are factored in. The only solution is to err on the side of caution and remain vigilant. Also watch out for other vehicles overtaking when it's not entirely safe to do so.

Even on the motorway you'll find people wandering across the roads and a generally relaxed attitude. As in most places the greatest danger comes from other drivers, not the roads. Mauritian drivers tend to have little consideration for each other, let alone for motorbikes. Buses are notorious for overtaking and then pulling in immediately ahead of other vehicles to pick up or drop off passengers; always use extra caution when a bus comes into sight. At night be aware that you'll face an assault course of ill-lit oncoming vehicles, totally unlit bikes and weaving pedestrians. If you sense that you've hit something while driving at night, proceed to the nearest police station. Motorcyclists should also be prepared for the elements, as sudden showers can come out of skies that were clear a second earlier.

Car Hire

To rent a car drivers must usually be over the age of 23 (some companies only require a minimum age of 21) and have held a driving licence for at least one year. Payment is generally made in advance. You can pay by credit card (Visa and MasterCard are the most widely accepted), though small companies might add a 3% 'processing fee' for this service. All foreigners are technically required to have an International Driving Licence. Few rental agencies enforce this, but it's safest to carry one as police can demand to see it.

Rates for the smallest hatchback start at around Rs 1000 a day (including insurance and unlimited mileage) with one of the local operators. Expect rates to start at Rs 1200 and beyond when using an international chain, though daily prices can even start as high as Rs 1600. On top of that you will be required to pay a refundable deposit, usually Rs 15,000; most companies will take an imprint of your credit card to cover this. Policies usually specify that drivers are liable for the first Rs 15,000 of damage in the event of an accident, but more comprehensive insurance is sometimes available for an extra cost.

Although there are dozens of operators on the island, it's best to book ahead during the high-season months (the European winter holidays). The following car-hire companies either have airport desks or can deliver to the airport.

ABC (☑ 216 8889; www.abc-carrental.com; Sir Seewoosagur Ramgoolam International Airport)

Avis (☑ 405 5200; www.avismauritius.com; Sir Seewoosagur Ramgoolam International Airport)

Budget (☑ 467 9700; www.budget.com.mu; Sir Seewoosagur Ramgoolam International Airport)

Claire & Sailesh Ltd (☑ 631 4625, 5754 6451; www.clairesaileshltd.com; Pointe d'Esny)

Europcar (☑ 637 3240; www.europcar.com; Sir Seewoosagur Ramgoolam International Airport)

Hertz (☑ 604 3021, 670 4301; www.hertz.com; Sir Seewoosagur Ramgoolam International Airport)

Kevtrav Ltd (☑ 465 4458; www.kevtrav.com; St Jean Rd, Quatre Bornes)

Ropsen (p101)

Sixt (☑ 427 1111; www.sixt.com; Sir Seewoosagur Ramgoolam International Airport)

CLIMATE CHANGE & TRAVEL

Every form of transport that relies on carbon-based fuel generates CO_2, the main cause of human-induced climate change. Modern travel is dependent on aeroplanes, which might use less fuel per kilometre per person than most cars but travel much greater distances. The altitude at which aircraft emit gases (including CO_2) and particles also contributes to their climate change impact. Many websites offer 'carbon calculators' that allow people to estimate the carbon emissions generated by their journey and, for those who wish to do so, to offset the impact of the greenhouse gases emitted with contributions to portfolios of climate-friendly initiatives throughout the world. Lonely Planet offsets the carbon footprint of all staff and author travel.

Motorcycle Hire

There are only a few places where you can hire motorbikes, which is a shame as this is a great way to explore the quiet coastal roads, especially in traffic-free Rodrigues. While you'll occasionally find a 125cc bike, most are 100cc or under; the smaller models are referred to as scooters.

Expect to pay upwards of Rs 500 per day (Rs 600 in Rodrigues). As with car hire, payment is requested in advance, along with a deposit of Rs 5000 or so.

Towns offering motorcycle hire include Grand Baie, Flic en Flac, Mahébourg and Port Mathurin. Your best bet is to ask around your hotel. You should be aware that most motorcycle hire is 'unofficial', so you may not be covered by insurance In event of a collision.

Parking

Parking is free and not a problem in most of Mauritius, though it's best not to leave your car in an isolated spot.

City parking, however, requires payment. There are supervised car parks in Port Louis, but elsewhere you'll have to park on the street, which in a handful of towns involves buying parking coupons – ask a local if you're not sure. Coupons are available from petrol stations and cost from Rs 50 for 10, with each coupon valid for 30 minutes. The same coupons can be used all over the island. Street parking is generally free at night and on weekends – the exact hours, which vary from one town to another, are indicated on signposts.

Road Rules

Local motorists seem to think they'll save battery power by not switching on their headlights, and the police are better at people control than traffic control. Traffic congestion can be heavy in Port Louis and, to a lesser extent, Grand Baie.

There are many pedestrian zebra crossings, but cross with care. If you cross expecting courtesy or that drivers will be worried about insurance, you'll get knocked over.

Driving is on the left and the speed limit varies from 30km/h in town centres to 110km/h on the motorway – speed limits are usually marked. Even so, not many people stick to these limits and the island has its fair share of accidents (and speed cameras). Remember also that the motorway has a series of roundabouts – bearing down on them at 110km/h is a dangerous pastime best avoided.

Drivers and passengers are required to wear seat belts. For lack of sufficient breathalysers, the alcohol limit (legally 0.5g/L) is defined by the police as one glass of beer.

TAXI

It's sometimes possible to imagine that every adult male in Mauritius is a taxi driver. Drivers will often shout out at travellers they see wandering around Port Louis, Flic en Flac or Grand Baie, while ranks outside hotels are usually overflowing. Negotiation is key: meters are rarely used and you'll usually be ripped off if you get into a taxi without agreeing on a price first. During the journey most drivers will tout for future business; if you aren't careful, you may find that you've agreed to an all-day island tour. If you aren't interested make this very clear, as many drivers won't take a half-hearted no for an answer.

Many guesthouse managers/owners have attempted to mitigate their guests' frustration with rip-offs by arranging prices with local taxi drivers. The quotes given under such arrangements, particularly those from small guesthouses, are often acceptable; they can usually arrange competitively priced airport pick-ups as well. Once you've got a feel for the rates, you can venture into independent bargaining. You'll find that prices are fairly standard – you may be able to knock off Rs 100 or Rs 200 here and there, though don't be crestfallen if you can't whittle the driver down to the exact price you're expecting (after all, they've had more practice at this taxi game than you!).

Taxis charge slightly more at night and the cheeky drivers may ask for an extra fee if you want the comfort of air-con. It's also worth remembering that some taxis charge around Rs 1 per minute waiting time. It seems minimal, but it adds up if you stop for lunch or do some sightseeing on foot. Your best bet is to negotiate a set fare with the driver that includes waiting time.

There's a taxi desk at the airport with set prices for just about anywhere on the island.

Taxi Hire

For around Rs 2000 to Rs 2500 you can hire a taxi for a full-day tour along one or two coasts of the island. You can cut costs by forming a group – the price should *not* be calculated per person. Once you've agreed on a price and itinerary, it helps to get the details down in writing. Although most drivers can speak both French and English, double-check before setting off to ensure you won't face a day-long communication barrier. If you're lucky you'll get an excellent and informative guide, but note that most drivers work on a commission basis with particular restaurants, shops and sights. If you want to go to the restaurant of your choice, you may have to insist on it. Small guesthouses can usually recommend a reliable driver.

Share Taxis

When individual fares are hard to come by, some taxis will cruise around their area supplementing the bus service. For quick, short-haul trips they pick up passengers waiting at the bus stops and charge just a little more than the bus. Their services are called 'share taxis' or 'taxi trains'. Mind you, if you flag down an empty taxi, you may have to pay the full fare.

Rodrigues

POP 42,396

Best Places to Eat

➡ La Belle Rodriguaise (p162)

➡ Chez Robert et Solange (p161)

➡ Le Marlin Bleu (p161)

➡ Mazavaroo (p161)

➡ Chez Paulina (p162)

Best Places to Stay

➡ Tekoma (p160)

➡ Bakwa Lodge (p160)

➡ La Belle Rodriguaise (p159)

➡ Pirate Lodge (p160)

➡ Kafe Marron (p159)

➡ Chez Claudine (p158)

Why Go?

Blissfully isolated more than 600km northeast of the mainland, this tiny volcanic outcrop surrounded by a massive turquoise lagoon is a stunning mountainous gem that barely feels connected to its big sister, Mauritius, let alone the wider world.

Often billed as the 'Mauritius of 25 years ago', Rodrigues actually bears little resemblance to its neighbour beyond the scenic strips of peach-tinged sand. The island's population is predominantly African and Creole – a far cry from the ethnic melting pot on Mauritius' main island – and you won't find a stalk of sugar cane anywhere on Rodrigues' hilly landscape. The pace of life, too, is undeniably slow, which gives the island its time-warped vibe. Great food, some fine natural sites and a host of activities round out an experience that lives long in the memory as one of those beautiful forgotten worlds in some remote corner of the globe.

When to Go

➡ November to February means high season and high prices; cyclones are possible from January. Accommodation and air tickets can be hard to come by, so book well in advance if travelling at this time.

➡ October, March and April are still considered high season in places, but there are generally fewer crowds. Rain is possible. Underwater visibility is especially good for diving and snorkelling at this time. All in all, it's a nice time to be on the island.

➡ May to September hails lower prices and milder temperatures; little chance of cyclones.

Port Mathurin

POP 6430

This tiny port must be one of the smallest, quietest, sleepiest regional capital cities on the planet. During the day the town has a friendly vibe, especially around the buzzing market stalls. Apart from its banks, supermarket and handful of restaurants, there's not much to do here and, apart from the Saturday market, the only reason to come is to get a taste of urban life, such as it is, Rodrigues-style.

◉ Sights & Activities

★ Saturday Market   MARKET

(Map p154; ☺5-10am) The Saturday market is as busy as Rodrigues gets and it's the best place on the island to shop for fresh produce and souvenirs. It's open the rest of the week but really gears up on Saturday, when much of the island turns out. It's next to the bridge near the post office. Turn up later than 10am and you'll wonder what all the fuss is about.

La Résidence   ARCHITECTURE

(Map p154; Rue de la Solidarité) One of the oldest buildings still standing in Port Mathurin, La Résidence dates from 1897, when it provided a fairly modest home for the British chief commissioner. Its facilities are now used as function rooms for the new Regional Assembly. As such it's closed to the public, though it is possible to get an idea of the structure from the veranda of the tourist office across the road.

🛌 Sleeping

Port Mathurin makes a convenient base if you're travelling by bus, but frankly the options in town lack the quality you'll find outside it and taxis rarely cost much. The main

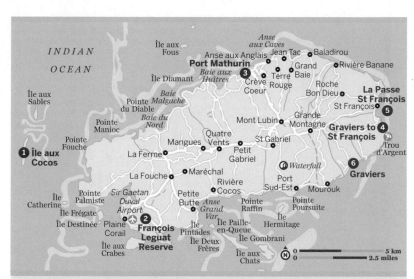

Rodrigues Highlights

❶ Île aux Cocos (p156)
Taking a boat ride out to the seabird colonies of this small, uninhabited slice of paradise.

❷ François Leguat Reserve (p155) Cavorting with hundreds of curious giant tortoises in a lovely setting.

❸ Saturday Market (p151) Getting up early in Port Mathurin and immersing yourself in the island's busiest market.

❹ Graviers to St François (p157) Hiking past Rodrigues' best beaches along the island's northeast coast.

❺ La Passe St François (p157) Diving the pristine waters off the island's east coast.

❻ La Belle Rodriguaise (p159) Eating the best in local cooking in Graviers, then sleeping by the sea.

RODRIGUES PORT MATHURIN

Rodrigues

TERRE ROUGE

ANSE AUX ANGLAIS

JEAN TAC

St François

INDIAN OCEAN

Port Mathurin

François Leguat Reserve

Trou d'Argent

Rodrigues

concentration of hotels and guesthouses is found 2km east of town at Anse aux Anglais.

Hébergement
Fatehmamode APARTMENT €
(Map p154; ☏ 831 2607, 5499 2020; www.heber gement-fatehmamode.com; Rue Max Lucchesi; per person without/with half board from Rs 500/800; ❄) Right in the centre of town, these no-frills rooms are about as cheap as things get on the island. Air-con is an option and rooms are basic with private bathroom.

Escale Vacances GUESTHOUSE €€
(Map p154; ☏ 831 2555; www.escale-vacances.com; Rue Johnston, Fond La Digue; s/d incl breakfast €65/100, incl half board €75/120; ❄ ❄) Located just outside the town centre, Port Mathurin's most upmarket option occupies a converted colonial mansion that feels somewhat like an old schoolhouse. Rooms are quiet and well appointed.

 Eating

Port Mathurin has a handful of restaurants, with more options east of town in Anse

aux Anglais. There are several small grocery stores on Rue de la Solidarité and Rue Mamzelle Julia. For quick eats, outlets on Rue de la Solidarité sell *pain fouré* (filled rolls) and noodles for a handful of rupees.

Aux Deux Frères MAURITIAN, INTERNATIONAL €
(Map p154; ☏ 831 0541; 1st fl, Patriko Bldg, Rue François Leguat; pizza from Rs 245, mains Rs 295-460; ◷ 8.30am-2.30pm Mon-Thu, 8.30am-2.30pm & 6.30-10pm Fri & Sat) Perched above a plaza of tour operators, Port Mathurin's slickest haunt serves local and international dishes in swish surrounds. The *marlin fumé avec gingembre* (smoked marlin with ginger) as a starter is small and simple but filled with taste. The restaurant also does pizza, pork brochettes and (when available) Creole sausages.

 Shopping

Care-Co ARTS & CRAFTS
(Map p154; Rue de la Solidarité; ◷ 8am-4pm Mon-Fri, to noon Sat) Care-Co sells coconut-shell items, honey and model boats made by people (mostly beekeepers) with disabilities.

Port Mathurin

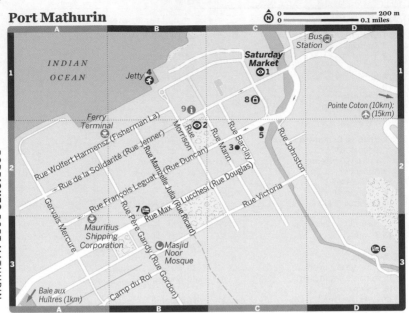

ℹ️ Information

Several banks flank Rue Max Lucchesi.

Free (if slow) wi-fi access is available outside the Alfred Northcoombs Building in central Port Mathurin. The building is home to the **Rodrigues Regional Library** (cnr Rue Morrison & Rue François Leguat; ⊙ 9am-4.30pm Mon-Fri, to 2pm Sat), which offers free wi-fi – hence the laptop-toting locals camped outside, even on weekends.

Discovery Rodrigues (Map p154; ☑ 832 0867; discoveryrodrigues@intnet.mu; Rue de la Solidarité; ⊙ 8am-4pm Mon-Fri, to noon Sat, to 10am Sun) Sharing an office and staff with the tourist office, this body oversees visits to Île aux Cocos. Although it organises tours there, it does not organise boat trips to the island.

Tourist Office (Map p154; ☑ 832 0867; www.tourism-rodrigues.mu; Rue de la Solidarité; ⊙ 8am-4pm Mon-Fri, to noon Sat, to 10am Sun) Small but helpful tourist office opposite La Résidence.

Port Mathurin Pharmacy (☑ 831 2279; Rue de la Solidarité; ⊙ 7.30am-4.30pm Mon-Fri, to 3pm Sat, to 11am Sun) The only pharmacy on the island.

ℹ️ Getting There & Away

Regular, old-school Ashok Leyland buses connect Port Mathurin with the rest of the island, but you may have to change buses in Mont Lubin, the island's high point, where all roads meet.

Around Rodrigues

Most of Rodrigues' more appealing corners lie beyond Port Mathurin, particularly around the southern and eastern coasts and the rugged interior

◉ Sights

★ Trou d'Argent   BEACH

(Map p152) One of the loveliest cove beaches anywhere in the Indian Ocean, this isolated spot, enclosed by low cliffs, is accessible only on foot on the coastal trail (p157) between St François and Graviers. Local legend has it that a pirate once hid his treasure here.

★ François Leguat
Reserve   WILDLIFE RESERVE

(Map p152; ☑ 832 8141; www.tortoisescavere serve-rodrigues.com; Anse Quitor; adult/child incl tortoises & cave Rs 470/235; ⊙ 9am-5pm, tours 9.30am, 10.30am, 1.30pm & 2.30pm) In 1691 François Leguat wrote that there were so many tortoises on Rodrigues that 'one can take more than a hundred steps on their shell without touching the ground'. Sadly the Rodrigues version of the giant tortoise became extinct, but this reserve is recreating the Eden described by the island's early explorers. Hundreds of tortoises from elsewhere (the outcome of a breeding program) roam the grounds, and more than 100,000 indigenous trees have been planted. Cave visits are also possible.

In the **caves**, spirited tour leaders point out quirky rock shapes and discuss the island's interesting geological history. Keep an eye out for the tibia bone of a solitaire bird that juts from the cavern's stone ceiling.

There's also a small enclosure with several giant fruit bats (the island's only endemic mammal) and a handful of recently arrived, critically endangered ploughshare tortoises from Madagascar. The on-site museum recounts the history and settlement of the island, with detailed information about the extinct Rodrigues solitaire, cousin of the dodo.

The reserve is in the island's southwest and is poorly signposted off the main road around 1.5km northeast of the airport.

Grande Montagne
Nature Reserve   NATURE RESERVE

(Map p152; ☑ 831 4558, 5773 6625; www.mauri-tian-wildlife.org; Grande Montagne; adult/child Rs 250/125; ⊙ 8am-3pm Mon-Fri, 8-11am Sat, tours

ISLAND TOURS

JP Excursions (Map p154; ☑ 831 1162, 5875 0730; www.jpexcursion-rodrigues. com; Rue Barclay) Professional outfit offering the full range of boat excursions, car rental, diving, fishing and kitesurfing.

Rotourco (Map p154; ☑ 831 0747; www. rotourco.com; Rue François Leguat) Offers boat tours to Île aux Cocos, as well as car rental (starting from Rs 1400 per day).

2000 Tours (☑ 832 4795; www.rod-rigues-2000tours.com) Local operator offering tours to Île aux Cocos, car rental, diving and kitesurfing.

Mireille (☑ 5492 8537; mireillesagor@ gmail.com) Arranges boat tours to Île aux Cocos and elsewhere, as well as hiking.

9.30am & 1.15pm Mon-Fri, 9.30am Sat) One of the last remaining stands of forest on Rodrigues, this nature reserve crowns the island's summit. The Mauritian Wildlife Foundation (p138) has planted more than 200,000 native plant species across more than 25 hectares, and the restoration of this ecosystem has ensured the survival of the Rodrigues fody and the Rodrigues warbler bird species, as well as the Rodrigues fruit bat. The MWF runs free guided tours weekdays and Saturdays – no need to book.

Otherwise trails pass through the forest – though they're not especially well marked, it's difficult to get too lost. Pick up the useful (and free) *Grande Montagne Nature Reserve Field Guide* at the entrance to help with plant and bird identification. The fine little **information centre** (Map p152; www.mauritian-wildlife.org; ⊙ 8am-3pm Mon-Fri), where guided tours of the reserve begin, has Rodrigues' most complete solitaire skeleton, as well as a skeleton of the extinct giant tortoises once endemic to the island. There's also a small shop.

Jardin des 5 Sens   GARDENS

(Map p152; ☑ 5722 5665; Montagne Bois Noir, Yvoir; adult/child incl tour & small tasting session €16/12; ⊙ 10am-6.30pm mid-Apr–mid-Sep, to 5.30pm mid-Sep–early Oct, last entry 1hr before closing time, tours 10am, 11am, 1pm, 2pm & 3pm) This pretty little botanical garden of indigenous Rodriguan plants is an interesting way to spend an hour, not to mention a good

ÎLE AUX COCOS CALLING

There are 17 small islands sprinkled around Rodrigues' lagoon and perhaps the most interesting of these is Île aux Cocos. Around 1.5km long, and 150m wide at its broadest point, Île aux Cocos is a nature reserve and the only island in the Indian Ocean on which four seabirds – the lesser noddy, brown noddy, fairy tern and sooty tern – all breed. The southern quarter of the island is fenced off as a restricted zone. Elsewhere there is a virgin quality to the place – the lesser noddies and fairy terns are remarkably tame, just as all wildlife (including the ill-fated dodo) was when the first sailors arrived on Mauritius and Rodrigues.

The reserve is overseen by Discovery Rodrigues (p154) – staff meet all boat arrivals and give a brief (and mostly French) overview of the island's more interesting features. The outfit does not, however, organise the boat trips – you will need to make arrangements through your hotel, a tour operator or directly with boat owners.

A trip to Île aux Cocos will cost around Rs 1500 per person if you organise it through your hotel, but it will cost significantly less (Rs 1000 to Rs 1200) if you go directly to the boat owner. This price includes the boat trip, park admission and a picnic lunch.

Most trips depart from **Pointe du Diable** (Map p152), though check with the boat owner when making the booking. If you don't have your own wheels, the owners may be able to arrange a pick-up from your hotel. The departure time could be anywhere from 7am to 10am depending on the tides, and the trip takes an hour each way. You'll probably end up spending around three hours on the island – bring your swimmers.

Boat owners we recommend include:

Rico François (☏875 5270) Departs Pointe du Diable.

Tonio Jolicouer (☏5875 5720) Departs Pointe du Diable.

Berraca Tours (☏831 2198; tropicalguy17@caramail.com) Departs Pointe du Diable.

Joe 'Cool' (☏5876 2826) Departs Pointe du Diable.

Christophe Meunier (☏5875 4442, 429 5045) Departs Anse aux Anglais. Christophe uses a sailing boat (rather than one with an outboard motor) and sometimes factors in extra time for snorkelling.

---

initiative. Time your visit to coincide with lunch at the attached Chez Jeannette (p162).

Caverne Patate
CAVE

(Map p152; tours Rs 120; ⊙tours 9am, 11am, 1pm & 3pm) Caverne Patate, in the island's south-western corner, is an impressive cave system with a few stalagmite and stalactite formations. Visit is by guided tour, during which a guide points out formations with uncanny resemblances to a dodo, Buckingham Palace and even Winston Churchill! The 700m tunnel is an easy walk but gets slippery in wet weather; wear shoes with good grip and take a light jacket. Watch for the spectacular white-tailed tropicbirds soaring overhead before you go underground.

The track to the caves is signposted off the road from La Ferme (on the main road into Rodrigues from the airport) to Petite Butte. Buses en route to La Fourche can drop you at the turn-off.

St Gabriel Church
CHURCH

(Map p152; off Chemin Parc du Nancy, Saint Gabriel) This surprisingly grand church in the middle of Rodrigues has one of the largest congregations in the Port Louis diocese. Constructed between 1936 and 1939, it was built by local volunteers who arduously lugged stone, sand and coral from all corners of the island. Christianity is an integral part of life on the island – hundreds upon hundreds of Rodriguans gather here every Sunday.

🏃 Activities

Birdwatching

Rodrigues is surprisingly well known among bird-watchers, primarily for the continued presence of two species: the Rodrigues warbler (there are now more than 4000 warblers, having recovered from a low of 30 in the 1970s) and the Rodrigues fody (six pairs in 1968, 8000 individuals today). They can be seen across the island, but your best chance to see them is while hiking in the Grande Montagne Nature Reserve (p155).

Diving

Rodrigues' marine environment is remarkably well preserved. The best dive sites (p32), including **La Passe St Francois** which teems with tuna, unicorn fish, groupers, turtles, rays, and jacks the size of small cars, lie off the eastern and southern coasts.

The main dive centres are all based in hotels, but nonguests are always welcome – just ring ahead. Figure on around Rs 1800 for a dive, including equipment.

As a general rule the best season for diving coincides with high season on the island. From October to December expect clear visibility, smooth seas, the possibility of whales, and water temperatures above 28°C. January and February are similar, but with the danger of cyclones. From March to September winds are generally stronger (though they usually ease in September) and water temperatures fall as low as 23°C.

Cotton Dive Centre   DIVING, KITESURFING
(Map p152; ☑ 831 8208, 831 8001; www.cottonbay resortandspa.com; Pointe Coton; ☉ closed Aug) A small PADI-accredited dive centre based at the Cotton Bay Resort & Spa, and run by French expats. Learn to dive packages are available; book ahead for all dives.

Bouba Diving   DIVING
(Map p152; ☑ 5920 0413, 5875 0573; www.bouba diving.com; Mourouk Ebony Hotel, Mourouk; 1/3 dives incl equipment Rs 1850/5270) Professionally run dive centre.

Snorkelling

There's plenty of good snorkelling around the lagoon, but it's usually an add-on to boat excursions, or something you arrange through your hotel by renting snorkelling gear. The most popular spots are on the boat excursion to Île aux Chats (p158), as well as offshore at St François, Anse aux Anglais and Port Sud-Est.

Fishing

Rod Fishing Club   FISHING
(Map p154; ☑ 875 0616; www.rodfishingclub.com; Terre Rouge) The island's leading deep-sea fishing experts make up the Rod Fishing Club, run by Yann Colas. Yann is skipper of the *Black Marlin,* which makes frequent jigging sorties from Port Mathurin. Book through the website and meet at the pier.

DON'T MISS

THE NORTHEASTERN COASTAL WALK

The island's most famous walk (No 4 on the *Carte Verte* map) is the classic, roughly two-hour coastal trail from **Graviers to St François** in the island's east. On the way you'll pass Rodrigues' most stunning stretches of sand, including Trou d'Argent (p155), one of the Indian Ocean's prettiest cove beaches which is the supposed location of a pirate's hidden booty.

If you're relying on public transport, we recommend beginning in Graviers – buses run to Graviers in the morning but are extremely scarce in the afternoon, when you're likely to have far better luck in St François.

Hiking

Hiking is the best way to uncover the island's natural treasures – most notably, its wild, undeveloped beaches. The difficult-to-find *Carte Verte de Rodrigues,* published by the Association Rodrigues Entreprendre Au Féminin, charts the island's eight most popular hikes and provides detailed information on how to access each trailhead using public transport.

When we last checked, the *Carte Verte* was available for purchase (Rs 100) at a kiosk in central Port Mathurin outside the Rodrigues Regional Library (p154). If you find it closed (which is often) or it's run out of stock (ditto), call ☑ 876 9170 and staff should be able to find you a copy of the map. Some hotels might also have one.

Kitesurfing

All the pros agree: Rodrigues is one of the best places in the world to kitesurf. **Nest Kitesurfing School** (Map p152; ☑ 5724 1773, 832 3180; www.thenestkitesurfing.com; Anse Mourouk) and **Tryst Kiteboarding School** (☑ 5875 8457; www.trystkiteboarding.com; 2hr group/private class per person €70/90) are the pick of the island's places. You could also try Cotton Dive Centre.

Some of the world's best kitesurfers descend on Rodrigues in late June or early July for the **Rodrigues International Kitesurfing Festival** (www.rodrigueskitesurf. com; ☉ Jun-Jul), which has been running since 2013.

ÎLE AUX CHATS & ÎLE HERMITAGE

A terrific way to see the southern coast of Rodrigues is to take a half-day boat excursion out into the lagoon. Numerous operators in Port Sud-Est, Mourouk and Graviers, and all hotels, can make the arrangements, which usually include an hour or two of snorkelling (in an area of surprisingly strong currents), a barbecue lunch on Île aux Chats – one of the larger islands of the eastern lagoon – and then a visit to Île Hermitage, a tiny island renowned for its beauty (and possible hidden treasure). Expect to pay around Rs 1000 to Rs 1200 per person.

Ziplining

Tyrodrig ADVENTURE SPORTS
(Map p152; ☑5499 6970; www.facebook.com/tyro drig.ilerodrigues; Montagne Malgache; zipline per person Rs 1000; ☺9am-noon & 1-5pm) If your idea of fun is zipping down a rope suspended over a canyon, then Tyrodrig is all yours. Five cables hang across the void, ranging from 110m to 420m, with a drop beneath you of between 50m and 100m. It's signposted off the main road between Mont Lubin and Grande Montagne. It claims to have the Indian Ocean's highest zipline.

★☆ Festivals & Events

Fête du Poisson CULTURAL
(☺1st week Mar) Rodrigues lives and breathes fish, and the Fête du Poisson marks the opening of the fishing season. It's celebrated with all sorts of festivities, including fishing expeditions – and lots of eating.

Festival Kréol CULTURAL
(☺Dec) The three-day Festival Kréol entails traditional Creole ceremonies and much dancing in the streets across Rodrigues.

🛏 Sleeping

The main concentration of hotels and guesthouses is found 2km east of Port Mathurin at Anse aux Anglais, at St François on the eastern coast and along the southern coast. Elsewhere the guesthouses in the quieter parts of the island offer the get-away-from-it-all experience par excellence.

La Cabane d'Ete APARTMENT €
(Map p152; ☑831 0747; www.lacabanedete.com; Baie Malagache; s/d incl breakfast €40/60) Adorable studio accommodation in Baie Malagache, southwest of Port Mathurin, is what's on offer here. The rooms have a hint of whitewash and bamboo about them, and the location is as far from tourist Rodrigues, such as it is, as you can get. Bookings can be made through Rotourco (p155) in Port Mathurin.

Chez Claudine GUESTHOUSE €
(Map p152; ☑831 8242; cbmoneret@intnet.mu; St François; per person incl half board Rs 1600) When St François was known for its end-of-the-world seclusion, this charming Tudor-style lodge was the only place to hang your hat. The well-maintained rooms have moved into a newer building out the back and are large, light and airy. Meals here are delicious, the owners are friendly and you're well placed for walks and beaches along the east coast.

La Paillote Creole GUESTHOUSE €
(Map p152; ☑5701 0448; www.facebook.com/lap aillottecreole; Graviers; per person incl breakfast/half board Rs 850/1100) Simple but excellent thatched rondavels with tiled floors set in well-maintained grounds win universal acclaim from budget travellers. The garden needs time to mature, but the owners are friendly and there's a wonderfully end-of-the-road feel here.

Residence Foulsafat GUESTHOUSE €
(Map p152; ☑831 1760; www.residencefoulsafat. com; Jean Tac; d incl half board €65) High in the hills with memorable views of the infinite blue, this friendly option has five houses, each with a unique design and theme. Our favourite is the adorable honeymooners' cottage with stone walls and attached gazebo covered with gingerbread trim.

Ti Pavillon GUESTHOUSE €
(Map p152; ☑875 0707; www.tipavillon.com; Anse aux Anglais; s/d Rs 1200/1700; ❄@🛜) This friendly spot, run by the same people that brought you Auberge du Lagon (p160), welcomes guests with wallet-pleasing prices and simple digs painted in bright primary colours. The common spaces are cluttered with wonderful bits and bobs.

Chinese lanterns and handmade woodcuts dangle overhead, tropical fish blow bubbles in the aquarium, furnishings are made from a ragtag assortment of tree stumps and patio furniture, and staircases seem to ramble off in different directions, much like an Escher drawing.

Piment Guesthouse
GUESTHOUSE €

(Map p152; ☏831 8260; www.ilerodriguesgitepiment.com; St François; per person incl half board Rs 1100; ❋ ❢) The rooms here are clean and large, if a little uninspiring, but some come with a kitchen. The family who owns the place is friendly, you're a five-minute walk from the beach and the whole establishment is blissfully quiet.

Chez Jeannette
GUESTHOUSE €

(Le Tropical; Map p152; ☏831 5860; www.gite-letropical.com; Montagne Bois Noir; per adult/child incl half board Rs 1400/700; ❢) Set high on a hill, this fine house, built partly of stone, has eight large, simple rooms that are blissfully quiet. The kitchen (p162) serves up fine food and there's even an on-site botanical garden (p155). The perfect mountain retreat as an overall place to stay, though the rooms are a little overpriced.

Auberge Lagon Bleu
GUESTHOUSE €

(Map p152; ☏831 0075; www.aubergelagonbleu.com; Caverne Provert; s/d/tr Rs 650/850/1100; ❋) Wicker baskets and vibrant artwork abound at this casual guesthouse on the road towards Jean Tac. Guests congregate in the sociable eating area tucked under tin roofing and drooping laundry lines. Colourful paintings on the walls spruce up the otherwise spartan bedrooms. It's an additional Rs 600 per person for half board.

★ La Belle Rodriguaise
GUESTHOUSE €€

(Map p152; ☏5875 0556; www.labellerodriguaise.com; Graviers; incl half board s Rs 2450-3350, d Rs 3800-5600; ❋ ❧) Laval and Françoise Baptiste's inviting seaside retreat has sun-drenched rooms in charming *case*-style abodes, all with wonderfully unobstructed sea views. Up the hill guests will find an amoeba-shaped pool and a breezy dining room set on a sweeping veranda. There's a real warmth to the welcome here, the food (p162) is outstanding and the whole place has a wonderfully remote feel.

Le Pandanus
GUESTHOUSE €€

(Map p152; ☏5440 2580; Baie Malgache; s/d from €46/80) This excellent little guesthouse along the northwestern coast is a real find. The rooms are more warmly decorated than most in this price category and the welcome is similarly warm. The sea views from most rooms are big, wide and wonderful.

Kafe Marron
GUESTHOUSE €€

(Map p152; ☏5706 0195; www.kafemarron.com; Pointe Coton; r Rs 2200-3500; Ⓟ❋❢) A block (or a rather long stone's throw through the *filao* trees) from Pointe Coton's quiet beach, Kafe Marron is a stylish little guesthouse that blends the traditional idea of a *chambre d'hôte* with the modern comforts of a quietly sophisticated B&B. Rooms have tiled floors, ample space and subtle designer touches. Run by Dorothy Lavendhomme, it's a terrific choice.

RODRIGUES AROUND RODRIGUES

CAFÉ MARRON: THE RAREST PLANT ON EARTH

In 1980 a teacher on Rodrigues asked his students to bring in a local plant as part of a school project. One student brought in a plant that baffled everyone. Finally experts at the UK's Kew Gardens identified the plant as café marron (*Ramosmania rodriguesii*), which was long thought extinct. Locals had for centuries used the plant as an aphrodisiac and as a treatment for sexually transmitted diseases, and news of its discovery leaked out. The plant was fenced off, but locals kept finding a way through. In 1986 an international operation was mounted: a cutting of the plant was flown from Rodrigues to London, where, within 24 hours, it was in Kew Gardens.

Cuttings were taken and it's from these that the Mauritian Wildlife Foundation has been able to grow more in its plant nursery. The plant is not yet out of danger – one of the plants in the Grande Montagne Nature Reserve (p155) was stolen (a younger, yet-to-flower replacement is labelled and can be seen alongside the main trail), as was another from the foundation's nursery. Even so, more than 50 have been successfully planted in the reserve. No other wild plants have ever been found, but – for the first time in living memory – the original plant recently began to grow fruit.

RODRIGUES AROUND RODRIGUES

Auberge du Lagon
GUESTHOUSE €€

(Map p152; ☎ 831 2825, 5875 0707; www.tipavillon. com; Jean Tac; s/d incl breakfast €50/63; ☒) Down a gravel track in Jean Tac, east of Anse aux Anglais, this fine guesthouse has big-horizon views and a sense of having left the world behind. The garden needs time to grow, but the rooms have a smart-casual look that blends simplicity with carefully chosen ochre and burnt-orange hues. There's also a breezy bar and an infinity pool.

Villas Vetiver
BUNGALOW €€

(Map p152; ☎ 5498 2870; www.villasvetiver.com; Jean Tac; r from €108; P☀☎☒) On its own promontory of land, and with nothing to interrupt the big-sea, big-sky views, Villas Vetiver has bungalows and a villa with simple wooden furnishings, tiled floors and a tremendous sense of light and space. The property could do with a few more trees, but it does capture that wild and bare look that's so characteristic of the island.

Koki Boner
BUNGALOW €€

(Map p152; ☎ 5916 6032, 5708 3742; www.face book.com/RodriguesVillaKokiBoner; Pointe Coton; s/d from €75/80; ☀☎☒) The two-bedroom bungalows here have a terrific location, and while they don't have a lot of character, they're modern and supremely comfortable. The beach is just across the road through the trees.

Le Kono Kono Bungalow Hotel
BUNGALOW €€

(Map p152; ☎ 831 0759; www.lekonokono.com; Jean Tac; s/d incl half board €58/92) The furnishings couldn't be simpler, but there's something that we like about this place, out in Jean Tac, east of Anse aux Anglais. There's a relaxed vibe, there are big-sky panoramas and the brick-walled, tiled-floored bungalows with pastel shades are tidy.

Coco Villas
GUESTHOUSE €€

(Map p152; ☎ 831 0449; www.rodrigues-cocovilla. com; Caverne Provert; per person incl half board Rs 1450-2000; ☀☎) Simple rooms at this family-run place make a quieter alternative to Anse aux Anglais just down the road. Rooms are nothing special, but the price is about right. Oh, and fabulous sunsets right outside your door.

Le Récif
GUESTHOUSE €€

(Map p152; ☎ 831 1804; www.lerecifhotel.com; Caverne Provert; s incl half board Rs 1400-3760, d incl half board Rs 2350-3760; ☀) Perched on the cliff just east of Anse aux Anglais, Le Récif has fabulous views from its balcony over the emerald lagoon. We reckon it's a touch overpriced in high season and it can have a vaguely abandoned air when things are quiet, but the rooms are large and the sunset views are hard to beat anywhere on the island.

★ Bakwa Lodge
HOTEL €€€

(Map p152; ☎ 832 3700; www.bakwalodge.com; Var Brulé, Mourouk; s/d from €125/220; P☀☎) One of the most beautiful places to stay on the island, this all-white oasis where the road ends in Mourouk is classy, understated luxury. Large and flooded with natural light, the rooms are decorated with offcuts from old wooden pirogues, and most have both indoor and outdoor showers. The lovely beach helps make up for the lack of a swimming pool.

★ Tekoma
HOTEL €€€

(Map p152; ☎ 483 4970; www.tekoma-hotel.com; Anse Ally, St François; s/d incl half board €310/359; ☀@☎☒) 🏊 Arguably the finest address on Rodrigues, this stunning place has supremely comfortable, free-standing cabins arrayed around a rocky headland that slopes down to a good beach, and there's a blissful sense of isolation. It also has the aim of being powered entirely by renewable energy, and the food is superb.

★ Pirate Lodge
HOTEL €€€

(Map p152; ☎ 831 8775; www.piratelodge. com; St François; ste incl breakfast from €150; ☒) These attractive four- to six-person apartments are set in a scenic palm grove visited by chirping birds. The outside design incorporates colourful Creole- and French-colonial-inspired details, while the interiors are stylish and sophisticated with classy knick-knacks dotting the living rooms and fully equipped kitchens.

Mourouk Ebony Hotel
HOTEL €€€

(Map p152; ☎ 832 3351; www.mouroukebonyhotel. com; Mourouk; s/d incl half board from €146/214; ☀☒) The Mourouk Ebony waits at the end of a wiggling mountain road, and is easily recognised from afar by its bright-orange roofing. The grounds feature gorgeous gardens full of orchids and wild-flowers that abut the rather lovely beach. The rooms are a little like Rodrigues itself: occasionally stylish, more often rustic and slightly faded.Gentle Creole beats waft over the lobby's hand-dyed wicker lounge chairs.

RODRIGUES CUISINE

The highlight of any visit to Rodrigues is sampling the unique local cuisine at one of the island's many *tables d'hôtes*. Rodriguans cook a variety of recipes that are quite different from those of their Mauritian neighbours – less emphasis is placed on spiciness and most meals are cooked with minimal amounts of oil. And while octopus dishes have colonised the mainland, the passion for (and most of the actual) *poulpe* or *ourite* comes from Rodrigues.

Meal prices at the island's best and most well-known *tables d'hôtes* range from Rs 400 to Rs 700. You should always call at least a day ahead to make a reservation.

A list of Rodrigues' must-eats, according to Françoise Baptiste, author, hostess and chef extraordinaire.

➡ *Ourite* – octopus salad with lemon juice, olive oil, pepper, onions and salt. The dried variety has a rather pungent taste and admittedly isn't for everyone.

➡ *Vindaye d'ourite* – boiled tender octopus flavoured with grated curcuma (such as ginger or turmeric), garlic, vinegar, lemon juice and a sprinkle of local spices.

➡ *Saucisses créole* – a variety of meats that are dried and cured locally.

➡ *La torte Rodriguaise* – a small cake of papaya, pineapple or coconut mixed with a cream made from a local root called *corn-floeur.*

Cotton Bay Hotel   HOTEL €€€

(Map p152; ☑ 831 8001; www.cottonbayresort andspa.com; Pointe Coton; s €175-285, d €200-375, ste €280-450, all incl half board; P ❄ ⊛ ≋) Still going strong after nearly 25 years in the business, charming Cotton Bay is the island's oldest hotel. The design scheme has an appealing Creole motif: floral trim, rustic wood furnishings, bamboo ceilings and tropically inspired prints adorn the rooms. Perks include a lovely pirogue-themed restaurant, outings on a private catamaran and endless streams of honey-tinged sand.

Les Cocotiers   HOTEL €€€

(Map p152; ☑ 831 1059; www.cocotiersrodrigues. com; Anse aux Anglais; s/d with half board from €99/149; ⊛ ⊛ ≋) A great choice at the end of the coastal road, this friendly resort comes with an airy restaurant, an inviting swimming pool and a popular dive centre. Vaco paintings adorn the walls in some rooms, and the beds have colourful duvets to match. Service can be patchy at reception.

✖ Eating

If you have your own wheels, there are plenty of good places to eat, though they're widely scattered around the island. St François and Pointe Coton on the island's east coast have a small but excellent selection of places.

★ Chez Robert et Solange   SEAFOOD €

(Map p152; ☑ 5733 1968; St François; mains Rs 50-400; ⊙ 11am-3pm Tue-Sun) This place is the essence of Rodrigues: fresh fish cooked in simple surroundings by the sea. It's 100m through the trees from the beach and with expertly cooked food. When you sit down, you'll be offered whatever it has (usually grilled chicken, grilled fish and octopus and papaya salads).

If you're going to splurge on lobster, do it here (around Rs 1500 per kilogram) if it has it.

Le Marlin Bleu   SEAFOOD €

(Map p152; ☑ 832 0701; Anse aux Anglais; mains Rs 275-550; ⊙ 10am-10.30pm Wed-Mon) The coolest, most sociable spot in Anse aux Anglais, this restaurant gets the thumbs up from expats and is dominated by larger-than-life Mega, the friendly owner who makes sure that everyone's having a good time. The food is excellent (we especially loved the octopus salad), with a good mix of seafood, pizza and local dishes.

Mazavaroo   MAURITIAN €

(Map p152; ☑ 5724 2282; St François; mains around Rs 300-650; ⊙ 11am-3pm Thu-Tue) Hikers tackling a scenic east-coast jaunt can take a break at this casual, lunch-only affair with painted pastel tables. Savour the home-cooked seafood (smoked marlin, grilled marlin, calamari, prawns and lobster) or house speciality *ceviché de thon* (like a tuna tartare).

Le Pandanus
MAURITIAN €

(Map p152; ☑5440 2580; Baie Malgache; mains Rs 250-380; ⊙noon-2.30pm) This gem of a place, one of a few out on the north-western coast, has an elevated dining room that looks straight out to sea. The meals are lovingly prepared and the usual *table d'hôte* hospitality and authenticity is at the heart of everything it does. The seafood is excellent, with octopus especially well prepared.

Chez Paulina
MAURITIAN €

(La Case Mama; Map p152; ☑5875 9201, 831 5845; Montagne Malgache; mains Rs 250-380) On the road down to Tyrodig, this terrific little place is often packed out at lunch time, especially on weekends. The price-to-quality ratio is particularly high and it does wonderful things on a shoestring with octopus, calamari and fish; its curries are especially worth trying.

Madame Larose
MAURITIAN €

(Map p152; ☑876 1350; Pointe Coton; mains Rs 280-650; ⊙noon-3pm & 6-10pm) On the road down to the beach in Pointe Coton, Madame Larose is a little local gem, with no-frills service and surrounds but good, honest cooking. Fresh fish, an above-average *salade d'ourite* (octopus salad), a mean chicken curry and good salads are among the dishes on offer.

★La Belle Rodriguaise
RODRIGUAN €€

(Map p152; ☑832 4040, 832 4359; www.labellerodriguaise.com; Graviers; 3-course meal Rs 800; ⊙11.30am-2.30pm) Perfected recipes by Françoise, author of a respected Rodriguan cookbook, are served on a breezy veranda with never-ending ocean views. Meals are mostly for guests of the hotel (p159), but ring ahead if you'd like to crash the party.

Chez Jeannette
RODRIGUAN €€

(Le Tropical; Map p152; ☑831 5860; www.gite-letropical.com; Montagne Bois Noir; meals Rs 450-600; ⊙11am-2pm & 7-9pm) Traditional Rodriguan flavours are what you'll get at this friendly guesthouse (p159) hidden in the hills. Dishes always feature an assortment of vegetables grown in the property's gardens.

🛍 Shopping

Miel Victoria
FOOD

(Map p152; ☑5876 4695, 5939 3634; off Chemin Parc du Nancy; ⊙9am-3pm Mon-Fri, 10am-2pm Sat) Rodrigues honey is renowned throughout the Indian Ocean and is often used by

Mauritius' finest chefs. It also makes a fabulous souvenir of a visit to the island and this is the easiest place to buy it. If you ask, they'll show you around the hives out the back.

ℹ Information

A growing number of hotels and guesthouses have wi-fi internet connections, but usually only in public areas. Mont Lubin and La Ferme have banks, and there's an ATM at the airport. There's also an **ATM** at the **police station** near Plaine Corail.

Queen Elizabeth Hospital (☑831 1628) The island's main hospital is at Crève Coeur, immediately east of Port Mathurin.

Understand Rodrigues

Rodrigues Today

Many in Rodrigues feel themselves ignored by policymakers on the main island of Mauritius and some are looking to take the next step. As such, complete independence remains a fervent desire for some and, in April 2010, the Muvman Independantis Rodriguais (MIR; Rodrigues Independent Movement) was launched when two candidates ran for government positions as 'Rodriguans' rather than 'Mauritians'. Although they were rebuffed the issue won't go away any time soon.

By 2012 the Rodrigues People's Organisation (OPR; Organisation du Peuple Rodriguais) had won back control of the regional assembly, and picked up two seats in broader Mauritian elections in 2014. As such, the independence voice remains occasionally noisy but is yet to make significant headway.

In the meantime Rodrigues' regional assembly is trying to tackle the overriding problems of population growth, poverty and critical water shortages. This third problem is a grave one, and there is year-round rationing. New hotels and many existing ones are being forced to look towards sustainable water options (including desalination), and it's an issue of long-term concern for the island.

History

Rodrigues is named after the Portuguese navigator Don Diégo Rodriguez, who was the first European to discover the uninhabited island in 1528. Dutch sailors were the next to pay a call, albeit very briefly, in 1601, followed a few years later by the French.

At first Rodrigues was simply a place where ships could take refuge from storms and replenish their supplies of fresh water and meat. Giant tortoises were especially prized since they could be kept alive on board for months. Over the years thousands were taken or killed until they completely died out. Rodrigues also had a big flightless bird, the solitaire, which went the same sorry way as its distant cousin, the dodo.

The first serious attempt at colonisation occurred in 1691 when Frenchman François Leguat and a band of seven Huguenot companions fled religious persecution at home in search of a 'promised land'. Crops grew well and the island's fauna and flora were a source of wonder. Even so, after two years, life on a paradise island began to pall, not least due to the lack of female company. With no boat of their own (the ship they arrived on failed to return as promised), Leguat and his friends built a craft out of driftwood and eventually made it to Mauritius.

In 1735 the French founded a permanent colony on Rodrigues with a small settlement at Port Mathurin, but the colony never really prospered. When the British – who wanted a base from which to attack French-ruled Mauritius – invaded in 1809, they were met with little resistance.

In 1967 Rodriguans distinguished themselves by voting against independence from Britain by a whopping 90% (the rest of Mauritius voted strongly in favour). It was a dramatic illustration of the difference in outlook between the two islands. Following independence Rodriguans continued to argue that their needs were significantly different from those of the rest of the country and that, in any case, they were being neglected by the central government.

The campaign was led by Serge Clair and his Organisation du Peuple de Rodrigues (OPR), founded in 1976. His patience and political skill eventually paid off. In 2001 it was announced that Rodrigues would be allowed a degree of autonomy, notably in socioeconomic affairs and in the management of its natural resources. The following year 18 councillors were elected; the Regional Assembly was formally inaugurated in 2002 with Serge Clair as chief commissioner.

Survival Guide

ℹ Getting There & Away

AIR

The island's main **Air Mauritius office** (☏ 831 1632; www.airmauritius.com; ADS Bldg, Rue Max Lucchesi) is in Port Mathurin. There is also an office at the **airport** (☏ 832 7700) that opens for arrivals and departures. It's a good idea to phone the airline the day before you leave, just to make sure there's been no change to the schedule. For most of the year there are just two flights a day. Whenever you travel, book early, as seats can be hard to come by if you leave it late.

There is a luggage limit of 15kg per person (unless you have an onward connection with an airline allowing more – note that the onward connection must be leaving within 24 hours), with excess charged at Rs 150 per kilogram.

SEA

The M/V *Anna* and M/S *Mauritius Trochetia* make the voyage from Port Louis to Rodrigues two to four times a month, docking at the **passenger terminal** (Map p154; Rue Wolfert Harmensz) in Port Mathurin. Services are operated by the Mauritius Shipping Corporation (p146) and take around 36 hours. Fares vary with the seasons and demand.

ℹ Getting Around

BICYCLE

If your hotel or guesthouse doesn't offer bike rental, contact Rotourco (p155) or one of the other travel agencies in Port Mathurin. The going

---

ARRIVING IN RODRIGUES

Flights arrive at **Sir Gaetan Duval airport** (Plaine Corail Airport; Map p152; ☏ 832 7888) at the southwestern tip of the island. A public bus runs between the airport and Port Mathurin roughly every 30 to 40 minutes from 6am to 4pm. The most hassle-free way to get to and from the airport is to pre-organise a ride with your accommodation of choice. Some hotels and guesthouses will include the price of a pick-up in their room rate. If they don't, expect to pay around €27 for a two-way transfer. If you're lucky enough to find a taxi waiting at the airport, figure on paying Rs 750 to Port Mathurin.

CLIMATE CHANGE & TRAVEL

Every form of transport that relies on carbon-based fuel generates CO_2, the main cause of human-induced climate change. Modern travel is dependent on aeroplanes, which might use less fuel per kilometre per person than most cars but travel much greater distances. The altitude at which aircraft emit gases (including CO_2) and particles also contributes to their climate change impact. Many websites offer 'carbon calculators' that allow people to estimate the carbon emissions generated by their journey and, for those who wish to do so, to offset the impact of the greenhouse gases emitted with contributions to portfolios of climate-friendly initiatives throughout the world. Lonely Planet offsets the carbon footprint of all staff and author travel.

rate is around Rs 200 to Rs 250 per day for a bike. Note that unless you're in it for the exercise, we recommend a scooter over a bicycle, as many of the interior roads can be discouragingly hilly.

BUS

The main **bus station** (Map p154; Anse aux Anglais Rd) is in Port Mathurin. In addition to the airport bus, the most useful routes are those to Grand Baie and Pointe Coton in the island's east, and to Gravier, Port Sud-Est and Rivière Cocos on the south coast. All apart from the Grand Baie buses pass through Mont Lubin in the centre of the island. Most buses operate every 30 to 60 minutes from about 7am to 4pm Monday to Saturday. Sunday services are fairly sporadic. Expect to pay Rs 15 to Rs 40 depending on your destination.

CAR & MOTORCYCLE

The road system in Rodrigues has improved enormously in recent years and sealed roads now lead to most parts of the island. Though 4WD vehicles are no longer strictly necessary, most hire cars are still sturdy pick-ups.

Car rental can be arranged through most hotels and guesthouses and local tour operators, who will deliver all over the island. Expect to pay at least Rs 1400 per day; the price is usually the same whether you have a sedan or a pick-up. Most importantly make sure you have sufficient petrol before setting off for the day as there are only three petrol stations on the island – **Mont Lubin** (Mont Lubin), **Port Mathurin** (Rue Max Lucchesi; ☉ 6am-6.30pm Mon-Sat, to 3pm Sun) and **near the airport** – though distances are small.

Three recommended rental agencies to contact in advance: JP Excursions, 2000 Tours and Rotourco (see p155).

If your hotel or guesthouse doesn't offer motorcycle or scooter rental, contact Rotourco or one of the other travel agencies in Port Mathurin. The going rate is around Rs 600 to Rs 650 per day for a scooter. It costs Rs 350 to fill a scooter's petrol tank.

TAXI

Most taxis on Rodrigues are 4WD pick-ups. Expect to pay between Rs 500 and Rs 1000 depending on location. You can also hire taxis by the day for an island tour; expect to pay Rs 2000 to Rs 3000.

JUSTIN FOULKES/LONELY PLANET ©

A Glimpse of Paradise

Beaches that defy all superlatives, wild landscapes that will forever be etched into your memory, ample adventure options, captivating festivals and a glimpse of history – it's impossible to be bored in Mauritius, Réunion and the Seychelles. Paradise found? You be the judge.

Contents
→ **Outdoor Adventures**
→ **History & Culture**
→ **Idyllic Beaches**
→ **The Ultimate Honeymoon**

Above Grand Anse beach (p307), La Digue

Outdoor Adventures

Sure, these divine islands strewn across the peacock-blue Indian Ocean were designed for lounging on a beach or luxuriating in sensuous nature. But when you've finished sipping your cocktail, you may want to get the blood flowing a little more. Plenty of adventure options are readily available.

Underwater Activities

Mauritius, Réunion and the Seychelles are a diver's mecca thanks to a combination of unique features. Healthy reefs, canyon-like terrain, shallow shelves, exciting shipwrecks, seamounts and quick shoreline drop-offs give snorkellers and divers almost instant access to a variety of environments. The water is warm and clear, and teeming with life from the tiniest juvenile tropical fish to the largest pelagic creature.

Canyoning

There's no better way to immerse yourself in grandiose scenery than by exploring the atmospheric canyons in the Cirque de Cilaos or Cirque de Salazie in Réunion; expect various jumps, leaps in crystal-clear natural pools and rappelling. In Mauritius, adventurers can abseil down the seven chutes at Tamarin Falls (p101).

Hiking

Criss-crossed with a network of paths ranging from simple nature trails to more challenging itineraries, Réunion has all the flavours of superlative hiking. Mauritius and Rodrigues also boast excellent walking options. The biggest surprise? The Seychelles. On top of world-renowned beaches, this archipelago offers divine coastal ambles and lovely jungle walks.

White-Water Rafting

The wealth of scenic rivers that decorates eastern Réunion make it a water lover's dream destination. Rivière des Marsouins, Rivière des Roches and Rivière Langevin offer top-class runs to get the blood racing.

1. Woman hiking on Praslin island (p298), Seychelles **2.** Rivière Langevin (p245), Réunion Island **3.** Freediving, Réunion island

3

History & Culture

Although many come to Réunion, Mauritius and the Seychelles for the incredible beaches and nature, these islands have rich and diverse cultures, influenced by the waves of migrants who gradually populated the islands. Culture buffs with a penchant for architecture and festivals will be in seventh heaven.

Multiculturalism

You'll see almost every shade of skin and hair imaginable, arising from a mixture of African, Indian, Chinese, Arab and French genes. Don't be surprised to see a cathedral, a Tamil temple, a mosque and a pagoda lying almost side by side.

Cultural & Religious Festivals

Fabulous festivals provide visitors with a peek into local culture. Divali, the Festival of Lights, is celebrated in all three islands in October or November. In Mauritius and Réunion, impressive fire-walking ceremonies take place in December or January. The Seychelles prides itself on its exuberant Festival Kréole.

1. Tamil temple Chapelle Front de Mer (p253), Ste-Suzanne 2. Eureka (p60), a unique Creole house in Moka 3. Festival Kréol (p24), Seychelles

Creole Architecture

Some wonderfully preserved colonial buildings can be found in Réunion, Mauritius and the Seychelles. From splendid plantation houses and captivating mansions to humble *cases créoles* (traditional Creole homes) and grand colonial buildings harking back to the French East India Company, there's much to be savoured.

Music & Dance

In this region of the Indian Ocean, from the smallest village to the largest city, music and dance are part of daily life. In June, top-name *maloya* (traditional Creole music from Réunion), *séga* (Creole music), salsa, reggae and electro performers from throughout the Indian Ocean and beyond gather in St-Pierre during the three-day Sakifo festival.

Idyllic Beaches

Believe the hype: the Seychelles and Mauritius have some of the most dreamy and dramatic beaches you'll find this side of Bora Bora. Take your pick!

Anse Cocos (La Digue)

Anse Cocos (p307) is a died-and-gone-to-heaven vision of a beach – a frost-white strip of sand fringed by turquoise waters. It can only be reached by foot, meaning that it always feels secluded.

Anse Lazio (Praslin)

Up on Praslin's northwestern coast, Anse Lazio (p298) consistently ranks in traveller surveys among the world's most beautiful beaches – it's bookended by granite piles, fringed with palms and bathed in waters so salty you'll float.

Anse Source d'Argent (La Digue)

OK, we thought the brochure spiel about Anse Source d'Argent (p307) being the most photogenic beach in the world was hype until we clapped eyes on its crystal-line waters and powder-soft sands. It's even more astounding in real life.

1. Anse Lazio (p298), Praslin **2.** Anse Source d'Argent (p307), La Digue **3.** Pointe d'Esny (p109), Mauritius

Pointe d'Esny (Mauritius)

This is it – the celebrity beach of southern Mauritius is Pointe d'Esny (p109). Immense, crystalline and glossy, it doesn't disappoint the bevy of swimmers and snorkellers who dabble in its gorgeous, lucent depths.

Rodrigues' East Coast

Between Graviers and St François on Rodrigues' east coast, the jagged coastline is regularly punctuated by appealing coves and stretches of gorgeous beach – the best is Trou d'Argent (p155). They're totally secluded and there's no road here.

Frégate (p319), Seychelles

The Ultimate Honeymoon

White-sand beaches. Secluded coves. Coral-coloured sunsets. Swish hotels. Hushed spas. It's not surprising that honeymooners and those seeking a glamorous tropical getaway have long had the Seychelles and Mauritius at the top of their wish lists.

Frégate (Seychelles)

If you want to live out that stranded-on-a-deserted-island fantasy, you've come to the right place. The 16 opulent villas at Frégate (p319) are so delicious you might not want to leave, except for a beauty treatment in the serene spa.

North Island (Seychelles)

Somewhere close to the pinnacle of Indian Ocean romance, sublime North Island (p318) is the ideal combination of blissful isolation, extraordinary natural beauty and faultless levels of luxury. Oh, and you'll have a butler, too.

Le Saint Géran (Mauritius)

Le Saint Géran (p124) is a sumptuous, impressive place that manages to get it right on so many levels – it's classy and stylish without being too formal, it's romantic without being too quiet and it's welcoming to families without allowing kids to run riot.

Praslin (Seychelles)

For couples in search of an intimate paradise, Château de Feuilles (p303) on Praslin is an extraordinary place to stay. Perched on a beautiful headland with stupendous vistas, this sweet hideaway has nine stone-walled villas dotted around manicured tropical gardens. The uber-romantic poolside restaurant and hilltop Jacuzzi add to the experience.

North Island (p318), Seychelles

Réunion

☎ 262 / POP 865,000

Best Places to Eat

➡ L'Instant Présent (p242)
➡ L'Eveil des Sens – Le Blue Margouillat (p202)
➡ Auberge Paysanne Le Palmier (p249)
➡ Villa Marthe (p220)
➡ Chez Éva Annibal (p256)

Best Places to Stay

➡ Senteur Vanille (p191)
➡ Rougail Mangue (p246)
➡ La Maison de Rosalie (p260)
➡ Diana Dea Lodge & Spa (p258)

Why Go?

Jutting out of the ocean like a basaltic shield cloaked in green, Réunion is a scenically magical island that enjoys a truly astonishing diversity of landscapes. Expect awesome mountains, emerald forests, tumbling waterfalls, soul-stirring panoramas, energetic coastal cities and a sprinkling of white- or black-sand beaches – not to mention the formidable Piton de la Fournaise, one of the world's most accessible active volcanoes. With its extraordinarily varied terrain, Réunion is a dream destination for lovers of the outdoors. Hiking is the number one activity, but paragliding, canyoning, mountain biking, rafting, diving, whale watching and horse riding are also readily available.

But it's not all about nature, landscapes and adrenaline – Réunion has its cultural gems as well, including stunning Creole architecture in cute-as-can-be villages as well as colourful religious buildings and festivals.

When to Go

➡ Réunion's climate experiences only two distinct seasons: the hot, rainy summer from December to April and the cool, dry winter from late April to November. Temperatures on the coast average 22°C in winter and 27°C in summer. In the mountains they drop to 11°C and 18°C, respectively.

➡ Peak tourist season is during the French school holidays from July to early September. From October through to the New Year holidays is also busy, but after this everything eases down during cyclone-prone February and March.

➡ The drier winter months are the most favourable for hiking, as some of the trails are simply impassable when it's wet. The east coast is considerably wetter than the west.

➡ Whale-watching season runs from June to October.

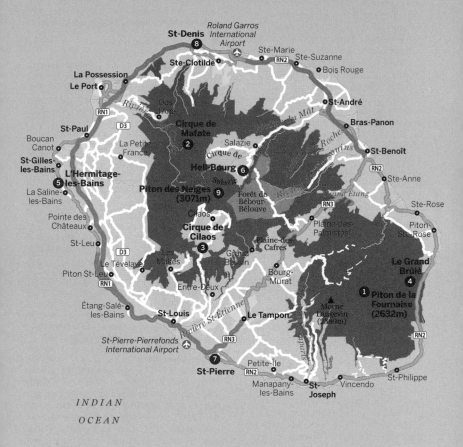

Réunion Highlights

1 **Piton de la Fournaise** (p229) Climbing up to the crater rim and staring down into the abyss.

2 **Cirque de Mafate** (p223) Hiking one of the Indian Ocean's greatest multi-day trails.

3 **Cirque de Cilaos** (p207) Canyoning within the island's most grandiose scenery.

4 **Le Grand Brûlé** (p250) Gazing over the moonscape of this black lava field.

5 **L'Hermitage-les-Bains** (p195) Immersing yourself in the island's steamy nightlife.

6 **Hell-Bourg** (p217) Strolling this picturesque town and soaking up its laid-back mountain atmosphere.

7 **St-Pierre** (p233) Embracing the town that is the heart and soul of Réunion.

8 **St-Denis** (p176) Going heritage hunting among the Creole buildings.

9 **Piton des Neiges** (p211) Huffing to the top for sensational views.

ST-DENIS

POP 145,300

Francophiles will feel comfortable in St-Denis (san-de-*nee*), the capital of Réunion. Except for the palms and flamboyant trees to remind you that you're somewhere sunnier (and hotter), St-Denis could be easily mistaken for a French provincial enclave, with a flurry of brasseries, bistros and *boulangeries*.

With most of Réunion's tourist attractions located elsewhere on the island, most visitors only stay long enough to rent a car before dashing off to more magnetic locations. But St-Denis warrants more than a fleeting glance. Scratch beneath the French polish and you'll soon realise that the city also has an undeniably Creole soul, with some delightful colonial and religious buildings and a casual multi-ethnic atmosphere.

If that's not enough, there are always epicurean indulgences. Sip a black coffee at a chic pavement cafe listening to a *séga* (traditional African music and dance) or *maloya* (traditional dance music of Réunion) soundtrack or indulge in fine dining at a gourmet restaurant.

History

St-Denis was founded in 1668 by the first governor Étienne Regnault, who named the settlement after a ship that ran aground here. But St-Denis didn't really start to develop until the governor Mahé de Labourdonnais moved the capital here from St-Paul in 1738; the harbour was in general more sheltered and easier to defend, and water more abundant.

The 19th century ushered in St-Denis' golden age. As money poured in from the sugar plantations, the town's worthies built themselves fine mansions, some of which can still be seen along Rue de Paris and in the surrounding streets. But in the late 1800s the bottom dropped out of the sugar market and the good times came to a stuttering end. St-Denis' fortunes only began to revive when it became the new departmental capital in 1946. To cope with the influx of civil servants, financiers and office workers, the city expanded rapidly eastwards along the coast and up the mountains behind. Even today the cranes are much in evidence as St-Denis struggles to house its ever-growing population.

◉ Sights

St-Denis is devoid of beach, but it has a gaggle of well-preserved colonial buildings harking back to the city's heyday in the 19th century.

The larger colonial piles are mainly strung out along Rue de Paris, Ave de la Victoire, Rue Pasteur and Rue Jean Chatel. It's also home to a smattering of impressive religious buildings.

★ Conseil Général de la Réunion – Direction de la Culture
HISTORIC BUILDING

(Villa du Département; Map p178; 18 Rue de Paris) Built in 1804 and one of the most elegant of St-Denis' Creole buildings, his villa has a superb *varangue* (veranda), finely crafted *lambrequins* (filigree-style decoration) and a manicured garden with a fountain.

Maison Carrère
MUSEUM

(Map p178; ☑ 0262 41 83 00; 14 Rue de Paris; €3; ☉ 9am-5pm Mon-Sat) This meticulously restored mansion dating from the 1820s is a beautiful example of Creole architecture, with its elaborate veranda and intricate *lambrequins* on the front of the eaves. The museum does an excellent job of explaining the city's colonial past. It also houses the tourist office.

Maison Kichenin
HISTORIC BUILDING

(Map p178; 42 Rue Labourdonnais) This perfectly preserved Creole mansion was built in the 1790s and is considered one of the oldest of its kind in St-Denis. The well-proportioned fountain in the garden is a highlight.

Musée Léon Dierx
MUSEUM

(Map p178; ☑ 0262 20 24 82; www.cg974.fr/culture; 28 Rue de Paris; adult/child €2/free; ☉ 9.30am-5pm Tue-Sun) Housed in the former bishop's palace, built in 1845, this museum hosts Réunion's most important collection of modern art. The more high-profile works may include paintings, sculptures and ceramics by Rousseau, Gauguin, Denis and Bernard (the works exhibited change every three months). You can also see a few paintings by the Réunionnais poet and painter Léon Dierx (1838–1912).

Mosquée Noor E Islam
MOSQUE

(Map p178; 121 Rue Maréchal Leclerc; ☉ 9am-noon & 2-4pm, closed to visitors during prayer times) One of St-Denis' most iconic buildings, the Grande Mosquée dominates the centre with its tall minaret. Its cool white-and-green interior is a haven of peace. The Islamic community in St-Denis is very traditional, so if you wish to visit, dress and behave with respect.

Le Barachois
WATERFRONT

(Map p178) This seafront park, lined by cannons facing out to sea, is a good place to catch the sea breeze in St-Denis. It has an area set aside for pétanque (a game similar to bowls), cafes and a monument to the Réunion-born aviator Roland Garros.

Jardin de l'État
GARDENS
(Botanical Gardens; Map p178; www.cg974.fr/culture; Rue Général de Gaulle; ☺7am-6pm) Created in 1763, the attractive Jardin de l'État, at the southern end of Rue de Paris, is a good place to recharge the batteries and be introduced to a variety of tropical plants and trees. The Musée d'Histoire Naturelle stands at the far end of the gardens.

Cathédrale de St-Denis
CHURCH
(Map p178; Place de la Cathédrale; ☺8am-5pm) Ambling down Ave de la Victoire, you'll come across the Tuscan-style Cathédrale de St-Denis, which was constructed between 1829 and 1832. As a cathedral this is a disappointment, since it looks more like a small New England mission church with its single, cream-plastered spire.

Maison Deramond-Barre
HISTORIC BUILDING
(Map p178; 15 Rue de Paris) This colonial structure dating from the 1830s was the family home of former French prime minister Raymond Barre and the birthplace of the poet and painter Léon Dierx. It's well worth a peek for its well-preserved architecture and harmonious proportions.

Former Hôtel de Ville
HISTORIC BUILDING
(Town Hall; Map p178; Rue de Paris) Many consider the neoclassical Former Hôtel de Ville, at the north end of Rue de Paris, to be the city's most beautiful building. It's certainly very imposing, with its regimented columns, balustrades, bright-yellow facade and jaunty clock tower.

Musée d'Histoire Naturelle
MUSEUM
(Map p178; ☑0262 20 02 19; www.cg974.fr/culture; Jardin de l'État; €2; ☺9.30am-5.30pm Tue-Sun) Go eye to eye with lemurs and other stuffed specimens in this museum located in the Jardin de l'État. Besides impressive lemurs, you'll see a good insect and bird collection on the 1st floor.

Préfecture
HISTORIC BUILDING
(Map p178; Place de la Préfecture) One of the grandest buildings in St-Denis, the Préfecture began life as a coffee warehouse in 1734 and later served as the headquarters of the French East India Company.

L'Artothèque
GALLERY
(Map p178; ☑0262 41 75 50; www.cg974.fr/culture; 26 Rue de Paris; ☺9.30am-5.30pm Tue-Sun) FREE This contemporary art gallery hosts changing exhibitions of works by local artists and those from neighbouring countries. It's housed in a handsome pale-yellow villa.

Palais Rontaunay
HISTORIC BUILDING
(Map p178; 5 Rue Rontaunay) Built in 1854, the Palais Rontaunay is a bourgeois villa that has preserved the elegant style of the 19th century.

Tamil Temple
HINDU TEMPLE
(Kovil Kalikambal Temple; Map p178; 259 Rue Maréchal Leclerc) St-Denis' small but wildly colourful Hindu temple stands out among a row of shops on a busy road in a slightly decrepit neighbourhood. Visitors are not allowed inside the temple.

Roland Garros Monument
STATUE
(Map p178; Place Sarda Garriga) On the waterfront, this statue honours the Réunion-born aviator Roland Garros, leaning nonchalantly on a propeller. Roland Garros was the first to fly across the Mediterranean in 1913.

Pagode Guan Di
BUDDHIST SITE
(Map p178; Rue Ste-Anne; ☺8.30-11am Mon, Wed & Sun) Blink and you'll miss this discreet pagoda, which is used by the Chinese community.

Notre-Dame de la Délivrance
CHURCH
(Map p178; Rte de la Montagne; ☺8am-6pm) Notre-Dame de la Délivrance (1893), which sits on the hillside across the usually dry Rivière St-Denis, is noteworthy for the statue of St Expédit just inside the door, dressed as a young Roman soldier.

🛏 Sleeping

Most hotels tend to be dull multistorey blocks that are designed with business travellers in mind. Budget beds are an endangered species and the choice of upmarket accommodation is surprisingly limited.

There is high demand throughout the year for accommodation, so advance booking is highly recommended.

Chez Nicole Maillot
B&B €
(☑0692 05 39 14, 0262 53 81 64; www.chambresdhotesnicolemaillot.jimdo.com; 54 Rue Nono Robert, La Confiance-les-Bas, Ste-Marie; d/tr incl breakfast €60/75; 🅿❄🛜🏊) From this B&B hidden in the hills above the airport, you can easily reach St-Denis (10km), the airport (5km) and the east coast, making it an ideal base. The three rooms, two of which have air-con, are nothing special, but it's the hush, the sea views, the tropical garden and the small pool that make this place special.

St-Denis

INDIAN OCEAN

LE BARACHOIS

Place Sarda Garriga

Place Général de Gaulle

Place de la Préfecture

Rivière St-Denis

Le Port (20km);
St-Gilles-les-Bains (35km)

RN1

Blvd Gabriel Macé

Rue de Nice

Rue Doret

Rue L'Amiral Lacaze

Rue Four à Chaux

Rue du Moulin à Vent

Rue Juliette Dodu

Rue des Sables

Rue Jules Auber

Blvd Joffre

Place Joffre

Place Étienne Regnault

Blvd Lancastel

St-Denis Pôle
d'Echanges
Océan

Car
Jaune

Rue Issop Ravate

Rue Laferrière

Rue Charles Gounod

Rue Alexis de Villeneuve

Rue Victor Mac-Auliffe

Rue Pasteur

Rue Labourdonnais

Rue de la Victoire

Rue Rontaunay

Place de la
Cathédrale

Ave de la Victoire

University

Rue Maréchal Leclerc

Rue Mal du Pavillon

Rue de la Compagnie

Place de la
Marie
(Town Hall)

Rue au Pont

Rue de la Boulangerie

Roland Garros
International (7.5km)

200 m
0.1 miles

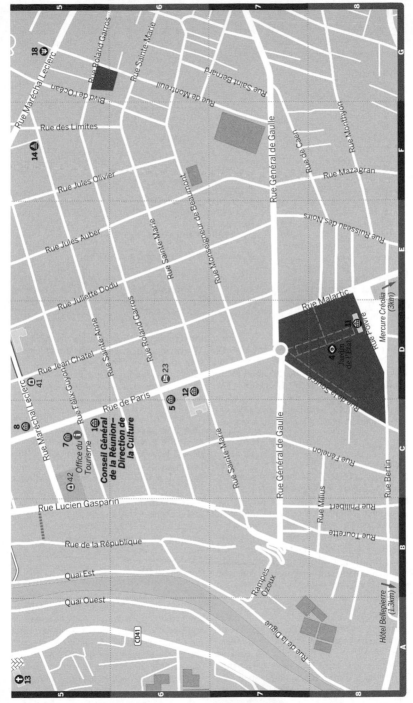

Rue Maréchal Leclerc

Blvd de l'Océan

Rue Roland Garros

Rue Sainte-Marie

Rue de Montreuil

Rue Saint Bernard

Rue des Limites

Rue Général de Gaulle

Rue de Caen

Rue Monthyon

Rue Jules Olivier

Rue Mazagran

Rue Jules Auber

Rue Ruisseau des Noirs

Rue Sainte-Marie

Rue Monseigneur de Beaumont

Rue Juliette Dodu

Rue Malartic

Mercure Créolia (3km)

Rue Roland Garros

Rue Sainte-Anne

Rue Poivre

11

4

Jardin de l'État

Jardin de l'État

Rue Jean Chatel

Rue Félix-Guyon

23

41

Rue de Paris

5   12

8

7   1

Office du Tourisme

Conseil Général de la Réunion– Direction de la Culture

42

Rue Sainte-Marie

Rue Général de Gaulle

Rue Lucien Gasparin

Rue Fénélon

Rue Bertin

Rue de la République

Rue Milius

Rue Philibert

Rue Tourette

Quai Est

Rampes Ozoux

Quai Ouest

Hôtel Bellepierre (1.3km)

Rue de la Digue

CD41

13

St-Denis

Phoenix　　　　　　　　　　HOTEL €

(Map p178; ☎0262 41 51 81; www.hotelphoenix.
re; 1 Rue du Moulin à Vent; d €52-57; ❋ ☎) This
little number is in a tranquil street within stumbling distance of the centre. The
rooms are neat and the bathrooms in
rooms 1, 4 and 5 have been upgraded. On
the whole, the place is clean and fair value
(for St-Denis). There's air-con from 7pm to
7am only.

★ La Maison d'Edith　　　　B&B €€

(Map p186; ☎0692 69 66 05; www.maisondedith.
com; 59 Chemin Commins, La Montagne; s/d incl
breakfast €100/120; P ☎ ☰) The owners are
passionate about Creole culture and have
renovated this mansion with a happy respect for the spirit of the place. Curl up with
your sweetie in one of the three rooms complete with period furniture, Creole ceilings
and rich fabrics. Best is the vast garden, with
ocean views and a superb swimming pool. A
great place to decompress.

La Villa des Cannes　　　　B&B €€

(Map p252; ☎0262 37 32 13, 0692 06 45 22; www.
lavilladescannes.com; 17 Lotissement Lisa, Chiendent,
Route du Paradis, Ste-Marie; d/q incl breakfast
€150/230; P ❋ ☎ ☰) Run by a widely travelled French couple, this boutique-style B&B
perched in the hills above Ste-Marie shelters

three rooms that are individually decorated
as well as a superb suite. The Sarkara room
may not be to everybody's taste, though; the
bathroom opens onto the bedroom (no door).
The glistening pool is the perfect remedy to a
day spent on twisty roads.

Central Hôtel　　　　　　　HOTEL €€

(Map p178; ☎0262 94 18 08; www.centralhotel.
re; 37 Rue de la Compagnie; s €74-104, d €84-
116, incl breakfast; P ❋ ☎) Comprising two
buildings, the Central gets by on its handy
location, a waddle away from restaurants,
bars and shops. It offers bland, fairly iden-
tical-looking hotel rooms without much
island flavour, but has private parking (12
spaces only) and neat bathrooms. Ask for a
room in the building equipped with a lift if
your suitcase is heavy. Skip breakfast.

Austral Hôtel　　　　　　　HOTEL €€

(Map p178; ☎0262 94 45 67; www.hotel-austral.fr; 20
Rue Charles Gounod; s €85-95, d €100-110; P ❋ @
☎ ☰) The rooms in this venerable establishment were modernised in 2018 and have the
requisite comforts. Location is tip-top, bathrooms are in good nick, facilities are good
and there's a small pool. There's limited private parking (arrive early to secure a space).
What's lacking? Charm and atmosphere.

Hôtel Bellepierre
HOTEL €€€

(☑ 0262 51 51 51; www.hotel-bellepierre.com; 91bis Allée des Topazes; s €170-227, d €192-245, incl breakfast; P ❄ 🛜 🛎) Life feels less hurried in this oasis of calm, perched on a hillside about 3km south of the centre. As you'd expect from a four-star establishment, rooms are spacious, well fitted out and comfortable. Those in the main building were refurbished in 2018. The pièce de résistance is the medium-sized pool, which seems to melt into the sea on the horizon.

Villa Angélique
BOUTIQUE HOTEL €€€

(Map p178; ☑ 0262 48 41 48; www.villa-angelique.fr; 39 Rue de Paris; d €160-190; ❄ 🛜) The closest thing St-Denis has to a boutique hotel, the Villa Angélique occupies a nicely renovated historic building and is just oozing with atmosphere. It's a modern twist on colonial decor: polished wood floors, beautiful wooden furniture, sparkling bathrooms and heavenly beds. There's a reputable on-site restaurant (open to all comers). One downside: there's no private parking.

Mercure Créolia
HOTEL €€€

(☑ 0262 94 26 26; www.exsel.re; 14 Rue du Stade, Montgaillard; d from €110-215; P ❄ 🛜 🛎) Mercure Créolia is located some 4km south of the city centre in a tranquil neighbourhood; your efforts in getting here are rewarded with splendid views over the coast. Rooms are functional and unflashy, and the decor is nothing special, but the setting and the relaxed-yet-professional feel more than make up for the slightly dated style. Amenities include a bar, a restaurant and a gym. The best asset is the pool, one of the biggest in Réunion.

Le Juliette Dodu
HOTEL €€€

(Map p178; ☑ 0262 20 91 20; www.hotel-juliettedodu.fr; 31 Rue Juliette Dodu; s €110-165, d €160-190, ste €215-250, incl breakfast; P ❄ 🛜 🛎) Live like a colonial administrator in this stylish 19th-century Creole building. Although the cheaper rooms feel claustrophobic and are unextraordinary, there are still enough vintage touches in the reception area – period furnishings, plump armchairs and old-fashioned tiles – to satisfy the snob within, with the added lure of a pool and a cosy restaurant (dinner only). Bonus: there's (limited) private parking.

🍴 Eating

Thanks to the French passion for gastronomy, St-Denis is heaven for food lovers, with a smorgasbord of eateries to suit all palates and budgets. Note that many bars also serve food.

★ La Saint-Georges
CRÊPES €

(Map p178; ☑ 0262 21 59 09; www.creperie-saint georges.fr; 5 Ruelle Edouard; crêpes €3-8, lunch menus €12-14) Wanna try something different? Not your average crêperie, La Saint-Georges is renowned for its gourmet crêpes and galettes made from top-notch ingredients. The industrial chic decor gives it a fresh, modern feel, and the crêpes are really first class. Where else could you savour a galette stuffed with tuna tartare and fresh vegetables?

Mafate Café
CAFE €

(Map p178; ☑ 0692 65 73 02; www.facebook.com/mafatecafe; 3 Rue Moulin à Vent; mains €6-14; ⏱ 8.30am-6pm Mon-Sat, 9am-1pm Sun; 🍴) This sweet spot hidden on a tranquil street north of the centre is perfect for a light lunch prepared with local, high-quality ingredients. It also serves tea, coffee, smoothies, pancakes, waffles and melt-in-the-mouth cakes. It's vegetarian-friendly.

Perlin Pain Pain
BAKERY €

(Map p178; ☑ 0262 23 01 21; www.perlinpainpain.re; 43 Rue de la Compagnie; sandwiches & snacks €3.50-16; ⏱ 5.30am-6.30pm Mon-Sat, to noon Sun; 🛜) One of the best bakery-delis in St-Denis, with a tantalising array of brioches, croissants, *macatias* (a variety of bun), sandwiches, burgers and bagels. It's also ideal for a refreshing cup of coffee or a quick and affordable sit-down lunch as you explore the city. Excellent breakfasts, too. There's a luminous dining room at the back.

Le Caudan
INDIAN €

(Map p178; ☑ 0262 94 39 00; 38 Rue Charles Gounod; mains €9-14; ⏱ 10am-2.30pm & 5-10pm Tue-Sat, 10am-2pm Sun) Tasty Indo-Mauritian snacks and ready-made meals are the order of the day at this under-the-radar neighbourhood venture set in a small Creole house with an appealing colourful interior. The homemade biryani is the speciality here. For dessert, try the *minsoob* (egg yolk with butter and cardamom). A cardamom tea will round things off nicely. Takeaways available.

L'Igloo
ICE CREAM €

(Map p178; ☑ 0262 21 34 69; www.liglooleffet glace.re; 67 Rue Jean Chatel; ice creams €2-13, mains €10-18; ⏱ 11.30am-midnight Mon-Sat, 3-11.30pm Sun; 🛜) Generous scoops and about 30 flavours are the trademarks of this drool-inducing ice-cream parlour in the heart of St-Denis. Take your mind off the somewhat tacky white-and-blue Antarctica murals by trying the Banana Split, with its deep, rich flavour; chocoholics will opt for the 'Palette aux 6 Chocolats', with six different chocolate flavours. Snacks and light meals are available at lunchtime.

★ Coffee Shop de Bourbon   CAFE €€

(Map p178; ☑ 0262 19 61 13; www.facebook.com/coffeeshop.re; 27bis Rue Alexis de Villeneuve; mains €8-24; ⊙ 7am-6.30pm Mon-Fri, 8am-7pm Sat, 9am-3pm Sun; 🐾) Smiley staff, slick decor, brisk service, good vibrations and plenty of healthy options on the menu ensure full tables at this bistro-cum-cafe. Indulge in breakfasts, salads, bruschettas, daily specials and a wealth of tempting desserts, including waffles and yummy cakes, as well as tea, coffee, smoothies and fruit juices.

Le Comptoir du Potager   FRENCH €€

(Map p178; ☑ 0692 85 59 31; www.facebook.com/AuComptoirDuPotager; 8bis Rue Labourdonnais; lunch menus €22-26, dinner menus €38-42; ⊙ noon-1.45pm Mon-Fri, 7.30-9.30pm Fri & Sat) For contemporary bistro cuisine, this boho-flavoured den is a winner. Pick from the small assortment of creative concoctions chalked on the board, and whatever you do, don't miss out on the exquisite homemade desserts. It fills up in the blink of an eye at lunchtime, so book a table or show up early.

La Calade   MEDITERRANEAN €€

(Map p178; ☑ 0262 20 32 32; www.facebook.com/LaCaladeRestaurant; 88 Rue Pasteur; mains €15-29; ⊙ noon-2pm & 7-10pm Tue-Sat; 🐾) The street entrance is rather discreet, but the French chef has received much attention since he opened his restaurant. Whether in the flowery garden or inside the elegant dining room, the food here is everything you'd want Mediterranean cuisine to be: super-fresh and packed with flavours. Tempting desserts, too.

L'Arto Carpe   FRENCH €€

(Map p178; ☑ 0262 21 55 48; www.facebook.com/artocarpe.re; 9 Ruelle Edouard; mains €13-24; ⊙ noon-2pm & 7-10pm Tue-Sat, bar 11am-11.45pm Tue-Sat; 🐾) Tucked in a pedestrianised alley behind the cathedral, this zinging restaurant built in a restored stone structure is a good choice if you're tired of heavy Creole classics. The concise menu involves seasonal, fresh ingredients, and dishes are imaginatively prepared and beautifully presented. Tapas (€6 to €11) are served from 6pm. It also doubles as a bar.

Le Roland Garros   BRASSERIE €€

(Map p178; ☑ 0262 41 44 37; 2 Place du 20 Décembre 1848; mains €17-22, lunch menu €17; ⊙ noon-midnight; 🐾) This St-Denis institu-

tion has the feel of a true Parisian bistro – packed, buzzing and full of attitude. It offers brasserie food that you wouldn't cross town for, but the menu covers enough territory to suit most palates. Its tartares and daily specials are well worth a try. Oh, and it's open on Sunday (a rarity in St-Denis).

Le Reflet des Îles   CREOLE €€

(Map p178; ☑ 0262 21 73 82; www.lerefletdesiles.com; 114 Rue Pasteur; mains €14-25; ⊙ noon-2pm & 7-9.30pm Mon-Sat) This eatery is the best place in St-Denis to try authentic Creole food by dipping into one of 15 cracking *carris* (curries) and *civets* (stews). There are also Western-style fish and meat dishes on offer if your tummy and palate are timid. The menu is translated into English – a rarity in Réunion. Most dishes cost less than €16.

La Fabrique   FUSION €€€

(Map p178; ☑ 0262 19 80 60; www.lafabriquerestaurant.re; 76 Rue Pasteur; mains €24-27, lunch menus €25-31, dinner menu €48; ⊙ noon-1.45pm Tue & Wed, noon-1.45pm & 7.45-9.30pm Thu-Sat; 🐾) Innovative cuisine reigns supreme under the stewardship of young chef Jehan Colson. With its intimate dining room, small terrace, industrial-chic decor and delicious cuisine, La Fabrique has honed the art of dining out to perfection. The menu is concise, but you can expect succulent concoctions prepared with top-of-the-line ingredients. The wine list is another hit, with well-chosen French tipples.

Le 144   INTERNATIONAL €€€

(Map p178; ☑ 0262 11 24 07; www.le-144.com; 12 Rue de Nice; mains €19-23, lunch menu €17; ⊙ noon-2pm & 7-10pm Tue-Fri, 7-10pm Sat, bar 11am-midnight Tue-Sat; 🐾) A surprisingly hip restaurant inside a Creole house complete with trendy, colourful interior, this cool culinary outpost is one of the most atmospheric spots in St-Denis and serves European-inspired dishes with a twist. Local gourmands rave about the tuna *tataki* (seared tuna) and the 'Burger 144', with raclette cheese.

L'Atelier de Ben   FUSION €€€

(Map p178; ☑ 0262 41 85 73; www.atelier-de-ben.com; 12 Rue de la Compagnie; mains €26-36, lunch menus €26-29; ⊙ noon-1.15pm & 7.30-9.15pm Tue-Fri, 7.30-9.15pm Sat) A true alchemist, the French chef Benoît Vantaux has got the magic formula right, fusing French with Creole and Asian to create stunning cuisine, perfectly matched with French tipples. Exquisite executions extend to the small dessert selection. Shame it doesn't have outdoor seating.

Drinking & Nightlife

Most of Réunion's action is down the coast at L'Hermitage-les-Bains and St-Pierre, but there are a handful of OK nightspots to keep you entertained in St-Denis. The most happening area is beside the cathedral, where more than half-a-dozen bars are concentrated in the span of only one or two blocks.

★ Le Passage du Chat Blanc   BAR
(Map p178; ☑ 0692 97 00 05; www.chatblanc.re; 26 Rue Jean Chatel; ☺ 5pm-midnight) A trendy crowd flocks to this popular bar with two entrances (one on Rue Jean Chatel, the other on Ruelle Edouard). Besides featuring a wide choice of beers and great cocktails (from €5), there's live music – house music, afro beat, rock, electro – or a DJ most nights of the week. Also serves pizzas.

Café Edouard   BAR
(Map p178; ☑ 0262 28 45 02; 13 Ruelle Edouard; ☺ 10am-11.30pm Mon-Sat; ☎) The place to hang out, this buzzy bar with outdoor tables has a great selection of beers and spirits. There's also well-priced bar food for lunch and dinner.

Le Prince Club   GAY
(Map p178; ☑ 0692 38 28 28; 108 Rue Pasteur; ☺ 11.30pm-4am Fri & Sat) A gay-friendly bar and club.

🛍 Shopping

The main shopping streets are the semi-pedestrianised Rue Maréchal Leclerc and Rue Juliette Dodu.

Boutique Pardon   CLOTHING
(Map p178; ☑ 0262 41 15 62; www.pardon.re; cnr Rue Maréchal Leclerc & Rue Jean Chatel; ☺ 9am-6.30pm Mon-Sat) Get glammed up at this trendsetting boutique stocking island-made shirts, T-shirts, dresses and accessories for men, women and kids.

Grand Marché   MARKET
(Map p178; 2 Rue Maréchal Leclerc; ☺ 8.30am-5.30pm Mon-Sat) This market has a mishmash of items for sale, including Malagasy wooden handicrafts, fragrant spices, woven baskets, embroidery, T-shirts, furniture and a jumble of knick-knacks.

ℹ Information

MEDICAL SERVICES
There are numerous well-stocked pharmacies around town.

Cabinet Médical de Garde Saint-Vincent
(☑ 0262 47 72 10; cnr Rue de Paris & Rue Maréchal Leclerc; ☺ 7pm-midnight Mon-Fri, from 2pm Sat, from 8am Sun) A small clinic (with two doctors) that's open outside regular business hours.

Centre Hospitalier Félix Guyon (☑ 0262 90 50 50; Allées des Topazes, Bellepierre) Réunion's main hospital has 24-hour medical and dental treatment and English-speaking staff.

TOURIST INFORMATION
Office du Tourisme (Map p178; ☑ 0262 41 83 00; www.ot-nordreunion.com; Maison Carrère, 14 Rue de Paris; ☺ 9am-6pm Mon-Sat; ☎) Housed in a historic building, the St-Denis tourist office has English-speaking staff and can provide plenty of information, maps and brochures. It also runs excellent cultural tours focusing on St-Denis' rich architectural heritage (€20, minimum two people) and biking tours (€25). Bookings for *gîtes de montagne* (mountain lodges) can also be made here. There's internet and wi-fi access (one hour free).

Gîtes de France (☑ 0262 90 78 78; www.gites-de-france-reunion.com) Information on *chambres d'hôtes* (family-run B&Bs).

ℹ Getting There & Away

AIR
Unless noted otherwise, the following airlines have offices in St-Denis. All airlines also have an office at the airport, which is usually open every day.

Air Austral (☑ 0825 01 30 12; www.airaustral.com; 4 Rue de Nice; ☺ 8.30am-5pm Mon-Fri, to 11.45am Sat)

Air France (☑ 3654; www.airfrance.com; 7 Ave de la Victoire; ☺ 9am-5pm Mon-Fri, 8.30am-noon Sat)

Air Madagascar (☑ 01 40 06 01 01; www.airmadagascar.com; 31 Rue Jules Auber; ☺ 8.15am-12.15pm & 1.30-5pm Mon-Thu, to 4pm Fri)

Air Mauritius (☑ 0262 94 83 83; www.airmauritius.com; 13 Rue Charles Gounod; ☺ 8.30am-12.30pm & 1.30-5.30pm Mon-Fri)

Corsair (☑ 3917; www.corsair.fr; 2 Rue Maréchal Leclerc; ☺ 9am-5.30pm Mon-Fri)

French Bee (☑ 0825 20 52 05; www.frenchbee.com) Doesn't have an office in St-Denis but is represented at the airport.

XL Airways (☑ 0892 69 21 23; www.xl.com) Doesn't have an office in St-Denis but is represented at the airport.

BUS
St-Denis Pôle d'Échanges Océan (Gare Routière; Map p178; ☑ 0810 12 39 74; www.

carjaune.re; Blvd Lancastel), the main long-distance bus station, is on the seafront. From here **Car Jaune** (Map p178; ✆ 0810 12 39 74; www.carjaune.re; Blvd Lancastel) operates various services. Information for Car Jaune, including all its routes and *horaires* (timetables) around the island and the airport bus service, is available from the information counter at the bus terminal. Some of the more useful routes include the following:

Line 02 West to St-Pierre via Le Port, St-Paul, St-Gilles-les-Bains, St-Leu, Étang-Salé-les-Bains and St-Louis (two hours, about 10 daily, fewer on Sunday).

Lines E1 or E2 East to St-Benoît via Ste-Suzanne, St-André and Bras-Panon (€2, one hour, about 16 daily, fewer on Sunday).

ZO (express) West to St-Pierre, direct (€5, one hour, about 12 daily except Sunday).

ZE (express) East to St-Benoît via the airport (€5, one hour, about three daily except Sunday).

❶ Getting Around

St-Denis is relatively small and getting around the centre on foot is a breeze.

Taxis around town are generally expensive. A trip across town will set you back at least €8.

During the day you should have no problem finding a taxi. It gets more difficult at night, when you might have to phone for one. A reliable company offering a 24-hour service is **Taxis Paille-en-Queue** (✆ 0262 29 20 29).

THE WEST

Welcome to Réunion's Sunshine Coast, or Réunion's Riviera, or the leeward coast. However you label it, say hello to this 45km-long string of seaside resorts and suburbs running from St-Paul to St-Louis. It has a wealth of developed tourist facilities and attractions, including the best of the island's beaches.

Sea, sand and sun are not the only raison d'être on the west coast. There's also a superfluity of activities on land and sea, including diving, whale watching, paragliding and mountain biking.

Despite the fact that tourist development has got a little out of hand to the south of St-Paul, it's easy to leave the Route des Tamarins that zips along the flanks of the mountains and explore the glorious hinterland and its bucolic offerings, with sugar-cane fields and cryptomeria forests swathing the slopes of the mountains, studded with character-filled villages.

St-Paul

POP 24,000

Try to visit St-Paul on a Friday or Saturday morning, when the local market is in full swing. This lively city also has a handful of architectural treats, including a few well-preserved colonial buildings along the seafront. The long black-sand beach is alluring but swimming is forbidden. For a dip in safer waters, head to nearby Boucan Canot.

◉ Sights

Cimetière Marin   CEMETERY
(Map p186; off RN1a) Most tourists who come to St-Paul visit the bright and well-kept Cimetière Marin, the cemetery at the southern end of town. It contains the remains of various famous Réunionnais, including the poet Leconte de Lisle (1818–94) and the pirate Olivier 'La Buse' Levasseur (The Buzzard), who was the scourge of the Indian Ocean from about 1720 to 1730.

Hindu Temple   HINDU TEMPLE
(Map p186; Rue St-Louis) Find this strikingly colourful temple dating from 1871 on a street running parallel to the seafront.

⬛ Sleeping

St-Paul has limited accommodation, which is why most visitors choose to stay in St-Denis, a mere 20-minute drive away (if there's no traffic jam), or in the resort towns of Boucan Canot or St-Gilles-les-Bains, a few kilometres to the south.

Kia Ora   B&B €€
(Map p186; ✆ 0262 25 31 68; www.kiaorarun.com; 204 Rue St-Louis; d €88, with shared bathroom €68, incl breakfast; ❋ ⬛ ⬛) Your well-travelled hosts keep their three *chambre d'hôte* (guest rooms) spick and span and serve delicious breakfasts on a terrace overlooking the pool. One room comes with private facilities, but note that the bathrooms don't have doors.

It's not far from the bus station – great for walkers who want to spend the night in St-Paul before heading to the Cirque de Mafate.

✖ Eating

While St-Paul is short on accommodation options, it has a surprisingly dynamic eating scene, with a good choice of restaurants, ranging from European gourmet dining to *camions-snacks* (snack vans). Make sure you save energy for the animated market on the seafront promenade. It's held all day on Friday and on Saturday morning. With heaps of local vegetables, fruits, spices and savoury snacks, it makes for a colourful experience.

La Magie des Glaces   ICE CREAM €
(Map p186; ☑ 0262 45 25 48; 1 Rue Edmond Albius; ice creams & crêpes €1.80-8.50; ☉ noon-6.30pm Tue-Sat, from 2pm Sun) St-Paul's premier ice-cream parlour will leave you a drooling mess. It serves up an excellent array of classic and exotic flavours, all prepared with high-quality ingredients. The passionfruit and geranium (yes!) are outstanding. It also whips up crêpes, pastries, chocolate mousse and macaroons. If only it had sea views, life would be perfect.

Le Grand Baie   FRENCH, CREOLE €€
(Map p186; ☑ 0262 22 50 03; www.facebook.com/restaurantlegrandbaie; 14 Rue des Filaos; mains €17-25; ☉ 11.45am-2pm & 7-10pm Tue-Sun) You're sure to find something to fill a gap at this haven of peace next to the Cimetière Marin, where the menu covers lots of salads as well as *métro* (French) and Creole dishes. With its vast decking terrace and first-class views of the bay, dining really does not get better than this.

Le Nature   CREOLE, BUFFET €€
(Map p186; ☑ 0262 71 45 89; 228 Rue Saint-Louis; lunch buffet €15; ☉ noon-2pm Mon-Sat; 🖘) Nature serves up a brilliant-value lunch buffet, consisting of about eight Creole dishes prepared from fresh simple ingredients. The setting is inviting, with a dining room embellished with colourful touches and a few outdoor tables. It also has a takeaway counter (from €5).

★ La Bas Ter La   FUSION €€€
(Map p186; ☑ 0262 57 10 51; 4 Rue Eugène Dayot; mains lunch €14-19, dinner €19-27; ☉ noon-1.30pm & 7.15-9pm Tue-Fri, 7.15-9pm Sat; 🖘) One of St-Paul's top tables, La Bas Ter La is tucked down a quiet street not far from the seafront. It offers excellent French cuisine with a refined twist, savoured in a stylishly modern dining room. The menu changes regularly. Book ahead.

La Barque   SEAFOOD €€€
(Map p186; ☑ 0692 23 20 01; www.labarque.re; 48 Rue de la Baie; mains €24-30; ☉ noon-2pm Tue, noon-2pm & 7-9pm Wed-Sat) This breezy fish restaurant, set within arm's reach of the crashing waves, is one of the best options around for a relaxed meal. The seafood dishes use what's available from the harbour, usually tuna and swordfish. Meat dishes also grace

the menu. There's a lush outdoor courtyard with a tiny pool and partial ocean views.

Le Jardin   EUROPEAN €€€
(Map p186; ☑ 0262 45 05 82; www.restaurantlejardin.re; 456 Rue St-Louis; mains €17-27; ☉ 11.30am-2pm & 7-9pm Mon, Tue & Thu-Sat) This surprisingly atmospheric restaurant at the northern end of town features an open-air dining room, a lounge area and a swimming pool, which will help you switch to 'relax' mode. Food-wise, it concocts French specialities. Warm and attentive service and a good place for a drink as well.

❶ Getting There & Away

St-Paul lies on Car Jaune's bus route between St-Denis and St-Pierre (€2). There are express buses every one to two hours in either direction (fewer on Sunday) and much more frequent nonexpress services. From St-Denis, the ride takes about 30 minutes. More information at www.carjaune.re.

The local bus company **Kar'Ouest** (Map p186; ☑ 0810 45 65 20; www.karouest.re; Chaussée Royale) operates fairly infrequent services from the central bus station to villages up in the hills such as Le Bernica, La Petite France (and further up towards Le Maïdo), Sans Souci (for the Canalisation des Orangers in the Cirque de Mafate) Villèle and Le Guillaume, among others. The fare is €2.

Dos d'Ane
POP 450
After braving St-Denis' busy streets and before tackling the seaside resorts further south, a drive up to the isolated village of Dos d'Ane, way up in the hills above Le Port (take the D1), will give you a breath of fresh air. It's an excellent base for hikes in the interior.

🛏 Sleeping & Eating

If you like peace, quiet and sigh-inducing views, you can spend a night or two at one of the B&Bs dotted around the village.

Auberge du Cap Noir –
Chez Raymonde   B&B €
(☑ 0262 32 00 82; 3 Allée Pignolet, Dos d'Ane; d/q incl breakfast €50/100; 🅿) Ideally sited on a hillside with swoony ocean views, this mellow, down-to-earth B&B offers four well-swept rooms at a price that won't make you flinch. Madame Pignolet knows her stuff when it comes to cooking lip-smacking Reunionnais specialties – her *mousse de*

Western Réunion

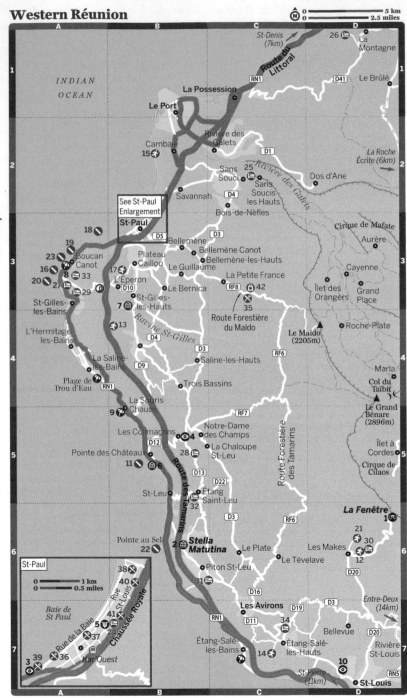

Western Réunion

patate au coulis de chocolat (sweet potato mousse with chocolate sauce) is simply divine (dinner is €20).

Les Acacias – Chez Axel et Patricia Nativel B&B €
(☏0262 32 01 47; 34 Rue Germain Elisabeth, Dos d'Ane; dm/with half board €20/40, d incl breakfast €48; 🅿🛜) If you like peace and quiet, you'll have few quibbles with this welcoming B&B. It's very simple but clean and the atmosphere is very relaxed. Digs are in two ordinary *chambres d'hôtes* and four spick-and-span six-bed dorms. The hearty evening meals (€20) go down well after a day's tramping, and the views over the northern coast from the terrace are stupendous.

❶ Getting There & Away

Your best bet is to explore the area with your own wheels. Follow the D1 from Rivière des Galets.

Les Hauts de St-Paul

A world away from the hurly-burly of the coast, the verdant Hauts de St-Paul is wonderful country for exploring off the beaten track. From St-Paul, use the D5 as a launch pad, then follow your nose (but bring a good map). You'll come across hamlets with such charming names as Sans Soucis les Hauts, Bois-de-Nèfles, Bellemène-les-Hauts, Le Guillaume, Le Bernica... It's as cute as it sounds! Start early morning to get the best views of the coast.

🛏 Sleeping

Accommodation options are thin on the ground in the area. Frankly, your best bet is to bunk down in a hotel or apartment in Boucan Canot or St-Gilles-les-Bains and explore the area on a day trip.

La Caz des Orangers GUESTHOUSE €
(Map p186; ☏0262 44 50 32, 0692 08 23 12; www.lacazdesorangers.com; 24 Impasse Cernot, Sans Soucis les Hauts; d incl breakfast €55, with shared bathroom €35; 🅿🛜) The main reason to stay at this no-frills yet practical establishment hidden in Sans Souci les Hauts, about 10km northeast of St-Paul, is if you're hiking to/from the Cirque de Mafate via the Canalisation des Orangers – the trailhead is just

400m uphill. The guesthouse has a large sitting room and plain bedrooms with minimalist decor; there are three more comfortable doubles in a separate building.

Add €15 for dinner. Note that guests can leave their car and luggage for free during their Mafate hiking trip. It costs €2 per day or €10 for overnight parking for nonguests.

ⓘ Getting There & Away

Unless you have a lot of time, you need a vehicle. Buses serve most places from St-Paul, but they aren't really convenient for the Hauts.

Le Maïdo

Be prepared for a visual shock: far above St-Paul and St-Gilles-les-Bains on the rim of the Cirque de Mafate, Le Maïdo is one of the most impressive viewpoints in Réunion. The lookout is perched atop the mountain peak at 2205m and offers stunning views down into the Cirque and back to the coast. You should arrive early in the day – by 7am if possible – if you want to see anything other than cloud.

Getting there is half the fun. The sealed Route Forestière du Maïdo winds all the way up to the viewpoint from **Le Guillaume** (14km) in the hills above St-Gilles-les-Bains, offering a scenic drive through majestic cryptomeria forests. You'll find a smattering of attractions along the way to keep you entertained.

A word of warning: expect traffic snarls on Sunday when hundreds of picnicking families set up base in the shade of trees along the road.

🏃 Activities

Hiking options abound near Le Maïdo. The peak is the starting point for the tough walk along the Cirque rim to the summit of **Le Grand Bénare** (2896m), another impressive lookout. Plan on six hours return. Hikers can also descend from Le Maïdo into the Cirque de Mafate via the Sentier de Roche-Plate.

🛏️ Sleeping & Eating

The village of La Petite France makes a convenient base for an early-morning start up to Le Maïdo.

Chez Rose Magdeleine   B&B €

(☑ 0262 32 53 50; 13 Chemin de l'École, La Petite France; d incl breakfast €45) Run by an affable Creole family, this good-value B&B is a really homey. It has few frills but the four rooms are immaculately clean, and the location, just off the main road in La Petite France, makes a convenient base for an early-morning start up to Le Maïdo. Evening meals are available on request (€22 to €25).

Chez Doudou et Alexandra   CREOLE €€

(Map p186; ☑ 0262 32 55 87; 394 Route du Maïdo, La Petite France; buffet €23; ☉ noon-2pm Tue-Sun) With its barnlike surrounds, Chez Doudou has a kind of ramshackle charm but has no views to speak of. The focus is on earthy regional food, so roll up for comforting Creole *carris* served with all the traditional accompaniments. It's full to bursting at weekends – reservations are advised.

🛍️ Shopping

La Petite France is famous for its traditional distilleries producing essential oils from geranium, cryptomeria and vetiver leaves (nice smell!). The distilleries also run small shops

---

DOWNHILL MOUNTAIN BIKING

The spectacular flanks of Le Maïdo will prove a sort of nirvana for mountain bikers who prefer sitting back and letting gravity do the work. The 35km, 2205m descent follows trails that wind through tamarind and cryptomeria forests and sugar-cane fields. Throughout the ride you're presented with astounding views of the lagoon and the coast.

Rando Réunion Passion (p191) is a professional set-up that offers a range of mountain-bike trips for riders of all levels. The most popular ride is the 'Classique du Maïdo' descent, from the lookout to the coast. If you're a beginner, fear not! You won't ride at breakneck speed, and various stops are organised along the way, where the guide will give you the lowdown on flora and fauna. Half-day packages including bike hire, transport to the start (by minivan, for an extra €5) and a guide cost around €60 per person (minimum four). Children over 12 are welcome. If you want to open up the throttle a little more, opt for the 'Maxi Cap Ouest' (€100) descent.

where you can stock up on perfumes, soaps and other natural health products. Stop off at some of the places scattered along the main road in La Petite France.

L'Alambic Bègue COSMETICS
(Map p186; ☑ 0692 64 58 25; http://alambicbegue. e-monsite.com; 403 Route du Maïdo, La Petite France; ☺ 8.30am-6pm) A long-standing distillery with an excellent reputation. It features a range of essential oils and health products.

❶ Getting There & Away

From the central bus station in St-Paul, Kar'Ouest (p185) runs three buses a day (Monday to Saturday) to the start of the Sentier de Roche Plate, the footpath into the Cirque de Mafate, which strikes off the road about 3km below the summit. The first bus up the hill leaves at 6am and the last one down is at 5.20pm (line 2, €2, one hour).

Boucan Canot

POP 3400

The 'Boucan' checklist: skimpy bikini, designer glasses (imitations may be sniggered at), sunscreen. This attitude-fuelled little resort town isn't dubbed the Réunionnais St-Tropez for nothing. Its beach is one of the most appealing on the island.

◎ Sights

Plage de Boucan Canot BEACH
(Map p186) Boucan Canot's main beach has been listed as one of Réunion's best, and once you get a glimpse of the gentle curve of the bright white sand, lined with palms and casuarina trees and framed with basalt rocks and cliffs, you'll see why. It gets packed on weekends. A 610m shark net, protecting a large bathing area, was installed off the beach in December 2015. Stick to the protected area (there's no barrier reef off Boucan Canot). It's not supervised.

Plage de Petit Boucan BEACH
At the southern end of Boucan Canot's main beach, you'll find this smaller, much quieter beach, but swimming is forbidden and there's no lifeguard.

🛏 Sleeping

Résidence Les Boucaniers APARTMENT €€
(☑ 0262 24 23 89; www.les-boucaniers.com; 29 Route de Boucan Canot; d €85; 🅿 ❋ 🛜) These self-catering studios and apartments have seen better days but the location, across the road from the beach, is hard to beat. Be sure

to book a unit with a sea view. Prices drop to €79 if you stay two nights or more.

Le Saint-Alexis Hotel & Spa RESORT €€€
(☑ 0262 24 42 04; www.hotelsaintalexis.com; 44 Route de Boucan Canot; d €170-290, ste from €290; 🅿 ❋ 🛜 🏊) Le Saint-Alexis is a quirkily laid-out resort at the southern tip of the main beach. The rooms are all arrayed around a central patio, which means that none of them have sea views. They're attractively decorated, although the ones in the angles lack natural light. Facilities include a small spa and a large, U-shaped pool that girdles the building.

Le Boucan Canot LUXURY HOTEL €€€
(☑ 0262 33 44 44; www.boucancanot.com; 32 Route de Boucan Canot; s €190-230, d €230-270, ste from €310, incl breakfast; 🅿 ❋ 🛜 🏊) This four-star establishment stretches over a rocky promontory at the northern end of the beach and gets plenty of sunshine, even in the late afternoon. Though nothing glam, the rooms, most of which were renovated in 2018, are bright and well-appointed and come with a sea view. Another highlight is the food; Le Cap restaurant offers fine à la carte dining.

🍴 Eating

La Case Bambou INTERNATIONAL €€
(☑ 0262592084; www.facebook.com/casebambou; 35 Route de Boucan Canot; mains €3-24; ☺ noon-2.30pm & 7-9.30pm) A long-standing favourite, the Bambou Bar has an arm-long menu. Order anything from pizzas and Creole staples to seafood, burgers, salads and meat dishes. It is also a fast-food outlet – head here for finger-licking crêpes, ice creams, waffles and sandwiches. Unsurprisingly, it's crowded on weekends.

Le Ti Boucan INTERNATIONAL €€
(☑ 0262 24 85 08; 32 Route de Boucan Canot; mains €14-22, lunch menu €14; ☺ 9am-9.30pm; 🛜) On the main strip, this cheerful place is a great spot to sample one of the various tartares on offer (try the tuna tartare with ginger). Meat-eaters may plump for the beef skewer or the grilled rib. Copious salads provide a tempting alternative. The service is friendly and the outside terrace is a delight.

La Boucantine FRENCH, CREOLE €€
(☑ 0692 66 48 94; 29 Route de Boucan Canot; mains €13-24; ☺ noon-2pm & 7-9.30pm Fri-Tue) One of the better (and slightly quieter) restaurants on this seaside strip, with an inviting terrace that affords lovely sea views.

WORTH A TRIP

MUSÉE DE VILLÈLE

The **Musée de Villèle** (Map p186; ☑0262 55 64 10; www.musee-villele.re; Domaine Panon-Desbassyns, St-Gilles-les-Hauts; €2; ☺9.30am-12.30pm & 1.30-5pm Tue-Sun) is set in the former home of the wealthy and very powerful Madame Panon-Desbassyns, a coffee and sugar baroness who, among other things, owned 300 slaves. The house, which is only accessible on a guided tour, was built in 1787 and is full of elegant period furniture. After the tour, wander the outbuildings and the 10-hectare park.

Legend has it that she was a cruel woman and that her tormented screams can still be heard from the hellish fires whenever Piton de la Fournaise is erupting. Exhibits include a clock presented to the Desbassyns by Napoleon; a set of china featuring Paul et Virginie, the love story by Bernardin de St-Pierre; and, last but not least, a portrait of Madame Panon-Desbassyns in a red turban looking surprisingly impish. Signs are in French and English. The museum is a 15-minute drive from St-Gilles-les-Bains.

High marks go to the *souris d'agneau confite aux épices* (lamb shank with spices) and the catch of the day. Mouthwatering desserts, too, including crêpes and chocolate cake.

Le Bistrot de Pépé Gentil　　BISTRO €€€
(☑0262 22 12 78; www.facebook.com/lebistrotdepepegentil; 15 Place des Coquillages; mains €25-31; ☺7-9.30pm Mon-Sat) This much-lauded venture with a vintage feel serves a range of culinary delights that deliciously represent French bistro cooking. The *ris de veau* (veal sweetbreads) and *filet de voilier* (sailfish fillet) are two specialities to look for, though the menu changes regularly according to markets and seasons.

ⓘ Getting There & Away

Car Jaune's lines 02 and T between St-Denis and St-Pierre run through the centre of Boucan Canot. The St-Denis–Boucan Canot trip (€2) takes about 50 minutes. For more information visit www.carjaune.re.

St-Gilles-les-Bains

POP 6500

The tourism machine shifts into overdrive in the large resort complex of St-Gilles-les-Bains, with its white sands, restaurants, bars and a boisterous atmosphere on weekends. During the week, however, the atmosphere is much more relaxed and you shouldn't have to fight for a space to lay your towel. There are numerous water activities on offer, from diving to whale watching.

◉ Sights

Plage des Roches Noires　　BEACH
(Map p192) Plage des Roches Noires, in the heart of town, is crowded and neatly striped

with sunbeds and parasols, but, beneath all this, it remains an attractive stretch of beach excellent for families, with shallow waters and plenty of restaurants. A shark net was installed off the beach in 2016 to increase safety. Watch for the warnings signs, though, and swim only in the supervised area. On the northern side of the Port de Plaisance.

Plage des Brisants　　BEACH
(Map p192) Plage des Brisants is a superb stretch of white sand on the southern side of the Port de Plaisance. That said, swimming is forbidden (yes, sharks). It's great for sunbathing.

Aquarium de la Réunion　　AQUARIUM
(Map p192; ☑0262 33 44 00; www.aquariumdelareunion.com; Îlot du Port; adult/child €9.50/6.50; ☺10am-5.30pm) In the modern Port de Plaisance complex, the quite engaging Aquarium de la Réunion houses a series of excellent underwater displays, including tanks with lobsters, barracudas, groupers and small sharks.

🏃 Activities

Whale Watching

From July (sometimes June) to October, whale watching has become increasingly popular in the St-Gilles area, with a number of operators, including dive shops, leading professional tours. Make sure to stick with operators with good environmental credentials.

★ Duocéan　　WHALE WATCHING
(☑0692 44 30 11; www.duocean.com; tours €60-90) When it comes to whale watching, this operator gets the best reviews for miles around. It's staffed with professional, experienced instructors who follow sustainable practices and never harass the cetaceans.

Boat Excursions

The best way to discover St-Gilles' iridescent lagoon is by joining a boat excursion. Various operators offer *promenades en mer* (boat excursions) and *observation sous-marine* (glass-bottomed tours) along the coast towards St-Leu or St-Paul. *Safaris dauphin* (dolphin encounters), whale-watching trips (from June or July to September or October), sunset cruises and day-long catamaran cruises are also available. Tours go every day but are weather-dependent.

Lady La Fée   BOATING

(Map p192; 0692 69 12 99; www.ladylafee.re; Port de Plaisance; half-day trip €60) This small outfit offers half- and full-day trips aboard a catamaran along the west coast. The itinerary is flexible. Sunset cocktail cruises cost €40.

Le Grand Bleu   BOATING

(Map p192; 0262 33 28 32; www.grandbleu.re; Îlot du Port; adult/child from €19/11) This reputable operator has the largest range of tours, from sunset cruises to whale- and dolphin-watching trips. Prices vary according to the duration of the cruise (the shortest tours last 75 minutes) and the type of boat.

Sealife – Visiobul   BOATING

(Map p192; 0262 24 49 57; www.facebook.com/visiobulreunion; Îlot du Port; adult/child from €13/8) Specialises in glass-bottomed boat tours. Also runs whale- and dolphin-watching trips as well as sunset cruises.

Diving

The waters off St-Gilles offer plenty of scope for diving, including the chance to explore a few wrecks (p34), whatever your level.

Bleu Marine Réunion   DIVING

(Map p192; 0262 24 22 00; www.bleu-marine-reunion.com; Port de Plaisance; introductory/single dive €65/50; 8am-5pm Tue-Sun) A fully fledged, well-organised dive shop offering a comprehensive menu of underwater adventures, including diving trips, snorkelling excursions (€30) and certification courses. Three-/six-dive packages are €144/280.

Ô Sea Bleu   DIVING

(Map p192; 0262 24 33 30; www.oseableu.com; Port de Plaisance; introductory/single dive €65/52; 8am-5pm) Professional dive shop that offers the full range of scuba activities. Four-/six-dive packages are €200/290. Snorkelling trips (€35), certification courses and dolphin-watching trips are also available. Add an extra €8 per dive for Nitrox dives.

Mountain Biking

The professional set-up **Rando Réunion Passion** (Map p192; 0262 45 18 67, 0692 21 11 11; www.vttreunion.com; 167 Rue du Général de Gaulle; tours €65-100) offers a range of mountain-bike trips for riders of all levels. The most popular ride is the Classique du Maïdo descent, from the Maïdo lookout to the coast. Experienced riders can opt for the Maxi Cap Ouest or La Méga. Add an extra €5 per person for transfers.

Sport Fishing

St-Gilles is a good base for fans of Ernest Hemingway. The waters off the west coast are a pelagic playpen for schools of marlin, swordfish, sailfish, shark and tuna. A fishing trip for four to six people costs around per half/full day €400/800. Two recommended outfits:

Réunion Fishing Club (Map p192; 0692 76 17 28; www.facebook.com/reunionfishingclub; Port de Plaisance; half-day tour €100; 7am-5pm) leads well-organised fishing trips while **Blue Marlin** (Map p192; 0692 65 22 35; www.bluemarlin.fr; Port de Plaisance; 7am-5pm) is a well-established operator whose prices vary according to the size of the party.

🛏 Sleeping

There's plenty of accommodation in the area, but almost everything is booked out during holiday periods and on weekends. The more appealing hotels and *chambres d'hôtes* are in the countryside just north of town or to the south in L'Hermitage-les-Bains. There's also a vast choice of holiday rentals.

Hôtel de la Plage   HOTEL €

(Map p192; 0262 24 06 37, 0692 80 07 57; www.hoteldelaplage.re; 20 Rue de la Poste; d €70-75, with shared bathroom s/d €45/65; ❄🛜) The highlights of this long-established and well-run hostel-like venture are its ultra-central (but noisy) location and colourful communal areas. The eight rooms are neat but vary in size, light and noisiness, so ask to see a couple before you settle on one. Rooms 114, 115 and 116 are the best. Book ahead.

⭐ Senteur Vanille   VILLA €€

(Map p186; 0262 24 04 88, 0692 78 13 05; www.senteurvanille.com; Route du Théâtre; bungalow €85-100, villa €160-200; P❄🛜) A true find for peace seekers, Senteur Vanille makes you feel like you've stepped into a Garden of Eden, with mango, lychee and papaya trees all over the grounds. Curl up in a vast, well-equipped villa (ideal for families)

St-Gilles-les-Bains

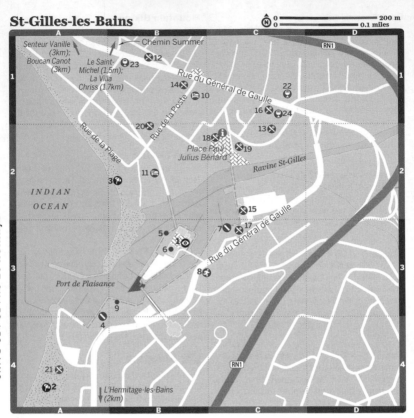

St-Gilles-les-Bains

or in a cute-as-can-be Creole bungalow. No swimming pool, but Boucan Canot beach is a 20-minute walk down a path.

La Villa Chriss　　　　　　　B&B **€€**

(Map p186; ☎ 0692 82 41 00; http://chambre-hote-luxe-reunion.com; Rue d'Anjou; s/d incl break-fast €130/140; **P ❄ 🛜 ⛱**) Run by Christine (hence the name), this boutique-style *maison d'hôte* (guesthouse), perched on the side of a hill, rejuvenates the weariest of travellers. It shelters two superb rooms that are decorated with a contemporary twist. A delicious gourmet breakfast is served by the pool, with mind-boggling views of the coast. Not suitable for children. Gay friendly.

★**Le Grand Bleu** HOTEL €€
(Map p192; ☑0262 02 60 60; www.hotel-legr andbleu.com; 46 Blvd Roland Garros; d €100-160; P❄🅿🛖) The latest addition to St-Gilles' accomodation scene, Le Grand Bleu brings a dash of modernity with 20 rooms done out in blue and white and sparkling bathrooms, a 50m Frisbee throw from the beach (but there are no views to speak of). Amenities include a well-regarded restaurant (menus from €17), a pool and a co-working space.

Le Saint-Michel HOTEL €€
(Map p186; ☑0262 33 13 33; www.hotelsaint michel.fr; 196 Chemin Summer; s €76, d €96-115, incl breakfast; P❄🅿🛖) This little number, amid a tropical garden on the outskirts of town, was in a transition phase when we visited. Bathrooms in the 15 rooms should have been modernised by the time you read this, and a new wing with 12 modern rooms should have been added. It's a two-minute drive to the centre and the beach.

🍴 Eating

St-Gilles has plenty of eating options, though standards tend to be more variable than elsewhere on the island.

As well as restaurants, you'll find several *camions-pizzas* (mobile pizza vans) on the main street; they're a good bargain and operate in the evening.

La Case Dic FAST FOOD €
(Map p192; ☑0692 54 35 33; www.facebook.com/ lacasedic; Place du Maré; mains €5-6) No misprint – mains cost no more than €6 at La Case Dic, which occupies a small booth inside the market. Not your average fast food outlet, it spins quality Creole meals at puny prices.

Le Glacier de Marie B ICE CREAM €
(Map p192; ☑0262 24 53 06; 13 Rue de la Poste; ice creams & snacks €3-11; ⏲1-7pm Tue, 11am-7pm Wed-Fri, 11am-7.30pm Sat & Sun) You'll lose all self-control at this drool-inducing ice-cream parlour. Amid a mind-boggling array of flavours, the sweet potato with honey screams 'try me'. The vanilla and pineapple are also

well worth a try. Other treats include pancakes, waffles and smoothies.

La Case à Pains BAKERY €
(Map p192; ☑0262 96 33 01; www.facebook.com/ lacaseapainsreunion; 29 Rue du Général de Gaulle; sandwiches from €5, lunch menu €5-8; ⏲6.30am-7pm) If you're toying with the idea of doing a beach picnic à la gourmet, it's worth stopping in here for some salads, pastries and well-prepared sandwiches. The signature offering is the *pain frotté à la vanille* (a variety of bread flavoured with vanilla). Also serves breakfast. Has outdoor tables.

Chez Loulou FAST FOOD €
(Map p192; ☑0262 24 40 41; 86 Rue du Général de Gaulle; mains €6-8; ⏲7am-1pm & 3-7pm Mon-Sat, 7am-1pm Sun) The most iconic Creole *case* (house) for kilometres around, with a distinctive turquoise facade on the main drag. It's famous for its belt-bustingly good samosas, *macatias* (a type of bun), croissants, cakes and tarts. Good sandwiches and takeaway meals at lunchtime, too.

Bistrot Case Créole BISTRO, CREOLE €€
(Map p192; ☑0262 24 28 84; www.facebook.com/ bistrotcasecreole; 57 Rue du Général de Gaulle; mains €15-23; ⏲noon-2pm & 7.30-9.30pm Tue-Fri, 7.30-9.30pm Sat) Familiar bistro fare with a local twist – salads, fish and meat dishes – won't inspire devotion, but the atmosphere is relaxed and service is efficient. At dinner it also lays on a Creole buffet featuring an assortment of six curries for €23. The weak point is its unassuming position on the main drag, with no sea views.

★**Le Saint-Michel** FRENCH, CREOLE €€€
(Map p186; ☑0262 33 13 33; www.hotelsaint michel.fr/the-restaurant; 196 Chemin Summer; mains €24-32, lunch menus €20-25, dinner menu €70; ⏲noon-1.30pm & 7.30-9.30pm) Part of the eponymous hotel, this is the gourmet choice in St-Gilles. With its enticing dining deck by the pool, charming welcome and delicious cuisine, Le Saint-Michel won't disappoint. The menu is a combination of high-brow, creative gastronomy and timeless classics such as beef fillet or half-cooked tuna steak. And there's always a great wine to match.

Bookings are essential to guarantee one of the prized tables near the pool.

★**Sauvage** INTERNATIONAL €€€
(Map p192; ☑0262 44 88 73; www.sauvage.re; Plage des Brisants; mains €15-28; ⏲noon-2.30pm & 7-9.30pm, bar 9am-10pm Sun-Thu, to 11pm Fri &

SHARK ATTACK PREVENTION

Shark attacks on surfers and swimmers have been a major issue in Réunion in recent years, especially off St-Leu, Boucan-Canot, St-Gilles-les-Bains, Trois-Bassins and Étang-Salé-les-Bains. Shark nets have been installed along Boucan-Canot and St-Gilles-les-Bains' beaches. Always swim in designated and supervised areas, and watch for the warning signs. Check the website of Centre de Ressources et d'Appui sur le Risque Requin (www.info-requin.re) for up-to-date information.

Sat) This sassy restaurant and bar directly on the beach is run by a dynamic crew who serve consistently delicious market-inspired cuisine. Throw in a congenial atmosphere, superb cocktails (from €8) and great tapas served from 6pm, and there's a lot to be said for letting a long, lazy afternoon here segue effortlessly into the evening.

Chez Marie
FRENCH, SEAFOOD €€€

(Map p192; ✆0262 24 98 87; Port de Plaisance; mains €13-25, menu €17; ◷noon-2.15pm) With its tiny terrace overlooking the harbour and simple yet well-prepared cuisine, this sweet lil' den is ideal for a quick and affordable sit-down lunch. The trademark here is freshness and great value for money. The octopus salad and swordfish in pineapple sauce both caught our eyes.

Le DCP
SEAFOOD €€€

(Map p192; ✆0262 33 02 96; 2 Place Paul Julius Bénard; mains €21-27; ◷noon-2pm & 7-9.30pm) Fish lovers will find nirvana here: this known-far-and-wide restaurant has a broad assortment of fish delivered daily from the harbour. Order it grilled, steamed, baked or raw. The tartares are reputedly the best on the island. It's near the tourist office.

Chez Nous
INTERNATIONAL €€€

(Map p192; ✆0262 24 08 08; www.facebook.com/ ChezNousRestaurant; 122 Rue du Général de Gaulle; mains €15-26; ◷noon-2pm & 7-11pm Mon-Fri, 7-11pm Sat & Sun) This bold bistro is beloved by all who come here. The blackboard menu features flavourful meat and fish dishes, some with an exotic twist, as well as salads. The service may see you twiddling your thumbs when it's crowded. It also has a bar area with a loungey vibe.

Chez Bobonne
FUSION €€€

(Map p192; ✆0262 39 27 96; 3 Rue St-Alexis; mains €22-34; ◷7.30-10pm Mon-Sat) Indulge in delicious French-inspired dishes at this fine-dining restaurant with contemporary decor and mood lighting. The small menu is chalked on the board and changes weekly. There's also a thoughtful wine list. It's tucked away from the main drag.

Drinking & Nightlife

St-Gilles is one of the top places in Réunion (on an equal footing with St-Pierre) for bar-hopping. The atmosphere is very Zoreilles (mainland French) – you could be mistaken for thinking you're in the French Côte d'Azur. Most places are scattered along Rue du Général de Gaulle and the chichi seafront. Most bars also serve food.

L'Etiquette
BAR

(Map p192; ✆0262 08 04 17; www.facebook.com/ letiquette974; 58 Rue du Général de Gaulle; ◷6.30-11.30pm Mon-Sat) L'Etiquette is part restaurant, part bar, but it's the bar section that grabbed our attention (and our euros), not least for its incredibly potent cocktails. Try its *ti punch* and you'll see what we mean.

Pinkananas
CLUB

(Map p192; ✆0692 65 75 95; www.facebook.com/ Pinkananas; 122 Rue du Général de Gaulle; ◷7pm-5am Tue-Sat) Kick off the night with a few shots at this atmospheric venue that draws the crowds on weekends.

Esko Bar
BAR

(Map p192; ✆0262 33 19 33; www.facebook.com/ eskobar.reunion; 131 Rue du Général de Gaulle; ◷7-11.30pm Mon-Sat) This chic venue has excellent cocktails, good tapas (from €6) and themed nights – check the website.

Information

Office du Tourisme (Map p192; ✆0262 42 31 31; www.ouest-lareunion.com; 1 Place Paul Julius Bénard; ◷10am-1pm & 2-6pm; ☏) Has helpful English-speaking staff. Free wi-fi. Does bookings for *gîtes de montagne*.

ℹ Getting There & Away

Car Jaune's nonexpress buses between St-Denis and St-Pierre (lines O2 and T) run through the centre of St-Gilles down Rue du Général de Gaulle. The trip to St-Denis (€2) takes at least one hour. More infomation at www.carjaune.re.

L'Hermitage-les-Bains

POP 6200

L'Hermitage has the bulk of the island's major resorts, a small selection of restaurant and entertainment options, and what is possibly Réunion's most scenic beach. Here, the island has the feel of a vacation destination.

⊙ Sights

Plage de L'Hermitage   BEACH

(Map p195; L'Hermitage-les-Bains) Lined with casuarina trees, Plage de L'Hermitage is an alluring place to fry in the sun. It is safe for swimming – it's protected by a barrier reef and is supervised by lifeguards – and extremely popular on weekends. Snorkelling is OK.

Le Jardin d'Eden   GARDENS

(Map p195; ☎ 0262 33 83 16; www.jardindeden.re; 155 RN1; adult/child €8/4; ☺10am-6pm) Appealing to a wider audience than just plant lovers and gardeners, Le Jardin d'Eden, across the main road from L'Hermitage, is definitely worth an hour or so for anyone interested in tropical flora. Sections of the gardens are dedicated to interesting concepts such as the sacred plants of the Hindus, medicinal plants, edible tropical plants, spices and aphrodisiac plants.

🛏 Sleeping

Camping Ermitage Lagon   CAMPGROUND €

(Map p195; ☎0262 96 36 70; www.camping ermitage.re; 60 Ave de Bourbon; camping per site 1-6 people €23-31; ℗ ☜) This camping ground has modern, functional facilities, including a restaurant, but is located near L'Hermitage's clubs, so it may not be quiet on weekends. There are lots of shady areas and you're within spitting distance of the beach. You can rent out a whole 'safari tent' for €40 to €52 during the week – quite a good deal by L'Hermitage standards.

L'Hermitage-les-Bains

RÉUNION L'HERMITAGE-LES-BAINS

Résidence Coco Island
GUESTHOUSE €

(Map p195; ☑ 0692 37 71 12, 0262 33 82 41; www.
cocoisland-reunion.com; 21 Ave de la Mer; d €49-
82; ❄ 🖥 ≋) This is a popular budget option,
with 23 unimaginative rooms of varying
size, shape and appeal – have a look before
committing. Cheaper rooms share toilets
but have cubicle showers plonked in the corner. All rooms have air-con. Guests can use
the communal kitchen and the heated pool
in the garden beside the reception. Prices
drop for stays longer than five nights. Bikes
are available for hire.

Les Bougainvilliers
GUESTHOUSE €

(Map p195; ☑ 0262 33 82 48; www.bougainvillier.
com; 27 Ruelle des Bougainvilliers; d €69-79;
🅿 ❄ 🖥 ≋) For something personal, try this
jolly, hospitably run little bolthole with 13
rooms. Firm mattresses, colourful walls, a
pool, plus a communal kitchen and a flower-
filled garden, all just a five-minute stroll
from the beach. And free bikes. The catch?
It's a wee bit compact – the pool almost licks
the terrace of the downstairs room.

Les Créoles
HOTEL €€

(Map p195; ☑ 0262 26 52 65; www.hotellescreoles.
com; 43 Ave de Bourbon; d €100-125; 🅿 ❄ 🖥 ≋)
On an island where affordable-but-beautiful
hotels are a rarity, this small-scale venture is
a safe bet. The comfortable, modern rooms
are arrayed around the swimming pool. It
feels a bit compact, but it provides a very
agreeable stay. Facilities include a bar (but
no restaurant). One quibble: it's not directly on the beach. Check out the website for
off-season discounts.

Le Récif
RESORT €€€

(Map p195; ☑ 0262 70 05 00; www.hotellerecif.
com; 50 Ave de Bourbon; d incl breakfast from
€220; 🅿 ❄ 🖥 ≋) While not luxurious, this
sprawling three-star resort consisting of various pavilions is a reliable base, especially if
you can score promotional rates. Furnishings and communal areas are quite tired,
so don't come expecting cutting-edge design. Its main selling points are its location,
a coconut's throw from the beach, and its
numerous amenities, including two pools, a
restaurant and a tennis court.

Lux
RESORT €€€

(Map p195; ☑ 0262 70 05 00; www.luxresorts.
com; 28 Rue du Lagon; d incl breakfast from €198;
🅿 ❄ 🖥 ≋) Lux pays elegant homage to luxurious colonial architecture, with a gaggle of
Creole-style villas scattered amid a sprawling

property at the very south end of the beach
at L'Hermitage. Facilities include three restaurants, a huge pool, a bar and direct beach
access. For the price, we'd expect a spa.

Eating

Most hotels have restaurants and happily accept nonguests dropping in for a meal. Don't
expect to have lunch or dinner on the beach –
in 2018, all beach restaurants were compelled
to close following a court decision. That said,
it's only a short drive north to St-Gilles-les-
Bains for a greater choice of options.

Snack Chez Herbert
CREOLE, SANDWICHES €

(Map p195; ☑ 0262 32 42 96; 40 Blvd Leconte de
Lisle; mains €4-8; ⏱ 11.30am-7pm Tue-Sun) This
popular joint is worth visiting for its cheap
and wholesome Creole staples. Snacks, salads, sandwiches and other nibbles are also
available. Take your plunder to the beach or
grab a (plastic) table on the shaded pavement and watch the pétanque players in
action just across the road.

Snack Chez Racine Jessica
CREOLE, SANDWICHES €

(Map p195; ☑ 0692 98 91 35; 42 Blvd Leconte de
Lisle; mains €3-8; ⏱ 11am-5pm Thu-Mon, to 3pm
Tue) Tasty, filling, cheap Creole food and voluminous sandwiches. No surprise that it's
popular. For a true local (if lowbrow) experience, try this modest eatery strategically positioned on a street running parallel to the
beach. Takeaway is available.

★ Le Manta
INTERNATIONAL €€€

(Map p195; ☑ 0262 33 82 44; www.le-manta.re; 18
Blvd Leconte de Lisle; mains €19-24; ⏱ noon-2pm
& 7-9.30pm; 🖥) Concealed in a wonderfully overgrown garden, this well-respected
restaurant has a great selection of fish and
meat dishes, as well as a few Creole classics
and salads. Toothsome specialities include
salade Manta, comprising smoked marlin
and tuna, and kangaroo fillet with Roque-
fort sauce. A few *carris* also grace the menu.
It's across the road from the beach.

🍷 Drinking & Nightlife

The unchallenged capital of Réunion's club
scene, L'Hermitage rocks on weekends.
The fun starts late – after midnight – and
places typically close around 5am. You
don't need to be completely dolled up but
if you're wearing shorts and flip-flops you'll
be turned away.

Beach Club
CLUB

(Map p195; ☑ 0692 40 01 38; www.facebook.com/beachclub974; 1 Rue des Îles Éparses; entry €15 incl one drink; ☺10pm-5am Sat & Sun) The Beach Club draws good-looking and well-dressed hordes looking to get down to salsa, Latin rock music and electro (among others).

La Villa Club
CLUB

(Map p195; ☑ 0692 60 19 00; www.facebook.com/villaclub974; 71 Ave de Bourbon; ☺11pm-5am Fri & Sat) L'Hermitage's top nightspot positively sizzles on a Friday and Saturday night when the dance floors are packed. Tropical, electro and dance music dominate the play list.

Le Loft
CLUB

(Map p195; ☑ 0262 24 81 06; www.facebook.com/leloftsaintgilles; 1 Rue des Îles Éparses; ☺10pm-5am Thu-Sat) A pulsating club playing a little bit of this and a little bit of that. Also has karaoke.

Moulin du Tango
CLUB

(Map p195; ☑ 0262 24 53 90; www.moulin-du-tango.re; 9 Ave de Bourbon; entry from €10; ☺10pm-5am Wed, Fri & Sat) Bump your hips with a mature crowd in this dance club famous for its themed nights.

❶ Getting There & Away

Car Jaune's nonexpress buses (lines O2 and T) between St-Denis (€2, one hour) and St-Pierre run through L'Hermitage. More information at www.carjaune.re.

La Saline-les-Bains

POP 2900

La Saline-les-Bains is getting increasingly popular along the west coast. It has a distinct atmosphere. Here it's more mellow, more alternative, more nonconformist. The eating and accommodation scene is now one of the best in Réunion.

◉ Sights

The main beach is a stellar stretch of white sand and is usually less crowded than its northern counterparts at St-Gilles or L'Hermitage. It has shallow, calm waters protected by a barrier reef, making it an ideal location for families.

Plage de la Souris Chaude
BEACH

(Map p186; La Souris Chaude) Not a fan of tan lines? Head due south and lay your towel on Plage de la Souris Chaude, which is a favourite among nudists (only just tolerated)

and gay men (head to the northern tip of the beach). It remains largely off the tourist radar, not least because it's a bit hard to find. Swimming is forbidden (and dangerous, because of sharks and currents).

Plage de Trou d'Eau
BEACH

(Map p198) At the southern end of the main beach, Plage de Trou d'Eau is a nice place to relax and have a safe swim in the lagoon, although it's not supervised. Paddleboard rental is available.

🏃 Activities

Stand-up paddleboarding is a great way to explore the lagoon at a gentle pace. **Ecole de Stand Up Paddle du Lagon** (Map p198; ☑ 0692 86 00 59, 0262 24 63 28; www.facebook.com/EcoleDeStandUpPaddleDuLagon; courses from €25; ☺by reservation) offers one- or two-hour courses run by a qualified instructor. The beachfront restaurant Planch'Alizé (p199) rents canoes, kayaks and paddleboats (from €6 per hour).

🛏 Sleeping

Le Vacoa
HOTEL €

(Map p198; ☑ 0262 24 12 48; www.levacoa.com; 54 Rue Antoine de Bertin; d €64-74; ✳🛜🌊) A five-minute stroll from the beach, this little two-storey *résidence hôtelière* (mini-resort) won't knock your socks off but it contains 15 modern, well-appointed (albeit hanky-sized) rooms arranged around a central courtyard. Expect a bit of road noise during the day. Precious perks include a kitchen for guests' use and a pocket-sized pool.

Dina Morgabine
HOTEL €€

(Map p198; ☑ 0262 61 88 88; www.dinamorgabine.com; 80bis Rue des Engagés, Bruniquel; d €115-165, q €195-280; 🅿✳🛜🌊) Its location near a roundabout about two kilometres away from the beach doesn't scream 'vacation' but this compact three-star establishment is a reliable port of call with neat rooms and lots of amenities, including a pool and a restaurant. Book a room with a sea view.

La Maison du Lagon
HOTEL €€

(Map p198; ☑ 0262 24 30 14; www.lamaisondulagon.com; 72 Rue Auge Lacaussade; s €80-125, d €100-135, incl breakfast, ste q €195; 🅿✳🛜🌊) This villa has a compact but respectable collection of various-sized rooms and apartments, but only four units have direct sea views. They all feel past their prime on the inside, but they are clean, and the location,

La Saline-les-Bains

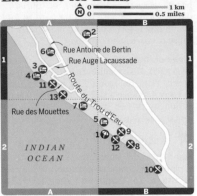

right by the beach, is tip-top. There's a small pool at the entrance of the property as well as a kitchenette.

Tip for couples: book the stand-alone Bungalow Plage (€115, without breakfast), which is a sweet spot. There's limited private parking (four spaces only).

Le Dalon Plage
BUNGALOW €€
(☎0262 34 29 77, 0692 04 94 26; www.ledalon. jimdo.com; 6 Allée des Tuits Tuits, La Souris Chaude; s/d incl breakfast €60/70, studio €75-85; P✲⛱) It's just a short amble from the Plage de la Souris Chaude to this exclusively gay cocoon. Guests are allowed (if not incited) to swim naked in the gleaming pool. Too

prudish? Slumber in one of the three fully equipped studios; the Kitouni is the brightest. There's also a small, plain room with shared bathroom in the owners' house.

Note that from early July to mid-August, this place is called Jardin de la Souris and welcomes non-gay visitors.

La Closerie du Lagon
APARTMENT €€
(Map p198; ☎0692 86 32 47, 0262 24 12 56; www. closerie-du-lagon.fr; 78ter Rue Lacaussade; d €113; P✲⛱) Alain and Charles are your kindly hosts at this ravishing abode, which consists of a 60-sq-m apartment with all mod cons in a peaceful property by the beach (but no sea views from the apartment). It's fully equipped. Intimate, chic and gay friendly. There's a two-night minimum stay. Bonus: free bikes and kayaks. Cash only.

★ La Villa de la Plage
B&B €€€
(Map p198; ☎0692 66 86 32, 0262 61 86 16; www. lavilladelaplage.fr; 52 Route du Trou d'Eau; d/bungalow incl breakfast €169/189; P✲⛱) You wouldn't guess it from the main road, but this efficiently-run B&B is one of the most atmospheric and relaxing places along the west coast. It features three colourful, impeccable rooms and a stand-alone bungalow in a lush garden that opens onto the beach. The icing on the cake? A lovely pool. Free kayaks, paddleboards and bikes. A sweet deal.

Ness by D-Ocean
HOTEL €€€
(Map p198; ☎0262 70 30 00; www.nessbyd ocean.com; 26 Route du Trou d'Eau; d €160-320; P✲⛱) Opened in 2019, this U-shaped venture facing the beach has six categories of rooms, including some awesome rooftop suites with sensational sea views. At the cheaper end of the scale, the Supérieures are much less impressive but get the job done, with clean lines, gleaming bathrooms and a kitchenette. Amenities include a spa, a pool, a bar and a restaurant.

✕ Eating

★ L'UniVert
EUROPEAN €€
(Map p198; ☎0262 61 54 36; www.facebook.com/ lunivert; 70 Route du Trou d'Eau; breakfast €8-15, mains €15-25; ⊗8-10.30am, noon-3pm & 5-10pm; ⛱) Overlooking the beach, this hip venture provides an enjoyable dining experience with healthy food, including a few veggie options, as well as mean breakfasts, tasty tapas and superb cocktails. It also scores high on atmosphere – it's trendy without being ostentatious.

La Bodega
EUROPEAN €€

(Map p198; ☑0262 35 66 69; www.facebook.com/labodega974; Plage de Trou d'Eau; mains €15-26; ☺noon-3pm & 6.30-9.30pm, bar 9am-10.30pm) Worth a mention for its breezy deck overlooking the lagoon, memorable sea views and jovial atmosphere, La Bodega serves a wide range of dishes, including tapas, salads and burgers, and there's a snack section if you prefer a sandwich or a waffle (from €3). More than the food, though, it's the beachside location that's the real draw. There's live music on Friday and Sunday evenings.

Planch'Alizé
EUROPEAN, SANDWICHES €€

(Map p198; ☑0262 24 62 61; www.facebook.com/PlanchAlize; 25 Rue des Mouettes; mains €14-25; ☺noon-2.30pm & 7-9pm Tue-Sat, noon-2.30pm Sun & Mon, bar 9am-late; ☏) This bustling little *paillotte* (beach restaurant) is noted for its reliable seafood as well as meat dishes, lavish salads and tempting desserts. It's also a fantastic spot for a drink any time of the day. Tapas are served after 5pm.

Live bands sometimes play here on Friday from 6.30pm. Sun lounges, snorkelling gear, kayaks and paddleboards are available for hire.

La Bonne Marmite
CREOLE €€

(Map p198; ☑0262 45 46 92; Route du Trou d'Eau; dinner buffet €21; ☺7.15-9.30pm Mon-Sat) Pounce on The Good Cooking Pot's excellent-value dinner buffet, which features 12 wholesome *carris* (curries) as well as grilled meat. You'll leave perfectly sated. It's a coconut's throw from the beach (with the sea just out of sight, alas).

Le Choka Bleu
EUROPEAN €€€

(Map p198; ☑0262 35 16 14; www.facebook.com/le.choka.bleu; 2 Route de St-Pierre; mains €24-30, menus €22-45; ☺noon-2pm & 6-10pm Wed-Sun, bar to 11.30pm; ☏) Large, well-spaced tables and high ceilings put diners in the right mood to settle down for a big night sampling the ambitious dishes on offer – mostly seafood and meat. Or you could simply park yourself with a cocktail on the concrete terrace to watch the sunset – soul-stirring. There are live bands on certain evenings (check the website).

Le Copacabana
FRENCH €€€

(Map p198; ☑0262 24 16 31; www.copacabana.re; 20 Rue des Mouettes; mains €20-30; ☺9-10.30am & noon-3pm, plus 7-10pm Fri & Sat, bar 9am-7pm; ☏) This trendy bar-restaurant has a peerless position right on the beach. Enjoy well-prepared fish and meat dishes as well as

excellent homemade desserts. Le Copa is also a fashionable spot for a night-time tipple or a refreshing fruit juice any time of the day. It also rents out sun lounges.

ⓘ Getting There & Away

Car Jaune's nonexpress buses between St-Denis and St-Pierre (lines O2 and T) run through La Saline-les-Bains (from St-Denis, €2, 1¼ hours). More at www.carjaune.re.

St-Leu
POP 33,600

Since the days of the sugar industry ended, forward-looking St-Leu has transformed itself into a mecca for outdoor enthusiasts. This is the place to get high – legally: no doubt you'll be tempted to join the paragliders who wheel down from the Hauts to the lagoon. Scuba divers also swear that the drop-offs here are the best on the island and, in season, whale-watching trips are very popular, too.

St-Leu has a smattering of handsome stone buildings dating from the French colonial era, such as the *mairie* (town hall) and the church opposite. Other attractions are the shady park along the seafront and a protected beach that is popular with families.

St-Leu is also optimally placed for explorations of the coast and forays into the Hauts. On weekends, it's also one of the liveliest towns along the coast, with live bands on the beach and good cheer.

⊙ Sights

Notre-Dame de la Salette
CHURCH

(Map p200; Sente la Salette) The little white chapel of Notre-Dame de la Salette, perched on the side of the hill to the east of town, was built in 1859 as a plea for protection against the cholera epidemic sweeping the entire island. Whether by luck or divine intervention, St-Leu was spared from the epidemic, and thousands of pilgrims come here each year on 19 September to offer their thanks.

Kelonia
MUSEUM

(Map p186; ☑0262 34 81 10; www.museesreunion.re/kelonia; 46 Rue du Général de Gaulle, Pointe des Châteaux; adult/child €8/5; ☺9am-5pm) Don't miss this ecologically conscious marine and research centre dedicated to sea turtles, about 2km north of St-Leu. It features exhibits, interactive displays and big tanks where you can get a close-up look at the five different varieties of turtle found in the waters around

St-Leu

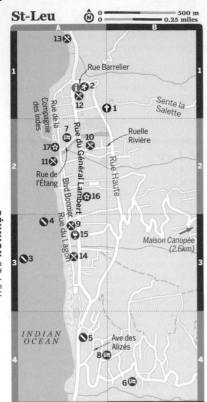

St-Leu

Réunion, especially the green turtle (*Chelonia mydas*). Guided tours are available.

Kids love the place but adults will also be blown away by this well-organised venture.

🏃 Activities

Diving

The dive spots off Pointe au Sel to the south of St-Leu (see p34) offer some of the best underwater landscapes in Réunion, while the lagoon closer to St-Leu is good for coral.

⭐ Scubananas –
Réunion Plongée   DIVING
(Map p200; ☑ 0692 85 66 37, 0262 34 77 77; www.reunionplongee.com; 375 Rue du Général Lambert; introductory/single dive €65/55; ⊙ 8.30am-4.30pm) A small outfit with good credentials. Four-/six-dive packages cost €210/310 and include equipment rental. Add €5 per dive for Nitrox dives. Between July and October, it also arranges well-organised whale-watching trips (€60). On the southern edge of St-Leu.

Excelsus   DIVING
(☑ 0262 34 73 65; www.excelsus-plongee.com; Impasse des Plongeurs, Pointe des Châteaux; introductory/single dive €65/55; ⊙ 8am-5pm) This efficient operation offers a full range of dives for all levels. Four-/10-dive packages cost €200/470. Prices include equipment rental. Nitrox dives are available at no extra cost.

Whale Watching

Most dive shops lead whale-watching tours between July and October when humpbacks swim near the coast. Scubananas – Réunion Plongée has good credentials.

🎊 Festivals & Events

Leu Tempo Festival   THEATRE
(www.lesechoir.com; ⊙ May) A very popular theatre festival in St-Leu. Also features dance, circus and music. Early May.

**Fête de Notre-Dame
de la Salette**   RELIGIOUS
(Festival of Notre Dame de la Salette; ⊙ Sep) Pilgrimage to the miracle-working Madonna at the chapel of Notre-Dame de la Salette (p199). Fair and street events over 10 days.

🛌 Sleeping

There aren't any resorts in St-Leu. Most accommodation here consists of a few little hotels in the backstreets or on the outskirts of town as well as holiday rentals. You'll need your own wheels to get to the beach.

Résidence Les Pêcheurs BUNGALOW €
(Map p200; ☑ 0262 34 91 25, 0692 85 39 84; http://les.pecheurs.pagesperso-orange.fr; 27 Ave des Alizés; d/q €58/99; P 🛜 🏊) Find this clean, friendly and well-run venture in a quiet neighbourhood on the southern edge of town. It consists of six bungalows with partial sea views. They're spacious, practical and well kitted out, but there's no air-con (only fans). There's no beach nearby, but guests can chill by the pool. Two nights minimum. Brilliant value.

Palais d'Asie APARTMENT €
(Map p200; ☑ 0262 34 80 41, 0692 86 48 80; lepalaisdasie974@gmail.com; 5 Rue de l'Étang; d €43-48, q €68; P ❄ 🛜 🏊) One of St-Leu's best bargains, though the 'Palais' bit is a gross misnomer. It's comfortably central, spitting distance from the beach and restaurants, and offers sparsely furnished but functional and clean rooms (some with kitchenettes) and secure private parking. And yes, it does have its own (tiny) swimming pool. Prices drop for stays longer than two nights.

There's also a much larger, brighter room with a terrace, that was added in 2019 (double from €75).

Iloha Seaview Hotel HOTEL €€
(☑ 0262 34 89 89; www.iloha.fr; 44 Rue Georges Pompidou, Route des Colimaçons, Pointe des Châteaux; d €110-200, bungalows €140-200; P ❄ 🛜 🏊) The Iloha is a very good all-round hotel-resort set in a sprawling property north of town. Its tidy rooms and simply designed bungalows offer a great choice for everyone from couples to families. Precious perks include two pools, two restaurants, a wellness centre and well-tended gardens. Of the 80 rooms, about 10 have ocean views. Check the website for special offers.

While the standard rooms, which were upgraded in 2018, feel a bit claustrophobic, the bungalows offer ample space.

⭐**Le Blue Margouillat** BOUTIQUE HOTEL €€€
(Map p200; ☑ 0262 34 64 00; www.blue-margouillat.com; Impasse Jean Albany; d €215-330, ste €435-615; P ❄ 🛜 🏊) This delightful hotel on the southern outskirts of St-Leu adds a welcoming touch of glam to the local hotel scene, with just 12 artfully designed rooms and two suites, an award-winning restaurant, an inviting pool and smashing views. That said, the odd layout of the bathrooms – no doors and no walls, only a thick curtain – may not be to everybody's taste.

🍴 Eating

L'Orange Givrée CAFETERIA €
(Map p200; ☑ 0262 70 50 03; 2 Rue Barrelier; mains €5-13; ⏱ 8.30am-3pm Mon-Sat) Blink and you'll miss the tiny entrance of this funky little den next to the tourist office. It whips up appetising salads, *plats du jour* (daily specials), sandwiches, bagels, fruit juices and other treats at wallet-friendly prices. Make sure you save room for the criminally addictive apple pie or brownie. Cash only.

⭐**Au Bout La Bas** EUROPEAN €€
(Map p200; ☑ 0262 55 98 72; 37 Rue du Lagon; mains €11-23; ⏱ noon-2pm & 7-9pm Tue-Sat) Brimming with good cheer, this tropical cocoon in a street running parallel to the seafront serves excellent food. A sampling of choices might include a burger with homemade fries, a copious salad, tuna tataki or a toothsome *tartine* (a slice of organic bread with toppings). The homemade desserts are every bit as devastatingly delicious as they sound. Mmm, the chocolate cake.

Sarah Beach INTERNATIONAL €€
(Map p200; ☑ 0262 10 23 37; www.facebook.com/restosb; 44 Rue du Général Lambert; mains €17-22; ⏱ noon-1.45pm & 7-9.30pm Thu-Mon) North of town, this restaurant has a great position overlooking the lagoon. With such appealing surroundings, many alfrescoholics would go back to this breezy veranda by the sea for the location alone, but the eclectic fare is tempting, too, especially the *pierrades* (a hot stone surface on which you cook thin strips of meat or fish), served at dinner.

Villa Vanille EUROPEAN €€
(Map p200; ☑ 0262 34 03 15; www.restaurant-lavillavanille.fr; 69 Rue du Lagon; mains €15-24; ⏱ 11.45am-2.15pm & 7-9.30pm) No plastic chairs at this zinging spot, but teak furnishings and an agreeable terrace. Villa Vanille has the most eclectic menu in town. Choose from frondy salads, excellent tuna tartares, meat dishes and locally produced ice creams. Lounge on the beach across the road once you've finished your meal – this is the life!

PARAGLIDING

St-Leu is one of the world's top spots for paragliding, with excellent uplifting thermals year-round. If you're new to dangling yourself in the air, you can tandem paraglide with one of the many operators offering flights. The most popular launch pad is at an altitude of 800m, high above the town. There's another launch pad at 1500m. The descent from the mountain is amazing, with heart-stopping views over the lagoon and the coast. Children over six are welcome.

Bourbon Parapente (Map p200; ☑0692 87 58 74; www.bourbonparapente.com; 4 Rue Haute; tandem flight €80-120; ⊗8am-5pm) An experienced outfit. Has a range of tandem flights lasting from 15 minutes to 35 minutes. Kids over five are welcome. There's a 10% discount if you book online.

Azurtech (☑0692 85 04 00; www.azurtech.com; Pointe des Châteaux; tandem flight €75-110; ⊗8am-5pm) A long-standing favourite. Has a range of tandem flights, including a 30-minute 'Must' flight, which comes recommended. Kids over five are welcome.

Le Zat SEAFOOD €€
(Map p200; ☑0262 42 20 92; 14 Rue de la Compagnie des Indes; mains €14-20; ⊗noon-2.45pm, bar 9am-4.30pm; ☜) Near the harbour and a Frisbee's throw from the beach, this unpretentious open-air joint majors in fish dishes as well as salads. Good homemade desserts, too. It's a supremely chilled place to sip a tropical potion while enjoying sea views.

★**L'Eveil des Sens –**
Le Blue Margouillat MODERN FRENCH €€€
(Map p200; ☑0262 34 64 00; www.blue-margouillat.com; Impasse Jean Albany; mains €32-49, menus €85-105; ⊗7.30-9pm Mon-Sat, noon-1pm & 7.30-9pm Sun) This elegant restaurant inside Le Blue Margouillat hotel is the top-end darling of the west coast. Marc Chappot's creative dishes are artfully prepared and presented, and all provide a burst of flavour. Another draw is the romantic setting: tables are set around the pool or on the colonial-style terrace. A memorable experience.

Il Etait Une Fois FRENCH €€€
(Map p200; ☑0692 68 96 19; 1 Ruelle Rivière; mains €24-30; ⊗7-9pm Tue-Sat) Tucked away on a side street running perpendicular to the main road, 'Once Upon a Time' offers something different. There's no menu, just a selection of the day's dishes depending on seasonal produce and the chef's mood. Its rustic, plant-filled terrace is also a welcoming place to eat.

🍷 Drinking & Nightlife

Le Zinc BAR
(Map p200; ☑0262 22 29 11; 228 Rue du Général Lambert; ⊗5pm-midnight Thu-Sun) Le Zinc is St-Leu's liveliest spot. Come for the good

fun, great mix of people, wicked cocktails and great music, with DJs or live bands every evening.

☆ Entertainment

St-Leu is especially popular for its *concerts sur la plage* (live bands on the beach) every weekend – don't miss it.

Rondavelle Les Filaos –
Chez Jean-Paul CONCERT VENUE
(Map p200; ☑0692 58 58 38; 17 Rue de la Compagnie des Indes; ⊗7.30am-8.30pm) Like bees to honey, St-Leusiens swarm on this modest, open-air bar close to the beach when live bands perform on Sunday evenings. Good blend of electro, *maloya* (traditional dance music), rock and jazz. During the day the 'Ronda' is esteemed for its cheap sandwiches, freshly squeezed fruit juices and cold beers.

Le Séchoir – Le K CONCERT VENUE
(Map p200; ☑0262 34 31 38; www.lesechoir.com; 209 Rue du Général Lambert) One of Réunion's venues for contemporary theatre, dance and music, as well as puppet shows, circus acts and other cultural activities. The organisers also put on open-air concerts and film shows in the area. Contact the tourist office to find out about the latest shows.

ℹ️ Information

Office du Tourisme (Map p200; ☑0262 34 63 30; www.ouest-lareunion.com; 1 Rue Barrelier; ⊗1.30-5.30pm Mon, 9am-noon & 1.30-5.30pm Tue-Fri, 9am-noon & 2-5pm Sat; ☜) At the north end of the main road passing through the centre of town. It has brochures galore and helpful, English-speaking staff. *Gîtes de montagne* can also be booked here. Free wi-fi.

ℹ️ Getting There & Away

Car Jaune's buses between St-Denis (€2, 1¼ hours) and St-Pierre (€2, 1¼ hours) run through the centre of St-Leu. The bus station is near the town hall. More information at www.carjaune.re.

Les Hauts de St-Leu

After getting active in St-Leu, there's no better way to wind down than by exploring the villages that cling to the sloping hills high above the town. The zigzagging roads are scenic to boot and the atmosphere wonderfully laid-back.

◎ Sights

To the north of St-Leu, take the D12, known as Route des Colimaçons – a series of S-curves – then veer due south on the D3 to **La Chaloupe St-Leu** before plunging back to the coast via **Piton St-Leu**, where the brightly painted **Hindu temple** is worth a gander. If you really want to get away from it all, you could continue to drive uphill from the village of **Les Colimaçons** until you reach the Route Forestière des Tamarins, which threads for 38km across the slopes from Le Tévelave to Le Maïdo – sensational. Whatever your itinerary, a GPS unit is essential as it's easy to get disoriented.

★ **Stella Matutina**   MUSEUM
(Map p186; ✆ 0262 34 59 60; www.museesreunion.re/musee/stella-matutina; 6 Allée des Flamboyants; adult/child €9/6; ⊙ 1-5.30pm Mon, 9.30am-4.45pm Tue-Sun) Réunion's most beloved museum is dedicated primarily to the sugar industry, but also provides fascinating insights into the history of the island, especially slavery and the colonial era. It includes a state-of-the-art 4D cinema. There's a shop and a cafeteria. It's about 4km south of St-Leu on the D11 to Piton St-Leu and Les Avirons.

Conservatoire Botanique National de Mascarin   GARDENS
(Map p186; ✆ 0262 24 92 27; www.cbnm.org; 2 Rue du Père Georges, Les Colimaçons; adult/child €7/5; ⊙ 9am-5pm Tue-Sun) Along the Route des Colimaçons, on the slopes north of St-Leu, this attractive garden is in the grounds of a 19th-century Creole mansion and contains an impressive collection of native plant species, all neatly labelled, as well as many from around the Indian Ocean. Spitting distance from the Conservatoire is the **Église du Sacré-Coeur**. This majestic church was built in 1875, using lava stones.

🛏️ Sleeping & Eating

There are several peaceful villages within 10km of St-Leu that offer accommodation in a relaxed, rural setting. Many places have a bird's-eye views down to the coast.

Maison Canopée   B&B
(Map p186; ✆ 0692 50 15 05; www.facebook.com/La.Maison.Canopee; 775 Chemin Dubuisson; d with shared bathroom €52-59; P 🐾) This is a solid choice, despite the fact that the two rooms share bathrooms and breakfast is extra (per person €10). The dearer room comes with sea views. Dinners can be arranged on request (€30).

**Le Balcon Créole –
Chez François et Michèle Huet**   B&B €
(Map p186; ✆ 0692 67 62 54, 0262 54 76 70; www.balcon-creole.fr; 202 Chemin Potier, Bras-Mouton; d incl breakfast €60; P 🐾) The four rooms here are sparkling, fresh and colourful, and provide a very cushy landing after a hard day's driving. The two ones at the front come with splendid sea views. When it comes to preparing fish dishes, the Huets know their stuff (dinner €25). It's signposted, uphill from the botanical garden.

Ask for the spacious Creole-style *gîte* (lodge/self-catering accommodation) in the flower-filled garden if you intend to stay more than four nights.

★ **Les Lataniers**   APARTMENT €€
(Map p186; ✆ 0692 25 13 38, 0262 34 74 45; www.les-lataniers.com; 136ter Rue Adrien Lagourgue, Piton St-Leu; d €90-145, q €125-160; P 🐾 🏊) An excellent surprise, with tasteful decor, a fantastic tropical garden and a stunning pool looking straight out to the sea. The nine apartments, three of which have ocean views, are huge, well appointed and sun-filled. There's a two-night minimum stay, and one-week stays are preferred. On the southern fringes of Piton St-Leu, toward Les Avirons.

Caz' Océane   B&B €€
(✆ 0692 74 63 94, 0262 54 89 40; www.chambredhotelslareunioncazoceane.com; 28 Chemin Mutel, Notre-Dame des Champs; s/d incl breakfast €70/90; P 🐾) Reached after innumerable twists and turns, this congenial B&B in the hamlet of Notre-Dame des Champs, a 30-minute drive from St-Leu, has four rooms and one apartment. They're nothing to write home about but they get the job done. The owners can cook some reputedly good evening meals (€30). Some English and German are spoken.

WORTH A TRIP

LE TÉVELAVE

Le Tévelave, about 10km up an impossibly twisty road in the hills above Les Avirons, is a gem of a village. It offers a real taste of rural life and is a great base for walkers. You can really feel a sense of wilderness and seclusion here, light years away from the bling and bustle of the coast. At the top of the village is the starting point for the Route Forestière des Tamarins, which leads through a cryptomeria forest and emerges 36km later below Le Maïdo. Picnic sites abound along the road. You'll need your own wheels to get to Le Tévelave as bus services are infrequent.

ℹ️ Getting There & Away

You'll need your own wheels to explore the *hauts* (hills) above St-Leu.

Étang-Salé-les-Bains

POP 14,000

Kilometres away from the hullabaloo around St-Gilles, Étang-Salé-les-Bains is a low-key resort more for locals than foreign tourists, though its superb black-sand beach is no longer a secret for in-the-know sunbathers and swimmers.

👁️ Sights

Plage de L'Étang-Salé-les-Bains
BEACH

The generous stretch of ash-coloured beach on the northern outskirts of town is great for sunbathing and swimming, and offers excellent sunset vistas. Most of the beach has a shallow bottom with a gradual slope. Swimming is forbidden outside the supervised area, which is marked by buoys.

Croc Parc
ZOO

(Map p186; ☑ 0262 91 40 41; www.crocparc.re; 1 Route Forestière; adult/child €12/10; ⊙ 10am-5pm) Wanna keep the kids happy? Take a small detour to this zoo, near Étang-Salé-les-Hauts (it's signposted). There are about 100 crocodiles at the complex, as well as iguanas, tortoises and lemurs. Feeding demonstrations are held at 4pm on Wednesdays and Sundays.

🏃 Activities

Very few visitors know that diving is available at Étang-Salé-les-Bains. The sites are almost untouched.

Plongée Salée
DIVING

(☑ 0262 91 71 23; www.plongeesalee.com; 5 Rue Motais de Narbonne; introductory dive €70-85, single dive €56) The owners of this reputable outfit take only small diving groups, with a selection of around 15 dive sites for all levels; see the schedule on the website. Certification courses are also on offer.

🛏️ Sleeping

Camping Municipal de l'Étang-Salé-les-Bains
CAMPGROUND €

(☑ 0262 91 75 86; www.camping-reunion.com; Rue Guy Hoarau; camping per site €22-28) There are 70 shady sites at this trim camping ground a short walk back from the beach. The ablution blocks are in good nick.

Zot Case
BUNGALOW €€

(Map p186; ☑ 0262 26 57 73, 0692 82 33 26; waro-lauret@wanadoo.fr; 3 Impasse des Alamandas, Route des Canots; bungalow per 2-3 nights from €270; P ❋ 🖥️ 🏊) This place is a bit tricky to find, tucked away in a side street in Étang-Salé-les-Hauts, but it's well worth the detour if you're after something quirky. Picture this: two lovely Creole houses (Zot Case en Natte and Zot Case en Dur) sheltering atmospheric rooms with parquet flooring – perfect for families or a group of friends. Longer stays are preferred.

Floralys & Roseaux des Sables
HOTEL €€

(☑ 0262 91 79 79; www.floralys.re; 2 Ave de l'Océan; d/q from €90/130; ❋ 🖥️ 🏊) This well-run three-star abode is set in an attractive 3-hectare garden beside the roundabout in the middle of town and a two-minute walk from the beach. It comprises two sections: the Floralys, with modern yet impersonal rooms set in a cluster of cottages, and the Roseaux des Sables, with upscale, fully equipped villas, at the far end of the property. It's a relaxing place, with plenty of shade, an on-site restaurant and a large pool, but it can be noisy on weekends.

🍴 Eating

You'll find a few *camions-snacks* along the beach as well as several popular eateries in the street running parallel to the beach.

Le Bambou
FRENCH, CREOLE €€

(☑ 0262 91 70 28; www.lebambou-restaurant.fr; 56 Rue Octave Bénard; mains €12-21; ⊙ 11.45am-9.30pm Mon-Sat, to 9pm Sun; 🖥️) This well-oiled machine near the main roundabout is known for its kilometre-long menu featuring lots of salads, burgers, pizzas, pasta dishes, crêpes, Creole classics, grilled meats and fish. The food ain't gourmet and doesn't claim to be, but if you need to fill a gap any time of the day, this is your baby.

ℹ Information

The **Office du Tourisme** (☏ 0820 20 32 20; www.sudreuniontourisme.fr; 74 Rue Octave Bénard; ⊙ 9am-noon & 1-4.30pm Mon-Sat; ⍐) is housed in the old train station on the roundabout that marks the town centre. *Gîtes de montagne* can be booked here. It also offers free wi-fi.

ℹ Getting There & Away

Car Jaune's nonexpress buses between St-Denis and St-Pierre (lines O2 and T, €2, about 20 daily, fewer on Sunday) run through Étang-Salé-les-Bains. From St-Denis, the ride takes about 1¼ hours. The town also lies on Car Jaune's coastal bus route (line S3) between St-Joseph and St-Paul. More information at www.carjaune.re.

Entre-Deux

POP 6260

The sweet little village of Entre-Deux, high in the hills 18km north of St-Pierre, got its name (which means 'between two') because it is situated on a ridge between two valleys: the Bras de Cilaos and the Bras de la Plaine. Entre-Deux is a delightful place to stay and get a taste of rural life, with plenty of cute Creole houses.

⊙ Sights

Entre-Deux has a wealth of *cases créoles,* traditional country cottages surrounded by well-tended and fertile gardens, many of which are being restored. There's also a strong tradition of local crafts, including natty slippers made from the leaves of an aloe-like plant called *choca.*

Espace Culturel
Muséographique
du Dimitile – Camp Marron   MUSEUM
(ECM; Map p208; ☏ 0692 39 73 26; http://ecm campmarron.e-monsite.com/; Le Dimitile; €2, audio guide €5; ⊙ by reservation) Just before the viewpoint of Le Dimitile, this modest yet well-organised museum does a good job of explaining *marronage* (the act of escaping plantation life) and tracing the history of slavery in Réunion. Sadly, its opening hours are unreliable; contact the tourist office in Entre-Deux or call ahead.

OFF THE BEATEN TRACK

ST-LOUIS

If St-Gilles and L'Hermitage are very Westernised and touristy, St-Louis, by contrast, falls below many travellers' radars. This is the heart of Tamil culture on the west coast, and it won't take long to feel that the city exudes an undeniably exotic atmosphere. It doesn't have anything fantastic to offer, but is certainly worth a quick stop to admire a handful of religious buildings, including a Tamil temple, a splendid mosque and the biggest church on the island.

Most people travel to St-Louis to catch the bus to Cilaos or to visit the **Sucrerie du Gol** (Map p186; ☏ 0262 91 05 47; www.tereos.re; Rond-Point du Gol; adult/ child €8/5; ⊙ 9am-9pm Tue-Sat, tours by reservation Jul-Dec), a sugar refinery that lies about 1.5km west of the centre.

Car Jaune buses between St-Denis and St-Pierre run through St-Louis. Buses to Cilaos (€2, 1½ hours) run from the bus station. More details at www. carjaune.re.

🏃 Activities

Le Dimitile   HIKING
(Map p208) The hike up the slopes of iconic Le Dimitile (1837m) is tough but you'll be rewarded with a sensational view over the Cirque de Cilaos. There are several options to reach the viewpoint and orientation table. The tourist office can provide information and sketch maps detailing the various routes.

The shortest route, called **Sentier de la Chapelle**, starts from the end of the D26 (there's a small parking area), about 10km from Entre-Deux, at an altitude of 1100m. Count on a five-hour return slog. It's mostly shady. On the way back, it's easier to follow the dirt road called Piste Jean Dubard, which is less slippery and will also take you back to the parking area.

To soak up the atmosphere, it's not a bad idea to overnight at one of the *gîtes* near the summit. Le Dimitile is also endowed with a strong historical significance; *marrons* (runaway slaves) took refuge in the area in the late 19th century.

Just before the viewpoint is Espace Culturel Muséographique du Dimitile.

Kreolie 4x4   TOURS
(☏ 0692 86 52 26; www.kreolie4x4.com; day trip incl lunch €100) This well-regarded outfit

organises excellent 4WD tours and specialises in day trips that include Entre-Deux and the viewpoint at Le Dimitile (1837m). Guides are informative, providing interesting titbits on the area's flora and fauna (in French).

✨ Festivals & Events

Fête du Choca   FAIR
(Festival of Choca; ☺ Jul) This festival celebrates crafts made from *choca* leaves; held in Entre-Deux.

🛏 Sleeping

Gîte Valmyr – Le Boucan des Cabris Marrons   GÎTE €
(Map p208; ☑ 0692 98 34 73; Le Dimitile; dm with half board €38; ☺ Wed-Sat, by reservation) Not far from the lookout that affords splendid views down into the Cirque de Cilaos, this is a great find for walkers and nature lovers. Digs are in basic three- to eight-bed huts. Run by Valmyr Talbot, who is a local character, this *gîte* is famous for its feisty atmosphere. Book ahead.

Gîte Émile   GÎTE €
(Map p208; ☑ 0692 67 24 54, 0262 57 43 03; Le Dimitile; dm incl half board €38) Up on Le Dimitile. Has basic accommodation in five- to 12-person dorms. It's usually open on weekends only. From the *gîte* to the viewpoint, it's a 30- to 45-minute walk.

Villa Oté   B&B €€
(Map p208; ☑ 0692 41 60 38, 0262 39 03 43; www.villaote.com; 29 Rue Maurice Berrichon; d incl breakfast €95; ℗ 🕸 ⛱) A beautifully manicured haven with delightful gardens and a great pool enclosed by charming guest quarters. The three rooms are individually designed and each one has its own entrance. One quibble: no air-con (only fans). The pool is accessible between 9.30am and 7pm. You can also use the Jacuzzi (€15). Dinner costs €27.

L'Échappée Belle   B&B €€
(☑ 0262 22 91 31, 0692 55 55 37; www.lechappee-belle.com; 13 Impasse du Palmier; d incl breakfast €110; ℗ 🕸 ⛱) Concealed behind high walls down a cul-de-sac near the *mairie* (town hall), this bright, contemporary five-room B&B has a number of points in its favour, not least its vast tropical garden and its pool – lovely for unwinding after a day's explorations. There's also a communal kitchen, a Jacuzzi (free) and a dining room in the garden. Downside: there's no air-con.

Le Dimitile   HOTEL €€€
(☑ 0262 39 20 00; www.hotel-ledimitile.com; 30 Rue Bras Long; d €170-190; ℗ 🕸 ⛱) Under new management since 2018, this beautifully manicured haven that comprises 18 rooms is back with a vengeance. Although it's still missing something like soul, it features small yet appealing rooms with cosy reds on the floors, natural stones and a lovely (heated) pool. The icing on the cake? An on-site restaurant (lunch menu €19, dinner €35-90).

🍴 Eating

Le Régal des Hauts   PIZZA, CREOLE €
(☑ 0692 72 81 45; 3 Rue Jean Lauret; mains €6-13; ☺ 11.30am-1.30pm & 6.30-9pm Tue-Sat, 6.30-9pm Sun & Mon) At dinner, wood-fired pizzas go down a treat at this lively joint near the town hall. They come either red or white (with or without tomato base), and are thin and relatively crispy. For something local, try the Victoria, with pineapple and chicken, or the Creole, with smoked sausage and spices. The menu is strong on Creole staples, too.

★ L'Arbre à Palabres   CREOLE, INTERNATIONAL €€
(☑ 0262 44 47 23; 29 Rue Césaire; mains €21-26; ☺ noon-1.30pm Wed-Thu & Sun, noon-1.30pm & 7-9pm Fri, 7-9pm Sat) For a menu that strays a little off the familiar sausage *rougail* (sausages cooked in tomato sauce) and chicken curry path, try this cute eatery in a Creole house, near the tourist office. The menu changes daily, according to what's available at the market. You can also dine in the cool shade of a massive lychee tree on the terrace.

Le Gadjak   CREOLE €€
(☑ 0692 41 03 69; 1 Rue Fortune Hoarau; mains €10-18; ☺ 11.45am-1.45pm & 6.30-8.30pm Mon, Tue & Thu, 11.45am-1.45pm Wed & Fri, 6.30-8.30pm Sat) Gadjak, smack dab in the centre, is a popular hangout serving Creole dishes as well as a few appetising French specialities (namely duck and *andouillette* – chitterling sausage) and tempting desserts. It also does takeaway (from €6). A great deal.

Le Longanis   CREOLE €€
(☑ 0262 39 70 56; www.le-longanis.com; 9bis Rue du Commerce; mains €11-15; ☺ 11.30am-1.45pm & 7-9pm Mon & Thu-Sat, 11.30am-1.45pm Tue & Sun) This typically Creole venue, right in the centre, whips up lip-smacking, dirt-cheap meals. Grab a dish from the daily specials, add a salad and you're sorted. Takeaway is available (€6).

ℹ Information

The **tourist office** (☑ 0262 39 69 80; www.ot-entredeux.com; 9 Rue Fortuné Hoarau;

⊗ 8am-noon & 1.30-5pm Mon-Sat) occupies a pretty *case créole* on the road into the village. Staff can arrange guided visits (usually in French) of the village (adult/child €15/7.50) and can provide leaflets on walks in the region (including climbing Le Dimitile) and on local artisans.

ℹ Getting There & Away

Car Jaune's line S5 operates a bus service (€2, three daily, 50 minutes to one hour) between Entre-Deux and the bus station in St-Pierre.

Les Makes

POP 650

One of Réunion's best-kept secrets, Les Makes has a wonderful bucolic atmosphere and a lovely setting. Snuggled into the seams of the Hauts, it's accessible via a tortuous secondary road from St-Louis (12km). At almost 1200m, breathing in the fresh alpine air here is enough therapy for a lifetime.

◎ Sights & Activities

★**La Fenêtre**   VIEWPOINT
(The Window; Map p186) It would be a sin to visit Les Makes and not take the forest road that leads to this viewpoint, another 10km further uphill. The view over the entire Cirque de Cilaos and the surrounding craggy summits that jab the skyline will be etched in your memory forever. La Fenêtre is also a wonderful picnic spot, and there are a few walking options in the area. Hint: arrive early, before it gets cloudy.

Observatoire Astronomique   OBSERVATORY
(Map p186; ☑0262 37 86 83; www.ilereunion.com/observatoire-des-makes; 18 Rue Georges Bizet, Les Makes; adult/child €10/5) Les Makes is an ideal area for stargazing. The Observatoire Astronomique offers stargazing programmes from 9pm to midnight. It's best to call ahead to confirm the programme is on.

Centre Équestre de la Fenêtre   HORSE RIDING
(Map p186; ☑0692 03 52 51; 31 Rue Montplaisir, Les Makes; per hour €18) This equestrian centre can arrange guided trips in the forests around Les Makes. It's a great way to soak up the scenery.

🍴 Sleeping & Eating

Le Vieil Alambic –
Chez Jean-Luc d'Eurveilher   B&B €
(Map p186; ☑0262 37 82 77; www.levieilalambic.com; 55 Rue Montplaisir; d incl breakfast €65; P 🛜) Should you fall under the spell of charming

Les Makes (no doubt you will), you can bunk down at this adorable B&B on the road to La Fenêtre, at an altitude of about 1000m. It features four tidy rooms (no views) that were given a lick of paint in 2018 and highly respected traditional meals (from €26). Prices drop by €5 if you stay two nights or more.

ℹ Getting There & Away

Getting to Les Makes by public transport is not really an option. You'll need your own wheels.

THE CIRQUES

Knitted together like a three leaf clover, the Cirques of Cilaos, Salazie and Mafate are Réunion's heart and soul. They're different in spirit from the rest of the island – more inward-looking, more secretive, and more traditional. The fast-paced and hedonistic coastal life seems light years away.

This rugged region is a fantastic playground for the stimulus-needy, with staggering mountain scenery, a mesh of well-marked trails and impressive canyons that beg to be explored. Even if you don't fancy outdoor adventures, it's worth visiting these awesomely photogenic amphitheatres just for the views.

The Cirques first began to be settled by *marrons* (runaway slaves) in the 18th century, and their descendants still inhabit some of the villages of the Cirques. The people residing here are adamantly tied to their traditional lifestyle.

Each Cirque has its own personality – try to include all three of them when planning your trip.

Cirque de Cilaos

The setting couldn't be more grandiose: imagine snaggle-toothed volcanic peaks, deep ravines and forests that are straight out of a fairy tale. At times, swirling banks of cloud add a touch of the bizarre. A sweet sprinkling of secluded hamlets top off this area's indisputable allure. For outdoorsy types, the Cirque de Cilaos is hard to beat.

To get here, clunk in your seatbelt and take a deep breath: the RN5, which connects St-Louis with Cilaos, 37km to the north, is Réunion's premier drive (and that is saying a lot). Snaking steeply around more than 400 twists and turns along the way up into the amphitheatre, it provides an endless stream of stunning vista-points. *Bon voyage!*

Cilaos

POP 5500

Cilaos is ensnared by scenery so mind-blowingly dramatic it's practically alpine. One name says it all: **Piton des Neiges** (3071m). The iconic peak towers over the town of Cilaos, acting like a magnet to hiking fiends. But there's no obligation to overdo it: a smattering of museums and plenty of short walks mean this incredible dose of natural magnificence can also be appreciated at a more relaxed pace.

The Cirques & Les Hautes Plaines

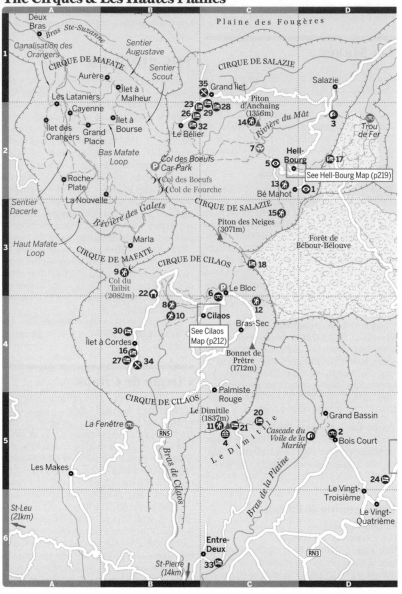

The largest settlement in any of the Cirques, Cilaos sits 1200m above sea level. Developed as a spa resort at the end of the 19th century, the town's fortunes still rest on tourism, particularly hiking and canyoning, backed up by agriculture and the bottled-mineral-water industry. The area is known for the production of lentils, embroidery and wine.

Cilaos fills up quickly on weekends. But despite its popularity there are no massive hotels or blaring discos, only low-key, small-scale operations.

◉ Sights

La Roche Merveilleuse VIEWPOINT
(Marvellous Rock; Map p208) Head to the Marvellous Rock for an eagle-eye panorama of Cilaos. It's accessible on foot or by road. From Cilaos, take the road to Bras-Sec. The turnoff to La Roche Merveilleuse is signposted on the left after about 2km. Bring a picnic – the setting is enchanting and there are a few *kiosques* (wooden shelters) to protect picnickers from any rain.

Maison de la Broderie MUSEUM
(Map p212; ☑0262 31 77 48; Rue des Écoles; adult/child €2/1; ⊙9.30am-noon & 2-5pm Mon-Sat, 9.30am-noon Sun) Entirely modernised in 2014, the Maison de la Broderie is home to an association of 30 or so local women dedicated to keeping Cilaos' embroidery tradition alive. They embroider and sell children's clothes, serviettes, place settings and tablecloths. It's laborious work: a single placemat takes between 12 and 15 days to complete. You can watch the women at work in the workshop upstairs.

🏃 Activities

Canyoning

Of the stellar spots for canyoning in Réunion, the Cilaos area tops the list, with three major canyons that draw action-seekers like bees to a honeypot: Canyons de Gobert, Fleurs Jaunes and Bras Rouge. All are very atmospheric; you can expect various jumps, leaps into natural pools and jaw-dropping rappelling. Access to the canyons involves a preliminary five- to 45-minute hike (and back). The time spent in the canyon is about three to five hours. The most suitable canyons for beginners and families are Canyon de Gobert and Mini Fleurs Jaunes (which is a section of Fleurs Jaunes). Fleurs Jaunes is a more aerial circuit, with seven rappels, including a 55m (yes!) rappel.

All canyoning trips are led by qualified instructors. Some of the major operators don't have offices but can be reached by phone.

Adrenal'île ADVENTURE SPORTS
(☑0692 75 04 00; www.adrenalile.com) A well-regarded operator. Qualified instructors will

RÉUNION CIRQUE DE CILAOS

Map

0 — 5 km
0 — 2.5 miles

St-André (6km)

Rivière des Roches

Rivière des Marsouins

Grand Étang

Cascade Biberon

RN3

Col de Bébour (1411m)

Plaine-des-Palmistes

📍31

🏕25

Petite Plaine

Plaine-des-Cafres 19

Col de Bellevue (1606m)

RN3

Route Forestière du Volcan

See Bourg-Murat Map (p227)

Bourg-Murat

RF5

See Piton de la Fournaise Map (p230)

La Grande Ferme

La Petite Ferme

Roche-Plate

Notre Dame de la Paix

Morne Langevin (2380m)

The Cirques & Les Hautes Plaines

take you along the most atmospheric canyons in the Cirque.

Cilaos Aventure ADVENTURE SPORTS

(☑0692 66 73 42; www.cilaosaventure.com; canyoning tours €55-80) This reliable outlet can arrange all kinds of canyoning trips in the area, including Fleurs Jaunes, Gobert and Bras Rouge. See the website for schedules.

Aparksa Montagne OUTDOORS

(☑0692 66 50 09; www.facebook.com/Aparksa Montagne; Cilaos; canyoning tours €50-70) For canyoning trips, guided walks (from €25) or excursions to lava tubes, this outfit has good credentials. The owner, Thomas Percheron is fluent in English.

Canyon Ric a Ric ADVENTURE SPORTS

(☑0692 86 54 85; www.canyonreunion.com; canyoning tours per person €55-80) Canyon Ric a Ric is one of the major canyoning operators in Réunion. Prices depend on the duration of the tour.

Bouisset Fabrice ADVENTURE SPORTS

(☑0692 66 22 73; bouisset.fabrice@wanadoo.fr; canyoning tours €55-70) Fabrice Bouisset is a qualified canyoning instructor and leads excellent canyoning trips around Cilaos, including Fleurs Jaunes.

Hiking

There are fabulous hiking options in the vicinity of Cilaos, including the climb up Piton des Neiges. There are well-marked trails suitable for all levels of fitness. The tourist office produces a small leaflet that gives an overview of the walks in the Cirque.

Col du Taïbit HIKING

(Map p208) An iconic climb to the pass that separates the Cirque de Cilaos from the Cirque de Mafate. From the pass you can walk down to Marla in the Cirque de Mafate in about 45 minutes. The starting point is signposted on the D242 (the road to Îlet à Cordes), 5km from Cilaos. About 4½ hours return, with 830m of altitude gain.

Le Kervéguen HIKING

(Map p208) This hike offers splendid views of the Cirque. The starting point is signposted on the D241 (the road to Bras-Sec), 5km from Cilaos. About five hours return.

Sentier Botanique WALKING

(Map p208) An easy 90-minute loop with a focus on local flora (most species are labelled). Perfectly suitable for families. It starts at La Roche Merveilleuse.

DON'T MISS

HIKING UP PITON DES NEIGES

The ascent to Réunion's highest point (3071m) is vigorous, but the 360-degree panorama at the summit is worth the effort. It's usually done in two days, with an overnight stay in **Gîte de la Caverne Dufour** (Map p208; ☑ 0692 67 74 26; dm €17-19, breakfast/dinner €6/22).

The trail starts at Le Bloc, between Cilaos and Bras-Sec (it's signposted), which you can reach by bus from Cilaos. From Le Bloc, it's a challenging ascent through a forest of cryptomeria (a cedar-like tree) to the Plateau du Petit Matarum, a flat area reached after about 1¼ hours. Here the forest changes to stunted giant heather bushes (knows as *branles*) cloaked in wisps of lichen. The next section is even more arduous than the previous one from Le Bloc, with steep gradients all the way from here to the *gîte* (lodge); allow another two hours from the Plateau du Petit Matarum to the *gîte*.

Because the summit of Piton des Neiges is usually cloaked in cloud by mid-morning, most people choose to stay overnight at the *gîte*, starting out for the peak before dawn. The path is clearly marked in white on the rock face. The climb takes about three hours return. The landscape becomes increasingly rocky the higher you climb, and the final section rises steeply over shifting cinders that make for slippery footing. At the summit there are few traces of vegetation, and the red, black and ochre rock leave little doubt about the mountain's volcanic origins. On a clear day, the whole island is spread out beneath you.

RÉUNION CIRQUE DE CILAOS

Bras Rouge
WALKING
(Map p208) An easy walk, amid great scenery, to the top of a waterfall. Plan on 2½ hours return.

La Chapelle
HIKING
(Map p208) This path connects Cilaos to a cave near a river (about five hours return).

Cycling & Mountain Biking
The Cirque de Cilaos, with its dramatic topography and great scenic roads, is superb terrain for experienced cyclists. Novices can ride to La Roche Merveilleuse (p209). The road to Bras-Sec is another stunner.

Tof Bike
MOUNTAIN BIKING
(Map p212; ☑ 0692 25 61 61; 29 Rue du Père Boiteau; half/full day €14/19; ◷ 8.30am-noon & 2.30-6pm Mon-Sat, to noon Sun) This outfit rents out mountain bikes in tip-top condition and gives advice on various circuits. A map is provided. Also rents out e-bikes (one hour/half day €10/30).

Rock Climbing
Rock climbing is becoming increasingly popular in Cilaos, where there is no shortage of awesome cliffs and gorges, particularly in the stunning Fleurs Jaunes area, which is home to dozens of mind-boggling ascents, graded four to eight (easy to difficult). For novices, there are also *falaise-écoles* (training cliffs that are specially equipped for beginners). **Run Évasion** (Map p212; ☑ 0262 31 83 57, 0692 61 28 60; www.runevasion.re; 23 Rue du Père Boiteau; canyoning tours €55-85; ◷ 8am-

noon & 2-6pm Mon-Sat, to 5pm Sun) and Cilaos Aventure employ qualified instructors. Plan on €55 per person.

✸ Festivals & Events

Fête de la Vigne
WINE
(Wine Harvest Festival; ◷ Jan) A popular wine fair, where local winemakers promote their products.

Fête des Lentilles
FOOD & DRINK
(Festival of Lentils; ◷ Oct) This agricultural fair held in Cilaos celebrates lentils through various exhibitions, conferences, tastings and recipe contests.

🛏 Sleeping

★ Gîte de la Chapelle
GÎTE €
(Map p212; ☑ 0692 09 27 30; etheve.valerie@orange.fr; 16 Rue de la Chapelle; dm/d with shared bathroom €18/36; ☜) This excellent budget option – by far our favourite *gîte* in town – is owner-run and it shows. It occupies an agreeable Creole house that was skilfully renovated in 2018 and shelters one double, three rooms sleeping four, and sparkling communal bathrooms. It feels much more modern, fresh and immaculate than other *gîtes* in town. There's a communal kitchen. Breakfast costs €6.

Au Cœur du Cirque
RENTAL HOUSE €
(Map p212; ☑ 0692 76 63 22; www.aucoeurducirque.com; 3a Route du Bras des Étangs; cottage for 1-6 people €80-120; ☐☜) This hidden treasure is one of Cilaos' best retreats. Au Cœur

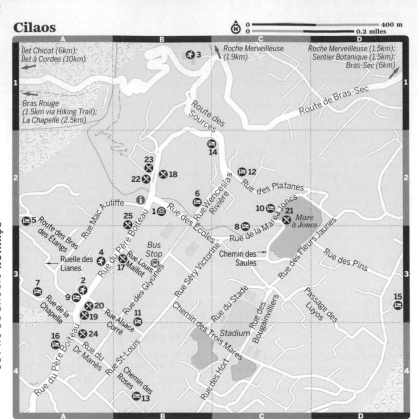

Cilaos

du Cirque is a cute-as-a-button cottage in a well-tended property blessed with sweeping Cirque views. Cocooned in a wonderfully private setting, it consists of a kitchen, sitting room, bathroom, terrace and two bedrooms – perfect for families, friends or couples. There's a two-night minimum stay; rates fall outside peak school holiday periods.

La Carte Postale
BUNGALOW €

(Map p212; ✆ 0693 50 10 33; http://colonia location.free.fr; 9 Rue de la Mare à Joncs; s/d incl breakfast €50/70; P 🖥) Two spick-and-span, self-contained Creole-style bungalows enjoy a spiffing location above Mare à Joncs (a small pond) with a picture-postcard view of the Cirque. The restaurant below is run by the same owners.

Le Bois de Senteur
B&B €

(Map p212; ✆ 0262 31 91 03, 0692 29 81 20; www. leboisdesenteur.com; 4 Chemin des Roses; d/q incl breakfast €60/80; P 🖥) This few-frills place in a peaceful cul-de-sac is brought to life

with lashings of colourful paint on the facade. Inside, the 10 rooms are modestly furnished and feel a tad compact. Ask for one of the upstairs rooms, which have balconies and afford dashing views of the Piton des Neiges (especially rooms 6, 7 and 9).

La Case Bleue
GÎTE €

(Map p212; ✆ 0692 65 74 96; www.gitecasebleu. e-monsite.com; 15 Rue Alsace Corré; dm/d €18/42) A good deal, this *gîte* occupies an attractive Creole house painted in blue. Expect a neat dorm (11 beds), back-friendly mattresses, salubrious bathrooms and a practical communal kitchen. There's also a modest double with its own entrance and bathrooms – ideal for couples, although it opens onto the dorm's terrace, which may be noisy if the *gîte* is full. Breakfast costs €6.

Clair de Lune
GÎTE €

(Map p212; ✆ 0692 00 57 54, 0692 82 47 13; 10 Rue Wenceslas Rivière; dm/d with shared bathroom incl breakfast €20/40; P) Run by Alex, who

Cilaos

knows a thing or 50 about Cilaos, this congenial spot has rooms of varying size and shape, with three- to seven-bed dorms and one double. Bathrooms are shared. The living area is a good place to swap tales with like-minded travellers. No wi-fi.

La Roche Merveilleuse   GÎTE €
(Map p212; 📞 0262 31 82 42; 1 Rue des Platanes; dm €18, d €45-50, with shared bathroom €42-45; P 🛜) This all-wood *gîte* looks like a Canadian chalet transplanted to Cilaos. Opt for one of the four snug doubles, which feel like cosy birds' nests. The real appeal is the panoramic view from the terrace.

Hôtel des Neiges   HOTEL €€
(Map p212; 📞 0262 31 72 33; www.hotel-des-neiges.com; 1 Rue de la Mare à Joncs; d €89-99; P 🛜🏊) One of Cilaos' few mid-range accommodation options, this abode has a range of well-maintained rooms in a two-storey, motel-like building. The decor is nothing special, but the relaxed feel and great amenities – two heated pools, a neat garden, a restaurant and a sauna – more than make up for the slightly dated sense of style. Frequent online promotional deals provide better value.

Otroiza   HOTEL €€
(Map p212; 📞 0262 31 50 12, 0692 05 25 93; www.otroiza.com; 3a Rue du Père Boiteau; d €80-90; P 🛜) This modernish hotel offers reasonably priced rooms with a clean modern design; pick of the bunch are the rooms at the back, with plenty of natural light and splendid mountain views. All come with attractive tiled bathrooms and excellent

bedding. There are only 10 rooms, which ensures intimacy.

Le Bois Rouge   B&B €€
(Map p212; 📞 0262 47 57 57, 0692 43 81 66; http://hotel-le-bois-rouge-maison-dhotes-de-charme-cilaos.business.site; 2 Route des Sources; s/d incl breakfast €99/119; P 🛜) Somewhere between a boutique hotel and B&B, the Bois Rouge has five stylish rooms with parquet flooring made of precious wood as well as cosy terraces. Angle for the Bois Noir, Ti Natte or Tamarin rooms, which offer the best views. Bonus: free transfers to the start of most hiking trails near Cilaos. Generous breakfasts, too.

★ Hôtel Tsilaosa   BOUTIQUE HOTEL €€€
(Map p212; 📞 0262 37 39 39; www.tsilaosa.com; Rue du Père Boiteau; d €140-185; P 🛜) This well-run four-star abode in a restored Creole home offers a smooth stay, with 22 rooms that are imaginatively decked out in local style; those upstairs have mountain views (rooms A, B, D, E and F are the best). There's a wine cellar in the basement where tastings of Cilaos and South African tipples can be organised. Also has a stunning rooftop Jacuzzi (€15).

Le Cilaos   HOTEL €€€
(Map p212; 📞 0262 31 85 85; www.leschenets-lecilaos.re; 40E Chemin des Trois Mares; s €97-117, d €147-182, ste €150-312, incl breakfast; P 🛜🏊) Cilaos' biggest hotel is in a transition period. Although the public areas have been spruced up, most rooms are still in need of a refurb – which should be completed by 2020. Room 108 and suites 114 to 117 have been modernised, though. Facilities include

---

DON'T MISS

CASCADE DU VOILE DE LA MARIÉE

On the southern outskirts of Salazie, along the road to Hell-Bourg and just north of the turnoff to Grand Îlet, are the spectacular waterfalls **Cascade du Voile de la Mariée** (Bridal Veil Falls; Map p208; Salazie) on your left. They drop in several stages from the often cloud-obscured heights into the ravine at the roadside. You get an even better view from the Grand Îlet road.

Musiques et Instruments de l'Océan Indien welcomed its first visitors, showcasing hundreds of musical instruments from Africa, India, China and Madagascar in a small yet state-of-the-art exhibition space. Don't miss the opportunity to embark on a musical and visual journey in this stunning museum.

Thermal Bath
RUINS

(Map p219) **FREE** Visitors can see the ruins of the old baths, which were in use until 1948. They are found in a ravine a 10-minute walk west of town (walk past Le Relais des Cimes hotel at the western end of Rue Général de Gaulle; it's signposted). It's a quiet and leafy spot.

Rivière du Mât
PICNIC AREA

(Map p208) From Îlet-à-Vidot, the asphalted road continues for about 2km to a small parking lot. From here, a steep footpath leads in about 15 minutes to the Rivière du Mât valley. Cross the footbridge and you'll soon reach a lovely picnic site by the river.

Bé Mahot
VILLAGE

(Map p208) About 3.5km from Hell-Bourg, Bé Mahot is a cute hamlet that's well worth visiting. With its clunky, colourful Creole houses clinging on the hillside and fantastic vistas of the Cirque, it's scenic to boot. There are several picnic sites along the road.

Îlet-à-Vidot
VILLAGE

(Map p208) The landscape surrounding the hamlet of Îlet-à-Vidot, about 2km from Hell-Bourg, is little short of breathtaking. The iconic, flat-topped Piton d'Enchaing, covered with thick vegetation, seems to stand guard over the village.

Maison Folio
HISTORIC BUILDING

(Map p219; ☎ 0262 47 80 98; 20 Rue Amiral Lacaze; entry €6, guided tour €5; ⊙ 9-11.30am & 2-5pm) One of the loveliest of Hell-Bourg's Creole houses is this typical 19th-century bourgeois villa almost engulfed by its densely planted garden. You can wander around the property or opt for the guided tour run by the owners. They show you around, pointing out the amazing variety of aromatic, edible, medicinal and decorative plants, and give insights into local culture. If the owners' son is around, he'll be happy to run a tour in English.

🏃 Activities

Hiking

Not surprisingly, the Hell-Bourg area is an adventure playground for hiking enthusiasts, with a good selection of day hikes. Hikers doing the Tour des Cirques route will have to pass through Hell-Bourg as they cross the Cirque de Salazie.

Hell-Bourg–Gîte de Bélouve About four hours return, with 570m of altitude gain. From Gîte de Bélouve (p233), you can continue to the Trou de Fer viewpoint (seven hours return from Hell-Bourg).

Piton d'Anchaing (Map p208) This soaring 1356m peak is a popular but challenging four-hour hike (return) from Îlet-à-Vidot, with 670m of altitude gain. Leave your car at the small parking area in Bras Marron (in Îlet-à-Vidot, follow the sign 'Piton d'Anchaing'). The trail starts by plunging down to a footbridge over Rivière du Mât, then stays fairly level for an hour or so, until it reaches the base of the Piton d'Anchaing. Now the climb really begins. At least one hour of switchback ascent along a narrow path brings you to the forested summit. You can do a 20-minute loop on the (flat) summit to make the most of the few viewpoints along the way (the best one is on the eastern side, with super views of the Cirque and the valley). Do not attempt this hike if it's wet.

Source Manouilh (Map p208) An exhilarating five- to six-hour loop, with a net altitude gain of about 600m.

Hell-Bourg–Gîte du Piton des Neiges A pleasant alternative to Cilaos if you're planning to hike up to Piton des Neiges. Expect a tough seven-hour climb (one way) via Cap Anglais, with a net altitude gain of 1470m.

Les Trois Cascades (Map p208) A short – about 90 minutes return – and relatively easy walk suitable for families, despite the initial steep section. It leads to a series of small waterfalls where you can take a dip.

Hell-Bourg

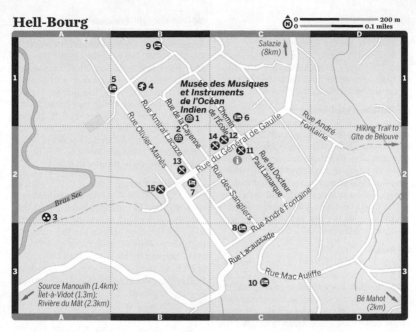

Hell-Bourg

Canyoning

The canyoning options available in the Cirque will make your spine tingle. Get wet at Trou Blanc, which is said to be the most 'aquatic' canyon in Réunion, with lots of *toboggans* (plunging down water-polished chutes) and leaps. Some sections are appropriately named 'The Washing Machine', 'The Bath' and 'The Aquaplaning'. Note that this canyon is not accessible during the rainiest months (from December to March).

Austral Aventure   ADVENTURE SPORTS
(Map p219; ☎0692 87 55 50; www.facebook.com/AustralAventureCanyonReunion; 42 Rue Amiral Laca-

ze; half-/full-day canyoning trips €55/75) This professional outfit has canyoning trips to Trou Blanc and Trou de Fer (from Hell-Bourg).

🛏 Sleeping

★La Mandoze   GÎTE €
(Map p219; ☎0262 47 89 65, 0692 65 65 28; 14 Chemin de l'École; dm €18, d with shared bathroom incl breakfast €45; 🅿🛜) This *gîte* set in a Creole house has all the hallmarks of a great deal: well-maintained dorms that can sleep six people, practical shared bathrooms, a tranquil location and a tab that won't burn a hole in your pocket. For those wanting

more privacy, three adjoining doubles, with wood-panelled walls, are available. They're compact but get the job done.

Breakfast (€6) and dinner (€22) are available. The owner, Patrick Manoro, is a mine of local knowledge and occasionally plays guitar for his guests in the evening.

Le Tableau d'Hell-Bourg GÎTE €
(Map p219; ☎0693 40 54 42; www.allonslareunion.com; 17 Impasse des Dahlias; d/q with shared bathroom €45/85; P 📶) With one double, two triples and one quadruple, all small but neat and tidy, this is an attractive choice for those who want something better than a dorm but cheaper than a hotel room. Another plus is the food (breakfast €6, dinner €20). It's north of the main drag, in a quiet area with lovely mountain views.

Le Relax CAMPGROUND €
(Map p208; ☎0692 66 58 89; 21 Chemin Bras-Sec, Îlet-à-Vidot; camping per site 1-2 people €11; P) Head to this homely campground in the hamlet of Îlet-à-Vidot, about 2km northwest of Hell-Bourg, if you're after a peaceful setting to pitch your tent within a grassy (and shady) property. The ablution block is in good nick and there's a kitchen for guests' use. No meal service, but there's a (modest) grocery store nearby.

The owner can take you to various scenic spots in the area and provide you with a wealth of information (alas, in French) about local plants and architecture.

Le Relais des Gouverneurs B&B €
(Map p219; ☎0262 47 76 21; www.relaisdesgouverneurs.fr; 2bis Rue Amiral Lacaze; d €70-85, q €100, incl breakfast; P 📶) This comfortably central B&B is a reliable option. The two Superieure rooms feature four-poster beds, wooden floors and clean bathrooms, while the Confort rooms are less spacious. Families can plump for the large Familiale units. The densely vegetated grounds add a lot of charm. Dinners (€25) are available if there's a minimum of six people.

Gîte du Piton d'Anchaing GÎTE €
(Map p219; ☎0693 60 66 43; www.facebook.com/gitedupitondanchaing; 33 Rue Olivier Manès; dm/d with shared bathroom €16/35; 📶) Occupying a cute Creole house on a tranquil street north of the main drag, this well-run *gîte* is a secure spot to hang your rucksack, with one tip-top and airy six-bed dorm, a clean double, well-scrubbed bathrooms and a nice communal area. Breakfast and dinner available.

★**Chambre d'Hôte des Agrumes** B&B €€
(Map p208; ☎0692 65 51 82; www.chambredhotesdesagrumes.fr; 7 Chemin Manouilh, Îlet-à-Vidot; d €90-110, q €180, incl breakfast; P 📶) If you're after hush and seclusion, these four standalone Creole-style bungalows scattered in an Eden-like garden are the answer. They're spacious and impeccably maintained, with spick-and-span bathrooms and a private terrace. Evening meals (€25) garner warm praise. Find this B&B in the hamlet of Îlet-à-Vidot, about 2.5km northwest of Hell-Bourg. There's a two-night minimum stay.

Les Jardins d'Héva HOTEL €€
(Map p219; ☎0262 47 87 87; www.jardinsdheva-ilereunion.com; 16 Rue Lacaussade; d incl breakfast €98; P 📶) This option perched on the southern outskirts of town has five colourful bungalows with a Creole flavour, each with two adjoining rooms. Three drawbacks: they don't have views of the Cirque, they lack intimacy (terraces are shared) and are starting to show their age. On the plus side, guests can access for free the mini spa featuring a sauna and a Jacuzzi.

There's an on-site restaurant if you're feeling too lazy to travel elsewhere, and a small gift shop. The owner, Alice Deligey, speaks English.

Le Relais des Cimes HOTEL €€
(Map p219; ☎0262 47 81 58; www.relaisdescimes.com; 67 Rue du Général de Gaulle; s €72-80, d €82-92, incl breakfast; P 📶) The rooms in the motel-like building lack character but they're fresh and tidy. Most upstairs rooms have mountain views. There's a couple of buildings across the street, which feature 11 rooms, including four atmospheric rooms that occupy two tastefully refurbished Creole houses; ask for the 'Chambres Case Créole'.

Eating

Hell-Bourg is synonymous with *chouchou*, a green, pear-shaped vegetable first imported from Brazil in 1834. It comes in salads, gratins and as *chouchou gateau* for dessert. You can stock up on basic provisions at the grocers and other food shops along the main road.

★**Villa Marthe** CREOLE
(Map p219; ☎0262 21 02 02; www.facebook.com/villamarthe974; 71 Rue du Général de Gaulle; mains €12-16; ⏰noon-2pm Mon-Fri, noon-2pm & 6.30-8.30pm Sat & Sun) This excellent restaurant serves hearty regional dishes including curries, stews and *bol renversé* (a bowl of

SENTIER SCOUT & SENTIER AUGUSTAVE

Taking the Sentier Scout trail down to Aurère in Bas Mafate and climbing back the next day by following the super scenic (but fairly dangerous in some sections) Sentier Augustave is undoubtedly one of the most exhilarating loops you can do in the Cirque de Mafate. In theory, you could tackle it in a single day, but we suggest spending the night in Aurère.

To get to the start of the Sentier Scout, take the *route forestière* (from Le Bélier) that leads to the car park below Col des Bœufs. Look for the small parking area (a few spaces) and the small sign 'Sentier Scout', about 2.3km before the car park, on your right. The trail begins dropping slowly in a thick forest. Further down, you'll walk on a spectacular, narrow ridge with panoramic vistas of the Cirque before descending to La Plaque and Îlet à Malheur, reached after about three hours. The final stretch between Îlet à Malheur and Aurère is very steep but short (about 30 minutes). Most of the run is shady and you'll be rewarded with sensational vistas of Piton Cabris, the tooth-shaped peak that lords over Aurère.

The next day, walk back to the *route forestière* by following the Sentier Augustave (in Aurère, look for the sign 'Bord Martin par Augustave') – allow four hours, with an elevation gain of about 600m. Be warned: this trail may be treacherous and is not suitable for people who suffer from vertigo – a young hiker fell to her death near Passerelle Marianne in January 2019 – and it shouldn't be tackled if it's wet. The first (and longest) part is a mild ascent along the cliffside – the trail is actually carved into the cliff face above the Bras Bémale canyon. Some sections are equipped with boardwalks, stairs, ladders and handrails tacked onto the sides of the cliff. You'll enjoy awesome vistas of the Bras Bémale gorge along the way. The second part consists of multiple crossings of Ravine Savon river, which may involve a bit of boulder-hopping (and getting your feet wet). The last section is a tedious uphill slog to the Bord Martin parking area on the *route forestière*. If you've left your car at the Sentier Scout trailhead, you'll need to walk another 800m up along the road to the Sentier Scout parking area.

RÉUNION CIRQUE DE SALAZIE

rice with various toppings) at very affordable prices. You'll need to get here early for lunch, especially if you want a (plastic) table on the shady terrace. Save a cranny for the delicious chocolate cake.

Snack-Bar Elisabeth Family FAST FOOD €
(Map p219; ☑ 0692 22 11 28; www.facebook.com/elisabethpro433; 15 Rue Amiral Lacaze; mains €4-10; ☺11am-5pm Wed-Sun) This well-run option in an appealing Creole house concentrates on a plain and simple menu – tacos, burgers, sandwiches and salads – but does it really well. It's also a great place for a post-hiking drink.

La Cascade Gourmande BAKERY €
(Map p219; ☑ 0262 47 85 40; 43 Rue du Général de Gaulle; sandwiches €3-4.50; ☺6am-6pm) This bakery whips up tasty sandwiches made with great ingredients, and bakes mouthwatering pastries, including *macatias*.

Les Jardins d'Héva CREOLE, BUFFET €€
(Map p219; ☑ 0262 47 87 87; 16 Rue Lacaussade; lunch buffet €15-18, dinner buffet €32; ☺12.15-1.30pm & 6.30-8pm Thu-Tue, 6.30-8pm Wed; 🛜) Les Jardins d'Héva rocks a superb setting: central Hell-Bourg at your feet, the jagged peaks of the Cirques in the distance, and a luminous dining room. Settle back and feast

on an assortment of well-prepared Creole staples, salads and homemade desserts. The lunch buffet is excellent value, while the dinner buffet includes drinks.

Le Relais des Cimes CREOLE €€
(Map p219; ☑ 0262 47 81 58; 67 Rue du Général de Gaulle; mains €13-18, menus €18-23; ☺noon-2pm & 7-8.30pm) At this Hell-Bourg stalwart the food has a temptingly pronounced regional flavour. Among the many winners are the Hell-Bourg trout, the chicken in coconut sauce and a good choice of generous *carris,* all served at affordable prices in rustic surrounds, featuring wooden ceilings and red tablecloths.

Le P'tit Koin Kréol CREOLE €€
(Map p219; ☑ 0692 36 66 78; 38 Rue du Général de Gaulle; mains €12-15; ☺noon-2.30pm) This well-regarded eatery in a cute Creole house off the main drag is a good place to sample authentic Réunionnais fare prepared mamastyle. Tour your taste buds with a *gratin de chouchou* or a tasty curry. It also does takeaway (€6 to €7).

Ti Chou Chou CREOLE €€
(Map p219; ☑ 0262 47 80 93; 42 Rue du Général de Gaulle; mains €13-23, menus €19-26; ☺11.30am-1.45pm & 6.30-7.45pm Sat-Wed, 11.30am-1.45pm

A GLIMPSE INTO THE CIRQUE DE MAFATE

If you have a day to spare, do not miss the opportunity to hike into the Cirque de Mafate. From the car park just below Col des Bœufs, it takes only two hours to descend to La Nouvelle via the atmospheric Plaine des Tamarins. La Nouvelle, which is dubbed 'the capital of Mafate', makes a great half-day hike, and you can have lunch there before climbing back to Col des Bœufs and the car park.

Not enough for you? If you're super fit and start at dawn, you can descend to La Nouvelle, spend an hour there before pressing on to Marla (allow another two hours). After having explored Marla for an hour or two, climb back to Col des Bœufs following the GR R3 (three hours from Marla, including a challenging 50-minute climb just after having crossed the Rivière des Galets) – a long but memorable day.

Thu) This small restaurant, with its appealing colourful facade on the main drag, is run by a friendly young team. Herbivores will opt for the *assiette ti chouchou*, which offers a combination of *chouchou, cresson* and *capucine* (all local vegetables). There's a shady terrace at the back. It's sometimes closed for dinner in low season.

❶ Information

There are no banks in Hell-Bourg, and there's only one ATM (at the post office).

Office du Tourisme (Map p219; ☑ 0262 47 89 89; www.reunionest.fr; 47 Rue du Général de Gaulle; ☉ 9am-noon & 1-5pm Mon-Sat; 🛜) has pamphlets on hiking options and bus schedules in the Cirque. Can also arrange bookings at *gîtes de montagne* and guided tours in English if given advance notice. Offers free wi-fi.

❶ Getting There & Away

Buses from Salazie to Hell-Bourg run about every two hours from 6.45am to 6.20pm (€2, about 20 minutes). In the opposite direction, there are services from 6.15am to 5.45pm. There are four buses in each direction on Sunday.

Grand Îlet & Col des Boeufs

This is a sweet, picturesque spot. About 17km west of Salazie, accessed by a scenic white-knuckle road, Grand Îlet really feels like the end of the line. The village sits at the base of the ridge separating the Cirque de Salazie and the Cirque de Mafate. Above the village is the mountain pass of Col des Bœufs, which forms the main pedestrian route between the two Cirques; access is via the village of **Le Bélier**, 3km above Grand Îlet, where you'll find the start of the tarred *route forestière* (forestry road) that leads to Col des Bœufs. The *route forestière* is dotted with a number of *kiosques* (picnic shelters) that are popular at weekends.

🛌 Sleeping

Ti Kaz Lontan   GÎTE, CAMPGROUND €
(Map p208; ☑ 0692 32 61 01, 0692 28 95 69; www.facebook.com/Mireille.corinne; 753 Route du Bélier, Casabois; dm €20, camping per person €5; 🅿🛜) This modest, family-run venture down the road to Le Bélier is a great option if you're counting the pennies, with a couple of well-kept four-bed dorms and a campground. If you don't have your own tent, you can rent a tent and a mattress (per person €12). Breakfast costs €5 and dinner will set you back €15.

Le Papangue   B&B €
(Map p208; ☑ 0692 60 30 67; nelson.boyer@wanadoo.fr; 6 Chemin Camp Pierrot; d incl breakfast €70; 🅿🛜) At the end of a long day's driving, it's a joy to snuggle into the freshly pressed linen of this B&B off the road to Le Bélier. There are three good-sized rooms, with parquet flooring and wood panelling on the walls. One quibble: two rooms face a concrete wall. A terrace was added in 2019.

Le Cimendef – Chez Noeline et Daniel Campton   B&B €
(Map p208; ☑ 0262 47 73 59; campton.cimendef @wanadoo.fr; 735 Route du Bélier, Casabois; d/ste incl breakfast €55/85; 🅿🛜) All four rooms are very simply laid out yet pleasing and are graced with ravishing views over the Cimendef (2226m). There's also an atmospheric suite featuring timber floor, a luminous bathroom (no door), Creole ceilings, an enticing orange colour scheme and your own terrace; prices for suites drop to €75 if you stay two nights or more. Dinner, available on certain evenings, is €25.

Le Guétali – Chez Liliane   B&B €
(Map p208; ☑ 0692 82 84 83; www.leguetali.com; 29 Chemin Camp-Pierrot; s/d/q incl breakfast €50/60/70; 🅿🛜) Five rooms with their own entrance occupy a large, colourful building that stands on a little knoll. The rooms are

spick and span, luminous and proffer ample mountain views. Our favourite is the Lilas. Liliane Bonnald, your affable host, is a good cook. Dinner costs €25. A great bet.

La Croisée des Sentiers   B&B €€

(Map p208; ☑ 0692 00 97 03, 0692 31 51 97; www.
facebook.com/lacroiseedessentiers; 21 Chemin du Stade; d/q incl breakfast €75/115; ☺ Feb-Dec; P ☀ ☎) A home away from home, this pert B&B occupies a modern house near the stadium. The four rooms, with their own entrance, are muted and tasteful, with crisp linen and glistening bathrooms. There's also a small but lovely pool in the garden. You are brilliantly placed for exploring the area. Note that no meals (except breakfast) are provided.

 Eating

**Snack Le Grand Îlet –
Chez Serge**   CREOLE €

(Map p208; ☑ 0262 47 71 19; 48 Rue du Père Mancel; mains €6-12; ☺ 11am-2pm & 6.30-8pm Fri-Wed) This wholly unpretentious, neon-lit eatery set in a modern house by the main road is worth stopping at for its short list of flavoursome daily specials (usually two), which may include sausage *rougail,* roasted chicken or shrimp *carri.* Everything's fresh and homemade. Takeaway meals are available (€6). Brilliant value.

ⓘ **Getting There & Away**

There are six buses a day (three on Sunday) from Salazie to Grand Îlet (45 minutes, €2) and Le Bélier (50 minutes, €2) between 6.45am (9.05am on Sunday) and 6.20pm. Heading back to Salazie, services depart from Le Bélier between around 5.45am and 5pm (7am to 5.20pm on Sunday), calling at Grand Îlet 10 minutes later.

From Le Bélier to Col des Bœufs (25 minutes, €2) there are two daily buses (line 82C). The tourist office in Hell-Bourg has timetables.

If you have your own car, you can leave it in the guarded car park (one/two days €3/12) at Le Petit Col, 6.5km up the *route forestière* and only 20 minutes' walk below the Col des Bœufs.

Cirque de Mafate

Surrounded by ramparts, criss-crossed with gullies and studded with narrow ridges, Cirque de Mafate is the wildest and the most remote of Réunion's Cirques. Nothing can prepare you for that first glimpse of this geological wonder, with its shifting colours, blissful serenity (except for the occasional whirring of choppers) and unsurpassed grandeur. No cars, no towns, no stress. Just soaring mountains, giddily deep ravines and a sprinkle of tiny hamlets where time seems to have stood still.

Apart from its impressive topography, what sets the Cirque de Mafate apart is its relative inaccessibility, despite being very close to the coastal fleshpots. No roads lead into the Cirque (although a *route forestière* runs right up to the pass at Col des Bœufs), so the villages that are scattered in this giant extinct volcano are accessible only by foot.

The Bas Mafate

The northern part of the Cirque de Mafate, called the Bas Mafate, has an end-of-the-world feeling that will appeal to those in search of hush. It is even more secluded (and that is saying something) and less 'touristy' than Haut Mafate (the southern part of the Cirque). Landscapes are spectacular, with

RÉUNION CIRQUE DE MAFATE

GEOGRAPHY OF THE CIRQUE MAFATE

Despite its remoteness and seclusion, the Cirque de Mafate is populated. In the valleys, plateaus and spurs that slice up the jaw-dropping terrain are scattered discreet little Creole settlements that retain a rough-diamond rural edge. Not much happens in these villages but it's hard not to fall under the spell of their phenomenal setting.

The southern part of the Cirque is called Haut Mafate (Higher Mafate) and receives the bulk of visitors. It comprises peaceful Marla, the highest hamlet of the Cirque at an altitude of 1621m; La Nouvelle, dubbed the 'capital of Mafate' and one of the main gateways to the Cirque, perched on a plateau at an altitude of 1421m; and Roche-Plate, at the foot of the imposing Maïdo.

The northern part of the Cirque is called Bas Mafate (Lower Mafate) and is considered even more secluded than Haut Mafate. It comprises Îlet à Bourse, Îlet à Malheur, Aurère, Grand Place, Cayenne, Les Lataniers and Îlet des Orangers. The two tiny communities of Grand Place and Cayenne lie above the rushing Rivière des Galets near the Cirque's main outlet.

LA NOUVELLE

The picturesque hamlet of La Nouvelle is the largest settlement in the Cirque de Mafate. Because of its good infrastructures and fairly easy access, it gets plenty of day trippers. Even if your time is limited, spend at least a day in La Nouvelle to get a feel for the Cirque de Mafate. Serious walkers will use La Nouvelle as a base before delving further into the Cirque.

La Nouvelle has a good selection of lodgings, some of which are really comfortable – for example, doubles with private facilities. If you're on a budget, you'll find the usual cramped dorms. One of the most reliable options is **Relais de Mafate** (✆ 0692 43 85 60; La Nouvelle; dm €17, d with shared bathroom €40, bungalow d/tr €60/80), a venture that has something for everybody and every budget. But the brightest option is **Tamaréo** (✆ 0692 32 08 28; www.letamareo.re; La Nouvelle; dm/s/d with shared bathroom incl half board €63/98/136), with shiny-clean four-bed dorms (towels are provided) and four cosy doubles. Oh, and there's a Jacuzzi (€10).

La Nouvelle can be reached on foot only. The easiest way to get to this village is from Col des Bœufs, a two-hour hike to the east.

precipitous mountain slopes and steep-sided valleys. If you want to immerse yourself in local culture and sample authentic rural Réunionnais life, the Bas Mafate is your answer.

🏃 Activities

Hiking in the area is phenomenal, with a splendid network of well-defined trails. One of the most popular options is to walk around the Bas Mafate Route (p45) over four days.

🛏 Sleeping & Eating

There's a good network of *gîtes* (private or run by the **Plateforme de Réservation – Île de la Réunion** (✆ 0810 16 00 00; www.explorelareunion.com)). A few places offer camp sites and all can prepare simple Creole meals for less than €25. You'll find drinking water at every *gîte*. Bring cash.

Chez Jean-Louis   GÎTE €
(✆ 0692 42 18 37; http://gite-chez-jean-louis.wifeo.com; Grand Place Les Hauts; dm/d with shared bathroom incl half board €45/90) The friendly owners rent one four-bed dorm and two doubles – be sure to book early. Excellent local food is served at dinner.

Chez Le Facteur   GÎTE €
(✆ 0692 03 83 93; www.chezlefacteur.com; Îlet des Orangers; dm/d with shared bathroom incl half board €40/80) A well-established *gîte,* with two doubles and two six-bed dorms.

Chez Marcel et Dominique Bilin   GÎTE €
(✆ 0692 27 80 13; Grand Place Les Hauts; dm/d with shared bathroom incl half board €45/100) A cosy *gîte*, with two neat doubles, one three-bed dorm and one seven-bed dorm. Excellent meals are served at dinner.

Gîte du Kanal   GÎTE €
(✆ 0693 90 57 12; Îlet des Orangers; dm incl half board €45) A cosy, well-run *gîte* with two six-bed dorms and one double (same price). Enjoy stupendous views.

ℹ Getting There & Away

The easiest way to get into the Bas Mafate is via Rivière des Galets. Catch any bus heading to the west or the south coast from St-Denis, and get off at 'Sacré Cœur' bus stop in Rivière des Galets, from where a 4WD taxi will pick you up (make sure you book in advance). Taxis from **4x4 Mafate** (www.4x4-mafate.fr) follow the floor of the Rivière des Galets valley and will drop you off at Deux Bras, which will spare you a monotonous stretch of about 9km. It costs €25 for one or two passengers, or €8 per person if there are at least three people. If you're driving, you can arrange parking with a taxi driver (count on €10 per day for the service). From Deux Bras, it takes approximately three hours to reach Aurère on foot.

Another option is from Sans Souci (accessible by bus from St-Paul, 12 daily, six on Sunday, €2) via the Canalisation des Orangers. From Sans Souci, it takes about four hours to reach the hamlet of Îlet des Orangers. Access is also possible from Le Maïdo (accessible by bus from St-Paul, three daily except Sunday) down to Roche-Plate, an arduous two- to three-hour descent.

The Haut Mafate

What's not to love in the Haut Mafate? Highlights include the forested Plaine des Tamarins, the deep valley of the Rivière des Galets, the waterfall at Trois Roches and the ruins of Maison Laclos, which is said to be the oldest dwelling in the Cirque. Of course, you'll also enjoy phenomenal views wherever you look.

AURÈRE

The tiny *îlet* (hamlet) of Aurère is perched Machu Picchu–like above the precipitous canyon of the Bras Bémale in the Cirque de Mafate. It's usually the first port of call for hikers who tackle the Bas Mafate loop. It's nothing more than a few colourful *cases* (Creole-style houses) but it offers plenty of rural charm in a magical setting.

The 'capital' of Bas Mafate, Aurère has an assortment of well-organised *gîtes* that mainly cater to hikers. Most can be booked by phoning the owners directly.

If you want to do Aurère in style, make a beeline for **Le Fanjan** (☑ 0692 09 18 86; www.facebook.com/lefanjan; Mafate; dm/ incl half board €45/120), a superb venture with four-bed dorms on the outskirts of the village – it's on the way to Îlet à Malheur. Well-run **Le Mafatais** (☑ 0692 07 84 71; Mafate; dm/s/d with shared bathroom incl half board €47/71/100) has doubles and a six-bed dorm, which open onto a neat garden. Larger five- to 11-bed dorms (and a grocery store) are found in **Le Poinsétia** (☑ 0262 55 02 33, 0692 08 92 20; Mafate; dm/s/d with shared bathroom incl half board €41/64/88; ☺ closed Tue & Wed), while there are four four-bed dorms, hearty Creole dishes and terrace views on offer at **Auberge Piton Cabris** (☑ 0262 43 36 83, 0692 26 33 59; Mafate; dm incl half board €42).

Aurère can be reached on foot only. Most visitors start from Rivière des Galets, a three-hour hike to the west. It can also be reached from Bord Martin in the Cirque de Salazie, following the Sentier Augustave or Sentier Scout trails.

The largest settlement is La Nouvelle, which has several shops, a school, a helipad and an interesting shingle-roofed chapel.

🏃 Activities

The area is truly stupendous for hiking, with countless trails allowing you to build your own itinerary. The most popular is the four-day Haut Mafate Route (p43). But if time is limited, simply spend a day in the Haut Mafate, in La Nouvelle (and Marla).

🛏 Sleeping & Eating

La Nouvelle, Marla and Roche-Plate are well endowed with *gîtes* (private or run by the Plateforme de Réservation – Île de la Réunion). La Nouvelle and Marla have the broadest range of accommodation options in all the Cirque. A few places have camp sites and most offer Creole meals (€20 to €25). Bring cash.

La Miellerie de Marla GÎTE €
(☑ 0692 03 20 99; www.mielleriedemarla.com; Marla; dm incl half board €47) A lovely, homely *gîte* on a ridge, with two four-bed dorms that are in tip-top condition. Meals are prepared with organic ingredients and bread is homemade. The owner is a beekeeper.

Auberge du Bronchard GÎTE €
(☑ 0692 20 83 86; Roche-Plate; dm/d with shared bathroom incl half board €42/97) A well-maintained *gîte* in Roche-Plate, with a

four-bed dorm, a six-bed dorm and two cute doubles. Also has a restaurant and grocery store.

★ Bois de Couleur B&B €€
(☑ 0693 11 70 00; bs.boisdecouleur@gmail.com; Marla; d incl breakfast €110) If you want to do Mafate in style, look no further than this well-run B&B on the northwestern outskirts of Marla. It features five surprisingly modern rooms with private facilities and lovely views. It feels a bit isolated, but that's part of the charm. Expect deer *carri* (curry) for dinner (there's a deer farm nearby); meals cost €28.

Snack Bar Le Marla FAST FOOD €
(☑ 0692 04 14 64; Marla; mains €10; ☺ 7am-9pm) Coming from La Nouvelle, this cool venture appears like a mirage at the entrance of Marla. Bliss! It serves sandwiches, *carris* (at lunchtime) and drinks. Also has dorms. Credit cards are accepted (minimum €10).

LES HAUTES PLAINES & THE VOLCANO

Réunion's only cross-island road passes through the Plaine-des-Cafres and the Plaine-des-Palmistes, collectively known as Les Hautes Plaines. At an altitude of about 1000m, the air is refreshingly crisp and often swathed in misty fog – a blessing if you're coming from the scorching coastal cities.

Barquisseau; r €40, with shared bathroom €30-35; P ✳ 🛜) The closest thing to a hostel you'll find in St-Pierre, this well-run place has spotlessly clean rooms and an optimal location near the seafront. Air-con is available in 12 rooms (out of 15); the cheaper ones are fan-cooled. Added perks include private parking (five spaces), a communal kitchen, and laundry service (€5). Prices drop by €5 if you stay two nights or more.

Ask for room 101, 102 or 103, with balcony. Towels are provided in the rooms equipped with private facilities; if you stay in one of the other rooms, there's a deposit of €5.

Chez Papa Daya
HOSTEL €

(Map p234; ☑ 0692 12 20 12, 0262 25 64 87; www.chezpapadaya.com; 27 Rue du Four à Chaux; s/d €35/45, with shared bathroom €30/35, q €65; P ✳ 🛜) Run by the affable Roger, this traveller-friendly stalwart shelters 20 simple, scrupulously clean rooms of varying sizes and shapes. What it lacks in style is made up for by an ace location, a waddle away from the seafront, shops, eateries, bars and clubs. Parking is available, but there are only six spaces. Facilities include a small kitchen (only accessible at breakfast).

Côté Lagon
B&B €€

(☑ 0693 92 53 01, 0262 45 63 28; www.cote-lagon.re; 79 Rue Amiral Lacaze, Terre Sainte; d incl breakfast €135-150; ✳ 🛜 🏊) Its sensational position across the road from the small beach in the Terre Sainte neighbourhood is the main drawcard here. The six rooms, which are done out in grey, taupe and chocolate shades, have a fresh, modern feel, but they are small and don't have sea views, and the property feels a tad compact. An added bonus is the postage-stamp-sized pool.

The included breakfast is served on a breezy terrace overlooking the beach. There's no private parking.

La Kazkifo
B&B €€

(Map p234; ☑ 0262 25 18 54, 0692 59 46 48; lakazkifo@outlook.fr; 7 Rue Amiral Lacaze, Terre Sainte; s/d incl breakfast €60/80; P ✳ 🛜 🏊) Lovely, clean *chambre d'hôte* with three trim and restful rooms with partial sea views in the attractive Terre Sainte neighbourhood. There's a tiny pool in the flowering garden. Top that off with the affable welcome of Yannick, who is also a good cook (dinner is available on request), and you have a great base for a few days.

Le Saint-Pierre
HOTEL €€

(Map p234; ☑ 0262 61 16 11; www.hotellesaintpierre.fr; 51 Ave des Indes; d €99-119, studio d €110-150; P ✳ 🛜 🏊) A stone's throw from the covered market and the seafront, this three-star abode has modern, stylish rooms in contemporary hues (has grey and taupe), balconies, comfy beds and walk-in showers. Hint: room 212 has two great terraces. Facilities include a bar-restaurant and a miniature pool. There are often good deals available on room rates; check the website or call the reception.

Lindsey Hotel
HOTEL €€

(Map p234; ☑ 0262 24 60 11; www.lindsey-hotel-reunion.fr; 21b Rue François Isautier; d €90-110; P ✳ 🛜 🏊) Tucked in a side street near the covered market, this pert venture in a large Creole-style building is perfectly poised for all of St-Pierre's attractions. The 18 rooms sport modern furnishings and feel fresh and comfortable. Rooms 7, 12 and 14 are the best, with balconies and city views. The small pool is an added bonus. Breakfast costs €10.

★ Villa Belle
B&B €€€

(☑ 0692 65 89 99; www.villabelle.e-monsite.com; 45 Rue Rodier; s €165-215, d €175-235, ste €310; P ✳ 🛜 🏊) Occupying a converted Creole mansion, this oh-so-chic *maison d'hôte* is the epitome of a refined cocoon, revelling quietly in minimalist lines, soothing colour accents and nice decorative touches. Our favourites are the two stand-alone Coloniale units, with their own little pond around the terrace. After a day of turf pounding, relax in the stress-melting pool. It's gay friendly.

Breakfast (€20 to €40) and dinner (€65) are available by request. Prices drop by 15% if you stay three nights or more.

Villa Delisle Hotel & Spa
CASINO HOTEL €€€

(Map p234; ☑ 0262 70 77 08; www.hotel-villadelisle.com; 42 Blvd Hubert Delisle; s €175-235, d €190-250 incl breakfast; P ✳ 🛜 🏊) Right on the seafront, this hotel with a heritage feel is full of vibrant colours and character. Rooms aren't lavish but are modestly stylish, and the Superior ones have balconies. Facilities include a restaurant, a bar, a small spa and a swimming pool.

✖ Eating

The excellent Creole, French, Italian and Asian restaurants make this town as pleasing to the belly as it is to the eye; you won't want to be skipping any meals here. Many bars also double up as restaurants. You'll also find plenty of fast food outlets along the beach.

Manciet
BAKERY €

(Map p234; ☑ 0262 25 06 73; 64 Rue Victor le Vigoureux; pastries from €1; ⏱ 6am-12.30pm & 2-6pm Tue-Sat, to noon Sun) This gourmet emporium is a veritable feast of perfectly presented pastries, cakes, pies and chocolates. And bread. And *macatias*. Simply divine.

Castel Glacier
ICE CREAM, CAFETERIA €

(Map p234; ☑ 0262 22 96 56; www.facebook.com/castelglacier; 38 Rue François de Mahy; ice creams €2.60-5, mains €13-17; ⏱ 11.45am-6pm Mon-Fri, noon-7pm Sat, 3-7pm Sun; 🐾) Generous scoops and about 40 flavours are the trademarks of this drool-inducing ice-cream parlour opposite the mosque. Also serves up snacks, well-presented salads and light meals at lunchtime, as well as crêpes any time of the day.

★ Ancre Terre et Mer
FRENCH €€

(Map p234; ☑ 0262 27 97 52; www.facebook.com/ancreterreetmer; 31 Rue Amiral Lacaze, Terre Sainte; mains €14-26, lunch menu €15-20; ⏱ noon-1.30pm & 7-9.45pm Tue & Thu-Sat, 7-9.45pm Wed) A hop and a skip from the seafront (but no views), this attractive garden restaurant has a seductively cosy terrace and serves up delectable burgers, tartares, risottos and a few salads. Something sweet to finish? Try the brownie with white chocolate ice cream.

★ La Kaz à Léa
INTERNATIONAL €€

(Map p234; ☑ 0262 25 04 25; 34 Rue François Isautier; mains €17-28, lunch menus €15-17; ⏱ noon-2pm & 7-9.30pm Mon-Sat; 🐾) This much-loved *case,* with its shady terrace and cosy dining room, is a soothing spot. It offers beautifully presented Creole, *métro* and Asian-inspired dishes as well as scrumptious homemade burgers. Desserts are delightful, especially the crème brûlée flavoured with vanilla. At €15, the three-course lunch menu is a steal. Lovely.

It also has a takeaway outlet next door that rustles up Creole staples (€6 to €8).

Snack Galam Massala
INDIAN €€

(Map p234; ☑ 0692 37 12 98; 5 Rue du Four à Chaux; mains €10-12; ⏱ 11am-2pm Tue-Sat) You wouldn't guess it from the humble surrounds, but this family-run place is praised for its lip-smacking biryanis and other tasty Indian staples, including beef or chicken tandoori. The menu changes daily, and features at least one vegetarian dish.

★ Ti Boui Boui
CREOLE, SEAFOOD €€

(☑ 0262 43 77 49; 48 Rue Amiral Lacaze, Terre Sainte; mains €16-25; ⏱ noon-1.30pm & 7-9.15pm Fri-Tue, noon-1.30pm Wed) This adorable Creole house has a spiffing location – it's right on the seashore in Terre Sainte (ask for a table with a sea view). Grab a dish from the daily specials, which may include curries and grilled swordfish, add a salad, and you're sorted.

L'Épicurieux
FUSION €€

(Map p234; ☑ 0262 83 84 66; www.facebook.com/lepicurieux974; 9 Rue Suffren; mains €16-24; ⏱ noon-2pm Mon-Wed, noon-2pm & 7-10pm Thu-Sat) You wouldn't guess it from the outside, but L'Épicurieux is a gourmand's playpen ensnared in a tropical garden complete with a small pool. A mix of local ingredients and European flavours is at work here. If it features on the chalkboard, try the risotto. Couples, take note: this place is particularly romantic at dinner.

La Lune dans le Caniveau
BISTRO €€

(Map p234; ☑ 0262 01 73 66; 1bis Rue Auguste Babet; mains €13-21; ⏱ 7-10pm Mon-Sat; 🚗) Stylishly decorated in a hip bistro style, this local treasure entices with simple yet inventive offerings that spoil your taste buds without spoiling your budget. The intimate dining room, though small, is cheerfully decorated and the kitchen turns out well-prepared fish and meat dishes as well as a few vegetarian options.

Belo Horizonte
FRENCH €€

(Map p234; ☑ 0262 22 31 95; www.restaurant-saint-pierre-belo.re; 10 Rue François de Mahy; mains €11-14; ⏱ noon-2pm Mon-Sat, 7-9.30pm Thu-Sat) Walls saturated in cheery coloured accents and other fancy decorative touches – some are covered with flip-flops – set the tone at this zinging joint where you can tuck into salads, pizzas, pasta dishes and daily specials. Excellent homemade desserts, too. The sun-dappled patio garden is enticing. You can also take away.

Kaz Nature
CAFETERIA €€

(Map p234; ☑ 0262 25 30 86; www.facebook.com/kaznature; 6 Rue François de Mahy; mains €10-18; ⏱ noon-2.30pm Mon-Sat; 🐾) This slick modern eatery does a brisk business with office workers – always a sign that you've found a good bargain. It speedily serves tasty wraps, crunchy salads and other healthy goodies. Also does takeaway.

RÉUNION ST-PIERRE

★ O'Baya FUSION €€€

(Map p234; ☑ 0262 59 66 94; www.facebook.com/
Elara.et.Grego; 7 Rue Auguste Babet; mains €19-
29; ☺noon-1.30pm & 7-9.30pm Tue-Fri, 7-9.30pm
Sat) Sick of stodgy *carris* (curries)? Then
head here for loveable fusion fare served
in a strong design-led interior. The menu
drips with panache and the chef prepares
succulent concoctions with top-of-the-line
ingredients. Both fish and meat dishes are
available. There's also an array of sweet
temptations, including melt-in-the-mouth
profiteroles.

Est Bento ASIAN €€€

(Map p234; ☑ 0262 02 08 03; 1ter Rue Auguste
Babet; mains €20-36; ☺noon-2pm & 7.30-9.30pm
Mon, Tue, Thu & Fri, 7.30-9.30pm Sat) Satisfy
those pangs for bento and other Asian
treats at this popular restaurant. Here you
can tuck into specialities that are hard to
find elsewhere – a godsend after too many
curries or French-inspired dishes. The
Japanese-style decor and brisk service add
to the appeal.

Le DCP SEAFOOD €€€

(Map p234; ☑ 0262 32 21 71; 38bis Blvd Hubert-Delisle; mains €21-27; ☺noon-2pm & 7-9.30pm) This
immutable seafood favourite on the seafront
gets the thumbs up for its choice of tartares
and carpaccios as well as fish dishes (usually tuna, swordfish and grouper) cooked to
crispy perfection. There's no outdoor seating, though.

Flagrant Délice FUSION €€€

(☑ 0692 87 28 03; www.leflagrantdelice.fr; 115 Rue
François de Mahy; mains €25-32, lunch menu €15-
23; ☺noon-1.30pm & 7.30-9.30pm Tue-Fri, 7.30-
9.30pm Sat) This inviting eatery housed in a
private villa is a gourmand's playpen, with
a tempting selection of imaginative dishes.
Be good to yourself with pork tenderloin in
pineapple sauce, toothfish steak with chori-
zo cream and luscious wines. The setting is
another draw: tables are arranged around a
small pool in a tropical garden.

🍷 Drinking & Nightlife

Night owls, rejoice: St-Pierre has a well-
established party reputation. It has a good
range of drinking options ranging from elegant cafes to lively waterfront bars and hole-
in-the-wall cocktail joints. The best buzz can
be found on the seafront. Most drinking
spots also serve food.

Le Five CLUB

(Map p234; ☑ 0692 97 02 22; www.five.re; 8 Rue
François de Mahy; ☺6pm-1am Wed & Thu, to 5am
Fri & Sat) One of the hottest spots in St-Pierre
when we dropped by. If you're after salsa, *ki-
zomba*, *séga* or some sexy tropical sounds,
look no further than Le Five. Early in the
evening it doubles as a bar and also serves
food and tapas.

Rouge BAR

(Map p234; ☑ 0262 59 10 40; 23 Rue François
Isautier; ☺6-11pm Mon-Sat) Although it also
doubles as a restaurant, it's the bar that we
recommend. With its potent cocktails (from
€8) served in a tastefully restored Creole
house, this is one of the most atmospheric
venues in town for a drink.

Long Board Café BAR

(Map p234; ☑ 0692 82 09 95; 18 Petit Blvd de la
Plage; ☺11am-1am Tue-Fri, from 5pm Sat & Sun)
Spiffing setting in a Creole house with a
terrace opening onto the seafront – this a
great place for quaffing a sunset beverage
(cocktails from €9). Offers live entertainment
and karaoke on selected evenings, usually on
Friday and Saturday. Also serves tapas.

Les Sal' Gosses BAR

(Map p234; ☑ 0262 96 70 36; 38 Blvd Hubert-
Delisle; ☺10.30am-midnight) This cool den on
the seafront hosts gigs from local bands –
usually on Wednesday or Thursday. Good
blend of jazz, soul and funk. Also has a
wide-ranging menu (but the food is only so-
so), tapas and billiards.

☆ Entertainment

Le Toit LIVE MUSIC

(Map p234; ☑ 0262 35 55 53; www.facebook.com/
Le-toit-338051396289084; 16 Rue Auguste Babet;
☺6pm-midnight Wed-Sat) Attracting mostly
Zoreilles (mainland French) regulars, this
lively bar is packed to the rafters on weekends. It hosts live bands on Thursday, Friday
and Saturday evenings (check the Facebook
page). Great-value beers and cocktails are
two more reasons to drop by. Skip the food.

ⓘ Information

Tourist Office (Map p234; ☑ 0820 20 32 20;
www.sudreuniontourisme.fr; Capitainerie,
Blvd Hubert-Delisle; ☺8am-6pm Mon-Sat, to
noon Sun) Has English-speaking staff and can
provide useful brochures and a town map. You
can book *gîtes de montagne* here and it can
also organise guided tours in English.

ℹ Getting There & Away

AIR

Air Mauritius and Air Austral operate daily flights between **Saint-Pierre-Pierrefonds International Airport** (Map p240; ☎ 0262 96 80 00; www.pierrefonds.aeroport.fr; Chemin de l'Aérodrome, Pierrefonds), 5km west of St-Pierre, and Mauritius.

Air Austral (☎ 0825 01 30 12; www.air-austral.com; 6 Blvd Hubert-Delisle; ☉ 9am-5pm Mon, 8.30am-5pm Tue-Fri, 8.30-11.45am Sat)

Air Mauritius (☎ 0262 80 88 10; www.airmauritius.com; 7 Rue François de Mahy; ☉ 9am-12.30pm & 1.30-5.30pm Mon-Fri, 9am-noon Sat)

BUS

St-Pierre is an important transport hub. **Car Jaune** (☎ 0810 12 39 74; www.carjaune.re) has a long-haul bus stop at the long-distance **bus station** (cnr Rue Presbytère & Luc Lorion) west of town.

Buses to/from St-Denis run frequently along the west coast via St-Louis and St-Gilles-les-Bains (1½ hours, €2) or direct via the Route des Tamarins if it's a Z'éclair service (line ZO, one hour, €5).

There are also three services a day to St-Benoît via Plaine-des-Palmistes (line S2, two hours, €2) and six services around the south coast through Manapany-les-Bains, St-Joseph and St-Philippe (line S1, 2½ hours, €2).

There are also three daily buses to Entre-Deux (line S5). For Cilaos, change in St-Louis.

THE WILD SOUTH

Aaaah, the Sud Sauvage (Wild South), where the unhurried life is complemented by the splendid scenery of fecund volcanic slopes, occasional beaches, waves crashing on the rocky shoreline and country roads that twist like snakes into the Hauts. In both landscape and character, the south coast is where the real wilderness of Réunion begins to unfold. Once you've left St-Pierre, a gentle splendour and a sense of escapism become tangible. The change of scenery climaxes with the Grand Brûlé, where black lava fields slice through the forest and even reach the ocean at several points.

St-Pierre to St-Joseph

Life – and travel – becomes more sedate as you head west through some of the south coast's delicious scenery. With only a few exceptions, urban life is left behind once

the road traverses **Grand Bois** and snakes its way along the coastline via **Grande Anse** and **Manapany-les-Bains**.

If you want to explore the Hauts, take the turnoff for Petite Île. From Petite Île, a scenic road wobbles slowly up to some charming villages. Continue uphill until the junction with the D3. If you turn left, you'll reach **Mont-Vert-les-Hauts**, approximately 5km to the west (and from there it's an easy drive downhill to the coast via Mont-Vert-les-Bas); if you turn right, you will cross **Manapany-les-Hauts** before reaching **Les Lianes** for St-Joseph.

◉ Sights & Activities

Plage de Grande Anse   BEACH
(Map p240; Grande Anse) Beach lovers should stop at Plage de Grande Anse, which is framed with basaltic cliffs and features a white-sand beach, a protected tide pool and picnic shelters. On weekends, the beach is often swamped with locals. Note that it's not safe to swim outside the tide pool due to unpredictable currents (and sharks).

Take the D30 that branches off the RN2 and winds down for about 2km to the beach.

Tide Pool   BEACH
(Map p240; Manapany-les-Bains) Find this lovely swimming spot at Manapany-les-Bains. There's no proper beach here (the shore is rocky) but there's a protected tide pool where you can splash about. It gets crowded on weekends.

L'Écurie du Relais   HORSE RIDING
(Map p240; ☎ 0262 56 78 67, 0692 00 42 98; www.ecuriedurelais.com; 75 Chemin Léopold Lebon, Manapany-les-Hauts; 1hr/day €25/120; ☉ Tue-Sun) Seeing the area from the saddle of a horse is a fun way to experience the visual appeal of the region, even if you're not an experienced rider. This well-established equestrian centre has guided trips in the Hauts as well as day tours to Grande Anse. The 90-minute ride (€34) takes you to rarely visited points in the Hauts with stunning views of Plaine-des-Grègues.

✿ Festivals & Events

Fête de l'Ail   FOOD & DRINK
(Festival of Garlic; ☉ Oct) A rural fair that celebrates garlic in Petite Île; held in October.

🛏 Sleeping

The area between St-Pierre and St-Joseph has a good range of lodging options, includ-

Southern Réunion

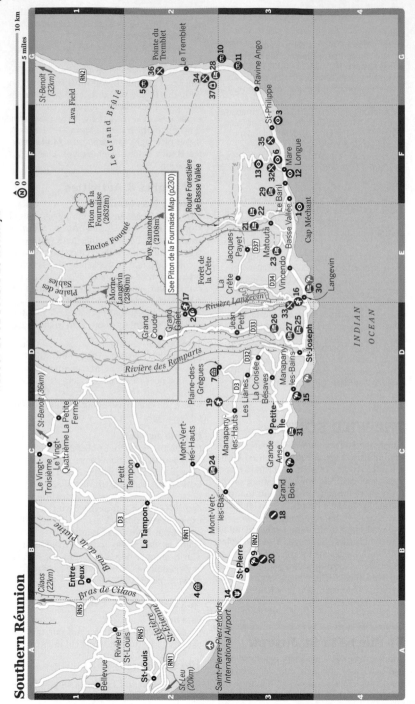

Southern Réunion

ing two hotels and a handful of great B&Bs and holiday rentals. Despite some signs on the road, many places are not easy to find. Check locations on the website (if there is one), use a GPS, or call ahead.

If you want to pamper yourself, opt for the Palm Hotel & Spa (p242).

★**La Cour Mont Vert**　　　　　B&B €
(☑ 0692 80 84 58, 0262 31 21 10; www.courmont vert.com; 18ter Chemin Roland Garros, Mont-Vert-les-Bas; d €70; P ⑤) Your heart will lift at the dreamy views over the coast; your body will rejuvenate with the Valatchy family's healthy meals (€27, certain evenings); your soul will find peace in the four button-cute Creole bungalows set in rural grounds awash with mangoes and lychees. Simply arrive, absorb and enjoy. Rates drop to €59 if you stay at least five nights.

There's a two-night minimum stay. No breakfast is served but there's a communal kitchen.

Gandalf Safari Camp　　　GUESTHOUSE €
(☑ 0262 58 45 59, 0692 40 78 39; www.gandalf safaricamp.de; 87 Blvd de l'Océan, Manapany-les-Bains; s €55-60, d €65-70, ste €125, incl breakfast; ❄@⑤) The German owners have long lived in Africa – hence the name. Their B&B features six rooms that are individually de-

signed, with such themes as Kreol, Malagasy, Arab, Chinese and Indian, but feel a tad compact due to the cubicle shower plonked in the corner. Good English is spoken. Air-con is extra (€5). Rates drop by €5 if you stay two nights.

The Malagasy room, complete with wooden masks and other delightful knick-knacks, is the best (and the most spacious). The Kreol is the cheapest, but its bathrooms are outside. There's also a larger suite. Perks include a kitchen for guests' use and a relaxing garden, plus 4WD tours can be organised (€70). It's a five-minute stroll from Manapany-les-Bains' tide pool. Cash only.

Vérémer　　　　　　　　　　B&B €
(Map p240; ☑ 0262 31 65 10, 0692 72 91 95; www. chambre-gite-veremer.com; 40 Chemin Sylvain Vitry, Petite Île; d incl breakfast €52-65, gîte d from €60; P ❄⑤⊠) Vérémer houses three few-frills but tidy rooms in two neat Creole buildings nestled in a well-tended tropical garden, with superlative views and a splendid pool that guests can use from breakfast to dinner (except Sunday afternoon). Grande Anse beach is 3.5km away. It's gay friendly.

The slightly dearer Mer room is on the small side but opens onto the garden and the pool and enjoys great sea views, while La Cour and La Verte rooms offer more privacy.

There's also a lovely *gîte* that can be rented for four nights or more.

L'Eau Forte
APARTMENT €

(☑ 0262 56 32 84; www.eau-forte.fr; 137bis Blvd de L'Océan, Manapany-les-Bains; d €50; ❋ 🕾) Bargain! Perfect for self-caterers, this fully equipped, spick-and-span villa has an ace location, on a velvety emerald hillside just above Manapany's tide pool, with sublime views of the rocky coastline. Don't fancy cooking? Find a restaurant a coin's toss down the road. There's a two-night minimum stay. Cash only. Book early.

Note that it's exposed to the noise of the surf when the sea is rough.

La Bulle Verte
B&B €€

(Map p240; ☑ 0262 33 58 80, 0692 87 94 90; www.labulleverte.re; 91 Chemin Piton Filaos, Mont-Vert-les-Hauts; d incl breakfast €85; ☉ Feb-Dec; P 🕾) If you're looking for the perfect compromise between style, atmosphere and seclusion, then look no further than this little slice of heaven immersed in greenery. The three cosy rooms are individually decorated and have great picture windows. Our favourite is the 'Cabane', sporting colourful touches, wooden beams and a great terrace.

Oh, and there's a Jacuzzi in the garden.

Soleil Couchant
HOTEL €€

(☑ 0262 52 40 17; lesoleilreunion@gmail.com; 2 Chemin de L'Araucaria, Mont-Vert-les-Bas; d €70-80; P ❋ 🕾 🌊) This small complex features three pavilions shaped like cubic Tetris pieces, which sit on a grassy patch of land. The 10 rooms are bright and tidy, but lack character. The real draws are the ocean vistas – straight from heaven – and the gleaming (heated) pool. There's an on-site restaurant, but food is only so so.

It's well worth opting for the rooms with panoramic views, especially rooms 1 and 2. Rooms 3, 4 and 5 also have ocean views.

Palm Hotel & Spa
LUXURY HOTEL €€€

(☑ 0262 56 30 30; www.palm.re; Grande Anse, Petite Île; d from €240-330, ste from €360, lodges from €550, incl breakfast; P ❋ 🕾 🌊) If you're really looking to push the boat out in the Wild South, then to be honest there's only this five-star resort. Peacefully reposed on a promontory overlooking the cerulean ocean, it sports well-furnished units that are designed with finesse but, frustratingly, only the three lodges face out towards the sea. From the hotel, a steep path leads down to Plage de Grande Anse.

Facilities include two pools, a luxurious spa and two gourmet restaurants (open to nonguests by reservation).

✖ Eating

For lunch, your best bet is to stop at a restaurant or snack bar near Plage de Grande Anse or Manapany-les-Bains. For dinner, order a meal at your B&B or hotel.

★ Chez Ti Fred
CREOLE

(☑ 0693 97 00 30; 15 Chemin Terrain Paulette, Petite Île; mains €15; ☉ noon-1pm & 7-8pm Tue, Wed, Fri & Sat, noon-1pm Sun) This few-frills but atmospheric haunt isolated among orchard trees and cane fields south of Petite Île is a great find. No culinary acrobatics here, just keep-the-faith Creole staples at affordable prices. We'll be back!

Les Badamiers
CREOLE €€

(☑ 0262 56 97 53; 22 Chemin Neuf, Grande Anse, Petite Île; mains €10-12; ☉ 11.45am-2pm Mon-Fri) This family-run eatery in a private house spins tasty *carris* and ace homemade desserts (Mmm, the crème brûlée and the *tarte Tatin* with papaya and cinnamon...). The menu is concise but everything is fresh, the atmosphere is reliably jovial and the prices incredibly good value for the area. The icing on the cake: a terrace with stupendous sea views.

It's about 100m away from the beginning of the road that descends to Grande Anse. No credit cards.

Chez Jo
INTERNATIONAL €€

(☑ 0262 31 48 83; 143 Blvd de L'Océan, Manapany-les-Bains; mains €13-22; ☉ 10am-5pm Mon-Thu & Sun, to 9pm Fri & Sat) In this buzzy eatery overlooking the tide pool in Manapany-les-Bains, you're bound to find something on the menu that takes your fancy. Treat yourself to grilled fish and meat dishes, salads or Creole staples, or just pop in for an exquisite fruit juice (€3.50 to €5). Good sandwiches (from €3.50) and takeaway meals, too.

★ L'Instant Présent
EUROPEAN €€€

(☑ 0262 09 33 64; www.facebook.com/instant.present.re; 129 Rue Mahé de la Bourdonnais, Petite Île; mains €20-25; ☉ 7-9pm Tue-Sat) Don't miss this soulful restaurant in the centre of Petite Île – it gets favourable word-of-mouth reviews along with our stamp of approval. The menu centres around Creole and French specialities with a creative twist. If you appreciate fine dining in pleasing surrounds, you won't leave disappointed. It also rents one double (€30) and one quadruple (€50), with a two-night minimum stay – bargain!

🛍 Shopping

Dekocéan ARTS & CRAFTS
(☑0692 04 05 25; www.dekocean.com; 41 Rue Joseph Suacot, Petite Île; ⊙10am-noon & 2-6pm Tue-Sat) Isabelle Biton specialises in porcelain painting. She paints Réunion-inspired designs (Creole *cases,* people, fruits, flowers and chameleons) on plates, cups and bowls.

Maison de l'Abeille FOOD
(☑0262 56 95 03; 68 Chemin Laguerre, Petite Île; ⊙9.30am-noon & 1.30-5pm Wed-Sat, to noon Sun) Not a craft shop but a bee farm, the Maison de L'Abeille sells natural products, including honey and gingerbread.

ℹ Information

Brochures and maps are available at the **Maison du Tourisme du Sud Sauvage** (Tourist Office; ☑0262 37 37 11; www.sudreuniontourisme.fr; 15 Allée du Four à Chaux, Manapany-les-Bains; ⊙9.30am-noon & 1-4.30pm Mon-Fri; 🛜). It also does bookings for *gîtes de montagne* and offers free wi-fi access.

ℹ Getting There & Away

Car Jaune's buses between St-Pierre and St-Benoît (line S1) run through Grande Anse and Manapany-les-Bains. More information at www.carjaune.re.

St-Joseph

POP 38,100
The Wild South's hub, modernish St-Joseph (say 'St-Jo' if you want to sound local) won't leap to the top of your list of preferred destinations in Réunion, but it offers useful services, including supermarkets and ATMs. While it oozes the kind of sunny languor you'd associate with the tropics, the bustling shopping streets at peak hours impart the energy (and stress) of a city.

🛏 Sleeping

Accommodation options are thin on the ground in St-Jo; most visitors tend to stay in B&Bs in the Hauts or in nearby Manapany-les-Bains.

La Case O' Gecko B&B €
(Map p240; ☑0262 58 30 47; www.facebook.com/ogecko974; 56B Rue Léon Dierx; s/d incl breakfast €45/65; 🅿❄🛜) Tucked in a side alley off Rue Léon Dierx, this venture harbours two tidy, if unexciting, rooms. One room has air-con, the other is fan-cooled. None have doors in the bathrooms, just curtains. An acceptable plan B.

L'Arpège Austral B&B €
(Map p240; ☑0692 70 74 12, 0262 56 36 89; http://arpegeaustral.minisite.fr; 53 Rue des Prunes; s/d incl breakfast €50/55; 🅿🛜) It's wonderful to be so near St-Joseph (2.5km), yet in such a serene spot. Sylvie, your hostess, offers two light-flooded rooms with sloping ceilings. They're quite simple but get the job done. For more privacy, the adjoining bungalow, decked out with a small private terrace, fits the bill. It's on the road to Grand Coude (follow the D33).

All units are fan-cooled (no air-con) and bathrooms in the two rooms have no doors, just curtains. Book in for a *table d'hôte* meal (€25) and you may sample a light *carri* on the shady terrace.

🍴 Eating

There's no shortage of places to eat at lunchtime, but if you happen to be in town for dinner, it feels almost deserted. There are a few snack bars and pizzerias that stay open in the evening, though.

Le Joséphin BAKERY €
(☑0262 01 04 61; 6 Rue du Général de Gaulle; sandwiches & salads €3-7; ⊙7am-6pm Tue-Sat) If you're planning a picnic, stop at this mouthwatering bakery, which sells tarts, pastries, breads and other treats. You'll also find sandwiches and salads. The streetside terrace allows for a dash of people-watching at lunchtime.

Le 4 Epices CREOLE €
(☑0262 47 84 66; 12 Rue du Général de Gaulle; mains €5-8; ⊙11.45am-1.30pm Mon-Sat) Literally a hole in the wall. There's only room for a few cramped tables, but there's no better lunchtime deal around. You can eat in or take away.

La Caz à Eva EUROPEAN €€€
(☑0262 47 58 95; 255bis Rue Raphaël Babet; mains €13-28; ⊙11.45am-1.45pm & 6.45-9pm Tue-Sat) No stodgy *carris* here – foodies saunter in for well-presented French-inspired fare with a creative bent, a respectable wine list and smart service. It's hidden in a cul-de-sac off the main drag.

ℹ Getting There & Away

St-Joseph lies on Car Jaune's coastal bus route between St-Pierre and St-Benoît (line S1). More information at www.carjaune.re.

WORTH A TRIP

RIVIÈRE DES REMPARTS

If you really want to get away from it all, check out the Rivière des Remparts, an easily overlooked splendour immediately north of St-Joseph. This valley – one of the wildest in the south – is accessible on foot (or by 4WD). The classic hike is along the river, up to the hamlet of Roche-Plate, about 18km to the north, and on to Nez de Bœuf on the road that leads to Piton de la Fournaise. Allow about four hours to reach Roche-Plate from St-Joseph, and another four hours to Nez de Bœuf.

You can break up your journey in Roche-Plate. Both the Gîte de la Rivière des Remparts – Morel Jacqueline and the Gîte Le Mahavel feature well-scrubbed dorms. Both are closed during the rainy season. Bookings are essential.

Note that 4WD transfers from St-Joseph can be arranged by the *gîtes* (return €150, up to 12 people), but the best way to get a feel for the valley is to explore it on foot.

Les Hauts de St-Joseph

Starting from St-Joseph you can cherry-pick an itinerary in the hinterland that takes in drowsy hamlets where locals all know each other, green-velvet mountains cloaked in layers of wispy cloud, rolling sugar-cane fields, twisting roads and panoramas to make the heart beat faster.

Follow the picturesque D3 that cuts inland before swinging northwestwards to Manapany-les-Hauts. You'll pass **Bésaves** and **Les Lianes**. You could also drive up to **Plaine-des-Grègues** (follow the D32, which branches off the D3 in La Croisée), the highest village of the area, which crouches in a bowl of mountains. This village is famed for its plantations of curcuma and vetiver, which are both used in perfumery.

◎ Sights

Maison du Curcuma　　　　　　　　MUSEUM
(Map p240; ☑ 0262 37 54 66; www.maisonducurcuma.fr; 14 Rue du Rond, Plaine-des-Grègues; ⊙ 9am-noon & 1.30-5pm) **FREE** Learn more about the virtues (and fragrances) of turmeric and vetiver at this small museum in a cute Creole house. It also sells delicious homemade marmalades and jams as well as locally grown spices.

✯✯ Festivals & Events

Fête du Safran　　　　　　　FOOD & DRINK
(Festival of Saffron; ⊙ Nov) A celebration of saffron held in Plaine-des-Grègues, near St-Joseph, in November.

🛏 Sleeping & Eating

Accommodation options are limited way up in the hills. Most visitors base themselves in St-Joseph, Grande Anse or Petite Île and drive up to Bésaves and Plaine-des-Grègues.

You won't find any restaurants in the area, just small grocery stores. For more options, consider driving down to St-Joseph or Petite Île.

Le Mahavel　　　　　　　　　　　GÎTE €
(Map p230; ☑ 0692 20 76 52; Roche-Plate; dm incl half board €43; ⊙ May–mid-Dec) This well-scrubbed *gîte* has four- to eight-bed dorms as well as a double. Bookings are essential.

**Gîte de la Rivière des Remparts –
Morel Jacqueline**　　　　　　　　　GÎTE €
(Map p230; ☑ 0692 68 35 32; Roche-Plate; dm incl half board €45; ⊙ May-Dec) A well-run *gîte* with 10- to 12-bed dorms. Bookings are essential.

ⓘ Getting There & Away

You'll need your own wheels to get to Bésaves, Les Lianes and Plaine-des-Grègues.

St-Joseph to Grand Coude

The timeless hamlet of Grand Coude, perched on a plateau at an altitude of 1300m, has a marvellous setting, with the soaring Morne Langevin (2380m) as the backdrop. Here you'll be smitten by the mellow tranquillity and laid-back lifestyle.

From St-Joseph, take the narrow D33, which passes through **Jean Petit** and twists its way across splendidly rugged scenery of looming peaks and deep gorges. Pull over for a picnic at **Petit Serré**, where a narrow ridge divides two valleys: the valley of the Rivière Langevin on your right and the valley of the Rivière des Remparts on your left. At one point the ridge is little wider than the road itself – you have the feeling of driving on a razor's edge!

At the end of the D33, about 15km north of St-Joseph, Grand Coude appears like a mirage.

◎ Sights

Le Labyrinthe En Champ Thé   GARDENS

(Map p230; ☑0692 60 18 88; www.enchampthe. com; 18 Rue Étienne Mussard, Grand Coude; adult/ child €5.50/4.50, guided tour €8.50/4.50; ⊙9am-noon & 1-5pm Mon-Sat, 9am-5pm Sun, guided tours 10am & 2pm by reservation) At the entrance of Grand Coude, Le Labyrinthe En Champ Thé is worth an hour or so for anyone interested in tropical flora, with an emphasis on tea and geranium. This botanical garden is the only place in Réunion where tea is cultivated. A 50g bag costs €10. You can also purchase syrups, jellies and essential oils made from geranium.

La Maison de Laurina   MUSEUM

(Map p230; ☑0692 68 78 72; www.lamaisondelaurina.fr; 24 Chemin de la Croizure, Grand Coude; €14; ⊙by reservation) Caffeine addicts should make a beeline for La Maison de Laurina, the owner of which grows a top-quality variety of coffee, the Bourbon Pointu. The admission price is a bit steep but it includes a two-hour visit to the plantation and tastings of various homemade delicacies flavoured with coffee (biscuits, liquor, rum). It's in Grand Coude.

⌐ Sleeping & Eating

Accommodation is limited to a handful of B&Bs along the D33.

There's nowhere to eat along the road to Grand Coude, so bring your own food if you're planning on being here for lunch. If you stay in a B&B, you can order dinner.

L'Eucalyptus –
Chez Marie-Claude Grondin   B&B €

(Map p230; ☑0692 68 78 72; 24 Chemin de la Croizure, Grand Coude; s/d incl breakfast €45/55; Pᐟ) Absolute peace and quiet prevail at this unfussy B&B. Choose between the dinky all-wood bungalow or one of the two simple rooms in a charming Creole building. Unwind in the generous garden, where coffee and geranium fill the air. Excellent Creole meals are served at dinner (€26) – you'll be treated to homemade desserts and veggies from the garden.

La Plantation   B&B €€

(Map p240; ☑0262 56 08 86, 0692 33 54 92; www. la-plantation.re; 124 Route de Jean Petit, Jean Petit;

d/ste incl breakfast €110/135; Pᐟᐟᐟᐟ) This upmarket B&B nestled amid sugar-cane fields has a small pool, an outdoor Jacuzzi and lush tropical garden with staggering views of the coast. There are three individually decorated rooms and two larger suites, all featuring handsomely designed bathrooms. Note that only one room comes with sea views. It's on the road to Grand Coude, about 5km from St-Joseph. Cash only.

At the end of the day, make sure you treat yourself to a copious *table d'hôte* (€28). Owner Eric can get by in English.

Au Lapin d'Or   B&B €€

(☑0692 66 89 20, 0262 56 66 48; sadehe.e.lucj@ gmail.com; 55bis Chemin Concession, Jean Petit; s/d incl breakfast €65/75; Pᐟ) Do you like rabbit? We dare ask because the owners of this pert little B&B (which translates as 'Golden Rabbit') in Jean Petit raise rabbits, meaning you'll enjoy them prepared Creole-style at dinner (€26). Accommodation-wise, the three rooms are outfitted with cheerful pastels and super clean bathrooms that don't have proper doors, just curtains. On the road to Grand Coude.

Don't miss out on the homemade *rhum tisane* (aromatic rum), best enjoyed under a gazebo in the garden.

ⓘ Getting There & Away

A few daily buses run between St-Joseph and Grand Coude, but it's much more convenient to explore the area with your own wheels.

St-Joseph to St-Philippe

The coastline between St-Joseph and St-Philippe is definitely alluring: a string of rocky coves and dramatic cliffs pounded by crashing waves and backed by steep hills clad with dense forests and undulating sugar-cane fields, with a few black-sand beaches thrown in for good measure.

Inland, it's no less spectacular. Follow the sinuous secondary roads that wiggle up to the Hauts (hills) and creep through beguiling settlements, which warrant scenic drives and have killer views over the ocean and plunging canyons.

Rivière Langevin

POP 1200

About 4km east of St-Joseph, you'll reach the coastal town of Langevin. From the coast, the Rivière Langevin valley slithers into the mountains. Come prepared: this scenic valley is extremely popular with picnicking families on Sunday.

◎ Sights & Activities

Cascade de la Grande Ravine WATERFALL
(Map p240) A narrow road follows the wide stony bed of the Rivière Langevin and leads to Cascade de la Grande Ravine, a majestic waterfall that drops into a broad pool. Admire it from a lookout by the road, about 9km from the junction with the coastal road.

Aquasens ADVENTURE SPORTS
(Map p240; ☑0692 20 09 03; www.aquasens.re; tours €55) This professional adventure centre runs fantastic guided *randonnées aquatiques* (a mix of walking, sliding, swimming and some serious jumping or plunging down water-polished chutes into natural pools) along the Rivière Langevin. Tours last from two to three hours, depending on the circuit. They can be undertaken by participants of all ages provided they can swim.

Adrenal'île ADVENTURE SPORTS
(Map p240; ☑0692 75 04 00; www.adrenalile.com; Rue de la Passerelle; tours €55) This reputable outfit offers canyoning trips along the Rivière Langevin. They're suitable to all levels of fitness.

Alpanes ADVENTURE SPORTS
(☑0692 77 75 30; www.alpanes.com; canyoning tours €55-95) Offers canyoning trips to Rivière Langevin.

🛏 Sleeping & Eating

There aren't any sleeping options in the Rivière Langevin valley. The nearest hotels and B&Bs are in St-Joseph, Manapany-les-Bains, Vincendo and Le Baril.

If you haven't brought a picnic, there's a bevy of cheap and cheerful eateries along the Rivière Langevin at the entrance to the valley. They're pretty much of a muchness and serve up Creole classics, which you can eat inside or take away.

Chez Malet CREOLE €
(Map p240; ☑0262 56 23 90, 0692 07 90 73; 114 Route de la Passerelle; mains €6-16; ⊙11.30am-2pm Sat-Thu) One of a number of popular eateries along the river, this ramshackle venture has a good terrace for a sandwich, a takeaway curry (from €6) or a beer. It's famed for its *thé dansant* (a party that's popular with senior citizens) on Wednesday and Sunday (from 9am).

ℹ Getting There & Away
You'll need your own wheels to explore the Rivière Langevin valley. Note that it's hard to find a parking space on weekends – come early.

Vincendo & Les Hauts

In Vincendo, few visitors get wind of the black-sand beach fringed by vacoa trees a few kilometres south of the RN2. Swimming is forbidden because there are some dangerous currents, but it's a great place for a picnic.

Back in the village, follow the D34 that goes uphill to the north and takes you to the hamlet of **La Crête**. From there, the D37 leads due east to another peaceful settlement, **Jacques-Payet**, before zigzagging downhill to the junction with the coastal road.

🛏 Sleeping & Eating

★Rougail Mangue GUESTHOUSE €
(Map p240; ☑0262 31 55 09, 0692 20 21 63; www.rougailmangue.com; 12 Rue Marcel Pagnol, Vincendo; s/d/tr/q €39/59/75/90, bungalows s/d €44/70; P❄☎≋) You'd never guess it from the road but this guesthouse is a great find. The ground floor is occupied by a smart lounge area, one six-bed room, two squeaky-clean quads and a cheery double that opens onto a well-tended garden. For more privacy, book the smallish yet cosy bungalow, with stupendous sea views. On the main road, between Langevin and Vincendo.

The coup de grâce is the glorious pool, with the ocean as a backdrop, and the outdoor Jacuzzi (€5). Air-con is extra (€5), except in the bungalow. Note that the bathroom in the bungalow has no door, just a curtain. Add €3 for breakfast (or €15 for a copious brunch), best enjoyed al fresco under a gazebo. There's also a kitchen. Book ahead.

La Table des Randonneurs GÎTE €
(☑0692 61 73 47; 17 Chemin des Barbadines, Jacques-Payet; dm/d incl breakfast €25/50, bungalow q €100; P) Way up in the hills, the 'Hikers' Table' is a safe bet, with two doubles (one of which has private facilities), one quad and one six-bed room in a modern house. They're down to earth, functional and simply furnished. There's also one self-contained bungalow that can sleep six people. No wi-fi. It's about 7km northeast of Vincendo (follow the D37).

The menu (€25 to €30) features local delicacies like smoked duck with *vacoa* and pork with palm hearts.

Ferme-Auberge Desprairies   B&B €
(☑ 0692 64 61 70, 0262 37 20 27; www.ferme-au berge-desprairies.com; 44 Route de Matouta, Matouta; d incl breakfast €50; ☐ ☎) One of the best things about this peaceful inn is the road to it, which travels through sugar-cane fields despite being only a couple of kilometres from the coast. The six rooms are strictly unmemorable but are kept tidy, and in this location, for this price, you won't hear anyone complaining. Rooms 1, 2 and 3 have sea views.

The owners also prepare delicious home-cooked meals (€22). Follow the D37 to the east to get here.

Îlet aux Palmistes   B&B €€
(Map p240; ☑ 0692 20 41 58, 0262 20 21 14; www. facebook.com/iletauxpalmistes; 25 Rue Claude Marion; s/d/q incl breakfast €60/75/110; ☐ ❋ ☎) What sets this *chambre d'hôte* apart are the stunning location amid sugarcane fields and the appealing architecture – no plain, concrete building, but a facade covered with wood. Its two rooms, one of which has air-con, are airy and comfortable and open onto a flowering garden. Meals (€28) come in for warm praise. There's also a communal kitchen.

Les Grands Monts   B&B €€
(☑ 0262 23 60 16, 0693 20 52 05; www.facebook. com/Les-Grands-Monts; 2A Impasse Sabine, Vincendo; d incl breakfast €145; ☐ ❋ ☎ ☎) Looking for a night at some place extra special? Make a beeline for this lovely *maison d'hôte* in a historic stone building. It shelters four spacious rooms that ingeniously blend volcanic stones and hardwoods. However, the open bathrooms in two rooms may not be to everyone's taste. The pool in the garden is a delight. Evening meals cost €35.

The Swiss owner, who took over in 2018, speaks English and German. It's in a cul-de-sac about 300m north of the RN2.

❶ Getting There & Away

Car Jaune's buses between St-Pierre and St-Benoît (line S1) run through Vincendo. More at www.carjaune.re. To get to the Hauts, you'll need your own wheels.

Basse-Vallée & Cap Méchant

The Basse-Vallée area is known for its production of baskets, bags (called *bertels*), hats

and other items from *vacoa* fronds. It's also famous for its rugged coastline, particularly Cap Méchant, one of the most extraordinary landscapes on the southern coast.

◉ Sights

Cap Méchant   NATURAL FEATURE
(Map p240) Cap Méchant is one of the eeriest landscapes in the south, with huge lava fields, windswept black cliffs, rows of *vacoa* trees and the mandatory picnic shelters. From the headland you can follow an excellent coastal path along the sea cliffs (bring sturdy shoes).

⌦ Sleeping

★**Gîte de Yoleine et Théophane**   GÎTE €
(Map p240; ☑ 0262 37 13 14, 0692 87 25 43; www. facebook.com/giteteophaneetyoleine; Route Forestière, Basse-Vallée; dm incl half board €51) One of southern Réunion's best-kept secrets, this rural paradise surrounded by forest and sugar-cane fields is a great place to come down a few gears. Way up in the hills, it shelters several six-bed dorms, each with its own bathroom. At dinner the super friendly owners will treat you with the freshest island ingredients.

Access is a bit tricky; it can be reached on foot (about 30 minutes) or with a normal car in dry weather via a scenic 2km dirt track from the Route Forestière (signed at the junction, about 5.5km above the village of Basse-Vallée).

Ferme-Auberge
Le Rond de Basse Vallée   INN €
(Map p240; ☑ 0692 69 65 51; Route Forestière, Basse-Vallée; d incl breakfast €50; ☐) Head up the Route Forestière to find this *ferme-auberge*, a great place to commune with nature. There are four simple rooms with functional bathrooms in a Creole-style building in harmony with the environment. The restaurant is across the road and features regional dishes with authentic flavours, including *vacoa*, a local speciality. A full meal will set you back €25.

Chambre d'Hôte
Le Puits des Français   B&B €€
(☑ 0692 36 26 16, 0262 28 57 50; huet.jacky@ hotmail.fr; 34 Rue Labourdonnais, Basse-Vallée; d incl breakfast €75; ☐ ❋ ☎ ☎) A hop from Cap Méchant, this abode features five bungalows arrayed around a tiny pool. They're comfortable but tightly packed together, so don't expect lots of privacy. Each bungalow has

its own strong chromatic vibration: electric blue, orange, green. The owner loves colour! Evening meals cost €28.

Coco Vanille B&B €€

(☑ 0262 93 18 76, 0692 94 51 12; www.coco-vanille.com; 68 Rue Labourdonnais, Basse-Vallée; d incl breakfast €68-75; ❄ ☎ ⬚) This laid-back B&B is a good deal with cool rooms, small bathrooms, a few fancy touches and a small breakfast terrace. The swimming pool in the tropical garden is a great addition when it's stifling hot. It's within walking distance of Cap Méchant. Dinner costs €22. No credit cards.

✖ Eating

Le Pinpin CHINESE, CREOLE €€

(☑ 0262 37 04 19; Rue du Cap Méchant, Cap Méchant; mains €12-18; ☉ 11.30am-2pm Thu-Tue) There's sure to be a dish on the extensive menu that suits your palate. Very popular with weekending families. It's known for its *palmiste* (palm hearts) specialities. On Sunday, the lunch buffet (€17) is wildly popular.

Le Cap Méchant CHINESE, CREOLE €€

(☑ 0692 85 39 28; Rue du Cap Méchant, Cap Méchant; mains €10-22; ☉ 11.30am-2pm Tue-Sun) Le Cap Méchant is mobbed at weekends but almost deserted on weekdays. It serves great *carris,* chop sueys and fish dishes.

L'Étoile des Mers CHINESE, CREOLE €€

(☑ 0262 37 04 60; Rue du Cap Méchant, Cap Méchant; mains €11-17; ☉ 11.30am-2pm) The food is a crowd-pleasing mix of Chinese dishes, Creole staples and *métro* classics.

ℹ Getting There & Away

Cap Méchant lies on Car Jaune's coastal bus route between St-Pierre and St-Benoît (line S1). More information at www.carjaune.re.

Le Baril

POP 2200

Le Baril is the last settlement before St-Philippe. Most people stop here for the Puits des Anglais, one of the most spectacular attractions along this stretch of coast.

◉ Sights

Puits des Anglais NATURAL FEATURE

(Wells of the British; Map p240; Le Baril) The main attraction in Le Baril is the Puits des Anglais, a splendid saltwater pool that has been constructed in the basaltic rock. It's mobbed at weekends but you'll have the whole place to yourself during the week.

🛏 Sleeping

Le Pinpin d'Amour B&B €

(Map p240; ☑ 0692 64 37 44, 0262 37 14 86; www.pinpindamour.com; 56 Chemin Paul Hoareau; d incl breakfast €65-75; ℗ ❄ @ ⬚) Spending a night at this original *chambre d'hôte* makes a good story to tell the folks back home. Your hosts have a passion for *vacoa* and *pinpin* (the palm's edible artichoke-like fruit), meaning you'll be guaranteed to taste them at dinner (€27 to €30). Accommodation-wise, the five appealing, if a bit itty-bitty and sombre, rooms sport pastel-coloured walls and honey-boarded floors.

The dearer rooms have a small veranda but no views to speak of. One quibble: the portable air-conditioners in the three rooms with air-con are a bit noisy. It's amid the sugar-cane fields above Le Baril, about 2km from the coastal road. There's a 10% discount for stays of two nights and more.

★ Le Four à Pain B&B €€

(☑ 0692 36 61 55; huet-jean-marc@hotmail.fr; 63C RN2; d incl breakfast €80; ℗ ❄ ⬚ ☎) Simplicity, character and a great welcome make Le Four à Pain special. Rooms, in two adorable Creole-style cottages, are light and fresh with contemporary decor, and have their own entrance. You're in a superb setting, with fine mature trees that shade a wonderfully quiet tropical garden. The coup de grâce is the lovely pool – pure bliss after a bout of sightseeing.

Don't miss out on the luscious dinners (€30) on certain evenings; you'll be guaranteed to sample palm-heart salad – the owner is a major producer in the south. It's off the main road.

Les Embruns du Baril HOTEL €€

(☑ 0262 20 07 17; www.facebook.com/lesembruns dubaril; RN2; d €100-130; ℗ ❄ ⬚ ☎) It's not the Ritz, but this three-star abode opened in 2018 offers a pleasant alternative to B&Bs, with 18 neat rooms, 16 of which have ocean views (tip: aim for room 15, which is the best). The on-site restaurant (mains from €15) gets good reviews. Note that wi-fi is available in the restaurant only.

✖ Eating

Apart from Warren Hastings, independent restaurants are scarce in Le Baril. Your best bet is to order a meal at your B&B.

Le Ti Vacoa
CREOLE, SANDWICHES €

(☑0692 92 20 24; Le Puits des Anglais, RN2; mains €4-8; ⊙10am-3pm & 4-9pm Tue-Sat, 10am-3pm Sun) This unfussy little kiosk could hardly be better situated: it overlooks the saltwater pool at Puits des Anglais. The menu concentrates on composed salads and a wide selection of appetising sandwiches (from €3).

Warren Hastings
CREOLE €€

(☑0692 52 03 82; 103A RN2; mains €16-24; ⊙11am-2pm & 6.30-9pm) The food looks as good as it tastes at this surprisingly upbeat cafe-bistro on the main road. It serves winningly fresh dishes prepared with local ingredients, including *palmiste* (palm hearts), and also doubles as a bar (believe us, the homemade rum is strong!). Find it on the eastern edge of Le Baril.

★ Auberge Paysanne
Le Palmier
CREOLE €€€

(Map p240; ☑0692 69 03 48; 21 Chemin Ceinture; menu €27; ⊙11.30am-1pm Sat-Thu, by reservation) Plenty of smiles from the owners, recipes plucked straight out of grandma's cookbook, a serene setting in the Hauts and partial sea views from the terrace – if you're after an authentic Creole experience, this place is hard to beat. Here you can eat local specialities that are hard to find elsewhere, such as chicken with palm hearts and papaya cake.

Note that it's not a walk-in restaurant – it's a private home that's open by reservation only. It's signposted from the main road.

❶ Getting There & Away

Car Jaune's buses between St-Pierre and St-Benoît (line S1, €2, about six daily) run through Le Baril. From St-Pierre, the ride takes about 50 minutes. More information at www.carjaune.re.

St-Philippe

POP 5100

The only town of consequence in the Wild South (along with St-Joseph), St-Philippe has a wonderfully down-to-earth, unfussy ambience. Although this friendly little town is devoid of overwhelming sights, it has a slew of (good) surprises up its sleeves and is optimally placed for explorations of the coast and forays into the Hauts. Oh, and St-Philippe lies in the shadow of Piton de la Fournaise.

◉ Sights

Sentier Botanique
de Mare Longue
GARDENS

(Map p240; Chemin Forestier) This pristine forest has an end-of-the-world feeling that will appeal to those in search of hush. From the car park you can tackle one of the three interpretative trails in the primary forest. It's inland between Le Baril and St-Philippe.

Le Jardin des Parfums
et des Épices
GARDENS

(Map p240; ☑0692 66 09 01; www.jardin-parfums-epices.com; 7 Chemin Forestier, Mare Longue; adult/child €6.10/3.05; ⊙tours 10.30am & 2.30pm) Inland between Le Baril and St-Philippe, don't miss the 3-hectare garden, Le Jardin des Parfums et des Épices. It contains over 1500 species in a natural setting in the Mare Longue forest, 3km west of St-Philippe. Knowledgeable and enthusiastic guides present the island's history, economy and culture through the plants; tours are in French and last 90 minutes.

Fishing Harbour
HARBOUR

(Map p240) With its handful of colourful fishing boats, the teensy fishing harbour is worth a peek.

✤ Festivals & Events

Fête du Vacoa
FAIR

(Festival of Vacoa; ⊙Aug) Vegetarians, rejoice: St-Philippe is the self-proclaimed capital of *vacoa* (screw-pine fronds). No joke – no less than 5000 visitors turn up to join St-Philippois townsfolk for the 10-day Fête du Vacoa in August.

⏣ Sleeping

★ Dan'n
Tan Lontan
BUNGALOW €

(☑0692 65 14 29, 0262 47 71 06; www.dantan lontan.com; 19 Allée des Palmiers; d €54-75; P ❄ ☎ ☎) Swap stress for bliss at this enticing venue in a splendid property five-minutes' walk from the centre. Handsome, well-thought-out and practical, the three Creole-style, fully equipped cottages are engaging places to stay. Relax in the lush garden, doze by the pool or enjoy a glass of something on your shady terrace. One of the area's best-kept secrets.

Note that the smaller bungalow is right by the pool, which limits the sense of privacy.

Le Palmier
B&B €

(☑0262 37 04 11, 0692 02 85 71; nicolelepalmier
@yahoo.fr; 8 Rue de la Pompe; s €46, d €52-62, incl
breakfast; P 🌸 🛜 🌊) It lacks excitement, maybe, but this friendly B&B down a little lane
at the east end of St-Philippe is a safe bet.
Rooms are ordinary, with immaculate tiles,
tiny bathrooms and colourful bedspreads.
Avoid the larger one at the back, which has
obstructed views. There's a communal kitch-
en for guests' use. Guests can use the pool
in front of the owners' house if they stay at
least two nights.

Au Domaine du Vacoa
B&B €

(☑0692 64 89 89, 0262 37 03 12; www.domainedu
vacoa.fr; 12 Chemin Vacoa; d incl breakfast €70;
P 🌸 🛜 🌊) This B&B in a pert little *case
créole* features two adjoining rooms enhanced with touches of colour, back-friendly
mattresses and spotless bathrooms. Au
Domaine du Vacoa's ultimate trump card,
though, is its small infinity pool with great
ocean views. At dinner (€26 to €28), warm
your insides with duck, *vacoa* and vegetables from the garden – all organic, of course.

🍴 Eating

La Mer Cassée
CREOLE €€

(Map p240; ☑0262 46 56 18; 101 RN2, Mare Longue; mains €10-15; ☺noon-1.30pm Thu-Tue) This
laid-back eatery is set in a small Creole
house along the main road (not so peaceful),
but there's outdoor seating across the road –
a few plastic tables under the shade of *vacoa* trees – and great ocean views. You won't
find more than three or four Creole dishes
on the chalkboard, but everything is fresh
and home made.

Marmite du Pêcheur
SEAFOOD €€

(☑0262 37 01 01; 18A RN2, Ravine Ango; mains
€15-31, Sun buffet €25; ☺noon-2pm Thu-Tue)
Can't stomach one more morsel of *carri
poulet* (chicken curry)? Then opt for this
eatery where cuisine is predominantly fishy:
crab, shrimps, fish, octopus and mussels,
climaxing with a gargantuan *marmite du
pêcheur* (€30), a kind of seafood stew. Alas,
no views. It's just off the main road, east of
St-Philippe.

ℹ️ Getting There & Away

Line S1 buses between St-Benoît (€2, 1¼ hours)
and St-Pierre (€2, one hour) stop at the town
hall in St-Philippe. More information at www.
carjaune.re.

Le Grand Brûlé

The crowning glory of the Wild South, the
arid, eerie landscape of Le Grand Brûlé is
a 6km-wide volcanic plain formed by the
main lava flow from the volcano. This is
where the action goes when the volcano is
erupting. The steep slopes above, known
as Les Grandes Pentes, have funnelled lava
down to the coast for thousands of years.

◉ Sights

Le Grand Brûlé Platform
VIEWPOINT

(Map p240; RN2) In April 2007, in one of the
most violent eruptions ever recorded, an impressive lava flow was formed, about 2km
north of Pointe du Tremblet. The road was
cut off for several months. It's a primal experience to drive through the barren moonscape that is this huge expanse of solidified,
pure-black lava field. It's forbidden to walk
across the lava flow, but a viewing platform
has been built just off the RN2.

Pointe de la Table
VIEWPOINT

(Map p240; RN2) In 1986 the lava unusually
flowed south of Le Grand Brûlé to reach the
sea at Pointe de la Table, a headland that lies
a few hundred metres north of Puits Arabe.
This eruption added over 30 hectares to the
island's area, more than 450 people had to
be evacuated and several homes were lost.
An interpretative trail has been set up and
makes for a lovely hike on the basaltic cliffs
pounded by the ocean.

Puits Arabe
VIEWPOINT

(Map p240) Leaving St-Philippe to the east,
you'll first come across Puits Arabe (Wells of
the Arabs), a hole that has been excavated in
the basaltic rock. It's a popular picnic site,
with shelters scattered amid rows of *vacoa*
trees.

🏃 Activities

Visitors to Réunion don't have to confine
themselves to exploring the surface of its
volcanic formations – at Le Grand Brûlé, it's
possible to go caving inside volcanic tubes
(elongated tunnels formed by the cooling
and rapid hardening of lava) and walk *under* the volcano.

Speleo Canyon
ADVENTURE SPORTS

(☑0692 11 50 13; www.speleocanyon.fr; tours €60-
75) Julien Dez is a qualified instructor with
lots of experience around Réunion. He can
arrange canyoning trips and guided treks as

well as guided excursions through the lava tubes of Le Grand Brûlé.

Envergure Réunion
ADVENTURE SPORTS

(☑ 0693 43 23 52; www.canyon-speleo.re; tours €50-75) A long-standing favourite for canyoning in southern Réunion and guided excursions through the lava tubes at Le Grand Brûlé.

Rougail Rando
ADVENTURE SPORTS

(Map p240; ☑ 0692 92 14 34; 1 RN2, Le Tremblet; tours from €50) Juanito specialises in guided excursions through the lava tubes at Le Grand Brûlé. Prices include gear rental.

🛏 Sleeping & Eating

There's only one accommodation option in Le Grand Brûlé area. You can base yourself in St-Joseph, St-Philippe or Ste-Rose and visit the area on a day trip.

A smattering of so-called 'restaurants' (in fact, private homes turned into casual eateries) are dotted along the RN2 between St-Philippe and Le Grand Brûlé.

Le Crabe Sous la Varangue
B&B €€

(Map p240; ☑ 0692 92 13 56, 0262 92 13 56; www.crabevarangue.canalblog.com; 1 RN2, Le Tremblet; s/d incl breakfast €65/80; P 🛜) This quirky B&B sits in isolated splendour on the main road between St-Philippe and Le Grand Brûlé. The two individually decorated rooms in the main house have pretty painted concrete floors and colourful walls, but are a bit sombre, while the third one occupies a cosy Creole house endowed with polished parquet floors. No air-con, but each room has a fan.

Dinner (€28) is only available on Friday and Saturday. The owner runs excursions to the lava tubes in Le Grand Brûlé.

★ Chez Moustache
CREOLE €€

(Map p240; ☑ 0692 33 27 03; 9 RN2, Le Tremblet; mains €12-17; ⏱ 11.30am-2.30pm Sat-Thu) A welcoming family-run outfit in a picturesque Creole house complete with a courtyard garden, Chez Moustache serves authentic Creole specialities at honest prices. The food is grounded in island tradition, as testified by the wood-fired oven. The menu changes nightly, and includes only four or five mains. Bad point: long service. It's about 5km south of the 2007 lava flow.

Le Vieux Port
CREOLE, SEAFOOD €€

(Map p240; ☑ 0692 15 79 31; 112 RN2, Le Tremblet; mains €15-22; ⏱ 11.30am-2.30pm Sun-Fri) A fine specimen of a restaurant, Le Vieux Port is ideally situated in a tropical garden about 500m south of the 2007 lava flow. It is strictly local cuisine – albeit of a refreshingly creative nature. Locals rave about the *rôti porc palmiste* (smoked pork with palm-heart salad) and the grilled fish. Takeaway is available. Reservations are advised on Sunday.

🛍 Shopping

Escale Bleue Vanille
FOOD

(Map p240; ☑ 0262 37 03 99; www.escale-bleue.fr; 7 RN2, Le Tremblet; guided tours €5; ⏱ 9am-5pm Mon-Sat) Learn how vanilla is prepared and purchase a sweet-scented vanilla pod at this small family-run operation.

ⓘ Getting There & Away

Le Grand Brûlé lies on Car Jaune's coastal bus route (line S1, about six daily, €2) between St-Pierre and St-Benoît. From St-Pierre, the ride takes about 1¼ hours. More information at www.carjaune.re.

THE EAST

The east coast is everything the west coast is not: low-key, unpretentious and luxuriant (yes, it *does* get much more rain). While this coast lacks the beaches of the west, the region makes up for it with spectacular waterfalls and fantastic picnic spots. The main produce of the area is sugar cane, but the region is also known for its vanilla plantations and fruit orchards.

This coastal stretch is also considered to be 'other', partially as it's the bastion of Tamil culture in Réunion. Here you'll find a distinctive atmosphere, with numerous temples and colourful religious festivals. For visitors it's an opportunity to discover a Réunion you never imagined.

Tourism in this area remains on a humble scale, with no star attractions. However, it's worth taking a few days to explore the quiet recesses of this less-visited part of the island where you can experience Réunion from a different perspective.

Ste-Suzanne

POP 20,500

The seaside town of Ste-Suzanne is usually glimpsed in passing by most tourists on the route down the coast, which is a shame because there are charming pockets in the area that beg discovery, including the splendid Rivière Ste-Suzanne, which is both a

Eastern Réunion

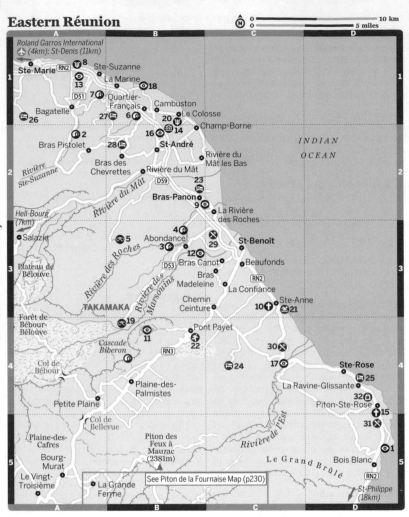

playground for outdoorsy types and a hotspot for sunbathers and picnickers.

◎ Sights

Bassin Boeuf WATERFALL

(Map p252) If you need to cool off, the Bassin Boeuf waterfall beckons with its enticing natural pools fringed with stone slabs, ideal for picnicking and sunbathing. Well worth the detour.

From Ste-Suzanne, follow the D51 towards Bagatelle for about 7km until the signpost 'Bassin Boeuf'. Leave your car at the small parking area and walk several minutes down a dirt road to the Rivière Ste-Suzanne. To get

to the waterfall, cross the river and follow the path on the right for about five minutes.

You can also access Bassin Nicole, another lovely waterfall that is downstream (it's visible from the dirt road leading to the Rivière Ste-Suzanne).

La Vanilleraie PLANTATION

(Map p252; ☎ 0262 23 07 26; www.lavanilleraie. com; Allée Chassagne, Domaine du Grand Hazier; tours adult/child €5/3; ☺ 8.30am-noon & 1.30-5pm Mon-Sat) At Domaine du Grand Hazier, a superb 18th-century sugar-planter's residence about 3km southwest of Ste-Suzanne, you'll find La Vanilleraie, where you can

Eastern Réunion

see vanilla preparation and drying processes and also purchase vanilla pods. Guided tours are available at 9am, 10am, 11am, 2pm, 3pm and 4pm. The manager speaks English.

Cascade Niagara   WATERFALL
(Map p252) Just beyond the church towards the southern end of town is a road signposted inland to Cascade Niagara, a 30m waterfall on the Rivière Ste-Suzanne. At the end of the road, about 2km further on, you wind up at the waterfall. On weekends it's a popular picnic site.

Cascade Délices   WATERFALL
(Map p252; Quartier-Français) In the Quartier-Français district, Cascade Délices is an easily accessed waterfall. It's only 4m high, but the junglelike setting will appeal to nature lovers, and you can dunk yourself in the cool water. It's signposted.

Lighthouse   LIGHTHOUSE
(Rue du Phare) Next to the tourist office, the small lighthouse – the only one on the island – is worth a gander. It was built in 1845 and is still in operation.

Chapelle Front de Mer   HINDU TEMPLE
(Map p252) Notable religious buildings in Ste-Suzanne include the Chapelle Front de Mer, an ornate Tamil temple built on a pebbly beach north of town (it's unsigned; follow the road to Domaine Grand Hazier/La Vannilleraie).

🛏 Sleeping & Eating

Ste-Suzanne doesn't have an abundance of sleeping options. With your own wheels, you may prefer to stay in St-Denis and visit the area on a day trip. The eating scene in Ste-Suzanne can optimistically be described as 'dull', but you're not far from St-Denis' gourmet restaurants.

Les Meublés de Dada   BUNGALOW €
(Map p252; ☏ 0692 87 39 33; www.les-meubles-de-dada.webnode.fr; 13 Chemin Rita Ah-Teng, Commune Carron; d €60; P ❄ 🛜) This well-designed, spacious (41 sq m) bungalow set in a well-tended tropical garden feels like a cosy doll's house and proffers ample coastal views. There's also a larger house that can sleep five people. It's a great deal for self-caterers and families, and a handy base for the east. There's a two-night minimum stay.

Le Pharest   GUESTHOUSE €
(☏ 0692 25 74 08, 0262 98 91 10; www.pharest-reunion.com; 22 Rue Blanchet; s €39-49, d €59-75, q €117, incl breakfast; P ❄ 🛜 ⛱) Near the lighthouse, this compact tropical cocoon offers five wooden bungalows that are set in an exuberant garden. They're fairly ramshackle and filled with wholly unpretentious furniture, but are kept in good nick. Precious perks include a small swimming pool and a restaurant (menu €22). What sets it apart,

VANILLA UNVEILED

The vanilla orchid was introduced into Réunion from Mexico around 1820, but early attempts at cultivation failed because of the absence of the Mexican bee that pollinates the flower and triggers the development of the vanilla pod. Fortunately for custard lovers everywhere, a method of hand-pollination was discovered in Réunion in 1841 by a 12-year-old slave, Edmond Albius. Vanilla was highly prized in Europe at the time and Albius' discovery ushered in an economic boom, at least for the French 'vanilla barons'.

The vanilla bubble burst, however, when synthetic vanilla – made from coal – was invented in the late 19th century. Réunion's vanilla industry was almost wiped out, but in recent years the growing demand for natural products has led to something of a revival. You'll now find vanilla 'plantations' hidden in the forests from Ste-Suzanne south to St-Philippe.

The majority of Réunion's crop is exported (Coca-Cola is the world's single biggest buyer), but vanilla is still a firm favourite in local cuisine. It crops up in all sorts of delicacies, from cakes and pastries to coffee, liqueurs, even vanilla duck and chicken. Best of all is the sublime flavour of a vanilla-steeped *rhum arrangé* (a mixture of rum, fruit juice, cane syrup and a blend of herbs and berries).

though, is the congenial atmosphere and the friendly welcome of Nadège and Patrick.

Air-con is extra (€3). If you stay three nights or more, it's worth opting for the fully equipped, spacious (51 sq m) *gîte* across the road (three nights for €225).

ℹ Information

The **tourist office** (☑ 0262 52 13 54; www.leb eaupays.com; 5 Rue du Phare; ◷ 9am-12.30pm & 1.30-5pm Mon-Sat; ☏) is near the lighthouse. *Gîtes de montagne* can be booked here.

ℹ Getting There & Away

Ste-Suzanne is served by Car Jaune buses running between St-Denis and St-Benoît (lines E1 and E2, €2, about 15 daily, less on Sunday). Buses between St-André and St-Denis (line E4) also stop at Ste-Suzanne. Buses stop at the town hall and at Quartier Français. From St-Denis, the ride takes about 45 minutes. More information at www.carjaune.re.

St-André

POP 56,600

St-André is the epicentre of Tamil culture in Réunion, and you'll see more women draped in vividly coloured saris than Zoreilles (mainland French) wearing designer glasses and trendy shirts. Busy streets transport you to a city somewhere in India with curry houses, sari shops and bric-a-brac traders. You'll definitely feel closer to Mumbai than Paris.

The mainly Tamil population in the area is descended from indentured labourers who were brought from India to work in the sugar-cane fields and factories after slavery was abolished in 1848.

◉ Sights

Sucrerie de Bois-Rouge   DISTILLERY

(Map p252; ☑ 0262 58 59 74; www.distilleriesav anna.com; 2 Chemin Bois Rouge; tour by reservation adult/child €12/8.50, distillery €8.50/5; ◷ 9am-6pm Mon-Sat Jan-Jun, to 8pm Jul-Dec) This sugar refinery is on the coast 3km north of St-André. During the cane harvest (July to early December) visitors are shown around the huge, high-tech plant, following the process from the delivery of the cut cane to the final glittering crystals. The two-hour tour includes the neighbouring distillery, where the by-products are made into rum. From January to June, you can only visit the distillery. There's a shop, Tafia et Galabé, where you can sip (and buy) the good stuff.

Children under seven years aren't allowed into the refinery. Wear closed shoes.

Temple of Colosse   HINDU TEMPLE

(Map p252; Chemin Agenor) Temple of Colosse is, by far, the most striking Tamil temple in Réunion. With its brightly painted decor, it's very photogenic. Since it's not open to the public, you'll have to content yourself with peering through the railings. It regularly hosts various Tamil ceremonies.

Plantation de
Vanille Roulof   PLANTATION

(Map p252; ☑ 0692 10 87 15; www.lavanilledelare union.com; 470 Chemin Deschanets; tours €4; ◷ 9am-4pm Mon-Sat, tours 11am, 2pm, 3pm & 4pm Mon-Sat) If you're after Réunion's Vanille Bourbon, head to this small family-run operation where you can buy vanilla pods at reasonable prices (40g for €30). You can also find out about the technique of 'marrying' the vanilla, a delicate operation in which the flowers are fertilised by hand.

Maison Martin Valliamé   HISTORIC BUILDING
(Map p252; 1590 Chemin du Centre; guided tour incl snacks €8.50; ⊙9am-12.30pm & 1.30-5pm Mon-Fri) This handsome colonial villa dates from 1925 and is worth a look. It's northeast of the centre. Guided tours in French are available on the hour from 10am to 4pm.

🛏 Sleeping & Eating

Poivre et Citronnelle   B&B €€
(Map p252; 📞0692 09 90 00; www.poivre-et-citron nelle.com; 204 Chemin Couturier; s/d incl break-fast €140/150; P❋令⊜) Run by a friendly *métro* couple, this B&B stands in a haven of tropical peace in a peaceful neighbourhood. The three adjoining rooms with their own entrance and terrace are colourful, while the fourth room upstairs affords great coastal views. Float in the sparkling pool (or in the Jacuzzi) or bask in the sunny garden.

Le Beau Rivage   CHINESE, CREOLE €€
(📞0262 46 08 66; 873 Chemin Agenor; mains €12-16; ⊙noon-1.45pm & 7-9pm Tue, Wed, Fri & Sat, noon-1.45pm Thu & Sun) True to its name (The Beautiful Shore), Le Beau Rivage has an enviable location on the seafront, beside the church ruins in Champ-Borne. That said, the dining room is overly dull; ask for a table near the windows. The cuisine is predominantly Chinese and Creole. Its good-value lunch buffet (€20) served on Sunday is very popular with Réunionnais families.

Le Velli   CREOLE €€
(📞0262 46 03 38; www.restaurantvelli.com; 336 Chemin Agenor; mains €15-25, menus €15-30; ⊙11.30am-2.30pm Mon-Fri & Sun) Dining at this inviting restaurant near the Temple of Colosse is all about having a good time enjoying the finer pleasures of life. The cuisine is resolutely Creole (with a refined twist), well prepared and well priced. Another draw is the shady courtyard at the back. Also does takeaway (from €6).

Kom La Kaz   CREOLE €€
(📞0692 61 49 10; 189 Rue Payet; mains €8-13; ⊙11.30am-1.30pm Mon-Sat) This rustic little place right in the centre serves well-prepared Creole dishes to eat in or take away.

❶ Information

There's a small but helpful **tourist office** (📞0262 46 16 16; www.reunionest.fr; Maison Martin Valliamé, 1590 Chemin du Centre;

⊙8.30am-12.30pm & 1.30-4pm Mon & Wed-Sat; 令). It has wi-fi access and can provide specific dates of Tamil festivals.

❶ Getting There & Away

Car Jaune buses from St-Denis to St-Benoît pass through St-André (€2, 50 minutes). If you're travelling to Salazie by bus (€2, 35 minutes), you will have to change here; there are six buses daily in each direction (three on Sunday). More details at www.carjaune.re.

Bras-Panon
POP 12,300

Bras-Panon is Réunion's vanilla capital, and most visitors come here to see (and smell!) the fragrant vanilla-processing plant. The town is also associated with a rare sprat-like delicacy known as *bichiques*. In early summer (around November or December) these are caught at the mouth of the Rivière des Roches as they swim upriver to spawn.

◉ Sights

**Bassin La Paix
& Bassin La Mer**   WATERFALL
(Map p252) A blissful site is Bassin La Paix, in the Rivière des Roches valley, about 2.5km west from Bras-Panon (it's signposted). From the car park, a path quickly

---

LITTLE INDIA

If you happen to be around Ste-Suzanne and St-André at certain periods of the year, you'll discover a very exotic side of the island, with lots of colourful festivals organised by the Tamil community.

If you're about, be sure to join in the heady hype of these local festivals. In January, don't miss Tamil **fire-walking ceremonies**, when participants enter a meditative state and then walk over red-hot embers as a sign of devotion to various deities. Thousands of goats are slaughtered as offerings and are distributed among the participants. Another must-see is the **Cavadee festival**, which usually takes place in January or February. In October or November, make a beeline for **Divali** (aka Dipavali), the Festival of Light. Dancers and decorated floats parade through the town centre. Visitors are welcome. Contact the tourist office in St-André for specific dates.

RÉUNION ST-BENOÎT

BELVÉDÈRE DE L'EDEN

A fabulous place to chill out is the aptly named viewpoint **Belvédère de l'Eden** (Map p252), in upcountry Bras-Panon. From Bras-Panon, take the road to St-André, then turn left onto the D59 (in the direction of Vincendo, Bellevue) for about 9km (follow the signs) until you reach a car park. From there, follow the meandering trail signed L'Eden. After about 20 minutes, you'll discover a wonderfully secluded picnic spot locals wish you hadn't. The views of the coast are incomparable.

leads down to a majestic waterfall tumbling into a large rock pool. It's an ideal picnic spot. For a more off-the-beaten-track experience, you can continue upstream to Bassin La Mer, another cascading delight that can be reached on foot only. The start of the trail is at the end of the car park.

It's an enjoyable (though exposed and hot) 40-minute walk. Reward yourself with a dip in the swimming holes at the bottom of the falls.

Coopérative de Vanille Provanille   FACTORY

(Map p252; ☑ 0262 51 70 12; www.provanille.fr; 21 RN2002; tours adult/child €6/free; ⊙ 8.30am-noon & 1.30-5pm) This working vanilla-processing plant offers an introduction to the process of producing Réunion's famous Vanille Bourbon via a 45-minute guided tour and a film on the history of vanilla cultivation. You'll find various vanilla products at the factory shop. It's worth a visit just for the dreamy smell.

✨ Festivals & Events

Fête des Bichiques   FOOD & DRINK

(Festival of Bichiques; ⊙ Oct) This rural fair celebrates the rare sprat-like delicacy known as *bichiques*. In Bras-Panon.

🛏 Sleeping

Chez Éva Annibal   INN €

(Map p252; ☑ 0262 51 53 76; 6 Chemin Rivière du Mât; d with shared bathroom incl breakfast €48; 🅿 ❄ 🛜) Set in a modern house, this inn has four functional but clean rooms with sloping ceilings and well-maintained communal facilities above the dining room. A good deal for the price.

Eating

There aren't many restaurants in Bras-Panon but you'll find a smattering of takeaway outlets offering Creole staples in the centre.

★ Chez Éva Annibal   CREOLE €€

(Map p252; ☑ 0262 51 53 76; 6 Chemin Rivière du Mât; meal €27; ⊙ noon-1pm & 7-8pm Mon-Sat, noon-1pm Sun) Chez Éva Annibal is something of an institution on the island. Pack a hearty thirst and giant-sized appetite before venturing into this plain but feisty inn. The Full Monty feast comprises rum, *gratin de légumes* (baked vegetables), fish curry, duck with vanilla, and cakes, all clearly emblazoned with a Creole Mama stamp of approval. Pity about the very ordinary dining room. Book ahead.

Le Ti' Piment   FRENCH, CREOLE €€

(☑ 0262 23 46 79; 1bis Rue Roberto; mains €13-22; ⊙ 11.40am-2pm & 6.40-9pm Tue-Sat, noon-2pm Sun) About 400m southeast of Coopérative de Vanille, Le Ti' Piment is a popular place serving French and Creole dishes in a pleasant, convivial space that combines style with informality. Look for chicken cooked with olives, deer stew and duck breast flambéed in rum. And desserts are satisfyingly sinful. Also does takeaway.

ℹ Getting There & Away

Car Jaune buses (lines E1 and E2, about 16 daily, €2) stop outside the vanilla cooperative en route between St-Denis and St-Benoît. From St-Denis, the ride takes about 45 minutes.

St-Benoît

POP 36,500

Sugar-cane fields, lychee and mango orchards, rice, spices, coffee... Great carpets of deep-green felt seem to have been draped over the lower hills that surround St-Benoît, a major agricultural and fishing centre.

Bar a few impressive religious buildings – a mosque, a church and a Tamil temple on the outskirts of town – St-Benoît is not overburdened with tourist sights. The area's best features lie elsewhere; turn your attention from the coast and plant it firmly on the cooler recesses of the hills and valleys to the west. The Rivière des Marsouins valley in particular is a delight, with its plunging waterfalls and luxuriant vegetation. Small wonder that Réunion's best white water is found here.

Sights

Grand Étang
LAKE

(Map p252) Around 12km southwest of St-Benoît along the road towards Plaine-des-Palmistes is the 3km road to Grand Étang (Big Pond). This pretty picnic spot lies at the bottom of an almost-vertical ridge separating it from the Rivière des Marsouins valley. Most people simply walk around the lake, following a well-defined path. It's muddy in places, but shouldn't take more than three hours from the car park, including a side trip to an impressive waterfall.

Takamaka Viewpoint
VIEWPOINT

(Map p252; D53) North of St-Benoît the D53 strikes southwest, following the Rivière des Marsouins 15km upstream to end beside the Takamaka viewpoint. Be prepared to fall on your knees in awe: despite a small power plant near the viewpoint, the overwhelming impression is of a wild, virtually untouched valley, its vertical walls cloaked with impenetrable forests. Here and there the dense green is broken by a silver ribbon of cascading water.

Activities

White-Water Rafting

The Rivière des Marsouins and Rivière des Roches offer magical white-water experiences for both first-time runners and seasoned enthusiasts.

Rafting Réunion
RAFTING

(Map p252; ☑ 0692 00 16 23; www.raftingreunion.fr; Bras-Canot; half-day excursions €40-50) A secure rafting operator with loads of experience. It runs half-day rafting trips on the Rivière des Marsouins and Rivière des Roches. Kids over six are welcome. Also offers *randonnées aquatiques* (guided excursions in the river, with a mix of walking and swimming).

Raft Aventures
RAFTING

(Map p252; ☑ 0692 70 36 46; www.runaventures. com; Bras-Canot; half-day trips €50) Specialises in rafting trips on the Rivière des Marsouins and Rivière des Roches.

Horse Riding

Ferme Équestre du Grand Étang
HORSE RIDING

(Map p252; ☑ 0262 50 90 03, 0692 86 88 25; riconourry@wanadoo.fr; RN3, Pont Payet; half/full day €55/130) The Ferme Équestre du Grand Étang, just beyond the Grand Étang turnoff, arranges half-day treks to the lake; the full-

OFF THE BEATEN TRACK

ÎLET BETHLÉEM

Very few visitors have heard about **Îlet Bethléem** (Map p252), a magical spot by the Rivière des Marsouins that locals would like to keep for themselves. Reached after a 15-minute walk from the car park, it features an old chapel (1858) – still a pilgrimage site – and a smattering of picnic shelters amid lush vegetation. It's also an excellent swimming spot, with lots of natural rock pools. Follow the D53 in the direction of Takamaka, then turn left after about 1km (it's signposted).

day trek includes lunch. It's also possible to arrange longer excursions to Bassin Boeuf or Bras Canot (one or two days). Ask for Fanou, who can speak English.

Sleeping & Eating

Longanis Lodge
VILLA €€

(☑ 0692 76 84 52; www.longanilodge.com; 95 Chem-in Harmonie, Abondance; d/q €115/155; P ⎙) The Longanis stuns with its modern architecture and bucolic setting by a river shaded by majestic *longani* trees. The villa can accommodate up to six people, so it's a fantastic deal for friends or families. There's no restaurant nearby, but the owner can prepare meals on request (€25). It's possible to reserve for a night or two, but longer stays are preferred.

If you stay three nights or more, add a flat fee of €40 for housekeeping. It's in Abondance, about 5km from St-Benoît (take the road to Takamaka).

★ La Cabane aux Épices
CREOLE €€

(Map p252; ☑ 0692 43 39 34; www.facebook.com/ lacabaneauxepices; 22 Chemin Maingard; mains €15-26; ⊙ 11.45am-1.15pm Mon-Sat) An excellent surprise, up in the hills above St-Benoît, 'The Spice Hut' specialises in grilled fish and meat dishes as well as tasty *carris*, all served in tempting, attractively presented morsels and with a smile. The menu changes daily and varies according to what's available at the market.

Le Beauvallon
SEAFOOD, CREOLE €€

(☑ 0262 50 42 92; Rue du Stade Raymond-Arnoux, Rivière des Roches; mains €12-24; ⊙ 11.30am-2.30pm) Le Beauvallon is well known to everyone in the area, not least for its location beside the mouth of the Rivière des Roches and its seasonal, scrumptious *carri bichiques* (curry made with a sprat-like delicacy). On the flip side, the vast dining room doesn't contain one whit of soul or character. Also does takeaway (from €6).

Le Régal' Est FRENCH, SEAFOOD €€
(✆0262 97 04 31; 9 Place Raymond Albius, St-Benoît; mains €13-30; ⊘11.30am-1.30pm Mon-Thu, 11.30am-1.30pm & 7-8.30pm Fri & Sat) This attractive venture located upstairs in the covered market serves a modern, creative fish and meat menu as well as Creole classics. Not all the dishes work, though.

★**Les Letchis** CREOLE €€€
(Map p252; ✆0262 50 39 77; www.facebook.com/lesletchis; 42 Îlet Danclas, Bras Canot; mains €20-30; ⊘11.30am-1.45pm Wed-Sun) Les Letchis has a fantastic location in a luxuriant garden by the Rivière des Marsouins. The menu is an ode to Creole classics and 'riverfood'; standouts include *carri bichiques* and braised duck. If you want to explore new culinary territories, try *rougail chevaquines* (a curry made from small freshwater prawns) or *carri anguilles* (eel curry). Reservations are advised.

It also has a trendy annexe called La Plantation River Beach, which specialises in light meals and cocktails and is open Friday and Saturday evenings and Sunday all day.

⊙ Getting There & Away

From St-Benoît a scenic road (the RN3) cuts across the Plaine-des-Palmistes to St-Pierre and St-Louis on the far side of the island. Alternatively, you can continue south along the coast road, passing through Ste-Anne, Ste-Rose, St-Philippe and St-Joseph to reach St-Pierre.

St-Benoît is a major transport hub. Bus services to and from St-Denis run approximately every half hour (€2, 1¼ hours). There are also two services linking St-Benoît and St-Pierre: line S2 (€2, two hours) follows the RN3 over the Plaine-des-Palmistes; line S1 (€2, 2½ hours) takes the coast road via St-Philippe, St-Joseph and Manapany-les-Bains. More information at www.carjaune.re.

Ste-Anne

POP 3800

Ste-Anne is an unpretentious town that's noted for its visually striking church. There's no beach, but if you're in the mood for a dip there are some enticing natural pools. It's about 5km south along the coast from St-Benoît.

⊙ Sights & Activities

Église CHURCH
(Map p252; Place de l'Église) You can't help but be dazzled by this surprisingly extravagant church that was erected in 1857. The facade of the building is covered in stucco depictions of fruit, flowers and angels. The overall effect is flamboyant rather than tasteful, and is reminiscent of the mestizo architecture of the Andes in South America.

Pont des Anglais BRIDGE
(Map p252) Between Ste-Anne and Ste-Rose is the graceful Pont des Anglais suspension bridge over the Rivière de l'Est, now bypassed by the main highway but open to pedestrians. It was claimed to be the longest suspension bridge in the world at the time of its construction in the late 19th century.

Bassin Bleu SWIMMING
(Map p252) If you need to cool off, there's no better place than Bassin Bleu, appropriately dubbed 'the lagoon of the east', at the mouth of a river, on the southern edge of town. It's a superb swimming spot, with crystal-clear water and big boulders. Take a plunge! Note that it's mobbed at weekends.

⊨ Sleeping & Eating

★**Diana Dea Lodge & Spa** BOUTIQUE HOTEL €€€
(Map p252; ✆0262 20 02 02; www.diana-dea-lodge.re; 94 Chemin Helvetia, Cambourg, Ste-Anne; d from €245, incl breakfast; P❋ ❡ ⌸) What a surprise it is to come upon a boutique hotel in such a remote location – Diana Dea Lodge is set high in the hills above Ste-Anne (it's signposted) and is reached after 12km of numerous twists and turns amid cane fields. It's also set apart by its design, which combines wood and stone.

Precious perks include a heated pool, a spa, a bar and a top-notch restaurant (open to nonguests by reservation) – not to mention astounding views of the coast. This is one of those special places that lingers in the mind for its serenity.

Les 5 Orangers CREOLE, CHINESE €€
(Map p252; ✆0692 11 60 48; www.facebook.com/Les5orangers; 12 Rampe des Chicots, Les Orangers; mains €8-13; ⊘9am-2pm & 6-9pm Wed-Sat, 9am-2pm Sun & Mon) You'll find solid Chinese and Creole fare and heaping portions at this welcoming no-frills joint on the main road in Les Orangers, between Ste-Anne and Ste-Rose. It doles out curries and stews, as well

as pork and chicken dishes, at eminently affordable prices.

L'Auberge Créole　　　　CHINESE, CREOLE €€

(☑0262 51 10 10; 1 Chemin Case; mains €10-28; ⊙11.30am-1.45pm & 6-8pm Tue-Sat, 11.30am-1.45pm Sun) At this respected venue, the menu roves from Creole dishes and *métro* classics to pizzas (evenings only) and Chinese specialities at prices that are more sweet than sour. Pity about the drab, neon-lit interior; take your order to go and eat under *vacoa* trees at Bassin Bleu.

ⓘ Information

There's a small **tourist office** (☑0262 47 05 09; www.reunionest.fr; Place de l'Église; ⊙9am-12.30pm & 1.30-5pm Mon-Sat; 🛜) beside the church. It has maps and brochures and does bookings for *gîtes de montagne*. Also offers wi-fi access.

ⓘ Getting There & Away

Ste-Anne is a stop on the coastal bus route (line S1) from St-Benoît to St-Pierre. More information at www.carjaune.re.

Ste-Rose

POP 6800

The small fishing community of Ste-Rose has its harbour at the inlet of La Marine. It's a great place to soak up the rural atmosphere, make the most of the unhurried pace of life and discover some superb landscapes nearby. South of Ste-Rose the first tongues of lava from Piton de la Fournaise start to make their appearance. Beyond Anse des Cascades, the main road continues south along the coast, climbs and then drops down to cross the 6km-wide volcanic plain known as Le Grand Brûlé.

⊙ Sights

At the picturesque **harbour** you'll see a **monument** to the young English commander Corbett, who was killed in 1809 during a naval battle against the French off the coast.

Further south you'll reach **La Cayenne**, which has a superb picnic area scenically perched on a cliff overlooking the ocean – well worth a pause.

Notre Dame des Laves　　　　CHURCH

(Map p252; Piton Ste-Rose) The lava flow from a 1977 eruption went through Piton Ste-Rose, split when it came to the church and reformed again on the other side. Many people see the church's escape as a miracle of divine intervention. A wooden log 'washed up' by the lava now forms the lectern inside the church, while the stained-glass windows depict various stages of the eruption.

It's about 4.5km south of Ste-Rose.

Anse des Cascades　　　　BAY

(Map p252) This scenic *anse* (bay) is beside the sea about 3km south of Piton Ste-Rose. The water from the hills drops dramatically into the sea near a traditional little fishing harbour. The coconut grove is splendid and is a hugely popular picnic spot, and there's a well-frequented restaurant close to the shore.

🛏 Sleeping

★**Matilona**　　　　B&B €

(☑0692 85 86 86; http://matilona.monsite-orange. fr; 84 Chemin du Petit Brûlé; s/d/q/studio incl breakfast €61/66/108/71; ⓟ❄🛜🔅) You wouldn't guess from outside, but this B&B housed in a converted supermarket (yes!) is a great find. Push the door open and you're in another reality: five simple yet inviting rooms and two studios with modern bathrooms, generously sized communal areas and a seductive garden overflowing with colourful plants. And a killer pool. Dinner (€30) is available several days a week.

Monsieur is a former chef, so you can expect to eat well. There's also a kitchen for guests' use. Prices drop by €5 if you stay two nights or more. Brilliant value.

Ferme-Auberge La Cayenne　　　　B&B €

(Map p252; ☑0262 47 23 46; www.ferme-auberge-lacayenne.fr; 317 Ravine Glissante; d €50; ⓟ🛜) This well-established guesthouse scores points for its location: it's perched above the sea, 1.5km south of Ste-Rose. The six rooms are small and utilitarian but the views of the swishing indigo waters from the balcony are nothing short of charming. One quibble: there's no air-con. The owner, Madame Narayanin, cooks beautifully (dinner €25 to €28), using mostly home-grown ingredients. Breakfast costs €7.

La Fournaise　　　　HOTEL €

(☑0262 47 03 40; www.hotellafournaise.fr; 154 RN2; d €69; ⓟ❄🛜🔅) This vaguely modernish venture on the main road is the only hotel in the area. It's an unexciting but reliable choice, with bare but serviceable rooms, an on-site restaurant (mains €13) and a pool. Go for a room with a sea view; the ones at the back (same price) overlook the parking lot.

★**La Maison de Rosalie** RENTAL HOUSE €€
(0692 29 34 34; rosalie.slowlife@gmail.com; 23 Chemin du Petit Brûlé; d/q €80/120; P 🛜) Relax and feel at home in this enchanting Creole house that has bags of charm and atmosphere. It's spacious, light and airy, with two bedrooms, spick-and-span bathrooms and a kitchen. It opens onto a vast garden dotted with plenty of tropical trees. A great choice. One downside: no air-con.

Cana Suc BUNGALOW €€
(📋0692 77 81 96; www.canasuc.re; 219 RN2; d incl breakfast €95, bungalow q 2 weekend/3 weekday nights €260/285; P🛜) This is an adorable nest with a row of three well-designed Creole bungalows opening onto expansive lawns and a flowery garden. One unit is a *chambre d'hôte,* while the two other ones are fully-equipped *gîtes* that are rented for longer stays.

✖ Eating

As everywhere along Réunion's east coast, the dining scene is pretty tame. You'll find a few eateries serving good Creole staples in the vicinity of Notre Dame des Laves church. If you stay at a B&B or at the only hotel in town, dinner is available on request.

Le Métis CREOLE €
(Map p252; 📋0692 57 77 33; 378bis RN2, Piton Ste-Rose; mains €9-12; ☺ 11.30am-2.30pm & 6.30-8.30pm Mon, Tue & Thu-Sat, 11.30am-8.30pm Sun) If you're looking for a quick food fix, check out the options at this family-run eatery opposite Notre Dame des Laves church. It specialises in tasty, freshly prepared Creole classics. Takeaway is available (€6 to €8).

Snack Chez Louiso FAST FOOD €
(📋0262 47 26 57; 46 Chemin de la Marine; sandwiches €3-4, mains €5-10; ☺11am-3pm Tue-Sun) Chez Louiso is a modest open-air eatery overlooking the harbour. The menu is limited to sandwiches and a couple of daily specials, but they're well prepared and sizzling-hot value. Grab a (plastic) table and soak up the great ocean views.

Restaurant Le Corail CREOLE €€
(Map p252; 📋0262 23 75 36; RN2, Piton Ste-Rose; sandwiches €3-5, mains €12-19; ☺11.30am-3pm) About 300m south of Notre Dame des Laves church, this colourful Creole house is your spot for Creole curries and stews as well as sandwiches. There's an inviting terrace but it overlooks the main road – expect some traffic noise during the day. Your best bet is to get takeaway (€6 to €8) – you'll find plenty of atmospheric spots along the coast.

Restaurant des Cascades BUFFET €€
(Map p252; 📋0262 47 20 42; Anse des Cascades; mains €10-26; ☺11.30am-2pm Sat-Thu) A local and tourist favourite, this beach restaurant in a lovely coconut grove bursts to the seams on weekends. It has a concise menu featuring Creole and meat dishes but the real clincher is the lunch buffet (€25, including starters, mains and a drink) .

🛍 Shopping

Domaine d'Aldachris FOOD
(Map p252; 📋0262 53 49 74; 371ter RN2, Piton Ste-Rose; ☺9am-4pm Sun-Thu) Just north of Piton Ste-Rose is this family-run operation where you can buy various tropical fruit products, including delicious jam, to-die-for cakes and different varieties of exceptionally sweet bananas. Everything is homemade and organic.

❶ Getting There & Away

Buses running from St-Benoît to St-Pierre (line S1, about six daily, €2) make handy stops near Notre Dame des Laves and Anse des Cascades. From St-Benoît, the ride takes about 35 minutes. More information at www.carjaune.re.

UNDERSTAND RÉUNION

Réunion Today

Réunion is one of the richest islands in the Indian Ocean. The standard of living is fairly high, and it's no surprise. As a French *département* (a French overseas territory), the island receives a lot of financial support from mainland France *(la métropole).* Despite this assistance, Réunion faces numerous challenges as it grapples with finding housing and job opportunities for its expanding population without compromising what makes the island so special – its extraordinary natural riches.

The New Coastal Road

This is the biggest infrastructure project in Europe (yes, Europe). After much controversy, the construction of the Nouvelle Route du Littoral is underway. This engineering feat involves the building of a new coastal highway between St-Denis and La La

Possession. The masterpiece of these herculean works is a 5400m-long offshore viaduct along the coastline. Currently, the existing Route du Littoral, the key artery connecting the capital to the northwest, is often closed due to landslides, causing mayhem for its estimated 60,000 daily motorists. With an estimated project-completion date of 2021 (and budget of €1.6 billion), these huge civil engineering works are expected to reduce congestion and sustain growth on the island but face strong opposition on fiscal and environmental grounds.

The Shark Crisis

In less than 10 years, Réunion has earned the grim distinction of being one of the most active shark-attack zones in the world. Since 2011, there have been 22 shark attacks around the island resulting in 10 deaths (seven surfers, two swimmers and one fisherman). All attacks bar two occurred along the west coast, between Boucan Canot and L'Étang-Salé-les-Bains. This resulted in a major crisis and lots of tension between the surfing community, local environmentalists and the local government about what measures should be taken. Finally, swimming and surfing have been banned around the island in all but a few places. By early 2016, two beaches devoid of barrier reefs – one in Boucan Canot and one in St-Gilles-les-Bains – were equipped with shark nets. In March 2016, surfers started to return to some of their favourite spots – but at their own risk. Swimmers should stick to the safe areas.

Tourism Stagnates

Tourism is a major source of income and a key economic sector in Réunion, but the island largely stays under the radar. While elsewhere in the Indian Ocean (especially in Mauritius and the Seychelles) tourism thrives, Réunion saw only around 500,000 tourists in 2017, despite the fact that 40% of the island was designated a Natural World Heritage Site in 2010. This prestigious recognition fostered high hopes but has not been synonymous with a higher influx of foreign tourists, despite a growing number of German visitors. The vast majority of visitors are French. There's a huge potential for growth – experts say that one million tourists per year could be an easy target – but there are a few hurdles: despite some publicity campaigns, Réunion remains under-promoted in Anglophone markets; English is not widely spoken on the island; the cost of flights is still prohibitive; and the lack of direct flights to European cities (bar Paris) is problematic – not to mention the negative publicity following the fatal shark attacks over the last few years. While visitors won't complain about the uncrowded beaches and world-class mountainscapes, boosting tourism remains a key economic hurdle for the island.

Structural Unemployment

Unemployment is Réunion's number-one problem, with the unemployment rate currently hovering around 28% (60% among people aged between 15 and 24), way above the French national average (about 9%). It's particularly problematic for women and young people without qualifications. This situation has led to simmering social unrest, peaking in a series of riots in Le Port in February 2012 and February 2013 and all around the island in November 2018 following the 'yellow vest' crisis in mainland France. Strikes – to put pressure on local government and employers and avoid job cuts – are common in the private sector. On an island with a rapidly increasing population and limited resources, the extent and persistence of local unemployment is a major challenge and solutions have yet to be found. Many Réunionnais have to leave their island to find a job in France. Small wonder that the construction of the Nouvelle Route du Littoral, a mammoth infrastructure project, is seen as an effective way to create jobs on the island.

An Ever-Growing Population

Estimates suggest that the population of Réunion will reach one million by 2030. With high levels of unemployment and an ever-growing population, the island is set for some fundamental challenges, and housing is emerging as one of them. Already there is tremendous pressure on land available for building. Most of the population is concentrated on the coastal strip, where the towns are gradually beginning to merge into one continuous urban 'ring'. Houses are also spreading slowly up the hillsides and traffic congestion is becoming a major headache. While the behemoth Route du Littoral construction project will ease some pressure off unemployment and congestion (eventually), Réunion needs to find sustainable, long-term solutions to these challenges.

History

Welcome to Paradise

The first visitors to the uninhabited island were probably Malay, Arab and European mariners, none of whom stayed. Then, in 1642, the French took the decision to settle the island, which at the time was called Mascarin. The first settlers arrived four years later, when the French governor of Fort Dauphin in southern Madagascar banished a dozen mutineers to the island.

On the basis of enthusiastic reports from the mutineers, King Louis XIV of France officially claimed the island in 1649 and renamed it Île Bourbon, after Colbert Bourbon, who had founded the French East India Company.

However appealing it seemed, there was no great rush to populate and develop the island. It was not until the beginning of the 18th century that the French East India Company and the French government took control of the island.

Coffee, Anyone?

Coffee was introduced between 1715 and 1730 and soon became the island's main cash crop. The island's economy changed dramatically. As coffee required intensive labour, African and Malagasy slaves were brought by the shipload. During this period, cereals, spices and cotton were also introduced as cash crops.

Like Mauritius, Réunion came of age under the governorship of the visionary Mahé de Labourdonnais, who served from 1735 to 1746. However, Labourdonnais treated Île de France (Mauritius) as a favoured sibling, and after the collapse of the French East India Company and the pressure of ongoing rivalry with Britain the governance of Île Bourbon passed directly to the French Crown in 1764.

A Brief British Interlude

The formerly productive coffee plantations were destroyed by cyclones very early in the 19th century, and in 1810, during the Napoleonic Wars, Bonaparte lost the island to the *habits rouges* (redcoats). Under British rule, sugar cane was introduced to Réunion and quickly became the primary crop. The vanilla industry, introduced in 1819, also grew rapidly. The British didn't stay long: just five years later, under the Treaty of Paris, the spoil was returned to the French as Île Bourbon. The British, however, retained their grip on Mauritius, Rodrigues and the Seychelles.

The French Return

In 1848 the Second Republic was proclaimed in France, slavery was abolished and Île Bourbon again became La Réunion. At the time, the island had a population of over 100,000 people, mostly freed slaves. Like Mauritius, Réunion immediately experienced a labour crisis and, like the British in Mauritius, the French 'solved' the problem by importing contract labourers from India, most of them Hindus, to work the sugar cane.

Réunion's golden age of trade and development lasted until 1870, with the country flourishing on the trade route between Europe, India and the Far East. Competition from Cuba and the European sugar-beet industry, combined with the opening of the Suez Canal (which short-circuited the journey around the Cape of Good Hope), resulted in an economic slump: shipping decreased, the sugar industry declined, and land and capital were further concentrated in the hands of a small French elite. Some small planters brightened their prospects by turning to geranium oil.

BLACK HISTORY

The late 18th century saw a number of slave revolts, and many resourceful Malagasy and African slaves, called *marrons*, escaped from their owners and took refuge in the mountainous interior. Some of them established private utopias in inaccessible parts of the Cirques, while others grouped together and formed organised communities with democratically elected leaders. These tribal chieftains were the true pioneers of the settlement of Réunion, but most ultimately fell victim to bounty hunters who were employed to hunt them down. The scars of this period of the island's history are still fresh in the population's psyche; perhaps from a sense of shame, there's surprisingly little record of the island's Creole pioneers except the names of several peaks (Dimitile, Enchaing, Mafate, Cimendef) where they were hunted down and killed.

After WWI, in which 14,000 Réunionnais served, the sugar industry regained a bit of momentum, but it again suffered badly through the blockade of the island during WWII.

Réunion Becomes a DOM

Réunion became a Département Français d'Outre-Mer (DOM; French Overseas Department) in 1946 and has representation in the French parliament. Since then there have been feeble independence movements from time to time but, unlike those in France's Pacific territories, these have never amounted to much. While the Réunionnais seemed satisfied to remain totally French, general economic and social discontent surfaced in dramatic anti-government riots in St-Denis in 1991.

The turn of the century marked a new era for Réunion; the local authorities managed to sign a few agreements with the French state, which confirmed the launching of subsidised *grands chantiers* (major infrastructure works), including the expressway called the Route des Tamarins and the Nouvelle Route du Littoral (an expressway between St-Paul and St-Denis).

Culture

Réunion is often cited as an example of racial and religious harmony, and compared with mainland France it is. While Marine Le Pen's far-right party wins 27% to 30% of the national vote, it doesn't exceed 3% in Réunion. Not that it's all hunky-dory. Réunion suffers from the same problems of a disaffected younger generation as in mainland Europe. But on the whole it's a pretty cohesive society, and the Réunionnais are quietly but justifiably proud of what they have achieved.

Daily Life

Contemporary Réunionnais are a thoroughly 21st-century people. The vast majority of children receive a decent standard of education and all islanders have access to the national health system, either in Réunion or in France. There are traffic jams, everyone has a mobile (cell) phone, and flashy cars are ubiquitous. But beneath this modern veneer, there are many more traditional aspects.

One of the strongest bonds unifying society, after the Creole language, is the importance placed on family life. It's particularly made evident at the *pique-nique du dimanche en famille* (Sunday family picnic). Religious occasions and public holidays are also vigorously celebrated, as are more personal family events, such as baptisms, first communions and weddings.

Though Réunion can't be mistaken for, say, Ibiza, Réunionnais share a zest for the fest. On weekends St-Gilles-les-Bains, L'Hermitage-les-Bains and St-Pierre are a magnet for Réunionnais from all over the island. The towns turn wild on those evenings as flocks of night owls arrive en masse to wiggle their hips and guzzle pints of Dodo beer and glasses of rum.

On a more mundane level, you'll quickly realise that the possession of a brand-new car is a sign of wealth and respect. The 'car culture' is a dominant trait; small wonder that traffic jams are the norm on the coastal roads. Many Réunionnais spend up to two hours daily in their car going to and from work! One favourite topic of conversation is the state of the roads, especially the tricky Route du Littoral between St-Paul and St-Denis, which is sometimes closed due to fallen rocks.

Another noticeable (though less immediately so) characteristic is the importance of *la di la fé* (gossip). If you can understand a little bit of French (or Creole), tune in to Radio Free Dom (www.freedom.fr) – you'll soon realise that gossip is a national pastime.

Despite the social problems that blight any culture, on the whole it's a society that lives very easily together.

Population

Cultural diversity forms an integral part of the island's social fabric. Réunion has the same population mix of Africans, Europeans, Indians and Chinese as Mauritius, but in different proportions. Cafres (people of African ancestry) are the largest ethnic group, comprising about 45% of the population. Malbars (Hindu Indians) comprise about 25% of the population, white Creoles (people of French ancestry) 15%, Europeans (also known as Zoreilles) 7%, Chinese 4% and Z'arabes (Muslim Indians) 4%.

The bulk of the island's population lives in coastal zones, with Malbars living predominantly in the east. The rugged interior is sparsely populated. Because the birth rate has remained quite high, a third of the population is under 20 years of age.

RÉUNION CULTURE

THE ODD CULT OF ST EXPÉDIT

You can't miss them. Red shrines honouring St Expédit are scattered all over the island, including on roadsides. St Expédit is one of Réunion's most popular saints, though some scholars argue there never was a person called Expédit. Whatever the truth, the idea was brought to Réunion in 1931 when a local woman erected a statue of the 'saint' in St-Denis' Notre-Dame de la Délivrance church in thanks for answering her prayer to return to Réunion. Soon there were shrines all over the island, where people prayed for the saint's help in the speedy resolution of all sorts of tricky problems.

Over the years, however, worship of the saint has taken on the sinister overtones of a voodoo cult: figurines stuck with pins are left at the saint's feet; beheaded statues of him are perhaps the result of unanswered petitions. The saint has also been adopted into the Hindu faith, which accounts for the brilliant, blood-red colour of many shrines. As a result the Catholic Church has tried to distance itself from the cult, but the number of shrines continues to grow.

Réunion also sees a continual tide of would-be immigrants. With a system of generous welfare payments for the unemployed, the island is seen as a land of milk and honey by those from Mauritius, the Seychelles and some mainland African countries. Since 2010 there has been significant immigration from the neighbouring Comoros and Mayotte Islands.

Gender Equality

Réunion is refreshingly liberal and equality between the sexes is the widely accepted norm. Divorce, abortion and childbirth outside marriage are all fairly uncontentious issues. However, it's not all rosy: women are poorly represented in local government and politics, and domestic violence is prevalent. This is closely connected to high rates of alcoholism.

Religion

An estimated 70% of the population belongs to the Catholic faith, which dominates the island's religious character. It's evidenced in the many saints' days and holidays, as well as in the names of towns and cities. Religious rituals and rites of passage play an important part in the lives of the people, and baptisms, first communions and church weddings are an integral part of social culture.

About a quarter of Réunionnais are Hindus, which is the dominant faith in the east. Traditional Hindu rites such as *teemeedee,* which features fire-walking, and *cavadee,* which for pilgrims entails piercing the cheeks with skewers, often take place. Muslims make up roughly 2%

of the population; as in Mauritius, Islam tends to be fairly liberal.

Interestingly, a great deal of syncretism between Hinduism, Islam and Catholicism has evolved over the years. In fact, many of the Malbar-Réunionnais participate in both Hindu and Catholic rites and rituals.

Apart from celebrating the Chinese New Year, the Sino-Réunionnais community (making up about 3% of the population) is not very conspicuous in its religious or traditional practices.

Religious tolerance is the norm. Mosques, churches, Hindu temples and pagodas can be found within a stone's throw of each other in most towns.

Arts

Literature

Few Réunionnais novelists are known outside the island and none are translated into English. One of the most widely recognised and prolific contemporary authors is the journalist and historian Daniel Vaxelaire. His *Chasseurs de Noires,* an easily accessible tale of a slave-hunter's life-changing encounter with an escaped slave, is probably the best to start with.

Jean-François Samlong, a novelist and poet who helped relaunch Creole literature in the 1970s, also takes slavery as his theme. *Madame Desbassayns* was inspired by the remarkable life story of a sugar baroness.

Other well-established novelists to look out for are Axel Gauvin, Jules Bénard, Jean Lods and Monique Agénor.

Music & Dance

Réunion's music mixes the African rhythms of reggae, *séga* (traditional slave music) and *maloya* with French, British and American rock and folk sounds. Like *séga*, *maloya* is derived from the music of the slaves, but it is slower and more reflective, its rhythms and words heavy with history, somewhat like New Orleans blues; fans say it carries the true spirit of Réunion. *Maloya* songs often carry a political message and up until the 1970s the music was banned for being too subversive.

Instruments used to accompany *séga* and *maloya* range from traditional homemade percussion pieces, such as the hide-covered *rouleur* drum and the maraca-like *kayamb*, to the accordion and modern band instruments.

The giants of the local music scene, and increasingly well known in mainland France, are Danyel Waro, Firmin Viry, Granmoun Lélé (deceased), Davy Sicard, Kaf Malbar, Lo Rwa Kaf (deceased) and the group Ziskakan. Women have also emerged on the musical scene, including Christine Salem and Nathalie Nathiembé. All are superb practitioners of *maloya*. Favourite subjects for them are slavery, poverty and the search for cultural identity. You'll also find a mix of *séga*, *maloya* and reggae, called *seggae* (look for René Lacaille and Ti Fock if you're interested).

As for Creole-flavoured modern grooves, the Réunionnais leave those to their tropical cousins in Martinique and Guadeloupe, although they make for popular listening in Réunion. It's all catchy stuff, and you'll hear it in bars, discos and vehicles throughout the islands of the Indian Ocean.

KABARS

If you're passionate about Creole music, try to attend a *kabar*. A *kabar* is a kind of impromptu concert or ball that is usually held in a courtyard or on the beach, where musicians play *maloya* (traditional dance music of Réunion). It's usually organised by associations, informal groups or families, but outsiders are welcome. There's no schedule; *kabars* are usually advertised by means of word of mouth, flyers or small ads in the newspapers. You can also enquire at the bigger tourist offices.

Architecture

The distinctive 18th-century Creole architecture of Réunion is evident in both the grand villas built by wealthy planters and other *colons* (settlers/colonists) and in the *ti' cases*, the homes of the common folk.

Local authorities are actively striving to preserve the remaining examples of Creole architecture around the island. You can see a number of beautifully restored houses in St-Denis and in the towns of Cilaos, Entre-Deux, Hell-Bourg and St-Pierre, among other places. They all sport *lambrequins* (filigree-style decorations), *varangues* (verandas) and other ornamental features.

Food & Drink

Réunion is a culinary delight: thanks to a mix of influences and prime fresh ingredients (plentiful seafood, succulent meat, spices, aromatic plants, and fruit and vegetables bursting with flavour), you're certain to eat well wherever you go. There's a balanced melange of French cuisine (locally known as *cuisine métro*) and Creole specialities and flavours, plus Indian and Chinese influences.

Staples & Specialities

It's impossible to visit Réunion without coming across *carri* (curry), which features on practically every single menu. The sauce comprises tomatoes, onions, garlic, ginger, thyme and saffron (or turmeric) and accompanies various kinds of meat, such as chicken *(carri poulet)*, pork *(carri porc)* and duck *(carri canard)*. Seafood *carris*, such as tuna *(carri thon)*, swordfish *(carri espadon)*, lobster *(carri langouste)* and freshwater prawn *(carri camarons)* are also excellent. Octopus curry, one of the best you'll eat, is called *civet zourite* in Creole.

Local vegetables can also be prepared *carri*-style – try *carri baba figue* (banana-flower *carri*) and *carri ti jaque* (jackfruit *carri*) – but they incorporate fish or meat. *Carris* are invariably served with rice, *grains* (lentils or haricot beans), *brèdes* (local spinach) and *rougail,* a spicy chutney that mixes tomato, garlic, ginger and chillies; other preparations of *rougail* may include a mixture of green mango and citrus. *Rougail saucisse* (sausages cooked in tomato sauce), served with rice and vegetables, is a Creole favourite. A common Tamil stew is *cabri massalé* (goat *carri*).

WHERE TO EAT & DRINK

Réunion has a fine range of eating options, and it's not necessary to book except on weekends. Dinners served at B&Bs should be booked the day before.

Restaurants The mainstay of Réunionnais dining and you're never far from one.

Tables d'hôte Home-cooked meals served at B&Bs.

Cafes Very popular in St-Denis and St-Pierre.

Takeaway outlets Serve cheap Creole staples.

Markets The best places to stock up on fresh fruits and vegetables.

Seafood lovers will be delighted to hear that the warm waters of the Indian Ocean provide an ample net of produce: lobster, prawns, *légine* (toothfish), swordfish, marlin, tuna and shark, among others. Freshwater prawns, usually served in *carri*, are highly prized.

Snacks include samosas, *beignets* (fritters) and *bonbons piments* (chilli fritters).

BREAKFASTS

Breakfast is decidedly French: *pain-beurre-confiture* (baguette, butter and jam) served with coffee, tea or hot chocolate is the most common offering. Added treats may include croissants, *pain au chocolat* (chocolate-filled pastry), brioches and honey.

DESSERTS

Desserts are equally exciting, with tropical fruit pies and jams, exotic sorbets and ice creams. If you like carb-laden cakes, you'll be happy. Each family has its own recipe for *gâteaux maison* (homemade cakes), which come in various guises. They are usually made from vanilla, banana, sweet potato, maize, carrot, guava... One favourite is *macatia* (a variety of bun), which can also be served at breakfast. You'll also find plenty of patisseries selling croissants and pastries. Baguettes can be bought from every street corner.

FRUITS

Fruits reign supreme in Réunion. Two iconic Réunionnais fruits are *litchis* (lychees) and *ananas Victoria* (pineapple of the Victoria variety). Local mangoes, passionfruit and papaya are also fabulously sweet. The local vanilla is said to be one of the most flavoursome in the world.

Drinks

Rum, rum, rum! Up in the hills, almost everyone will have their own family recipe for *rhum arrangé*, a heady mixture of local rum and a secret blend of herbs and spices. In fact, not all are that secret. Popular concoctions include *rhum faham*, a blend of rum, sugar and flowers from the faham orchid; *rhum vanille*, made from rum, sugar and fresh vanilla pods; and *rhum bibasse*, made from rum, sugar and tasty *bibasse* (medlar fruit). The family *rhum arrangé* is a source of pride for most Creoles; if you stay in any of the rural *gîtes* or *chambres d'hôtes* you can expect the proprietor to serve up their version with more than a little ceremony.

Réunion being French territory, wine is unsurprisingly taken seriously. Along with French wines, you'll find a good choice of South African reds and whites. The island also has a small viniculture in Cilaos, where you can do a tasting.

The local brand of beer, Bourbon (known as Dodo), is sold everywhere. It is a fairly light, very drinkable beer. Other local beers include the Picaro, which comes as a pale ale and an amber ale. Foreign beers are also available, including the Belgian Kékette. For a refresher, nothing beats a fresh fruit juice or a glass of Cilaos, a high-quality sparkling water from Cirque de Cilaos.

The French take their coffee seriously and it's a passion that hasn't disappeared just because they're now in the Indian Ocean. A cup of coffee can take various forms but the most common is a small, black espresso called simply *un café*.

Vegetarians & Vegans

Vegetarians won't go hungry. Réunionnais love vegetables, eating them in salads or in gratins (a baked dish). You'll certainly come across *chouchou* (choko; a speciality in the Cirque de Salazie), lentils (a speciality in the Cirque de Cilaos), *bois de songe* (a local vegetable that looks like a leek) and *vacoa* (screw-pine fronds), not to mention *bringelles* (aubergines) and *baba figue* (banana flower). Salads, rice and fruits are ubiquitous. In Chinese restaurants, menus feature vegetarian dishes, such as chop suey and noodles. Most supermarkets have vegetarian fare, too, and *chambre d'hôte* owners will be happy to cook vegetarian dishes if you let them know well in advance.

Environment

Réunion lies about 220km southwest of Mauritius, at the southernmost end of the great Mascareignes volcanic chain. Réunion's volcano, Piton de la Fournaise, erupts with great regularity, spewing lava down its southern and eastern flanks. The last major eruption occurred in 2015, with almost 2½ months of continuous volcanic activity.

The Land

There are two major mountainous areas on Réunion. The older of the two covers most of the western half of the island. The highest mountain is Piton des Neiges (3071m), an alpine-class peak. Surrounding it are three immense and splendid amphitheatres: the Cirques of Cilaos, Mafate and Salazie. These long, wide, deep hollows are sheer-walled canyons filled with convoluted peaks and valleys, the eroded remnants of the ancient volcanic shield that surrounded Piton des Neiges.

The smaller of the two mountainous regions lies in the southeast and continues to evolve. It comprises several extinct volcanic cones and one that is still very much alive, Piton de la Fournaise (2632m). This rumbling peak still pops its cork relatively frequently in spectacular fashion. In 2007 lava flows reached the sea and added another few square metres to the island. Since 1998 there have been spectacular eruptions almost every second year – attractions in their own right. No one lives in the shadow of the volcano, where lava flowing down to the shore has left a remarkable jumbled slope of cooled black volcanic rock, known as Le Grand Brûlé.

These two mountainous areas are separated by a region of high plains, while the coast is defined by a gently sloping plain that varies in width. Numerous rivers wind their way down from the Piton des Neiges range, through the Cirques, cutting deeply into the coastal plains to form spectacular ravines.

Animals

The animals that you are likely to see are introduced hares, deer, geckoes, rats and, if you're lucky, chameleons. Tenrecs (called *tang* in Creole), which resemble hedgehogs, are a species introduced from Madagascar.

The most interesting creepy crawlies are the giant millipedes – some as long as a human foot – which loll around beneath rocks in more humid areas. Other oversized creatures are the yellow-and-black *Nephila* spiders whose massive webs are a common sight. You'll also find the *Heteropoda venatoria* or huntsman spider, called *babouk* in Creole.

As far as birdlife is concerned, of the original 30 species endemic to the island, only nine remain. The island's rarest birds are the *merle blanc* (cuckoo shrike) – locals call it the *tuit tuit*, for obvious reasons – and the black petrel. Probably the best chance of seeing – or, more likely, hearing – the *tuit tuit* is directly south of St-Denis, near the foot of La Roche Écrite.

Bulbuls, which resemble blackbirds (with yellow beaks and legs but grey feathers) and are locally known as *merles,* are also common. Birds native to the highlands include the *tec-tec* or Réunion stonechat, which inhabits the tamarind forests. There's also the *papangue* (Maillardi buzzard), a protected hawk-like bird that begins life as a little brown bird and turns black and white as it grows older. It is Réunion's only surviving bird of prey and may be spotted soaring over the ravines.

The best-known seabird is the white *paille-en-queue* (white-tailed tropicbird), which sports two long tail plumes.

DARE TO TRY

If you're a gastronomic adventurer, start your culinary odyssey with *salade de palmiste,* a delectable salad made from the bud of the palmiste palm tree, known as the 'heart of palm'. The palm dies once the bud is removed, earning this wasteful salad delicacy the title 'millionaire's salad'. For something a bit more unusual, try *carri bichiques* (curry made with a sprat-like delicacy), which is dubbed *le caviar réunionnais* (Réunionnais caviar). You might need to seek out *larves de guêpes* (wasps' larvae), another local delicacy that is available from April to October. Fried and salted, they reputedly increase sexual stamina.

You may also want to learn the terms for *carri pat' cochons* (pig's trotter *carri*) and *carri anguilles* (eel *carri*) so you don't accidentally order them in a restaurant. Réunionnais also drool over *carri tang* (tenrec curry, a small Malagasy hedgehog-like creature), which you're not likely to find served in restaurants.

UNESCO WORLD HERITAGE SITE

Réunion's landscapes and natural riches are so unique that in 2010, Unesco designated over 40% of the island a Natural World Heritage Site under the title 'Pitons, Cirques & Remparts'. This is an exceptional recognition of the island's phenomenally appealing mountainscapes and its remarkable biodiversity. Other natural sites in the world that have been awarded such a distinction include the Galapagos Islands, the Great Barrier Reef and the Grand Canyon National Park.

Mynahs, introduced at the end of the 18th century to keep grasshoppers under control, are common all over the island, as are the small, red cardinal-like birds known as fodies.

The best spots to see birdlife are the Forêt de Bébour-Bélouve above Hell-Bourg, and the wilderness region of Le Grand Brûlé at the southern tip of the island.

Plants

Thanks to an abundant rainfall and marked differences in altitude, Réunion has some of the most varied plant life in the world. Parts of the island are like a grand botanical garden. Between the coast and the alpine peaks you'll find palms, screw pines (also known as pandanus or *vacoa*), casuarinas *(filaos)*, vanilla, spices, other tropical fruit and vegetable crops, rainforest and alpine flora.

Réunion has no less than 700 indigenous plant species, 150 of which are trees. Unlike Mauritius, large areas of natural forest still remain. It's estimated that 30% of the island is covered by native forest.

Gnarled, twisted and sporting yellow, mimosa-like flowers, the *tamarin des Hauts* (mountain tamarind tree) is a type of acacia and is endemic to Réunion. One of the best places to see these ancient trees is in the

THE SEOR

You'll find information on local birds and where to spot them on the website of the Société d'Études Ornithologiques de la Réunion (SEOR; www.seor.fr), an organisation working to save some of the island's rarest species.

Forêt de Bébour-Bélouve, east of the Cirque de Salazie.

At the other extreme, the lava fields around the volcano exhibit a barren, moonlike surface. Here the various stages of vegetation growth, from a bare new lava base, are evident. The first plant to appear on lava is the heather-like plant the French call *branle vert (Philippia montana)*. Much later in the growth cycle come tamarind and other acacia trees.

Afforestation has been carried out mainly with the Japanese cryptomeria, *tamarin des Hauts,* casuarina and various palms.

Like any tropical island, Réunion has a wealth of flowering species, including orchid, hibiscus, bougainvillea, vetiver, geranium, frangipani and jacaranda.

National Parks

It is estimated that nearly a third of the 25km-long lagoon along the west coast from Boucan Canot south to Trois Bassins has already suffered damage from a variety of causes: sedimentation, agricultural and domestic pollution, cyclones, fishing and swimmers. To prevent the situation deteriorating further, a marine park was set up in 1997. In addition to educating local people on the need to keep the beaches and the water clean, marine biologists have been working with local fishers and various water-sports operators to establish protection zones. A fully fledged nature reserve – the Réserve Naturelle Marine de la Réunion (www.reservemarinereunion.fr) – was created in 2007.

Part of the interior of the island is protected, too. The Parc National des Hauts de la Réunion (www.reunion-parcnational.fr) was established in early 2007, resulting in half of Réunion's total land area now being under protection. There's a tightly regulated core area of 1000 sq km, including the volcano, the mountain peaks and the areas around Mafate and Grand Bassin, surrounded by a buffer zone of some 700 sq km to encompass most of the ravines.

Environmental Issues

The central problem confronting Réunion is how to reconcile environmental preservation with a fast-growing population in need of additional housing, roads, jobs, electricity, water and recreational space.

Despite the establishment of the Parc National des Hauts de la Réunion and the Réserve Naturelle Marine de la Réunion, the island is facing major issues, all related to two massive engineering works. The 'smaller' is the Route des Tamarins, which was completed in 2009. This 34km expressway that slices across the hills above St-Gilles-les-Bains required numerous bridges over the ravines. According to local environmentalists, the road cut across the only remaining savannah habitat on the island.

The second major engineering project is the Nouvelle Route du Littoral (new coastal highway). Due to be completed in 2021, this expressway will link capital St-Denis to La Possession and will be built on columns rising out of the ocean. The scheme has been met with anger by environmentalists, who claim that such major infrastructure works will have a negative impact on marine life. They have started to file lawsuits to derail the project. However, local authorities claim this project is vital for the economy and development of the island.

SURVIVAL GUIDE

ℹ Directory A-Z

ACCESSIBLE TRAVEL

Independent travel is difficult for anyone who has mobility problems in Réunion. Only upmarket hotels have features specifically suited to wheelchair use. That said, most restaurants are wheelchair accessible.

Negotiating the streets of most towns in a wheelchair is frustrating given the lack of adequate equipment, and most outdoor attractions and historic places don't have trails suited to wheelchair use. Some notable exceptions are Kelonia (p199) in St-Leu, the Musée de Villèle (p190) in St-Gilles-les-Hauts, the Cité du Volcan (p226) in Bourg-Murat and Stella Matutina (p203) museum near St-Leu. With a bit of extra warning, some riding stables, dive centres and other sports operators, including paragliding centres, can cater for people with disabilities. Forêt de Bébour-Bélouve (p233) also has a 30-minute trail that's accessible to people with disabilities.

Download Lonely Planet's free Accessible Travel guides from http://lptravel.to/Accessible Travel.

ACCOMMODATION

It's wise to book well in advance, particularly in high season (both the mainland France and local school holidays, particularly July, August and from mid-December to mid-January). If you're planning a hiking trip in September, October or

PRACTICALITIES

Newspapers Daily regional newspapers include French-language *Journal de l'Île de la Réunion* (www.clicanoo.re) and *Le Quotidien* (www.lequotidien.re), both good for features and events listings.

TV One government channel, Réunion 1re, as well as the independent Antenne Réunion and Canal + Réunion; most programming comes from mainland France.

Radio Tune in to Réunion 1re, Kreol FM or Radio Free Dom for local news (in French and Creole).

Smoking Prohibited in indoor public places and on public transport but is allowed in outdoor restaurants and on beaches. As with elsewhere, the trend is towards prohibition, so expect restrictions to increase over time.

Weights & Measures Réunion uses the metric system.

November, it's also imperative to book *gîtes de montagne* as early as possible.

Hotels Range from two-star ventures to a few luxury resorts.

Gîtes Range from basic mountain lodges to more comfortable options.

B&Bs These small, family-run houses provide good value. More luxurious versions are more like a boutique hotel.

Meublés de Tourisme & Locations Saisonnières Rental houses. A great choice for self-caterers.

Camping

Bad news for those who want to spend their holiday under canvas: there are only two official camping grounds, on the southwest coast at Étang-Salé-les-Bains and L'Hermitage-les-Bains. You'll also find a couple of *camping chez l'habitant* (informal, privately run camping grounds) in Îlet-à-Vidot and Bébour-Bélouve. The Cirque de Mafate also features a few simple camping spots.

You can camp for free in some designated areas in the Cirques, but only for one night at a time. Setting up camp on Piton de la Fournaise (the volcano) is forbidden for obvious reasons.

Chambres d'Hôtes

Chambres d'hôtes are the French equivalent of B&Bs. They are normally tucked away in the hills or in scenic locations and offer a window into a more traditional way of life. Options include everything from restored Creole houses or modern buildings to rooms in family houses. On

RÉUNION DIRECTORY A-Z

the whole standards are high, and rooms are generally good value. B&B rates are from around €50 for a double room. Upmarket versions are more like boutique hotels. Breakfast is always included.

Many *chambres d'hôtes* also offer *tables d'hôtes* (hearty evening meals) at around €20 to €32 per person (set menu), but this must be reserved in advance (usually the day before). This is a fantastic way to meet locals and sample the local cuisine.

Chambres d'hôtes can be booked by phoning the owners directly.

Gîtes de Montagnes

Gîtes de montagne are basic mountain cabins or lodges, operated by the local authorities through the Plateforme de Réservation – Île de la Réunion (p224). It is possible to organise a walking holiday using the *gîtes de montagne* only.

The *gîtes de montagne* in Réunion are generally in pretty good condition. Thanks to solar power, they all have electricity (in the communal areas only), and usually provide warm showers.

Gîtes de montagne must be booked and paid for in advance, and charges are not refundable unless a cyclone or a cyclone alert prevents your arrival. In practice, you won't be denied access if you just turn up without your voucher, but you may not have a bed if it's full. Last-minute reservations may be accepted, as there are often last-minute cancellations.

You can book (by phone or online) through the Plateforme de Réservation – Île de la Réunion Tourisme or through any tourist office on the island, including those in St-Denis, Cilaos, Salazie, Hell-Bourg, St-Gilles-les-Bains, St-Pierre, St-Leu,

St-André, Ste-Anne, and Bourg-Murat. It's highly recommended that you book well in advance, especially during the busy tourist seasons, as there's only a limited number of places available. One night's accommodation without food costs between €16 and €20 per person.

When staying in a *gîte de montagne,* you have to call the *gîte* at least one day ahead to book your meals (or you can ask for this to be done for you when you make the original booking). Dinner costs from €16 to €20, and usually consists of hearty *carris* (curries). Breakfast costs around €7 and normally consists of coffee, bread and jam. Payment is made directly to the caretaker, in cash.

Sleeping arrangements usually consist of bunk beds in shared rooms, so be prepared for the communal living that this entails, although the more recently built *gîtes* usually have a few private rooms. Sheets and blankets are provided, though you might want to bring a sheet sleeping bag (a sleep sheet).

It's not a bad idea to also bring along toilet paper and a torch (flashlight). It can get quite chilly at night, so warm clothing will be in order. Some places will let you cook, but many kitchens are so basic that you probably won't bother.

On arrival and departure you must 'book' in and out with the manager, who will collect your voucher and payment for meals. In theory, you're not meant to occupy a *gîte* before 3pm or remain past 10am.

Gîtes d'Étape

Gîtes d'étapes, sometimes simply called *gîtes,* are privately owned and work in roughly the same way as the *gîtes de montagne,* offering dorm beds and meals. Some places even have doubles. One main difference is that you can book these places directly with the owners. There are numerous *gîtes d'étapes* in the Cirque de Mafate, and others dotted around the island; most are in the vicinity of walking trails. The host will often offer meals or cooking facilities.

Local tourist offices can provide lists of *gîtes d'étapes* in their area.

Meublés de Tourisme & Apartments

Meublés de tourisme and apartments (also known as *locations saisonnières*) are private houses and lodges that families and groups can rent for self-catering holidays, normally by the week or weekend (but increasingly with only a two-night minimum stay, sometimes even one night in low season). There are dozens of *meublés de tourisme* and apartments scattered all over the island.

Most offer lodging for four or more people, with facilities of varying standards. Costs vary from around €60 to €100 per night. If you average out the per-person, per-week price and factor in cooking several meals in the house, *gîte* stays can actually be quite economical. Plus, the *gîte* owner often lives nearby and can be a mine of local information.

Apartments, *locations saisonnières* and *meublés de tourisme* can be booked online or by phoning the owners directly. A deposit of some sort is usually required in advance.

Hotels

If you're after serious cosseting and ultraposh digs, you might be looking at the wrong place. Most hotels on the island are rated as one-, two- or three-star, and lots are unclassified. There is only a sprinkling of four- and five-star hotels.

Hotels are found in St-Denis and around the beach resorts of the west coast, though you'll also find some in the attractive mountain towns of Cilaos and Hell-Bourg.

Booking Services

Centrale d'Information et de Réservation Régionale – Île de la Réunion Tourisme (www.explorelareunion.com) Wide range of options from the official website.

Allons La Réunion (www.allonslareunion.com) A good overview of lodging options.

Gîte de France (www.gites-de-france-reunion.com) B&Bs, *gîtes* and apartments.

Lonely Planet (www.lonelyplanet.com/reunion/hotels) Recommendations and bookings.

CHILDREN

➡ Réunion is an eminently suitable destination if you're travelling with the kids in tow. With its abundance of beaches, picnic spots and outdoor activities, plus its healthy food, it offers plenty to do for travellers of all ages in a generally hazard-free setting.

➡ Most locals have a number of children themselves and will not be troubled by a rowdy child at the next table.

➡ There are excellent medical facilities in the main cities.

➡ For more information, see Lonely Planet's *Travel with Children*.

Practicalities

➡ A few hotels offer kids clubs and many places provide cots for free and additional beds for children at a small extra cost. Most *chambres d'hôtes* welcome children.

➡ Many restaurants have children's menus with significantly lower prices.

➡ Nappies (diapers) are readily available.

➡ Breastfeeding in public is not a problem.

➡ The main car-hire companies can supply safety seats at additional cost.

ELECTRICITY

220V, 50Hz AC, using European-style two-round pins.

EMBASSIES & CONSULATES

Since Réunion isn't independent, only a few countries have diplomatic representation.

Belgium Consulate (☏ 0262 97 99 10; chatel@groupechatel.com; 80 Rue Adolphe Pegoud, Ste-Marie)

German Consulate (☏ 0692 73 68 98; st-denis@hk-diplo.de; 64 Ave Eudoxie Nonge, Ste-Clotilde)

Madagascar Consulate (☏ 0262 72 07 30; consulat-madrun@wanadoo.fr; 29 Rue St Joseph Ouvrier, St-Denis)

Seychelles Consulate (☏ 0262 57 26 38; hrop@wanadoo.fr; 67 Chemin de Kerveguen, Le Tampon)

Swiss Consulate (☏ 0262 52 56 41; reunion@honorarvertretung.ch; 3bis Impasse Tapioca, Bois Rouge)

INTERNET ACCESS

Many midrange and all top-end hotels offer wi-fi access, as do B&Bs, many cafes, restaurants and most tourist offices, usually without charge. In hotels, coverage may be restricted to public areas. The connection is generally good.

LEGAL MATTERS

➡ French police have wide powers of search and seizure and can ask you to prove your identity at any time.

➡ Foreigners must be able to prove their legal status in France (eg passport, visa, residency permit) without delay.

➡ If the police stop you for any reason, be polite and remain calm. Verbally (and of course physically) abusing a police officer can lead to a hefty fine.

➡ People who are arrested are considered innocent until proven guilty, but can be held in custody until trial.

➡ Possession and use of drugs is strictly illegal and penalties are severe.

LGBT+ TRAVELLERS

French laws concerning homosexuality prevail in Réunion, which means there is no legal discrimination against homosexual activity and homophobia is relatively uncommon. People are fairly tolerant, though by no means as liberal as

RÉUNION DIRECTORY A-Z

EATING PRICE RANGES

The following price ranges refer to a main course. The service charge is included in the bill.

€ less than €10

€€ €10 to €20

€€€ more than €20

in mainland France; open displays of affection may be regarded with disdain, especially outside St-Denis.

Throughout the island, but particularly on the west coast, there are restaurants, bars, operators and accommodation places that make a point of welcoming gays and lesbians. Certain areas are the focus of the gay and lesbian communities, among them St-Denis, St-Pierre and La Saline-les-Bains.

MONEY

ATMs in major towns; credit cards widely accepted except in *chambres d'hôtes* (B&Bs) and mountain lodges.

Moneychangers

➜ All banks in Réunion have dropped their foreign-exchange facilities in favour of ATMs.

➜ The only *bureau de change* on the island is in St-Denis.

➜ As a general strategy, it's sensible to bring a fair supply of euros with you and to top up from the ATMs.

Exchange Rates

For current exchange rates, see www.xe.com.

Australia	A$1	€0.63
Canada	C$1	€0.66
Japan	¥100	€0.80
Mauritius	Rs 100	€2.53
NZ	NZ$1	€0.59
UK	UK£1	€1.13
USA	US$1	€0.88

Tipping

Tipping is not expected in Réunion.

OPENING HOURS

Banks 8am–4pm, Monday to Friday or Tuesday to Saturday.

Bars 10am–midnight (or when the last customer leaves).

Clubs 10pm–4am Friday and Saturday.

Government offices 8.30am–noon and 2pm–5pm Monday to Thursday, to 3pm Friday.

Restaurants 11.30am or noon–1.30pm or 2pm, and 6.30pm or 7pm–9.30pm; often closed on one or two days of the week.

Shops and businesses 8.30am–5pm or 6pm Monday to Saturday, often with a break from noon–1pm or 2pm. Some shops close on Monday.

PUBLIC HOLIDAYS

Most of Réunion's offices, museums and shops are closed during *jours fériés* (public holidays).

New Year's Day 1 January

Easter Monday March/April

Labour Day 1 May

Victory Day 1945 8 May

Ascension Day late May or June

Bastille Day (National Day) 14 July

Assumption Day 15 August

All Saints' Day 1 November

Armistice Day 1918 11 November

Abolition of Slavery Day 20 December

Christmas Day 25 December

SAFE TRAVEL

➜ Overall, Réunion is relatively safe compared with most Western countries, but occasional robberies do occur.

➜ Don't leave anything of value in a rental car or on the beach and ensure that your room or bungalow is securely locked.

➜ Violence is rarely a problem, and muggings are almost unheard of. Intoxicated people are the most likely troublemakers.

➜ Unfortunately Réunion has a bad record when it comes to road safety, which means that you must drive defensively at all times. Potential dangers include drunk drivers, excessive speed, twisting roads and blind bends.

Swimming

➜ Swimmers should always be aware of currents and riptides. Seek advice before entering the water.

➜ Shark attacks on surfers or swimmers have been a problem over the last few years. Always heed any advice, such as shark warning signs, that you might come across, and stick to the lifeguard-patrolled beaches in St-Gilles-les-Bains, St-Leu, L'Hermitage-les-Bains, La Saline-les-Bains, Étang-Salé-les-Bains and St-Pierre. Swim only inside lagoons and protected areas. In an effort to improve the safety of swimmers and surfers, shark nets were installed off Les Roches Noires beach in St-Gilles-les-Bains and Boucan Canot beach in early 2016.

TELEPHONE

➜ All telephone numbers throughout Réunion consist of 10 digits; landline numbers start with 0262, and mobile-phone numbers start with 0692 or 0693.

➜ If calling a Réunion landline or mobile number from abroad (bar France), you'll need to dial your country's international-access code, Réunion's country code (262), then the local number minus the initial 0. Calling abroad from Réunion, dial 00 for international access, then the country code, then the area code and local number.

➜ There are no area codes in Réunion.

Mobile Phones

➜ For mobile phones, Réunion uses the GSM 900/1800 system, which is compatible with

Europe and Australia, but incompatible with North American GSM 1900.

➜ The network covers most towns and villages throughout the island, including the Cirque de Mafate.

➜ If your GSM phone has been 'unlocked', it is also possible to buy a SIM card with either of the two local network operators: Orange (www.orange.re) and SFR (www.sfr.re). Recharge cards are readily available, or you can top up your credit by phone or online. When buying a SIM card, you'll need to bring along your passport.

TOURIST INFORMATION

There are generally *offices du tourisme* (tourist offices) in most main towns across the island. Most of them have at least one staff member who speaks English. Tourist-office staff provide maps, brochures and the magazines *Ileenile* (www.ile-en-ile.com) and *Guide Run,* which are useful directories of hotels, restaurants and other places of interest to visitors.

Île de la Réunion Tourisme (IRT; www.reunion.fr) Réunion's regional tourist office has a fantastic website with easy-to-browse information on activities, attractions and places to stay, among others.

VISAS

Though Réunion is a French department, it's not part of the Schengen treaty. The visa requirements for entry to Réunion are almost the same as for France, bar a few exceptions. For EU nationals, a national ID or a passport suffices. Citizens of a number of other Western countries, including Australia, the USA, Canada and New Zealand, do not need visas to visit Réunion as tourists for up to three months.

Other nationals should check with the French embassy or consulate nearest your home address to find out if you need a visa. For example, South African citizens need a visa to enter mainland France but don't require a visa for Réunion. For up-to-date information on visa requirements see www.diplomatie.gouv.fr.

ⓘ Getting There & Away

Although it's just a tiny speck in the Indian Ocean, Réunion is fairly straightforward to get to, though access is limited to flights only. Flights and tours can be booked online at lonely planet.com/bookings.

ENTERING THE COUNTRY

Entering Réunion is usually hassle free, with no visas required for many nationalities. Customs searches are generally quick and easy if they occur at all.

ARRIVING IN RÉUNION

Roland Garros International Airport (St-Denis) There's no shuttle-bus service between the airport and St-Denis. Taxis from just outside the airport cost from €25 (from €30 at night) to central St-Denis. The ride takes about 20 minutes.

Saint-Pierre-Pierrefonds International Airport (St-Pierre) A taxi ride to St-Pierre costs about €15 and takes no more than 10 minutes.

AIR

Direct flights connect Réunion with China, Comoros, France, India, Madagascar, Mauritius, Mayotte, Thailand, the Seychelles and South Africa. For further afield, you'll need to take a connecting flight from South Africa, Mauritius, Asia or France.

Airports & Airlines

Réunion has two international airports. The vast majority of flights come into **Roland Garros International Airport** (☑ 0262 28 16 16; www.reunion.aeroport.fr; Ste-Marie) about 10km east of St-Denis. Coming from Mauritius, you have the option of landing at Saint-Pierre-Pierrefonds International Airport (p239), in the south of the island near St-Pierre.

Air Austral (p183) is the national carrier. It has a good safety record and a decent international network.

ⓘ Getting Around

BICYCLE

The traffic, the haste of most motorists and the steep and precarious nature of the mountain roads mean that those considering cycling as a form of transport in Réunion should be prepared for some hair-raising and potentially dangerous situations.

BUS

Réunion's major towns and many of the little ones in between are linked by bus. The island's bus service is known as Car Jaune (www.carjaune.re) and has distinctive yellow buses. The main bus station is on Blvd Lancastel on the St-Denis seafront.

DEPARTURE TAX

Departure tax is included in the price of a ticket.

Buses on most routes run between about 6am and 7pm Monday to Saturday, with a limited number of services on Sunday. You can buy a ticket from the driver as you board (except in the main bus stations, where you get them at vending machines). To get the bus to stop, you ring the bell or clap your hands twice loudly.

Car Jaune provides regional minibus services for several areas on the island; they run from St-Benoît, St-Joseph, Ste-Rose, St-Leu and St-Paul. These convoluted local routes can be fairly confusing, particularly if you don't speak much French. Of most use to travellers are the buses from St-André to Salazie, Salazie to Hell-Bourg, Grand Îlet and Le Bélier, and the buses from St-Louis to Cilaos, Îlet à Cordes and Bras-Sec.

CAR & MOTORCYCLE

Travelling by car is by far the most convenient way to get around the island.

Hire

Car hire is extremely popular in Réunion, and rates are very reasonable. Rates start at €35 per day (including third-party liability insurance and unlimited kilometres) and can drop to as low as €25 per day if you rent for several weeks. Most companies require a credit card, primarily so that you can leave a deposit.

Most companies stipulate that the driver must be at least 21 (sometimes 23) years of age, have held a driving licence for at least a year, and have a passport or some other form of identification. EU citizens can drive on their national driving licence; drivers from elsewhere need an international driving licence.

Collision-damage waivers (CDW, or *assurance tous risques*) are not included and vary greatly from company to company. The *franchise* (excess) for a small car is usually around €800. You can reduce it to zero (or at least to half) by paying a daily insurance supplement.

Arranging your car rental before you leave home is usually cheaper than a walk-in rental.

All major firms have a desk at the airports. There are also plenty of independent operators around the island. They are cheaper than international companies but their rental cars are usually older. Most offer delivery to the airport for a surcharge. Reputable ones include the following:

Auto-Europe (www.autoeurope.com)

Cool Location (☑ 0262 41 86 24; www.cool-location.fr; 43 Rue Jules Auber, St-Denis)

Degrif' Loc – Bonne Route (☑ 0262 26 29 44, 0692 05 18 32; www.degrifloc.re; 136 chemin Calebasse, La Rivière St-Louis)

Europcar (☑ 0262 93 14 15; www.europcar-reunion.com; Roland Garros International Airport)

ITC Tropicar (☑ 0262 24 01 01; www.itctropicar.re) Has offices in St-Pierre, St-Gilles-les-Bains and at the airport.

Mik Location (☑ 0262 30 60 66; www.mik-location.com) Offices in St-Denis and St-Pierre.

Multi Auto (☑ 0693 39 85 00, 0262 48 83 82; www.multiauto.re) In Ste-Clotilde, St-André, St-Paul and at the airport.

Petrol stations are very easy to find. A litre of unleaded costs around €1.50. Most stations accept credit cards.

Road Conditions

The road system on the island is excellent and well signposted. Inaugurated in June 2009, the Route des Tamarins is a 34km, four-lane expressway that connects St-Paul to Étang-Salé and branches onto the existing RN1. It creates a direct route between the two biggest cities, St-Denis in the north and St-Pierre in the south. The massive New Coastal Road (Nouvelle Route du Littoral) between St-Denis and La Possession is due to open in 2021.

Routes départementales, the names of which begin with the letter D (or RD), are tertiary local roads, many of them very tortuous (use your horn!).

There are some gorgeous runs, cruising along the island's dramatic roads. Exhilarating views aside, motoring around Réunion can be fairly hair-raising on occasion. Heading into the mountains via the Cirques roads is a magnificent experience, but roads are narrow; hairpin bends *(lacets)* are tortuous and blind; and rocky outcrops or sugar-cane fields often prevent you spotting oncoming traffic. Use your horn to announce your presence. Avoid driving at night and allow extra time to reach your destination.

Road Rules

Like mainland France, Réunion keeps to the right side of the road. Speed limits are clearly indicated and vary from 50km/h in towns to 110km/h on dual carriageways. Drivers and passengers are required to wear seatbelts. The blood-alcohol content limit is 0.5g/L.

Seychelles

☏ 248 / POP 94,633

Best Places to Eat

➜ La Grande Maison (p294)

➜ Café des Arts (p305)

➜ Le Domaine's Combava (p316)

➜ Del Place (p297)

➜ Kafe Kreol (p293)

Best Places to Stay

➜ Maia Luxury Resort & Spa (p296)

➜ North Island (p318)

➜ Fregate Island Private (p320)

➜ Desroches Island Resort (p322)

➜ Devon Residence (p293)

Why Go?

Mother Nature was unbelievably generous with the Seychelles, a fabled paradise whose islands lie scattered across the Indian Ocean. Spellbinding beaches are the main attraction, and what beaches! Exquisite ribbons of sand lapped by turquoise waters and backed by lush hills, palm trees and Dali-esque boulders. Beyond the beach, diving and snorkelling are brilliant in the warm waters amid abundant marine life, while few places on the planet do ocean-side luxury quite like the Seychelles. Mahé is the largest island and entry point to the Seychelles, with some fabulous resorts, restaurants and beaches, not to mention the small capital city of Victoria. But it's also the busiest island, with glorious Praslin and La Digue a short boat ride away. Even further out, there are real lost-world islands to be found.

When to Go

➜ From December to March, the trade winds bring warmer, wetter airstreams from the northwest. From June to September the southeast trades usher in cooler, drier weather but the winds whip up the waves and you'll want to find protected beaches. The turnaround periods (April to May and October to November), which are normally calm and windless, are ideal. Temperatures range between 24°C and 32°C throughout the year.

➜ Rainfall varies considerably from island to island and from year to year. Mahé and Silhouette, the most mountainous islands, get the highest rainfall.

➜ Accommodation can be hard to find during the peak seasons from December to January and July to August. The Seychelles lies outside the cyclone zone.

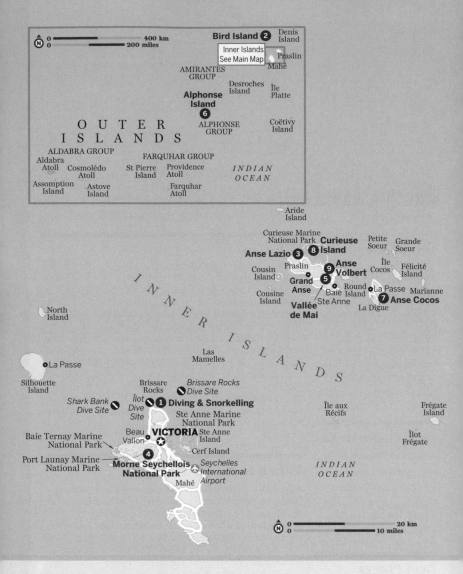

Seychelles Highlights

1 Mahé (p286) Diving and snorkelling among the dense varieties of marine life off Mahé island.

2 Bird Island (p319) Embracing nature on this gorgeous tropical isle.

3 Anse Lazio (p298) Lazing on one of the world's most alluring beaches.

4 Morne Seychellois National Park (p290) Exploring mountain forest and coastal mangroves.

5 Vallée de Mai (p298) Walking under the coco de mer palms in this jungle paradise.

6 Alphonse Island (p321) Living out your deserted island fantasy on this coral islet.

7 Anse Cocos (p307) Flopping on this near perfect beach after a short hike.

8 Curieuse Island (p305) Swimming, picnicking and greeting giant tortoises.

9 Anse Volbert (p298) Paddleboarding along this palm-studded beach.

MAHÉ

By far the largest and most developed of the Seychelles islands, Mahé is home to the country's capital, Victoria, and to about 90% of the Seychelles' population. As such it's both as busy as the Seychelles gets, and home to the largest selection of resorts and activities, from the hiking possibilities across the rugged interior of Morne Seychellois National Park to diving pristine sites and snorkelling within sight of whale sharks in or just beyond the glorious bays caressed by gorgeously multihued waters. The west coast, from top to bottom, is one long string of stunning beaches and outstanding accommodation, but there are plenty of secret gems elsewhere. And wherever you're based, paradise lies close at hand – a bus or car ride of no more than 20 minutes will bring you to fabulous natural attractions.

Victoria

POP 25,896

Welcome to one of the world's smallest capital cities. Victoria may be the country's main economic, political and commercial hub, and it may be home to about a third of the Seychelles' population, but it retains the air of a provincial town. While it may not fulfil all fantasies about tropical paradise, the city still has a little charm and a little promise when you scratch beneath the surface. There's a bustling market, a terrific new history museum, manicured botanical gardens (p278) and a fistful of attractive old colonial buildings sidling up alongside modern structures and shops. It's also a good place to grab last-minute gifts before heading home.

Oh, and there's the setting. Victoria is set against an impressive backdrop of towering granite mountains.

◎ Sights

The beautifully restored National Museum of History beside the clock tower is an appealing example of Creole architecture. Other architectural highlights include the colonial buildings that are scattered along Francis Rachel and Albert Sts. Other examples of traditional Creole architecture include Kaz Zanana and the Marie-Antoinette (p281) restaurant.

★ **National Museum of History**   MUSEUM
(Map p282; Independence Ave, Old Courthouse; adult/child Rs 150/free; ⊙ 9am-noon Mon, to 5pm Tue-Fri, to 2pm Sat) Housed in Victoria's restored colonial-era Supreme Court building (1885), this terrific museum opened in late 2018. While the architecture itself is worth admiring, the museum's exhibitions are outstanding. Downstairs is an informative journey through 300 years of Seychelles history, with plenty of information to put the model ships, old cannons and other historical pieces in context. Upstairs focuses on Creole culture, with displays on music, clothing, fishing and architecture.

★ **Sir Selwyn**
Selwyn-Clarke Market   MARKET
(Map p282; Market St; ⊙ 5.30am-5pm Mon-Fri, to noon Sat) No trip to Victoria would be complete without a wander through the covered market. It's small by African standards, but it's a bustling, colourful place nonetheless. Alongside fresh fruit and vegetables, stalls sell souvenirs such as local spices and herbs, as well as the usual assortment of *pareos* (sarongs) and shirts. Early morning is the best time to come, when fishmongers display an astonishing variety of seafood, from parrotfish to barracuda. It's at its liveliest on Saturday.

★ **Kaz Zanana**   GALLERY
(Map p282; ☑ 4325534; Revolution Ave; ⊙ 8.30am-4.30pm Mon-Fri, 10am-2pm Sat) **FREE** This gallery, in a traditional Creole wooden structure built in 1915 and restored in the 1980s, exhibits the work of George Camille, one of the Seychelles' best-loved painters. It's a short uphill walk from the main downtown area. The artworks are for sale.

Cathedral of the
Immaculate Conception   CHURCH
(Map p282; Olivier Maradan St; ⊙ sunset-sunrise) This imposing cathedral is noteworthy for its elegant portal and colonnaded facade – the interior nave is long and airy with some stained-glass windows.

Domus   ARCHITECTURE
(Map p282; Olivier Maradan St) The extravagant facade of the building immediately west of the cathedral belongs to the Domus – built in 1934 as a residence for Swiss missionaries, it's now the Roman Catholic priests' residence and a national monument.

Clock Tower   MONUMENT
(Map p282; cnr Francis Rachel St & Independence Ave) The focal point of the city centre is this downsized replica of the clock tower on

Mahé

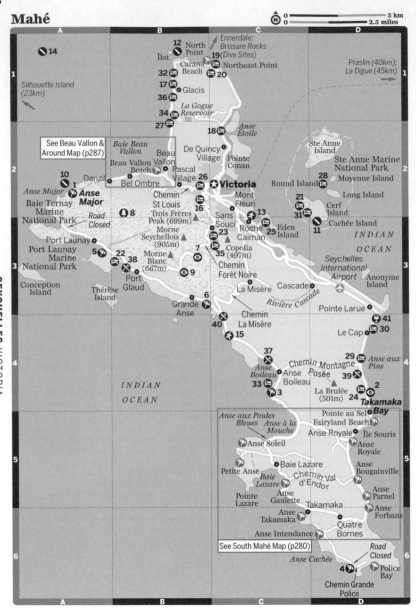

SEYCHELLES VICTORIA

London's Vauxhall Bridge. It was brought to Victoria in 1903 when the Seychelles became a Crown colony.

Botanical Gardens
GARDENS
(Map p282; ☑ 4670500; Rs 100; ⊗ 8am-5pm) The manicured botanical gardens, full of streams and birdsong, are about a 10-minute walk south of the centre. Star attractions are the coco de mer palms lining the main alley. There's also a spice grove, a pen of giant tortoises, a patch of rainforest complete with fruit bats, and a cafeteria.

Mahé

☞ Tours

Victoria can be a good place to organise boat trips or excursions, with a few reputable travel agencies dotted around the town centre.

Marine Charter Association   BOATING
(MCA; Map p282; ☑ 4322126; mca@seychelles.net; 5th Jun Ave) Marine Charter Association runs glass-bottom boat tours to Ste Anne Marine National Park for €90/50 per adult/child.

Creole Travel Services   TOURS
(Map p282; ☑ 2297000; www.creoletravelservices. com; Albert St; ☺ 8am-4.40pm Mon-Fri, to noon Sat) This reputable travel agency offers the full range of services, including ticketing, car hire and tours around Mahé and to other islands. Also shelters a bureau de change and sells ferry tickets to Praslin.

Mason's Travel   TOURS
(Map p282; ☑ 4288888; www.masonstravel.com; Revolution Ave; ☺ 8am-4.30pm Mon-Fri, to noon

Sat) A well-established travel agency. Offers a wide array of tours around Mahé and to other islands.

Sleeping

We can't think why you'd make Victoria your Mahé base – most people visit the capital on a day trip and then return to sleep by the sea or high in the mountains. With the exception of the Hilltop Boutique Hotel (p281), Victoria's range of accommodation is slim, with one of the best choices on nearby Eden Island (p283).

Calypha
Guesthouse   GUESTHOUSE €
(Map p278; ☑ 4241157; Off North Coast Rd, Ma Constance; s/d incl breakfast €45/70; ❄ 🐾) This family-run guesthouse, about 3km north of Victoria in a not-so-attractive area, won't be the most memorable stay of your trip but is OK for a night's kip. The six rooms are in

South Mahé

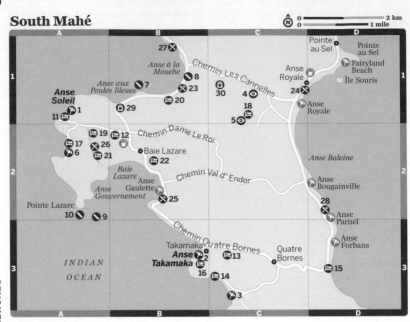

South Mahé

sore need of TLC but are otherwise in reasonable condition. Note that air-con is extra (€10 per day). Creole-style dinners are available on request (€15). Cash only.

Beau Séjour   GUESTHOUSE €€
(Map p278; ☏4226144; Curio Rd, Bel Air; r incl breakfast €95; P✳︎🛜) A guesthouse with style, this is a lovely place to dawdle in and soak up the tranquil charm from the foot

of the Trois Frères – the location is one of the best in northern Mahé. It's sparkling clean and has character in abundance. Only rooms 1 and 5 have a view (other rooms are at the back). Meals on request.

★ **Hilltop Boutique Hotel** BOUTIQUE HOTEL €€€
(Map p278; ☑ 2526870; www.facebook.com/hill topboutiquehotel; Serret Rd; r €160; P ❋ ☎) Comfortable rooms, most with elevated views out over Victoria, make this a fine choice up the hill from the town centre. You've one of Victoria's best restaurants, Marie-Antoinette, right next door, and the wood-and-wicker rooms are large and light-filled. Friendly service, too, and great breakfasts. Wi-fi comes and goes a little.

✕ Eating

Papagalo CREOLE €
(Map p282; ☑ 4321144; www.facebook.com/papa galo.sc; Francis Rachel St; mains Rs 30-70; ⊙ noon-9pm Mon-Sat) Downstairs from Sam's Pizzeria, this wildly popular takeaway place serves up hearty Creole staples in a cafeteria-style display cabinet – point to what you want, wait for staff to weigh it and you're half-way to a fine picnic at the place of your choosing. Dishes change daily, but often include pineapple chicken, lentils or chow mein.

Le Rendevous Cafe CAFE €
(Map p282; ☑ 4610200; Quincy St; mains Rs 85-175; ⊙ 8am-6pm Mon-Sat; ❋ ☑) This charming oasis of a 1st-floor cafe rises above the din of downtown Victoria. It serves smoothies and fresh juices, good coffee, and light meals such as wraps, sandwiches and salads – we enjoyed the vanilla tea and the quinoa and bean salad. Service is friendly, and the air-con everything you'd hope for on a hot day.

★ **Marie-Antoinette** CREOLE €€
(Map p278; ☑ 4266222; Serret Rd; set menu Rs 285; ⊙ noon-2.45pm & 6-8.45pm Mon-Sat) Marie-Antoinette isn't just a restaurant, it's an experience, especially at dinner. It occupies a beautiful, wood-and-iron colonial Seychellois mansion. Bring an empty stomach – the *menu* (set menu of the day) includes battered parrotfish and aubergine fritters, grilled fish, tuna steak, chicken curry, fish stew, rice and salad, and hasn't changed since the 1970s. It's off the road to Beau Vallon.

Legend has it that Henry Morton Stanley stayed here in the 1870s on his return journey from Africa, where he found Dr Livingstone; the house was once known as Livingstone's Cottage.

The Market Bistro INTERNATIONAL €€
(Map p282; ☑ 4225451; Market St; breakfast Rs 120-245, mains Rs 175-365; ⊙ 8am-4pm Mon-Sat) The food is fresh and tasty at this appealing eatery, in the southwestern corner of the market (p277) (upstairs). Typical dishes include smoked-fish salad, tiger prawns kebab or red snapper fillet.

News Café CAFETERIA €€
(Map p282; ☑ 4322999; Albert St, Trinity House; mains Rs 170-300; ⊙ 8.30am-5pm Mon-Fri, to 3pm Sat) This cheerful cafe-bar overlooking the main drag is an excellent venue to enjoy breakfast (muesli!) and read the newspapers, or to take a lunchtime break from town. Wraps, paninis and pasta share the menu with roast chicken or pork, salads (try the octopus with mango) and seafood *brochettes*. For dessert, it has to be the ginger cream brûlée with cinnamon.

Sam's Pizzeria PIZZA €€
(Map p282; ☑ 4323495; Francis Rachel St; pizza from Rs 175, mains Rs 175-350; ⊙ 11am-2.30pm & 6-10pm) Walls here are adorned with paintings by local artist George Camille, which

---

CHEAP EATS IN VICTORIA

Although Victoria does have some appealing places for a sit-down meal, there's a real tradition here of buying cheap and cheerful takeaway meals in the market area and taking them back to your desk (if you're a local worker) or to the picnic beach of your choice (if you're a visitor). Our pick of the places is:

Papagalo Be prepared to queue for simple, hearty local dishes sold by weight.

Smoke Roast House (Map p282; ☑ 2781480; Market St; mains Rs 20-65; ⊙ 10am-7pm Mon-Sat) One of the most popular places for cheap octopus curry within sight of the market entrance.

Lai Lam Food Shop (Map p282; Benezet St; mains Rs 35-70; ⊙ noon-4pm Mon-Fri) Roast chicken or smoked fish in the same block as the market.

Taste of Italy (Map p282; Market St; mains Rs 57-184; ⊙ 8.30am-5pm Mon-Fri, to 2pm Sat) Home-cooked Italian staples served for sit-down or takeaway.

Victoria

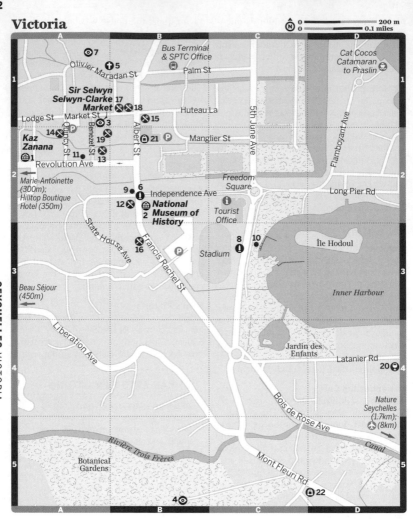

SEYCHELLES VICTORIA

gives the place a splash of style. Get things going with pizza cooked in a wood-fired oven, salad, pasta or grilled fish and meat. And yes, it's open on Sunday – a rarity in Victoria. Takeaway is available.

Coco Blu INTERNATIONAL €€€
(Le Cafe de l'Horloge; Map p282; ☑ 4323556; Francis Rachel St; mains Rs 250-540; ⊙9am-10pm Mon-Sat) The decor of this 1st-floor eatery overlooking the clock tower is easy on the eye, a mix of stylish and quirky, and the vantage point is good for people-watching. A change in name and ownership has done the

food here the world of good – the octopus salad is among the best we tasted.

Otherwise, the extensive menu takes in fish, meat, salad, pizza and ice cream.

Drinking & Nightlife

There's nowhere in downtown Victoria that we recommend for an evening drink – like port cities the world over, its bars are rough-and-ready places where you need to keep your wits about you. For any nightlife to speak of, head for Eden Island or Beau Vallon (p290) instead.

Victoria

Level Three Bar BAR
(Map p282; Latanier Rd; ⊙5pm-late Mon-Fri) Despite the odd location in a nondescript building near the harbour, Level Three Bar is worth considering for its affordable cocktails (Rs 150) and its cool atmosphere. There's karaoke on Friday evening.

🛍 Shopping

Seychelles Island Foundation GIFTS & SOUVENIRS
(SIF; Map p282; ☑4321735; www.sif.sc; Mont Fleuri Rd, Victoria; ⊙9am-4pm Mon-Fri) If you want to buy a *coco fesse* (the fruit of the coco de mer palm), head to the Seychelles Island Foundation, which has some stock and will issue you the required export permit. Be prepared to fork out about €200. Its work centres on habitat restoration on the Aldabra Atoll, as well as managing Vallée de Mai (p298) on Praslin.

Camion Hall ARTS & CRAFTS
(Map p282; Albert St; ⊙9am-5pm Mon-Sat) Head to this small shopping mall right in the centre for creative and interesting locally made arts and crafts.

❶ Information

Tourist Office (Map p282; ☑4610800; www.seychelles.travel; Independence Ave; ⊙8am-4pm Mon-Fri, 9am-noon Sat) Has a few brochures and decent maps of Mahé, Praslin and La Digue.

❶ Getting There & Away

Cat Cocos Catamaran to Praslin (Map p282; ☑4324843; www.seychelles-ferry-tickets.

com; Victoria Port) Ferries to/from Praslin and La Digue.

Bus Terminal & SPTC Office (Seychelles Public Transport Corporation; Map p282; ☑4280280, 4325252; www.sptc.sc; Palm St; ⊙8am-4pm Mon-Fri) Buses to all points of the island.

Eden Island

Opened for business in 2012 and fast becoming one of the coolest places on Mahé, Eden Island has a luxury hotel, a yacht marina, the east coast's best bar (p284), good restaurants and a modern shopping mall. With waterside villas on sale – it's the only place in the Seychelles where foreigners are permitted to buy land – it's already becoming a smart alternative to Victoria. There are times here when you won't feel like you're in the Seychelles at all, but it will appeal to those who like the whole luxury marina vibe.

🛏 Sleeping

★**Eden Bleu Hotel** LUXURY HOTEL €€€
(Map p278; ☑4399100; www.edenbleu.com; Eden Island; s/d from €310/345; ❄@🖻🎝) The closest hotel to the airport, the Eden Bleu overlooks the sedate marina on Eden Island. Its stylish rooms have Nespresso machines and in-room Apple TV. The high levels of comfort compensate a little for the lack of a beach – it's more business hotel than beach resort – but it does fill an important niche and does so exceptionally well.

The breakfast buffet is top-notch, and while there's the merest hint of things starting to age a little, that's us being incredibly picky.

SEYCHELLES EDEN ISLAND

✕ Eating

Eden Island's waterside restaurants are garnering a reputation for high-end quality and sophistication, although the could-be-anywhere atmosphere won't appeal to many. There is also a handful of ice-cream parlours, juice bars and even a supermarket scattered around the shopping mall.

The Maharajas INDIAN €€
(Map p278; ☑ 4346829; www.themaharajassey chelles.com; Eden Island; mains Rs 145-375; ☺ noon-10.30pm) Our pick for the Seychelles' best Indian restaurant, Maharajas has views of the yacht harbour and the mountains of Mahé beyond. The cooking is assured, the service attentive. Try the *tandoori jhinga* (tandoori jumbo prawns from the clay oven).

Tamassa INTERNATIONAL €€
(Map p278; ☑ 4346880; www.facebook.com/ Tamassarestaurant; Eden Plaza; mains Rs 210-400; ☺ 11am-11pm) A curious mix of pizza, pasta and Chinese food ranges across the menu here, but you're on safe ground if you order something local – the octopus curry is simply sublime. It's a touch away from the other restaurants, and gets less busy as a result.

Bravo INTERNATIONAL €€
(Map p278; ☑ 4346020; Eden Island; mains Rs 200-800; ☺ noon-late Mon-Sat) This open-air restaurant overlooking the marina at Eden Island provides an agreeable dining experience with mostly Italian food. Everything's pretty good, but if you want a recommendation, go for the Mega Burger or the seared tuna salad. Save some room for an ice cream with chocolate sauce.

Spar Supermarket SUPERMARKET €€
(Map p278; Ground fl, Eden Plaza; ☺ 8am-8pm Mon-Sat, to 6pm Sun) One of the best supermarkets on Mahé.

🍷 Drinking & Nightlife

★ **The Boardwalk** LOUNGE
(Map p278; ☑ 4346622; Eden Island; ☺ 8am-midnight Mon-Thu, to 1am or later Fri & Sat) As good for a morning coffee as a late-night cocktail, this slice of sophistication could be the coolest place on the island. With wicker sofas on a pontoon out on the water and downbeat tunes keeping things mellow, it's our pick for the best bar in the country.

Chatterbox Cafe CAFE
(Map p278; ☑ 4346136; www.facebook.com/Chatter boxsey; Eden Plaza; ☺ 8am-9pm Mon-Thu, to 10pm Fri & Sat, 9am-8pm Sun) The pick of Eden Island's cafes, Chatterbox does excellent coffee and always has a buzz about it – locals come out to the island just for a coffee here. It also offers breakfasts, burgers, salads, pastries and pizza, but we love it for the range and quality of the coffees; iced coffees are served, too.

🛍 Shopping

Eden Art Gallery ART
(Map p278; ☑ 2514707; Shop 103, Eden Plaza; ☺ 10.30am-6.30pm Mon-Fri, to 2pm Sat) This large showroom sells local artworks and photography, framed and unframed, with mostly prints and some original work. It's sometimes has temporary exhibitions.

Giraffe BOOKS
(Map p278; ☑ 4346972; Ground fl, Eden Plaza; ☺ 10am-1pm & 1.45-5.15pm Mon-Fri, 10am-2pm Sat) The Seychelles has very few bookshops, which is why this place is a real find. It may be small, but there's a good mix of fiction, nonfiction and kids' books.

ℹ Information

Eden Pharmacy (☑ 2501500; Eden Plaza; ☺ 9am-7pm Mon-Fri, 10am-3pm Sat) This well-stocked pharmacy is on the ground floor of the Eden Plaza shopping mall.

ℹ Getting There & Away

Eden Island is connected to the main Mahé island via a bridge, around 4km south of Victoria.

There's no public transport to Eden Island, but a taxi to/from downtown Victoria should cost no more than Rs 180.

Ste Anne Marine National Park

Ste Anne Marine National Park, off Victoria, consists of six islands, two of which rank among the more accessible Seychelles islands – day trippers are permitted to land on **Cerf Island** and **Moyenne Island**. There's good snorkelling and any Mahé tour operator can arrange a snorkelling day trip here.

Of the other islands, the largest of the six, and only 4km east of Victoria, is **Ste Anne Island**, which has ravishing beaches. **Round Island** was once home to a leper colony, but these days it's better known for the offshore snorkelling and seriously alluring beaches. For more than a decade there have been plans for a luxury resort on **Long Island** – Pelangi Resorts took up the lease in 2015. At the time of research, plans were still on the drawing board. The smallest island of the lot, **Cachée**, lies southeast of Cerf. It's uninhabited.

 ## Activities

The swimming and snorkelling here are excellent, although the coral has been damaged by silting from construction works in the bay. There are superb beaches, but expect some algae. Note that park authorities charge a fee of €10 (free for children under 12 years) to enter the marine park. Tour operators include this in their prices.

Cerf Island Explorer   DIVING
(Map p278; 2570043; palblanchard@hotmail.com; Cerf Island; Mon-Sat by reservation) For diving inside Ste Anne Marine National Park, contact Cerf Island Explorer, a small outfit run by Marseillais Philippe Blanchard, who provides personalised service at affordable prices (€70/85 for a single/introductory dive). Dedicated snorkelling trips cost €45 (two people minimum). If you're not staying in the park, he can arrange pickups from Eden Island.

Sleeping & Eating

Although most visitors arrive on day trips by boat, there are a handful of luxury resorts on the islands (and a couple of upper-midrange options) within the national park itself. These make fabulous escapist alternatives to staying on the mainland.

⭐ Fairy Tern Chalets   APARTMENT €€€
(Map p278; 4321733; www.fairyternchalet.sc; Cerf Island; d €155;) Run by an affable South African couple, this is a great place to get away from it all; it's the most reasonable option within Ste Anne Marine National Park. Digs are in two squeaky-clean, spacious bungalows overlooking the beach. For when you don't fancy cooking, the restaurant at L'Habitation Cerf Island is a five-minute walk away. Free canoes.

JA Enchanted Island Resort   RESORT €€€
(Map p278; 4672727; www.jaresortshotels.com/en/seychelles/ja-enchanted-island-resort; Round Island; villa incl breakfast from €630;) The epitome of a luxurious island retreat, this Round Island resort, within Ste Anne Marine National Park, has stunning, spacious villas turned out in a classical style. The balcony bathtub in one is our pick for the best bathtub-with-a-view anywhere in the Seychelles. Private pools, a first-rate

TREASURE ISLAND?

Moyenne Island has a rather unusual backstory. The island was uninhabited for most of the first half of the 20th century, but was purchased for £8000 by former UK newspaper editor Brendon Grimshaw. Grimshaw, the island's only full-time inhabitant, spent 50 years transforming it, hacking back the jungle but replanting more than 16,000 trees in a bid to create his very own tropical paradise. He also set up a breeding programme for Aldabra tortoises and transformed Moyenne into a nature reserve, charging day visitors for the privilege of visiting. Local legend asserts that pirate treasure lies buried on the island – Grimshaw excavated two sites and found evidence of human-made hiding places but no loot – and two graves found on the island are believed to be those of pirates. When Grimshaw died in 2012, his dream was realised when the Seychelles' government incorporated Moyenne into Ste Anne Marine National Park.

restaurant and a sense of utter exclusivity round out a rather impressive package.

Cerf Island Resort   RESORT €€€
(Map p278; 4294500; www.cerf-resort.com; Cerf Island; s/d with half board from €405/530;) This venture strikes a perfect balance between luxury, seclusion and privacy (there are only 24 villas), on a hillside. This is a romantic resort, extremely quiet and popular with honeymooners, and the rooms have a lovely wood-and-bamboo design scheme. Facilities include a small pool and a spa. One grumble: the beach lacks the wow factor.

L'Habitation Cerf Island   HOTEL €€€
(Map p278; 2781311; www.facebook.com/habicerf; Cerf Island; d/ste with half board from €245/275;) This comfortable little colonial-style hotel is right on the beach, and just a 10-minute boat ride from Victoria. It has a tranquil, convivial and homey atmosphere with 12 sunny rooms, two villas and lovely gardens (but not much shade). The restaurant serves superfresh seafood. Prices drop for stays longer than three nights.

Villa de Cerf   VIILLA €€€
(Map p278; 2523161; www.villadecerf.com; Cerf Island; r with half board from €190;) This establishment occupies an elegant Creole

mansion with an unparalleled location on the beach. Stay four nights and you get the third free.

ⓘ Getting There & Away

Unless you're staying in one of the luxury resorts and can therefore arrange a boat transfer, the only way to get to the park and its islands is on an organised boat tour.

Beau Vallon & the North Coast

Beau Vallon, 3km from Victoria on Mahé's northwest coast, has the island's longest and, some would say, best beach. While it may be overbuilt by Seychellois standards, you'll find it remarkably low-key and quiet if you've experienced other tropical destinations. The seaside ambience, with fishers selling fresh fish late in the afternoon in the shade of *takamaka* trees, adds a dash of real life.

North of Beau Vallon, there's some great scenery up the coast to **Glacis** and **North Point**. With your own wheels, it's a scenic drive on a narrow road that hugs the coastline, with intermittent, lovely views over secluded coves at the foot of the cliffs.

West of Beau Vallon, the coastal road passes **Bel Ombre**, which has some good accommodation options and a little fishing harbour, and ends at **Danzil**, where La Scala (p290) restaurant lies. From there, you can walk to Anse Major (p294). Ah, Anse Major...

⊙ Sights

★ **Beau Vallon Beach**   BEACH
(Map p287) A beautiful semi-circle of sand backed by palms and *takamaka* trees, Beau Vallon beach is Mahé's most popular. The swimming is excellent, but there can be strong waves from June to November. For day visitors, beach bed rental costs Rs 75/150/225 per one/two/four hours, or Rs 325 per day.

🏄 Activities

As with elsewhere in the Seychelles, diving (see p37) and snorkelling are the main activities; the latter can often be combined with a trip on a glass-bottom boat. Parasailing is also a highlight here.

★ **Beau Vallon Aquatic Sports Center**   WATER SPORTS
(Map p287; ☑2515558, 2594367; Beau Vallon Beach; s/tandem parasail €50/70, 20-min jet ski €50; ☺variable) There's no better view of

west-coast Mahé than from a parasail pulled by a boat out over the bay. It can also set you up with jet skis and tube rides.

Boat House Spa   SPA
(Map p287; ☑2785661; www.facebook.com/boat housespaseychelles; North Coast Rd; 1-hr massage from Rs 700; ☺10am-7pm Mon-Fri, to 6pm Sat) Just in case you needed help relaxing here in the Seychelles, this well-run spa does all the necessaries – massages, facials, manicures, pedicures and body scrubs. We didn't try them all, but we'd be very happy to do so, and they're sure to be good if the massages are anything to go by.

Diving

Underwater Centre/Dive Seychelles   DIVING
(Map p287; ☑4345445, 4247165; www.divesey chelles.com.sc; Berjaya Resort, Beau Vallon; full-gear dive from €60; snorkelling 2/4 hrs €25/45) This dive centre is in the Berjaya Resort. Certification courses and dive packages are available. In conjunction with MCSS (www.mcss.sc), it organises whale-shark spotting off Mahé's west coast in September and October and also offers snorkelling.

Blue Sea Divers   DIVING
(Map p287; ☑2526051; www.blueseadivers.com; Beau Vallon; introductory dives from €95, single dives from €55; ☺daily) This French-run operation offers the full slate of diving adventures, including introductory dives, single dives, certification courses and various dive and snorkelling packages. It also runs cruises around the Seychelles aboard the splendid liveaboard dive boat *Galatea* (www.divingcruises.com), which started operating in June 2013.

Snorkelling & Boat Tours

The bay of Beau Vallon hosts a few good snorkelling spots, especially along the rocky shore up the coast to North Point. It's also the main launching pad for boat excursions and snorkelling trips to **Baie Ternay** at the northwestern tip of the island, where the reefs are healthy and marine life plentiful. Full-day excursions include entry fees to the park, barbecue lunch and snorkelling gear. The best season is from April to October. A group of four to six people is required. Contact a recommended operator (or ask your hotel or guesthouse to do it for you).

At the Berjaya Resort, Underwater Centre/Dive Seychelles fits snorkelling (€25/45 for two/four hours) in during its dive outings to Îlot (p37), Baie Ternay Marine Na-

Beau Vallon & Around

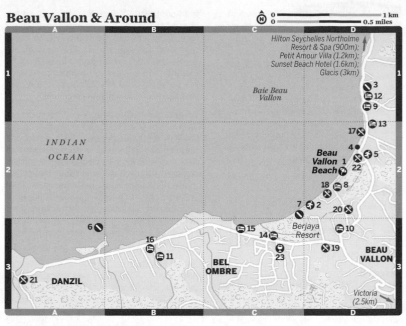

N
0 ————————— 1 km
0 ————————— 0.5 miles

Hilton Seychelles Northolme
Resort & Spa (900m);
Petit Amour Villa (1.2km);
Sunset Beach Hotel (1.6km);
Glacis (3km)

Baie Beau
Vallon

INDIAN
OCEAN

Beau
Vallon
Beach

Berjaya
Resort

BEL
OMBRE

BEAU
VALLON

DANZIL

Victoria
(2.5km)

SEYCHELLES BEAU VALLON & THE NORTH COAST

Beau Vallon & Around

tional Park and the lighthouse. It also rents snorkelling gear (€10 per day).

Blue Marlin   BOATING
(Map p287; ☑ 2510269, 2516067; Beau Vallon; full-day trip €95) Full-day boat trips, which include a bbq lunch on Thérèse Island and snorkelling at Baie Ternay Marine National Park.

Teddy's Glass Bottom Boat   BOATING
(☑ 2511125, 2511198; teddysgbb@yahoo.com; half-/full-day trip €65/95; ☺ by reservation) Good cre-

dentials. Runs glass-bottom trips to Baie Ternay and Ste Anne Marine National Park that include swimming and snorkelling stops.

**Dolphin Nemo
Glass Bottom Boat**   BOATING
(Map p287; ☑ 2596922; dolphinnemo10@gmail.com; Beau Vallon; full-day trip €95; ☺ by reservation) Does the standard tours to Ste Anne Marine National Park and Baie Ternay. It has a small kiosk on the beach in Beau Vallon.

CARANA BEACH

Here's a secret, only known to locals (whisper it softly): Carana Beach. This tiny, dreamlike cove lapped by lapis lazuli waters offers a small patch of sand framed by big boulders, with a couple of palm trees leaning over the shore. It's at Northeast Point. Officially the beach is open to the public, but you may need to contact the Carana Beach Hotel to arrange access.

🛏 Sleeping

Beau Vallon and Bel Ombre offer the widest range of accommodation in north Mahé, with a good mix of luxury resorts and self-catering villas set on or just back from the lovely beach.

Casadani
HOTEL €

(Map p287; ☑4248481; www.casadani-seychelles. com; Bel Ombre; s/d incl breakfast €80/95; P❄🛜) Soothingly positioned on a velvety emerald hillside just above the coastal road, this popular venture is a good deal if you can score a room with a sea view. The 25 rooms are well appointed yet utilitarian, but you'll be too busy soaking up the fabulous views from the vast shared terrace to mind. Car and boat hire are possible.

Beau Vallon Residence
APARTMENT €

(Map p287; ☑2516067; www.beauvallonresidence. sc; Beau Vallon; s/d/q €55/65/90; P❄🛜) Beau Vallon Residence has one self-contained apartment that can sleep four people, and it's very well kept and priced. It's not on the beach and there's no view, but you're in a quiet property, close to shops and banks. And Beau Vallon beach is just a five- to 10-minute stroll down the road. Excellent value. Book early.

Ocean View Guesthouse
APARTMENT €€

(Map p287; ☑2578025; www.oceanview-guest house.com; Bel Ombre; r incl breakfast €105-135; P❄) A great-value port of call. Above the road in Bel Ombre, this jolly good villa shelters four immaculate rooms with balcony. The upstairs ones offer splendid views of the bay. The cheaper Vakwa room, at the back, has no view. It's a 20-minute walk to Beau Vallon beach.

Carana Hilltop Villa
VILLA €€

(Map p278; ☑2781601; www.caranahilltopvilla. com; Off North Coast Rd, Glacis; r/f incl break-

fast from €110/140; ❄🛜🛁) This place high above Mahé's north coast gets rave reviews from travellers and we're inclined to agree with their assessment. The 11 rooms spread across two villas are large and lovingly cared for, and the pool is larger than in most such places. You'll need a vehicle to stay here, but that's true of many places on Mahé.

Diver's Lodge Guesthouse
GUESTHOUSE €€

(Map p287; ☑4261222; Mare Anglaise; d incl breakfast €90-140; P❄🛜) Just above the main coast road, next to a **dive centre** (Map p287; ☑4261106; www.bigbluedivers.net; Mare Anglaise; ⊙Mon-Sat) 🤿, these four rooms in a modern villa are large, pathologically clean and equipped to a high standard. The ones upstairs are significantly dearer but offer fleeting glimpses of the ocean through the foliage of exotic trees. Dinner can be arranged on request.

Beach House
APARTMENT €€

(Map p287; ☑2522010; www.choiceseychelles. com/beach-house.html; Mare Anglaise; s incl breakfast €75-105, d incl breakfast €90-115; ❄🛜) In an area where economical options are on the verge of extinction, the Beach House represents reasonable value. The four functional and spacious rooms ensure a decent night's sleep for guests keen to roll out of bed and onto Beau Vallon beach, just across the road.

Yarrabee
APARTMENT €€

(Map p278; ☑4261248; www.seychelles-yarrabee. com; Glacis; studios €80-150; ❄🛜) Two fully equipped studios and a three-bedroom unit with heavenly views of the bay. It's near a tiny beach and a small supermarket. Excellent value.

Georgina's Cottage
GUESTHOUSE €€

(Map p287; ☑4247016; www.georginas-cottage. com; Beau Vallon; r incl breakfast €90-120; ❄🛜) This friendly operation has catered to budget travellers for years. Since its serious makeover back in 2012, it has featured dearer but more comfortable rooms in an attractive Creole building. Its location is hard to beat: a 20m Frisbee throw from the beach, and also close to dive centres, restaurants and shops. Eddy, the manager, is full of local info.

★ Carana Beach Hotel
LUXURY HOTEL €€€

(Map p278; ☑4383333; www.caranabeach.com; North Coast Rd, Glacis; s/d from €397/424; 🛜🛁) Perched alongside one of northern Mahé's most beautiful beaches, the Carana Beach Hotel has rooms with a boutique feel; all come with Nespresso machines and some come with private plunge pool. Muted colour schemes, understated contemporary flair and extraordinary views add up to one of Mahé's best places to stay.

★ Hilton Seychelles Northolme Resort & Spa
RESORT €€€

(Map p278; ☑4299000; www.hilton.com; Glacis; villas €350-1400; P❄@🗑🏊) This gorgeous villa-only property is the smallest Hilton in the world and we love it all the more for it. There's a quiet sophistication and intimacy about the place, and the villas are exceptional – we'd move in and stay forever at their new Grand Ocean Pool Villas with big-sky views, private swimming pools and stunning design if we could.

★ H Resort Beau Vallon
RESORT €€€

(Map p287; ☑4387000; www.hresortseychelles. com; Beau Vallon; ste/villa from €450/1050; P❄@🗑🏊) One of the most attractive properties in Beau Vallon, H Resort has supremely comfortable suites and villas that make appealing use of wood, wicker and linen. The site is draped along the southern end of beautiful Beau Vallon beach, but sheltered by the trees. Good restaurants, excellent service and stylish public areas round out a terrific package.

Le Méridien Fisherman's Cove
RESORT €€€

(Map p287; ☑4677000; www.marriott.com; Bel Ombre; d incl breakfast from €400; P❄🗑🏊) A reliable resort with a staggering bow-shaped lobby and 70 stylish, modern rooms – bathrooms are not separate from bedrooms. Rooms are tightly packed together but face the sea and are buffered by lush gardens. The atmosphere is more convivial than intimate. Facilities include two restaurants, a bar, a spa and a pool. One minus: the beach is disappointingly thin.

Lilot Beach Chalets
CHALET €€€

(Map p278; www.lilot-beach-chalets.com; Off North Coast Rd, Glacis; r from €299) Fronting directly onto one of Mahé's prettiest coves, these chalets are down off the main road and yet a world away. The accommodation is large and the wooden floors are a lovely touch; we could spend hours here just sitting on one of the balconies...

Petit Amour Villa
VILLA €€€

(Map p278; ☑2578039; www.petitamourvilla. com; Glacis; d/ste incl breakfast from €203/280; P❄@🗑🏊) Consistently positive reviews are hardly surprising given what's on offer here – fabulous views and simply magnificent rooms that range from classic luxury

to a refined combination of dark wood and contrasting colours. Meals are excellent. There's a minimum three-night stay.

Apartments Sables d'Or
APARTMENT €€€

(Map p287; ☑4247404; www.sables-dor.sc; Beau Vallon; 1-/2-bedroom apt from €295/409; ❄🗑) Lovely, modern, self-catering apartments right on Beau Vallon's gorgeous beach make this one of the best choices on this corner of Mahé. The owners are a mine of information about the island and there are numerous restaurants a short walk away.

Bliss
BOUTIQUE HOTEL €€€

(Map p278; ☑2711187, 4261369; www.bliss-mahe. net; North Coast Rd, Glacis; d/ste with half board from €250/400; P❄🗑🏊) The Bliss Seaside building shelters eight rooms decorated with natural materials and ocean views that will leave you speechless. The Hillside rooms, in a building across the road, are much less inspiring, despite the lush tropical garden. Amenities include a pool, two good restaurants, a little spa and a great wooden sun deck with direct access to a small beach.

✖ Eating

Baobab Pizzeria
PIZZA €

(Map p287; ☑4247167; Beau Vallon; pizza Rs 135-175, mains Rs 90-185; ⊙noon-3.30pm & 6.30-9.30pm Tue-Sun) Madame Michel presides over this unpretentious, sand-floored eatery right on the beach – it's been around for years and is a local institution. After a morning spent in the waves, re-energise with a piping-hot pizza, a plate of pasta or fish and chips.

Leo's Food Bus
FOOD TRUCK €

(Map p287; ☑2767671; Beau Vallon Beach; mains Rs 50-200; ⊙noon-9pm) One of the more permanent food stalls that sets up along the Beau Vallon foreshore, Leo's is a reliable choice for simple, no-nonsense burgers, sausage

---

WHALE-SHARK SPOTTING

Between August and October it's common to see whale sharks offshore from Mahé's north and west coasts. Underwater Centre/Dive Seychelles (p286) runs dedicated snorkelling trips focusing on whale sharks in September and October (€140 to €150), though don't expect to touch them – guidelines state you should keep at least 4m away. It also runs whale-shark monitoring programmes.

and chips, fish steak with rice, and the like. Also does a handful of pizza varieties.

★ Rockpool
INTERNATIONAL €€

(Map p278; ☑ 2525858; North Coast Rd, Glacis; mains Rs 280; ☺ 12.30-9.30pm) The views here, next to Bliss (p289) hotel, are rather special and there's a real classy-but-casual atmosphere; they haven't tried to cram in too many tables, for example. The menu offers a mix of seafood (fish *Parmigiana* or whole grilled fish) and Mediterranean dishes (Italian-style meatballs, home-made lasagne and chicken gyros). Bring your swimmers and plan to be here at sunset.

Da Lydia
GELATO, CAFE €€

(Map p287; ☑ 2711321; Bel Ombre Rd, Beau Vallon; mains Rs 30-175; ☺ 10am-7pm Mon-Sat) Modern and brightly lit, this lovely corner cafe does terrific gelato and ice-cream sundaes, as well as snacks (pastries and crépes), a few mains and light meals (pasta, salads, sandwiches and paninis), and breakfasts.

Coral Asia
SUSHI €€

(Map p287; ☑ 4291000; Coral Strand Hotel, Beau Vallon; 4 nigiri from Rs 110, set menus Rs385-765; ☺ noon-10pm) On an open-sided elevated platform above the beach at the Coral Strand Hotel, Coral Asia does excellent sushi. We especially love the sashimi and nigiri platter that includes 10 pieces for a very reasonable Rs 385. Service can be hit or miss, but you'll enjoy the views while waiting for food.

La Scala
ITALIAN €€€

(Map p287; ☑ 4247535; Danzil; mains Rs 200-475; ☺ 7.15-10pm Mon-Sat) An old favourite of visitors and locals alike, this restaurant specialises in quality Italian homemade pasta (the *gnocchi della casa* tastes particularly good, despite the dated decor) and good seafood amid the low-lit ambience on the breezy terrace overlooking the sea. The tiramisu will

---

BAZAR LABRIN

On Wednesday evening don't miss Bazar Labrin, which injects a bit of vitality and excitement into the Beau Vallon area. Numerous food and craft stalls take positions along the seafront, with impromptu live bands or sound systems. It's popular with local families and flirting youngsters. For tourists, it's a great opportunity to catch local vibes.

---

finish you off sweetly. It's at the end of the coast road near Danzil.

La Perle Noire
INTERNATIONAL €€€

(Map p287; ☑ 4620220; Beau Vallon; mains Rs 790-590; ☺ 6.30-9.30pm Mon-Sat) The 'Black Pearl' scores high on atmosphere, with an eye-catching nautical theme and seafaring paraphernalia liberally scattered around the dining rooms. The food – mostly fish and meat dishes with an Italian twist – gets good reviews from the many repeat visitors.

Drinking & Nightlife

Beau Vallon is the most 'happening' (by Seychellois standards, which isn't saying much) area on Mahé. The bars at Le Méridien Fisherman's Cove (p289) and Hilton Seychelles Northolme (p289) are great for a sunset cocktail.

Tequila Boom
CLUB

(Map p287; ☑ 2525127; Bel Ombre; ☺ 11pm-5am Fri & Sat) The pick of the predominantly local nightclubs, this place along the main road in Bel Ombre, close to Beau Vallon, plays local music that'll have you up and dancing in no time.

ⓘ Getting There & Away

Buses leave regularly from Victoria for Beau Vallon (Rs 10; 15 to 30 minutes), either straight over the hill via St Louis, or the long way round via Glacis. The last bus to Victoria leaves at around 7.30pm; it's a Rs 200 taxi ride if you miss it.

Morne Seychellois National Park

While the dazzling coastline of Mahé is undoubtedly the island's main attraction, its mountainous interior is a dramatic landscape that's wonderful to explore. The splendid Morne Seychellois National Park encompasses an impressive 20% of the land area of Mahé and contains a wide variety of habitats, from coastal mangrove forests up to the country's highest peak, the Morne Seychellois (905m). Choked in thick forest, the enigmatic central part of the park is virtually deserted and can only be reached by walking trails; the trailheads are mostly accessible by road. Up here, you don't have to go very far before the outside world starts to feel a long, long way away.

TOP NATURE WALKS IN THE MORNE SEYCHELLOIS NATIONAL PARK

There are excellent walks in the Morne Seychellois National Park, with a number of hiking trails through the jungle-clad hills. These are detailed in a series of leaflets that are available at the botanical gardens (p278) in Victoria. Once you move beyond the trailheads, the trails are poorly signed, so it's not a bad idea to hire a guide, who will also provide natural and cultural insights. **Jacques Barreau** (☑ 2579191) and **Basile Beaudoin** (☑ 2514972) lead hiking and birdwatching trips into the park and charge around €80 to €100 for an informative half-day's walk, including transport. You can also contact **Terence Belle** (☑ 2722492), but he only works on Saturday and Sunday. Bring plenty of water.

Tea Factory to Morne Blanc

The imposing white bulk of Morne Blanc (667m) and its almost-sheer 500m face make a great hiking destination. Although the track is only 1200m long each way, it is quite steep – climbing 230m from start to finish. Plan on roughly 45 minutes to an hour for the ascent. The reward is a tremendous view over the west coast and the islands of Thérèse and Conception. The path starts 250m up the road from the tea factory (p292) on the cross-island road from Victoria to Port Glaud. Along the trail watch for the pendulous jackfruit plant and endemic bird species such as the Seychelles sunbird, Seychelles bulbul and the undeniably lovely blue pigeon; white-tailed tropicbirds soar high above the summit. You'll descend back the way you came.

Danzil to Anse Major

The 2.5km walk to this secluded beach takes you along a coast fringed by impressive glacis rock formations. The path starts at the end of the road at Danzil, heading west from Beau Vallon, a few hundred metres further up from La Scala restaurant. It's a fairly easy one-hour romp, but most of the path is exposed to the sun. Before descending to the beach, the path goes past a lookout that affords fantastic vistas of Anse Major (p294). The beach is blissfully quiet, and good for swimming, though there can be strong currents. Return by the same route.

Copolia

This is the most popular walk on Mahé, and one of the easiest high-country walks. It also has a pleasant Indiana Jones feel – you walk almost all the way amid a thick jungle, with lots of interesting fauna and flora. Now is your chance to spot leaf insects and the *Sooglossus gardineri*, the smallest frog on earth. Watch also for the distinctive (and carnivorous) pitcher plants close to the trail's highest point. The trail starts on the cross-island Chemin Forêt Noire about 5km above Victoria. It's only just over 1km to the granite platform of Copolia (497m), but the final section is quite steep; allow roughly two hours there and back. The views of Victoria and Ste Anne Marine National Park are sensational.

Trois Frères

Trois Frères (Three Brothers) refers to the three cliffs that tower over Victoria. The path is signed from the Sans Souci forest station on the Chemin Forêt Noire, about 4km from Victoria. The first part of the walk, up to a kiosk from where you get ample views, is fairly easy and can be covered in about one hour. The second leg, to the cross on the summit (699m), is tricky to follow and involves some scrambling – take a guide. Still game? Allow an extra two hours to reach the summit. You have to descend the same way.

⊙ Sights

Although hiking is the main attraction in Morne Seychellois, you could also follow the sinuous road that cuts a swathe through the heart of the park with some splendid views opening up en route. Both Mission Lodge and the Tea Factory (p292) are accessible along the road, and both have superb views.

Mission Lodge   HISTORIC SITE
(Venn's Town; Map p278; Off Sans Souci Rd; ⊙ 9am-5.30pm) FREE Close to the highest point you can reach on Mahé by road, Mission Lodge has a superb lookout with spectacular views of central Mahé and the west coast, and some low-slung stone ruins slowly returning to the forest (a school was built here by the

London Missionary Society in the 19th century to care for slave children who had been dumped on the island after the abolition of slavery). Queen Elizabeth II took tea in the small pavilion in 1972.

SeyTé Tea Factory   FARM
(Map p278; ☑4378221; Sans Souci Rd; Rs 25; ⊙7am-4pm Mon-Fri) At the working tea factory, about 3km past Port Glaud, 20-minute tours take you through the tea-making process. It's best to visit before noon, when you can see the whole process from drying to packing. There's also a gift shop where you can sample and purchase the fragrant SeyTé and citronnelle. There are fine west-coast views from the car park and you can watch the spectacular white-tailed tropicbirds take flight from here.

🛏 Sleeping & Eating

★Copolia Lodge   B&B €€€
(Map p278; ☑2761498; www.copolialodge.com; Bel Air, Sans Souci; d incl breakfast €195-275; P✷🛜🏊) Copolia Lodge is magical, if you don't mind the sense of isolation – it's a 15-minute drive uphill from Victoria. Poised on a greenery-shrouded promontory, this very well-run villa offers cracking views of the coastal plain and Ste Anne Marine National Park. It sports six bright, immaculate rooms with clean lines, ample space and lots of amenities, including a superb pool.

Excellent meals (€30) are available on request. It's just across the road from the Copolia (p291) trailhead.

The Station   GUESTHOUSE €€€
(Map p278; ☑4224203, 2581611; www.thestationseychelles.com; Sans Souci; r from €195; 🛜) High on the hill, this wellbeing spa and hotel is utterly different to anywhere else on the island. Whitewashed rooms, lovely views from the public areas and free yoga classes are the hallmarks here. There's an on-site restaurant and lovely little shop selling essential oils and the like.

★The Station   CAFE €€
(Map p278; ☑4225709; Sans Souci; mains Rs 155-265, 3-course Sat lunch Rs 450; ⊙10am-5pm) With gorgeous views and a healthy ethic when it comes to cooking, The Station is a lovely place to stop high atop the island. Dishes range from salads, soups and bruschetta to meze and savoury pancakes; yummy desserts, too. The adults-only 'Letting Go Saturdays' is fast becoming an island institution.

ⓘ Getting There & Away

A few buses per day connect Port Glaud and Port Launay with Victoria.

The road over the mountains from Victoria to Port Glaud, which cuts through the Morne Seychellois National Park, is a stunning scenic drive. Take the Bel Air Rd, which branches off Revolution Ave, and continue on Sans Souci Rd.

East Coast

The east coast has some stunning corners, including the gorgeous beaches of Fairyland, Anse Royale, Anse Bougainville, Anse Parnel and Anse Forbans, further south. There are also some good snorkelling spots off Anse Royale itself, plus spice and flower gardens and a rum distillery. But beyond that, much of the east coast is given over to housing, so there are only a few spots that fit the picture-postcard ideal.

◉ Sights

★Takamaka Bay   DISTILLERY
(Map p278; ☑4283716, 2597454; www.takamaka.sc; La Plaine St André, East Coast Rd, Le Cap; guided tours Rs 150, tasting only Rs 100; ⊙8.30am-4pm Mon-Fri, tours 11.30am & 1.30pm) On this popular tour you learn the story behind the island's main distillery and about the rum-making process. The tour runs for between 30 and 45 minutes and concludes with a tasting and an opportunity to purchase bottles of rum. There is also a forest walk and a small stand of sugar cane. It features a highly regarded restaurant (p294).

Kot Man-Ya   GARDENS
(Map p280; ☑371190; Chemin Les Canelles; adult/child Rs 150/75; ⊙8am-5pm) Worth a look if you're in the area, this lovely vivid garden, overseen by a retired Seychelles diplomat, has all manner of exotic, tropical flowers on display. It nicely complements Le Jardin du Roi, not far away. A few tortoises roam the grounds.

Le Jardin du Roi   GARDENS
(Map p280; ☑4371313; Enfoncement, Anse Royale; adult/child Rs 125/free; ⊙10am-5.30pm) Located 2km up in the hills above Anse Royale, this lush spice garden owes its existence to Pierre Poivre, the French spice entrepreneur. There is a self-guided walk around the 35-hectare orchard-crossed-with-forest. The planter's house contains a one-room museum and there's a pleasant cafe-restaurant

with smashing views down to the coast. Homemade jams, marmalade and spices are available at the gift shop.

🛏 Sleeping

The east coast may not be the sexiest part of the island, but we've unearthed a smattering of excellent-value (by Seychellois standards), family-run ventures from where you can easily reach the western coast, by bus or by car.

Jamelah Apartments   APARTMENT €
(Map p278; ☑ 4410819, 2523923; jamelah@intel vision.net; East Coast Rd, Le Cap; d €70, apt €80-110, incl breakfast; [P][✳][🛜]) This reliable option is run by Florie, who has great insight into budget travellers' needs. The two serviceable rooms (each with balcony and sea views) are a cast-iron bargain. If you're travelling with kids, opt for one of the four self-contained apartments in a separate building. They face a small 'beach', adequate for a waist-high dip at high tide.

Lalla Panzi Beach Guesthouse   GUESTHOUSE €
(Map p278; ☑ 4376411; www.lalla-panzi-beach. com; Le Cap; r incl breakfast €60; [✳][🛜]) Lalla Panzi is not the beachfront paradise you were dreaming of, but it's a neat property leading down to the sea. This friendly guesthouse offers four scrupulously clean rooms arranged around a cosy lounge; rooms 2 and 3 have sea views. Furnishings are slightly dated and the decor is a tad kitsch, but that's part of the charm.

★ Devon Residence   VILLA €€
(Map p278; ☑ 2512721; www.devon.sc; Off East Coast Rd, La Plaine St Andre; villas €100-150; [P][✳][🛜]) No, you're not hallucinating, the view is real. Poised on a greenery-shrouded hillside, the five villas overlook Anse Royale – full frame. They're extremely well appointed, spacious, bright and immaculate. A flotilla of perks, including free transfers to/from the airport, daily cleaning, free wi-fi, TV and washing machine, make this one of the best-value stays you'll have. Bonus: the owner rents cars at unbeatable rates (you'll need wheels to stay here).

Koko Grove Chalets   CHALET €€
(Map p280; ☑ 2585986; www.kokogrove.nl; Anse Royale; chalets €100-155; [P][✳][🛜]) If you're after hush and seclusion, then these three timbered chalets, outstandingly positioned in the velvety emerald hills above Anse Royale, are the answer. The three units are self-contained, with cosy living areas and private verandas overlooking the tiny swimming pool, with the ocean as a backdrop. It's 400m north of Le Jardin du Roi.

There's a store 400m down the road – useful if you're preparing your own food. If you don't fancy cooking, the owners can prepare excellent Creole meals.

Chalets d'Anse Forban   BUNGALOW €€€
(Map p280; ☑ 4366111; www.forbans.com; South Coast Rd, Anse Forbans; 2-person bungalow €161-185, 4-person bungalow €250-370; [P][✳][🛜]) Tranquillity: this family-friendly place has 12 sparkling-clean, fully equipped bungalows that are well spaced out; recent furniture and mattresses; expansive lawns; a lovely beach with good swimming; and fishers selling their catch on the beach in the afternoon. Add a few sun loungers and a nearby store, and you have a great deal. There's a minimum stay of three nights.

🍴 Eating

Pomme Canelle Restaurant   CREOLE €
(Map p278; East Coast Rd, Domaine de Val des Prés; Mon-Sat/Sun buffet Rs 200/250; ⊙ 10am-9pm) Occupying one of a number of heritage Creole buildings in this complex of artisan stalls, the Pomme Canelle serves up a well-priced Creole buffet with cooling breezes (these old Creole buildings were built to maximise natural 'air-con') that is particularly popular for a weekend lunch.

★ Kafe Kreol   INTERNATIONAL €€
(Map p280; ☑ 2606464; www.facebook.com/kafe kreol; East Coast Rd, Anse Royale; breakfast Rs 35-250, mains Rs 270-480, pizzas Rs 200-320; ⊙ 9am-9.30pm) One of the east coast's best seaside restaurants, stylish and breezy Kafe Kreol combines beachside charm, good service and terrific food; the octopus curry is outstanding, the tuna is cooked just right and the pizzas are excellent. Try local Slow Turtle Cider, or locally made Shark's ice cream, then wander down to the beach to cap off a near-perfect afternoon.

Le Jardin du Roi   CAFE €€
(Map p280; ☑ 4371313; Anse Royale; mains Rs 150-325; ⊙ 10am-4.30pm) The setting is wonderful at this cafe-restaurant up in the hills at the spice garden, and it puts you in the mood for a fruit juice or a crunchy salad. Seafood and sandwiches also feature on the menu, alongside octopus with saffron, cinnamon and coconut. The crêpes are simple but excellent – ask for a sprinkling of cinnamon.

Les Dauphins Heureux Café-Restaurant
CREOLE €€

(Map p280; ☑ 4430100; Anse Royale; pizza from Rs 190, mains Rs 215-340; ⊗ 8.30am-10pm Mon-Sat, from 1pm Sun) A classic beachfront setting with a shady terrace and a tropical garden characterises this classy eatery with a modernish feel. Choose between subtly flavoured fish, seafood, curries and meat dishes – we enjoyed the grilled fish with papaya. Head here on Sundays for the excellent Creole buffet (adult/child Rs 450/250) served at lunchtime.

Surfers Beach Restaurant
CREOLE €€

(The Beach House; Map p280; ☑ 2783703; www.surfersbeach.sc; Anse Parnel; pizzas from Rs 165, mains Rs 250-575; ⊗ noon-9.30pm) In a terrific location overlooking the seductive beach at Anse Parnel (although overhanging branches now obscure much of the view), Surfers Beach is a heart-stealing, open-air joint. Linger over salads, grilled fish or octopus curry while enjoying the caress of the breeze on your face.

★ La Grande Maison
CREOLE €€€

(Map p278; ☑ 2522112; www.facebook.com/LGM sey; East Coast Rd, Takamaka Distillery, La Plaine St Andre; lunch tapas Rs 60-120, dinner mains Rs 350-550; ⊗ noon-3pm & 7-9.30pm Tue-Sat) At Takamaka Bay (p292), La Grande Maison is the home kitchen of Christelle Verheyden, arguably the country's most talented chef. The atmosphere, in a restored and airy colonial home, is a fine backdrop for Verheyden's exquisite tastes built around the best local (often organic) ingredients and fine-dining sensibility. Verheyden is also a sommelier: the wines are as excellent as the cooking.

🍷 Drinking & Nightlife

Katiolo
CLUB

(Map p278; ☑ 4375453; East Coast Rd, Anse Faure; men/women Rs 100/50; ⊗ 10.30pm-late Wed, Fri & Sat) The east coast is home to one of Mahé's most popular nightclubs. Despite outward appearances, it's a fairly hip venue, so dress up rather than down.

🛍 Shopping

Domaine de Val des Prés
ARTS & CRAFTS

(Map p278; East Coast Rd, Anse aux Pins; ⊗ 9.30am-5pm Mon-Sat) The Domaine de Val des Prés at Anse aux Pins consists of a cluster of craft shops grouped around a 19th-century plantation house with a few bits of memorabilia. The rather motley assortment of crafts on offer includes model boats, pottery, paintings, clothing and products fashioned from the hugely versatile coconut tree.

ⓘ Getting There & Away

Buses leave regularly from Victoria for the east coast. The last bus to Victoria leaves Anse Royale around 7.30pm.

West Coast

The west coast is very easy on the eye. There are one or two sights to aim for, but it's the beaches and coastal scenery that are the star attractions. Wilder than the east, this is the part of Mahé where green hills tumble past coconut-strewn jungles before sliding gently into translucent waters.

There's only a handful of settlements, including the fishing villages of **Anse Boileau**, **Grande Anse** and **Port Glaud**. If it really is isolation you're after, continue north on the narrow coastal road to **Baie Ternay**, a blissful, end-of-the-road kind of place.

The west coast is easily accessed from the east coast via several scenic roads that cut through the mountainous interior.

⊙ Sights

★ Anse Major
BEACH

(Map p278) One of the most beautiful beaches on Mahé, Anse Major is only accessible on foot from Danzil – few visitors to the Seychelles make it here. The setting is a match for any beach in the Seychelles, although swimming can be dangerous.

★ Anse Soleil
BEACH

(Map p280) The idyllic little beach of Anse Soleil is a pocket-sized paradise. You can pause here for lunch – there's a beach **restaurant** (Map p280; ☑ 4361700; Anse Soleil; mains Rs 250-420; ⊗ noon-3pm) – but beware, you may never want to leave. It's accessible via a secondary road (it's signposted).

Anse Takamaka
BEACH

(Map p280) The gently curving Anse Takamaka is a gorgeous strand for walking unfettered on white sand and gaping at sunsets. Facilities include **Chez Batista's** (Map p280; ☑ 4366300; www.chezbatista.com; Anse Takamaka; mains Rs 110-785, buffet Rs 375-450; ⊗ 12.30-8pm Mon-Sat, 1-5pm Sun) bar-restaurant.

Anse Port Launay
BEACH

(Map p278) Close to the **Constance Ephelia** (Map p278; ☑ 4395000; www.constancehotels.com; Port Launay; d with half board from €415; [P][❄][🛜][🏊]), just 50m beyond Port Launay Bus Terminal, this gorgeous circle of sand can feel like paradise with its overhanging trees, turquoise waters and lovely views.

Petite Anse
BEACH

(Map p280) This pristine curve of white sand is accessible via the Four Seasons Resort (p296); wait at the gate and a buggy will take you down to the beach. Come late afternoon: as the sun lowers, the sky deepens to orange. This beach just might be heaven, despite the fact that it has been partly privatised by the hotel. Visitors can use the hotel's beach-restaurant for food and drink.

Grande Anse
BEACH

(Map p278) Grande Anse is an immense swathe of sand that glimmers with a fierce but utterly enchanting beauty. No other beach provides the same opportunities for long, solitary walks. It's not suitable for swimming, though, due to strong currents.

Anse Intendance
BEACH

(Map p280) A top-end resort lines the northern portion of this high-profile beach. The southern end is almost deserted and offers good swimming and snorkelling. The sunset views are some of the best in the Seychelles. From the police station at Quatre Bornes, take the 1.7km concrete road that leads down to Anse Intendance.

Anse Petite Police & Police Bay
BEACH

(Map p278) From the village of Quatre Bornes, a road leads to Police Bay, a splendid, blissfully isolated spot at the southern tip of the island. Sadly, the currents are too dangerous for swimming, but the beaches are great places to watch the surf (bring a picnic).

🏃 Activities

Dive Resort Seychelles
DIVING

(Map p280; ☑ 4372057; www.scubadiveseychelles. com; Anse à la Mouche; ⊗ Mon-Sat) This well-regarded venture takes beginners and experienced divers to some truly impressive dive sites off the southwestern coast. An introductory/single dive costs €100/60.

Turquoise Horse Trails
HORSE RIDING

(Map p278; ☑ 2638850; www.turquoisehorse trails.com; West Coast Rd, Barbarons; 40-min/1- /2-hr trail ride €60/90/160; ⊗ 8am-5pm Tue-Sun) Trail rides along the beach or up into the forest make for a fabulous excursion that gives you a whole new perspective on the Seychelles' gorgeous topography. It caters to all levels of experience, but advance bookings are essential.

🛏 Sleeping

La Rocaille
BUNGALOW €

(Map p280; ☑ 2524238; lelarocaille@gmail.com; Anse Gouvernement Rd, Anse Soleil; d €70; 🅿) This is a pleasant find, but there's only one unit, on the hill that separates Anse Gouvernement from Anse Soleil. It's simple but well kept, and the grounds are nice enough, with lots of vegetation and birdsong. You'll need a car if you're staying here. There's no air-con.

★ Anse Takamaka View
APARTMENT €€

(Map p280; ☑ 2510007; www.atv.sc; Takamaka; bungalows €90-170; 🅿 ❄ 🛜 🏊) No photo retouching on the website – we guarantee that the views from the terrace are *that* terrific, the pool (complete with a pool bar) *that* scintillating, and the three bungalows *that* roomy and comfortable. Run by a Seychellois/German couple, this wonderfully peaceful property is a winner. Meals (€18) are available twice a week. The minimum stay is three nights.

★ La Maison Soleil
APARTMENT €€

(Map p280; ☑ 2712677; www.maisonsoleil.info; Anse Soleil Rd; ste €110-230; 🅿 ❄ 🛜) Seeking a relaxing cocoon with homey qualities without the exorbitant price tag? Run by artist Andrew Gee, whose gallery is just next door, this champ of a self-catering option has all the key ingredients, with tasteful apartments, prim bathrooms and a colourful garden. Anse Soleil is within walking distance.

Anse Soleil Beachcomber
HOTEL €€

(Map p280; ☑ 4361461; www.ansesoleilbeach comber.com; Anse Soleil; s/d incl breakfast from €110/130; 🅿 ❄ 🛜) This family-run hotel, among rocks on the idyllic cove of Anse Soleil, has location sorted. The clean and simple rooms with private terraces are less exciting than the location, but the flowery grounds add charm. Rooms 6, 7 and 8 open onto the sea, but the more recent Premier rooms, slightly set back from the shore, are much larger.

Chez Batista's
BUNGALOW €€

(Map p280; ☑ 4366300; www.chezbatista.com; Anse Takamaka; d €82-106, ste from €165, incl breakfast; 🅿 ❄ 🛜) Your only concern here: whether to frolic on the beach *now* or first sip a cocktail at the restaurant. This long-standing venue on Takamaka beach features 11 bland, sometimes retro but acceptable rooms (no sea views) and some suites overlooking the water. The property feels a bit crowded and service can be irregular but the idyllic location's the pull.

La Residence
APARTMENT €€

(Map p280; ☑4371733; www.laresidence.sc; Anse à la Mouche; studios/villas €90/186; P ❅ ☎) Perched on a hillside, the five fully equipped studios and three villas are roomy, straightforward and tidy, if a touch old-fashioned. The buildings are functional rather than filled with noticeable character, but there are good views from the terrace (despite the odd power line).

Blue Lagoon Chalets
APARTMENT €€

(Map p280; ☑4371197; www.seychelles.net/b lagoon; West Coast Rd, Anse à la Mouche; d €145; P ❅ ☎) The friendly owner here offers four well-cared-for holiday units that are peppered across a well-tended park, a hop across the road from the seashore. They sleep up to four people and are fully equipped.

Anse Soleil Resort
APARTMENT €€

(Map p280; ☑4361090; www.ansesoleil.sc; Anse Soleil; 1-/2-bedroom apt incl breakfast €100/150; P ❅ ☎) Run by a hospitable family, this discreet number has just four self-catering apartments; the Kitouz is the best, but all are well equipped, nicely laid out and spacious, and come with a large terrace from where you can soak up the view over Anse

---

SEXY COCONUTS

The *coco fesse* (the fruit of the coco de mer palm) is often described as the sexiest fruit on earth. Given the peculiar buttocks-like shape of these sensual fruits, they have been the source of many legends and erotic lore, and greatly excited the 17th-century sailors who first stumbled upon them after months at sea. Before 1768 the coconuts, which were occasionally found floating in the Indian Ocean, were believed to grow in a magic garden at the bottom of the sea. This rare palm grows naturally only in the Seychelles.

Only female trees produce the erotically shaped nuts, which can weigh over 30kg. The male tree possesses a decidedly phallic flower stem of 1m or longer, adding to the coco de mer's steamy reputation.

Harvesting the nuts is strictly controlled by the Seychelles Island Foundation (p283), an NGO that manages the Vallée de Mai on behalf of the government.

à la Mouche (if you can ignore the power lines). Meals (€15) are available on request.

★ Maia Luxury Resort & Spa
RESORT €€€

(Map p278; ☑4390000; www.tsogosun.com/maia; West Coast Rd, Anse Louis; d incl breakfast €2200; P ❅ @ ☎ ≋) One of Mahé's most exclusive hotels, this place will render you speechless – you'll never want to leave. Overlooking glorious Anse Louis, it's truly beautiful, with great expanses of white beach, palm-shaded landscaped grounds, a splendid infinity pool and 30 gorgeous villas – each with its own pool. Nothing is too much trouble for the obliging staff.

★ Four Seasons Resort
RESORT €€€

(Map p280; ☑4393000; www.fourseasons.com/seychelles; Petite Anse; d incl breakfast from €975; P ❅ ☎ ≋) With its stadium-sized villas perched on a hillside, swoony ocean views, sense of privacy and lovely spa, this five-star bigwig, opened in 2009, is a fab place for honeymooners and loved-up couples. The bedrooms and bathrooms are massive, and masterpieces of understatement despite luxuries such as works of art adorning the walls, teak furnishings, high-quality linen and king-size beds.

Banyan Tree
RESORT €€€

(Map p280; ☑4383500; www.banyantree.com; Off Intendance Rd, Anse Intendance; d incl breakfast from €680; P ❅ ☎ ≋) The Banyan Tree is a gorgeous property. Three highlights: the spa, possibly the most attractive on Mahé (and that's no small claim); a fabulous location on a greenery-shrouded hillside with heavenly views of the sea; and 54 wonderfully roomy and stylish villas that get plenty of sunshine, even in late afternoon.

Valmer Resort
BUNGALOW €€€

(Map p280; ☑4381555; www.valmerresort.com; Baie Lazare; d from €190; P ❅ ☎ ≋) A cluster of well-organised villas and bunaglows cascades down a hillside cloaked in green, each enjoying stupendous ocean views. Apart from the four ordinary 'garden studios', which are just off the main road, the 17 units are sun-filled, capacious and tasteful. A hit is the pool, built at the foot of a big granite boulder. There's an on-site restaurant (by the pool).

✖ Eating

★ Oscars - The Bar & Grill
SEAFOOD €€

(Map p280; ☑2773919; West Coast Rd; mains Rs 200-450; ☺10am-9pm) For fresh fish, grilled just the way it should be, Oscars is a terrific choice. There's grouper, sailfish, marlin and red snapper, but the best order is yellow-fin tuna seared, served rare and marinated in the house concoction of herbs and spices. Sidle up to the bar or, better still, occupy one of the garden tables with terrific coastal views.

La Gaulette Food Bar
SEAFOOD €€

(Map p280; ☑2781183; https://lagauletterestau rant.business.site; South Coast Rd, Anse Gaulette; mains Rs 140-375; ☺11.30am-9pm Tue-Sun) Grilled tuna, seafood pasta, ginger prawns. A range of cocktails, ciders and juices. An absence of wi-fi and a beach across the road. Everyone's different, but this place ticks a whole lot of boxes for us when it comes to south-coast bliss.

Maria's Rock Cafeteria
INTERNATIONAL €€

(Map p280; ☑4361812; Anse Gouvernement Rd, Anse Soleil; mains Rs 215-295; ☺noon-9pm Wed-Mon) Now here's something different. Maria, the Seychellois spouse of artist Antonio Filippin, runs this quirky restaurant beside her husband's **studio** (Map p280; ☑2510977; Baie Lazare; ☺10am-7pm Wed-Sat & Mon). The cavernous interior is discombobulating, with granite tabletops and concrete walls sprayed with paint. Food-wise, it majors on fish and meat dishes, grilled at your table on a stone plate. Skip the pancakes.

Veranda Cafe
CAFE €€

(Map p278; ☑2853865; West Coast Rd, Barbarons; mains Rs 250-400; ☺11am-6pm) True to its name, Veranda Cafe offers classy but casual veranda dining with good coffee, snacks and light meals, pizzas and burgers, as well as more substantial mains such as garlic prawns with feta and parsley or local curries and fish. Indoors there's a lovely **shop** (Map p278; ☑4378132; www.pineapplestudio.sc; West Coast Rd, Barbarons; ☺11am-4.30pm Mon-Sat).

Chez Plume
INTERNATIONAL €€

(Map p278; ☑4355050; www.aubergeanseboileau. com; West Coast Rd, Anse Boileau; mains Rs 215-490; ☺noon-9.30pm Tue-Sat, to 3pm Sun, 6-9.30pm Mon) A west-coast veteran, Chez Plume can still hold its own among the new crop of places. It serves local specialities such as Creole black pudding, octopus or crab curry, and the intriguing *capitaine blanc* with passionfruit sauce. There's an extensive wine list covering South Africa and Europe, a range of beers and generally good service.

Anchor Café – Islander Restaurant
INTERNATIONAL €€

(Map p280; ☑4371289; Anse à la Mouche; lunch mains Rs 150-350, dinner mains Rs 180-800; ☺noon-9pm Mon-Sat; ☜) This family-run restaurant takes its cooking seriously. Its champion dishes include blackened fish, a range of Creole curries (including lobster curry), grilled fish snapper, plus the obligatory catch of the day. A few vegetarian options also grace the menu. Eat al fresco near a huge anchor in the garden and enjoy the amazing sunset over the bay.

★ Del Place
CREOLE, EUROPEAN €€€

(Map p278; ☑2814111; www.delplaceseychelles. com; Port Glaud; mains Rs 265-790; ☺11am-4pm & 6-9pm) This delightful spot weds cafe-cool to excellent cooking. The centrepiece is local seafood: octopus straight from the lagoon, baked red snapper in banana leaf, seafood platters and Creole curries, including the rarely seen crab curry. Throw in great salads (such as palm heart), local tapas, cool cocktails and beautiful beach views and it adds up to our favourite west-coast venue.

🛍 Shopping

The glorious southwest seems to be an endless source of inspiration for a number of artists, and you'll find small galleries signposted all the way along the coast road.

Michael Adams' Studio
ART

(Map p280; ☑4361006; www.michaeladamsart. com; South Coast Rd, Anse à la Mouche; ☺by appointment) Visit the studio of Michael Adams MBE, where silkscreen prints burst with the vivid life of the forests. They are irresistible and highly collectable, so bring plenty of rupees if you're thinking of buying. Even if you don't ring ahead and you're driving by, stop in – it could be open, though don't count on it.

Tom Bowers
ART

(Map p280; ☑4371518; artworks@seychelles.net; Chemin Les Cannelles; ☺by reservation) This British-born artist creates some truly amazing bronze sculptures and his works, such as the **Liberty Monument** (Map p282; 5th Jun Ave) in Victoria, are increasingly being commissioned for public places. If you haven't called ahead, turn up at the gate and ring the bell to see if the artist is in residence.

❶ Getting There & Away

Buses leave regularly from Victoria for the west coast. The last bus to Victoria leaves Quatre Bornes in the south around 7.30pm.

SEYCHELLES WEST COAST

PRASLIN

A wicked seductress, Praslin has lots of temptations: stylish lodgings, tangled velvet jungle that's ripe for exploration, curving hills dropping down to gin-clear seas, gorgeous stretches of silky sand edged with palm trees and a slow-motion ambience. No, you're not dreaming – this is the Seychelles you dreamed of when you first imagined this tropical archipelago.

Lying about 45km northeast of Mahé, the second-largest island in the Seychelles is closer to the sleepiness of La Digue than the relative hustle and bustle of Mahé. Like Mahé, Praslin is a granite island, with a ridge of small mountains running east–west along the centre, and the svelte interior, especially the Vallée de Mai, is fascinating for its flora and birdlife. Its combination of manageable size (you're never more than an hour's drive from anywhere else on the island) and gorgeous beaches makes Praslin a fine choice for your Seychelles holiday.

◎ Sights

★ Anse Lazio   BEACH
(Map p300) Anse Lazio, on the northwest tip of the island, is picture-perfect everywhere you look and often turns up in lists of the world's most beautiful beaches. The long beach has lapis lazuli waters with great waves, a thick fringe of palm and *takamaka* trees, and granite boulders at each extremity. There's some good snorkelling among the rocks along the arms of the bay and there's a beachside restaurant. Despite its popularity, it never feels crowded, but watch your valuables here.

★ Anse Volbert   BEACH
(Map p300) This long, gently arching beach is among the most popular strands on the island. It's great for safe swimming and sunbathing, and it's also good for water sports. There are plenty of facilities, including restaurants and hotels. A small islet – Chauve-Souris – floats offshore. You can swim to it for snorkelling.

★ Vallée de Mai   NATIONAL PARK
(Map p300; www.sif.sc; adult/child under 12 Rs 350/free; ⊙ 8.30am-5.30pm, last tickets at 4.30pm) 🌿 Gorgeous World Heritage–listed Vallée de Mai is one of only two places in the world where the rare coco de mer palm grows in its natural state (the other being nearby Curieuse (p305) Island). It's also a birding hotspot: watch for the endemic Seychelles

bulbul, the lovely blue pigeon, the Seychelles warbler and the endangered black parrot, of which there are between 520 and 900 left in the wild. It's a real slice of Eden.

Three hiking trails (plus a number of connecting minor subtrails) lead through this primeval, emerald-tinged forest, which remained totally untouched until the 1930s. The shortest is about 1km and the longest is 2km and all are clearly marked and easy going – perfect for families. As you walk amid the forest, the atmosphere is eerie, with the monstrous leaves of the coco de mer soaring 30m to a sombre canopy of huge fronds. Signs indicate some of the other endemic trees to look out for (there are more than 50 other indigenous plants and trees), including several varieties of pandanus (screw pines) and latanier palms. This is also home one of only two populations of the giant bronze gecko, and 14 endemic reptile and amphibian species.

There are free guided visits at 9am and 2pm, but we recommend taking a private guide for a 1½- to two-hour guided walk (Rs 1000 per group) through the forest – you'll miss so much if you go it alone.

There's an informative **visitor centre** (Map p300; 📞 4236220; www.sif.sc; Vallée de Mai; ⊙ 8.30am-4.30pm), cafe and excellent shop on-site.

Anse La Blague   BEACH
(Map p300) Head to Anse La Blague on the east coast if you're after a secluded picnic spot. Very few tourists make it to this isolated beach, which feels like the world's end. It has no facilities, other than shady *takamaka* trees to hang your towel on. You might come across a few fishers with their catch of *cordonnier* (jobfish).

Anse Marie-Louise   BEACH
(Map p300) At the island's southern tip, Anse Marie-Louise is a pretty spot. There are no facilities and no parking lot; just pull over at the side of the road and voila – you're at the beach. Continuing along the coastal road to the west, you'll find numerous coves and other beaches.

🏃 Activities

Whether you're an experienced diver or a novice slapping on fins for the first time, you'll find superb dive sites (see p37) off Praslin. The best snorkelling spots can be found at Anse Lazio, around St Pierre Islet and off Baie Laraie on Curieuse (p305).

It's not a bad idea to rent a kayak and explore Anse Volbert at your leisure and paddle around Chauve Souris Island. Sagittarius Taxi Boat handles rentals (from €15 per hour).

White Tip Dive Centre
DIVING

(Map p300; ☑ 4232282, 2514282; www.whitetip divers.com; Anse Volbert) At the eastern end of **Paradise Sun Hotel** (Map p300; ☑ 4293293; www.tsogosun.com/paradise-sun; Anse Volbert; d from €608; P ❄ ☎ ☎), this small, professional outfit has years of experience diving the sites around Praslin and La Digue. It charges very reasonable rates (by Seychellois standards). An introductory dive is €85 while single dives cost from €55. Packages, certification courses and snorkelling trips are also available.

Sagittarius Taxi Boat
BOATING

(Map p300; ☑ 2512137, 2861201; www.facebook. com/sagittariustaxiboatexcursions; Anse Volbert; ☺ 9am-5pm) The alternative to an all-inclusive boat excursion is to charter your own boat from Anse Volbert. Sagittarius Taxi Boat, on the beach beside the Paradise Sun Hotel, charges €40 for Curieuse (p305); Curieuse with St Pierre costs €45.

Octopus Dive Centre
DIVING

(Map p300; ☑ 4232602; www.octopusdiver.com; Anse Volbert) This dive school is very experienced after more than a decade running dives around the island. An introductory dive is only €90. A standard dive runs upwards of €60. Also offers dive packages, certification courses and snorkelling trips.

🛏 Sleeping

Anse Volbert, with its restaurants and other tourist facilities, makes a good base. Grand Anse is busier and less attractive, and there are some decent options within walking distance of the Baie Ste Anne jetty. Halfway between Anse Lazio and Anse Volbert, Anse Possession is convenient to both and is a good, quiet base, although the beach is not Praslin's best. Always book your accommodation well in advance.

🛏 Grand Anse & Anse Kerlan

Sunset Cove Villa
APARTMENT €€

(Map p300; ☑ 2513048; www.sunset-cove-villa. com; Anse Kerlan; r €75-150; P ❄) Pinch yourself – you're just steps from the sea. OK, there's no proper beach here because of erosion, but the setting is truly appealing. Digs are in two comfortable, well-equipped and light-filled houses. No meal service, but there's a small supermarket nearby.

Seashell Self Catering
APARTMENT €€

(Map p300; ☑ 2513764; csetheve@hotmail.com; Anse Kerlan; d €85; P ❄ ☎) This sturdy house built from granite stones scores goals with a combination of affordable rates and a handy position – the sea is just 100m away, though the beach is not that great because of erosion and seaweed. The two large, spotless studios are pleasantly furnished, with tiled floors, sparkling bathrooms, good bedding and a terrace. Both have a kitchenette.

★ Constance Lémuria
RESORT €€€

(Map p300; ☑ 4281281; www.constancehotels.com; Anse Kerlan; d incl breakfast from €575; P ❄ @ ☎ ☎) Praslin's top-drawer establishment occupies the island's northwest tip. If you're not bowled over by the voluminous foyer and marvellous spa, you will be by the three-tiered infinity pool, three gorgeous beaches and expansive grounds where the villas blend in among the rocks and water features. Facilities include three restaurants, a kids' club and an 18-hole golf course (open to non-guests).

Villas de Mer
HOTEL €€€

(Map p300; ☑ 4233972; www.villasdemerho tel.com; Grand Anse; d incl breakfast from €207; P ❄ ☎ ☎) Villas de Mer is a lower top-end option with good accommodation for its price following a full refit. Here the 10 brightly painted rooms occupy two rows of low-slung buildings facing each other. A highlight is the restaurant, which has a fabulous beach frontage and serves fresh seafood. The atmosphere is relaxed and friendly.

Praslin

Aride Island (10km);
Aride Bank (Dive Site)

Anse
Badamier

Roche
Canon

Curieuse
(172m)

Anse
St José

Anse
Georgette

**Anse
Lazio**

36

Petite
Anse
Kerlan

17

23 1

28

Anse
Boudin

21

Anse
Takamaka

42

Grand Fond
(340m)

31

33

20   44

34   12

Praslin
Airport

**GRAND
ANSE**

35   43

18

6

37

Cousin Island
Special Reserve

Cousin
Island

9

Pasquière Track

INDIAN

OCEAN

Anse Citron

Cousine Island (2km);
South Cousine Island
(Dive Site)

Dhevatara
Beach Hotel
BOUTIQUE HOTEL €€€

(Map p300; ☑4237333; www.dhevatara.com/
Praslin-Island.html; Grand Anse; d from €548;
P❋⊚☎) Dhevatara is sleek and imaginative, a boutique-like luxury venture loaded
with more cool than any other on the island. With only 10 rooms divided into two
categories (garden views and ocean views),
it's a great choice for couples. Rooms are
not huge but are individually designed; the
ones upstairs get more natural light. Facilities include a spa.

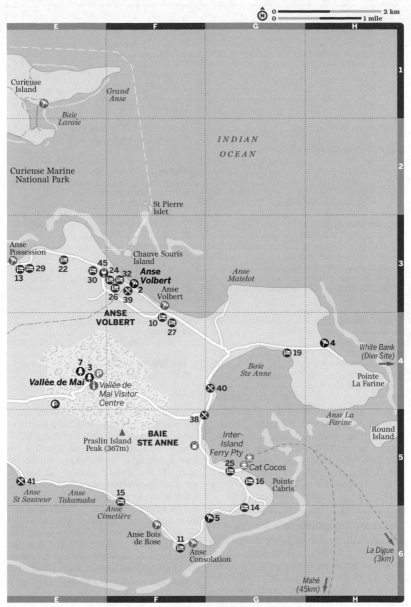

Castello Beach Hotel HOTEL €€€

(Map p300; ☎4298900; www.castellobeachhotel. com; Anse Kerlan; s/d from €199/238; P✳@ 🛜🌊) This four-star, suites-only hotel has large rooms, an above-average restaurant and a lovely sunset-facing location on a small stretch of sand. Wood floors and wicker fur-

nishings give it a nicely casual feel, although not many of the suites have beach views.

Islander Guesthouse APARTMENT €€€

(Map p300; ☎4233224, 2781224; www.islander-seychelles.com; Anse Kerlan; d/apt incl breakfast €170/243; P✳🛜) The good people at the

Praslin

Islander are not setting out to win any 'best in its class' awards with their establishment but its virtue is the good condition of the rooms, and you'll be made to feel at home. The four bungalows (eight rooms in total) are unpretentious but clean and the property opens onto Anse Kerlan. Air-con is extra (€8). There's an on-site restaurant.

Anse Consolation Area

Bonnen Kare Beach Villa APARTMENT €€
(Map p300; ☑4322457; bonnenkare@gmail.com; Anse Consolation; d/q €120/220; ⊕) A lovely option for a group of friends or a family, this secluded four-room villa opening onto an idyllic sandy cove really fulfils the dreams of a private beach getaway. Don't fancy cooking? The maid can prepare meals on request. No air-con. Wi-fi costs €8 per day.

**Coco de Mer Hotel &
Black Parrot Suites** RESORT €€€
(Map p300; ☑4290555; www.cocodemer.com; Anse Bois de Rose; s/d incl breakfast from €386/455;

P⊛☎☀) The exclusive Black Parrot Suites, perched on a headland with fantastic ocean views, affords serious cosseting and a hideaway: the 12 stylish suites and adjoining spa appeal to couples (no children under 14). Along the shore, resort-like Coco de Mer has 40 tastefully refurbished rooms, a gym and a lovely saltwater pool out over the water.

The beach is average – it's shallow and tides can cause a build-up of seaweed between May and October – but you can cool off in the other pool in the shape of a *coco fesse*. Friendly staff are another highlight. All in all, a great recommendation for unpretentious and low-key luxury.

Baie Ste Anne &
Pointe Cabris

Le Port Guest House GUESTHOUSE €
(Map p300; ☑4232262; www.leportguesthouse seychelles.com; Baie Ste Anne; d/q from €80/125; ⊛) Not far from the jetty, this friendly guesthouse has three comfortable, fuss-free rooms,

two of which enjoy partial sea views. The area doesn't scream 'vacation' but Anse Volbert (p298) is easy to reach by bus. Good value.

Iles des Palmes
RESORT €€

(Map p300; ☏2711051; www.ilesdespalmes.com; d/q bungalows Rs180/275; ❄☀🌐🏊) On a quiet stretch of road that branches off towards Anse La Blague from the East Coast road between Anse Volbert and Baie Ste Anne, Iles des Palmes has large, wood-furnished bungalows right by the water. The beach is nothing special, but the kayaking is good here – and ask about exploring the neighbouring forest on foot.

★Château de Feuilles
LUXURY HOTEL €€€

(Map p300; ☏4290000; www.chateaudefeuilles. com; Pointe Cabris; d incl breakfast €499-895; P❄☀🌐🏊) Paradise awaits in this bijou hideaway on a beautiful headland near Baie Ste Anne. Nine luxurious, stone-walled villas are ingeniously deployed over several acres of tropical gardens. A serene symphony of earth tones and natural textures, elegant furnishings, sensational views, high-class amenities (including complimentary car), an uberromantic poolside restaurant and a hilltop Jacuzzi – every detail is spot on. Three-night minimum.

Colibri Guest House
BUNGALOW €€€

(Map p300; ☏4294200; www.colibrihotel-praslin. com; Pointe Cabris; d/apt incl breakfast from €166/199; P❄☀🌐🏊) A good deal close to Baie Ste Anne. Features a clutch of A-framed bungalows and villas on a verdant hillside with glorious views over La Digue. The bungalows are slightly hipper than the no-frills Chalets Côté Mer, a sister property next door. Aim for the Colibri, Magpie, Fairytern, Katiti or Kato, which are the best laid out. The cheaper units are fan-cooled. Minimum three nights.

🛏 Anse Volbert Area

Les Lauriers
BUNGALOW €€

(Map p300; ☏4232241; www.laurier-seychelles. com; Anse Volbert; s/d/f incl breakfast from €100/130/190; P❄☀🌐) A pleasant oasis, despite the lack of sea views and the odd landscaping of the compound. Run by friendly Edwin and Sybille, it features six uncomplicated and smallish, neat rooms as well as eight spacious bungalows with more being built when we last visited. It's well worth opting for half board (from €175 for two), given the attached high-quality restaurant.

Rosemary's Guest House
GUESTHOUSE €€

(Map p300; ☏4232176; Anse Volbert; r incl breakfast from €125; ❄☀🌐) Relaxed and friendly, this homey place features two types of rooms. The four fan-cooled rooms in the two older buildings feel a bit tired but are tidy, while the four with air-con occupy a modern building overlooking the beach. Though the property feels a tad compact, the location is ace. Herbert is a fabulous host.

★Le Duc de Praslin
HOTEL €€€

(Map p300; ☏4232252; www.leduc-seychelles. com; Anse Volbert; s/d incl breakfast from €255/330; P❄☀🌐🏊) This little island of subdued glamour, a *coco fesse*'s throw from the beach, is one of the most appealing options on Praslin. The generously sized, sensitively furnished rooms have all mod cons and orbit around an alluring pool and a nicely laid-out tropical garden. Another plus is the excellent Café des Arts (p305). If only the rooms had ocean views.

★Acajou Beach Resort
RESORT €€€

(Map p300; ☏4385300; www.acajouseychelles. com; Côte D'Or; s/d from €337/392; P❄@🌐🏊) 🌿 Beautiful rooms decked out in wood and white linen and set in a lush tropical garden are the highlights of this excellent resort close to Anse Volbert. It all fronts onto a gorgeous beach, plus there's a good spa and three restaurants. Half the resort's electricity needs come from solar power and it has a range of eco initiatives.

Les Villas D'Or
VILLA €€€

(Map p300; ☏4232777; www.lesvillasdorsey-chelles.com; Côte D'Or; d/q from €308/605; P❄@🌐🏊) Beautifully appointed, self-catering villas separated from the sea only by a lush garden strewn with palms are the hallmarks of this excellent property. There are 10 villas, two of which are suitable for families. It's close to Anse Volbert.

🛏 Anse Possession Area

Chalets Anse Possession
APARTMENT €

(Map p300; ☏4232180; chesca2207@hotmail.com; Anse Possession; d/q incl breakfast from €68/120; P❄☀) Four two-bedroom villas are set in lush greenery off the coast road. Although not the height of luxury, they're clean, comfy, roomy and serviceable – perfect for the traveller who's not fussy. Meals (from €15) can be served on request. The owners can pick you up at the jetty. Excellent value.

Marine Park Cottage　　BUNGALOW €€
(Map p300; ☑ 2511174; Anse Possession; bungalow
€90-200; ❋ 🕾) Free-standing stone bungalows just across the road from the beach –
it's a simple, time-honoured recipe for a
memorable Praslin stay. The stone walls add
character to an otherwise simple package,
but the bungalows are excellent value for the
price and the location is brilliant. The beach
is not Praslin's best.

La Domaine de La Reserve　　HOTEL €€€
(Map p300; ☑ 4298000; www.domainedelareser
ve.sc/en; Anse Petit Cour; r incl breakfast €374;
❋ 🕾 ≋) Surrounding the pretty beach of
Anse Petite Cour and with views of Curieuse
Island, La Domaine is a fine choice, at once
secluded and handy for anything on the east
coast – including Anse Lazio. Rooms can be
a little stark, but they're supremely comfortable. There are two restaurants on site.

Anse Lazio Area

Maison du Soleil　　VILLA €
(Map p300; ☑ 2508230; jeanlouis@seychelles.
net; Zimbabwe; d €60-95) Almost too good to
be true. A location scout's dream, this self-
catering villa perched on a hilltop offers
million-dollar views of Curieuse and Praslin's northern coastline. There's a second
villa further down the hill. OK, both are very
modestly furnished, there's no air-con (and
no wi-fi) and you need wheels to stay here,
but those are the only gripes.

Jardin Marron　　APARTMENT €€
(Map p300; ☑ 2740710; jardinmarron@gmail.com;
Anse Boudin; apt from €115; ❋ 🕾) These self-
catering apartments get rave reviews from
travellers and a fair proportion of repeat
visitors, and we can understand why. The
rooms are bright and comfortable with a mix
of modern style and dated wood furnishings.
But they're kept clean, the views from some
are brilliant, and service is above average.

★ Raffles Praslin　　RESORT €€€
(Map p300; ☑ 4296000; www.raffles.com/pras
lin; Anse Takamaka; d incl breakfast from €890;
🅿 ❋ @ 🕾 ≋) Luxurious villas, each with its
own private plunge pool and many with uninterrupted views of paradise, make this one
of the premier properties on Praslin. You can
count on a sublime two-tiered infinity pool,
seven excellent restaurants, a luxury spa and
great service. The beach here is excellent,
but you're close to Anse Lazio.

**Le Chevalier
Bay Guesthouse**　　GUESTHOUSE €€€
(Map p300; ☑ 4232322; www.lechevalierbay.com;
Anse Lazio; d/f incl breakfast from €175/245; 🅿 ❋)
Imagine staying within a stone's throw of
one of the world's most beautiful beaches.
Just through the trees from Anse Lazio, the
rooms here are simple and a bit sterile, but
the location is fantastic. Alas, no sea views
because of the foliage of *takamaka* trees.

Eating

Since most people eat in their hotels or
guesthouses, there are relatively few independent restaurants on Praslin, although
there are still some good choices. Most hotels have restaurants that are open to all
comers (by reservation).

Grand Anse & Anse Kerlan

Vero's Butchery　　FOOD TRUCK €
(Map p300; ☑ 2590922; Anse Kerlan; mains Rs 40-
85; ⊙ 8.30am-5pm Mon-Sat, 8am-11pm Sun) Simple but appealing. This roadside food truck
serves up lamb curry, stir-fried fish fillet or
roasted spare ribs as well as a handful of fast-
food staples such as hamburgers and chips
and the like. It's all cooked while you wait.

**Breeze Garden &
The Fish Restaurant**　　INTERNATIONAL €€
(Map p300; ☑ 4237000; Grand Anse; mains Rs
200-430; ⊙ 1-9.30pm) In a verdant property near the west coast's main **church** (Map
p300), Breeze Garden has agreeably green
surroundings and offers salads, curries, pasta dishes and pizzas; try the swordfish kebab
or Creole octopus curry. Takeaway is also
available and there's a less appealing cafe.

Capricorn　　SEAFOOD €€
(Map p300; ☑ 4233224; Anse Kerlan; mains Rs
290-840; ⊙ 12.30-3pm & 6-9.30pm Mon-Sat) At
Anse Kerlan, Capricorn is the good on-site
restaurant at Islander (p301). It's famous for
its 'octopus Patrick-style' (octopus in a saffron sauce), roasted octopus or steamed crab
with ginger and spices, as well as homemade
desserts.

★ Restaurant Paradisier　　INTERNATIONAL €€€
(Map p300; ☑ 4237537; Grand Anse; pizza from
Rs 190, mains Rs 380-450; ⊙ noon-3pm & 6-9pm)
Considered one of the best restaurants in
Grand Anse, this place concocts Creole classics, copious sandwiches and tasty pizzas
that you can enjoy in an atmospheric garden
terrace complete with wrought-iron furnishings. Dishes are classy, from linguini with

CURIEUSE ISLAND

Curieuse Island is a granite island 1.5km off Praslin's north coast. A leper colony from 1833 until 1965, Curieuse is today used as a breeding centre for giant Aldabra tortoises. The wardens at the **Giant Tortoise Farm** (Curieuse Island; ⊙ hours vary) show visitors around the pens, after which you're free to explore the rest of the island. Nearby **Baie Laraie** is a fantastic place for swimming and snorkelling. From Baie Laraie, a path leads to **Anse St José**, where you can visit the **Doctor's House** (Anse José, Curieuse Island; ⊙ variable) `FREE`; it contains a small historical museum. If you fancy a dip after your picnic, the beach is lovely: a stretch of pristine pale golden sand fringed with lofty palm trees and framed by massive granite boulders.

Most visitors to Curieuse Island arrive on an organised tour, usually in combination with **Cousin Island** and **St Pierre Islet**. Tours are arranged through Praslin's hotels or any tour operator. Day trips cost around €130/65 for an adult/child including lunch, landing fees and the marine-park entry fee. The alternative is to charter your own boat from Anse Volbert (p298). Sagittarius Taxi Boat (p299), on the beach beside the Paradise Sun Hotel, charges €40 for Curieuse, including fees; Curieuse with St Pierre costs €50. You'll also find taxi boats at Anse Possession, or you could contact Edwin at Les Lauriers (p303), whose tours get rave reviews from travellers.

clams to grilled Charlois striploin or French black mussels in white wine. If only it had beach frontage, life would be perfect.

Baie Ste Anne & Pointe Cabris

ISPC Supermarket SUPERMARKET €
(Map p300; Baie Ste Anne; ⊙ 9am-6pm Mon-Fri, to 1pm Sat) As much a deli as a small supermarket, this fab place sells wines and cheeses alongside generally high-quality groceries. Perfect for a Praslin picnic.

Cool Licks CREOLE €
(Map p300; Baie Ste Anne; mains Rs 60-100; ⊙ 10am-10pm Tue-Sun) This popular roadside eatery is a terrific place for simple Creole street food or even takeaways. Barbecue spare ribs, fish and sausage and more dominate the menu but there are also prawn sticks, burgers and fresh juices. The shaded tables have a loyal following around lunchtime so grab one if you can.

La Buse Restaurant SEAFOOD €€
(Iles des Palmes; Map p300; ☑ 2711051; mains Rs 285-750; ⊙ noon-3pm & 6-9pm) In a pretty spot along a coast road that runs out to Anse La Blague (p298), this pool- and beach-side restaurant serves good steaks, whole grouper and jambalaya, a New Orleans dish that combines seafood with meat and local spices.

★**Les Rochers** SEAFOOD €€€
(Map p300; ☑ 2514034, 4233803; Anse St Sauveur; mains Rs 450-1150; ⊙ 12.30-3.30pm & 6-9.30pm Tue-Sat) The approach to seafood is all about

freshness and interfering as little as possible with the ingredients: just the way we like it. A few Creole inflections liven things up a little, but we really like the grilled prawns or fish. And somehow it all tastes better at the outdoor tables on the rocks overlooking the beach and beyond.

Anse Volbert Area

Gelateria de Luca ICE CREAM, PIZZERIA €€
(Map p300; ☑ 4232706; Anse Volbert; lunch specials & pizza from Rs 150, mains Rs 150-450, ice cream 1/2 scoops Rs 20/40; ⊙ 9am-9.30pm) Praslin's prime ice-cream parlour does some interesting flavours such as crème caramel, as well as a mean *coppa tropicale;* takeaway scoop sizes could be larger. It also whips up pasta, pizza and various snacks at lunchtime, while dinner is a more formal affair, with dishes such as pan-roasted chicken with cinnamon, pork spare ribs and crab curry.

Village du Pecheur SEAFOOD €€
(Map p300; ☑ 2611111; www.thesunsethotelgroup. com; Anse Volbert; sandwiches from Rs 105, mains Rs 180-395; ⊙ 11am-9pm) Classy decor, a sandy floor that segues effortlessly onto lovely Anse Volbert (p298), and dishes such as seafood curry flavoured with cinnamon leaf and served with Creole chutney and rice, or octopus curry with coconut milk, make this an excellent choice for those keen to eat by the sea.

★**Café des Arts** INTERNATIONAL €€€
(Map p300; ☑ 4232170; Anse Volbert; lunch mains from Rs 280, dinner mains Rs 440-650;

FINDING THE BLUE PIGEON

Found only in the Seychelles, the Seychelles Blue Pigeon is most commonly seen on Praslin. We've had luck in finding it in the Vallée de Mai (p298), but it's also easy to spot perched on the power lines along the coast road on the west side of the island between Les Rochers and the road that comes down to the coast from Vallée de Mai.

⊘noon-2.30pm & 6-9.30pm Tue-Sun) Praslin's most stylish restaurant is in the Le Duc de Praslin hotel. Flickering candles, colourful paintings, swaying palms, a breezy terrace and the sound of waves washing the beach will rekindle even the faintest romantic flame. The food is refined; flavourful Seychellois favourites are whipped into eye-pleasing concoctions such as red-snapper fillet in passionfruit sauce or marinated chicken with tropical fruits. It's more casual at lunchtime, with wraps, sandwiches and pasta. There's also a reputable art gallery.

✖ Anse Lazio Area

★ PK's @ Pasquière
& Gastropub   INTERNATIONAL €€
(Map p300; ☑4236242; Anse Boudin; mains Rs 200-525; ⊘11am-8.30pm Mon-Sat) You can see this place from the coastal road thanks to its distinctive position in a secluded hillside property with pretty coastal views. Tables are widely spaced and the menu has a lightness of touch missing from many of its peers. The meat or seafood dishes are all heartily recommended, but we especially like the seafood platter. Great value.

Bonbon Plume   SEAFOOD €€€
(Map p300; ☑4232136; Anse Lazio; mains Rs 285-1150; ⊘noon-3.30pm) Tourist trap or front-row seat for paradise? Both perhaps. With such a location – the palm-thatched canopy is right on the beach at gorgeous Anse Lazio – tables are in high demand: ring ahead if you want your feet in the sand. Try the sautéed crab with garlic, the fabulous grilled prawns or the grilled catch of the day.

Bigger premises were being built when we visited, but we hope it doesn't lose that end-of-the-road, feet-in-the-sand feel.

Le Chevalier   INTERNATIONAL €€€
(Map p300; ☑4232322; www.lechevalierbay.com; Anse Lazio; mains Rs 350-550; ⊘8am-3.30pm &

7-10pm) OK, Le Chevalier is not right on the beach, but the setting is appealing nonetheless and you're *very* close to glorious Anse Lazio. The menu offers lots of variety from the octopus curry or garlic calamari to lighter salads; the lobster lunch for two (Rs 1500) is outstanding.

☕ Drinking & Nightlife

Chill Out Tapas Lounge Bar   BAR
(Map p300; ☑4294800; 1st fl, Cafe des Arts, Anse Volbert; ⊘6pm-1am Tue-Thu, to 2am Fri & Sat, 1-8pm Sun) Upstairs from Cafe des Arts, this supercool beach-side spot is Praslin's (and perhaps even the Seychelles') trendiest bar. The resident DJ runs things on Wednesdays, Saturdays and chilled-out Sundays and the dress code is long pants for men (except on Sundays) and no flip-flops.

ℹ Information

You'll find several banks and bureaux de change in Grand Anse, Baie Ste Anne and Anse Volbert. All banks have ATMs and exchange facilities.

ℹ Getting There & Away

Praslin Airport (Map p300; ☑4284666; www.seychellesairports.travel; Grand Anse) is 3km north of Grand Anse and has more than a dozen daily flights to/from Mahé. The return fare for the 20-minute flight is about €132.

Regular ferry services connect Praslin with Mahé and La Digue. The port is in Baie Ste Anne.

BOAT

Cat Cocos (Map p300; www.cat-cocos-seychelles.com; Baie Ste Anne; ⊘ticket office 7am-5.30pm) has catamaran connections between Praslin and Mahé (adult/child one-way from €50/25, one hour, at least three daily) and La Digue (adult/child one-way from €14/7, 15 minutes, one to two daily).

For La Digue, Inter-Island Ferry Pty (p317) runs a catamaran between Praslin and La Digue (15 minutes, five to seven daily).

ℹ Getting Around

BICYCLE

You can hire bikes through your accommodation. Depending on where you're staying, rental might be free or cost Rs 150 per day.

BUS & TAXI

Praslin has a decent bus service (Rs 10) as well as the usual taxis. A taxi ride from the Baie Ste Anne jetty to Anse Volbert or Grand Anse will set you back Rs 300.

CAR

A car is a great way to see the island. There are many local car-hire companies, but no international companies – make the arrangements through your hotel or guesthouse. Expect to pay about €50 per day for the smallest car. Cars can be delivered to your hotel, the airport or the jetty.

SHUTTLES TO ANSE LAZIO

Given that the beach at Grand Anse is only so-so, some accommodation options in the area offer their guests a free daily shuttle to/from Anse Lazio (p298) several times per week – ask before you go to the expense of hiring a car.

LA DIGUE

A marvel. A simple word but one that conveys so many aspects of the Seychelles' third-most inhabited island. The coastline, one bewitching bay after another, is studded with heart-palpitatingly gorgeous beaches. The hilly interior is cloaked with tangled jungle, tall trees and wild hiking trails. Yet, miraculously, despite being just a 15-minute ferry journey from Praslin, the vast majority of it is untouched by development. You don't have to look further than Anse Marron – it's one of the planet's most beautiful beaches but accessible by foot only. And even where infrastructure exists – around the sleepy tropical port in La Passe and La Réunion – everything is so laid-back that visiting feels like a step back in time. One of the most charming elements is that the preferred method of transport for locals (and visitors alike) is the old-fashioned bicycle, with trucks, taxis and electric carts left to make guest appearances.

☉ Sights

★ Anse Marron   BEACH

(Map p309) Perhaps the most stunning natural pool and beach combo on the planet, Anse Marron sits nestled behind Gaudíesque granite boulders at the remote southern tip of La Digue. The tiny inlet is truly a hidden morsel of tranquillity, with its sheltered, crystal-clear waters providing a surreal location for a swim or snorkel. The sand on this fantastically wild beach is blindingly white, and the fact that it's a difficult journey to reach by foot only adds to its allure.

★ Anse Source d'Argent   BEACH

(Map p309; ☉6am-6.30pm) Famed for being one of the most photographed beaches on the planet, Anse Source d'Argent is a sight to behold. Its dazzling white sands are lapped by shallow emerald waters, backed by some of La Digue's most beautiful granite boulders and shaded by craning coconut palms.

Unless you want to wade through watery depths, you'll need to pass through the old L'Union Estate coconut plantation to access the beach, which means paying Rs115 (valid for a day).

The beach is justifiably popular, so the sands can get crowded with beach goers, particularly as the beach area shrinks at hide tide. Coming in the early morning and returning in the late afternoon is a great way to avoid many of the island's day visitors (keep your entrance ticket). As the sun starts to descend you can walk around or curl up under the shade of the trees and feel like you have this uninhabited piece of paradise all to yourself.

During the day a couple of shacks sell fruit and refreshments, and there are transparent kayaks for rent.

★ Nid d'Aigle   VIEWPOINT

(Eagle's Nest; Map p309) Nid d'Aigle, the highest point on La Digue (333m), commands sensational views out over the island, as well as out to Mahé, Praslin, Curieuse, Félicité, Grande Soeur, Petite Soeur and even Frégate. It's an effort to hike here, but the view is worth every step.

Anse Cocos   BEACH

(Map p309) This wonderfully scenic beach of salt-white sand and turquoise water curves gracefully between distant granitic outcrops. What sets it apart from others on this stretch of coast is the beachfront shade offered by casuarina trees and craning palms. It's a fantastic place to flop, and given the effort required to hike here, it's also one of the quietest options. Rip currents are an issue for swimming, but the northern tip of the beach has some protected pools for a dip.

Grand Anse   BEACH

(Map p309) On the southeast coast is La Digue's longest beach, Grand Anse. It's a stunning place to sun yourself, and while busier than nearby Petite Anse and Anse Cocos (both accessed by foot only), it sees fewer visitors than Anse Source d'Argent simply because it's further from La Passe. Two caveats: swimming can be dangerous because of the strong offshore currents during the southeast monsoon, from April to October; and apart from a massive casuarina tree, there's not much shade.

La Digue

Petite Anse   BEACH

(Map p309) This dramatic crescent of bleached white sand sits between Grande Anse and Anse Cocos on La Digue's southeast coast. Although less than a 300m walk (along a well-defined trail) from the northern end of Grande Anse, Petite Anse receives a fraction of the sunbathers. Its only downsides are the lack of shade (some vendors do set up palm frond shelters, however) and the strong riptides that make it dangerous for swimming.

Anse Sévère   BEACH

(Map p309) Easily accessible on the northern outskirts of La Passe, Anse Sévère is a great beach to spend a day on. Set alluringly behind stands of *takamaka* trees, its jade waters are kid-friendly (due to the barrier reef) and there is some good snorkelling to boot. Throw in a shack for some tasty lunch and several fresh juice stalls and you're laughing. Don't leave before you've soaked up the sunset.

**L'Union Estate &
Copra Factory**   HISTORIC SITE

(Map p309; L'Union; Rs 115; ☉6am-6.30pm) At one time, the main industry on La Digue was coconut farming, centred on L'Union Estate coconut plantation south of La Passe. These days L'Union Estate is run as an informal 'theme park', which harbours the Old Plantation House, vanilla plantations, a colonial-era graveyard, a boatyard and the obligatory pen of giant tortoises. You'll need to pass through the property to get to Anse Source d'Argent.

Anse Patates   BEACH

(Map p309) Petite, picture perfect and ideal for a splash or snorkel, this boulder-framed beach sits tucked into the northern tip of the island. As it's within sight of camera-toting cyclists and pedestrians on the road above, Anse Patates isn't the ideal spot for a peaceful afternoon of lounging.

Notre Dame de L'Assomption   CHURCH

(Map p310; La Réunion) With its striking yellow facade and white trim, this unmissable Catholic church is well worth a gander, particularly on Sunday mornings when it is bursting at the seams with a devout congregation. The sound of the rousing hymns radiates beyond its stone walls.

Veuve Reserve   WILDLIFE RESERVE

(Map p310; ☎2783114; La Réunion; adult/child SR150/free; ☉information centre 8am-4pm Mon-Fri) La Digue is one of the last refuges of the black paradise flycatcher, which locals call the *veuve* (widow). This small forest reserve, which has been set aside to protect its natural habitat, is thought to now shelter over a dozen pairs (after 11 males and nine females were translocated to Curieuse in late 2018). The male has long black tail feathers. Other species include terrapins, fruit bats and moorhens. There are several walking trails punctuated with interpretive panels about flora. There's also a small information centre.

🏃 Activities

Boat Excursions

Taking a boat excursion to nearby **Île Cocos**, **Félicité** and **Grande Soeur** will be one of the main highlights of your visit to the Seychelles and it's well worth the expense. Full-day tours typically stop to snorkel off Félicité, Grande Soeur and Petite Soeur, with some also including Île Cocos.

La Digue

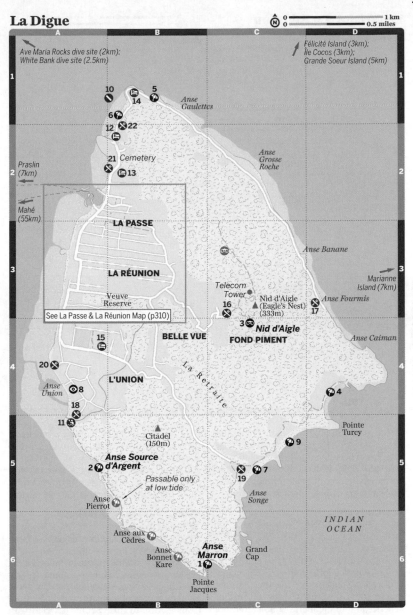

0 —— 1 km
0 —— 0.5 miles

Ave Maria Rocks dive site (2km);
White Bank dive site (2.5km)

Félicité Island (3km);
Île Cocos (3km);
Grande Soeur Island (5km)

Anse Gaulettes

Praslin (7km)

Mahé (55km)

Anse Grosse Roche

LA PASSE

LA RÉUNION

Veuve Reserve

See La Passe & La Réunion Map (p310)

Anse Banane

Marianne Island (7km)

Telecom Tower

Nid d'Aigle (Eagle's Nest) (333m)

Anse Fourmis

BELLE VUE

Nid d'Aigle
FOND PIMENT

Anse Caiman

L'UNION

Anse Union

La Retraite

Pointe Turcy

Citadel (150m)

Anse Source d'Argent

Passable only at low tide

Anse Pierrot

Anse Songe

INDIAN OCEAN

Anse aux Cèdres

Anse Bonnet Kare

Anse Marron

Grand Cap

Pointe Jacques

Cemetery

SEYCHELLES LA DIGUE

Mason's Travel   CRUISE
(Map p310; ☑ 4234227; www.masonstravel.
com; La Passe; half-/full-day cruise per person Rs
1000/2100; ☺ 8am-4.30pm Mon-Fri, to noon Sat)
Half-day boat excursions depart daily with
swimming and snorkelling around the islands of Félicité and Grande Soeur. Less frequent full-day options are also possible.

Diving & Snorkelling
La Digue has excellent access to a range of
fantastic dive sites (p37), including the iconic
White Bank. Snorkelling is also top-notch.

La Passe & La Réunion

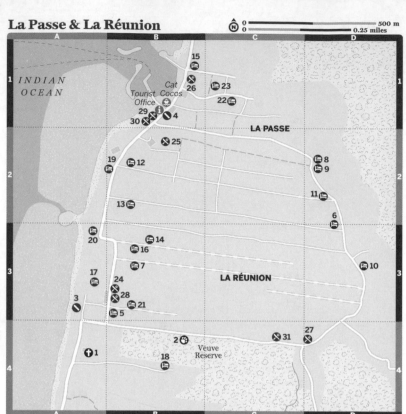

INDIAN OCEAN

LA PASSE

LA RÉUNION

Veuve Reserve

Sweet spots around the island include Anse Sévère and Anse Patates. Île Cocos and Félicité seem to be tailored to the expectations of avid snorkellers, with glassy turquoise waters and a smattering of healthy coral gardens. All boat tours include snorkelling stops.

Azzurra Pro Dive
DIVING

(Map p310; ☑ 2605500; www.ladigue.sc/dive-center.html; La Réunion; tank dives from €72; ☉ 8am-4pm) This PADI-certified dive centre organises a variety of dive trips and certification courses. Morning trips (€132) include two separate tank dives, while the afternoon option (€72) involves a single dive. Snorkellers can join the morning and afternoon excursions for €55 and €35 respectively (plus €14 for equipment rental). Based at La Digue Island Lodge (p314).

Trek Divers
DIVING

(Map p310; ☑ 2513066; www.trekdivers.com; La Passe; ☉ by reservation) This small dive outfit is run by Christophe Condé, who has plen-

ty of experience. Daily half-day trips (€120) include two dives at different sites, while weekly full-day excursions for snorkellers and divers cost €100, plus €35 per tank-dive (up to three). Courses from 'Discover Scuba' (€90) to PADI Divemaster (€750) are offered.

Hiking, Surfing & Kayaking

★ Sunny Trail Guide
ADVENTURE

(☑ 2525357; www.sunnytrailguide.net; La Passe; ☉ by reservation) Run by Robert Agnes, this outfit offers a wide range of hikes for all levels, as well as kayak tours and surfing lessons. Costs vary depending on the activity and the size of the party, but a hike from Grande Anse to Anse Source d'Argent with lunch at Anse Marron is €40 per person. Transfers, fruits and snacks are included.

★ Crystal Water Kayaks
KAYAKING

(Map p309; ☑ 2747457; www.facebook.com/crystal waterkayaks; per person €35) It's one thing to kayak around La Digue; it's totally another to do so in a transparent kayak that reveals the

La Passe & La Réunion

aquatic treasures that lurk beneath. Various 2.5-hour guided tours take in Anse Source d'Argent and Anse Pierrot or Anse Sévère and Anse Patates. Others visit Félicité and Île Cocos. Guests can also hire the kayaks (or SUPs) for independent paddling (Rs 300 per hour).

Paradise Tours HIKING, KAYAKING
(☑2580533; henrybibi1990@hotmail.com; per person from €40; ☉ by reservation) Henry Bibi is very knowledgeable about local flora and fauna and runs informative day walks with snacks and transport included. Trips include Anse Marron (taking in Grande Anse and Anse Source d'Argent), Anse Cocos and ruins on the Nid d'Aigle ridge. He also runs kayak tours.

⌂ Sleeping

Noticeably devoid of large resorts, La Digue is instead the realm of self-catering apartments, quiet villas and family guesthouses, all of which are located in or around La Passe and La Réunion. Most are in the midrange bracket. Discounts are usually offered for longer stays, but book ahead as many lodgings are already full months in advance. Credit cards may not be accepted by some smaller places; check when booking.

★ **Pension Michel** BUNGALOW €€
(Map p310; ☑4234003; www.pensionmichel.sc; La Réunion; s/d/tr incl breakfast €90/105/145; ❋☎) Loungers, hammocks and other areas of quiet respite are just a few of the treats found in this pension's lovely garden. And set

between the flowers, shrubs and trees are some beautiful little white bungalows, with peaceful verandas and vibrant trimmings of yellow and green. Rooms are flooded with light, as well as being comfy and clean.

★ **Maison Charme de L'Île** APARTMENT €€
(Map p309; ☑2512542; maisoncharmedelile@gmail.com; L'Union; d €140; ❋☎❄) Maison Charme de L'île offers home-style comfort, friendly staff and a super-quiet location for an affordable price. A two-minute bike ride from the waterfront, the four roomy, light-drenched, lovingly kept apartments have been styled with flair (even the kitchens), and there's a tiny corner pool to beat the heat. Each unit has a front veranda and small backyard.

Cabanes des Anges APARTMENT €€
(Map p310; ☑4234112; www.cabanesdesanges.sc; La Réunion; s/d/tr incl breakfast €135/165/225, apt €165-205; ❋☎❄) This peaceful place is set around a shapely pool and deck area. There are three rooms (two doubles and a triple), as well as six one-bedroom apartments that feature open-plan kitchens with bar seats, satellite TVs and large verandas. Everything has been designed with a cool contemporary crispness. Bedrooms are big and flooded with light, with tiled floors and shiny-clean bathrooms.

Bel Amie Self Catering GUESTHOUSE €€
(Map p310; ☑4234749, 2572207; www.belleamieselfcatering.com; La Réunion; d €80-100; ❋☎) The five colourful rooms in its charming two-storey

HIKING ON LA DIGUE

Exploring La Digue's recesses by foot will enable you to experience the best of what this little island has to offer. Tracks are not always well defined and are thus difficult to find and to follow; it's advisable to go with a guide – Sunny Trail Guide (p310), Paradise Tours (p311) and **Coco Trail** (☎2535447; www.cocotrailguide.com; per person €35-40; ⏲by reservation) are reliable options.

Nid d'Aigle

Tackling Nid d'Aigle (p307), the highest point on La Digue (333m), is more of a challenge than ever. With the central section of the island-topping ridge heavily overgrown, it means making a much steeper ascent. From the steps leading up to the doorway of Bellevue (p315) restaurant, you'll see a trail off to the right signposted as 'To the Mountain'. Within a minute or two there is an inconspicuous fork in the path (so keep your eyes peeled at the treeline); the less trodden one to the right leads up to Nid d'Aigle. While it's only 300m to the summit, it climbs more than 100m in elevation over this distance, some of it over large rocks, some up slippery paths. When you reach an intersection on the ridge turn right and Nid d'Aigle (no sign) is less than a minute away. Stand on the rocks and soak up your rewards.

If you'd like a more gentle climb (with imperceptibly less lofty views), take the option to the left at the fork above Bellevue. This slightly longer route also leads to a ridge-top path, from where you'll need to turn left. From there you'll soon see the telecom tower, and further on you'll find some ruins of old buildings and some large sculpted boulders that make ideal viewpoints. This path continues down to La Passe, but to continue on this way requires a guide as it is heavily overgrown.

Grand Anse to Anse Cocos

From Loutier Coco (p315) restaurant, it's an easy 400m walk to Petite Anse (p308) – simply stroll along Grand Anse (p307) and then up and over the ridge on the fairly well-defined path. Once at Petite Anse, the path to Anse Cocos (p307) starts immediately and moves inland from behind the juice stands at the southern end of the beach. From there it's another 900m to the wonders of Anse Cocos.

Grand Anse to Anse Marron (& on to Anse Source d'Argent)

From Anse Source d'Argent, a memorable adventure consists of climbing up the granite hills that loom above the southwest coast before getting down to **Anse Pierrot**, from where you can continue along the shore to **Anse aux Cèdres** and **Anse Bonnet Kare** (and back to Anse Source d'Argent along the shore). The beauty of these stunning swathes of sand lies in the fact that they're totally secluded and there's no road here. It's an arduous climb to reach the top of the granite hills but the panoramic views will be etched in your memory forever. It's a half-day excursion. It's also possible to continue as far as Anse Marron and up to Grand Anse.

chalet are a bargain, particularly the two huge, vaulted-ceiling options upstairs, both of which share a lovely balcony. There is a communal kitchen to help keep costs down further. Families can link various rooms together.

Kot Babi Guesthouse GUESTHOUSE **€€**
(Map p310; ☎4234747, 2514338; www.kotbabi.sc; La Passe; d/q €85/105, 1/3-bed apt €110/255; ❄📶) In the heart of La Passe, but set back off the main drag, Kot Babi offers a few rooms in its traditional mansion house, as well as a handful of self-catering cottages in its garden. Families are well catered to, with both a quad family room and separate family chalet (€130, plus €25 per child).

Kaz Digwa Self Catering APARTMENT **€€**
(Map p310; ☎2575457, 2513684; kazdigwa@gmail.com; La Réunion; d/q €110/160; ❄📶) Serviceable and cosy are the watchwords at this welcoming abode that comprises two wooden chalet-like bungalows with shady wraparound verandas. Set in a beautifully manicured garden, complete with a hammock between two palms, the chalets are well appointed, relaxing and spacious – the larger one has two bedrooms – and the kitchens are brilliantly equipped. If you're too lazy to cook, meals are possible. Children below the age of six are free, while those up to 10 are charged just €10 per night. Additional adults or older kids are charged €25.

Domaine Les Rochers APARTMENT €€
(Map p310; ☑4235334; www.domainelesrochers. com; La Réunion; d €135-190; ✴ 🛜) Found down a lovely palm-lined road on the edge of La Réunion and La Passe, this verdant place offers four large, well-thought-out apartments with open-plan bedroom-sitting-rooms, immaculate en suites and well-equipped kitchens. There are also two separate rooms available in Villa Palmier, which share a kitchen (families can combine them for €240), and a smaller self-catering bungalow.

Veronic Guesthouse APARTMENT €€
(Map p310; ☑4234743, 2592463; seyladigue@ya hoo.com; La Passe; d/q €90/180; ✴ 🛜) A good option for budget-conscious travellers, the cute, comfy and clean bungalows here feature simple kitchens, shared laundry facilities, TVs and homely furnishings. There is a larger family suite, with two bedrooms (both with en suites) and an open-plan kitchen.

Cocotier du Rocher APARTMENT €€
(Map p310; ☑2514889, 4234489; www.cocotier durocher.com; La Réunion; d €150-185; ✴ 🛜) Although prettily decorated with local stone, wood and the odd sea shell, the real charm of this place is how the four bungalows (eight rooms in total) are embedded in blooming tropical gardens. Relax on your roomy veranda, complete with loungers and dining table, in privacy. Rooms are fully equipped with kitchens and kept scrupulously clean. Most rooms (bar Koko Zerm and Koko Sek) have an additional single bed, which can accommodate a child. Breakfast is available upon request.

Bois d'Amour APARTMENT €€
(Map p310; ☑2529290, 4234490; www.boisd amour.de; La Réunion; d/q €110/160; 🛜) Privacy is put on a premium at Bois d'Amour, with just three beautifully designed and constructed wooden chalets (six rooms in total) spread out in its Eden-like garden of tropical flowers and exotic fruit trees. They're amply sized, equipped with kitchens, cleaned daily and have fans instead of air-con. For families, the two-bedroom/-bathroom Kokover chalet is perfect. Add an extra €12 per person for breakfast.

La Diguoise B&B €€
(Map p310; ☑4234713, 2510332; www.diguoise. com; La Passe; d incl breakfast €125-220; ✴ 🛜 🏊) An expansive, lush garden and lovely pool are the highlights of this well-run venture. The rooms in the two main houses are scru-pulously clean and a healthy size. There are also two smaller, less exciting rooms in a low-rise building at the back of the garden. Several rooms can accommodate families (€50 extra per child aged two to 12).

Calou Guest House GUESTHOUSE €€
(Map p310; ☑4234083, 2781327; www.calouguest house.com; La Passe; d incl breakfast €105; ✴ 🛜 🏊) This well-established venture continues to go from strength to strength, adding two new rooms with an extra bed for kids, and updating the other four doubles with hard-wood floors, raised ceilings, large closets and bathrooms featuring design touches such as inlaid stone surrounds. There's also a three-bedroom family house (€50 per person) at the top of the rambling property.

There's a quirky covered pool up the steps from the open-air bar, though guests can also use the more attractive pool next door at Chalets de Palma. A double with half board is an attractive option for €120.

Chalets de Palma GUESTHOUSE €€
(Map p310; ☑4234083; www.chaletsdepalma.com; La Réunion; d incl breakfast €135-140; ✴ 🛜 🏊) Beneath the bougainvillea-draped arch welcoming you at Chalets de Palma is a delightful little pool and eight simple rooms found in four red-roofed bungalows. All rooms are clean and well organised (satellite TV, air-con, a private terrace, daily cleaning). The larger 'superior' options feature sliding glass doors and can accommodate an additional adult or child.

L'Océan Hotel HOTEL €€
(Map p309; ☑2594303; www.hotellocean.sc; Anse Patates; d incl breakfast €140; ✴ 🛜) We could talk about the local artwork on the walls, or about how the spacious rooms are squeaky clean (albeit a bit dated), but all you'll care about is the staggering ocean views. All eight rooms (and their private balconies) proffer similar vistas, though those from the two top rooms (7 and 8) are the best.

Fleur de Lys BUNGALOW €€
(Map p310; ☑4234459; www.fleurdelysseychelles. com; La Passe; d €135; ✴ 🛜) A chilled, sleepy vibe permeates this group of eight Cre-ole-style bungalows and the grassy garden that connects them all. However, beneath the green tin roofs are vibrant, light-filled interiors, with wicker furniture, kitchenettes and spotless bathrooms. Breakfast is available for €12 per person.

★ Le Nautique

GUESTHOUSE €€€

(Map p310; ☑4234700; http://lenautique.sc/
ladigue; La Réunion; d incl breakfast €245-345;
❄ 🌐 ≋) Although this small boutique offering opened in 2018, owner Natasha's
family has longstanding roots on the island.
Together with her Australian husband Stu-
art, the pair have created a fantastic retreat
that feels both casual and luxurious. The
Creole-style cottages with gabled roofs and
shady verandahs have airy, nautical-themed
rooms that would sit comfortably on the
pages of *House & Garden* magazine.

★ Le Domaine de L'Orangeraie
Resort & Spa

HOTEL €€€

(Map p309; ☑4299999; www.orangeraie.sc; La
Passe; d incl breakfast from €400; ❄ 🌐 ≋) This
dramatic 63-suite resort climbs its way up
the tree-covered slope that overlooks the
harbour, with spacious, well-appointed villas nestled among giant granite boulders. Its
two restaurants, bar area and private pool
are all on the oceanfront, which is just a skip
across the road from reception. The spa, with
staggering views, sits at the top of the hill.

The Villa de Charme (double from €500)
and Villa de Charme Elégance (double
from €700) are truly stunning, each full of
warm woods, signature stone walls, vaulted
thatched ceilings, theatrical mosquito nets,
massive fabric prints and grand bathrooms.
However, the 20 'Garden Villa' suites and
eight Jardin Suite Residences – both featuring sprawling, contemporary interiors, complete with nightclub-esque lighting effects
and low ceilings – lack the same tropical
fairy-tale appeal.

★ Anse Sévère Beach Villas

APARTMENT €€€

(Map p309; ☑235009; severe@seychelles.sc;
Anse Sévère; d €230-250, q €300; ❄ 🌐) Across
the road from Anse Sévère (and one of the
island's sweetest juice stalls), these three villas host six self-catering apartments. Apart
from Number 6 in the original small villa,
the five new arrivals feature spacious open-
plan layouts with log-post beds, well-kitted
out kitchens and plenty of stone mosaics.
Numbers 4 and 5 have the best views and
the most private verandahs.

★ La Digue Holiday Villa

APARTMENT €€€

(Map p310; ☑2514047, 4235265; www.ladigueholi
dayvilla.com; La Réunion; d €185; ❄ 🌐 ≋) These
six stylish apartments nestled in a magnificently landscaped plot are decorated with
the design-conscious in mind: a cheerful

mix of wood and stone, sparkling kitchens,
quality fixtures, and a soothing yellow and
green palette. To top it off, there's a pool in
the flowering garden. Breakfast can be arranged for €10 per person. Anse Coco (room
1) is the most private.

Villa Charme De L'Île

APARTMENT €€€

(Map p310; ☑2512542; villacharmedelile@gmail.
com; La Passe; d €200; ❄ 🌐 ≋) The new sister
property to longstanding favourite Maison
Charme De L'Île, Villa features five spacious
self-catering apartments around a rather
lovely pool. The open-plan interiors are bright
and crisp, and everything from the bleached
wood furniture and artwork to the royal blue
and turquoise accents is ocean themed. The
modern bathrooms are lovely and large, and
feature freestanding soaker tubs.

Le Repaire

BOUTIQUE HOTEL €€€

(Map p310; ☑2550594, 4234332; www.lerepaire
seychelles.com; La Réunion; d incl breakfast €245-
300; ❄ 🌐 ≋) Design-savvy travellers will
enjoy the stylish furniture, boldly coloured
feature walls, soothing tones and vibrant
George Camille artwork in the spacious
rooms. Outside is a lovely garden, a couple
of petite pools and a spiffing seaside location
(albeit one that's no good for swimming).

It's worth paying the extra €30/55 for a
sea-view/beachfront superior room (Bwa De
Roz and Voloutye are our top picks). Some
rooms, especially the Bodanmyen, feel too
close to the on-site restaurant.

La Digue Island Lodge

RESORT €€€

(Map p310; ☑4292525; www.ladigue.sc; La Réunion; d incl half-board €275-480; ❄ 🌐 ≋) Set
along a beautiful section of Anse Réunion, this resort has a variety of revamped
A-frame chalets and rooms. The best budget
options are in the charming Yellow House, a
colonial mansion at the back of the carefully
manicured gardens. The most alluring are
the towering beach chalets, which stare out
to sea and feature ultramodern, semi-open
plan bathrooms of dark stone.

The garden A-frame chalets, like those on
the beach, have ladder-accessed mezzanine
levels that accommodate one child (free up to
the age of 12). The two-bedroom options in the
atmospheric plantation beach house are great
for larger families. Amenities are solid, with
two restaurants, two bars, a spa and pool. The
beach's shallow waters are handy for parents,
but not ideal for proper swimming.

Château St Cloud
HOTEL €€€

(Map p310; ☑4295400; www.chateaustcloud.sc; La Réunion; s/d incl breakfast from €150/€200; ✳☎☲) Both eclectic and peaceful, this long-standing favourite has three room categories squeezed into its green confines. There's also a cavernous restaurant and a lovely little pool surrounded by towering palms. Pick of the bunch are the superior rooms, which are dotted on a forest-clad hillside, while the four deluxe rooms, set in a former colonial building, are super-spacious and marry modern and Creole design influences.

✗ Eating

STC
SUPERMARKET

(Map p310; ☑4234024; La Réunion; ☻8.30am-6pm Mon-Fri, to 2pm Sat, to 1pm Sun) The best-stocked supermarket on the island. It sells almost everything self-caterers could want.

★ Rey & Josh Cafe Takeaway
CREOLE €

(Map p310; ☑2563601; La Réunion; mains Rs 60-70; ☻noon-8pm) The newest takeaway on the block and the best of the bunch according to many locals. Although the menu is limited, the seafood curries are a tasty bargain. There are a handful of outdoor picnic tables to dine at.

Mi Mum's Takeaway
CREOLE €

(Map p310; La Passe; mains Rs 50-80; ☻11.30am-3pm & 6-9pm Mon-Sat) Given it's still thriving despite the nightclub it's set beside having long since deceased says everything you need to know. Order a tasty, budget-friendly veg curry wrap in a chapati or a fish curry, burger or pizza, then sit at one of the cloth-covered tables next to the defunct pool table and eat under the black, star-covered ceiling. Its soft-service ice cream (Rs 15) is heavenly on a hot day.

Takamaka Café
CREOLE, SANDWICHES €

(Map p309; Anse Sévère; mains Rs 50-180; ☻9am-4pm Mon-Sat) This little shack, with creatively hewn tables and chairs under the trees at Anse Sévère, serves up simple sandwiches, seafood salads and fruit platters. Fresh juices (Rs 100) and cocktails (Rs125 to 175) are also on the menu. Be warned: food runs out by 2pm.

★ Chez Jules Restaurant
CREOLE, SEAFOOD €€

(Map p309; ☑2510384, 4234287; Anse Banane; mains Rs 230-575; ☻8.30am-8.30pm Mon-Sat, to 6pm Sun) This beachfront-roadside shack may be on the casual side, but it serves up some of the finest meals on the island. The

octopus curry and tuna steak with coconut sauce are both particularly divine. Feel free to rock up for breakfast (omelettes and fresh juices and smoothies) or lunch, but you'll need to book in for dinner by 3pm. Cash only.

★ Bellevue
CREOLE €€

(Map p309; ☑2527856; Belle Vue; mains Rs 150-200, dinner Rs 500; ☻noon-3pm, sunset dinner 6.30pm, bar 10am-6pm) It's a hell of a hike or cycle to get to this eagle's eyrie, but you'll be amply rewarded with cardiac-arresting views. At lunchtime, it serves up the usual Creole seafood suspects at very reasonable prices. Dinner is a more romantic affair, and should be booked ahead; the set price includes transfers to La Passe. A good deal.

Old Pier Café
CREOLE €€

(Map p309; Anse Union; mains Rs 130-250; ☻9am-6pm) Find some shade at a table beneath the large tree or under this cafe's sloping roof, then sink your feet into the seaside sand and your teeth into a light meal. The most atmospheric restaurant within L'Union Estate & Copra Factory (p308) serves open sandwiches, salads and seafood straight off the grill. It's also a great place for a cool drink or sunset cocktail; happy hour runs from 4pm to 6pm (cocktails Rs 100).

Zerof
CREOLE, BUFFET €€

(Map p310; ☑4234439; La Réunion; mains Rs 150-300, buffet incl service Rs 385; ☻8-10am, noon-3pm & 5.30-9pm) Zerof is a great spot to savour a variety of traditional Creole meals, particularly on Wednesday, Friday and Sunday evenings when it lays on an excellent buffet. Book in advance for the buffet.

Gregoire's Pizzeria
PIZZA €€

(Map p310; ☑4292557; La Réunion; mains Rs 93-240; ☻11am-2pm & 6-10pm) Bubbling thin-crust pizzas straight from the brick oven are the name of the game here – they are some of the best in town. Takeaway is available at lunch till 3pm.

Loutier Coco
CREOLE €€

(Map p309; ☑2514762; www.facebook.com/loutier coco; Grand Anse; mains Rs 150-300, lunch buffet Rs 300; ☻11am-3.30pm, bar to 5pm) The ocean breezes blowing off Grand Anse flow straight through the cool confines of Loutier Coco. It's famous for its lunchtime buffets of grilled fish, traditional Creole curries and salads, fruit and coffee, though this spread is only put on when ordered ahead by larger groups – it's worth calling to time your visit for one.

Tarosa CREOLE, INTERNATIONAL €€

(Map p310; La Passe; mains Rs 170-350; ⊙ 7.30-10am, noon-3pm & 6-9pm) This casual outdoor restaurant offers seafront dining in the heart of La Passe. The menu features Creole specials (smoked fish salad and seafood coconut curries), as well as burgers, pasta dishes and Indian fare (the biryani is a good choice for vegetarians). Just outside the restaurant's gates is its takeaway – join the queue (if there isn't one, it's closed or sold out) and choose from a selection of bargain friendly curries, grilled or fried fish and vegetable noodles (mains Rs 50 to 65).

Lanbousir SEAFOOD €€

(Map p309; www.facebook.com/lanboursir; Anse Union; mains Rs 185-300; ⊙ 12.30-3pm) The flavour-filled smoke wafting from this ramshackle eatery should be enough to lure you onto one of its off-kilter picnic tables for a filling lunch after (or before) working your tan at nearby Anse Source d'Argent. Run by a gang of affable ladies, it serves up seafood salads, a variety of lip-smacking curries and grilled fish, prawns and octopus. It's within L'Union Estate & Copra Factory (p308).

La Digue Pizzeria PIZZA, INTERNATIONAL €€

(Map p310; ☑ 2617721; La Passe; pizzas Rs 125-200; ⊙ 11am-10pm Tue-Thu & Sun, to 11pm Fri & Sat) A restaurant of two parts, La Digue Pizzeria is both a takeaway joint and formal sit-down restaurant. The latter opens after 6pm and serves decent seafood salads and a variety of local and international dishes. Upstairs is the cheaper takeaway, which does a brisk trade in average pizzas and sloppier versions of the burgers and chips served downstairs. It's out of sight from the main drag in the Mills Complex, but it's well signposted.

★**Le Nautique** INTERNATIONAL €€€

(Map p310; ☑ 4234700; http://lenautique.sc/la digue; La Réunion; mains Rs 195-425; ⊙ noon-3pm & 7-9.30pm) Small, but perfectly formed, the elevated deck of this open-air dining room overlooks the ocean and provides a romantic setting for a dinner that won't disappoint. The red snapper fillet topped with a banana sauce (its signature dish) bursts with sweet flavours, as does the 'Trio of Fish' (tuna, jobfish and red snapper) with candied orange. Reservations are a must.

★**Le Domaine's Combava** INTERNATIONAL €€€

(Map p309; ☑ 4299999; www.orangeraie.sc; La Passe; mains lunch Rs 250-410, dinner Rs 350-850; ⊙ noon-3.30pm & 7-9pm) Surrounded by water features and ocean views, this elegant open-air restaurant within Le Domaine de L'Orangeraie Resort & Spa (p314) offers fine dining, a cool setting and attentive service. It's particularly atmospheric in the evening. Lunch dishes range from succulent ceviche and Thai curries to pizza and burgers, while dinner serves up perfectly prepared seafood and meat dishes with both Creole and international flavours.

★**Le Repaire** ITALIAN €€€

(Map p310; ☑ 4234332; www.lerepaireseychelles.com; La Réunion; mains Rs 165-495; ⊙ 7-9am, 12.30-2.30pm & 7-10pm) Le Repaire stands apart by serving incredibly well-executed Italian classics. The Italian chef imports some key ingredients from his homeland, so the pastas, risottos and pizzas all pop with old-world flavour. The meat and seafood dishes, such as pan-seared tuna rolled in black sesame seeds, are also succulent successes.

Santosha INTERNATIONAL €€€

(Map p309; ☑ 4299999; www.orangeraie.sc; La Passe; buffet breakfast/dinner Rs 500/910; ⊙ 7.30-9.30am & 7.30-9.30pm) Within Le Domaine de L'Orangeraie Resort (p314), this buffet restaurant sits strikingly on the water's edge. Each night has a different theme, whether Creole, Indian, Mediterranean, Asian, BBQ or simply seafood. The breakfast spread is the best on the island and is certainly worth the splurge if you're feeling hungry.

**The Fish Trap Bar
& Restaurant** INTERNATIONAL €€€

(Map p310; ☑ 2616100; fishtraprestaurant@seychelles.net; La Passe; mains Rs 235-500; ⊙ 7.30am-11pm; 🛜) In a great location on the water's edge, with tables inside, on the deck and spread out on the beach, this pretty-in-pastels restaurant is a tourist staple in La Passe. The menu runs the gamut from seafood to meat dishes and salads to Creole staples, with large main portions and overflowing baskets of French fries. It's also a great place to linger over a fruity cocktail (from Rs 150) as the sun sinks low on the horizon.

ℹ Information

Tourist Office (Map p310; ☑ 4234393; www.seychellesladigue.com; La Passe; ⊙ 8am-noon & 1-4pm Mon-Fri, 9am-noon Sat) Provides basic information and helps organise tours.

Logan Hospital (☑ 4234255; La Passe) Offers basic health-care services. It's not well signposted, but it's a mustard yellow single-storey building at the southern end of La Passe.

ℹ️ Getting There & Away

The island is easily reached by boat from both Mahé and Praslin. La Dique is only about 5km from Praslin.

Inter-Island Ferry Pty (Map p300; 📱 4232329; www.iif-catrose.com; one-way adult/child €15/7.50) operates a catamaran service between Praslin and La Digue. There are around seven departures daily (five on Sunday) between 7am (9am on Sunday) and 5.15pm (5.45pm on Friday, Saturday and Sunday) from Praslin and between 7.30am (9.30am on Sunday) and 5.45pm (6.15pm on Friday, Saturday and Sunday) from La Digue. The crossing takes approximately 15 minutes.

Cat Cocos (Map p310; 📱 4324843; www.cat-cocos-seychelles.com; La Passe; ⏰ 6am-8pm) runs a once- or twice-daily service between La Digue and Mahé (€64); it makes a brief stop in Praslin en route.

Tickets for both companies can be purchased directly online or from the **Seychelles Port Authority** (📱 4234393; La Passe; ⏰ 6am-8pm) ticket window near the jetty on La Digue.

ℹ️ Getting Around

BICYCLE

There are a few surfaced roads on the island. Given that it is less than 5km from north to south, by far the best – and most enjoyable – way to get around is on foot or bicycle. There are loads of bikes to rent. Operators have outlets near the pier, or you can book through your hotel or guesthouse. Most places charge between Rs 100 and Rs 150 per day. **Tati's Bicycle Rental** (La Passe; per day Rs 150; ⏰ 7am-6pm) is a reliable option.

With the sun setting around 6pm, it's best to bring a head torch to navigate the darkness (and to be seen by others) when on two wheels.

OTHER INNER ISLANDS

Apart from Mahé, Praslin and La Digue, the other main islands making up the Inner Islands group include Bird, North, Silhouette, Félicité, Frégate and Denis Islands. These widely scattered islands are all run as exclusive island retreats. If you want to live out that stranded-on-a-deserted-island fantasy, consider staying at one of these private island resorts.

Apart from the sense of exclusivity, what makes these hideaways so special is their green ethos. They're all involved in pioneering conservation projects and are sanctuaries for various rare species.

Silhouette

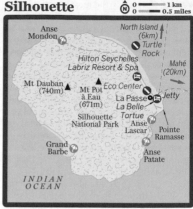

Silhouette

A truly magnificent and wild hideaway, the mountainous island of Silhouette is famed for its biological diversity. So much so that in 2010 more than 90% of it was permanently protected as Silhouette National Park – a bold move by the government given it's the country's third-largest granitic island after Mahé and Praslin. There's a small research station based in the village of La Passe that's open to visitors; it focuses on the conservation of giant tortoises and the monitoring of sea turtles and bats. Hikes, such as the one to the majestic sands and rocks of Anse Mondon, offer you further chances to understand and witness the island's rich ecosystems and wildlife. The island dive centre opens up the remarkable underwater world for exploration.

🏃 Activities

Day visits to the island can be arranged through the Hilton Seychelles Labriz for Rs 1500, which includes lunch, use of facilities and boat transfer.

Eco Center   DIVING
(Map p317; https://eco-center.jimdo.com; La Passe; ⏰ 9am-6pm Mon Sat) This five-star PADI dive centre offers a full range of certification courses and access to the best dive sites in the area.

🛏️ Sleeping & Eating

Hilton Seychelles Labriz
Resort & Spa   RESORT €€€
(Map p317; 📱 4293949; www.hiltonseychelles labriz.com; La Passe; d incl breakfast from €350;

❄☎✉) ✐ Possibly the most affordable private-island resort in the Seychelles, the five-star Hilton Seychelles Labriz comprises 111 villas of varying levels of opulence. Most of them are spread along a narrow beach, providing ocean views and direct access – some also feature private plunge pools. There are no less than eight restaurants, including one in the historic Grann Kaz plantation house.

Its food and agricultural program is one of many reasons Labriz has won several environmental and sustainability awards in recent years. The list of activity facilities is prolific, with a tennis court (and coach), spa, kids' adventure centre, gym and nearby dive centre (p317). There are also guides for nature walks through the national park to sites such as Anse Mondon. One minus: the main beach is too shallow for proper swimming at low tide.

La Belle Tortue
BOUTIQUE HOTEL €€€

(Map p317; ✒2569708; www.labelletortue.com; La Passe; d with half board €515-750; ❄☎) This upscale venture is a more intimate alternative to a resort, with seven rooms in three modern villas set along the shore of a lovely sandy bay. Each is roomy, light filled and beautifully attired, with rich hardwood floors, elegant furnishings and slate-filled bathrooms. The downstairs rooms can be expanded into suites by incorporating an adjacent lounge.

❶ Getting There & Away

Most guests come to Silhouette by boat from Belle Ombre on Mahé. These transfers are free for Hilton guests, but €125 return for each person staying at La Belle Tortue.

North Island

North Island is the last word in exclusivity and its boutique resort is universally lauded as a milestone in the 'couture castaway' Indian Ocean experience. It's little wonder the Duke and Duchess of Cambridge chose it for their honeymoon. Honouring the environment is paramount here (the island is now plastic free), and the Noah's Ark program continues to restore native vegetation and nurture critically endangered species. Wildlife is everywhere and nature trails wind through fertile forests, connecting its three scenic summits – Grand Palos, Bernica and Spa Hill – with four pristine beaches where soft white sands flirt with azure waters. It's

not uncommon to see eagle rays and turtles swimming in the shallows from shore. Few people ever get to set foot here, but those that do will always long to return.

🛏 Sleeping & Eating

★ North Island
RESORT €€€

(✒4293100; www.north-island.com; d with full board €7590; ❄☎✉) ✐ It's easy to understand why North Island regularly features on lists of the world's top hotels. The natural island environment is staggeringly beautiful, as are the 11 ultra-luxurious villas that embrace it. Wrapped around private pools, each villa majestically juxtaposes smoothly hewn logs with glass, stone and flowing fabrics. The warmth and hospitality of staff, which includes a butler, is unparalleled.

The cavernous bathrooms, much like the bedroom and separate library, are so full of light that it often feels like you're outside when you're not. A separate kitchen near the covered al-fresco dining area is full of all the nibbles and drinks you could desire, though you'll be hard pressed not to be totally fulfilled by the offerings from the resort's chef.

With an accredited dive centre, water sports, gym, award-winning spa, yoga instructor and resident ecologist (for educational hikes) there are plenty of enriching ways (other than flopping on the beach) to spend your days.

❶ Getting There & Away

All guests come to North Island by helicopter. Transport is handled directly by the resort and is arranged in conjunction with accommodation.

Denis

There's a white-sand beach lapped by luxuriously warm waters, a shimmering lagoon with every hue from lapis lazuli to turquoise, plus palm and casuarina trees leaning over the shore. Welcome to Denis, a coral island that lies about 95km northeast of Mahé.

There are nature walks along scenic pathways as well as fishing, snorkelling and diving trips that will keep you active. Wildlife lovers will enjoy it here too; although Denis is small – barely 1.3km in length and 1.75km at its widest point – it's a sanctuary for a variety of species, including giant tortoises, magpie robins, paradise flycatchers and Seychelles warblers. From July to December you may see turtles laying eggs on the beach.

🛏 Sleeping & Eating

Denis Private Island   RESORT €€€

(📞 4288963; www.denisisland.com; s/d with full board from €1205/1310; ❄@📶) 🍴 Impressive Denis Private Island is essentially *Swiss Family Robinson* meets stylish travel magazine. The 25 villas are just steps from the dazzling white beach. They have a gorgeous feel, with lots of wood, quality furnishings and elegant showers – not to mention the outdoor bathroom. Diving and fishing are catered for amply, and the entire place feels eerily empty even at full capacity.

Food is organic and prepared from produce and livestock that has been nurtured on the island farm. The international clientele is mainly made up of couples, but families are also welcome (children free; 12 to 17 years €195). All guests get around by bicycle or on foot, and refreshingly there are no TVs or in-room wi-fi. You also won't find a pool, but who needs one when there's such an unbelievable beach on your doorstep?

🛈 Getting There & Away

Denis Island is serviced by charter planes and helicopters from Mahé. Transport is handled directly by Denis Private Island resort and is arranged in conjunction with accommodation.

Bird Island

Bird is the ultimate in ecotourism and bird life-viewing. Some 1.5 million sooty terns nest here, as well as thousands of fairy terns and common noddies who descend on this coral island en masse between April and October. You just have to sit on your verandah and birds will come to land on your head. Hawksbill turtles breed on the island's beaches between November and March, while their land-bound relatives lumber around the interior. Green turtles also use the sandy shores for their nests. If you don't mind the constant birdsong (and whiff of droppings), Bird Island is also a great place to decompress, with two fantastic beaches and a wonderfully relaxing atmosphere.

🛏 Sleeping & Eating

Bird Island Lodge   LODGE €€€

(📞 4323322, 4224925; www.birdislandseychelles.com; s/d/tr with full board from €347/451/670; ☺closed Dec; 📶) 🍴 No TV. No air-con. No phones. No pool. Just you, masses of birds, 24 giant turtles, the inky-blue ocean and sensational beaches. Enjoy this slice of untouched paradise in one of the 24 simple yet genuinely ecofriendly and agreeably designed chalets. They rest in a leafy plot, a thong's throw from the beach.

Food is a definite plus, with copious meals using local ingredients and fresh seafood. Activities available include snorkelling, kayaking, shore fishing and dolphin-spotting (between September and November as well as in March and April). You can also join an ecotour of the island with the resident conservationist Robbie Bression – a memorable experience. You'll probably come across Esmeralda, one of the largest tortoises in the world – a 300kg monster of a specimen. All in all, this is one of the most affordable private islands in the Seychelles.

🛈 Getting There & Away

Bird Island is approximately 100km north of Mahé and is serviced by daily flights from Mahé (€415 per person return). These are arranged directly with the Bird Island Lodge.

Frégate

Fairy-tale Frégate is a private island where guests' supreme comfort and enjoyment is as catered to as the environment and wildlife. The result of the latter is a sky full of tropical birds, an endemic forest crawling with a few thousand giant tortoises, and a pristine shoreline providing successful nesting grounds for two species of endangered sea turtles. There are well-demarcated wilderness trails to explore alone or with the island's resident conservationist, and no less than seven white-sand beaches that will have you grinning ear to ear (Anse Maquereau and Anse Victorin are regularly voted among the world's best). Fishing, diving and snorkelling are also possibilities off its shores. Unsurprisingly, this exclusive place has become a hideaway for celebs and millionaires who find serenity in the Fregate Island Private resort. But for those with a biological education, it's an incredibly rewarding place to volunteer in its wide-ranging conservation program.

⊙ Sights & Activities

★ Anse Maquereau   BEACH

Quite possibly the world's most beautiful beach, petite Anse Maquereau is flanked by granitic monoliths, backed by palms and caressed by waters of the deepest blue. But with so few guests on the island, it's often yours alone – and you can keep it that way if you turn the sign atop the steps from 'Beach free' to 'Beach in use' before heading down.

No matter when your feet hit the sand, you'll find a cooler full of ice cold drinks waiting (it's just that kind of place). If your beverage of choice isn't chilling, there's a phone direct to the bar.

★**Fregate Island Private** VOLUNTEERING
(☑4397100, In Germany +49 (0) 6924 754 9425; www.fregate.com) The island's conservation team is often looking for qualified volunteers to help with the monitoring of giant tortoises, nesting sea turtles, endemic birds and invertebrates. Volunteers must commit to six months and have a tertiary qualification in biological sciences. You'll need to cover the cost of your international flights and a medical check, but the rest is covered.

Mont Signal VIEWPOINT
The rocky crown of the island (125m) proffers incredible views west, and is a surreal spot for sunset. It's a 1.6km return hike along a well-marked trail that is signposted on the paved path that crosses the centre of the island.

🛌 Sleeping & Eating

★**Fregate Island Private** RESORT €€€
(☑in Germany +49 (0) 6924 754 9425, 4397100; www.fregate.com; d with full board from €5160; ✳@🎧🏊) 🏄 Perched on a hillside and patrolled by some of the island's 3500 free-roaming giant tortoises, this breathtaking resort is home to 16 elegant villas that each feature staggering water views, a large infinity pool, Jacuzzi, personal butler and no less than 400-sq-m of space to luxuriate in.

The vistas in your villa follow you from the entrance hall into the immaculate glass-walled bedroom, where you can watch the horizon brighten at dawn from the comfort of your huge bed. On the opposite side of the villa is the lounge, which manages to blend chic style with bare-foot comfort – its soft sofas are perfect for air-con ocean gazing when the sun chases you inside.

Meals can be taken in your villa, on the beach, in the main restaurant or in the 'tree house' that sits up in the forest canopy. The quality and variety of dishes (from Wagyu steaks and sushi to Thai curries and pizza) are off the chart. There are activities aplenty, ranging from nature walks, swimming, fishing, diving and snorkelling. Soothing treatments are always available from the resort's Rock Spa.

ℹ Getting There & Away

Most guests come to Frégate Island by helicopter (20 minutes) from Mahé. Transport is handled directly by the resort and is arranged in conjunction with accommodation.

Félicité

Another speck of Seychelles paradise in the Indian Ocean, this 2.68-sq-km granitic island floats in sparkling turquoise waters a few kilometres east of La Digue. The aquatic riches along its reef-lined shores, particularly Anse La Cour, have made it popular snorkelling site for boat excursions from La Digue. For island guests, Grande Anse is a stunning place to soak up some sun, whereas the deeper waters at sheltered Anse Peniche are ripe for swimming.

Not always considered utopia, Félicité was where the British exiled Abdullah Muhammad Shah II, the 26th Sultan of Perak, in the late 19th century. The island eventually became a coconut plantation before later being abandoned. Since late 2016 it has been home to the five-star resort Six Senses Zil Pasyon. In the decade preceding the opening, ecologists worked hard to remove non-native vegetation and facilitate the return of endemic birds, tortoises and turtles, a process that continues today.

⊙ Sights & Activities

Grande Anse BEACH
This ribbon of white sand is the most beautiful beach on Félicité, though shallow waters make swimming difficult. It's also the least visited, simply because it's the furthest from the resort. At the far end there's a lovely hammock strung between a couple of palms waiting for you. Enjoy.

Anse La Cour SNORKELLING
The reef directly off this beach is one of the area's best snorkelling sites. Turtle sightings are common.

🛌 Sleeping

★**Six Senses Zil Pasyon** RESORT €€€
(☑4671000; www.sixsenses.com/resorts/zilpasyon; Félicité Island; d with full board from €2440; ✳🎧🏊) 🏄 By focusing on connecting its properties and guests with nature, Six Sens-

es has climbed to the top of the luxury hotel brand rankings. Looking at Zil Pasyon, it's easy to see why. The sleek wood-filled villas, each with their own infinity pool, blend seamlessly into the rocky, jungle-clad landscape and offer guests their own private slice of paradise.

The interiors are decked out with warm wood on both the floors and the vaulted ceilings, while white linens, woven wall coverings and teal rugs and cushions add softer textures and vibrancy. Wall-to-wall bi-fold doors let the outside in, connecting the large deck and outdoor dining area with the bedroom. The slate-filled bathrooms proffer views, some from a swing beside the bath, and all feature Japanese toilets with all their bells and squirting whistles. The only downside is that none of the villas have direct beach access, though all but one of them (number 2) have spectacular ocean views, even the less expensive 'hideaway' options.

Activities available to guests include kayaking, stand-up paddleboarding, snorkelling, nature walks and treatments in the magical rock-topping spa.

✕ Eating

The sole eating options on Félicité are the two restaurants at Six Senses Zil Pasyon: Island Café and Ocean Kitchen. The standard of fare is outstanding, with many of the organic ingredients sourced locally. Guests can also dine in their villa or at one of several scenic private sites around the island. Dining here as a day visitor is possible, but it must be booked well in advance.

❶ Getting There & Away

Helicopter transfers to/from Mahé cost €920, while boat transfers to/from Praslin are €180. Both options are arranged by Six Senses Zil Pasyon and take up to four passengers.

OUTER ISLANDS

The Amirantes Group lies about 250km southwest of Mahé. Its main island is Desroches. Another 200km further south, the Alphonse Group is another cluster of coral islands that provides some of the best saltwater fly-fishing in the world.

The Aldabra Group is the most remote of the Outer Island groups. It includes Aldabra Atoll, which is a Unesco World Heritage Site and nature reserve and lies more than 1000km from Mahé. Aldabra Atoll is home

to about 150,000 giant tortoises, and flocks of migratory birds fly in and out in their thousands. Aldabra Atoll is only accessible to scientists and volunteers as government permission is required to visit; check with the Seychelles Island Foundation (www.sif.sc) for the information. However, visiting Wizard Island and Astove Island in the Aldabra Group's Cosmoledo Atoll and Astove Atoll, respectively, are now a possibility.

Alphonse Island

Alphonse, about 400km southwest of Mahé, is a small, thickly vegetated island that's surrounded by a vast lagoon and healthy reef gardens. It does have some great beaches, but the main drawcard is fly fishing. The clear waters of the sandbanks that shelve the lagoon's perimeters are made for battles with the bonefish, giant trevally, triggerfish and other species. Alphonse is also increasingly promoting its diving potential, which is unrivalled in the country (if not in the Indian Ocean). The best thing is that it also appeals to romantics and families in search of a no-fuss hideaway.

🛏 Sleeping & Eating

Alphonse Island Resort   RESORT €€€
(⌨ in South Africa +27 82 496 4570; www.alphonse-island.com; Alphonse Group; r per person with full board US$900-1975; ☺ Nov-Apr; 🕷 🛜 ⊠)
🮥 This laid-back establishment seduces those who stay here with a row of 22 cosy A-framed beach bungalows and five villas that have direct access to the lagoon. With wooden furnishings and modern amenities, they represent a nicely judged balance between comfort, rustic charm and tropical atmosphere. Various fishing and diving packages are available, and snorkelling trips can be arranged.

❶ Getting There & Away

There are regular chartered flights between Alphonse and Mahé. Transport is handled directly by the Alphonse Island Resort and is arranged in conjunction with accommodation.

Desroches

The last section of an ancient volcanic caldera to keep its head above water, this sliver of Indian Ocean bliss literally sits on the edge of an abyss. And it's for this reason that this island, some 230km southwest of Mahé, is renowned for its diving and fishing – big wall dives and deep-sea fish are a stone's throw away. But you don't have to get wet to experience the aquatic treasures, it's possible to see sharks, turtles and rays from its shores. People call the phenomenon 'dry snorkelling'. The beaches are good, though they don't justify a 'fly and flop' type holiday, but rather one based around oceanic activities.

Sleeping & Eating

★ **Desroches Island Resort** RESORT €€€
(☑ 4229400; www.fourseasons.com/seychelles
desroches; d incl breakfast €1189-2271; ❄ 🛜 🏊) Reborn in 2018 under the Four Seasons name, this completely overhauled five-star 71-room resort resides at the western end of the island. The airy bungalows, villas and oversized suites all feature private pools, and the contemporary interiors – lined with warm woods, cream linens and elegant furnishings from far and wide – are a lesson in restrained opulence. The dining options are first class, with the Claudine restaurant serving fresh seafood, salads, pizza and more, and the Lighthouse eatery featuring everything from sushi and Alaskan king crab to dry-aged French steaks. There's also a deli for midday cravings or picnics.

Blue Safari Seychelles (☑ in South Africa +27 82 496 4570; www.bluesafari.com) has a base here and offers diving, snorkelling, fishing, kayaking and stand-up paddleboarding. There is also a Discovery Centre that showcases the flora and fauna found onshore and off, with a marine educator on hand who gives lectures.

ℹ Getting There & Away

There are daily charter flights between Mahé and Desroches (35 minutes, return €460), which are organised by Desroches Island Resort.

UNDERSTAND SEYCHELLES

Seychelles Today

The Seychelles has come a long way since independence, and it prides itself on having attained stability and a certain prosperity. Standards of health, education and housing have steadily improved, and the country enjoys the highest annual per-capita income in Africa. After years of communist rule, the Seychelles has evolved towards a free-market economy in order to attract foreign investors. For all the stability, the winds of (peaceful) political change are in the air, while environmental issues loom large.

Winds of Change

The Seychelles continues to be one of Africa's star economic performers. Annual economic growth consistently hovers around 5% – it reached 5.3% in 2017 – while annual GDP per capita sat at a very respectable US$29,300 in 2017, higher than in Russia, Greece and Croatia. All of which should add up to a good news story for a popular government, right? Not quite. In presidential elections held in December 2015, incumbent James Michel held on by the barest of margins (a mere 193 votes, winning just 50.02% of the popular vote). Any suggestion that the result was a blip in the ruling party's popularity came crashing down 10 months later, in September 2016, when the opposition coalition, the LDS, won 19 out of 33 parliamentary seats in elections for the National Assembly. It was the Seychelles' equivalent of a political earthquake, representing as it did the first defeat in four decades for the ruling party. With the next presidential elections just around the corner in 2020, the Seychelles could be on the cusp of a whole new era. That these changes have occurred peacefully, through the ballot box, is widely seen as a sign of the country's political maturity and should augur well for the future.

A Fragile Environment

Like so many island nations, the Seychelles has a particular interest in the impact of climate change. With 85% of its population and tourism developments occurring along the country's coastline, the Seychelles is particularly susceptible to rising sea levels caused by global warming. A leading scientific study published in the journal *Science Advances* in 2018 named the Seychelles alongside the Maldives and Hawaii as islands where fresh groundwater supplies could be under serious threat by 2050. Check out http://global floodmap.org/Seychelles for an idea of the impact of rising waters on the Seychelles – an 18-inch rise, for example, would flood nearly a quarter of the country's population. To its credit, the Seychelles government has been active in advocating for change in international forums; they even have their own climate change ambassador. And in February 2018, the Seychelles announced the creation of a marine reserve in return for the forgiveness of a portion of its national debt, a move seen as a model for conservation projects elsewhere. Still, even optimists in Seychelles understand that their future is not entirely in their own hands.

History

Like Mauritius and Réunion, the Seychelles had no indigenous population predating the European colonisers, and until the 18th century it was uninhabited. The islands were first spotted by Portuguese explorers, but the first recorded landing was by a British East India Company ship in 1609. Pirates and privateers used the Seychelles as a temporary base during lulls in their marauding.

The Colonial Period

In 1742 Mahé de Labourdonnais, the governor of what is now Mauritius, sent Captain Lazare Picault to investigate the islands. Picault named the main island after his employer (and the bay where he landed after himself) and laid the way for the French to claim possession of the islands 12 years later.

It took a while for the French to do anything with their possession. It wasn't until 1770 that the first batch of 21 settlers and seven slaves arrived on Ste-Anne Island. After a few false starts, the settlers began growing spices, cassava, sugar cane and maize.

In the early 19th century, the British began taking an interest in the Seychelles. Not willing to die for their colony, the French didn't resist British attacks and the Seychelles became a British dependency in 1814. The British did little to develop the islands except increase the number of slaves. After abolition in 1835, freed slaves from around the region were also brought here. Over the decades that followed, the islands were used as a holding pen for numerous political prisoners and exiles. However, because few British settled here, the French language and culture remained dominant.

In 1903 the Seychelles became a crown colony administered from London. It promptly went into the political and economic doldrums until 1964, when two political parties were formed. France Albert René,

a young lawyer, founded the Seychelles People's United Party (SPUP). A fellow lawyer, James Mancham, led the new Seychelles Democratic Party (SDP).

Independence

Mancham's SDP, made up of business people and planters, won the elections in 1966 and 1970. René's SPUP fought on a socialist and independence ticket. In June 1975 a coalition of the two parties gave the appearance of unity in the lead-up to independence, which was granted a year later. Mancham became the first president of the Republic of Seychelles and René the prime minister.

The flamboyant Sir Jim – as poet and playboy James Mancham was known – placed all his eggs in one basket: tourism. He became a jet-setter, flying around the world with a beautiful socialite on each arm, and he put the Seychelles on the map.

The rich and famous poured in for holidays and to party, party, party. Adnan Khashoggi and other Arab millionaires bought large tracts of land, while film stars and celebrities came to enhance their romantic, glamorous images.

According to René and the SPUP, however, the wealth was not being spread evenly and the country was no more than a rich person's playground. René stated that poor Creoles were little better off than slaves.

The René Era

In June 1977, barely a year after independence, René and a team of Tanzanian-trained rebels carried out an almost bloodless coup while Mancham was in London attending a Commonwealth Conference. In the following years, René consolidated his position by deporting many supporters of the outlawed SDP. Opposed to René's one-party socialist state, these *grands blancs* (white landowners) set up 'resistance movements' in Britain, South Africa and Australia.

The country fell into disarray as the tourist trade dried to a trickle. The 1980s saw a campaign of civil disruption by supporters of the SDP, two army mutinies and more foiled coup attempts.

Finally, facing growing international criticism and the threatened withdrawal of foreign aid, René pulled a political about-face in the early 1990s; he abandoned one-party rule and announced the return to a multiparty democracy.

Elections were held in 1992 under the watchful eye of Commonwealth observers. René and his renamed Seychelles People's Progressive Front (SPPF) won 58.4% of the votes; Mancham, who had returned to the Seychelles, fielded 33.7% for his SDP and claimed the results were rigged.

René maintained his grip on power, while the SDP's star continued to wane. Even Mancham himself abandoned the SDP in favour of the centrist Seychelles National Party (SNP) in 1999. In the 2002 elections, the SNP, led by Anglican priest Wavel Ramkalawan, confirmed its stand as the main opposition party by winning more than 42% of the vote.

The Long Road to Democracy

In April 2004 René finally relinquished the presidency to the former vice president, James Michel, who had stood by René through thick and thin. After a close race with opposition leader Wavel Ramkalawan, Michel won the 2006 presidential election, gaining 53.5% of the vote.

Michel has not seemed willing to cede his power to any of his opponents; he prematurely dissolved the National Assembly in March 2007, following the boycott of assembly proceedings by the opposition party. The ensuing general elections in May 2007 returned 18 SPPF members against seven members of Ramkalawan's SNP opposition party (exactly the same numbers as before the dissolution). Though these elections were held democratically, the opposition claimed that the government bought votes.

On the economic front, in 2008 the highly indebted country was forced to turn to the IMF for assistance. A package of reforms was passed, including the free floating of the rupee, the abolition of all exchange restrictions and massive cuts in public spending. Debt was frozen and the economy quickly rebounded.

Elections in 2015 saw the government retain power but with a greatly reduced majority, leading many to wonder whether the ruling party's four decades at the helm might be under threat.

Culture

Like its neighbours Mauritius and Réunion, the Seychelles is often cited as an example of racial and religious harmony, and compared with most countries it is. There's not much anticolonial feeling evident – it has long been replaced with a sense of national pride that developed after independence. There's even a lingering fondness for such British institutions as afternoon tea, while French cultural influence has waned somewhat, mainly because it is regarded as rather elitist.

Lifestyle

Thanks to the islands' close links with Europe, the contemporary face of the Seychelles is surprisingly modern. The main island of Mahé can be a rather sophisticated place, characterised as much by Western-style clothing, brand-new cars, mobile phones and modern houses as by any overt signs of traditional Creole culture. But beneath this strongly Westernised veneer, many aspects of traditional Creole culture survive. They live on in dance, music, hospitality, ancient beliefs, the language, the carefree attitude and in many other day-to-day ways of doing things.

Most Seychellois are Catholic, but marriage is a curiously unpopular institution. This is partly because marriage is considered to be a relic of slavery, when marriages simply didn't take place and the institution has never really taken hold in the centuries since. Getting married is also expensive and is beyond the means of poorer Seychellois. As a result, an estimated 75% of children are born out of wedlock. There's no taboo about illegitimacy, however.

ⓘ ETIQUETTE

Although largely informal in their everyday dealings, Seychellois do observe some (unspoken) rules of etiquette.

Greetings Shake hands with men and women when meeting for the first time and when saying goodbye.

Clothing Although beachwear is fine for the beaches, you will cause offence and may experience pestering if you dress in skimpy clothing elsewhere. Nude bathing is forbidden.

Island time Impatience will get you nowhere in the Seychelles, where time flows with the tides.

Photographing people Always respect the wish of locals. Ask permission to photograph and don't insist or snap a picture if permission is denied.

Population

The population of the Seychelles is more strongly African than in Mauritius or Réunion, but the Seychellois remain a mosaic of French, African, Indian, Chinese and Arab heritage. Creole culture, itself a melting pot of influences, reigns supreme, whereas distinct Indian and Chinese communities make up only a tiny proportion of the ethnic mix. As for the *grands blancs* (white landowners), most were dispossessed in the wake of the 1977 coup.

As in Mauritius and Réunion, it is the Creole language, cuisine and culture that helps bind the Seychelles' society. Nearly 90% of the population speaks Creole as their first language, though most also speak English – the language of government and business – and French.

About 90% of Seychellois live on Mahé and nearly a third of these are concentrated in and around the capital. Most of the remaining 10% live on Praslin and La Digue, while the other islands are either uninhabited or home to tiny communities.

Religion

About three-quarters of Seychellois are Roman Catholic, 6% are Anglican and around 4% belong to the rapidly expanding evangelical churches. The remainder belong to the tiny Hindu, Muslim and Chinese communities largely based in Victoria.

Most people are avid churchgoers. On a Sunday, Victoria's Catholic and Anglican cathedrals, as well as the smaller churches scattered around the main islands, are full to bursting.

There is also a widespread belief in the supernatural and in the old magic of spirits known as *gris gris*. Sorcery was outlawed in 1958, but a few *bonhommes* and *bonnefemmes di bois* (medicine men and women) still practise their cures and curses and concoct potions for love, luck and revenge.

Arts

Literature

Among the most important local authors writing in Creole are the poet-playwright Christian Sevina, short-story author and playwright Marie-Thérèse Choppy, poet Antoine Abel and mystery writer Jean-Joseph Madeleine. Unfortunately their works are not yet available in English.

In fact, there is surprisingly little English-language fiction about these islands. Most authors go in for travelogues and autobiographies. The one exception is long-time resident Glynn Burridge, who mixes fact and fiction in his short stories. They are published locally in two volumes under the title *Voices: Seychelles Short Stories* (2014) and are available in bookshops in Victoria.

Music & Dance

The Indian, European, Chinese and Arabic backgrounds of the Seychellois are reflected in their music. Musicians from the Seychelles have their own take on musical genres from Africa and elsewhere – *seggae* is a fusion of Mauritian *séga* and reggae, while the African rhythms of *moutia* (a dance) have been blended with reggae to form *mouggae*. Local percussion music is known as *kanmtole*.

Patrick Victor and Jean-Marc Volcy are two of the Seychelles' best-known musicians, playing Creole pop and folk music. Victor is known for combining native folk beats with Kenyan *benga* to produce what's known as *montea*. Other local stars are Emmanuel Marie and the late Raymond Lebon, whose daughter Sheila Paul made it into the local charts with an updated rendering of her father's romantic ballads.

For a window on modern Seychelles music, pick up *Seychelles – Nouvelle Tendances* (2018), which includes tracks by Patrick Victor and Jean-Marc Volcy, among others.

Visual Arts

Over recent decades, more and more artists have settled in the Seychelles and spawned a local industry catering to souvenir-hungry tourists. While shops are full of stereotypical scenes of palm trees and sunsets, there are also some innovative and talented artists around.

Michael Adams is the best-known and most distinctive contemporary artist. George Camille is another highly regarded artist who takes his inspiration from nature. Other notable artists are Barbara Jenson on La Digue and **Gerard Devoud** (Map p280; ✒ 4381515; Baie Lazare; ⊙ 10am-7pm) at Baie Lazare on Mahé's west coast.

Look out, too, for works by Leon Radegonde, who produces innovative abstract collages; Andrew Gee, who specialises in silk paintings and watercolours of fish; and Christine Harter, who creates sun-drenched paintings. The painter and sculptor Egbert Marday produces powerful sketches of fisherfolk and plantation workers, but is perhaps best known for the statue of a man with a walking cane, situated outside the courthouse on Victoria's Independence Ave. Lorenzo Appiani produced the sculptures on the roundabouts at each end of 5th June Ave in Victoria.

Food & Drink

The real beauty of Seychellois cuisine is its freshness and simplicity. Meat lovers, come prepared: it is heavily influenced by the surrounding ocean, with fish appearing as the main ingredient in many dishes. Cultural influences are also distinctive, with a blend of European (mostly French and Italian) and African gastronomic influences.

Staples & Specialities

Fish, fish, FISH! And rice. This is the most common combination (*pwason ek diri* in Creole patois) in the Seychelles, and we won't complain – fish is guaranteed to be served ultrafresh and literally melts in your mouth. You'll devour bourgeois, capitaine, shark, job, parrotfish, caranx, grouper and tuna, among others. To bring variety, they are cooked in innumerable guises: grilled, steamed, minced, smoked, stewed, salted, baked, wrapped in a banana leaf; the list goes on and on.

Seafood lovers will have found their spiritual home in the Seychelles, with lobster, crab, shellfish (especially *trouloulou* and *teck teck*, two local varieties of shells) and octopus widely available.

The Seychelles is dripping with tropical fruit, including mango, banana, breadfruit, papaya, coconut, grapefruit, pineapple and carambola. Mixed with spices, they make wonderful accompaniments, such as the flavourful *chatini* (chutney). Vanilla, cinnamon and nutmeg are used to flavour stews and other preparations.

Gastronomes might consider trying *civet de chauve souris* (bat curry), which is considered a delicacy. La Grande Maison (p294) is a good place to try this rather disconcerting idea. You'll also find meat, mostly beef and chicken, but it's imported.

Drinks

Freshly squeezed juices and coconut water are the most natural and thirst-quenching drinks around. If you want to put some wobble in your step, Seybrew, the local brand of beer, is sold everywhere. Eku, another locally produced beer, is a bit harder to find. Wine is available at most restaurants.

The rums produced by Takamaka Bay (p292), on the East Coast of Mahé, ranks among the best in the Indian Ocean.

Where to Eat & Drink

There's a full gamut of restaurant types, from funky shacks and fast-food outlets to ritzy restaurants. Larger hotels have a choice of restaurants, with one always serving buffets (usually Creole or seafood). There is not a vast selection of street snacks to choose from in the Seychelles, but street vendors sell fresh fruit and fish – a good option if you're self-catering. Grocery stores are also widely available. The market in Victoria is another good place to stock up on fresh food.

Many visitors to the Seychelles opt for packages that include breakfast and dinner at their hotel. If you'd prefer to sample local specialities, enjoy the Seychelles' many fine eateries, feast on views and share a beach picnic with the locals, you'll find that bed-and-breakfast deals will allow you more flexibility.

Vegetarians & Vegans

Restaurant menus in the Seychelles are dominated by fish, seafood and meat dishes, though there are actually a few salad and pasta options that are meat-free. If you're self-catering, you'll have much more choice, with a good selection of fruits and vegetables.

Environment

The Seychelles is an archipelago that lies about 1600km off the east coast of Africa and just south of the equator. For such a small country it supports a large variety of flora and fauna. Because of the islands' isolation and the comparatively late arrival of humans, many species here are endemic to the Seychelles. The country is a haven for wildlife, particularly birds and tropical fish.

The Land

The Seychelles is made up of 115 islands, of which the central islands (including Mahé, Praslin and La Digue) are granite; the outlying islands are coral atolls. The granite islands, which do not share the volcanic nature of Réunion and Mauritius, appear to be peaks of a huge submerged plateau that was torn away from Africa when the continental plates shifted about 65 million years ago.

Animals

Common mammals and reptiles include fruit bats or flying foxes, geckos, skinks and tenrecs (a hedgehog-like mammal imported from Madagascar). There are also some small snakes, but they are not dangerous.

More noteworthy is the fact that giant tortoises, which feature on the Seychelles' coat of arms, are now found only in the Seychelles and the Galápagos Islands (off Ecuador). The French and English wiped out the giant tortoises from all the Seychelles islands except Aldabra, where happily more than 100,000 still survive. Many have been brought to the central islands, where they munch their way around hotel gardens, and there is a free-roaming colony on Curieuse Island.

Almost every island seems to have some rare species of bird: on Frégate, Cousin, Cousine and Aride there are magpie robins (known as *pie chanteuse* in Creole); on Cousin, Cousine and Aride you'll find Seychelles warblers; La Digue, Denis and Curieuse have the *veuve* (paradise flycatcher); and Praslin has black parrots. The bare-legged scops owl and the Seychelles kestrel live on Mahé, and Bird Island is home to millions of sooty terns.

Plants

The coconut palm and the casuarina are the Seychelles' most common trees. There are a few banyans and you're also likely to see screw pines, bamboo and tortoise trees (so named because the fruit looks like the tortoises that eat it).

There are about 80 endemic plant species. Virgin forest now exists only on the higher parts of Silhouette Island and Mahé, and in the Vallée de Mai on Praslin, which is one of only two places in the world where the giant coco de mer palm grows wild. The other is nearby Curieuse Island.

In the high, remote parts of Mahé and Silhouette Island, you may come across the insect-eating pitcher plant, which either clings to trees and bushes or sprawls along the ground.

National Parks

The Seychelles currently boasts two national parks and seven marine national parks, as well as several other protected areas under government and NGO management. In all, about 46% of the country's total land mass is now protected as well as some 45 sq km of ocean, with the latter figure expected to rise over the coming years.

Environmental Issues

The Seychelles has a generally good record for protecting its natural environment. As early as 1968, Birdlife International got the ball rolling when it bought Cousin Island and began studying some of the country's critically endangered species. This was followed in the 1970s with legislation to establish national parks and marine reserves.

Despite a largely positive record on environmental protection, the government has made some controversial choices, In 1998 it authorised a vast land-reclamation project on Mahé's northeast coast to provide much-needed space for housing. More recently, the construction of Eden Island, an artificial island with luxury properties off Mahé's east coast, has also raised concerns. Both projects have caused widespread silting, marring the natural beauty of this coast indefinitely, though the alternative was to clear large tracts of forest. A difficult choice.

Tourism has had a similarly mixed effect. Every year, more resort hotels and lodges pop up, most notably on formerly pristine beaches or secluded islands. Sure, they have nothing on the concrete-and-glass horrors of, say, Hawaii or Cancun, but they still necessitate additional support systems, including roads and numerous vehicle trips, not to mention cutting down vegetation and making demands on precious resources such as water. On the other hand, tourist dollars provide much-needed revenue for funding conservation projects. Local attitudes have also changed as people have learned to value their environment through public education campaigns.

Impetus for environmental protection is coming from NGOs operating at both community and government levels. They have notched up some spectacular successes, such as the Magpie Robin Recovery Program, funded by the Royal Society for the Protection of Birds and Birdlife International. From just 23 magpie robins languishing on Frégate Island in 1990, there are now nearly 250 living on Frégate, Cousin, Denis and Cousine Islands. Similar results have been achieved with the Seychelles warbler on Cousin, Cousine and Aride Islands.

As part of these projects, a number of islands have been painstakingly restored to their original habitat by replacing alien plant and animal species with native varieties. Several islands have also been developed for ecotourism, notably Frégate, Bird, Denis, North, Silhouette and Alphonse Islands. The visitors not only help fund conservation work, but it is also easier to protect the islands from poachers and predators if they are inhabited. With any luck, this marriage of conservation and tourism will point the way to the future

The coral reefs that encircle many of the Seychelles' islands are seen as barometers of the health of the local marine environment, and the news is worrying. Increasing sea-surface temperatures, caused by the phenomenon known as El Niño, can have devastating effects; an El Niño event in 2016 caused widespread coral bleaching and a massive reduction in coral coverage. A similar event in 1998 saw the bleaching of 90% of reefs in the Seychelles. While the reefs are of great significance for their own sakes, in the Seychelles the flow-on effects for tourism and fisheries, both major income earners for the Seychellois, don't bear thinking about.

SLEEPING PRICE RANGES

The following price ranges refer to a double room with bathroom but without breakfast.

€ less than €75

€€ €75–€150

€€€ more than €150

SURVIVAL GUIDE

 Directory A-Z

ACCESSIBLE TRAVEL

Most luxury hotels conform to international standards for disabled access, and it's usually possible to hire an assistant if you want to take an excursion. Apart from that, special facilities for travellers with disabilities are few and far between in the Seychelles, and no beach is equipped with wheelchair access.

Download Lonely Planet's free Accessible Travel guides from http://lptravel.to/Accessible Travel.

ACCOMMODATION

Accommodation should always be booked in advance, particularly during peak periods (Christmas to New Year and Easter) and high season (December to March, and July and August).

Self-catering accommodation Self-catering villas or apartments can be excellent alternatives to hotels. Many are by the sea and range from basic to luxurious.

Hotels and resorts The choice here is vast. Top-end resorts often blend opulent bungalows into the natural setting. You can expect restaurants, bars, swimming pool and sometimes a spa.

Private island resorts These ultra-exclusive options fulfil desert-island fantasies, and the pampering on offer is legendary. All have an eco bent.

Guesthouses & Self-Catering Accommodation

No, you don't need to remortgage the house to visit the Seychelles if you stay in one of the numerous cheaper guesthouses or self-catering establishments on Mahé, Praslin and La Digue. Self-catering options are private homes, villas, residences, studios or apartments that are fully equipped and can be rented by the night, although some have a minimum stay of two or three nights. The distinction between self-catering options and guesthouses is slim. Typically, rooms in guesthouses don't come equipped with a kitchen, and breakfast is usually offered. That said, at most self-catering ventures, breakfast and dinner can be arranged on request. Standards are generally high: even in the cheapest guesthouse you can expect to get a room with a private bathroom and air con, as well as a daily cleaning service. Both options are generally excellent value, especially for families or groups of friends. Most cost between €80 and €200. Many offer discounts for extended stays.

They also offer good opportunities for cultural immersion. They're mostly family-run operations and provide a much more personal, idiosyncratic experience than hotels.

Resorts & Hotels

There's no shortage of uberluxurious options that seem to have sprung straight from the pages of a glossy designer magazine, with luxurious villas oozing style and class, and fabulously lavish spas in gorgeous settings.

For those whose budget won't stretch quite this far, there are also a few good-value, mid-range affairs around Mahé, Praslin and La Digue, with prices around €250 for a double.

Note that hotels commonly offer internet specials well below the advertised rack rates. It is also well worth checking with travel agents about hotel-and-flight holiday packages, which usually come cheaper.

Expect to pay €180 per person per night (including half board) at the very minimum. Prices quickly climb all the way up to €1000 per person per night.

Virtually all the hotels charge higher rates during peak periods.

All-inclusive, full-blown resorts featuring a wide range of recreational facilities and entertainment programs are quite rare in the Seychelles.

Private Island Resorts

If you want to combine escapism with luxury, the Seychelles offers a clutch of ultraexclusive hideaways that almost defy description. They include Alphonse, Bird, Desroches, Félicité, Silhouette, North, Frégate and Denis Islands. This is where you are really buying into the dream. They offer every modern convenience but still preserve that perfect tropical-island ambience – the Robinson Crusoe factor – and feature an atmosphere of romance, rejuvenation and exotic sensuality. Each private-island resort has its own personality and devotees. There's minimal contact with the local people, though.

Expect to pay between a cool €450 to a whopping €7500 a night, full board.

Booking Services

Seychelles Travel (www.seychelles.travel) Has a list of accommodation options.

Seyvillas (www.seyvillas.com) Hotels and self-catering villas, placing the accent on originality and authentic hospitality.

Seychelles Bons Plans (www.seychellesbonsplans.com) A selection of well-run and well-priced establishments.

Seychelles Resa (www.seychelles-resa.com) Look for special offers.

CHILDREN

➡ The Seychelles is a very child- and family-friendly place.

➡ Most hotels cater for all age groups, offering babysitting services, kids' clubs and activities especially for teenagers.

EATING PRICE RANGES

The following price ranges refer to a standard main course, including service charges and taxes.

€ less than Rs 150

€€ Rs 150–300

€€€ more than Rs 300

➡ While children will happily spend all day splashing around in the lagoon, boat trips around the islands should also appeal.

➡ Communing with giant tortoises is a sure-fire hit and visiting some of the nature reserves can be fun.

➡ Finding special foods and other baby products can be difficult, especially outside Victoria, so you might want to bring your favourite items with you.

ELECTRICITY

The Seychelles uses 220V, 50Hz AC; plugs in general use are type G.

EMBASSIES & CONSULATES

Countries with diplomatic representation in the Seychelles include the following:

British High Commission (☑ 4283666; www.gov.uk/world/organisations/high-commission-victoria; Francis Rachel St, 3rd fl, Oliaji Trade Centre, Victoria; ⊗ 8.30am-noon Mon-Thu)

French Embassy (☑ 4225513; www.sc.ambafrance.org/-Francais-; 1st fl, Immeuble La Ciotat, Mont Fleuri Rd, Victoria; ⊗ 8am-noon & 1-5pm Mon-Thu)

German Honorary Consulate (☑ 4601100; germanconsul@natureseychelles.org; Nature Seychelles, Roche Caiman, PO Box 1310, Mahé; ⊗ 8am-4pm Mon-Fri)

US Consular Agency (☑ 4225256; https://mu.usembassy.gov/u-s-citizen-services/u-s-consular-agency-victoria-seychelles; Francis Rachel St, 2nd fl, Oliaji Trade Centre, Victoria; ⊗ 8.30am-12.30pm Tue-Thu)

INTERNET ACCESS

➡ There is a small number of internet cafes in Victoria, but fewer with each passing year. Outside the capital, internet cafes are harder to find.

➡ Many midrange and all top-end hotels offer wi-fi, as do self-catering establishments and some restaurants and cafes. In some cases wi-fi access is restricted to public areas and is not free of charge.

➡ If you will be in the Seychelles for a while, consider buying a USB stick (dongle) from local mobile provider Cable & Wireless (p331), which

PRACTICALITIES

Newspapers Key newspapers include the government-controlled daily *Seychelles Nation* (www.nation.sc) and the daily *Today in Seychelles* (www.today-inseychelles.com).

TV Seychelles Broadcasting Corporation (www.sbc.com) broadcasts in English, French and Creole. BBC World, France 24 and CNN are available on satellite.

Radio SBC runs the main radio station and 24-hour music station, Paradise FM. BBC World Service and Radio France International (RFI) available in Mahé.

Smoking Prohibited in indoor public places, at workplaces and on public transport; allowed in outdoor restaurants, on beaches and in some hotel rooms.

Weights & Measures The Seychelles uses the metric system.

and transport – are quoted in euros and can be paid in euros (and less frequently in US dollars). In restaurants, prices are quoted in rupees but you can also pay in euros.

Credit cards Widely accepted.

Local currency The Seychelles rupee (Rs), which is divided into 100 cents (¢). Bank notes come in denominations of Rs 10, Rs 25, Rs 50, Rs 100 and Rs 500; there are coins of Rs 1, Rs 5, 1¢, 5¢, 10¢ and 25¢.

Tipping Not generally practised in the Seychelles and is never an obligation.

Exchange Rates

For current exchange rates, see www.xe.com.

Australia	A$1	Rs 9.24
Canada	C$1	Rs 10.30
Europe	€1	Rs 15.21
Japan	¥100	Rs 12.79
NZ	NZ$1	Rs 8.79
UK	UK£1	Rs 16.63
USA	US$1	Rs 13.62

you can then load with airtime and plug into your laptop.

➜ Connections are still fairly slow by Western standards.

LGBT+ TRAVELLERS

In 2016, the Seychelles parliament decriminalised sex between men (female-female sex was never considered a crime), same-sex marriage is recognised by law, and LGBT+ couples are legally permitted to adopt. Although community attitudes are somewhat more conservative than these laws suggest, the Seychellois are generally tolerant of gay and lesbian relationships as long as couples don't flaunt their sexuality in public; open displays of affection could raise eyebrows. We've never heard of any problems arising from same-sex couples sharing rooms during their holidays. There is no open gay or lesbian scene in the Seychelles.

For more, check out the following:

Gay Seychelles Guide 2019 (www.travelgay.com/gay-seychelles-guide/) Less a guide than a high-level overview of the legal situation and community attitudes.

Global Gayz – Seychelles (www.globalgayz.com/gay-seychelles/) Similar in its focus on high-level issues rather than a gay guide to the islands.

MONEY

ATMs You'll find ATMs on Mahé, Praslin and La Digue.

Cash Euros are the best currency to carry. Prices for most tourist services – including accommodation, excursions, diving, car hire

OPENING HOURS

Banks 8.30am–2pm Monday to Friday, 8.30-11am Saturday

Government offices 8am–4pm or 5pm Monday to Friday

Restaurants 11am–2pm or 3pm and 6pm–9pm daily

Shops and businesses 8am–5pm Monday to Friday, 8am–noon Saturday

PUBLIC HOLIDAYS

New Year 1 and 2 January

Good Friday March/April

Easter Day March/April

Labour Day 1 May

Liberation Day 5 June

Corpus Christi 10 June

National Day 18 June

Independence Day 29 June

Assumption 15 August

All Saints' Day 1 November

Immaculate Conception 8 December

Christmas Day 25 December

SAFE TRAVEL

➜ Beaches in the Seychelles are beauties but some change dramatically with the seasons. They can be tranquil and flat as a lake at certain times of the year, and savage with incredible surf and mean rip currents at other periods. Most beaches are not supervised.

➜ If you hire a car, don't leave anything valuable in it. If you must do so, hide everything well out of sight. Wherever possible, park in a secure car park or at least somewhere busy.

➡ Never leave your valuables unattended on the beach.

➡ When sunbathing or walking around a coconut grove, beware of falling coconuts – they can cause severe head injuries.

TELEPHONE

➡ The telephone system is efficient and reliable.

➡ Telephone cards are available from **Cable & Wireless** (4284063; www.cwseychelles.com; Francis Rachel St; per hour Rs 40; 7.30am-4.30pm Mon-Fri, 8am-noon Sat). Local calls within and between the main islands, as well as international calls, cost around Rs 4 per minute.

➡ When phoning the Seychelles from abroad, you'll need to dial the international code for the Seychelles (248), followed by the seven-digit local number.

➡ There are no area codes.

➡ Calling abroad from the Seychelles, dial 00 for international access, then the country code, area code and local number.

➡ If you have an unlocked GSM phone, you can use a local SIM card (Rs 50) purchased from either Cable & Wireless or **Airtel** (4610615; www.africa.airtel.com/seychelles; Huteau Lane; 8.30am-4pm Mon-Fri, to noon Sat). When buying a SIM card you'll need to bring along your passport.

TIME

The Seychelles is on GMT plus four hours. When it's noon in Victoria, it's 8am in London, 9am in Paris, 3am in New York and 6pm in Sydney. The Seychelles does not operate a system of daylight saving; being equatorial, its sunset and sunrise times vary only slightly throughout the year.

TOURIST INFORMATION

The very well-organised Seychelles Tourism Bureau (www.seychelles.travel) is the only tourist information body in the Seychelles. The head office is in Victoria (p283) and it has an office on La Digue (p316). On Praslin, the Vallée de Mer Visitor Centre (p298) covers only the national park.

VISAS

Visas are not required for most Western nationals for stays of up to three months. They just need a valid passport.

VOLUNTEERING

Want to get involved in turtle tagging, whale shark monitoring or researching certain animal species? The following all have volunteer programs.

Nature Seychelles (Map p278; 4601100; www.natureseychelles.org; Roche Caiman) Has volunteering opportunities on Cousin Island.

Seychelles Island Foundation (p283) If you want to buy a coco fesse (the fruit of the coco de mer palm), head to the Seychelles Island Foundation, which has some stock and will issue you the required export permit. Be prepared to fork out about €200. Their work centres on habitat restoration on the Aldabra Atoll, as well as managing Vallée de Mai on Praslin.

Marine Conservation Society Seychelles (MCSS; www.mcss.sc) Has various volunteering opportunities, including whale shark monitoring and turtle tagging.

Fregate Island Private (p320) Help monitor giant tortoises, nesting sea turtles, endemic birds and invertebrates.

ℹ Getting There & Away

ENTERING THE COUNTRY

Entering the Seychelles is usually hassle-free, with no visas required for many nationalities. Customs searches are generally quick and easy if they occur at all.

Initial entry is granted for the period of the visit (with a maximum of three months) and proof of a planned and paid-for departure is required. Immigration officers will also require that you mention the name, address and phone number of the place where you are staying in the Seychelles; they may even ask for proof of a hotel (or other accommodation) booking.

AIR

Direct flights connect the Seychelles with China, France, Germany, Kenya, India, Madagascar, Mauritius, Réunion, South Africa, Sri Lanka and the UAE. For further afield, you'll need to take a connecting flight from South Africa, Europe or the Middle East.

Airports & Airlines

The **Seychelles International Airport** (Map p278; 4384400; www.seychellesairports.sc),

ARRIVING IN THE SEYCHELLES

Seychelles International Airport
(Mahé) The Seychelles' only international airport is located on Mahé, about 8km south of Victoria. Big hotels provide transport to and from the airport. Taxis from just outside the airport cost from Rs 500 to Beau Vallon. The ride takes about 25 minutes.

DEPARTURE TAX

Departure tax is included in the price of a ticket.

about 8km south of Victoria, is the only international airport in the Seychelles.

Air Seychelles (☑ 4391000; www.air seychelles.com; Independence Ave, Victoria; ☺ 8am-4pm Mon-Fri, to noon Sat) is the national carrier with a good safety record. It has a fairly limited international network, but has a code-share agreement with Etihad Airways.

❶ Getting Around

AIR

Air Seychelles takes care of all inter-island flights, whether scheduled or chartered. The only scheduled services are between Mahé and Praslin, with around 25 flights per day in each direction. The fare for the 20-minute hop is about €132 return. The luggage limit is only 20kg. Air Seychelles also flies to Bird, Denis, Frégate and Desroches Islands, but on a charter basis; bookings for these flights are handled directly by hotels on the island.

La Digue and Silhouette Island (and all other islands) can be reached by helicopter.

Note that Mahé is the only hub for flights within the Seychelles.

BICYCLE

Bicycles are the principal form of transport on La Digue. On Praslin you can rent bikes at Anse Volbert or through your accommodation. Mahé is a bit hilly for casual cyclists and most visitors rent cars, so bike rental is hard to find there.

BOAT

Travel by boat is very easy between Mahé, Praslin and La Digue, with regular and efficient ferry services. In high season it's advisable to book your ticket at least a day in advance with the ferry company, through a travel agent or online at www.seychellesbookings.com.

For all other islands you have to charter a boat or take a tour.

BUS

Good news: if you have time, you don't really need to rent a car to visit the islands.

Mahé

An extensive bus service operates throughout Mahé. Destinations and routes are usually marked on the front of the buses. There is a flat rate of Rs 6 whatever the length of the journey; pay the driver as you board. Bus stops have

signs and shelters and there are also markings on the road.

Timetables and maps of each route are posted at the terminus in Victoria, where you can also pick up photocopied timetables (Rs 5) at the SPTC office (p283). All parts of the island are serviced, but for many trips, you'll have to change buses in the capital.

Praslin

Praslin boasts a relatively efficient bus service. The basic route is from Anse Boudin to Mont Plaisir (for Anse Kerlan) via Anse Volbert, Baie Ste Anne, Vallée de Mai, Grand Anse and the airport. Buses run in each direction every hour (every half-hour between Baie Ste Anne and Mont Plaisir) from 6am to 6pm. Anse Consolation and Anse La Blague are also serviced. For Anse Lazio, get off at Anse Boudin and walk to the beach (about 20 minutes; 1km). There is a flat fare of Rs 7.

CAR

If you want to control your own destiny, your best bet is to rent a car. Most of the road network on Mahé and Praslin is sealed and in good shape. More of a worry are the narrow bends and the speed at which some drivers – especially bus drivers – take them.

Drive on the left, and beware of drivers with fast cars and drowsy brains – especially late on Friday and Saturday nights. On Mahé the speed limit is supposed to be 40km/h in built-up areas, 65km/h outside towns and 80km/h on the dual carriageway between Victoria and the airport. On Praslin the limit is 40km/h throughout the island.

On La Digue and all other islands there are no car-rental companies – all tourists get around on foot or by bike.

Car Hire

There are any number of car-rental companies on Mahé and quite a few on Praslin. Due to healthy competition, the cheapest you're likely to get on Mahé is about €40 to €45 a day for a small hatchback. Rates on Praslin are about €5 to €10 higher. You can book through your hotel or guesthouse. Most apartment and guesthouse owners have negotiated discounts with car-rental outlets for their clients. A number of companies also have offices at the airport.

Drivers must be over 23 years old and have held a driving licence for at least a year. Most companies accept a national licence.

TAXI

Taxis operate on Mahé and Praslin and there are even a handful on La Digue. They are not metered. Agree on a fare before departure.

Survival Guide

Health

As long as you stay up to date with your vaccinations and take some basic preventive measures, you'd have to be pretty unlucky to encounter any serious health hazards in Mauritius, Réunion or the Seychelles. The islands have a fair selection of tropical diseases on offer, but you're much more likely to get a bout of diarrhoea or a sprained ankle than an exotic disease.

Chikungunya epidemics have been an issue in the region in the past, so check the latest before travelling, and at the time of writing there was an outbreak of dengue fever in Mauritius.

BEFORE YOU GO

Planning

A little planning before departure, particularly for pre-existing illnesses, will save you a lot of trouble later. Before a long trip, get a check-up from your dentist and your doctor if you require regular medication or have a chronic illness, eg high blood pressure or asthma. You should also organise spare contact lenses and glasses (and take your optical prescription with you); get a first-aid and medical kit together; and arrange necessary vaccinations.

Travellers can register with the International Association for Medical Assistance

to Travellers (www.iamat. org). Its website can help travellers find a doctor who has recognised training. You might also consider doing a first-aid course (contact the Red Cross or St John International) or attending a remote medicine first-aid course, such as that offered by the Royal Geographical Society (https://wildernessmedical training.co.uk/).

If you are bringing medications with you, carry them in their original containers, clearly labelled. A signed and dated letter from your physician describing all medical conditions and medications, including generic names, is also a good idea. If carrying syringes or needles, be sure to have a physician's letter documenting their medical necessity.

Health Insurance

Find out in advance whether your insurance plan will make payments directly to providers or will reimburse you later for health expenditures (in many countries doctors expect payment in cash). It is vital to ensure that your travel insurance will cover outdoor activities, including paragliding, diving and canyoning, as well as the emergency transport required to get you to a good hospital – or all the way home – by air and with a medical attendant if necessary. Not all insur-

ance policies cover this, so be sure to check the contract carefully. If you need medical care, your insurance company may be able to help locate the nearest hospital or clinic, or ask at your hotel. In an emergency, contact your embassy or consulate.

Medical Checklist

It is a very good idea to carry a medical and first-aid kit with you, to help yourself in case of minor illness or injury. Following is a list of items you should consider packing.

➡ antidiarrhoeal drugs (eg loperamide)

➡ acetaminophen (paracetamol) or aspirin

➡ anti-inflammatory drugs (eg ibuprofen)

➡ antihistamines (for hay fever and other allergic reactions)

➡ antibacterial ointment (eg Bactroban) for cuts and abrasions (prescription only)

➡ steroid cream or hydrocortisone cream (for allergic rashes)

➡ bandages, gauze, gauze rolls

➡ adhesive or paper tape

➡ scissors, safety pins, tweezers

➡ thermometer

➡ pocket knife

➡ DEET-containing insect repellent for the skin

➜ sunblock

➜ oral rehydration salts

➜ iodine tablets (for water purification)

➜ syringes and sterile needles (if travelling to remote areas)

Useful Resources

There is a wealth of travel health advice available on the internet – www.lonelyplanet. com is a good place to start. The World Health Organization publishes a superb book called *International Travel and Health,* which is revised annually and is available online for free at www.who. int/ith. The following are other health-related websites of general interest:

Centers for Disease Control and Prevention (www.cdc.gov)

Fit for Travel (www.fitfortravel. scot.nhs.uk)

MD Travel Health (https://red planet.travel/mdtravelhealth)

You may also like to consult your government's travel-health website, if one is available:

Australia (https://smartraveller. gov.au/guide/all-travellers/ health/)

Canada (www.phac-aspc.gc.ca)

USA (www.cdc.gov/travel)

IN MAURITIUS, RÉUNION & SEYCHELLES

Availability & Cost of Health Care

Health care in Mauritius and Réunion is generally excellent; the Seychelles is pretty good by African standards, but some travellers have been critical of the standard of the public health system. Generally, public hospitals offer the cheapest service, but may not have the most up-

to-date equipment and medications; private hospitals and clinics are more expensive but tend to have more advanced drugs and equipment and better-trained medical staff.

Infectious Diseases

It's a formidable list, but a few precautions go a long way.

Chikungunya

This viral infection transmitted by certain mosquito bites was traditionally rare in the Indian Ocean until 2005 when an epidemic hit Réunion, Mauritius and the Seychelles. The unusual name means 'that which bends up' in the East African language of Makonde, a reference to the joint pain and physical distortions it creates in sufferers. Chikungunya virus is rarely fatal, but it can be, and it's always unpleasant. Symptoms are often flu-like, with joint pain, high fever and body rashes being the most common.

It's important not to confuse it with dengue fever. If you're diagnosed with Chikungunya virus expect to be down for at least a week, possibly longer. The joint pain can be horrendous and there is no treatment; those infected need simply to rest inside (preferably under a mosquito net to prevent reinfection), taking gentle exercise to avoid joints stiffening unbearably. The best way to avoid it is to avoid mosquito bites, so

bring plenty of repellent, use the anti-mosquito plug-ins wherever you can and bring a mosquito net if you're really thorough.

Dengue Fever

Dengue fever (or breakbone fever) is present in the Seychelles with outbreaks on the islands of Mahé and Praslin as recently as 2018. It also reappeared in Réunion in 2018, with more than 6000 people infected. Although the risk to travellers remains small, it is recommended that you take precautions to avoid being bitten by mosquitos. It's a particular concern in urban areas, especially after heavy rains and anywhere with standing or stagnant water. Mosquitoes that carry the virus are active from dawn until dusk.

Dengue fever causes a feverish illness with headache and muscle pains similar to those experienced with a bad, prolonged attack of influenza. There might be a rash. Mosquito bites should be avoided whenever possible. Self-treatment: paracetamol and rest.

Hepatitis A

Hepatitis A is spread through contaminated food (particularly shellfish) and water. It causes jaundice and, though it is rarely fatal, it can cause prolonged lethargy and delayed recovery. If you've had hepatitis A, you shouldn't drink alcohol for up to six months afterwards, but once you've recovered there won't be any long-term problems.

The first symptoms include dark urine and a yellow colour to the whites of the eyes. Sometimes a fever and abdominal pain might be present. Hepatitis A vaccine (Avaxim, VAQTA, Havrix) is given as an injection: a single dose will give protection for up to a year, and a booster after a year gives 10-year protection. Hepatitis A and typhoid vaccines can also be given as a single-dose vaccine (Hepatyrix or Viatim).

Hepatitis B

Hepatitis B is spread through infected blood, contaminated needles and sexual intercourse. It can also be passed from an infected mother to the baby during childbirth. It affects the liver, causing jaundice and occasionally liver failure. Most people recover completely, but some people might be chronic carriers of the virus, which could lead eventually to cirrhosis or liver cancer. Those visiting high-risk areas for extended periods, or those with increased social or occupational risk, should be immunised. Many countries now include hepatitis B as part of routine childhood vaccinations. It is given singly or can be given at the same time as hepatitis A (Hepatyrix). A course will give protection for at least five years. It can be given over four weeks or six months.

Leptospirosis

Cases of leptospirosis have been reported in Réunion. It spreads through the excreta of infected rodents, especially rats. It can cause hepatitis and renal failure, which might be fatal. Symptoms include flu-like fever, headaches, muscle aches and red eyes, among others. Avoid swimming or walking in stagnant waters.

Malaria

There is no risk of malaria in the Seychelles; the risk is extremely low in Réunion and Mauritius.

Rabies

Rabies is spread by receiving bites or licks on broken skin by an infected animal. The risk is mainly from dogs. It is always fatal once the clinical symptoms start (which might be up to several months after an infected bite), so post-bite vaccination should be given as soon as possible. Post-bite vaccination prevents the virus from spreading to the central nervous system, and is necessary whether or not you were vaccinated before the bite. If you have not already been vaccinated, you will need a course of five injections starting 24 hours after being bitten or as soon as possible after the injury. If you have been vaccinated, you will need fewer post-bite injections (three injections over a month), and have more time to seek medical help.

Travellers' Diarrhoea

Although it's not inevitable that you will get diarrhoea while travelling in the region, it's certainly possible. Sometimes dietary changes, such as increased spices or oils, are the cause. To avoid diarrhoea, only eat fresh fruits or vegetables if cooked or peeled, and be wary of dairy products that might contain unpasteurised milk. Although freshly cooked food is often a safe option, plates or serving utensils might be dirty, so you should be highly selective when eating food from street vendors (make sure that cooked food is piping hot all the way through).

If you develop diarrhoea, be sure to drink plenty of fluids, preferably an oral rehydration solution containing water (lots), and some salt and sugar. A few loose stools don't require treatment, but if you start having more than four or five stools a day, you should start taking an antibiotic (usually a quinoline drug, such as ciprofloxacin or norfloxacin) and an antidiarrhoeal agent (such as loperamide) if you are not within easy reach of a toilet. However, if diarrhoea is bloody, persists for more than 72 hours or is accompanied by fever, shaking chills or severe abdominal pain, you should seek medical attention

Yellow Fever

Although yellow fever is not a problem in the region, travellers should still carry a certificate as evidence of vaccination if they have recently been in an infected country. For a list of these countries, visit the website of the World Health Organization (www.who.int/ith) or the Centers for Disease Control and Prevention (www.cdc.gov). A traveller without a legally required, up-to-date certificate may be vaccinated and detained in isolation at the place of entry for up to 10 days or possibly repatriated.

Diving Health & Safety

Health Requirements

Officially a doctor should check you over before you do a course and fill out a form of diving-related health questions. In practice most dive schools will let you dive or do a course if you complete a medical questionnaire, but the check-up is still a good idea. This is especially so if you have any problem at all with your breathing, ears or sinuses. If you are an asthmatic, have any other chronic breathing difficulties or any inner-ear problems, you shouldn't do any diving.

Decompression Sickness

This is a very serious condition – usually, though not always, associated with diver error. The most common symptoms are unusual fatigue or weakness, skin itch, pain in the arms, legs (joints or mid-limbs) or torso, dizziness and vertigo, local numbness, tingling or paralysis and shortness of breath.

The most common causes of decompression sickness (or the 'bends' as it is commonly known) are diving too deep, staying at depth for too long or ascending too quickly. This results in nitrogen coming out of solution in the blood and forming bubbles, most commonly in the bones and particularly in the joints or in weak spots such as healed fractured sites.

Note that your last dive should be completed 24 hours before flying in order to minimise the risk of residual nitrogen in the blood that can cause decompression injury.

The only treatment for decompression sickness is to put the patient into a recompression chamber. There are recompression chambers in Mauritius, Réunion and Seychelles.

Insurance

In addition to normal travel insurance, it's a very good idea to take out specific diving cover, which will pay for evacuation to a recompression facility and the cost of hyperbaric treatment in a chamber. Divers Alert Network (www.diversalert network.org) is a nonprofit diving-safety organisation. It provides a policy that covers evacuation and recompression.

Environmental Hazards

Heat Exhaustion

This condition occurs following heavy sweating and excessive fluid loss with inadequate replacement of fluids and salt, and is particularly common in hot climates when taking unaccustomed exercise before full acclimatisation. Symptoms include headache, dizziness and tiredness. Dehydration is already happening by the time you feel thirsty – aim to drink sufficient water to produce pale, diluted urine. Self-treatment is by fluid replacement with water and/or fruit juice, and cooling by cold water and fans. The treatment of the salt-loss component consists of consuming salty fluids as in soup, and adding a little more table salt to foods than usual.

Heatstroke

Heat exhaustion is a precursor to the much more serious condition of heatstroke. In this case there is damage to the sweating mechanism, with an excessive rise in body temperature; irrational and hyperactive behaviour; and eventually loss of consciousness and death. Rapid cooling by spraying the body with water and fanning is ideal. Emergency fluid and electrolyte replacement is usually also required by intravenous drip.

Insect Bites & Stings

Mosquitoes in the region can carry chikungunya virus and dengue fever, plus they (and other insects) can cause irritation and infected bites.

To avoid these, take the same precautions as you would for avoiding malaria, including wearing long pants and long-sleeved shirts, using mosquito repellent, avoiding highly scented perfumes or aftershaves, etc. Bee and wasp stings cause major problems only to those who have a severe allergy to the stings (anaphylaxis), in which case carry an adrenaline (epinephrine) injection.

Leeches may be present in damp rainforest conditions; they attach themselves to your skin to suck your blood. Salt or a lighted cigarette end will make them fall off. Ticks can cause skin infections and other more serious diseases. If a tick is found attached, press down around the tick's head with tweezers, grab the head and gently pull upwards.

Marine Life

A number of Indian Ocean species are poisonous or may sting or bite. Watch out above all for sea urchins. Other far rarer creatures to look out for include the gaudy lionfish with its poisonous spined fins, and the cleverly camouflaged – and exceptionally poisonous – stonefish, which lives camouflaged amid coral formations. Some shells, such as the cone shell, can fire out a deadly poisonous barb. The species of fire coral, which looks like yellowish brush-like coral growths, packs a powerful sting if touched.

Shark attacks on surfers have been a major issue in Réunion, especially off Boucan Canot, St-Gilles-les-Bains, Trois Bassins and Étang-Salé-les-Bains. Stick to supervised and protected beaches. In the Seychelles, two fatal shark attacks on swimmers were reported in 2011; both occurred at Anse Lazio. Still, the risk of shark attacks remains extremely small.

Language

Along with the local Creoles, French is spoken (and official) in all three destinations included in this book. You'll find that menus on the islands are mostly in French, with English variations in some cases.

CREOLES

The Creoles spoken in Mauritius, Réunion and Seychelles are a blend of French and an assortment of African languages, with some regional variations. Seychelles Creole is similar to that of Mauritius, but differs significantly from the Creole spoken in Réunion. Note also that the Creole spoken in Mauritius and Seychelles is more comprehensible to French people than that of Réunion, even though Réunion itself is thoroughly French.

Mauritius

The official languages of Mauritius are English and French. English is used mainly in government and business. French is the spoken language in educated and cultural circles, and is used in newspapers and magazines. You'll probably find that most people will first speak to you in French and only switch to English once they realise you're an English speaker. Most Indo-Mauritians speak Bhojpuri, derived from a Bihari dialect of Hindi.

There are major differences between the pronunciation and usage of Creole and standard French. Here are some basic phrases you may find handy.

WANT MORE?

For in-depth language information and handy phrases, check out Lonely Planet's *French Phrasebook*. You'll find it at **shop.lonelyplanet.com**, or you can buy Lonely Planet's iPhone phrasebooks at the Apple App Store.

How are you?	*Ki manière?*
Fine, thanks.	*Mon byen, mersi.*
I don't understand.	*Mo pas comprend.*
OK.	*Correc.*
Not OK.	*Pas correc.*
he/she/it	*li*
Do you have ...?	*Ou éna ...?*
I'd like ...	*Mo oulé ...*
I'm thirsty.	*Mo soif.*
Cheers!	*Tapeta!*
Great!	*Formidabe!*

Réunion

French is the official language of Réunion, but Creole is the most widely spoken language. Few people speak English.

Keep in mind that a word that means one thing in French can mean something completely different in Creole, and where a word does have the same meaning, it's usually pronounced differently in Creole. Creole also has a number of *bons mots* and charming idioms, which are often the result of Hindi, Arab and Malagasy influences or misinterpretations of the original French word. For example, *bonbon la fesse* (bum toffee) is a suppository, *conserves* (preserves) are sunglasses, and *cœur d'amant* (lover's heart) is a cardamom seed. *Coco* is your head, *caze* is your house, *marmaille* is your child, *baba* is your baby, *band* means 'family', *le fait noir* means 'night', and *mi aime jou* means 'I love you'.

There are two basic rules of Creole pronunciation: r is generally not pronounced (when it is, it's pronounced lightly), and the soft j and ch sounds of French are pronounced as 'z' and 's' respectively. For example, *manzay* is the Creole equivalent of French 'manger' (to eat), *zamais* is used for 'jamais' (never), and you'll hear *sontay* instead of 'chanter' (to sing).

NUMBERS

1	*un*	un
2	*deux*	der
3	*trois*	trwa
4	*quatre*	ka·trer
5	*cinq*	sungk
6	*six*	sees
7	*sept*	set
8	*huit*	weet
9	*neuf*	nerf
10	*dix*	dees
20	*vingt*	vung
30	*trente*	tront
40	*quarante*	ka·ront
50	*cinquante*	sung·kont
60	*soixante*	swa·sont
70	*soixante-dix*	swa·son·dees
80	*quatre-vingts*	ka·trer·vung
90	*quatre-vingt-dix*	ka·trer·vung·dees
100	*cent*	son
1000	*mille*	meel

Seychelles

English and French are the official languages of the Seychelles. Most people speak both, although French Creole (known as Kreol Seselwa) is the lingua franca. Kreol Seselwa was 'rehabilitated' and made semi-official in 1981, and is increasingly used in newspapers and literature. These days, most Seychellois will use English when speaking to tourists, French when conducting business, and Creole in the home.

Seychelles Creole is similar to that of Mauritius and Martinique, but differs remarkably from that of Réunion. The soft pronunciation of certain French consonants is hardened and some syllables are dropped completely. The soft *j* becomes 'z', for example. The following Creole phrases can get you started:

Good morning./ Good afternoon.	*Bonzour.*
How are you?	*Comman sava?*
Fine, thanks.	*Mon byen, mersi.*
What's your name?	*Ki mannyer ou appel?*
My name is ...	*Mon appel ...*
Where do you live?	*Koté ou resté?*
I don't understand.	*Mon pas konpran.*
I like it.	*Mon kontan.*
Where is ...?	*Ol i ...?*
How much is that?	*Kombyen sa?*
I'm thirsty.	*Mon soif.*
Can I have a beer, please?	*Mon kapa ganny en labyer silvouplé?*

FRENCH

The pronunciation of French is pretty straightforward for English speakers as the sounds used in spoken French can almost all be found in English. There are just a couple of exceptions: nasal vowels (represented in our pronunciation guides by o or u followed by an almost inaudible nasal consonant sound m, n or ng), the 'funny' *u* (ew in our guides) and the deep-in-the-throat *r*. Bearing these few points in mind and reading our pronunciation guides as if they were English, you'll be understood just fine.

In the following phrases we have included masculine and femine forms where necessary, separated by a slash and indicated with the abbreviations 'm/f'.

Basics

Hello.	*Bonjour.*	bon·zhoor
Goodbye.	*Au revoir.*	o·rer·vwa
Excuse me.	*Excusez-moi.*	ek·skew·zay·mwa
Sorry.	*Pardon.*	par·don
Yes./No.	*Oui./Non.*	wee/non
Please.	*S'il vous plaît.*	seel voo play
Thank you.	*Merci.*	mair·see
You're welcome.	*De rien.*	der ree·en

How are you?
Comment allez-vous?   ko·mon ta·lay·voo

Fine, and you?
Bien, merci. Et vous?   byun mair·see ay voo

My name is ...
Je m'appelle ...   zher ma·pel ...

What's your name?
Comment vous appelez-vous?   ko·mon voo·za·play voo

Do you speak English?
Parlez-vous anglais?   par·lay·voo ong·glay

I don't understand.
Je ne comprends pas.   zher ner kom·pron pa

Accommodation

Do you have any rooms available?
Est-ce que vous avez des chambres libres?   es·ker voo za·vay day shom·brer lee·brer

How much is it per night/person?
Quel est le prix par nuit/personne?   kel ay ler pree par nwee/per·son

Is breakfast included?
Est-ce que le petit déjeuner est inclus?   es·ker ler per·tee day·zher·nay ayt en·klew

campsite	*camping*	korn·peeng
dorm	*dortoir*	dor·twar
guesthouse	*pension*	pon·syon
hotel	*hôtel*	o·tel
youth hostel	*auberge de jeunesse*	o·berzh der zher·nes
a ... room	*une chambre ...*	ewn shom·brer ...
single	*à un lit*	a un lee
double	*avec un grand lit*	a·vek un gron lee
twin	*avec des lits jumeaux*	a·vek day lee zhew·mo
with (a) ...	*avec ...*	a·vek ...
air-con	*climatiseur*	klee·ma·tee·zer
bathroom	*une salle de bains*	ewn sal der bun
window	*fenêtre*	fer·nay·trer

Directions

Where's ...?
Où est ...?   oo ay ...

What's the address?
Quelle est l'adresse?   kel ay la·dres

Could you write the address, please?
Est-ce que vous pourriez écrire l'adresse, s'il vous plaît?   es·ker voo poo·ryay ay·kreer la·dres seel voo play

Can you show me (on the map)?
Pouvez-vous m'indiquer (sur la carte)?   poo·vay·voo mun·dee·kay (sewr la kart)

at the corner	*au coin*	o kwun
behind	*derrière*	dair·ryair
in front of	*devant*	der·von
far (from)	*loin (de)*	lwun (der)
left	*gauche*	gosh
near (to)	*près (de)*	pray (der)
opposite ...	*en face de ...*	on fas der ...
right	*droite*	drwat
straight ahead	*tout droit*	too drwa

Eating & Drinking

What would you recommend?
Qu'est-ce que vous conseillez?   kes·ker voo kon·say·yay

What's in that dish?
Quels sont les ingrédients?   kel son lay zun·gray·dyon

I'm a vegetarian.
Je suis végétarien/ végétarienne.   zher swee vay·zhay·ta·ryun/ vay·zhay·ta·ryen (m/f)

I don't eat ...
Je ne mange pas ...   zher ner monzh pa ...

Cheers!
Santé!   son·tay

That was delicious.
C'était délicieux!   say·tay day·lee·syer

Please bring the bill.
Apportez-moi l'addition, s'il vous plaît.   a·por·tay·mwa la·dee·syon seel voo play

I'd like to reserve a table for ...	*Je voudrais réserver une table pour ...*	zher voo·dray ray·zair·vay ewn ta·bler poor ...
(eight) o'clock	*(vingt) heures*	(vungt) er
(two) people	*(deux) personnes*	(der) pair·son

Key Words

appetiser	*entrée*	on·tray
bottle	*bouteille*	boo·tay
breakfast	*petit déjeuner*	per·tee day·zher·nay
children's menu	*menu pour enfants*	mer·new poor on·fon
cold	*froid*	frwa
delicatessen	*traiteur*	tray·ter
dinner	*dîner*	dee·nay
dish	*plat*	pla
food	*nourriture*	noo·ree·tewr
fork	*fourchette*	foor·shet
glass	*verre*	vair
grocery store	*épicerie*	ay·pees·ree
highchair	*chaise haute*	shay zot
hot	*chaud*	sho
knife	*couteau*	koo·to
local speciality	*spécialité locale*	spay·sya·lee·tay lo·kal
lunch	*déjeuner*	day·zher·nay
main course	*plat principal*	pla prun·see·pal
market	*marché*	mar·shay
menu (in English)	*carte (en anglais)*	kart (on ong·glay)
plate	*assiette*	a·syet
spoon	*cuillère*	kwee·yair
wine list	*carte des vins*	kart day vun
with/without	*avec/sans*	a·vek/son

Meat & Fish

beef	*bœuf*	berf
chicken	*poulet*	poo·lay
crab	*crabe*	krab
lamb	*agneau*	a·nyo
oyster	*huître*	wee·trer
pork	*porc*	por

snail	*escargot*	es·kar·go
squid	*calmar*	kal·mar
turkey	*dinde*	dund
veal	*veau*	vo

red wine	*vin rouge*	vun roozh
tea	*thé*	tay
(mineral) water	*eau (minérale)*	o (mee·nay·ral)
white wine	*vin blanc*	vun blong

Fruit & Vegetables

apple	*pomme*	pom
apricot	*abricot*	ab·ree·ko
asparagus	*asperge*	a·spairzh
beans	*haricots*	a·ree·ko
beetroot	*betterave*	be·trav
cabbage	*chou*	shoo
cherry	*cerise*	ser·reez
corn	*maïs*	ma·ees
cucumber	*concombre*	kong·kom·brer
grape	*raisin*	ray·zun
lemon	*citron*	see·tron
lettuce	*laitue*	lay·tew
mushroom	*champignon*	shom·pee·nyon
peach	*pêche*	pesh
peas	*petit pois*	per·tee pwa
(red/green) pepper	*poivron (rouge/vert)*	pwa·vron (roozh/vair)
plum	*prune*	prewn
potato	*pomme de terre*	pom der tair
pumpkin	*citrouille*	see·troo·yer
shallot	*échalote*	eh·sha·lot
spinach	*épinards*	eh·pee·nar
strawberry	*fraise*	frez
tomato	*tomate*	to·mat
vegetable	*légume*	lay·gewm

Other

bread	*pain*	pun
butter	*beurre*	ber
cheese	*fromage*	fro·mazh
egg	*œuf*	erf
honey	*miel*	myel
jam	*confiture*	kon·fee·tewr
pasta/noodles	*pâtes*	pat
pepper	*poivre*	pwa·vrer
rice	*riz*	ree
salt	*sel*	sel
sugar	*sucre*	sew·krer
vinegar	*vinaigre*	vee·nay·grer

Drinks

beer	*bière*	bee·yair
coffee	*café*	ka·fay
(orange) juice	*jus (d'orange)*	zhew (do·ronzh)
milk	*lait*	lay

Emergencies

Help!
Au secours! — o skoor

Leave me alone!
Fichez-moi la paix! — fee·shay·mwa la pay

I'm lost.
Je suis perdu/perdue. — zhe swee·pair·dew (m/f)

Call a doctor.
Appelez un médecin. — a·play un mayd·sun

Call the police.
Appelez la police. — a·play la po·lees

I'm ill.
Je suis malade. — zher swee ma·lad

It hurts here.
J'ai une douleur ici. — zhay ewn doo·ler ee·see

I'm allergic to ...
Je suis allergique ... — zher swee za·lair·zheek ...

Where are the toilets?
Où sont les toilettes? — oo son ley twa·let

Shopping & Services

I'd like to buy ...
Je voudrais acheter ... — zher voo·dray ash·tay ...

Can I look at it?
Est-ce que je peux le voir? — es·ker zher per ler vwar

I'm just looking.
Je regarde. — zher rer·gard

I don't like it.
Cela ne me plaît pas. — ser·la ner mer play pa

How much is it?
C'est combien? — say kom·byun

It's too expensive.
C'est trop cher. — say tro shair

Can you lower the price?
Vous pouvez baisser le prix? — voo poo·vay bay·say ler pree

There's a mistake in the bill.
Il y a une erreur dans la note. — eel ya ewn ay·rer don la not

ATM	*guichet automatique de banque*	gee·shay o·to·ma·teek der bonk
credit card	*carte de crédit*	kart der kray·dee
internet cafe	*cybercafé*	see·bair·ka·fay
post office	*bureau de poste*	bew·ro der post
tourist office	*office de tourisme*	o·fees der too·rees·mer

Time & Dates

What time is it?
Quelle heure est-il? — kel er ay til

It's (eight) o'clock.
Il est (huit) heures. — il ay (weet) er

It's half past (10).
Il est (dix) heures et demie. — il ay (deez) er ay day·mee

morning	matin	ma·tun
afternoon	après-midi	a·pray·mee·dee
evening	soir	swar

yesterday	hier	yair
today	aujourd'hui	o·zhoor·dwee
tomorrow	demain	der·mun

Monday	lundi	lun·dee
Tuesday	mardi	mar·dee
Wednesday	mercredi	mair·krer·dee
Thursday	jeudi	zher·dee
Friday	vendredi	von·drer·dee
Saturday	samedi	sam·dee
Sunday	dimanche	dee·monsh

January	janvier	zhon·vyay
February	février	fayv·ryay
March	mars	mars
April	avril	a·vreel
May	mai	may
June	juin	zhwun
July	juillet	zhwee·yay
August	août	oot
September	septembre	sep·tom·brer
October	octobre	ok·to·brer
November	novembre	no·vom·brer
December	décembre	day·som·brer

Transport

boat	bateau	ba·to
bus	bus	bews
plane	avion	a·vyon
train	train	trun

first	premier	prer·myay
last	dernier	dair·nyay
next	prochain	pro·shun

I want to go to ...
Je voudrais aller à ... — zher voo·dray a·lay a ...

Does it stop at ...?
Est-ce qu'il s'arrête à ...? — es·kil sa·ret a ...

At what time does it leave/arrive?
À quelle heure est-ce qu'il part/arrive? — a kel er es kil par/a·reev

Can you tell me when we get to ...?
Pouvez-vous me dire quand nous arrivons à ...? — poo·vay·voo mer deer kon noo za·ree·von a ...

I want to get off here.
Je veux descendre ici. — zher ver day·son·drer ee·see

a ... ticket	un billet ...	un bee·yay ...
1st-class	de première classe	der prem·yair klas
2nd-class	de deuxième classe	der der·zyem las
one-way	simple	sum·pler
return	aller et retour	a·lay ay rer·toor
aisle seat	côté couloir	ko·tay kool·war
delayed	en retard	on rer·tar
cancelled	annulé	a·new·lay
platform	quai	kay
ticket office	guichet	gee·shay
timetable	horaire	o·rair
train station	gare	gar
window seat	côté fenêtre	ko·tay fe·ne·trer

I'd like to hire a ...	Je voudrais louer ...	zher voo·dray loo·way ...
4WD	un quatre-quatre	un kat·kat
car	une voiture	ewn vwa·tewr
bicycle	un vélo	un vay·lo
motorcycle	une moto	ewn mo·to

child seat	siège-enfant	syezh·on·fon
diesel	diesel	dyay·zel
helmet	casque	kask
mechanic	mécanicien	may·ka·nee·syun
petrol/gas	essence	ay·sons
service station	station-service	sta·syon·ser·vees

Is this the road to ...?
C'est la route pour ...? — say la root poor ...

(How long) Can I park here?
(Combien de temps) Est-ce que je peux stationner ici? — (kom·byun der tom) es·ker zher per sta·syo·nay ee·see

The car/motorbike has broken down (at ...)
La voiture/moto est tombée en panne (à ...). — la vwa·tewr/mo·to ay tom·bay on pan (a ...).

I have a flat tyre.
Mon pneu est à plat. — mom pner ay ta pla

I've run out of petrol.
Je suis en panne d'essence. — zher swee zon pan day·sons

I've lost my car keys.
J'ai perdu les clés de ma voiture. — zhay per·dew lay klay der ma vwa·tewr

Behind the Scenes

SEND US YOUR FEEDBACK

We love to hear from travellers – your comments keep us on our toes and help make our books better. Our well-travelled team reads every word on what you loved or loathed about this book. Although we cannot reply individually to your submissions, we always guarantee that your feedback goes straight to the appropriate authors, in time for the next edition. Each person who sends us information is thanked in the next edition – the most useful submissions are rewarded with a selection of digital PDF chapters.

Visit **lonelyplanet.com/contact** to submit your updates and suggestions or to ask for help. Our award-winning website also features inspirational travel stories, news and discussions.

Note: We may edit, reproduce and incorporate your comments in Lonely Planet products such as guidebooks, websites and digital products, so let us know if you don't want your comments reproduced or your name acknowledged. For a copy of our privacy policy visit lonelyplanet.com/privacy.

OUR READERS

Many thanks to the travellers who used the last edition and wrote to us with helpful hints, useful advice and interesting anecdotes:

David Kozma, Elisabetta Galliani, Melanie Astor, Peter Williams, Roman Hauser, Stephan Brox, Rudolf Marek, Stephan Brox

WRITER THANKS
Matt Phillips

A huge thanks to Lonely Planet for inspiring my travel, and for investing their time and resources in me over the years. This dream assignment wouldn't have been possible without the backing of Jen Carey or the support at home from Amanda Pirie. As always, a big shout out to my family who've always been there for me, through thick and thin. And to all the Seychellois who greeted me with warmth and a smile, a sincere thank you – I'll be back!

Jean-Bernard Carillet

Heaps of thanks to the commissioning and production team at Lonely Planet, especially Matt, for his trust and support, and to the editorial and cartography teams. In Réunion, a special mention goes to my friends Jean-Paul, Isabelle and Anaïs, who it was a pleasure to meet again. And how could I forget my daughter Eva, who had already shared some of my Réunion adventures during a previous trip? We'll be back.

Anthony Ham

Thanks as always to Matt Phillips, long-time collaborator and wise Africa head, for his ongoing faith and for sending me to such glorious places. Thanks to our lovely Norwegian friends in Beau Vallon. To Marina, Carlota and Valentina – so happy to share these places with you, *con todo mi amor*. And to Jan, for always keeping the home fires burning and being the faithful follower of my journeys.

ACKNOWLEDGEMENTS

Climate map data adapted from Peel MC, Finlayson BL & McMahon TA (2007) 'Updated World Map of the Köppen-Geiger Climate Classification', *Hydrology and Earth System Sciences*, 11, 1633–44.

Cover photograph: Seychelles beach; IM_photo/Shutterstock ©

BEHIND THE SCENES

THIS BOOK

This 10th edition of Lonely Planet's *Mauritius, Réunion & Seychelles* guidebook was curated by Matt Phillips and researched and written by Matt, Jean-Bernard Carillet and Anthony Ham. The previous two editions were also written by Jean-Bernard and Anthony. This guidebook was produced by the following:

Destination Editor Matt Phillips

Senior Product Editor Elizabeth Jones

Regional Senior Cartographer Diana Von Holdt

Product Editor Kate Kiely

Cartographer Anthony Phelan

Book Designer Mazzy Prinsep

Assisting Editors Andrew Bain, Hannah Cartmel, Samantha Cook, Michelle Coxall, Barbara Delissen, Samantha Forge, Shona Gray, Victoria Harrison, Gabrielle Innes, Charlotte Orr, Fergus O'Shea, Gabrielle Stefanos

Assisting Cartographers Hunor Csutoros, Valentina Kremenchutskaya

Assisting Book Designer Jessica Rose

Cover Researcher Brendan Dempsey-Spencer

Thanks to Sasha Drew, Genna Patterson

Index

Map Legend

Sights

- Beach
- Bird Sanctuary
- Buddhist
- Castle/Palace
- Christian
- Confucian
- Hindu
- Islamic
- Jain
- Jewish
- Monument
- Museum/Gallery/Historic Building
- Ruin
- Shinto
- Sikh
- Taoist
- Winery/Vineyard
- Zoo/Wildlife Sanctuary
- Other Sight

Activities, Courses & Tours

- Bodysurfing
- Diving
- Canoeing/Kayaking
- Course/Tour
- Sento Hot Baths/Onsen
- Skiing
- Snorkelling
- Surfing
- Swimming/Pool
- Walking
- Windsurfing
- Other Activity

Sleeping

- Sleeping
- Camping
- Hut/Shelter

Eating

- Eating

Drinking & Nightlife

- Drinking & Nightlife
- Cafe

Entertainment

- Entertainment

Shopping

- Shopping

Information

- Bank
- Embassy/Consulate
- Hospital/Medical
- Internet
- Police
- Post Office
- Telephone
- Toilet
- Tourist Information
- Other Information

Geographic

- Beach
- Gate
- Hut/Shelter
- Lighthouse
- Lookout
- Mountain/Volcano
- Oasis
- Park
- Pass
- Picnic Area
- Waterfall

Population

- Capital (National)
- Capital (State/Province)
- City/Large Town
- Town/Village

Transport

- Airport
- Border crossing
- Bus
- Cable car/Funicular
- Cycling
- Ferry
- Metro station
- Monorail
- Parking
- Petrol station
- Subway station
- Taxi
- Train station/Railway
- Tram
- Underground station
- Other Transport

Routes

- Tollway
- Freeway
- Primary
- Secondary
- Tertiary
- Lane
- Unsealed road
- Road under construction
- Plaza/Mall
- Steps
- Tunnel
- Pedestrian overpass
- Walking Tour
- Walking Tour detour
- Path/Walking Trail

Boundaries

- International
- State/Province
- Disputed
- Regional/Suburb
- Marine Park
- Cliff
- Wall

Hydrography

- River, Creek
- Intermittent River
- Canal
- Water
- Dry/Salt/Intermittent Lake
- Reef

Areas

- Airport/Runway
- Beach/Desert
- Cemetery (Christian)
- Cemetery (Other)
- Glacier
- Mudflat
- Park/Forest
- Sight (Building)
- Sportsground
- Swamp/Mangrove

Note: Not all symbols displayed above appear on the maps in this book

OUR STORY

A beat-up old car, a few dollars in the pocket and a sense of adventure. In 1972 that's all Tony and Maureen Wheeler needed for the trip of a lifetime – across Europe and Asia overland to Australia. It took several months, and at the end – broke but inspired – they sat at their kitchen table writing and stapling together their first travel guide, *Across Asia on the Cheap*. Within a week they'd sold 1500 copies. Lonely Planet was born.

Today, Lonely Planet has offices in Franklin, London, Melbourne, Oakland, Dublin, Beijing and Delhi, with more than 600 staff and writers. We share Tony's belief that 'a great guidebook should do three things: inform, educate and amuse'.

OUR WRITERS

Matt Phillips

Seychelles Raised in sunny Tsawwassen (just south of Vancouver) and now at home on the banks of the Thames in Hammersmith, London, Matt loves pushing his boundaries and exploring areas of the world that challenge him. His first such trip was to India, which inspired his love of life, and his second was a solo overland adventure from South Africa to Morocco. The latter thrust him out of a career working as a geologist in underground gold mines and into a life of travel writing. He has happily never looked back. Matt has travelled to more than 70 countries across Africa, Asia, Europe, Australia and the Americas to research and write about everything from epic adventures to responsible travel.

Jean-Bernard Carillet

Réunion Jean-Bernard is a Paris-based freelance writer and photographer who specialises in Africa, France, Turkey, the Indian Ocean, the Caribbean and the Pacific. He loves adventure, remote places, islands, outdoors, archaeological sites and food. His insatiable wanderlust has taken him to 114 countries across six continents, and it shows no sign of waning. It has inspired lots of articles and photos for travel magazines and some 70 Lonely Planet guidebooks, both in English and in French.

Anthony Ham

Mauritius, Rodrigues, Seychelles Anthony is a freelance writer and photographer who specialises in Spain, East and Southern Africa, the Arctic and the Middle East. When he's not writing for Lonely Planet, Anthony writes about and photographs Spain, Africa and the Middle East for newspapers and magazines in Australia, the UK and US.

In 2001, after years of wandering the world, Anthony finally found his spiritual home when he fell irretrievably in love with Madrid on his first visit to the city. Less than a year later, he arrived there on a one-way ticket, with not a word of Spanish and not knowing a single person in the city. When he finally left Madrid ten years later, Anthony spoke Spanish with a Madrid accent, was married to a local and Madrid had become his second home. Now back in Australia, Anthony continues to travel the world in search of stories. Anthony also wrote and researched the Planning and Survival chapters.

Published by Lonely Planet Global Limited
CRN 554153
10th edition – Dec 2019
ISBN 978 1 78657 497 8
© Lonely Planet 2019   Photographs © as indicated 2019
10 9 8 7 6 5 4 3 2 1
Printed in China